A NIETZSCHE COMPENDIUM

A NIETZSCHE COMPENDIUM

Beyond Good and Evil, On the Genealogy of Morals, Twilight of the Idols, The Antichrist, and *Ecce Homo*

FRIEDRICH NIETZSCHE

EDITED AND WITH AN INTRODUCTION
BY DAVID TAFFEL

BARNES & NOBLE
NEW YORK

THE BARNES & NOBLE
LIBRARY OF ESSENTIAL READING

Introduction and Suggested Reading
© 2008 by Barnes & Noble, Inc.

Beyond Good and Evil originally published in 1886; *On the Genealogy of Morals* originally published in 1887; *Twilight of the Idols* originally published in 1889; *The Antichrist* originally published in 1895; and *Ecce Homo* originally published in 1908.

This 2008 edition published by Barnes & Noble, Inc.

Barnes & Noble, Inc.
122 Fifth Avenue
New York, NY 10011

ISBN: 978-0-7607-9110-3

Printed and bound in Canada

15 17 19 20 18 16 14

CONTENTS

INTRODUCTION

THIS CONVENIENT NEW COMPENDIUM CONTAINS THE FIVE MOST philosophically significant of Nietzsche's post-*Thus Spoke Zarathustra* writings. In his characteristically idiosyncratic literary biography, *Ecce Homo*, Nietzsche writes that the books he composed after his renowned *Zarathustra* are "fish hooks" for catching readers who share his sense that a cataclysmic shift in human psychology has just occurred. Alas, Nietzsche laments, in his time there were "no fish." No one else had heard the ominous splitting of history in two with the advent of *nihilism*—the uncanny and pervasive feeling that life is devoid of all meaning, purpose, and value—that so profoundly affected Nietzsche he could do nothing else with his life but articulate this event. "Nihilism is at our door," Nietzsche famously wrote. Do we perceive it yet? After more than a century, do we recognize that the psychological landscape in which we move about is the very one described by Nietzsche? How many of us, even after thoroughly reading his books, see that if we burrow deep enough into the intractable dilemmas of our age, we discover at their roots Nietzsche's preoccupation: "The aim is lacking: 'Why' finds no answer. . ."? It is often said that Nietzsche is self-contradicting, confusing, and even incomprehensible. Yet the books gathered together in this volume articulate his distinct perspective at least as clearly and consistently as most other influential philosophers in the history of the West have articulated theirs. Moreover, these works are written in a beautifully stylized and frequently poetic language that dispenses with virtually all technical jargon. Each of Nietzsche's sentences and paragraphs, as well as his whole books, are masterfully crafted works of art in addition to being intellectual lightening bolts that lay bare with every flash a radically new way of grasping reality, the world, and ourselves. Why, then, the persistent lament about Nietzsche's obscurity? Perhaps the fault for this lies not so much in Nietzsche's writings as in ourselves. Perhaps it is due to the fact that we are in denial about the possible existence of the reality Nietzsche describes. We couldn't continue with life as usual if we truly took him seriously, yet not knowing how otherwise to proceed, we simply "don't understand him." This, however, would not be the case if we were "fish" like those Nietzsche seeks to catch with his last major works. Such fish already have gills for the oxygen of the reality Nietzsche describes. In fact, they are anxiously seeking entry to that reality, for they have an intuition that only there will they breathe freely. In the hope that there are by now many such fish, this introduction to Nietzsche's five most straightforward elaborations of his perspective attempts to bait his hooks with a brief account of several of Nietzsche's key themes and their direct relevance to easily recognizable features of our contemporary social and cultural reality.

Friedrich Nietzsche was born in 1844, in Saxony, Germany. His father, a protestant minister, died while Nietzsche was still a youth, and as a result he was raised predominantly by three powerful women: his mother, aunt, and sister. He was a brilliant student and a prodigy in the burgeoning field of philology (the analysis of the grammar, syntax, and vocabulary of ancient languages), receiving the position of full professor at the philology department of the University of Basel, Switzerland, at the unprecedented age of twenty-four. His courses, however, were in subjects too arcane to attract many students and lifelong health problems increased during his tenure at Basel to the point of forcing him to step down permanently in 1879. His first book, *The Birth of Tragedy Out of the Spirit of Music*, published in 1872, propounded a groundbreaking reinterpretation of pre-Socratic, ancient Greek culture which ultimately supplanted the romanticized ideal of "ancient Greece" that had held sway in European intellectual circles since the Renaissance. Nietzsche's most conventionally academic book, *The Birth of Tragedy* was nonetheless controversial and earned its author an enduring reputation as a gifted but unduly contentious writer and thinker. His subsequent publications (which include *Untimely Meditations; Human, All Too Human; The Dawn; The Gay Science; Thus Spoke Zarathustra; Beyond Good and Evil;* and *The Genealogy of Morals*) would do little in Germany during his productive lifetime but cement this reputation. Nietzsche suffered a complete mental breakdown in late 1888 that reduced him to a near vegetative state for his remaining eleven years of life. However, in the

period immediately preceding this breakdown he was at his most prolific, producing numerous major works between 1886 and 1889, four of
which were penned in 1888 alone. By the time he died in 1900, his works
were already becoming internationally recognized as masterpieces of
philosophy and literature, prompting his custodian-sister, Elisabeth
Förster-Nietzsche, to publish a complete edition of his writings in 1901
that contained a first, short version of *The Will to Power*, hastily assembled
from Nietzsche's notebooks at his sister's behest and in accordance with
an outline for the proposed work that Nietzsche had discarded. The facts
that Nietzsche's sister was married to a well-known anti-Semite and was
reported to have told Hitler he was the embodiment of her brother's
ideal are largely responsible for the unwarranted historical association of
Nietzsche's thought with Nazism that has greatly prejudiced the reception
of his philosophy until this day. This is especially unfortunate since the
works Nietzsche completed with his own hand have long been very widely
available and offer a sufficiently comprehensive account of his thought to
serve as a corrective to any distortions for which either *The Will to Power* or
any of Nietzsche's sister's actions may have been responsible.

Nietzsche's writings have had an enormous impact on European cul-
ture, decisively influencing Sigmund Freud, Max Weber, Thomas Mann,
Albert Camus, the Symbolists and Surrealists, Ludwig Wittgenstein, Martin
Heidegger, Jean-Paul Sartre, and Michel Foucault, just to name a few.
British and American cultures have proven less openly welcoming to
Nietzsche's influence, but through European scholars' immigration to both
countries following the rise of Nazism as well as through English-language
writers and poets such as Joseph Conrad and T. S. Elliot, his impact on
the English-speaking world has also been deep and wide, if somewhat
subterranean. One need merely look at the number of library shelves
groaning under the weight of Nietzsche commentaries to gauge his
enduring appeal.

The five books included in this compendium, though each quite different from the others and totally unique, are all cut from the same cloth
in terms of philosophical content. Nietzsche's views on all decisive points
had become settled before he began writing *Zarathustra* (first part published in 1883), and thus each one of his succeeding books functions as a
different window onto the same essential set of insights. *Beyond Good and
Evil* (1886) is intended as a prosaic presentation of the main themes
treated more symbolically and poetically in *Zarathustra*: namely, how a
hypocritically self-righteous interpretation of everything in the world has

insinuated itself into all aspects of modern intellectual life and what getting "beyond" this interpretation entails and requires. *On The Genealogy of Morals* (1887) describes in three polemical essays how the denial of the goodness of our everyday world and everything that belongs to it came to be the dominant standpoint and at what expense. In *The Twilight of the Idols* (written in 1888 and, like the following two books, completed by Nietzsche but published after his mental demise), Nietzsche's tone becomes more strident, as would increasingly be the case in his last works. This brief book finds Nietzsche slinging "arrows" seemingly haphazardly in many directions, yet the work as a whole attains a remarkable continuity and unity. Almost all the major themes of Nietzsche's late works, such as "the will to power," "the eternal return of the same," and "the revaluation of all values," are touched upon here and often very precisely, succinctly, and seemingly effortlessly elucidated. Of *Twilight*, Nietzsche once commented, "This work is my philosophy in a nutshell. . . ."[1] *The Antichrist* (written in 1888) is the first and only completed volume of what Nietzsche projected to be a four-part work titled *The Revaluation of All Values*, the successor to his abandoned *Will to Power* project. In it, Nietzsche sets his sights on Christianity—which he carefully distinguishes from what he understands the historical Jesus to have represented and taught—and he attacks it with perhaps the most persuasive anti-Christian arguments that have ever been written. It is no book for fainthearted believers. Finally, *Ecce Homo* (written in 1888) is Nietzsche's self-styled autobiography. It illuminates Nietzsche's concept of the person who affirms the absolute goodness of everyday existence by presenting Nietzsche himself as an example of this type, and it also contains book-by-book accounts of his works that offer important insights into what Nietzsche regarded as their significance. Taken together and read straight through, these books offer the reader a definitive account of Nietzsche's perspective as he intended it to be presented and a sweeping attack upon everything the modern Western world holds to be good about itself.

Turning to a closer engagement with the substance of Nietzsche's texts, it is important to note that Nietzsche's use of bombastic sounding catch-phrases for some of his most central ideas has been at least partly responsible for his thought being so easily misunderstood and wrongly appropriated. For this reason a clarification of some of the most important of these phrases and their place in Nietzsche's overarching philosophy should serve as a more useful introduction to the books contained in this volume than a more extensive sketch of the contents of each one. It could be fairly said that the most frequently abused of all Nietzsche's shorthand slogans for his most important insights is "the will to power." In the posthumously assembled collection of excerpts from Nietzsche's late notebooks titled *The Will to Power*, the term "will to power" is used in a more technical and philosophically systematic way than it is in the five works completed by Nietzsche and contained here. In fact, the philosophy contained in the book *The Will to Power* and the notebooks from which its content is drawn is much closer to a full-blown philosophical system than anything one finds in the works Nietzsche intended for publication. The meaning of the slogan "will to power" in the works contained in this volume is deceptively simple: it stands for the human condition as it is now, always has been, and always will be. What makes this idea deceptively simple is that by positing the human condition as essentially unchanging, Nietzsche has in one stroke challenged the general assumption that mankind makes some sort of progress through the course of history. In this context, two of Nietzsche's other most important insights and their respective slogans, "the eternal return of the same" and "the revaluation of all values," come into the picture as corollaries and elaborations of the idea of "will to power." For if there is no progress in human history, then we do not confront something new in the human condition in different historical eras, but rather we continually encounter different incarnations of the same basic reality and the same basic human dynamic—i.e., *an eternal return of the same.* Moreover, insofar as the common objective of Christianity and modern science has been to affect man and the world in such a way that a more perfect future condition (either here or in the hereafter) could be secured, and as a result the dominant mode of evaluating everything has been in terms of whether it helped or hindered the realization of that more perfect condition, Nietzsche's challenging the reality of any such ideal forces upon us both a need to consider different possible criteria for evaluating everything and an obligation to consider the consequences of having measured everything in terms of a nonexistent ideal for more than two millennia. Together these comprise the task of a *revaluation of all values.* Finally, since the reigning interpretation has been one that injected a moral hue into all of its evaluations, Nietzsche's rejection of the universal validity of this mode of evaluation makes him a challenger of the notion that traditional concepts of "good" and "evil" are legitimate measures of the value of things—in other words, he becomes, in his own acerbic terms, "an immoralist." Moreover, anyone who frees himself from the need to judge everything from a moralistic perspective, conformity to which has up to now been universally pushed upon the individual by society through all imaginable overt and covert means, places him or herself in the same condition as Nietzsche's "free-spirits"—i.e., those who are able to fashion values for themselves and to evaluate each aspect of their experience by the criterion of whether or not it promotes their self-realization and the fulfillment of their unique human potential.

One way of further illuminating the radical new perspective imminent in the web of interwoven Nietzschean themes and slogans just described is by relating it to the "prophetic tradition" of social criticism that derives its name from the Old Testament prophets and is sometimes also said to include Jesus Christ. The ancient Hebrew prophets decried the situation of mankind during their era, pointing out the persistent cruelty of man against man, the use of physical and psychological force to maintain adherence to social orders that were extremely hierarchical in all respects and radically inequitable. They characterized relations between people as cruel struggles between opposing forces trying to gain advantage over and dominate one another. To this reality they opposed an idealized one in which human relationships were to be ruled by compassion and love, and where social, political, and economic injustices were to be minimized or eliminated. We hear many voices calling for movement toward such a society in our time and almost all of us have some sympathy with them. But Nietzsche in effect takes a big black marker and puts an "X" over the ideal world that is set against our own everyday one by the prophets and their present-day progeny. It is an illusion. It will not come to pass in this reality or the next. It is a lie that is used by some people to manipulate others into behaving in a way that benefits the former and deceives the latter into thinking it benefits them also.

What, according to Nietzsche, is undeniably real? The everyday world the prophets and their successors condemn is the undeniably real. Yes, it has many vile and horrific aspects, but we should not allow that to drive us into denial of the fact that this is the reality we face, the reality we must come to terms with if we want to be intellectually honest with ourselves. There is no "outside," no "beyond" the reality the prophets decry. As the only world there is, the prophets' attitude toward it is one of life-denial and negation, which Nietzsche characterizes as "No-saying." Moreover, the No-sayers have elevated their life-denying assessment of the one and only reality to the status of highest moral standpoint. Everything that denies the value of this reality is "good." Everything that thrives in, bolsters, and says Yes to life as it actually is, is "evil." The mere acknowledgement and acceptance of the actually existing state of affairs is stigmatized as morally reprehensible.

For Nietzsche, the real challenge men and women face today is the one they have always faced: to find a way to comport themselves toward the reality of the world they confront with playfulness, joy, and high spirits, despite its fearful aspects. He does not underestimate the difficulty of this task but maintains that once we have recognized that our ideals of the future or "beyond" are narcotics with which we numb ourselves to the undeniably real pain of existence and blind ourselves to what is nonetheless beautiful, good, strong, and true in it, we are faced with a choice: living with this knowledge and needing to find a life-affirming way to do so or anesthetizing ourselves once again. Nietzsche's revaluation of all values places the value of honesty—in particular, "intellectual honesty" or honesty with oneself—high up in the new table of values, and from the perspective of this valuation, the advocates of continued "sleep"—the No-sayers—automatically drop to the bottom rung of Nietzsche's human hierarchy. It is they who desire mankind to be a real mediocrity, cowering from the present in the hope of a future of weak-willed ease. Against them Nietzsche opposes the immoralists and free-spirits who reject the notions that the present is somehow deficient for human fulfillment and that the morally ambiguous abundance of life as it is must be suppressed and denied for ethical reasons. Rather, such life-affirming individuals suspect a non-moral motivation behind the deeds of those who say No to this life: they suffer from it too much to acknowledge that it is the one and only life there is. Such sufferers always exist, says Nietzsche. They are probably always in the majority. And that depressing fact must also be accepted by the Yes-sayers as an essential part of the reality that eternally returns. Nietzsche's objection to those who suffer from life too much is not that they are weak or have any less right to exist or do what they must to survive than anyone else, but rather that at least since the advent of Christianity they have universalized their own type. It is human nature, they claim, to suffer inexorably from this life and aspire to escape it into some ideal future or beyond. And insofar as the born No-sayers have been effective in propagating this message, they have made those few individuals born with the rare capacity to say Yes to this life believe in the truth of the life-denying viewpoint and see themselves as fellow sufferers. These few potential "lucky hits" have been stunted in their cradles. All their Yes-saying characteristics have been morally stigmatized. The incipient Yes-sayers' innate strengths and natural advantages have been blunted or turned against them, used to tie the Yes-sayers down and keep them from discerning that for them there is an alternative to life-denial. They have the potential to be real, everyday life-affirming beings, but the No-sayers have convinced them that no such beings are possible in the world today. It is for suppressing the emergence and self-discovery of the life-affirming few that Nietzsche resents and attacks the life-denying majority with such venom. To belong to the herd is fine for herd members, but to demand that everybody be a herd member, to will that all humanity become herd—this is an outrageous swindle of unprecedented proportions. For Nietzsche, "bad taste!"

As thus described, Nietzsche's philosophy is highly contentious. One might well wonder just how it is that a philosopher spewing such pungent notions should come to be not only among the most famous thinkers of our time but also among the most influential. For, as was noted above, it is indisputable that Nietzsche has become exceedingly influential over the course of the past century. Leaving aside for the moment his purely literary appeal, it is worth considering why Nietzsche's ideas are being found ever-increasingly persuasive by experts in the disciplines to which they relate. The answer to this question lies in the often-overlooked fact that Nietzsche was an acknowledged linguistic genius, a first-rate expert in "philology" (literally, "love of the word [or speech]"). While he may not have read closely many of the celebrated tomes of modern philosophy, he mastered at a very early age all the classics and many of the obscurities of Western literature up through the Renaissance. That meant his understanding of human consciousness was the product of a deep and profound grasp of the birth of highly articulate speech (with the ancient Greeks) and its development and change up through the emergence of modern Western languages. He may not have known the nuances of every passage in Hegel's *Logic*, but he very likely knew the nuances of every line of Greek tragedy better than Hegel did. Though Nietzsche doesn't overly celebrate himself as an initiator of what is now called "the linguistic turn" in philosophy, it is in connection with the intellectual revolution brought about by this turn (in which Nietzsche did play a key role) that his philosophy has become so persuasive. Nietzsche discovers a new level on which to approach philosophical issues, moving beyond argumentative discourse over concepts and values to the analysis of the language used to express concepts and values and the study of how this language emerged and sometimes changed quite radically over time. Suddenly, following Nietzsche, *the* philosophical issue ceases to be the accuracy of what is said in a given statement (about the world, God, the soul, truth, etc.) and instead becomes what are the possible reasons why a specific person at a specific time might have made precisely this kind of statement and/or found it to be persuasive. This is a radical shift indeed. Once scientific analysis of language revealed that it is inherently fluid and that "truth" is an attribute of certain uses of language, not something to do with the relation between statements and an independent reality to which they refer, the "truth" of a given statement became no longer as philosophically significant as the reasons for asserting and holding something to be true. By being among the first to think through the radical consequences of this discovery, Nietzsche transposed the whole of Western philosophical and cultural history into a new key and shifted the philosophical quest from the search for goodness and truth to the search for the largely unconscious reasons for claiming and believing that something is good or true. Exploration of the ramifications of this intellectual revolution with regard to what kinds of knowledge are accessible to human inquiry is among the central concerns of contemporary philosophy and social science. And in this context, no one has been more effective at calling into question what was previously regarded as most certain, good, and true than Friedrich Nietzsche. It is for this reason, as well as because of the intrinsic beauty of his writings and attraction of his counterintuitive but powerfully stated views, that Nietzsche has become a towering figure in the Western philosophical tradition and that the works contained in this compendium will remain timeless masterpieces of the highest intellectual and cultural importance.

David Taffel is the author of *Nietzsche Unbound: The Struggle for Spirit in the Age of Science* and the managing editor of *The Conversationalist*, a global news and culture website. He has a Ph.D. in philosophy from the New School for Social Research, where his dissertation was awarded the Hans Jonas Memorial Prize for Philosophy.

BEYOND GOOD AND EVIL

TRANSLATED BY

HELEN ZIMMERN

CONTENTS

INTRODUCTION TO
THE TRANSLATION

HERE, IN SPITE OF ITS NAME, IS ONE OF THE MOST SERIOUS, PROFOUND, AND original philosophical works. It offers a feast of good things to the morally and intellectually fastidious, which will take long to exhaust. There is really something new in the book—much that is new! Burke says, in his *Reflexions on the Revolution in France* (p. 128), "We [Englishmen] know that we have made no discoveries, and we think that no discoveries are to be made in morality." The latter statement, which still represents the general views of Englishmen, is now proved to be entirely mistaken. Discoveries have now been made in the realm of morals, which are perhaps even more *practically* important than all the discoveries in physical science; and it is to Nietzsche especially that we are indebted for those discoveries, which are set forth, in part at least, in this volume—the very discoveries, in fact, which Burke himself required, in order to give a satisfactory answer to the French Revolutionists.

As, however, many who might otherwise appreciate the book, may stumble over its name at the threshold, it should perhaps be explained that the astounding and portentous designation, *Beyond Good and Evil*, applies to it properly only from the false point of view of its pseudo-moral opponents; as, however, it is a very striking expression, such as is always wanted for the title of a book, it has been appropriated for the purpose, notwithstanding the fact that to ordinary minds, and in ordinary language, it implies the very reverse of what the book teaches. Of course, there is a certain amount of truth in the designation, and therefore a justification for it: Nietzsche's position is beyond the spurious "good" and the spurious "evil" of the prevalent slave-morality, which deterio-rates humanity; but he takes a firm stand on the genuine "good" and the genuine "bad" of master-morality, which promotes the advancement of the human race. This is so obvious from a glance at the book that it is scarcely necessary to refer to Nietzsche's express statement of the fact in the *Genealogy of Morals*, i. 17. He there says expressly, with reference to "the dangerous watchword inscribed on the outside of his last book: *Beyond Good and Evil*" "at any rate, it does *not* mean, 'Beyond Good and Bad.'"

(When so many reproaches have been unjustly heaped upon Nietzsche and his disciples, under the false pretence that they repudiate true moral-ity, it is difficult to resist the opportunity to turn round upon those maligners parenthetically, and point out who it is that is really beyond good and bad from the true moral standpoint—is it perhaps those very maligners themselves, whom Nietzsche with his acuteness has touched on the quick? The Kirkcaldyan gospel of *The Wealth of Nations*, under which we all live more or less, and which in puerile fashion the political econo-mists still repeat almost by rote, not only implicitly disregards morals, but on many occasions boldly and explicitly professes to have nothing to do with them, in fact, professes to be altogether beyond good and bad in the ordinary sense of these words. [See, for example, Walker's works on *Political Economy*, and many other writers on the subject.] And is not this *Political Economy* the unquestioned creed of almost all the non-Socialists who condemn Nietzsche? Even the Königsbergian gospel, with its *Sublime Moral Law*, and its *Categorical Imperative*, has allied and adjusted itself to the Kirkcaldyan gospel of universal, insatiable, exclusively individualistic, and absolutely unscrupulous Mammonism. The Benthamites, the Spencerites, and the Neo-Hegelianites or Greenites, have had still less difficulty in forming an alliance with Mammonism, even in its worst aspects. All those "good people," therefore, who are so ready to condemn others, have actually themselves taken up a position beyond good and bad in the dis-reputable sense of these terms, unlike Nietzsche, who occupies the only justifiable position from the true moral standpoint.)

One or two of the leading points in Nietzsche's philosophy should perhaps be mentioned—but we cannot touch on the numerous details, which may, however, often be deduced from the leading principles here indicated:

1. Nietzsche especially makes the highest excellence of society the ethical end; whereas almost all other moralists adopt "ends" which lead

directly or indirectly, to the degeneration of society. As a necessary consequence, he favours a true aristocracy as the best means for elevating the human race to supermen.

2. Instead of advocating "equal and inalienable rights to life, liberty, and the pursuit of happiness," for which there is at present such an outcry (a regime which necessarily elevates fools and knaves, and lowers the honest and intelligent), Nietzsche advocates simple *justice*—to individuals and families according to their *merits*, according to their *worth* to society; *not* equal rights, therefore, but unequal rights, and inequality in advantages generally, approximately proportionate to deserts: consequently therefore, a genuinely superior ruling class at one end of the social scale, and an actually inferior ruled class, with slaves at its basis, at the opposite social extreme.

3. Unlike social evolutionists generally, who either stop short in their quest, or neglect Newton's rule of philosophising, which prohibits the assigning of superfluous, unknown, or imaginary causes, Nietzsche explains social phenomena by familiar, natural causes, assigning to them a human, all-too-human origin, and accounting for them especially, like Larochefoucauld, as a result of the self-interest and self-preservative instinct of individuals and classes—that is to say, practically, in conformity to the true principles of evolution, which recognise in everything a conscious or subconscious will to persist and evolve—a matter which Darwin certainly overlooked too much in his imperfect attempts to explain moral and social evolution.

4. One of Nietzsche's most important services has been to furnish a true philosophy of the more modern period of history, during the last two thousand years. As "the first psychologist of Christianity," he has successfully accounted for the anomalous phenomenon of the Christian religion—the special embodiment of slave-morality—by showing that it is an artful device, consciously and subconsciously evolved for the self-preservation and advantage of the inferior classes of society, who have thus, to the detriment of the race, gained an abnormal and temporary ascendency over the better class of men, to whom the mastership belongs, under the sway of the normally prevailing pagan or master-morality which favours the advance of mankind.

Nietzsche, therefore, differs radically from most of the leaders of English thought with regard to the great questions of ethics and religion. Spencer, Huxley, Alfred R. Wallace, Leslie Stephen, A. J. Balfour, Benjamin

Kidd, Frederic Harrison, Grant Allen, T. H. Green, Andrew Lang, and their followers, though differing in many points among themselves, seem all to have a strong instinctive aversion to recognise self-interest as a leading factor in the evolution of morals and religion; indeed, some of the mystifiers among them, especially Green's time-serving followers, with their fixed idea of a dotard Deity (or God-aping devil?) devolving himself as fast as possible into constitutionalism, democracy, and anarchy, would almost sooner gaze on the Gorgon's head than contemplate the possibility of such an illuminating, ready, and natural explanation. Most of those leaders of English thought are also equally averse to recognise that the true ethical end *must be* the highest excellence of society. It would involve in many people such an upsetting of their intellectual furniture to admit Nietzsche's new ideas—it would also involve ultimately the upsetting of cherished institutions which are profitable to them, or to which they have become satisfactorily adjusted: many responsible people, therefore, prefer to barricade their intellects against such new and danger-threatening ideas, which are far more revolutionary, or rather counterrevolutionary, than Socialism! The great mass even of cultured people in England seem unable to cross the *pontes asinorum* of morals: they cannot grasp the related facts that what is good for one is *not* necessarily good for society at large, and that many people, in spite of Socrates, instinctively *choose the bad*, when it is most profitable to themselves. All popular and superficial writers, however, and all demagogues, take for granted the opposite doctrines—namely, that whatever is advantageous to any person, be he the most wicked and worthless creature on the face of the earth, is therefore necessarily for the good of the whole community; and that everyone instinctively chooses the right course as soon as he knows it.

Some English writers, however, approximate pretty closely to Nietzsche on some of the points in his philosophy: for example, Emerson, Carlyle, Kingdon Clifford, Samuel Butler, Sir Alfred Lyall, Stuart-Glennie, Karl Pearson, and doubtless many others. None of these writers have, however, elaborated the whole subject as Nietzsche has done. Bernard Shaw, as is well known, has also many points in common with Nietzsche. F. C. S. Schiller should likewise be named here, whose *Pragmatism*, about which there is so much noise at present, has obviously been largely influenced by Nietzsche's writings. H. G. Wells' semi-serious writings seem like a coarse and crooked refraction of the ideas of Nietzsche.

To be sure, all prudent, worldly wise men follow more or less approximately the practise which Nietzsche teaches, notwithstanding the opposite principles which they perhaps profess to hold: they do not willingly allow equal rights to knaves and fools to do as they like, much less are they willing to practise self-sacrifice for the sake of the most worthless specimens of humanity. Not even the special champions and forlorn hope of these ideas—the secularists, "rationalists," ethiculturists and "philanthropists"— are inclined to practise themselves to any great extent, the slave-morality which they preach to others. There is nowadays, also, a healthy tendency in the clergy of the established churches to send people to hell for wickedness, rather than for unbelief as was done formerly, and is still done by the evangelical party. The great majority of people, however, hold, or pretend to hold, principles which are altogether inconsistent with their practise— in fact they are not rational beings in the realm of morals (or are their "principles" meant only for the practise of other people but not for themselves?). The great advance which Nietzsche has made is that he has *harmonised moral theory and practise,* and *rationalised morality.*

As regards its relation to Nietzsche's other works, this book was meant on the one hand to explain more clearly in prose form the ideas expressed poetically and somewhat obscurely in his previous book, *Thus Spake Zarathustra;* and on the other hand, as its subtitle indicates, it was meant as a prologue or prelude to his great, never-completed work on which he was then engaged, *The Will to Power: An Attempt at a Transvaluation of All Values.* The circumstances under which the work was written are very fully set forth in chapter 30 (pp. 588–635) of *Das Leben Nietzsches.* With the exception of the epode, the book was written partly in the summer of 1885 at Sils-Maria, and partly in the following winter at Nice. It was during this period that Nietzsche's sister was married and went with her husband to Paraguay, thus leaving her brother more solitary than ever. The spirit of solitude which broods over the book, discloses itself especially in the last chapter. The manuscript was sent to the printer in June 1886, and the book was published in the September following at Nietzsche's own expense.

Nietzsche was personally acquainted with Miss Helen Zimmern—her important book on Schopenhauer brought her under his notice—and, as appears from his letters, he had her in view as a translator of his works: this led her to undertake the task of rendering this volume into English. A good deal of labour has been spent in making the version as satisfactory as possible by further revision. We here take the opportunity to thank Mr. Alfred E. Zimmern of New College, Oxford, and a German friend of his, Mr. W. Drechsler, Rhodes Scholar of Worcester College, for reading very carefully some of the first proofs and suggesting improvements. Dr. Oscar Levy has also read many of the proofs and made valuable suggestions.

The friends of the cause are, however, still further indebted to Dr. Oscar Levy—whose name is well known to students of Nietzschean literature by his book, *The Revival of Aristocracy*—for enabling the publication of Nietzsche's works to be resumed once more. His patronage of the cause stands out in pleasing contrast to the indifference and hostility to Nietzsche of some of the English professional "philosophers," who should have been the first to welcome the new knowledge, had they been true men.

THOMAS COMMON
23rd August 1907

PREFACE

Supposing that Truth is a woman—what then? Is there not ground for suspecting that all philosophers, insofar as they have been dogmatists, have failed to understand women—that the terrible seriousness and clumsy importunity with which they have usually paid their addresses to Truth, have been unskilled and unseemly methods for winning a woman? Certainly she has never allowed herself to be won; and at present every kind of dogma stands with sad and discouraged mien—*if*, indeed, it stands at all! For there are scoffers who maintain that it has fallen, that all dogma lies on the ground—nay more, that it is at its last gasp. But to speak seriously, there are good grounds for hoping that all dogmatising in philosophy, whatever solemn, whatever conclusive and decided airs it has assumed, may have been only a noble puerilism and tyronism; and probably the time is at hand when it will be once and again understood *what* has actually sufficed for the basis of such imposing and absolute philosophical edifices as the dogmatists have hitherto reared: perhaps some popular superstition of immemorial time (such as the soul-superstition, which, in the form of subject- and ego-superstition, has not yet ceased doing mischief); perhaps some play upon words, a deception on the part of grammar, or an audacious generalisation of very restricted, very personal, very human—all-too-human facts. The philosophy of the dogmatists, it is to be hoped, was only a promise for thousands of years afterwards, as was astrology in still earlier times, in the service of which probably more labour, gold, acuteness, and patience have been spent than on any actual science hitherto: we owe to it, and to its "super-terrestrial" pretensions in Asia and Egypt, the grand style of architecture. It seems that in order to inscribe themselves upon

11

the heart of humanity with everlasting claims, all great things have first to wander about the earth as enormous and awe-inspiring caricatures: dogmatic philosophy has been a caricature of this kind—for instance, the Vedanta doctrine in Asia, and Platonism in Europe. Let us not be ungrateful to it, although it must certainly be confessed that the worst, the most tiresome, and the most dangerous of errors hitherto has been a dogmatist error—namely, Plato's invention of Pure Spirit and the Good in Itself. But now when it has been surmounted, when Europe, rid of this nightmare, can again draw breath freely and at least enjoy a healthier—sleep, we, *whose duty is wakefulness itself*, are the heirs of all the strength which the struggle against this error has fostered. It amounted to the very inversion of truth, and the denial of the *perspective*—the fundamental condition—of life, to speak of Spirit and the Good as Plato spoke of them; indeed one might ask, as a physician: "How did such a malady attack that finest product of antiquity, Plato? Had the wicked Socrates really corrupted him? Was Socrates after all a corrupter of youths, and deserved his hemlock?" But the struggle against Plato, or—to speak plainer, and for the "people" —the struggle against the ecclesiastical oppression of millenniums of Christianity (for Christianity is Platonism for the "people"), produced in Europe a magnificent tension of soul, such as had not existed anywhere previously; with such a tensely strained bow one can now aim at the furthest goals. As a matter of fact, the European feels this tension as a state of distress, and twice attempts have been made in grand style to unbend the bow: once by means of Jesuitism, and the second time by means of democratic enlightenment—which, with the aid of liberty of the press and newspaper-reading, might, in fact, bring it about that the spirit would not so easily find itself in "distress!" (The Germans invented gunpowder— all credit to them! But they again made things square—they invented printing.) But we, who are neither Jesuits, nor democrats, nor even sufficiently Germans, we *good Europeans*, and free, *very* free spirits—we have it still, all the distress of spirit and all the tension of its bow! And perhaps also the arrow, the duty, and, who knows? *The goal to aim at. . . .*

Sils-Maria, Upper Engadine,
June 1885

CHAPTER ONE

PREJUDICES OF PHILOSOPHERS

1

THE WILL TO TRUTH, WHICH IS TO TEMPT US TO MANY A HAZARDOUS enterprise, the famous Truthfulness of which all philosophers have hitherto spoken with respect, what questions has this Will to Truth not laid before us! What strange, perplexing, questionable questions! It is already a long story; yet it seems as if it were hardly commenced. Is it any wonder if we at last grow distrustful, lose patience, and turn impatiently away? That this Sphinx teaches us at last to ask questions ourselves? *Who* is it really that puts questions to us here? *What* really is this "Will to Truth" in us? In fact we made a long halt at the question as to the origin of this Will—until at last we came to an absolute standstill before a yet more fundamental question. We inquired about the *value* of this Will. Granted that we want the truth: *why not rather* untruth? And uncertainty? Even ignorance? The problem of the value of truth presented itself before us—or was it we who presented ourselves before the problem? Which of us is the Oedipus here? Which the Sphinx? It would seem to be a rendezvous of questions and notes of interrogation. And could it be believed that it at last seems to us as if the problem had never been propounded before, as if we were the first to discern it, get a sight of it, and *risk raising* it. For there is risk in raising it, perhaps there is no greater risk.

2

How could anything originate out of its opposite? For example, truth out of error? Or the Will to Truth out of the will to deception? Or the generous deed out of selfishness? Or the pure

13

sun-bright vision of the wise man out of covetousness? Such genesis is impossible; whoever dreams of it is a fool, nay, worse than a fool; things of the highest value must have a different origin, an origin of *their own*—in this transitory, seductive, illusory, paltry world, in this turmoil of delusion and cupidity, they cannot have their source. But rather in the lap of Being, in the intransitory, in the concealed God, in the "Thing-in-itself"—*there* must be their source, and nowhere else!

This mode of reasoning discloses the typical prejudice by which metaphysicians of all times can be recognised, this mode of valuation is at the back of all their logical procedure; through this "belief" of theirs, they exert themselves for their "knowledge," for something that is in the end solemnly christened "the Truth." The fundamental belief of metaphysicians is *the belief in antitheses of values*. It never occurred even to the wariest of them to doubt here on the very threshold (where doubt, however, was most necessary); though they had made a solemn vow, "*de omnibus dubitandum.*" For it may be doubted, firstly, whether antitheses exist at all; and secondly, whether the popular valuations and antitheses of value upon which metaphysicians have set their seal, are not perhaps merely superficial estimates, merely provisional perspectives, besides being probably made from some corner, perhaps from below—"frog perspectives," as it were, to borrow an expression current among painters. In spite of all the value which may belong to the true, the positive, and the unselfish, it might be possible that a higher and more fundamental value for life generally should be assigned to pretence, to the will to delusion, to selfishness, and cupidity. It might even be possible that *what* constitutes the value of those good and respected things, consists precisely in their being insidiously related, knotted, and crocheted to these evil and apparently opposed things—perhaps even in being essentially identical with them. Perhaps! But who wishes to concern himself with such dangerous "Perhapses!" For that investigation one must await the advent of a new order of philosophers, such as will have other tastes and inclinations, the reverse of those hitherto prevalent—philosophers of the dangerous "Perhaps" in every sense of the term. And to speak in all seriousness, I see such new philosophers beginning to appear.

3

Having kept a sharp eye on philosophers, and having read between their lines long enough, I now say to myself that the greater part of conscious thinking must be counted amongst the instinctive functions, and it is so even in the case of philosophical thinking; one has here to learn anew, as one learned anew about heredity and "innateness." As little as the act of birth comes into consideration in the whole process and procedure of heredity, just as little is "being-conscious" *opposed* to the instinctive in any decisive sense; the greater part of the conscious thinking of a philosopher is secretly influenced by his instincts, and forced into definite channels. And behind all logic and its seeming sovereignty of movement, there are valuations, or to speak more plainly, physiological demands, for the maintenance of a definite mode of life. For example, that the certain is worth more than the uncertain, that illusion is less valuable than "truth": such valuations, in spite of their regulative importance for *us*, might notwithstanding be only superficial valuations, special kinds of *niaiserie*, such as may be necessary for the maintenance of beings such as ourselves. Supposing, in effect, that man is not just the "measure of things. . . ."

4

The falseness of an opinion is not for us any objection to it: it is here, perhaps, that our new language sounds most strangely. The question is, how far an opinion is life-furthering, life-preserving, species-preserving, perhaps species-rearing; and we are fundamentally inclined to maintain that the falsest opinions (to which the synthetic judgements a priori belong), are the most indispensable to us; that without a recognition of logical fictions, without a comparison of reality with the purely *imagined* world of the absolute and immutable, without a constant counterfeiting of the world by means of numbers, man could not live—that the renunciation of false opinions would be a renunciation of life, a negation of life. *To recognise untruth as a condition of life*: that is certainly to impugn the traditional ideas of value in a dangerous manner, and a philosophy which ventures to do so, has thereby alone placed itself beyond good and evil.

5

That which causes philosophers to be regarded half-distrustfully and half-mockingly, is not the oft-repeated discovery how innocent they are—how often and easily they make mistakes and lose their way, in short, how childish and childlike they are—but that there is not enough honest dealing with them, whereas they all raise a loud and virtuous outcry when the problem of truthfulness is even hinted at in the remotest manner. They all pose as though their real opinions had been discovered and attained through the self-evolving of a cold, pure, divinely indifferent dialectic (in contrast to all sorts of mystics, who, fairer and foolisher, talk of "inspiration"); whereas, in fact, a prejudiced proposition, idea, or "suggestion," which is generally their heart's desire abstracted and refined, is defended by them with arguments sought out after the event. They are all advocates who do not wish to be regarded as such, generally astute defenders, also, of their prejudices, which they dub "truths"—and *very* far from having the conscience which bravely admits this to itself; very far from having the good taste of the courage which goes so far as to let this be understood, perhaps to warn friend or foe, or in cheerful confidence and self-ridicule. The spectacle of the Tartuffery of old Kant, equally stiff and decent, with which he entices us into the dialectic byways that lead (more correctly mislead) to his "categorical imperative"—makes us fastidious ones smile, we who find no small amusement in spying out the subtle tricks of old moralists and ethical preachers. Or, still more so, the hocus-pocus in mathematical form, by means of which Spinoza has as it were clad his philosophy in mail and mask—in fact, the "love of *his* wisdom," to translate the term fairly and squarely—in order thereby to strike terror at once into the heart of the assailant who should dare to cast a glance on that invincible maiden, that Pallas Athene: how much of personal timidity and vulnerability does this masquerade of a sickly recluse betray!

6

It has gradually become clear to me what every great philosophy up till now has consisted of—namely, the confession of its originator, and a species of involuntary and unconscious autobiography; and moreover that the moral (or immoral) purpose in every philosophy has constituted the true vital germ out of which the entire plant has always grown. Indeed, to understand how the abstrusest metaphysical assertions of a philosopher have been arrived at, it is always well (and wise) to first ask oneself: "What morality do they (or does he) aim at?" Accordingly, I do not believe that an "impulse to knowledge" is the father of philosophy; but that another impulse, here as elsewhere, has only made use of knowledge (and mistaken knowledge!) as an instrument. But whoever considers the fundamental impulses of man with a view to determining how far they may have here acted as *inspiring* genii (or as demons and cobolds), will find that they have all practised philosophy at one time or another, and that each one of them would have been only too glad to look upon itself as the ultimate end of existence and the legitimate *lord* over all the other impulses. For every impulse is imperious, and as *such*, attempts to philosophise. To be sure, in the case of scholars, in the case of really scientific men, it may be otherwise—"better," if you will; there there may really be such a thing as an "impulse to knowledge," some kind of small, independent clockwork, which, when well wound up, works away industriously to that end, *without* the rest of the scholarly impulses taking any material part therein. The actual "interests" of the scholar, therefore, are generally in quite another direction—in the family, perhaps, or in money-making, or in politics; it is, in fact, almost indifferent at what point of research his little machine is placed, and whether the hopeful young worker becomes a good philologist, a mushroom specialist, or a chemist; he is not *characterised* by becoming this or that. In the philosopher, on the contrary, there is absolutely nothing impersonal; and above all, his morality furnishes a decided and decisive testimony as to *who he is*—that is to say, in what order the deepest impulses of his nature stand to each other.

7

How malicious philosophers can be! I know of nothing more stinging than the joke Epicurus took the liberty of making on Plato and the Platonists: he called them *Dionysiokolakes*. In its original sense, and on the face of it, the word signifies "Flatterers of Dionysius"—consequently, tyrants' accessories and lick-spittles; besides this, however, it is as much as to say, "They are all *actors*, there is nothing genuine about them" (for *Dionysiokolax* was a popular name for an actor). And the latter is really the malignant reproach that Epicurus cast upon Plato: he was annoyed by the grandiose manner, the mise-en-scène style of which Plato and his scholars were masters—of which Epicurus was not a master! He, the old schoolteacher of Samos, who sat concealed in his little garden at Athens and wrote three hundred books, perhaps out of rage and ambitious envy of Plato, who knows! Greece took a hundred years to find out who the garden-god Epicurus really was. Did she ever find out?

8

There is a point in every philosophy at which the "conviction" of the philosopher appears on the scene; or, to put it in the words of an ancient mystery:

Adventavit asinus,
Pulcher et fortissimus.

9

You desire to *live* "according to Nature?" Oh, you noble Stoics, what
fraud of words! Imagine to yourselves a being like Nature, boundlessly
extravagant, boundlessly indifferent, without purpose or consideration,
without pity or justice, at once fruitful and barren and uncertain: imagine
to yourselves *indifference* as a power—how *could* you live in accordance
with such indifference? To live—is not that just endeavouring to be otherwise than this Nature? Is not living valuing, preferring, being unjust, being
limited, endeavouring to be different? And granted that your imperative,
"living according to Nature," means actually the same as "living according
to life"—how could you do *differently?* Why should you make a principle
out of what you yourselves are, and must be? In reality, however, it is quite
otherwise with you: while you pretend to read with rapture the canon of
your law in Nature, you want something quite the contrary, you extraordinary stage-players and self-deluders! In your pride you wish to dictate your
morals and ideals to Nature, to Nature herself, and to incorporate them
therein; you insist that it shall be Nature "according to the Stoa," and
would like everything to be made after your own image, as a vast, eternal
glorification and generalisation of Stoicism! With all your love for truth,
you have forced yourselves so long, so persistently, and with such hypnotic rigidity to see Nature *falsely,* that is to say, Stoically, that you are no
longer able to see it otherwise—and to crown all, some unfathomable
superciliousness gives you the Bedlamite hope that *because* you are able to
tyrannise over yourselves—Stoicism is self-tyranny—Nature will also allow
herself to be tyrannised over: is not the Stoic a *part* of Nature? . . . But this
is an old and everlasting story: what happened in old times with the Stoics
still happens today, as soon as ever a philosophy begins to believe in itself.
It always creates the world in its own image; it cannot do otherwise; philosophy is this tyrannical impulse itself, the most spiritual Will to Power,
the will to "creation of the world," the will to the *causa prima.*

10

The eagerness and subtlety, I should even say craftiness, with which the
problem of "the real and the apparent world" is dealt with at present
throughout Europe, furnishes food for thought and attention; and he
who hears only a "Will to Truth" in the background, and nothing else,
cannot certainly boast of the sharpest ears. In rare and isolated cases, it
may really have happened that such a Will to Truth—a certain extravagant
and adventurous pluck, a metaphysician's ambition of the forlorn hope—

has participated therein: that which in the end always prefers a handful of "certainty" to a whole cartload of beautiful possibilities; there may even be puritanical fanatics of conscience, who prefer to put their last trust in a sure nothing, rather than in an uncertain something. But that is Nihilism, and the sign of a despairing, mortally wearied soul, notwithstanding the courageous bearing such a virtue may display. It seems, however, to be otherwise with stronger and livelier thinkers who are still eager for life. In that they side *against* appearance, and speak superciliously of "perspective," in that they rank the credibility of their own bodies about as low as the credibility of the ocular evidence that "the earth stands still," and thus, apparently, allowing with complacency their securest possession to escape (for what does one at present believe in more firmly than in one's body?) who knows if they are not really trying to win back something which was formerly an even *securer* possession, something of the old domain of the faith of former times, perhaps the "immortal soul," perhaps "the old God," in short, ideas by which they could live better, that is to say, more vigorously and more joyously, than by "modern ideas?" There is *distrust* of these modern ideas in this mode of looking at things, a disbelief in all that has been constructed yesterday and today; there is perhaps some slight admixture of satiety and scorn, which can no longer endure the bric-à-brac of ideas of the most varied origin, such as so-called Positivism at present throws on the market; a disgust of the more refined taste at the village-fair motleyness and patchiness of all these reality-philosophasters, in whom there is nothing either new or true, except this motleyness. Therein it seems to me that we should agree with those sceptical anti-realists and knowledge-microscopists of the present day; their instinct, which repels them from *modern* reality, is unrefuted ... what do their retrograde bypaths concern us! The main thing about them is *not* that they wish to go "back," but that they wish to get *away* therefrom. A little *more* strength, swing, courage, and artistic power, and they would be *off*—and not back!

11

It seems to me that there is everywhere an attempt at present to divert attention from the actual influence which Kant exercised on German philosophy, and especially to ignore prudently the value which he set upon himself. Kant was first and foremost proud of his Table of Categories; with it in his hand he said: "This is the most difficult thing that could ever be undertaken on behalf of metaphysics." Let us only understand this "could be!" He was proud of having *discovered* a new faculty in man, the faculty of synthetic judgement a priori. Granting that he deceived himself in this matter; the development and rapid flourishing of German philosophy depended nevertheless on his pride, and on the eager rivalry of the younger generation to discover if possible something—at all events "new faculties"—of which to be still prouder! But let us reflect for a moment— it is high time to do so. "How are synthetic judgements a priori *possible?*" Kant asks himself—and what is really his answer? *"By means of a means* (faculty)" but unfortunately not in five words, but so circumstantially, imposingly, and with such display of German profundity and verbal flourishes, that one altogether loses sight of the comical *niaiserie allemande* involved in such an answer. People were beside themselves with delight over this new faculty, and the jubilation reached its climax when Kant further discovered a moral faculty in man—for at that time Germans were still moral, not yet dabbling in the "Politics of hard fact." Then came the honeymoon of German philosophy. All the young theologians of the Tübingen institution went immediately into the groves—all seeking for "faculties." And what did they not find—in that innocent, rich, and still youthful period of the German spirit, to which Romanticism, the malicious fairy, piped and sang, when one could not yet distinguish between "finding" and "inventing!" Above all a faculty for the "transcendental"; Schelling christened it, intellectual intuition, and thereby gratified the most earnest longings of the naturally pious-inclined Germans. One can do no greater wrong to the whole of this exuberant and eccentric movement (which was really youthfulness, notwithstanding that it disguised itself so boldly in hoary and senile conceptions), than to take it seriously, or even treat it with moral indignation. Enough, however—the world grew older, and the dream vanished. A time came when people rubbed their foreheads, and they still rub them today. People had been dreaming, and first and foremost—old Kant. "By means of a means (faculty)" he had said, or at least meant to say. But, is that—an answer? An explanation? Or is it not rather merely a repetition of the question? How does opium induce sleep? "By means of a means (faculty)," namely the *virtus dormitiva*, replies the doctor in Molière,

> *Quia est in eo virtus dormitiva,*
> *Cujus est natura sensus assoupire.*

But such replies belong to the realm of comedy, and it is high time to replace the Kantian question, "How are synthetic judgements a priori possible?" by another question, "Why is belief in such judgements *necessary?*" in effect, it is high time that we should understand that such judgements must be *believed* to be true, for the sake of the preservation of creatures like ourselves; though they still might naturally be *false* judgements! Or, more plainly spoken, and roughly and readily—synthetic judgements a priori should not "be possible" at all; we have no right to them; in our mouths they are nothing but false judgements. Only, of course, the belief in their truth is necessary, as plausible belief and ocular evidence belonging to the perspective view of life. And finally, to call to mind the enormous influence which "German philosophy"—I hope you understand its right to inverted commas (goosefeet?) has exercised throughout the whole of Europe, there is no doubt that a certain *virtus dormitiva* had a share in it; thanks to German philosophy, it was a delight to the noble idlers, the virtuous, the mystics, the artists, the three-fourths Christians, and the political obscurantists of all nations, to find an antidote to the still overwhelming sensualism which overflowed from the last century into this, in short—*"sensus assoupire. . . ."*

12

As regards materialistic atomism, it is one of the best refuted theories that have been advanced, and in Europe there is now perhaps no one in the learned world so unscholarly as to attach serious signification to it, except for convenient everyday use (as an abbreviation of the means of expression)—thanks chiefly to the Pole Boscovich: he and the Pole Copernicus have hitherto been the greatest and most successful opponents of ocular evidence. For whilst Copernicus has persuaded us to believe, contrary to all the senses, that the earth does *not* stand fast, Boscovich has taught us to abjure the belief in the last thing that "stood fast" of the earth—the belief in "substance," in "matter," in the earth-residuum, and particle - atom: it is the greatest triumph over the senses that has hitherto been gained on earth. One must, however, go still further, and also declare war, relentless war to the knife, against the "atomistic requirements" which still lead a dangerous afterlife in places where no one suspects them, like the more celebrated "metaphysical requirements": one must also above all give the finishing stroke to that other and more portentous atomism which Christianity has taught best and longest, the *soul-atomism*. Let it be permitted to designate by this expression the belief which regards the soul as something indestructible, eternal, indivisible, as a monad, as an *atomon: this* belief ought to be expelled from science! Between ourselves, it is not at all necessary to get rid of "the soul" thereby, and thus renounce one of the oldest and most venerated hypotheses—as happens frequently to the clumsiness of naturalists, who can hardly touch on the soul without immediately losing it. But the way is open for new acceptations and refinements of the soul-hypothesis; and such conceptions as "mortal soul," and "soul as subjective multiplicity," and "soul as social structure of the instincts and passions," want henceforth to have legitimate rights in science. In that the *new* psychologist is about to put an end to the superstitions which have hitherto flourished with almost tropical luxuriance around the idea of the soul, he is really, as it were, thrusting himself into a new desert and a new distrust—it is possible that the older psychologists had a merrier and more comfortable time of it; eventually, however, he finds that precisely thereby he is also condemned to *invent*—and, who knows? Perhaps to *discover* the new.

13

Psychologists should bethink themselves before putting down the instinct of self-preservation as the cardinal instinct of an organic being. A living thing seeks above all to *discharge* its strength—life itself is *Will to Power*; self-preservation is only one of the indirect and most frequent *results* thereof. In short, here, as everywhere else, let us beware of *superfluous* teleological principles! One of which is the instinct of self-preservation (we owe it to Spinoza's inconsistency). It is thus, in effect, that method ordains, which must be essentially economy of principles.

14

It is perhaps just dawning on five or six minds that natural philosophy is only a world-exposition and world-arrangement (according to us, if I may say so!) and *not* a world-explanation; but insofar as it is based on belief in the senses, it is regarded as more, and for a long time to come must be regarded as more—namely, as an explanation. It has eyes and fingers of its own, it has ocular evidence and palpableness of its own: this operates fascinatingly, persuasively, and *convincingly* upon an age with fundamentally plebeian tastes—in fact, it follows instinctively the canon of truth of eternal popular sensualism. What is clear, what is "explained"? Only that which can be seen and felt—one must pursue every problem thus far. Obversely, however, the charm of the Platonic mode of thought, which was an *aristocratic* mode, consisted precisely in *resistance to* obvious sense-evidence—perhaps among men who enjoyed even stronger and more fastidious senses than our contemporaries, but who knew how to find a higher triumph in remaining masters of them: and this by means of pale, cold, grey conceptional networks which they threw over the motley whirl of the senses—the mob of the senses, as Plato said. In this overcoming of the world, and interpreting of the world in the manner of Plato, there was an *enjoyment* different from that which the physicists of today offer us—and likewise the Darwinists and antiteleologists among the physiological workers, with their principle of the "smallest possible effort," and the greatest possible blunder. "Where there is nothing more to see or to grasp, there is also nothing more for men to do"—that is certainly an imperative different from the Platonic one, but it may notwithstanding be the right imperative for a hardy, labourious race of machinists and bridge-builders of the future, who have nothing but *rough* work to perform.

15

To study physiology with a clear conscience, one must insist on the fact that the sense-organs are *not* phenomena in the sense of the idealistic philosophy; as such they certainly could not be causes! Sensualism, therefore, at least as regulative hypothesis, if not as heuristic principle. What? And others say even that the external world is the work of our organs? But then our body, as a part of this external world, would be the work of our organs! But then our organs themselves would be the work of our organs! It seems to me that this is a complete *reductio ad absurdum*, if the conception *causa sui* is something fundamentally absurd. Consequently, the external world is *not* the work of our organs?

16

There are still harmless self-observers who believe that there are "immediate certainties"; for instance, "I think," or as the superstition of Schopenhauer puts it, "I will"; as though cognition here got hold of its object purely and simply as "the thing in itself," without any falsification taking place either on the part of the subject or the object. I would repeat it, however, a hundred times, that "immediate certainty," as well as "absolute knowledge" and the "thing in itself," involve a *contradictio in adjecto*; we really ought to free ourselves from the misleading significance of words! The people on their part may think that cognition is knowing all about things, but the philosopher must say to himself:

When I analyse the process that is expressed in the sentence, "I think," I find a whole series of daring assertions, the argumentative proof of which would be difficult, perhaps impossible: for instance, that it is *I* who think, that there must necessarily be something that thinks, that thinking is an activity and operation on the part of a being who is thought of as a cause, that there is an "ego," and finally, that it is already determined what is to be designated by thinking—that I *know* what thinking is. For if I had not already decided within myself what it is, by what standard could I determine whether that which is just happening is not perhaps "willing" or "feeling?" In short, the assertion "I think," assumes that I *compare* my state at the present moment with other states of myself which I know, in order to determine what it is; on account of this retrospective connexion with further "knowledge," it has at any rate no immediate certainty for me.

In place of the "immediate certainty" in which the people may believe in the special case, the philosopher thus finds a series of metaphysical questions presented to him, veritable conscience questions of the intellect, to wit: "From whence did I get the notion of 'thinking?' Why do I believe in cause and effect? What gives me the right to speak of an 'ego,' and even of an 'ego' as cause, and finally of an 'ego' as cause of thought?" He who ventures to answer these metaphysical questions at once by an appeal to a sort of *intuitive* perception, like the person who says, "I think, and know that this, at least, is true, actual, and certain"—will encounter a smile and two notes of interrogation in a philosopher nowadays. "Sir," the philosopher will perhaps give him to understand, "it is improbable that you are not mistaken, but why should it be the truth?"

17

With regard to the superstitions of logicians, I shall never tire of emphasising a small, terse fact, which is unwillingly recognised by these credulous minds—namely, that a thought comes when "it" wishes, and not when "I" wish; so that it is a *perversion* of the facts of the case to say that the subject "I" is the condition of the predicate "think." *One* thinks; but that this "one" is precisely the famous old "ego," is, to put it mildly, only a supposition, an assertion, and assuredly not an "immediate certainty." After all, one has even gone too far with this "one thinks"—even the "one" contains an *interpretation* of the process, and does not belong to the process itself.

One infers here according to the usual grammatical formula—"To think is an activity; every activity requires an agency that is active; consequently. . . ." It was pretty much on the same lines that the older atomism sought, besides the operating "power," the material particle wherein it resides and out of which it operates—the atom. More rigorous minds, however, learnt at last to get along without this "earth-residuum," and perhaps someday we shall accustom ourselves, even from the logician's point of view, to get along without the little "one" (to which the worthy old "ego" has refined itself).

18

It is certainly not the least charm of a theory that it is refutable; it is precisely thereby that it attracts the more subtle minds. It seems that the hundred-times-refuted theory of the "free will" owes its persistence to this charm alone; someone is always appearing who feels himself strong enough to refute it.

19

Philosophers are accustomed to speak of the will as though it were the best-known thing in the world; indeed, Schopenhauer has given us to understand that the will alone is really known to us, absolutely and completely known, without deduction or addition. But it again and again seems to me that in this case Schopenhauer also only did what philosophers are in the habit of doing—he seems to have adopted a *popular prejudice* and exaggerated it. Willing—seems to me to be above all something *complicated*, something that is a unity only in name—and it is precisely in a name that popular prejudice lurks, which has got the mastery over the inadequate precautions of philosophers in all ages. So let us for once be more cautious, let us be "unphilosophical": let us say that in all willing there is firstly a plurality of sensations, namely, the sensation of the condition "*away from which* we go," the sensation of the condition "*towards which* we go," the sensation of this "*from*" and "*towards*" itself, and then besides, an accompanying muscular sensation, which, even without our putting in motion "arms and legs," commences its action by force of habit, directly we "will" anything. Therefore, just as sensations (and indeed many kinds of sensations) are to be recognised as ingredients of the will, so, in the second place, thinking is also to be recognised; in every act of the will there is a ruling thought; and let us not imagine it possible to sever this thought from the "willing," as if the will would then remain over! In the third place, the will is not only a complex of sensation and thinking, but it is above all an *emotion*, and in fact the emotion of the command. That which is termed "freedom of the will" is essentially the emotion of supremacy in respect to him who must obey: "I am free, 'he' must obey"—this consciousness is inherent in every will; and equally so the straining of the attention, the straight look which fixes itself exclusively on one thing, the unconditional judgement that "this and nothing else is necessary now," the inward certainty that obedience will be rendered— and whatever else pertains to the position of the commander. A man who *wills* commands something within himself which renders obedience, or which he believes renders obedience. But now let us notice what is the strangest thing about the will—this affair so extremely complex, for which the people have only one name. Inasmuch as in the given circumstances we are at the same time the commanding *and* the obeying parties, and as the obeying party we know the sensations of constraint, impulsion, pressure, resistance, and motion, which usually commence immediately after the act of will; inasmuch as, on the other hand, we are accustomed to disregard this duality, and to deceive ourselves about it by means of the synthetic term "I": a whole series of erroneous conclusions, and consequently of false judgements about the will itself, has become attached to the act of willing—to such a degree that he who wills believes firmly that willing *suffices* for action. Since in the majority of cases there has only been exercise of will when the effect of the command—consequently obedience, and therefore action—was to be *expected*, the *appearance* has translated itself into the sentiment, as if there were there a *necessity of effect*; in a word, he who wills believes with a fair amount of certainty that will and action are somehow one; he ascribes the success, the carrying out of the willing, to the will itself, and thereby enjoys an increase of the sensation of power which accompanies all success. "Freedom of Will"—that is the expression for the complex state of delight of the person exercising volition, who commands and at the same time identifies himself with the executor of the order—who, as such, enjoys also the triumph over obstacles, but thinks within himself that it was really his own will that overcame them. In this way the person exercising volition adds the feelings of delight of his successful executive instruments, the useful "underwills" or under-souls—indeed, our body is but a social structure composed of many souls—to his feelings of delight as commander. *L'effet c'est moi*: what happens here is what happens in every well-constructed and happy commonwealth, namely, that the governing class identifies itself with the successes of the commonwealth. In all willing it is absolutely a question of commanding and obeying, on the basis, as already said, of a social structure composed of many "souls"; on which account a philosopher should claim the right to include willing-as-such within the sphere of morals—regarded as the doctrine of the relations of supremacy under which the phenomenon of "life" manifests itself.

20

That the separate philosophical ideas are not anything optional or autonomously evolving, but grow up in connexion and relationship with each other; that, however suddenly and arbitrarily they seem to appear in the history of thought, they nevertheless belong just as much to a system as the collective members of the fauna of a Continent—is betrayed in the end by the circumstance: how unfailingly the most diverse philosophers always fill in again a definite fundamental scheme of *possible* philosophies. Under an invisible spell, they always revolve once more in the same orbit; however independent of each other they may feel themselves with their critical or systematic wills, something within them leads them, something impels them in definite order the one after the other— to wit, the innate methodology and relationship of their ideas. Their thinking is in fact far less a discovery than a re-recognising, a remembering, a return and a homecoming to a far-off, ancient common-household of the soul, out of which those ideas formerly grew: philosophising is so far a kind of atavism of the highest order. The wonderful family resemblance of all Indian, Greek, and German philosophising is easily enough explained. In fact, where there is affinity of language, owing to the common philosophy of grammar—I mean owing to the unconscious domination and guidance of similar grammatical functions—it cannot but be that everything is prepared at the outset for a similar development and succession of philosophical systems; just as the way seems barred against certain other possibilities of world-interpretation. It is highly probable that philosophers within the domain of the Ural-Altaic languages (where the conception of the subject is least developed) look otherwise "into the world," and will be found on paths of thought different from those of the Indo-Germans and Mussulmans, the spell of certain grammatical functions is ultimately also the spell of *physiological* valuations and racial conditions. So much by way of rejecting Locke's superficiality with regard to the origin of ideas.

21

The *causa sui* is the best self-contradiction that has yet been conceived, it is a sort of logical violation and unnaturalness; but the extravagant pride of man has managed to entangle itself profoundly and frightfully with this very folly. The desire for "freedom of will" in the superlative, metaphysical sense, such as still holds sway, unfortunately, in the minds of the half-educated, the desire to bear the entire and ultimate responsibility for one's actions oneself, and to absolve God, the world, ancestors, chance, and society therefrom, involves nothing less than to be precisely this *causa sui*, and, with more than Munchausen daring, to pull oneself up into existence by the hair, out of the slough of nothingness. If any one should find out in this manner the crass stupidity of the celebrated conception of "free will" and put it out of his head altogether, I beg of him to carry his "enlightenment" a step further, and also put out of his head the contrary of this monstrous conception of "free will": I mean "non-free will," which is tantamount to a misuse of cause and effect. One should not wrongly *materialise* "cause" and "effect," as the natural philosophers do (and whoever like them naturalise in thinking at present), according to the prevailing mechanical doltishness which makes the cause press and push until it "effects" its end; one should use "cause" and "effect" only as pure *conceptions*, that is to say, as conventional fictions for the purpose of designation and mutual understanding—*not* for explanation. In "being-in-itself" there is nothing of "causal-connexion," of "necessity," or of "psychological non-freedom"; there the effect does *not* follow the cause, there "law" does not obtain. It is *we* alone who have devised cause, sequence, reciprocity, relativity, constraint, number, law, freedom, motive, and purpose; and when we interpret and intermix this symbol-world, as "being in itself," with things, we act once more as we have always acted—*mythologically*. The "non-free will" is mythology; in real life it is only a question of *strong* and *weak* wills. It is almost always a symptom of what is lacking in himself, when a thinker, in every "causal-connexion" and "psychological necessity," manifests something of compulsion, indigence, obsequio-usness, oppression, and non-freedom; it is suspicious to have such feelings— the person betrays himself. And in general, if I have observed correctly, the "non-freedom of the will" is regarded as a problem from two entirely opposite standpoints, but always in a profoundly *personal* manner: some will not give up their "responsibility," their belief in *themselves*, the personal right to *their* merits, at any price (the vain races belong to this class); others on the contrary, do not wish to be answerable for anything, or blamed for anything, and owing to an inward self-contempt, seek *to get out of the business*, no matter how. The latter, when they write books, are in the habit at present of taking the side of criminals; a sort of socialistic sympathy is their favourite disguise. And as a matter of fact, the fatalism of the weak-willed embellishes itself surprisingly when it can pose as "*la religion de la souffrance humaine*"; that is *its* "good taste."

22

Let me be pardoned, as an old philologist who cannot desist from the mischief of putting his finger on bad modes of interpretation, but "Nature's conformity to law," of which you physicists talk so proudly, as though—why, it exists only owing to your interpretation and bad "philology." It is no matter of fact, no "text," but rather just a naïvely humanitarian adjustment and perversion of meaning, with which you make abundant concessions to the democratic instincts of the modern soul! "Everywhere equality before the law—Nature is not different in that respect, nor better than we": a fine instance of secret motive, in which the vulgar antagonism to everything privileged and autocratic—likewise a second and more refined atheism—is once more disguised. "*Ni dieu, ni maître*"—that, also, is what you want; and therefore "Cheers for natural law!" is it not so? But, as has been said, that is interpretation, not text; and somebody might come along, who, with opposite intentions and modes of interpretation, could read out of the same "Nature," and with regard to the same phenomena, just the tyrannically inconsiderate and relentless enforcement of the claims of power—an interpreter who should so place the unexceptionalness and unconditionalness of all "Will to Power" before your eyes, that almost every word, and the word "tyranny" itself, would eventually seem unsuitable, or like a weakening and softening metaphor—as being too human; and who should, nevertheless, end by asserting the same about this world as you do, namely, that it has a "necessary" and "calculable" course, *not*, however, because laws obtain in it, but because they are absolutely *lacking*, and every power effects its ultimate consequences every moment. Granted that this also is only interpretation—and you will be eager enough to make this objection? Well, so much the better.

23

All psychology hitherto has run aground on moral prejudices and timidities, it has not dared to launch out into the depths. Insofar as it is allowable to recognise in that which has hitherto been written, evidence of that which has hitherto been kept silent, it seems as if nobody has yet harboured the notion of psychology as the Morphology and *Development-doctrine of the Will to Power*, as I conceive of it. The power of moral prejudices has penetrated deeply into the most intellectual world, the world apparently most indifferent and unprejudiced, and has obviously operated in an injurious, obstructive, blinding, and distorting manner. A proper physio-psychology has to contend with unconscious antagonism in the heart of the investigator, it has "the heart" against it: even a doctrine of the reciprocal conditionalness of the "good" and the "bad" impulses, causes (as refined immorality) distress and aversion in a still strong and manly conscience—still more so, a doctrine of the derivation of all good impulses from bad ones. If, however, a person should regard even the emotions of hatred, envy, covetousness, and imperiousness as life-conditioning emotions, as factors which must be present, fundamentally and essentially, in the general economy of life (which must, therefore, be further developed if life is to be further developed), he will suffer from such a view of things as from seasickness. And yet this hypothesis is far from being the strangest and most painful in this immense and almost new domain of dangerous knowledge; and there are in fact a hundred good reasons why everyone should keep away from it who *can* do so! On the other hand, if one has once drifted hither with one's bark, well! Very good! Now let us set our teeth firmly! Let us open our eyes and keep our hand fast on the helm! We sail away right *over* morality, we crush out, we destroy perhaps the remains of our own morality by daring to make our voyage thither—but what do *we* matter! Never yet did a *profounder* world of insight reveal itself to daring travellers and adventurers, and the psychologist who thus "makes a sacrifice"—it is *not* the *sacrifizio dell' intelletto,* on the contrary! Will at least be entitled to demand in return that psychology shall once more be recognised as the queen of the sciences, for whose service and equipment the other sciences exist. For psychology is once more the path to the fundamental problems.

CHAPTER TWO

THE FREE SPIRIT

24

O SANCTA SIMPLICITAS! IN WHAT STRANGE SIMPLIFICATION AND FALSIFICATION man lives! One can never cease wondering when once one has got eyes for beholding this marvel! How we have made everything around us clear and free and easy and simple! How we have been able to give our senses a passport to everything superficial, our thoughts a godlike desire for wanton pranks and wrong inferences! How from the beginning, we have contrived to retain our ignorance in order to enjoy an almost inconceivable freedom, thoughtlessness, imprudence, heartiness, and gaiety—in order to enjoy life! And only on this solidified, granite-like foundation of ignorance could knowledge rear itself hitherto, the will to knowledge on the foundation of a far more powerful will, the will to ignorance, to the uncertain, to the untrue! Not as its opposite, but—as its refinement! It is to be hoped, indeed, that *language*, here as elsewhere, will not get over its awkwardness, and that it will continue to talk of opposites where there are only degrees and many refinements of gradation; it is equally to be hoped that the incarnated Tartuffery of morals, which now belongs to our unconquerable "flesh and blood," will turn the words round in the mouths of us discerning ones. Here and there we understand it, and laugh at the way in which precisely the best knowledge seeks most to retain us in this *simplified,* thoroughly artificial, suitably imagined and suitably falsified world: at the way in which, whether it will or not, it loves error, because, as living itself, it loves life!

25

After such a cheerful commencement, a serious word would fain be heard; it appeals to the most serious minds. Take care, ye philosophers and friends of knowledge, and beware of martyrdom! Of suffering "for the truth's sake!" even in your own defence! It spoils all the innocence and fine neutrality of your conscience; it makes you headstrong against objections and red rags; it stupefies, animalises, and brutalises, when in the struggle with danger, slander, suspicion, expulsion, and even worse consequences of enmity, ye have at last to play your last card as protectors of truth upon earth—as though "the Truth" were such an innocent and incompetent creature as to require protectors! And you of all people, ye knights of the sorrowful countenance, Messrs Loafers and Cobweb-spinners of the spirit! Finally, ye know sufficiently well that it cannot be of any consequence if *ye* just carry your point; ye know that hitherto no philosopher has carried his point, and that there might be a more laudable truthfulness in every little interrogative mark which you place after your special words and favourite doctrines (and occasionally after yourselves) than in all the solemn pantomime and trumping games before accusers and law-courts! Rather go out of the way! Flee into concealment! And have your masks and your ruses, that ye may be mistaken for what you are, or somewhat feared! And pray, don't forget the garden, the garden with golden trellis-work! And have people around you who are as a garden— or as music on the waters at eventide, when already the day becomes a memory. Choose the *good* solitude, the free, wanton, lightsome solitude, which also gives you the right still to remain good in any sense whatsoever! How poisonous, how crafty, how bad, does every long war make one, which cannot be waged openly by means of force! How *personal* does a long fear make one, a long watching of enemies, of possible enemies! These pariahs of society, these long-pursued, badly persecuted ones— also the compulsory recluses, the Spinozas or Giordano Brunos—always become in the end, even under the most intellectual masquerade, and perhaps without being themselves aware of it, refined vengeance-seekers and poison-brewers (just lay bare the foundation of Spinoza's ethics and theology!), not to speak of the stupidity of moral indignation, which is the unfailing sign in a philosopher that the sense of philosophical humour has left him. The martyrdom of the philosopher, his "sacrifice for the sake of truth," forces into the light whatever of the agitator and actor lurks in him; and if one has hitherto contemplated him only with artistic curiosity, with regard to many a philosopher it is easy to understand the dangerous desire to see him also in his deterioration (deteriorated into a "martyr," into a stage- and tribune-bawler). Only, that it is necessary with such a desire to be clear *what* spectacle one will see in any case—merely a satiric play, merely an epilogue farce, merely the continued proof that the long, real tragedy *is at an end*, supposing that every philosophy has been a long tragedy in its origin.

26

Every select man strives instinctively for a citadel and a privacy, where he is *free* from the crowd, the many, the majority—where he may forget "men who are the rule," as their exception; exclusive only of the case in which he is pushed straight to such men by a still stronger instinct, as a discerner in the great and exceptional sense. Whoever, in intercourse with men, does not occasionally glisten in all the green and grey colours of distress, owing to disgust, satiety, sympathy, gloominess and solitariness, is assuredly not a man of elevated tastes; supposing, however, that he does not voluntarily take all this burden and disgust upon himself, that he persistently avoids it, and remains, as I said, quietly and proudly hidden in his citadel, one thing is then certain: he was not made, he was not predestined for knowledge. For as such, he would one day have to say to himself: "The devil take my good taste! But 'the rule' is more interesting than the exception—than myself, the exception!" And he would go *down*, and above all, he would go "inside." The long and serious study of the *average* man—and consequently much disguise, self-overcoming, familiarity, and bad intercourse (all intercourse is bad intercourse except with one's equals): that constitutes a necessary part of the life-history of every philosopher; perhaps the most disagreeable, odious, and disappointing part. If he is fortunate, however, as a favourite child of knowledge should be, he will meet with suitable auxiliaries who will shorten and lighten his task; I mean so-called cynics, those who simply recognise the animal, the commonplace and "the rule" in themselves, and at the same time have so much spirituality and ticklishness as to make them talk of themselves and their like *before witnesses*—sometimes they wallow, even in books, as on their own dung-hill. Cynicism is the only form in which base souls approach what is called honesty; and the higher man must open his ears to all the coarser or finer cynicism, and congratulate himself when the clown becomes shameless right before him, or the scientific satyr speaks out. There are even cases where enchantment mixes with the disgust—namely, where by a freak of nature, genius is bound to some such indiscreet billy-goat and ape, as in the case of the Abbé Galiani, the profoundest, acutest, and perhaps also filthiest man of his century—he was far profounder than Voltaire, and consequently also, a good deal more silent. It happens more frequently, as has been hinted, that a scientific head is placed on an ape's body, a fine exceptional understanding in a base soul, an occurrence by no means rare, especially amongst doctors and moral physiologists. And whenever any one speaks without bitterness, or rather quite innocently of man, as a belly with two requirements, and a head with one; whenever any one sees, seeks and *wants* to see only hunger, sexual instinct, and vanity as the real and only motives of human actions; in short, when any one speaks "badly"—and not even "ill"—of man, then ought the lover of knowledge to hearken attentively and diligently; he ought, in general, to have an open ear wherever there is talk without indignation. For the indignant man, and he who perpetually tears and lacerates himself with his own teeth (or, in place of himself, the world, God, or society), may indeed, morally speaking, stand higher than the laughing and self-satisfied satyr, but in every other sense he is the more ordinary, more indifferent, and less instructive case. And no one is such a *liar* as the indignant man.

27

It is difficult to be understood, especially when one thinks and lives *gangas-rotogati*[1] among those only who think and live otherwise—namely, *kurmagati*,[2] or at best "froglike," *mandeikagati*[3] (I do everything to be "difficultly understood" myself!) and one should be heartily grateful for the goodwill to some refinement of interpretation. As regards "the good friends," however, who are always too easy-going, and think that as friends they have a right to ease, one does well at the very first to grant them a playground and romping-place for misunderstanding—one can thus laugh still; or get rid of them altogether, these good friends—and laugh then also!

28

What is most difficult to render from one language into another is the *tempo* of its style, which has its basis in the character of the race, or to speak more physiologically, in the average *tempo* of the assimilation of its nutriment. There are honestly meant translations, which, as involuntary vulgarisations, are almost falsifications of the original, merely because its lively and merry *tempo* (which overleaps and obviates all dangers in word and expression) could not also be rendered. A German is almost incapacitated for *presto* in his language; consequently also, as may be reasonably inferred, for many of the most delightful and daring nuances of free, free-spirited thought. And just as the buffoon and satyr are foreign to him in body and conscience, so Aristophanes and Petronius are untranslatable for him. Everything ponderous, viscous, and pompously clumsy, all long-winded and wearying species of style, are developed in profuse variety among Germans—pardon me for stating the fact that even Goethe's prose, in its mixture of stiffness and elegance, is no exception, as a reflexion of the "good old time" to which it belongs, and as an expression of German taste at a time when there was still a "German taste," which was a rococo-taste *in moribus et artibus*. Lessing is an exception, owing to his histrionic nature, which understood much, and was versed in many things; he who was not the translator of Bayle to no purpose, who took refuge willingly in the shadow of Diderot and Voltaire, and still more willingly among the Roman comedy-writers—Lessing loved also free-spiritism in the *tempo*, and flight out of Germany. But how could the German language, even in the prose of Lessing, imitate the *tempo* of Machiavelli, who in his *Principe* makes us breathe the dry, fine air of Florence, and cannot help presenting the most serious events in a boisterous *allegrissimo*, perhaps not without a malicious artistic sense of the contrast he ventures to present—long, heavy, difficult, dangerous thoughts, and a *tempo* of the gallop, and of the best, wantonest humour? Finally, who would venture on a German translation of Petronius, who, more than any great musician hitherto, was a master of *presto* in invention, ideas, and words? What matter in the end about the swamps of the sick, evil world, or of the "ancient world," when like him, one has the feet of a wind, the rush, the breath, the emancipating scorn of a wind, which makes everything healthy, by making everything *run*! And with regard to Aristophanes—that transfiguring, complementary genius, for whose sake one *pardons* all Hellenism for having existed, provided one has understood in its full profundity *all* that there requires pardon and trans-figuration; there is nothing that has caused me to meditate more on *Plato's* secrecy and sphinx-like nature, than the happily preserved *petit fait* that under the pillow of his deathbed there was found no "Bible," nor anything Egyptian, Pythagorean, or Platonic—but a book of Aristophanes. How could even a Plato have endured life—a Greek life which he repudiated—without an Aristophanes!

29

It is the business of the very few to be independent; it is a privilege of the strong. And whoever attempts it, even with the best right, but without being *obliged* to do so, proves that he is probably not only strong, but also daring beyond measure. He enters into a labyrinth, he multiplies a thousandfold the dangers which life in itself already brings with it; not the least of which is that no one can see how and where he loses his way, becomes isolated, and is torn piecemeal by some minotaur of conscience. Supposing such a one comes to grief, it is so far from the comprehension of men that they neither feel it, nor sympathise with it. And he cannot any longer go back! He cannot even go back again to the sympathy of men!

30

Our deepest insights must—and should—appear as follies, and under certain circumstances as crimes, when they come unauthorisedly to the ears of those who are not disposed and predestined for them. The exoteric and the esoteric, as they were formerly distinguished by philosophers—among the Indians, as among the Greeks, Persians, and Mussulmans, in short, wherever people believed in gradations of rank and *not* in equality and equal rights—are not so much in contradistinction to one another in respect to the exoteric class, standing without, and viewing, estimating, measuring, and judging from the outside, and not from the inside; the more essential distinction is that the class in question views things from below upwards—while the esoteric class views things *from above downwards.* There are heights of the soul from which tragedy itself no longer appears to operate tragically; and if all the woe in the world were taken together, who would dare to decide whether the sight of it would *necessarily* seduce and constrain to sympathy, and thus to a doubling of the woe? . . . That which serves the higher class of men for nourishment or refreshment, must be almost poison to an entirely different and lower order of human beings. The virtues of the common man would perhaps mean vice and weaknesses in a philosopher; it might be possible for a highly developed man, supposing him to degenerate and go to ruin, to acquire qualities thereby alone, for the sake of which he would have to be honoured as a saint in the lower world into which he had sunk. There are books which have an inverse value for the soul and the health according as the inferior soul and the lower vitality, or the higher and more powerful, make use of them. In the former case they are dangerous, disturbing, unsettling books, in the latter case they are herald-calls which summon the bravest to *their* bravery. Books for the general reader are always ill-smelling books, the odour of paltry people clings to them. Where the populace eat and drink, and even where they reverence, it is accustomed to stink. One should not go into churches if one wishes to breathe *pure* air.

31

In our youthful years we still venerate and despise without the art of *nuance*, which is the best gain of life, and we have rightly to do hard penance for having fallen upon men and things with Yea and Nay. Everything is so arranged that the worst of all tastes, *the taste for the unconditional*, is cruelly befooled and abused, until a man learns to introduce a little art into his sentiments, and prefers to try conclusions with the artificial, as do the real artists of life. The angry and reverent spirit peculiar to youth appears to allow itself no peace, until it has suitably falsified men and things, to be able to vent its passion upon them: youth in itself even, is something falsifying and deceptive. Later on, when the young soul, tortured by continual disillusions, finally turns suspiciously against itself—still ardent and savage even in its suspicion and remorse of conscience: how it upbraids itself, how impatiently it tears itself, how it revenges itself for its long self-blinding, as though it had been a voluntary blindness! In this transition one punishes oneself by distrust of one's sentiments; one tortures one's enthusiasm with doubt, one feels even the good conscience to be a danger, as if it were the self-concealment and lassitude of a more refined uprightness; and above all, one espouses upon principle the cause *against* "youth." A decade later, and one comprehends that all this also was still-youth!

32

Throughout the longest period of human history—one calls it the prehistoric period—the value or non-value of an action was inferred from its *consequences*; the action in itself was not taken into consideration, anymore than its origin; but pretty much as in China at present, where the distinction or disgrace of a child redounds to its parents, the retro-operating power of success or failure was what induced men to think well or ill of an action. Let us call this period the *pre-moral* period of mankind; the imperative, "know thyself!" was then still unknown. In the last ten thousand years, on the other hand, on certain large portions of the earth, one has gradually got so far, that one no longer lets the consequences of an action, but its origin, decide with regard to its worth: a great achievement as a whole, an important refinement of vision and of criterion, the unconscious effect of the supremacy of aristocratic values and of the belief in "origin," the mark of a period which may be designated in the narrower sense as the *moral* one: the first attempt at self-knowledge is thereby made. Instead of the consequences, the origin—what an inversion of perspective! And assuredly an inversion effected only after long struggle and wavering! To be sure, an ominous new superstition, a peculiar narrowness of interpretation, attained supremacy precisely thereby: the origin of an action was interpreted in the most definite sense possible, as origin out of an *intention*; people were agreed in the belief that the value of an action lay in the value of its intention. The intention as the sole origin and antecedent history of an action: under the influence of this prejudice moral praise and blame have been bestowed, and men have judged and even philosophised almost up to the present day. Is it not possible, however, that the necessity may now have arisen of again making up our minds with regard to the reversing and fundamental shifting of values, owing to a new self-consciousness and acuteness in man—is it not possible that we may be standing on the threshold of a period which to begin with, would be distinguished negatively as *ultra-moral*: nowadays when, at least amongst us immoralists, the suspicion arises that the decisive value of an action lies precisely in that which is *not intentional*, and that all its intentionalness, all that is seen, sensible, or "sensed" in it, belongs to its surface or skin—which, like every skin, betrays something, but *conceals* still more? In short, we believe that the intention is only a sign or symptom, which first requires an explanation—a sign, moreover, which has too many interpretations, and consequently hardly any meaning in itself alone: that morality, in the sense in which it has been understood hitherto, as intention-morality, has been a prejudice, perhaps a prematureness or preliminariness, probably something of the same rank as astrology and alchymy, but in any case something which must be surmounted. The surmounting of morality, in a certain sense even the self-surmounting of morality—let that be the name for the long secret labour which has been reserved for the most refined, the most upright, and also the most wicked consciences of today, as the living touchstones of the soul.

33

It cannot be helped: the sentiment of surrender, of sacrifice for one's neighbour, and all self-renunciation - morality, must be mercilessly called to account, and brought to judgement; just as the aesthetics of "disinterested contemplation," under which the emasculation of art nowadays seeks insidiously enough to create itself a good conscience. There is far too much witchery and sugar in the sentiments "for others" and "*not* for myself," for one not needing to be doubly distrustful here, and for one asking promptly: "Are they not perhaps—*deceptions?*" That they *please*—him who has them, and him who enjoys their fruit, and also the mere spectator—that is still no argument in their *favour*, but just calls for caution. Let us therefore be cautious!

34

At whatever standpoint of philosophy one may place oneself nowadays, seen from every position, the *erroneousness* of the world in which we think we live is the surest and most certain thing our eyes can light upon: we find proof after proof thereof, which would fain allure us into surmises concerning a deceptive principle in the "nature of things." He, however, who makes thinking itself, and consequently "the spirit," responsible for the falseness of the world—an honourable exit, which every conscious or unconscious *advocatus dei* avails himself of—he who regards this world, including space, time, form, and movement, as falsely *deduced*, would have at least good reason in the end to become distrustful also of all thinking; has it not hitherto been playing upon us the worst of scurvy tricks? And what guarantee would it give that it would not continue to do what it has always been doing? In all seriousness, the innocence of thinkers has something touching and respect-inspiring in it, which even nowadays permits them to wait upon consciousness with the request that it will give them *honest* answers: for example, whether it be "real" or not, and why it keeps the outer world so resolutely at a distance, and other questions of the same description. The belief in "immediate certainties" is a *moral naïveté* which does honour to us philosophers; but—we have now to cease being "*merely* moral" men! Apart from morality, such belief is a folly which does little honour to us! If in middle-class life an ever-ready distrust is regarded as the sign of a "bad character," and consequently as an imprudence, here amongst us, beyond the middle-class world and its Yeas and Nays, what should prevent us being imprudent and saying: the philosopher has at length a *right* to "bad character," as the being who has hitherto been most befooled on earth—he is now under *obligation* to distrustfulness, to the wickedest squinting out of every abyss of suspicion. Forgive me the joke of this gloomy grimace and turn of expression; for I myself have long ago learned to think and estimate differently with regard to deceiving and being deceived, and I keep at least a couple of pokes in the ribs ready for the blind rage with which philosophers struggle against being deceived. Why *not?* It is nothing more than a moral prejudice that truth is worth more than semblance; it is, in fact, the worst proved supposition in the world. *So* much must be conceded: there could have been no life at all except upon the basis of perspective estimates and semblance's; and if, with the virtuous enthusiasm and stupidity of many philosophers, one wished to do away altogether with the "seeming world"—well, granted that *you* could do that—at least nothing of your "truth" would thereby remain! Indeed, what is it that forces us in general to the supposition that there is an essential opposition of "true" and "false?" Is it not enough to suppose degrees of seemingness, and as it were lighter and darker shades and tones of semblance—different *valeurs*, as the painters say? Why might not the world *which concerns us*—be a fiction? And to any one who suggested: "But to a fiction belongs an originator?" might it not be bluntly replied: *Why?* May not this "belong" also belong to the fiction? Is it not at length permitted to be a little ironical towards the subject, just as towards the predicate and object? Might not the philosopher elevate himself above faith in grammar? All respect to governesses, but is it not time that philosophy should renounce governess-faith?

35

O Voltaire! O humanity! O idiocy! There is something ticklish in "the truth," and in the *search* for the truth; and if man goes about it too humanely—"*il ne cherche le vrai que pour faire le bien*"—I wager he finds nothing!

36

Supposing that nothing else is "given" as real but our world of desires and passions, that we cannot sink or rise to any other "reality" but just that of our impulses—for thinking is only a relation of these impulses to one another: are we not permitted to make the attempt and to ask the question whether this which is "given" does not *suffice*, by means of our counterparts, for the understanding even of the so-called mechanical (or "material") world? I do not mean as an illusion, a "semblance," a "representation" (in the Berkeleyan and Schopenhauerian sense), but as possessing the same degree of reality as our emotions themselves—as a more primitive form of the world of emotions, in which everything still lies locked in a mighty unity, which afterwards branches off and develops itself in organic processes (naturally also, refines and debilitates)—as a kind of instinctive life in which all organic functions, including self-regulation, assimilation, nutrition, secretion, and change of matter, are still synthetically united with one another—as a *primary form* of life? In the end, it is not only permitted to make this attempt, it is commanded by the conscience of *logical method*. Not to assume several kinds of causality, so long as the attempt to get along with a single one has not been pushed to its furthest extent (to absurdity, if I may be allowed to say so): that is a morality of method which one may not repudiate nowadays—it follows "from its definition," as mathematicians say. The question is ultimately whether we really recognise the will as *operating*, whether we believe in the causality of the will; if we do so—and fundamentally our belief *in this* is just our belief in causality itself—we *must* make the attempt to posit hypothetically the causality of the will as the only causality. "Will" can naturally only operate on "will"—and not on "matter" (not on "nerves," for instance): in short, the hypothesis must be hazarded, whether will does not operate on will wherever "effects" are recognised—and whether all mechanical action, inasmuch as a power operates therein, is not just the power of will, the effect of will. Granted, finally, that we succeeded in explaining our entire instinctive life as the development and ramification of one fundamental form of will—namely, the Will to Power, as *my* thesis puts it; granted that all organic functions could be traced back to this Will to Power, and that the solution of the problem of generation and nutrition—it is one problem—could also be found therein: one would thus have acquired the right to define *all* active force unequivocally as *Will to Power*. The world seen from within, the world defined and designated according to its "intelligible character"—it would simply be "Will to Power," and nothing else.

37

"What? Does not that mean in popular language: God is disproved, but not the devil?" On the contrary! On the contrary, my friends! And who the devil also compels you to speak popularly!

38

As happened finally in all the enlightenment of modern times with the French Revolution (that terrible farce, quite superfluous when judged close at hand, into which, however, the noble and visionary spectators of all Europe have interpreted from a distance their own indignation and enthusiasm so long and passionately, *until the text has disappeared under the interpretation*), so a noble posterity might once more misunderstand the whole of the past, and perhaps only thereby make *its* aspect endurable. Or rather, has not this already happened? Have not we ourselves been—that "noble posterity?" And, insofar as we now comprehend this, is it not— thereby already past?

39

Nobody will very readily regard a doctrine as true merely because it makes people happy or virtuous—excepting perhaps the amiable "Idealists," who are enthusiastic about the good, true, and beautiful, and let all kinds of motley, coarse, and good-natured desirabilities swim about promiscuously in their pond. Happiness and virtue are no arguments. It is willingly forgotten, however, even on the part of thoughtful minds, that to make unhappy and to make bad are just as little counter-arguments. A thing could be *true*, although it were in the highest degree injurious and dangerous; indeed, the fundamental constitution of existence might be such that one succumbed by a full knowledge of it—so that the strength of a mind might be measured by the amount of "truth" it could endure—or to speak more plainly, by the extent to which it *required* truth attenuated, veiled, sweetened, damped, and falsified. But there is no doubt that for the discovery of certain *portions* of truth the wicked and unfortunate are more favourably situated and have a greater likelihood of success; not to speak of the wicked who are happy—a species about whom moralists are silent. Perhaps severity and craft are more favourable conditions for the development of strong, independent spirits and philosophers than the gentle, refined, yielding good-nature, and habit of taking-things easily, which are prized, and rightly prized in a learned man. Presupposing always, to begin with, that the term "philosopher" be not confined to the philosopher who writes books, or even introduces *his* philosophy into books! Stendhal furnishes a last feature of the portrait of the free-spirited philosopher, which for the sake of German taste I will not omit to underline —for it is *opposed* to German taste. "*Pour être bon philosophe*," says this last great psychologist, "*il faut être sec, clair, sans illusion. Un banquier, qui a fait fortune, a une partie du caractère requis pour faire des découvertes en philosophie, c'est-à-dire pour voir clair dans ce qui est.*"

40

Everything that is profound loves the mask; the profoundest things have a hatred even of figure and likeness. Should not the *contrary* only be the right disguise for the shame of a God to go about in? A question worth asking! It would be strange if some mystic has not already ventured on the same kind of thing. There are proceedings of such a delicate nature that it is well to overwhelm them with coarseness and make them unrecognisable; there are actions of love and of an extravagant magnanimity after which nothing can be wiser than to take a stick and thrash the witness soundly: one thereby obscures his recollection. Many a one is able to obscure and abuse his own memory, in order at least to have vengeance on this sole party in the secret: shame is inventive. They are not the worst things of which one is most ashamed: there is not only deceit behind a mask—there is so much goodness in craft. I could imagine that a man with something costly and fragile to conceal, would roll through life clumsily and rotundly like an old, green, heavily hoped wine-cask: the refinement of his shame requiring it to be so. A man who has depths in his shame meets his destiny and his delicate decisions upon paths which few ever reach, and with regard to the existence of which his nearest and most intimate friends may be ignorant; his mortal danger conceals itself from their eyes, and equally so his regained security. Such a hidden nature, which instinctively employs speech for silence and concealment, and is inexhaustible in evasion of communication, *desires* and insists that a mask of himself shall occupy his place in the hearts and heads of his friends; and supposing he does not desire it, his eyes will some day be opened to the fact that there is nevertheless a mask of him there—and that it is well to be so. Every profound spirit needs a mask; nay, more, around every profound spirit there continually grows a mask, owing to the constantly false, that is to say, *superficial* interpretation of every word he utters, every step he takes, every sign of life he manifests.

41

One must subject oneself to one's own tests that one is destined for independence and command, and do so at the right time. One must not avoid one's tests, although they constitute perhaps the most dangerous game one can play, and are in the end tests made only before ourselves and before no other judge. Not to cleave to any person, be it even the dearest—every person is a prison and also a recess. Not to cleave to a fatherland, be it even the most suffering and necessitous—it is even less difficult to detach one's heart from a victorious fatherland. Not to cleave to a sympathy, be it even for higher men, into whose peculiar torture and helplessness chance has given us an insight. Not to cleave to a science, though it tempt one with the most valuable discoveries, apparently specially reserved for *us*. Not to cleave to one's own liberation, to the voluptuous distance and remoteness of the bird, which always flies further aloft in order always to see more under it—the danger of the flier. Not to cleave to our own virtues, nor become as a whole a victim to any of our specialities, to our "hospitality" for instance, which is the danger of dangers for highly developed and wealthy souls, who deal prodigally, almost indifferently with themselves, and push the virtue of liberality so far that it becomes a vice. One must know how *to conserve oneself*—the best test of independence.

42

A new order of philosophers is appearing; I shall venture to baptise them by a name not without danger. As far as I understand them, as far as they allow themselves to be understood—for it is their nature to *wish* to remain something of a puzzle—these philosophers of the future might rightly, perhaps also wrongly, claim to be designated as "*tempters!* " This name itself is after all only an attempt, or, if it be preferred, a temptation.

43

Will they be new friends of "truth," these coming philosophers? Very probably, for all philosophers hitherto have loved their truths. But assuredly they will not be dogmatists. It must be contrary to their pride, and also contrary to their taste, that their truth should still be truth for everyone— that which has hitherto been the secret wish and ultimate purpose of all dogmatic efforts. "My opinion is *my* opinion: another person has not easily a right to it"—such a philosopher of the future will say, perhaps. One must renounce the bad taste of wishing to agree with many people. "Good" is no longer good when one's neighbour takes it into his mouth. And how could there be a "common good!" The expression contradicts itself; that which can be common is always of small value. In the end things must be as they are and have always been—the great things remain for the great, the abysses for the profound, the delicacies and thrills for the refined, and, to sum up shortly, everything rare for the rare.

44

Need I say expressly after all this that they will be free, *very* free spirits, these philosophers of the future—as certainly also they will not be merely free spirits, but something more, higher, greater, and fundamentally different, which does not wish to be misunderstood and mistaken? But while I say this, I feel under *obligation* almost as much to them as to ourselves (we free spirits who are their heralds and forerunners), to sweep away from ourselves altogether a stupid old prejudice and misunderstanding, which, like a fog, has too long made the conception of "free spirit" obscure. In every country of Europe, and the same in America, there is at present something which makes an abuse of this name: a very narrow, prepossessed, enchained class of spirits, who desire almost the opposite of what our intentions and instincts prompt—not to mention that in respect to the *new* philosophers who are appearing, they must still more be closed windows and bolted doors. Briefly and regrettably, they belong to the *levellers*, these wrongly named "free spirits"—as glib-tongued and scribe-fingered slaves of the democratic taste and its "modern ideas": all of them men without solitude, without personal solitude, blunt honest fellows to whom neither courage nor honourable conduct ought to be denied; only, they are not free, and are ludicrously superficial, especially in their innate partiality for seeing the cause of almost *all* human misery and failure in the old forms in which society has hitherto existed—a notion which happily inverts the truth entirely! What they would fain attain with all their strength, is the universal, green-meadow happiness of the herd, together with security, safety, comfort, and alleviation of life for everyone; their two most frequently chanted songs and doctrines are called "Equality of Rights" and "Sympathy with all Sufferers"—and suffering itself is looked upon by them as something which must be *done away with*. We opposite ones, however, who have opened our eye and conscience to the question how and where the plant "man" has hitherto grown most vigorously, believe that this has always taken place under the opposite conditions, that for this end the dangerousness of his situation had to be increased enormously, his inventive faculty and dissembling power (his "spirit") had to develop into subtlety and daring under long oppression and compulsion, and his Will to Life had to be increased to the unconditioned Will to Power: we believe that severity, violence, slavery, danger in the street and in the heart, secrecy, stoicism, tempter's art and devilry of every kind— that everything wicked, terrible, tyrannical, predatory, and serpentine in man, serves as well for the elevation of the human species as its opposite: we do not even say enough when we only say *this much*; and in any case we find ourselves here, both with our speech and our silence, at the *other* extreme of all modern ideology and gregarious desirability, as their antipodes perhaps? What wonder that we "free spirits" are not exactly the most communicative spirits? That we do not wish to betray in every respect *what* a spirit can free itself from, and *where* perhaps it will then be driven?

And as to the import of the dangerous formula, *Beyond Good and Evil*, with which we at least avoid confusion, we *are* something else than "*libres-penseurs*" "*liberi pensatori*," "freethinkers," and whatever these honest advocates of "modern ideas" like to call themselves. Having been at home, or at least guests, in many realms of the spirit; having escaped again and again from the gloomy, agreeable nooks in which preferences and prejudices, youth, origin, the accident of men and books, or even the weariness of travell seemed to confine us; full of malice against the seductions of dependency which lie concealed in honours, money, positions, or exaltation of the senses; grateful even for distress and the vicissitudes of illness, because they always free us from some rule, and its "prejudice," grateful to the God, devil, sheep, and worm in us; inquisitive to a fault, investigators to the point of cruelty, with unhesitating fingers for the intangible, with teeth and stomachs for the most indigestible, ready for any business that requires sagacity and acute senses, ready for every adventure, owing to an excess of "free will"; with anterior and posterior souls, into the ultimate intentions of which it is difficult to pry, with foregrounds and backgrounds to the end of which no foot may run; hidden ones under the mantles of light, appropriators, although we resemble heirs and spendthrifts, arrangers and collectors from morning till night, misers of our wealth and our full-crammed drawers, economical in learning and forgetting, inventive in scheming; sometimes proud of tables of categories, sometimes pedants, sometimes night-owls of work even in full day; yea, if necessary, even scarecrows—and it is necessary nowadays, that is to say, inasmuch as we are the born, sworn, jealous friends of *solitude*, of our own profoundest midnight and midday solitude: such kind of men are we, we free spirits! And perhaps *ye* are also something of the same kind, ye coming ones? Ye *new* philosophers?

CHAPTER THREE

THE RELIGIOUS MOOD

45

THE HUMAN SOUL AND ITS LIMITS, THE RANGE OF MAN'S INNER EXPERIENCES hitherto attained, the heights, depths and distances of these experiences, the entire history of the soul *up to the present time*, and its still unexhausted possibilities: this is the preordained hunting-domain for a born psychologist and lover of a "big hunt." But how often must he say despairingly to himself: "A single individual! Alas, only a single individual! And this great forest, this virgin forest!" So he would like to have some hundreds of hunting assistants, and fine trained hounds, that he could send into the history of the human soul, to drive *his* game together. In vain: again and again he experiences, profoundly and bitterly, how difficult it is to find assistants and dogs for all the things that directly excite his curiosity. The evil of sending scholars into new and dangerous hunting-domains, where courage, sagacity, and subtlety in every sense are required, is that they are no longer serviceable just when the "*big* hunt," and also the great danger commences—it is precisely then that they lose their keen eye and nose. In order, for instance, to divine and determine what sort of history the problem of *knowledge and conscience* has hitherto had in the souls of *homines religiosi*, a person would perhaps himself have to possess as profound, as bruised, as immense an experience as the intellectual conscience of Pascal; and then he would still require that wide-spread heaven of clear, wicked spirituality, which, from above, would be able to oversee, arrange, and effectively formulise this mass of dangerous and painful experiences. But who could do me this service! And who would have time to wait for such servants! They evidently appear too rarely, they are so improbable at all times! Eventually one must do everything *oneself* in order to know something; which means that one has *much* to do! But a curiosity like mine is once for all the most agreeable of vices—pardon me! I mean to say that the love of truth has its reward in heaven, and already upon earth.

46

Faith, such as early Christianity desired, and not infrequently achieved in the midst of a sceptical and southernly free-spirited world, which had centuries of struggle between philosophical schools behind it and in it, counting besides the education in tolerance which the *imperium Romanum* gave—this faith is *not* that sincere, austere slave-faith by which perhaps a Luther or a Cromwell, or some other northern barbarian of the spirit remained attached to his God and Christianity; it is much rather the faith of Pascal, which resembles in a terrible manner a continuous suicide of reason—a tough, long-lived, wormlike reason, which is not to be slain at once and with a single blow. The Christian faith from the beginning, is sacrifice: the sacrifice of all freedom, all pride, all self-confidence of spirit; it is at the same time subjection, self-derision, and self-mutilation. There is cruelty and religious Phœnicianism in this faith, which is adapted to a tender, many-sided, and very fastidious conscience; it takes for granted that the subjection of the spirit is indescribably *painful*, that all the past and all the habits of such a spirit resist the *absurdissimum*, in the form of which "faith" comes to it. Modern men, with their obtuseness as regards all Christian nomenclature, have no longer the sense for the terribly superlative conception which was implied to an antique taste by the paradox of the formula, "God on the Cross." Hitherto there had never and nowhere been such boldness in inversion, nor anything at once so dreadful, questioning, and questionable as this formula: it promised a trans-valuation of all ancient values. It was the Orient, the *profound* Orient, it was the Oriental slave who thus took revenge on Rome and its noble, light-minded toleration, on the Roman "Catholicism" of non-faith; and it was always, not the faith, but the freedom from the faith, the half-stoical and smiling indifference to the seriousness of the faith, which made the slaves indignant at their masters and revolt against them. "Enlightenment" causes revolt: for the slave desires the unconditioned, he understands nothing but the tyrannous, even in morals; he loves as he hates, without *nuance*, to the very depths, to the point of pain, to the point of sickness—his many *hidden* sufferings make him revolt against the noble taste which seems to *deny* suffering. The scepticism with regard to suffering, fundamentally only an attitude of aristocratic morality, was not the least of the causes, also, of the last great slave-insurrection which began with the French Revolution.

47

Wherever the religious neurosis has appeared on the earth so far, we find it connected with three dangerous prescriptions as to regimen: solitude, fasting, and sexual abstinence—but without it being possible to determine with certainty which is cause and which is effect, or *if* any relation at all of cause and effect exists there. This latter doubt is justified by the fact that one of the most regular symptoms among savage as well as among civilised peoples is the most sudden and excessive sensuality; which then with equal suddenness transforms into penitential paroxysms, world-renunciation, and will-renunciation: both symptoms perhaps explainable as disguised epilepsy? But nowhere is it *more* obligatory to put aside explanations: around no other type has there grown such a mass of absurdity and superstition, no other type seems to have been more interesting to men and even to philosophers—perhaps it is time to become just a little indifferent here, to learn caution, or, better still, to look away, *to go away*. Yet in the background of the most recent philosophy, that of Schopenhauer, we find almost as the problem in itself, this terrible note of interrogation of the religious crisis and awakening. How is the negation of will *possible?* How is the saint possible? That seems to have been the very question with which Schopenhauer made a start and became a philosopher. And thus it was a genuine Schopenhauerian consequence, that his most convinced adherent (perhaps also his last, as far as Germany is concerned), namely, Richard Wagner, should bring his own lifework to an end just here, and should finally put that terrible and eternal type upon the stage as Kundry, *type vécu*, and as it loved and lived, at the very time that the mad-doctors in almost all European countries had an opportunity to study the type close at hand, wherever the religious neurosis—or as I call it, "the religious mood"—made its latest epidemical outbreak and display as the "Salvation Army." If it be a question, however, as to what has been so extremely interesting to men of all sorts in all ages, and even to philosophers, in the whole phenomenon of the saint, it is undoubtedly the appearance of the miraculous therein—namely, the immediate *succession of opposites*, of states of the soul regarded as morally antithetical: it was believed here to be self-evident that a "bad man" was all at once turned into a "saint," a good man. The hitherto existing psychology was wrecked at this point; is it not possible it may have happened principally because psychology had placed itself under the dominion of morals, because it *believed* in oppositions of moral values, and saw, read, and *interpreted* these oppositions into the text and facts of the case? What? "Miracle" only an error of interpretation? A lack of philology?

48

It seems that the Latin races are far more deeply attached to their Catholicism than we Northerners are to Christianity generally, and that consequently unbelief in Catholic countries means something quite different from what it does among Protestants—namely, a sort of revolt against the spirit of the race, while with us it is rather a return to the spirit (or nonspirit) of the race. We Northerners undoubtedly derive our origin from barbarous races, even as regards our talents for religion—we have *poor* talents for it. One may make an exception in the case of the Celts, who have therefore furnished also the best soil for the Christian infection in the north: the Christian ideal blossomed forth in France as much as ever the pale sun of the north would allow it. How strangely pious for our taste are still these later French sceptics, whenever there is any Celtic blood in their origin! How Catholic, how un-German does Auguste Comte's Sociology seem to us, with the Roman logic of its instincts! How Jesuitical, that amiable and shrewd cicerone of Port-Royal, Sainte-Beuve, in spite of all his hostility to Jesuits! And even Ernest Renan: how inaccessible to us Northerners does the language of such a Renan appear, in whom every instant the merest touch of religious thrill throws his refinedly voluptuous and comfortably couching soul off its balance! Let us repeat after him these fine sentences—and what wickedness and haughtiness is immediately aroused by way of answer in our probably less beautiful but harder souls, that is to say, in our more German souls! *Disons donc hardiment que la religion est un produit de l'homme normal, que l'homme est le plus dans le vrai quand il est le plus religieux et le plus assuré d'une destince infinie. . . . C'est quand il est bon qu'il veut que la virtu corresponde à un order éternel, c'est quand il contemple les choses d'une manière désintéressée qu'il trouve la mort révoltante et absurde. Comment ne pas supposer que c'est dans ces moments-là, que l'homme voit le mieux?* . . . These sentences are so extremely *antipodal* to my ears and habits of thought, that in my first impulse of rage on finding them, I wrote on the margin, "*la niaiserie religieuse par excellence!*" until in my later rage I even took a fancy to them, these sentences with their truth absolutely inverted! It is so nice and such a distinction to have one's own antipodes!

49

That which is so astonishing in the religious life of the ancient Greeks is the irrestrainable stream of *gratitude* which it pours forth—it is a very superior kind of man who takes *such* an attitude towards nature and life. Later on, when the populace got the upper hand in Greece, *fear* became rampant also in religion; and Christianity was preparing itself.

50

The passion for God: there are churlish, honest-hearted, and importunate kinds of it, like that of Luther—the whole of Protestantism lacks the southern *delicatezza*. There is an Oriental exaltation of the mind in it, like that of an undeservedly favoured or elevated slave, as in the case of St. Augustine, for instance, who lacks in an offensive manner, all nobility in bearing and desires. There is a feminine tenderness and sensuality in it, which modestly and unconsciously longs for a *unio mystica et physica*, as in the case of Madame de Guyon. In many cases it appears, curiously enough, as the disguise of a girl's or youth's puberty; here and there even as the hysteria of an old maid, also as her last ambition. The Church has frequently canonised the woman in such a case.

51

The mightiest men have hitherto always bowed reverently before the saint, as the enigma of self-subjugation and utter voluntary privation —why did they thus bow? They divined in him—and as it were behind the questionableness of his frail and wretched appearance the superior force which wished to test itself by such a subjugation; the strength of will, in which they recognised their own strength and love of power, and knew how to honour it: they honoured something in themselves when they honoured the saint. In addition to this, the contemplation of the saint suggested to them a suspicion: such an enormity of self-negation and anti-naturalness will not have been coveted for nothing—they have said, inquiringly. There is perhaps a reason for it, some very great danger, about which the ascetic might wish to be more accurately informed through his secret interlocutors and visitors? In a word, the mighty ones of the world learned to have a new fear before him, they divined a new power, a strange, still unconquered enemy: it was the "Will to Power" which obliged them to halt before the saint. They had to question him.

52

In the Jewish Old Testament, the book of divine justice, there are men, things, and sayings on such an immense scale, that Greek and Indian literature has nothing to compare with it. One stands with fear and reverence before those stupendous remains of what man was formerly, and one has sad thoughts about old Asia and its little out-pushed peninsula Europe, which would like, by all means, to figure before Asia as the *Progress of Mankind.* To be sure, he who is himself only a slender, tame house-animal, and knows only the wants of a house-animal (like our cultured people of today, including the Christians of "cultured" Christianity), need neither be amazed nor even sad amid those ruins—the taste for the Old Testament is a touchstone with respect to "great" and "small": perhaps he will find that the New Testament, the book of grace, still appeals more to his heart (there is much of the odour of the genuine, tender, stupid beadsman and petty soul in it). To have bound up this New Testament (a kind of *rococo* of taste in every respect) along with the Old Testament into one book, as the Bible, as *The Book in Itself,* is perhaps the greatest audacity and "sin against the Spirit" which literary Europe has upon its conscience,

53

Why Atheism nowadays? "The father" in God is thoroughly refuted; equally so "the judge," "the rewarder." Also his "free will": he does not hear—and even if he did, he would not know how to help. The worst is that he seems incapable of communicating himself clearly; is he uncertain? This is what I have made out (by questioning, and listening at a variety of conversations) to be the cause of the decline of European theism; it appears to me that though the religious instinct is in vigorous growth—it rejects the theistic satisfaction with profound distrust.

54

What does all modern philosophy mainly do? Since Descartes—and indeed more in defiance of him than on the basis of his procedure—an *attentat* has been made on the part of all philosophers on the old conception of the soul, under the guise of a criticism of the subject and predicate conception—that is to say, an *attentat* on the fundamental presupposition of Christian doctrine. Modern philosophy, as epistemological scepticism, is secretly or openly *anti-Christian,* although (for keener ears, be it said) by no means antireligious. Formerly, in effect, one believed in "the soul" as one believed in grammar and the grammatical subject: one said, "I" is the condition, "think" is the predicate and is conditioned—to think is an activity for which one *must* suppose a subject as cause. The attempt was then made, with marvellous tenacity and subtlety, to see if one could not get out of this net—to see if the opposite was not perhaps true: "think" the condition, and "I" the conditioned; "I," therefore, only a synthesis which has been *made* by thinking itself. *Kant* really wished to prove that, starting from the subject, the subject could not be proved—nor the object either: the possibility of an *apparent existence* of the subject, and therefore of "the soul," may not always have been strange to him—the thought which once had an immense power on earth as the Vedanta philosophy.

55

There is a great ladder of religious cruelty, with many rounds; but three of these are the most important. Once on a time men sacrificed human beings to their God, and perhaps just those they loved the best—to this category belong the firstling sacrifices of all primitive religions, and also the sacrifice of the Emperor Tiberius in the Mithra-Grotto on the Island of Capri, that most terrible of all Roman anachronisms. Then, during the moral epoch of mankind, they sacrificed to their God the strongest instincts they possessed, their "nature"; *this* festal joy shines in the cruel glances of ascetics and "anti-natural" fanatics. Finally, what still remained to be sacrificed? Was it not necessary in the end for men to sacrifice everything comforting, holy, healing, all hope, all faith in hidden harmonies, in future blessedness and justice? Was it not necessary to sacrifice God himself, and out of cruelty to themselves to worship stone, stupidity, gravity, fate, nothingness? To sacrifice God for nothingness—this paradoxical mystery of the ultimate cruelty has been reserved for the rising generation; we all know something thereof already.

56

Whoever, like myself, prompted by some enigmatical desire, has long endeavoured to go to the bottom of the question of pessimism and free it from the half-Christian, half-German narrowness and stupidity in which it has finally presented itself to this century, namely, in the form of Schopenhauer's philosophy; whoever, with an Asiatic and super-Asiatic eye, has actually looked inside, and into the most world-renouncing of all possible modes of thought—beyond good and evil, and no longer like Buddha and Schopenhauer, under the dominion and delusion of morality—whoever has done this, has perhaps just thereby, without really desiring it, opened his eyes to behold the opposite ideal: the ideal of the most world-approving, exuberant and vivacious man, who has not only learnt to compromise and arrange with that which was and is, but wishes to have it again *as it was and is*, for all eternity, insatiably calling out *da capo*, not only to himself, but to the whole piece and play; and not only to the play, but actually to him who requires the play—and makes it necessary; because he always requires himself anew—and makes himself necessary. What? And this would not be—*circulus vitiosus dens?*

57

The distance, and as it were the space around man, grows with the strength of his intellectual vision and insight: his world becomes profounder; new stars, new enigmas, and notions are ever coming into view. Perhaps everything on which the intellectual eye has exercised its acuteness and profundity has just been an occasion for its exercise, something of a game, something for children and childish minds. Perhaps the most solemn conceptions that have caused the most fighting and suffering, the conceptions "God" and "sin," will one day seem to us of no more importance than a child's plaything or a child's pain seems to an old man; and perhaps another plaything and another pain will then be necessary once more for "the old man"—always childish enough, an eternal child!

58

Has it been observed to what extent outward idleness, or semi-idleness, is necessary to a real religious life (alike for its favourite microscopic labour of self-examination, and for its soft placidity called "prayer," the state of perpetual readiness for the "coming of God") I mean the idleness with a good conscience, the idleness of olden times and of blood, to which the aristocratic sentiment that work is *dishonouring*—that it vulgarises body and soul—is not quite unfamiliar? And that consequently the modern, noisy, time-engrossing, conceited, foolishly proud laboriousness educates and prepares for "unbelief" more than anything else? Amongst these, for instance, who are at present living apart from religion in Germany, I find "freethinkers" of diversified species and origin, but above all a majority of those in whom laboriousness from generation to generation has dissolved the religious instincts; so that they no longer know what purpose religions serve, and only note their existence in the world with a kind of dull astonishment. They feel themselves already fully occupied, these good people, be it by their business or by their pleasures, not to mention the "Father-land," and the newspapers, and their "family duties"; it seems that they have no time whatever left for religion; and above all, it is not obvious to them whether it is a question of a new business or a new pleasure—for it is impossible, they say to themselves, that people should go to church merely to spoil their tempers. They are by no means enemies of religious customs; should certain circumstances, state affairs perhaps, require their participation in such customs, they do what is required, as so many things are done—with a patient and unassuming seriousness, and without much curiosity or discomfort; they live too much apart and outside to feel even the necessity for a *for* or *against* in such matters. Among those indifferent persons may be reckoned nowadays the majority of German Protestants of the middle classes, especially in the great laborious centres of trade and commerce; also the majority of laborious scholars, and the entire University personnel (with the exception of the theologians, whose existence and possibility there always gives psychologists new and more subtle puzzles to solve). On the part of pious, or merely church-going people, there is seldom any idea of *how much* goodwill, one might say arbitrary will, is now necessary for a German scholar to take the problem of religion seriously; his whole profession (and as I have said, his whole workmanlike laborious-ness, to which he is compelled by his modern conscience) inclines him to a lofty and almost charitable serenity as regards religion, with which is occasionally mingled a slight disdain for the "uncleanliness" of spirit which he takes for granted wherever any one still professes to belong to the Church. It is only with the help of history (*not* through his own per-sonal experience, therefore) that the scholar succeeds in bringing himself to a respectful seriousness, and to a certain timid deference in presence of religions; but even when his sentiments have reached the stage of gratitude towards them, he has not personally advanced one step nearer to that which still maintains itself as Church or as piety; perhaps even the contrary. The practical indifference to religious matters in the midst of which he has been born and brought up, usually sublimates itself in his case into circumspection and cleanliness, which shuns contact with reli-gious men and things; and it may be just the depth of his tolerance and humanity which prompts him to avoid the delicate trouble which toler-ance itself brings with it. Every age has its own divine type of naïveté, for the discovery of which other ages may envy it: and how much naïveté— adorable, childlike, and boundlessly foolish naivete—is involved in this belief of the scholar in his superiority, in the good conscience of his tolerance, in the unsuspecting, simple certainty with which his instinct treats the religious man as a lower and less valuable type, beyond, before, and *above* which he himself has developed—he, the little arrogant dwarf and mob-man, the sedulously alert, head-and-hand drudge of "ideas," of "modern ideas!"

59

Whoever has seen deeply into the world has doubtless divined what wisdom there is in the fact that men are superficial. It is their preservative instinct which teaches them to be flighty, lightsome, and false. Here and there one finds a passionate and exaggerated adoration of "pure forms" in philosophers as well as in artists: it is not to be doubted that whoever has *need* of the cult of the superficial to that extent, has at one time or another made an unlucky dive *beneath* it. Perhaps there is even an order of rank with respect to those burnt children, the born artists who find the enjoyment of life only in trying to *falsify* its image (as if taking wearisome revenge on it); one might guess to what degree life has disgusted them, by the extent to which they wish to see its image falsified, attenuated, ultrified, and deified; one might reckon the *homines religiosi* amongst the artists, as their *highest* rank. It is the profound, suspicious fear of an incurable pessimism which compels whole centuries to fasten their teeth into a religious interpretation of existence: the fear of the instinct which divines that truth might be attained *too soon*, before man has become strong enough, hard enough, artist enough.... Piety, the *Life in God*, regarded in this light, would appear as the most elaborate and ultimate product of the *fear* of truth, as artist-adoration and artist-intoxication in presence of the most logical of all falsifications, as the will to the inversion of truth, to untruth at any price. Perhaps there has hitherto been no more effective means of beautifying man than piety; by means of it man can become so artful, so superficial, so iridescent, and so good, that his appearance no longer offends.

60

To love mankind *for God's sake*—this has so far been the noblest and remotest sentiment to which mankind has attained. That love to mankind, without any redeeming intention in the background, is only an *additional* folly and brutishness, that the inclination to this love has first to get its proportion, its delicacy, its grain of salt and sprinkling of ambergris from a higher inclination: whoever first perceived and "experienced" this, however his tongue may have stammered as it attempted to express such a delicate matter, let him for all time be holy and respected, as the man who has so far flown highest and gone astray in the finest fashion!

61

The philosopher, as *we* free spirits understand him—as the man of the greatest responsibility, who has the conscience for the general development of mankind—will use religion for his disciplining and educating work, just as he will use the contemporary political and economic conditions. The selecting and disciplining influence—destructive, as well as creative and fashioning—which can be exercised by means of religion is manifold and varied, according to the sort of people placed under its spell and protection. For those who are strong and independent, destined and trained to command, in whom the judgement and skill of a ruling race is incorporated, religion is an additional means for overcoming resistance in the exercise of authority—as a bond which binds rulers and subjects in common, betraying and surrendering to the former the conscience of the latter, their inmost heart, which would fain escape obedience. And in the case of the unique natures of noble origin, if by virtue of superior spirituality they should incline to a more retired and contemplative life, reserving to themselves only the more refined forms of government (over chosen disciples or members of an order), religion itself may be used as a means for obtaining peace from the noise and trouble of managing *grosser* affairs, and for securing immunity from the *unavoidable* filth of all political agitation. The Brahmins, for instance, understood this fact. With the help of a religious organisation, they secured to themselves the power of nominating kings for the people, while their sentiments prompted them to keep apart and outside, as men with a higher and super-regal mission. At the same time religion gives inducement and opportunity to some of the subjects to qualify themselves for future ruling and commanding: the slowly ascending ranks and classes, in which, through fortunate marriage customs, volitional power and delight in self-control are on the increase. To them religion offers sufficient incentives and temptations to aspire to higher intellectuality, and to experience the sentiments of authoritative self-control, of silence, and of solitude. Asceticism and Puritanism are almost indispensable means of educating and ennobling a race which seeks to rise above its hereditary baseness and work itself upward to future supremacy. And finally, to ordinary men, to the majority of the people, who exist for service and general utility, and are only so far entitled to exist, religion gives invaluable contentedness with their lot and condition, peace of heart, ennoblement of obedience, additional social happiness and sympathy, with something of transfiguration and embellishment, something of justification of all the commonplaceness, all the meanness, all the semi-animal poverty of their souls. Religion, together with the religious significance of life, sheds sunshine over such perpetually harassed men, and makes even their own aspect endurable to them; it operates upon them as the Epicurean philosophy usually operates upon sufferers of a higher order, in a refreshing and refining manner, almost *turning suffering to account*, and in the end even hallowing and vindicating it. There is perhaps nothing so admirable in Christianity and Buddhism as their art of teaching even the lowest to elevate themselves by piety to a seemingly higher order of things, and thereby to retain their satisfaction with the actual world in which they find it difficult enough to live—this very difficulty being necessary.

62

To be sure—to make also the bad counter-reckoning against such religions, and to bring to light their secret dangers—the cost is always excessive and terrible when religions do *not* operate as an educational and disciplinary medium in the hands of the philosopher, but rule voluntarily and *paramountly*, when they wish to be the final end, and not a means along with other means. Among men, as among all other animals, there is a surplus of defective, diseased, degenerating, infirm, and necessarily suffering individuals; the successful cases, among men also, are always the exception; and in view of the fact that man is *the animal not yet properly adapted to his environment*, the rare exception. But worse still. The higher the type a man represents, the greater is the improbability that he will *succeed*; the accidental, the law of irrationality in the general constitution of mankind, manifests itself most terribly in its destructive effect on the higher orders of men, the conditions of whose lives are delicate, diverse, and difficult to determine. What, then, is the attitude of the two greatest religions above-mentioned to the *surplus* of failures in life? They endeavour to preserve and keep alive whatever can be preserved; in fact, as the religions *for sufferers*, they take the part of these upon principle; they are always in favour of those who suffer from life as from a disease, and they would fain treat every other experience of life as false and impossible. However highly we may esteem this indulgent and preservative care (inasmuch as in applying to others, it has applied, and applies also to the highest and usually the most suffering type of man), the hitherto *paramount* religions—to give a general appreciation of them—are among the principal causes which have kept the type of "man" upon a lower level— they have preserved too much *that which should have perished.* One has to thank them for invaluable services; and who is sufficiently rich in gratitude not to feel poor at the contemplation of all that the "spiritual men" of Christianity have done for Europe hitherto! But when they had given comfort to the sufferers, courage to the oppressed and despairing, a staff and support to the helpless, and when they had allured from society into convents and spiritual penitentiaries the broken-hearted and distracted: what else had they to do in order to work systematically in that fashion, and with a good conscience, for the preservation of all the sick and suffering, which means, in deed and in truth, to work for *the deterioration of the European race?* To *reverse* all estimates of value—*that* is what they had to do! And to shatter the strong, to spoil great hopes, to cast suspicion on the delight in beauty, to break down everything autonomous, manly, conquering, and imperious—all instincts which are natural to the highest and most successful type of "man"—into uncertainty, distress of conscience, and self-destruction; forsooth, to invert all love of the earthly and of supremacy over the earth, into hatred of the earth and earthly things— *that* is the task the Church imposed on itself, and was obliged to impose, until, according to its standard of value, "unworldliness," "unsensuousness," and "higher man" fused into one sentiment. If one could observe the strangely painful, equally coarse and refined comedy of European Christianity with the derisive and impartial eye of an Epicurean god, I should think one would never cease marveling and laughing; does it not actually seem that some single will has ruled over Europe for eighteen centuries in order to make a *sublime abortion* of man? He, however, who, with opposite requirements (no longer Epicurean) and with some divine hammer in his hand, could approach this almost voluntary degeneration and stunting of mankind, as exemplified in the European Christian (Pascal, for instance), would he not have to cry aloud with rage, pity, and horror: "Oh, you bunglers, presumptuous pitiful bunglers, what have you done! Was that a work for your hands? How you have hacked and botched my finest stone! What have *you* presumed to do!" I should say that Christianity has hitherto been the most portentous of presumptions. Men, not great enough, nor hard enough, to be entitled as artists to take part in fashioning man; men, not sufficiently strong and far-sighted to *allow*, with sublime self-constraint, the obvious law of the thousandfold failures and perishings to prevail; men, not sufficiently noble to see the radically different grades of rank and intervals of rank that separate man from man: *such* men, with their "equality before God," have hitherto swayed the destiny of Europe; until at last a dwarfed, almost ludicrous species has been produced, a gregarious animal, something obliging, sickly, mediocre, the European of the present day.

→ CHAPTER FOUR ←

APOPHTHEGMS AND INTERLUDES

63
HE WHO IS A THOROUGH TEACHER TAKES THINGS SERIOUSLY—AND EVEN himself—only in relation to his pupils.

64
"Knowledge for its own sake"—that is the last snare laid by morality: we are thereby completely entangled in morals once more.

65
The charm of knowledge would be small, were it not that so much shame has to be overcome on the way to it.

65A
We are most dishonourable towards our God: he is not *permitted* to sin.

66
The tendency of a person to allow himself to be degraded, robbed, deceived, and exploited might be the diffidence of a God amongst men.

67
Love to one only is a barbarity, for it is exercised at the expense of all others. Love to God also!

68
"I did that," says my memory. "I could not have done that," says my pride, and remains inexorable. Eventually—the memory yields.

69

One has regarded life carelessly, if one has failed to see the hand that—
kills with leniency.

70

If a man has character, he has also his typical experience, which
always recurs.

71

The Sage as Astronomer. So long as thou feelest the stars as an "above
thee," thou lackest the eye of the discerning one.

72

It is not the strength, but the duration of great sentiments that makes
great men.

73

He who attains his ideal, precisely thereby surpasses it.

73A

Many a peacock hides his tail from every eye—and calls it his pride.

74

A man of genius is unbearable, unless he possess at least two things
besides: gratitude and purity.

75

The degree and nature of a man's sensuality extends to the highest alti-
tudes of his spirit.

76

Under peaceful conditions the militant man attacks himself.

77

With his principles a man seeks either to dominate, or justify, or honour,
or reproach, or conceal his habits: two men with the same principles probably seek fundamentally different ends therewith.

78

He who despises himself, nevertheless esteems himself thereby, as
a despiser.

79

A soul which knows that it is loved, but does not itself love, betrays its sediment: its dregs come up.

80

A thing that is explained ceases to concern us. What did the God mean who gave the advice, "Know thyself!" Did it perhaps imply: "Cease to be concerned about thyself! Become objective!" And Socrates? And the "scientific man?"

81

It is terrible to die of thirst at sea. Is it necessary that you should so salt your truth that it will no longer—quench thirst?

82

"Sympathy for all"—would be harshness and tyranny for *thee*, my good neighbour!

83

Instinct. When the house is on fire one forgets even the dinner. Yes, but one recovers it from amongst the ashes.

84

Woman learns how to hate in proportion as she—forgets how to charm.

85

The same emotions are in man and woman, but in different *tempo*; on that account man and woman never cease to misunderstand each other.

86

In the background of all their personal vanity, women themselves have still their impersonal scorn—for "woman."

87

Fettered Heart, Free Spirit. When one firmly fetters one's heart and keeps it prisoner, one can allow one's spirit many liberties: I said this once before. But people do not believe it when I say so, unless they know it already.

88

One begins to distrust very clever persons when they become embarrassed.

89

Dreadful experiences raise the question whether he who experiences them is not something dreadful also.

90

Heavy, melancholy men turn lighter, and come temporarily to their surface, precisely by that which makes others heavy—by hatred and love.

91

So cold, so icy, that one burns one's finger at the touch of him! Every hand that lays hold of him shrinks back! And for that very reason many think him red-hot.

92

Who has not, at one time or another—sacrificed himself for the sake of his good name?

93

In affability there is no hatred of men, but precisely on that account a great deal too much contempt of men.

94

The maturity of man—that means, to have reacquired the seriousness that one had as a child at play.

95

To be ashamed of one's immorality is a step on the ladder at the end of which one is ashamed also of one's morality.

96

One should part from life as Ulysses parted from Nausicaa—blessing it rather than in love with it.

97

What? A great man? I always see merely the play-actor of his own ideal.

98

When one trains one's conscience, it kisses one while it bites.

99

The Disappointed One Speaks. "I listened for the echo and I heard only praise."

100

We all feign to ourselves that we are simpler than we are; we thus relax ourselves away from our fellows.

101

A discerning one might easily regard himself at present as the animalisation of God.

102

Discovering reciprocal love should really disenchant the lover with regard to the beloved. "What! *She* is modest enough to love even you? Or stupid enough? Or—or——"

103

The Danger in Happiness. "Everything now turns out best for me, I now love every fate: who would like to be my fate?"

104

Not their love of humanity, but the impotence of their love, prevents the Christians of today—burning us.

105

The *pia fraus* is still more repugnant to the taste (*the "piety"*) of the free spirit (the "pious man of knowledge") than the *impia fraus*. Hence the profound lack of judgement, in comparison with the church, characteristic of the type "free spirit"—as *its* non-freedom.

106

By means of music the very passions enjoy themselves.

107

A sign of strong character, when once the resolution has been taken, to shut the ear even to the best counter-arguments. Occasionally, therefore, a will to stupidity.

108

There is no such thing as moral phenomena, but only a moral interpretation of phenomena.

109

The criminal is often enough not equal to his deed: he extenuates and maligns it.

110

The advocates of a criminal are seldom artists enough to turn the beautiful terribleness of the deed to the advantage of the doer.

111

Our vanity is most difficult to wound just when our pride has been wounded.

112

To him who feels himself preordained to contemplation and not to belief, all believers are too noisy and obtrusive; he guards against them.

113

"You want to prepossess him in your favour? Then you must be embarrassed before him."

114

The immense expectation with regard to sexual love, and the coyness in this expectation, spoils all the perspectives of women at the outset.

115

Where there is neither love nor hatred in the game, woman's play is mediocre.

116

The great epochs of our life are at the points when we gain courage to rebaptise our badness as the best in us.

117

The will to overcome an emotion, is ultimately only the will of another, or of several other, emotions.

118
There is an innocence of admiration: it is possessed by him to whom it has not yet occurred that he himself may be admired some day.

119
Our loathing of dirt may be so great as to prevent us cleaning ourselves— "justifying" ourselves.

120
Sensuality often forces the growth of love too much, so that its root remains weak, and is easily torn up.

121
It is a curious thing that God learned Greek when he wished to turn author—and that he did not learn it better.

122
To rejoice on account of praise is in many cases merely politeness of heart—and the very opposite of vanity of spirit.

123
Even concubinage has been corrupted—by marriage.

124
He who exults at the stake, does not triumph over pain, but because of the fact that he does not feel pain where he expected it. A parable.

125
When we have to change an opinion about any one, we charge heavily to his account the inconvenience he thereby causes us.

126
A nation is a detour of nature to arrive at six or seven great men. Yes, and then to get round them.

127
In the eyes of all true women science is hostile to the sense of shame. They feel as if one wished to peep under their skin with it—or worse still, under their dress and finery.

128

The more abstract the truth you wish to teach, the more must you allure the senses to it.

129

The devil has the most extensive perspectives for God; on that account he keeps so far away from him: the devil, in effect, as the oldest friend of knowledge.

130

What a person *is* begins to betray itself when his talent decreases—when he ceases to show what he *can do*. Talent is also an adornment; an adornment is also a concealment.

131

The sexes deceive themselves about each other: the reason is that in reality they honour and love only themselves (or their own ideal, to express it more agreeably). Thus man wishes woman to be peaceable: but in fact woman is *essentially* unpeaceable, like the cat, however well she may have assumed the peaceable demeanour.

132

One is punished best for one's virtues.

133

He who cannot find the way to *his* ideal, lives more frivolously and shamelessly than the man without an ideal.

134

From the senses originate all trustworthiness, all good conscience, all evidence of truth.

135

Pharisaism is not a deterioration of the good man; a considerable part of it is rather an essential condition of being good.

136

The one seeks an accoucheur for his thoughts, the other seeks someone whom he can assist: a good conversation thus originates.

137

In intercourse with scholars and artists one readily makes mistakes of opposite kinds: in a remarkable scholar one not infrequently finds a mediocre man; and often even in a mediocre artist, one finds a very remarkable man.

138

We do the same when awake as when dreaming: we only invent and imagine him with whom we have intercourse—and forget it immediately.

139

In revenge and in love woman is more barbarous than man.

140

Advice as a Riddle. "If the band is not to break, bite it first—secure to make!"

141

The belly is the reason why man does not so readily take himself for a God.

142

The chastest utterance I ever heard: "*Dans le véritable amour c'est l'âme qui enveloppe le corps.*"

143

Our vanity would like what we do best to pass precisely for what is most difficult to us. Concerning the origin of many systems of morals.

144

When a woman has scholarly inclinations there is generally something wrong with her sexual nature. Barrenness itself conduces to a certain virility of taste; man, indeed, if I may say so, is "the barren animal."

145

Comparing man and woman generally, one may say that woman would not have the genius for adornment, if she had not the instinct for the *secondary* role.

146

He who fights with monsters should be careful lest he thereby become a monster. And if thou gaze long into an abyss, the abyss will also gaze into thee.

147

From old Florentine novels—moreover, from life: *Buona femmina e mala femmina vuol bastone.* Sacchetti, November 86.

148

To seduce their neighbour to a favourable opinion, and afterwards to believe implicitly in this opinion of their neighbour—who can do this conjuring trick so well as women?

149

That which an age considers evil is usually an unseasonable echo of what was formerly considered good—the atavism of an old ideal.

150

Around the hero everything becomes a tragedy; around the demigod everything becomes a satyr-play; and around God everything becomes—what? Perhaps a "world"?

151

It is not enough to possess a talent: one must also have your permission to possess it; eh, my friends?

152

"Where there is the tree of knowledge, there is always Paradise": so say the most ancient and the most modern serpents.

153

What is done out of love always takes place beyond good and evil.

154

Objection, evasion, joyous distrust, and love of irony are signs of health; everything absolute belongs to pathology.

155

The sense of the tragic increases and declines with sensuousness.

156

Insanity in individuals is something rare—but in groups, parties, nations, and epochs it is the rule.

157

The thought of suicide is a great consolation: by means of it one gets successfully through many a bad night.

158

Not only our reason, but also our conscience, truckles to our strongest impulse—the tyrant in us.

159

One *must* repay good and ill; but why just to the person who did us good or ill?

160

One no longer loves one's knowledge sufficiently after one has communicated it.

161

Poets act shamelessly towards their experiences: they exploit them.

162

"Our fellow-creature is not our neighbour, but our neighbour's neighbour": so thinks every nation.

163

Love brings to light the noble and hidden qualities of a lover—his rare and exceptional traits: it is thus liable to be deceptive as to his normal character.

164

Jesus said to his Jews: "The law was for servants; love God as I love him, as his Son! What have we Sons of God to do with morals!"

165

In Sight of every Party. A shepherd has always need of a bell-wether—or he has himself to be a wether occasionally.

166

One may indeed lie with the mouth; but with the accompanying grimace one nevertheless tells the truth.

167

To vigorous men intimacy is a matter of shame—and something precious.

168

Christianity gave Eros poison to drink; he did not die of it, certainly, but degenerated to Vice.

169

To talk much about oneself may also be a means of concealing oneself.

170

In praise there is more obtrusiveness than in blame.

171

Pity has an almost ludicrous effect on a man of knowledge, like tender hands on a Cyclops.

172

One occasionally embraces someone or other, out of love to mankind (because one cannot embrace all); but this is what one must never confess to the individual.

173

One does not hate as long as one disesteems, but only when one esteems equal or superior.

174

Ye Utilitarians—ye, too, love the *utile* only as a *vehicle* for your inclinations—ye, too, really find the noise of its wheels insupportable!

175

One loves ultimately one's desires, not the thing desired.

176

The vanity of others is only counter to our taste when it is counter to our vanity.

177

With regard to what "truthfulness" is, perhaps nobody has ever been sufficiently truthful.

178

One does not believe in the follies of clever men: what a forfeiture of the rights of man!

179

The consequences of our actions seize us by the forelock, very indifferent to the fact that we have meanwhile "reformed."

180

There is an innocence in lying which is the sign of good faith in a cause.

181

It is inhuman to bless when one is being cursed.

182

The familiarity of superiors embitters one, because it may not be returned.

183

"I am affected, not because you have deceived me, but because I can no longer believe in you."

184

There is a haughtiness of kindness which has the appearance of wickedness.

185

"I dislike him." Why? "I am not a match for him." Did anyone ever answer so?

CHAPTER FIVE

THE NATURAL HISTORY
OF MORALS

186

THE MORAL SENTIMENT IN EUROPE AT PRESENT IS PERHAPS AS SUBTLE, belated, diverse, sensitive, and refined, as the *Science of Morals* belonging thereto is recent, initial, awkward, and coarse-fingered: an interesting contrast, which sometimes becomes incarnate and obvious in the very person of a moralist. Indeed, the expression, *Science of Morals* is, in respect to what is designated thereby, far too presumptuous and counter to *good* taste—which is always a foretaste of more modest expressions. One ought to avow with the utmost fairness *what* is still necessary here for a long time, *what* is alone proper for the present: namely, the collection of material, the comprehensive survey and classification of an immense domain of delicate sentiments of worth, and distinctions of worth, which live, grow, propagate, and perish—and perhaps attempts to give a clear idea of the recurring and more common forms of these living crystallisations—as preparation for a *theory of types* of morality. To be sure, people have not hitherto been so modest. All the philosophers, with a pedantic and ridiculous seriousness, demanded of themselves something very much higher, more pretentious, and ceremonious, when they concerned themselves with morality as a science: they wanted to *give a basis* to morality—and every philosopher hitherto has believed that he has given it a basis; morality itself, however, has been regarded as something "given." How far from their awkward pride was the seemingly insignificant problem—left in dust and decay—of a description of forms of morality, notwithstanding that the finest hands and senses could hardly be fine enough for it! It was precisely owing to moral philosophers knowing the moral facts imperfectly, in an arbitrary epitome, or an accidental abridgment—perhaps as the morality of their environment, their position, their church, their *Zeitgeist*, their climate and zone—it was precisely because they were badly instructed with regard to nations, eras, and past ages, and were by no means eager to know about these matters, that they did not even come in sight of the real problems of morals—problems which only disclose themselves by a comparison of *many* kinds of morality. In every *Science of Morals* hitherto, strange as it may sound, the problem of morality itself has been *omitted*; there has been no suspicion that there was anything problematic there! That which philosophers called "giving a basis to morality," and endeavoured to realise, has, when seen in a right light, proved merely a learned form of good *faith* in prevailing morality, a new means of its *expression*, consequently just a matter-of-fact within the sphere of a definite morality, yea, in its ultimate motive, a sort of denial that it is *lawful* for this morality to be called in question—and in any case the reverse of the testing, analysing, doubting, and vivisecting of this very faith. Hear, for instance, with what innocence—almost worthy of honour—Schopenhauer represents his own task, and draw your conclusions concerning the scientificalness of a *Science* whose latest master still talks in the strain of children and old wives: "The principle," he says (page 136 of the *Grundprobleme der Etkik*[1]), "the axiom about the purport of which all moralists are *practically* agreed: *neminem laede, immo omnes quantum potes juva*—is *really* the proposition which all moral teachers strive to establish, . . . the *real* basis of ethics which has been sought, like the philosopher's stone, for centuries." The difficulty of establishing the proposition referred to may indeed be great—it is well known that Schopenhauer also was unsuccessful in his efforts; and whoever has thoroughly realised how absurdly false and sentimental this proposition is, in a world whose essence is Will to Power, may be reminded that Schopenhauer, although a pessimist, *actually*—played the flute . . . daily after dinner: one may read about the matter in his biography. A question by the way: a pessimist, a repudiator of God and of the world, who *makes a halt* at morality—who assents to morality, and plays the flute to *laede-neminem* morals, what? Is that really—a pessimist?

187

Apart from the value of such assertions as "there is a categorical imperative in us," one can always ask: What does such an assertion indicate about him who makes it? There are systems of morals which are meant to justify

their author in the eyes of other people; other systems of morals are
meant to tranquillise him, and make him self-satisfied; with other systems
he wants to crucify and humble himself; with others he wishes to take
revenge; with others to conceal himself; with others to glorify himself and
gain superiority and distinction; this system of morals helps its author to
forget, that system makes him, or something of him, forgotten; many a
moralist would like to exercise power and creative arbitrariness over mankind; many another, perhaps, Kant especially, gives us to understand by
his morals that "what is estimable in me, is that I know how to obey—and
with you it *shall* not be otherwise than with me!" In short, systems of morals are only a *sign language of the emotions.*

188

In contrast to *laisser-aller,* every system of morals is a sort of tyranny
against "nature" and also against "reason"; that is, however, no objection,
unless one should again decree by some system of morals, that all kinds
of tyranny and unreasonableness are unlawful. What is essential and
invaluable in every system of morals, is that it is a long constraint. In
order to understand Stoicism, or Port-Royal, or Puritanism, one should
remember the constraint under which every language has attained to
strength and freedom—the metrical constraint, the tyranny of rhyme and
rhythm. How much trouble have the poets and orators of every nation
given themselves! Not excepting some of the prose writers of today, in
whose ear dwells an inexorable conscientiousness—"for the sake of a
folly," as utilitarian bunglers say, and thereby deem themselves wise—
"from submission to arbitrary laws," as the anarchists say, and thereby
fancy themselves "free," even free-spirited. The singular fact remains,
however, that everything of the nature of freedom, elegance, boldness,
dance, and masterly certainty, which exists or has existed, whether it be
in thought itself, or in administration, or in speaking and persuading, in
art just as in conduct, has only developed by means of the tyranny of such
arbitrary law; and in all seriousness, it is not at all improbable that precisely this is "nature" and "natural"—and *not laisser-aller!* Every artist
knows how different from the state of letting himself go, is his "most
natural" condition, the free arranging, locating, disposing, and construct-
ing in the moments of "inspiration"—and how strictly and delicately he
then obeys a thousand laws, which, by their very rigidness and precision,
defy all formulation by means of ideas (even the most stable idea has, in
comparison therewith, something floating, manifold, and ambiguous in it).

The essential thing "in heaven and in earth" is, apparently (to repeat it once more), that there should be long *obedience* in the same direction; there thereby results, and has always resulted in the long run, something which has made life worth living; for instance, virtue, art, music, dancing, reason, spirituality—anything whatever that is transfiguring, refined, foolish, or divine. The long bondage of the spirit, the distrustful constraint in the communicability of ideas, the discipline which the thinker imposed on himself to think in accordance with the rules of a church or a court, or conformable to Aristotelian premises, the persistent spiritual will to interpret everything that happened according to a Christian scheme, and in every occurrence to rediscover and justify the Christian God: all this violence, arbitrariness, severity, dreadfulness, and unreasonableness, has proved itself the disciplinary means whereby the European spirit has attained its strength, its remorseless curiosity and subtle mobility; granted also that much irrecoverable strength and spirit had to be stifled, suffocated, and spoilt in the process (for here, as everywhere, "nature" shows herself as she is, in all her extravagant and *indifferent* magnificence, which is shocking, but nevertheless noble). That for centuries European thinkers only thought in order to prove something—nowadays, on the contrary, we are suspicious of every thinker who "wishes to prove something"—that it was always settled beforehand what *was to be* the result of their strictest thinking, as it was perhaps in the Asiatic astrology of former times, or as it is still at the present day in the innocent, Christian-moral explanation of immediate personal events "for the glory of God," or "for the good of the soul": this tyranny, this arbitrariness, this severe and magnificent stupidity, has *educated* the spirit; slavery, both in the coarser and the finer sense, is apparently an indispensable means even of spiritual education and discipline. One may look at every system of morals in this light: it is "nature" therein which teaches to hate the *laisser-aller*, the too great freedom, and implants the need for limited horizons, for immediate duties—it teaches the *narrowing of perspectives*, and thus, in a certain sense, that stupidity is a condition of life and development. "Thou must obey someone, and for a long time; *otherwise* thou wilt come to grief, and lose all respect for thyself"—this seems to me to be the moral imperative of nature, which is certainly neither "categorical," as old Kant wished (consequently the "otherwise"), nor does it address itself to the individual (what does nature care for the individual!) but to nations, races, ages, and ranks, above all, however, to the animal "man" generally, to *mankind*.

189

Industrious races find it a great hardship to be idle: it was a master stroke of *English* instinct to hallow and begloom Sunday to such an extent that the Englishman unconsciously hankers for his week- and workday again: as a kind of cleverly devised, cleverly intercalated *fast*, such as is also frequently found in the ancient world (although, as is appropriate in southern nations, not precisely with respect to work). Many kinds of fasts are necessary; and wherever powerful impulses and habits prevail, legislators have to see that intercalary days are appointed, on which such impulses are fettered, and learn to hunger anew. Viewed from a higher standpoint, whole generations and epochs, when they show themselves infected with any moral fanaticism, seem like those intercalated periods of restraint and fasting, during which an impulse learns to humble and submit itself—at the same time also to *purify* and *sharpen* itself; certain philosophical sects likewise admit of a similar interpretation (for instance, the Stoa, in the midst of Hellenic culture, with the atmosphere rank and overcharged with aphrodisiacal odours). Here also is a hint for the explanation of the paradox, why it was precisely in the most Christian period of European history, and in general only under the pressure of Christian sentiments, that the sexual impulse sublimated into love (*amor-passion*).

190

There is something in the morality of Plato which does not really belong to Plato, but which only appears in his philosophy, one might say, in spite of him: namely, Socratism, for which he himself was too noble. "No one desires to injure himself, hence all evil is done unwittingly. The evil man inflicts injury on himself; he would not do so, however, if he knew that evil is evil. The evil man, therefore, is only evil through error; if one free him from error one will necessarily make him—good." This mode of reasoning savours of the *populace*, who perceive only the unpleasant consequences of evil-doing, and practically judge that "it is *stupid* to do wrong"; while they accept "good" as identical with "useful and pleasant," without further thought. As regards every system of utilitarianism, one may at once assume that it has the same origin, and follow the scent: one will seldom err. Plato did all he could to interpret something refined and noble into the tenets of his teacher, and above all to interpret himself into them—he, the most daring of all interpreters, who lifted the entire Socrates out of the street, as a popular theme and song, to exhibit him in endless and impossible modifications—namely, in all his own disguises and multiplicities. In jest, and in Homeric language as well, what is the Platonic Socrates, if not—

πρόσθε Πλάτων ὄπιθέν τε Πλάτων μέσση τε Χίμαιρα.

191

The old theological problem of "Faith" and "Knowledge," or more plainly, of instinct and reason—the question whether, in respect to the valuation of things, instinct deserves more authority than rationality, which wants to appreciate and act according to motives, according to a "Why," that is to say, in conformity to purpose and utility—it is always the old moral problem that first appeared in the person of Socrates, and had divided men's minds long before Christianity. Socrates himself, following, of course, the taste of his talent—that of a surpassing dialectician —took first the side of reason; and, in fact, what did he do all his life but laugh at the awkward incapacity of the noble Athenians, who were men of instinct, like all noble men, and could never give satisfactory answers concerning the motives of their actions? In the end, however, though silently and secretly, he laughed also at himself: with his finer conscience and introspection, he found in himself the same difficulty and incapacity. "But why"—he said to himself—"should one on that account separate oneself from the instincts! One must set them right, and the reason *also*—one must follow the instincts, but at the same time persuade the reason to support them with good arguments." This was the real *falseness* of that great and mysterious ironist; he brought his conscience up to the point that he was satisfied with a kind of self-outwitting: in fact, he perceived the irrationality in the moral judgement. Plato, more innocent in such matters, and without the craftiness of the plebeian, wished to prove to himself, at the expenditure of all his strength—the greatest strength a philosopher had ever expended—that reason and instinct lead spontaneously to one goal, to the good, to "God"; and since Plato, all theologians and philosophers have followed the same path—which means that in matters of morality, instinct (or as Christians call it, "Faith," or as I call it, "the herd") has hitherto triumphed. Unless one should make an exception in the case of Descartes, the father of rationalism (and consequently the grandfather of the Revolution), who recognised only the authority of reason: but reason is only a tool, and Descartes was superficial.

192

Whoever has followed the history of a single science, finds in its development a clue to the understanding of the oldest and commonest processes of all "knowledge and cognisance": there, as here, the premature hypotheses, the fictions, the good stupid will to "belief," and the lack of distrust and patience are first developed—our senses learn late, and never learn completely, to be subtle, reliable, and cautious organs of knowledge. Our eyes find it easier on a given occasion to produce a picture already often produced, than to seize upon the divergence and novelty of an impression: the latter requires more force, more "morality." It is difficult and painful for the ear to listen to anything new; we hear strange music badly. When we hear another language spoken, we involuntarily attempt to form the sounds into words with which we are more familiar and conversant—it was thus, for example, that the Germans modified the spoken word *arcubalista* into *armbrust* (crossbow). Our senses are also hostile and averse to the new; and generally, even in the "simplest" processes of sensation, the emotions *dominate*—such as fear, love, hatred, and the passive emotion of indolence. As little as a reader nowadays reads all the single words (not to speak of syllables) of a page—he rather takes about five out of every twenty words at random, and "guesses" the probably appropriate sense to them—just as little do we see a tree correctly and completely in respect to its leaves, branches, colour, and shape; we find it so much easier to fancy the chance of a tree. Even in the midst of the most remarkable experiences, we still do just the same; we fabricate the greater part of the experience, and can hardly be made to contemplate any event, *except* as "inventors" thereof. All this goes to prove that from our fundamental nature and from remote ages we have been—*accustomed to lying.* Or, to express it more politely and hypocritically, in short, more pleasantly—one is much more of an artist than one is aware of. In an animated conversation, I often see the face of the person with whom I am speaking so clearly and sharply defined before me, according to the thought he expresses, or which I believe to be evoked in his mind, that the degree of distinctness far exceeds the *strength* of my visual faculty—the delicacy of the play of the muscles and of the expression of the eyes *must* therefore be imagined by me. Probably the person put on quite a different expression, or none at all.

193

Quidquid luce fuit, tenebris agit: but also contrariwise. What we experience in dreams, provided we experience it often, pertains at last just as much to the general belongings of our soul as anything "actually" experienced; by virtue thereof we are richer or poorer, we have a requirement more or less, and finally, in broad daylight, and even in the brightest moments of our waking life, we are ruled to some extent by the nature of our dreams. Supposing that someone has often flown in his dreams, and that at last, as soon as he dreams, he is conscious of the power and art of flying as his privilege and his peculiarly enviable happiness; such a person, who believes that on the slightest impulse, he can actualise all sorts of curves and angles, who knows the sensation of a certain divine levity, an "upwards" without effort or constraint, a "downwards" without descending or lowering—without *trouble*! How could the man with such dream-experiences and dream-habits fail to find "happiness" differently coloured and defined, even in his waking hours! How could he fail—to long *differently* for happiness? "Flight," such as is described by poets, must, when compared with his own "flying," be far too earthly, muscular, violent, far too "troublesome" for him.

194

The difference among men does not manifest itself only in the difference of their lists of desirable things—in their regarding different good things as worth striving for, and being disagreed as to the greater or less value, the order of rank, of the commonly recognised desirable things: it manifests itself much more in what they regard as actually *having* and *possessing* a desirable thing. As regards a woman, for instance, the control over her body and her sexual gratification serves as an amply sufficient sign of ownership and possession to the more modest man; another with a more suspicious and ambitious thirst for possession, sees the "questionableness," the mere apparentness of such ownership, and wishes to have finer tests in order to know especially whether the woman not only gives herself to him, but also gives up for his sake what she has or would like to have— only *then* does he look upon her as "possessed." A third, however, has not even here got to the limit of his distrust and his desire for possession: he asks himself whether the woman, when she gives up everything for him, does not perhaps do so for a phantom of him; he wishes first to be thoroughly, indeed, profoundly well known; in order to be loved at all he ventures to let himself be found out. Only then does he feel the beloved one fully in his possession, when she no longer deceives herself about him, when she loves him just as much for the sake of his devilry and concealed insatiability, as for his goodness, patience, and spirituality. One man would like to possess a nation, and he finds all the higher arts of Cagliostro and Catalina suitable for his purpose. Another, with a more refined thirst for possession, says to himself: "One may not deceive where one desires to possess"—he is irritated and impatient at the idea that a mask of him should rule in the hearts of the people: "I must, therefore, *make* myself known, and first of all learn to know myself!" Amongst helpful and charitable people, one almost always finds the awkward craftiness which first gets up suitably him who has to be helped, as though, for instance, he should "merit" help, seek just *their* help, and would show himself deeply grateful, attached, and subservient to them for all help. With these conceits, they take control of the needy as a property, just as in general they are charitable and helpful out of a desire for property. One finds them jealous when they are crossed or forestalled in their charity. Parents involuntarily make something like themselves out of their children—they call that "education"; no mother doubts at the bottom of her heart that the child she has born is thereby her property, no father hesitates about his right to subject it to *his own* ideas and notions of worth. Indeed, in former times fathers deemed it right to use their discretion concerning the life or death of the newly born (as amongst the ancient Germans). And like the father, so also do the teacher, the class, the priest, and the prince still see in every new individual an unobjectionable opportunity for a new possession. The consequence is. . . .

195

The Jews—a people "born for slavery," as Tacitus and the whole ancient world say of them; "the chosen people among the nations," as they themselves say and believe—the Jews performed the miracle of the inversion of valuations, by means of which life on earth obtained a new and dangerous charm for a couple of millenniums. Their prophets fused into one the expressions "rich," "godless," "wicked," "violent," "sensual," and for the first time coined the word "world" as a term of reproach. In this inversion of valuations (in which is also included the use of the word "poor" as synonymous with "saint" and "friend") the significance of the Jewish people is to be found; it is with *them* that the *slave-insurrection in morals* commences.

196

It is to be *inferred* that there are countless dark bodies near the sun—such as we shall never see. Amongst ourselves, this is an allegory; and the psychologist of morals reads the whole star-writing merely as an allegorical and symbolic language in which much may be unexpressed.

197

The beast of prey and the man of prey (for instance, Caesar Borgia) are fundamentally misunderstood, "nature" is misunderstood, so long as one seeks a "morbidness" in the constitution of these healthiest of all tropical monsters and growths, or even an innate "hell" in them—as almost all moralists have done hitherto. Does it not seem that there is a hatred of the virgin forest and of the tropics among moralists? And that the "tropical man" must be discredited at all costs, whether as disease and deterioration of mankind, or as his own hell and self-torture? And why? In favour of the "temperate zones"? In favour of the temperate men? The "moral"? The mediocre? This for the chapter: *Morals as Timidity*.

198

All the systems of morals which address themselves to individuals with a view to their "happiness," as it is called—what else are they but suggestions for behaviour adapted to the degree of *danger* from themselves in which the individuals live; recipes for their passions, their good and bad propensities, insofar as such have the Will to Power and would like to play the master; small and great expediencies and elaborations, permeated with the musty odour of old family medicines and old-wife wisdom; all of them grotesque and absurd in their form—because they address themselves to "all," because they generalise where generalisation is not authorised; all of them speaking unconditionally, and taking themselves unconditionally; all of them flavoured not merely with one grain of salt, but rather endurable only, and sometimes even seductive, when they are over-spiced and begin to smell dangerously, especially of "the other world." That is all of little value when estimated intellectually, and is far from being "science," much less "wisdom"; but, repeated once more, and three times repeated, it is expediency, expediency, expediency, mixed with stupidity, stupidity, stupidity—whether it be the indifference and statuesque coldness towards the heated folly of the emotions, which the Stoics advised and fostered; or the no-more-laughing and no-more-weeping of Spinoza, the destruction of the emotions by their analysis and vivisection, which he recommended so naïvely; or the lowering of the emotions to an innocent mean at which they may be satisfied, the Aristotelianism of morals; or even morality as the enjoyment of the emotions in

a voluntary attenuation and spiritualisation by the symbolism of art, perhaps as music, or as love of God, and of mankind for God's sake—for in
religion the passions are once more enfranchised, provided that . . . ; or,
finally, even the complaisant and wanton surrender to the emotions, as
has been taught by Hafis and Goethe, the bold letting-go of the reins, the
spiritual and corporeal *licentia morum* in the exceptional cases of wise old
codgers and drunkards, with whom it "no longer has much danger." This
also for the chapter: *Morals as Timidity*.

199

Inasmuch as in all ages, as long as mankind has existed, there have also
been human herds (family alliances, communities, tribes, peoples, states,
churches), and always a great number who obey in proportion to the small
number who command—in view, therefore, of the fact that obedience has
been most practised and fostered among mankind hitherto, one may reasonably suppose that, generally speaking, the need thereof is now innate
in everyone, as a kind of *formal conscience* which gives the command: "Thou
shalt unconditionally do something, unconditionally refrain from something"; in short, "Thou shalt." This need tries to satisfy itself and to fill its
form with a content; according to its strength, impatience, and eagerness,
it at once seizes as an omnivorous appetite with little selection, and accepts
whatever is shouted into its ear by all sorts of commanders—parents, teachers, laws, class prejudices, or public opinion. The extraordinary limitation
of human development, the hesitation, protractedness, frequent retrogression, and turning thereof, is attributable to the fact that the herd-instinct
of obedience is transmitted best, and at the cost of the art of command. If
one imagine this instinct increasing to its greatest extent, commanders
and independent individuals will finally be lacking altogether; or they will
suffer inwardly from a bad conscience, and will have to impose a deception
on themselves in the first place in order to be able to command: just as if
they also were only obeying. This condition of things actually exists in
Europe at present—I call it the moral hypocrisy of the commanding class.
They know no other way of protecting themselves from their bad conscience than by playing the role of executors of older and higher orders (of
predecessors, of the constitution, of justice, of the law, or of God himself),
or they even justify themselves by maxims from the current opinions of the
herd, as "first servants of their people," or "instruments of the public weal."
On the other hand, the gregarious European man nowadays assumes an air
as if he were the only kind of man that is allowable; he glorifies his qualities,

such as public spirit, kindness, deference, industry, temperance, modesty, indulgence, sympathy, by virtue of which he is gentle, endurable, and useful to the herd, as the peculiarly human virtues. In cases, however, where it is believed that the leader and bell-wether cannot be dispensed with, attempt after attempt is made nowadays to replace commanders by the summing together of clever gregarious men: all representative constitutions, for example, are of this origin. In spite of all, what a blessing, what a deliverance from a weight becoming unendurable, is the appearance of an absolute ruler for these gregarious Europeans—of this fact the effect of the appearance of Napoleon was the last great proof: the history of the influence of Napoleon is almost the history of the higher happiness to which the entire century has attained in its worthiest individuals and periods.

200

The man of an age of dissolution which mixes the races with one another, who has the inheritance of a diversified descent in his body—that is to say, contrary, and often not only contrary, instincts and standards of value, which struggle with one another and are seldom at peace—such a man of late culture and broken lights, will, on an average, be a weak man. His fundamental desire is that the war which is *in him* should come to an end; happiness appears to him in the character of a soothing medicine and mode of thought (for instance, Epicurean or Christian); it is above all things the happiness of repose, of undisturbedness, of repletion, of final unity—it is the "Sabbath of Sabbaths," to use the expression of the holy rhetorician, St. Augustine, who was himself such a man. Should, however, the contrariety and conflict in such natures operate as an *additional* incentive and stimulus to life—and if, on the other hand, in addition to their powerful and irreconcilable instincts, they have also inherited and indoctrinated into them a proper mastery and subtlety for carrying on the conflict with themselves (that is to say, the faculty of self-control and self-deception), there then arise those marvellously incomprehensible, and inexplicable beings, those enigmatical men, predestined for conquering and circumventing others, the finest examples of which are Alcibiades and Caesar (with whom I should like to associate the *first* of Europeans according to my taste, the Hohenstaufen, Frederick the Second), and amongst artists, perhaps Lionardo da Vinci. They appear precisely in the same periods when that weaker type, with its longing for repose, comes to the front; the two types are complementary to each other, and spring from the same causes.

201

As long as the utility which determines moral estimates is only gregarious utility, as long as the preservation of the community is only kept in view, and the immoral is sought precisely and exclusively in what seems dangerous to the maintenance of the community, there can be no "morality of love to one's neighbour." Granted even that there is already a little constant exercise of consideration, sympathy, fairness, gentleness, and mutual assistance, granted that even in this condition of society all those instincts are already active which are latterly distinguished by honourable names as "virtues," and eventually almost coincide with the conception "morality": in that period they do not as yet belong to the domain of moral valuations—they are still *ultra-moral.* A sympathetic action, for instance, is neither called good nor bad, moral nor immoral, in the best period of the Romans; and should it be praised, a sort of resentful disdain is compatible with this praise, even at the best, directly the sympathetic action is compared with one which contributes to the welfare of the whole, to the *res publica.* After all, "love to our neighbour" is always a secondary matter, partly conventional and arbitrarily manifested in relation to our *fear of our neighbour.* After the fabric of society seems on the whole established and secured against external dangers, it is this fear of our neighbour which again creates new perspectives of moral valuation. Certain strong and dangerous instincts, such as the love of enterprise, foolhardiness, revengefulness, astuteness, rapacity, and love of power, which up till then had not only to be honoured from the point of view of general utility—under other names, of course, than those here given—but had to be fostered and cultivated (because they were perpetually required in the common danger against the common enemies), are now felt in their dangerousness to be doubly strong—when the outlets for them are lacking—and are gradually branded as immoral and given over to calumny. The contrary instincts and inclinations now attain to moral honour; the gregarious instinct gradually draws its conclusions. How much or how little dangerousness to the community or to equality is contained in an opinion, a condition, an emotion, a disposition, or an endowment—that is now the moral perspective; here again fear is the mother of morals. It is by the loftiest and strongest instincts, when they break out passionately and carry the individual far above and beyond the average, and the low level of the gregarious conscience, that the self-reliance of the community is destroyed; its belief in itself, its backbone, as it were, breaks; consequently these very instincts will be most branded and defamed. The lofty independent spirituality, the will to stand alone, and even the cogent reason, are felt to be dangers; everything that elevates the individual above the herd, and is a source of fear to the neighbour, is henceforth called *evil*; the tolerant, unassuming, self-adapting, self-equalising disposition, the *mediocrity* of desires, attains to moral distinction and honour. Finally, under very peaceful circumstances, there is always less opportunity and necessity for training the feelings to severity and rigour; and now every form of severity, even in justice, begins to disturb the conscience; a lofty and rigorous nobleness and self-responsibility almost offends, and awakens distrust, "the lamb," and still more "the sheep," wins respect. There is a point of diseased mellowness and effeminacy in the history of society, at which society itself takes the part of him who injures it, the part of the *criminal*, and does so, in fact, seriously and honestly. To punish, appears to it to be somehow unfair—it is certain that the idea of "punishment" and "the obligation to punish" are then painful and alarming to people. "Is it not sufficient if the criminal be rendered *harmless*? Why should we still punish? Punishment itself is terrible!" With these questions gregarious morality, the morality of fear, draws its ultimate conclusion. If one could at all do away with danger, the cause of fear, one would have done away with this morality at the same time, it would no longer be necessary, it *would not consider itself* any longer necessary! Whoever examines the conscience of the present-day European, will always elicit the same imperative from its thousand moral folds and hidden recesses, the imperative of the timidity of the herd: "we wish that some time or other there may be *nothing more to fear*!" Some time or other—the will and the way *thereto* is nowadays called "progress" all over Europe.

202

. Let us at once say again what we have already said a hundred times, for people's ears nowadays are unwilling to hear such truths—*our* truths. We know well enough how offensively it sounds when anyone plainly, and without metaphor, counts man amongst the animals; but it will be accounted to us almost a *crime*, that it is precisely in respect to men of "modern ideas" that we have constantly applied the terms "herd," "herd-instincts," and such like expressions. What avail is it? We cannot do otherwise, for it is precisely here that our new insight is. We have found that in all the principal moral judgements Europe has become unanimous, including likewise the countries where European influence prevails: in Europe people evidently *know* what Socrates thought he did not know, and what the famous serpent of old once promised to teach—they "know" today what is good and evil. It must then sound hard and be distasteful to the ear, when we always insist that that which here thinks it knows, that which here glorifies itself with praise and blame, and calls itself good, is the instinct of the herding human animal: the instinct which has come and is ever coming more and more to the front, to preponderance and supremacy over other instincts, according to the increasing physiological approximation and resemblance of which it is the symptom. *Morality in Europe at present is herding-animal morality*; and therefore, as we understand the matter, only one kind of human morality, beside which, before which, and after which many other moralities, and above all *higher* moralities, are or should be possible. Against such a "possibility," against such a "should be," however, this morality defends itself with all its strength; it says obstinately and inexorably: "I am morality itself and nothing else is morality!" Indeed, with the help of a religion which has humoured and flattered the sublimest desires of the herding-animal, things have reached such a point that we always find a more visible expression of this morality even in political and social arrangements: the *democratic* movement is the inheritance of the Christian movement. That its *tempo*, however, is much too slow and sleepy for the more impatient ones, for those who are sick and distracted by the herding-instinct, is indicated by the increasingly furious howling, and always less disguised teeth-gnashing of the anarchist dogs, who are now roving through the highways of European culture. Apparently in opposition to the peacefully industrious democrats and Revolution-ideologues, and still more so to the awkward philosophasters and fraternity-visionaries who call themselves Socialists and want a "free society," those are really at one with them all in their thorough and instinctive hostility to every form of society other than that of the *autonomous* herd (to the extent even of repudiating the notions "master" and "servant"—*ni dieu ni maître*, says a socialist formula); at one in their tenacious opposition to every special claim, every special right and privilege (this means ultimately opposition to *every* right, for when all are equal, no one needs "rights" any longer); at one in their distrust of punitive justice (as though it were a violation of the weak, unfair to the *necessary* consequences of all former society); but equally at one in their religion of sympathy, in their compassion for all that feels, lives, and suffers (down to the very animals, up even to "God"—the extravagance of "sympathy for God" belongs to a democratic age); altogether at one in the cry and impatience of their sympathy, in their deadly hatred of suffering generally, in their almost feminine incapacity for witnessing it or *allowing* it; at one in their involuntary beglooming and heart-softening, under the spell of which Europe seems to be threatened with a new Buddhism; at one in their belief in the morality of *mutual* sympathy, as though it were morality in itself, the climax, the *attained* climax of mankind, the sole hope of the future, the consolation of the present, the great discharge from all the obligations of the past; altogether at one in their belief in the community as the *deliverer*, in the herd, and therefore in "themselves."

203

We, who hold a different belief—we, who regard the democratic movement, not only as a degenerating form of political organisation, but as equivalent to a degenerating, a waning type of man, as involving his mediocrising and depreciation: where have we to fix our hopes? In *new philosophers*—there is no other alternative: in minds strong and original enough to initiate opposite estimates of value, to transvalue and invert "eternal valuations"; in forerunners, in men of the future, who in the present shall fix the constraints and fasten the knots which will compel millenniums to take *new* paths. To teach man the future of humanity as his *will*, as depending on human will, and to make preparation for vast hazardous enterprises and collective attempts in rearing and educating, in order thereby to put an end to the frightful rule of folly and chance which has hitherto gone by the name of "history" (the folly of the "greatest number" is only its last form)—for that purpose a new type of philosophers and commanders will some time or other be needed, at the very idea of which everything that has existed in the way of occult, terrible, and benevolent beings might look pale and dwarfed. The image of such leaders hovers before *our* eyes: is it lawful for me to say it aloud, ye free spirits? The conditions which one would partly have to create and partly utilise for their genesis; the presumptive methods and tests by virtue of which a soul should grow up to such an elevation and power as to feel a *constraint* to these tasks; a transvaluation of values, under the new pressure and hammer of which a conscience should be steeled and a heart transformed into brass, so as to bear the weight of such responsibility; and on the other hand the necessity for such leaders, the dreadful danger that they might be lacking, or miscarry and degenerate: these are *our* real anxieties and glooms, ye know it well, ye free spirits! These are the heavy distant thoughts and storms which sweep across the heaven of *our* life. There are few pains so grievous as to have seen, divined, or experienced how an exceptional man has missed his way and deteriorated; but he who has the rare eye for the universal danger of "man" himself *deteriorating*, he who like us has recognised the extraordinary fortuitousness which has hitherto played its game in respect to the future of mankind—a game in which neither the hand, nor even a "finger of God" has participated! He who divines the fate that is hidden under the idiotic unwariness and blind confidence of "modern ideas," and still more under the whole of Christo-European morality—suffers from an anguish with which no other is to be compared. He sees at a glance all that could still *be made out of man* through a favourable accumulation and augmentation of human powers and arrangements; he knows with all the knowledge of his conviction how unexhausted man still is for the greatest possibilities, and how often in the past the type man has stood in presence of mysterious decisions and new paths: he knows still better from his painfulest recollections on what wretched obstacles promising developments of the highest rank have hitherto usually gone to pieces, broken down, sunk, and become contemptible. The *universal degeneracy of mankind* to the level of the "man of the future"—as idealised by the socialistic fools and shallow-pates—this degeneracy and dwarfing of man to an absolutely gregarious animal (or as they call it, to a man of "free society"), this brutalising of man into a pigmy with equal rights and claims, is undoubtedly *possible!* He who has thought out this possibility to its ultimate conclusion knows *another* loathing unknown to the rest of mankind—and perhaps also a new *mission!*

CHAPTER SIX

WE SCHOLARS

204

AT THE RISK THAT MORALISING MAY ALSO REVEAL ITSELF HERE AS THAT which it has always been—namely, resolutely *montrer ses plaies*, according to Balzac—I would venture to protest against an improper and injurious alteration of rank, which quite unnoticed, and as if with the best conscience, threatens nowadays to establish itself in the relations of science and philosophy. I mean to say that one must have the right out of one's own *experience*—experience, as it seems to me, always implies unfortunate experience? To treat of such an important question of rank, so as not to speak of colour like the blind, or *against* science like women and artists ("Ah! This dreadful science!" sigh their instinct and their shame, "it always *finds things out!*"). The declaration of independence of the scientific man, his emancipation from philosophy, is one of the subtler after-effects of democratic organisation and disorganisation: the self-glorification and self-conceitedness of the learned man is now everywhere in full bloom, and in its best springtime—which does not mean to imply that in this case self-praise smells sweetly. Here also the instinct of the populace cries, "Freedom from all masters!" and after science has, with the happiest results, resisted theology, whose "handmaid" it had been too long, it now proposes in its wantonness and indiscretion to lay down laws for philosophy, and in its turn to play the "master"—what am I saying! To play the *philosopher* on its own account. My memory—the memory of a scientific man, if you please! Teems with the naïvetés of insolence which I have heard about philosophy and philosophers from young naturalists and old physicians (not to mention the most cultured and most conceited of all learned men, the philologists and schoolmasters, who are both the one and the other by profession). On one occasion it was the specialist and the Jack Horner who instinctively stood on the defensive against all synthetic tasks and capabilities; at another time it was the industrious worker who had got a scent of *otium* and refined luxuriousness in the internal economy of the philosopher, and felt himself aggrieved and belittled thereby. On another occasion it was the colour-blindness of the utilitarian, who sees nothing in philosophy but a series of *refuted* systems, and an extravagant expenditure which "does nobody any good." At another time the fear of disguised mysticism and of the boundary-adjustment of knowledge became conspicuous, at another time the disregard of individual philosophers, which had involuntarily extended to disregard of philosophy generally. In fine, I found most frequently, behind the proud disdain of philosophy in young scholars, the evil after-effect of some particular philosopher, to whom on the whole obedience had been foresworn, without, however, the spell of his scornful estimates of other philosophers having been got rid of—the result being a general ill-will to all philosophy. (Such seems to me, for instance, the after-effect of Schopenhauer on the most modern Germany: by his unintelligent rage against Hegel, he has succeeded in severing the whole of the last generation of Germans from its connexion with German culture, which culture, all things considered, has been an elevation and a divining refinement of the *historical sense*; but precisely at this point Schopenhauer himself was poor, irreceptive, and un-German to the extent of ingeniousness.) On the whole, speaking generally, it may just have been the humanness, all-too-humanness of the modern philosophers themselves, in short, their contemptibleness, which has injured most radically the reverence for philosophy and opened the doors to the instinct of the populace. Let it but be acknowledged to what an extent our modern world diverges from the whole style of the world of Heraclites, Plato, Empedocles, and whatever else all the royal and magnificent anchorites of the spirit were called; and with what justice an honest man of science *may* feel himself of a better family and origin, in view of such representatives of philosophy, who, owing to the fashion of the present day, are just as much aloft as they are down below—in Germany, for instance, the two lions of Berlin, the anarchist Eugen Dühring and the amalgamist Eduard von Hartmann. It is especially the sight of those hotch-potch philosophers, who call themselves "realists," or "positivists," which is calculated to implant a dangerous distrust in the soul of a young and ambitious scholar: those philosophers, at the best, are themselves but scholars and specialists, that is very evident! All of them are persons who have been vanquished and *brought back again* under the dominion of science, who at one time or another claimed more from themselves, without having a right to the "more" and its responsibility —and who now, creditably, rancorously and vindictively, represent in word and deed, *disbelief* in the master-task and supremacy of philosophy. After all, how could it be otherwise? Science flourishes nowadays and has the good conscience clearly visible on its countenance; while that to which the entire modern philosophy has gradually sunk, the remnant of philosophy of the present day, excites distrust and displeasure, if not scorn and pity. Philosophy reduced to a "theory of knowledge," no more in fact than a diffident science of epochs and doctrine of forbearance: a philosophy that never even gets beyond the threshold, and rigorously *denies* itself the right to enter—that is philosophy in its last throes, an end, an agony, something that awakens pity. How could such a philosophy—*rule!*

205

The dangers that beset the evolution of the philosopher are, in fact, so manifold nowadays, that one might doubt whether this fruit could still come to maturity. The extent and towering structure of the sciences have increased enormously, and therewith also the probability that the philosopher will grow tired even as a learner, or will attach himself somewhere and "specialise": so that he will no longer attain to his elevation, that is to say, to his superspection, his circumspection, and his *despection.* Or he gets aloft too late, when the best of his maturity and strength is past; or when he is impaired, coarsened, and deteriorated, so that his view, his general estimate of things, is no longer of much importance. It is perhaps just the refinement of his intellectual conscience that makes him hesitate and linger on the way; he dreads the temptation to become a dilettante, a millepede, a milleantenna; he knows too well that as a discerner, one who has lost his self-respect no longer commands, no longer *leads;* unless he should aspire to become a great play-actor, a philosophical Cagliostro and spiritual rat-catcher—in short, a misleader. This is in the last instance a question of taste, if it has not really been a question of conscience. To double once more the philosopher's difficulties, there is also the fact that he demands from himself a verdict, a Yea or Nay, not concerning science, but concerning life and the worth of life—he learns unwillingly to believe that it is his right and even his duty to obtain this verdict, and he has to seek his way to the right and the belief only through the most extensive (perhaps disturbing and destroying) experiences, often hesitating, doubting, and dumbfounded. In fact, the philosopher has long been mistaken and confused by the multitude, either with the scientific man and ideal scholar, or with the religiously elevated, desensualised, desecularised visionary and God-intoxicated man; and even yet when one hears anybody praised, because he lives "wisely," or "as a philosopher," it hardly means anything more than "prudently and apart." Wisdom: that seems to the populace to be a kind of flight, a means and artifice for withdrawing successfully from a bad game; but the *genuine* philosopher—does it not seem so to *us*, my friends? Lives "unphilosophically" and "unwisely," above all, *imprudently*, and feels the obligation and burden of a hundred attempts and temptations of life—he risks *himself* constantly, he plays *this* bad game.

206

In relation to the genius, that is to say, a being who either *engenders* or *produces*—both words understood in their fullest sense—the man of learning, the scientific average man, has always something of the old maid about him; for, like her, he is not conversant with the two principal functions of man. To both, of course, to the scholar and to the old maid, one concedes respectability, as if by way of indemnification—in these cases one emphasises the respectability—and yet, in the compulsion of this concession, one has the same admixture of vexation. Let us examine more closely: what is the scientific man? Firstly, a commonplace type of man, with commonplace virtues: that is to say, a non-ruling, non-authoritative, and non-self-sufficient type of man; he possesses industry, patient adaptableness to rank and file, equability and moderation in capacity and requirement; he has the instinct for people like himself, and for that which they require—for instance: the portion of independence and green meadow without which there is no rest from labour, the claim to honour and consideration (which first and foremost presupposes recognition and recognisability), the sunshine of a good name, the perpetual ratification of his value and usefulness, with which the inward *distrust* which lies at the bottom of the heart of all dependent men and gregarious animals, has again and again to be overcome. The learned man, as is appropriate, has also maladies and faults of an ignoble kind: he is full of petty envy, and has a lynx-eye for the weak points in those natures to whose elevations he cannot attain. He is confiding, yet only as one who lets himself go, but does not *flow*; and precisely before the man of the great current he stands all the colder and more reserved—his eye is then like a smooth and irresponsive lake, which is no longer moved by rapture or sympathy. The worst and most dangerous thing of which a scholar is capable results from the instinct of mediocrity of his type, from the Jesuitism of mediocrity, which labours instinctively for the destruction of the exceptional man, and endeavours to break—or still better, to relax—every bent bow. To relax, of course, with consideration, and naturally with an indulgent hand—to *relax* with confiding sympathy: that is the real art of Jesuitism, which has always understood how to introduce itself as the religion of sympathy.

207

However gratefully one may welcome the *objective* spirit—and who has not been sick to death of all subjectivity and its confounded *ipsissimosity*! In the end, however, one must learn caution even with regard to one's gratitude, and put a stop to the exaggeration with which the unselfing and depersonalising of the spirit has recently been celebrated, as if it were the goal in itself, as if it were salvation and glorification—as is especially accustomed to happen in the pessimist school, which has also in its turn good reasons for paying the highest honours to "disinterested knowledge." The objective man, who no longer curses and scolds like the pessimist, the *ideal* man of learning in whom the scientific instinct blossoms forth fully after a thousand complete and partial failures, is assuredly one of the most costly instruments that exist, but his place is in the hand of one who is more powerful. He is only an instrument; we may say, he is a *mirror*—he is no "purpose in himself." The objective man is in truth a mirror: accustomed to prostration before everything that wants to be known, with such desires only as knowing or "reflecting" imply—he waits until something comes, and then expands himself sensitively, so that even the light footsteps and gliding past of spiritual beings may not be lost on his surface and film. Whatever "personality" he still possesses seems to him accidental, arbitrary, or still oftener, disturbing; so much has he come to regard himself as the passage and reflexion of outside forms and events. He calls up the recollection of "himself" with an effort, and not infrequently wrongly; he readily confounds himself with other persons, he makes mistakes with regard to his own needs, and here only is he unrefined and negligent. Perhaps he is troubled about the health, or the pettiness and confined atmosphere of wife and friend, or the lack of companions and society— indeed, he sets himself to reflect on his suffering, but in vain! His thoughts already rove away to the *more general* case, and tomorrow he knows as little as he knew yesterday how to help himself. He does not now take himself seriously and devote time to himself: he is serene, *not* from lack of trouble, but from lack of capacity for grasping and dealing with *his* trouble. The habitual complaisance with respect to all objects and experiences, the radiant and impartial hospitality with which he receives everything that comes his way, his habit of inconsiderate good nature, of dangerous indifference as to Yea and Nay: alas! There are enough of cases in which he has to atone for these virtues of his! And as man generally, he becomes far too easily the *caput mortuum* of such virtues. Should one wish love or hatred from him—I mean love and hatred as God, woman, and animal understand them—he will do what he can, and furnish what he can. But one must not be surprised if it should not be much—if he should show himself just at this point to be false, fragile, questionable, and deteriorated. His love is constrained, his hatred is artificial, and rather *un tour de force*, a slight ostentation and exaggeration. He is only genuine so far as he can be objective; only in his serene totality is he still "nature" and "natural." His mirroring and eternally self-polishing soul no longer knows how to affirm, no longer how to deny; he does not command; neither does he destroy. "*Je ne méprise presque rien*"—he says, with Leibnitz; let us not overlook nor undervalue the *presque!* Neither is he a model man; he does not go in advance of anyone, nor after either; he places himself generally too far off to have any reason for espousing the cause of either good or evil. If he has been so long confounded with the *philosopher*, with the Caesarean trainer and dictator of civilisation, he has had far too much honour, and what is most essential in him has been overlooked—he is an instrument, something of a slave, though certainly the sublimest sort of slave, but nothing in himself—*presque rien!* The objective man is an instrument, a costly, easily injured, easily tarnished, measuring instrument and mirroring apparatus, which is to be taken care of and respected; but he is no goal, no outgoing nor upgoing, no complementary man in whom the *rest* of existence justifies itself, no termination—and still less a commencement, an engendering, or primary cause, nothing hardy, powerful, self-centred, that wants to be master; but rather only a soft, inflated, delicate, movable potter's-form, that must wait for some kind of content and frame to "shape" itself thereto—for the most part a man without frame and content, a "selfless" man. Consequently, also, nothing for women, *in parenthesi*.

208

When a philosopher nowadays makes known that he is not a sceptic —I hope that has been gathered from the foregoing description of the objective spirit? People all hear it impatiently; they regard him on that account with some apprehension, they would like to ask so many, many questions . . . indeed among timid hearers, of whom there are now so many, he is henceforth said to be dangerous. With his repudiation of scepticism, it seems to them as if they heard some evil-threatening sound in the distance, as if a new kind of explosive were being tried somewhere, a dynamite of the spirit, perhaps a newly discovered Russian *nihiline*, a pessimism *bonce voluntatis*, that not only denies, means denial, but—dreadful thought! *Practises* denial. Against this kind of "good will"—a will to the veritable, actual negation of life—there is, as is generally acknowledged nowadays, no better soporific and sedative than scepticism, the mild, pleasing, lulling poppy of scepticism; and Hamlet himself is now prescribed by the doctors of the day as an antidote to the "spirit," and its underground noises. "Are not our ears already full of bad sounds?" say the sceptics, as lovers of repose, and almost as a kind of safety police, "this subterranean Nay is terrible! Be still, ye pessimistic moles!" The sceptic, in effect, that delicate creature, is far too easily frightened; his conscience is schooled so as to start at every Nay, and even at every sharp, decided Yea, and feels something like a bite thereby. Yea! And Nay! They seem to him opposed to morality; he loves, on the contrary, to make a festival to his virtue by a noble aloofness, while perhaps he says with Montaigne: "What do I know?" Or with Socrates: "I know that I know nothing." Or: "Here I do not trust myself, no door is open to me." Or: "Even if the door were open, why should I enter immediately?" Or: "What is the use of any hasty hypotheses? It might quite well be in good taste to make no hypotheses at all. Are you absolutely obliged to straighten at once what is crooked? To stuff every hole with some kind of oakum? Is there not time enough for that? Has not the time leisure? Oh, ye demons, can ye not at all *wait?* The uncertain also has its charms, the Sphinx, too, is a Circe, and Circe, too, was a philosopher"—Thus does a sceptic console himself; and in truth he needs some consolation. For scepticism is the most spiritual expression of a certain many-sided physiological temperament, which in ordinary language is called nervous debility and sickliness; it arises whenever races or classes which have been long separated, decisively and suddenly blend with one another. In the new generation, which has inherited as it were different standards and valuations in its blood, everything is disquiet, derangement, doubt, and tentative; the best powers operate restrictively, the very virtues prevent each other growing and becoming strong, equilibrium, ballast, and perpendicular stability are lacking in body and soul. That, however, which is most diseased and degenerated in such nondescripts is the *will*; they are no longer familiar with independence of decision, or the courageous feeling of pleasure in willing—they are doubtful of the "freedom of the will" even in their dreams. Our present-day Europe, the scene of a senseless, precipitate attempt at a radical blending of classes, and *consequently* of races, is therefore sceptical in all its heights and depths, sometimes exhibiting the mobile scepticism which springs impatiently and wantonly from branch to branch, sometimes with gloomy aspect, like a cloud overcharged with interrogative signs—and often sick unto death of its will! Paralysis of will; where do we not find this cripple sitting nowadays! And yet how bedecked oftentimes! How seductively ornamented! There are the finest gala dresses and disguises for this disease; and that, for instance, most of what places itself nowadays in the showcases as "objectiveness," "the scientific spirit," "*l'art pour l'art*," and "pure voluntary knowledge," is only decked-out scepticism and paralysis of will—I am ready to answer for this diagnosis of the European disease. The disease of the will is diffused unequally over Europe; it is worst and most varied where civilisation has longest prevailed; it decreases according as "the barbarian" still—or again—asserts his claims under the loose drapery of Western culture. It is therefore in the France of today, as can be readily disclosed and comprehended, that the will is most infirm; and France, which has always had a masterly aptitude for converting even the portentous crises of its spirit into something charming and seductive, now manifests emphatically its intellectual ascendency over Europe, by being the school and exhibition of all the charms of scepticism. The power to will and to persist, moreover, in a resolution, is already somewhat stronger in Germany, and again in the North of Germany it is stronger than in Central Germany; it is considerably stronger in England, Spain, and Corsica, associated with phlegm in the former and with hard skulls in the latter—not to mention Italy, which is too young yet to know what it wants, and must first show whether it can exercise will; but it is strongest and most surprising of all in that immense middle empire where Europe as it were flows back to Asia—namely, in Russia. There the power to will has been long stored up and accumulated, there the will—uncertain whether to be negative or affirmative—waits threateningly to be discharged (to borrow their pet phrase from our physicists). Perhaps not only Indian wars and complications in Asia would be necessary to free Europe from its greatest danger, but also internal subversion, the shattering of the empire into small states, and above all the introduction of parliamentary imbecility, together with the obligation of everyone to read his newspaper at breakfast. I do not say this as one who desires it; in my heart I should rather prefer the contrary—I mean such an increase in the threatening attitude of Russia, that Europe would have to make up its mind to become equally threatening—namely, *to acquire one will,* by means of a new caste to rule over the Continent, a persistent, dreadful will of its own, that can set its aims thousands of years ahead; so that the long spun-out comedy of its petty-stateism, and its dynastic as well as its democratic many-willedness, might finally be brought to a close. The time for petty politics is past; the next century will bring the struggle for the dominion of the world— the *compulsion* to great politics.

209

As to how far the new warlike age on which we Europeans have evidently entered may perhaps favour the growth of another and stronger kind of scepticism, I should like to express myself preliminarily merely by a para- ble, which the lovers of German history will already understand. That unscrupulous enthusiast for big, handsome grenadiers (who, as King of Prussia, brought into being a military and sceptical genius—and there- with, in reality, the new and now triumphantly emerged type of German), the problematic, crazy father of Frederick the Great, had on one point the very knack and lucky grasp of the genius: he knew what was then lacking in Germany, the want of which was a hundred times more alarming and serious than any lack of culture and social form—his ill-will to the young Frederick resulted from the anxiety of a profound instinct. *Men were lack- ing;* and he suspected, to his bitterest regret, that his own son was not man enough. There, however, he deceived himself; but who would not have deceived himself in his place? He saw his son lapsed to atheism, to the *esprit,* to the pleasant frivolity of clever Frenchmen—he saw in the back- ground the great bloodsucker, the spider scepticism; he suspected the incurable wretchedness of a heart no longer hard enough either for evil or good, and of a broken will that no longer commands, is no longer *able* to command. Meanwhile, however, there grew up in his son that new kind of harder and more dangerous scepticism—who knows *to what extent* it was encouraged just by his father's hatred and the icy melancholy of a will condemned to solitude? The scepticism of daring manliness, which is closely related to the genius for war and conquest, and made its first entrance into Germany in the person of the great Frederick. This scepti- cism despises and nevertheless grasps; it undermines and takes possession; it does not believe, but it does not thereby lose itself; it gives the spirit a dangerous liberty, but it keeps strict guard over the heart. It is the *German* form of scepticism, which, as a continued Fredericianism, risen to the highest spirituality, has kept Europe for a considerable time under the dominion of the German spirit and its critical and historical distrust. Owing to the insuperably strong and tough masculine character of the great German philologists and historical critics (who, rightly estimated, were also all of them artists of destruction and dissolution), a *new* conception of the German spirit gradually established itself—in spite of all Romanticism in music and philosophy—in which the leaning towards masculine scepticism was decidedly prominent: whether, for instance, as fearlessness of gaze, as courage and sternness of the dissecting hand, or as resolute will to dangerous voyages of discovery, to spiritualised North Pole expeditions under barren and dangerous skies. There may be good grounds for it when warm-blooded and superficial humanitarians cross themselves before this spirit, *cet esprit fataliste, ironique, méphislophélique*, as Michelet calls it, not without a shudder. But if one would realise how characteristic is this fear of the "man" in the German spirit which awakened Europe out of its "dogmatic slumber," let us call to mind the former conception which had to be overcome by this new one—and that it is not so very long ago that a masculinised woman could dare, with unbridled presumption, to recommend the Germans to the interest of Europe as gentle, good-hearted, weak-willed, and poetical fools. Finally, let us only understand profoundly enough Napoleon's astonishment when he saw Goethe: it reveals what had been regarded for centuries as the "German spirit." "*Voilà un homme!*" that was as much as to say: "But this is a *man!* And I only expected to see a German!"

210

Supposing, then, that in the picture of the philosophers of the future, some trait suggests the question whether they must not perhaps be sceptics in the last-mentioned sense, something in them would only be designated thereby—and *not* they themselves. With equal right they might call themselves critics; and assuredly they will be men of experiments. By the name with which I ventured to baptise them, I have already expressly emphasised their attempting and their love of attempting: is this because, as critics in body and soul, they will love to make use of experiments in a new, and perhaps wider and more dangerous sense? In their passion for knowledge, will they have to go further in daring and painful attempts than the sensitive and pampered taste of a democratic century can approve of?

There is no doubt: these coming ones will be least able to dispense with the serious and not unscrupulous qualities which distinguish the critic from the sceptic: I mean the certainty as to standards of worth, the conscious employment of a unity of method, the wary courage, the standing-alone, and the capacity for self-responsibility; indeed, they will avow among themselves a *delight* in denial and dissection, and a certain considerate cruelty, which knows how to handle the knife surely and deftly, even when the heart bleeds. They will be *sterner* (and perhaps not always towards themselves only) than humane people may desire, they will not deal with the "truth" in order that it may "please" them, or "elevate" and "inspire" them—they will rather have little faith in "*truth*" bringing with it such revels for the feelings. They will smile, those rigorous spirits, when anyone says in their presence: "that thought elevates me, why should it not be true?" or: "that work enchants me, why should it not be beautiful?" or: "that artist enlarges me, why should he not be great?" Perhaps they will not only have a smile, but a genuine disgust for all that is thus rapturous, idealistic, feminine, and hermaphroditic; and if anyone could look into their inmost heart, he would not easily find therein the intention to reconcile "Christian sentiments" with "antique taste," or even with "modern parliamentarism" (the kind of reconciliation necessarily found even amongst philosophers in our very uncertain and consequently very conciliatory century). Critical discipline, and every habit that conduces to purity and rigour in intellectual matters, will not only be demanded from themselves by these philosophers of the future; they may even make a display thereof as their special adornment—nevertheless they will not want to be called critics on that account. It will seem to them no small indignity to philosophy to have it decreed, as is so welcome nowadays, that "philosophy itself is criticism and critical science—and nothing else whatever!" Though this estimate of philosophy may enjoy the approval of all the Positivists of France and Germany (and possibly it even flattered the heart and taste of *Kant*: let us call to mind the titles of his principal works), our new philosophers will say, notwithstanding, that critics are instruments of the philosopher, and just on that account, as instruments, they are far from being philosophers themselves! Even the great Chinaman of Königsberg was only a great critic.

211

I insist upon it that people finally cease confounding philosophical workers, and in general scientific men, with philosophers—that precisely here one should strictly give "each his own," and not give those far too much,

these far too little. It may be necessary for the education of the real philosopher that he himself should have once stood upon all those steps
upon which his servants, the scientific workers of philosophy, remain
standing, and *must* remain standing: he himself must perhaps have been
critic, and dogmatist, and historian, and besides, poet, and collector,
and traveller, and riddle-reader, and moralist, and seer, and "free spirit," and
almost everything, in order to traverse the whole range of human values
and estimations, and that he may *be able* with a variety of eyes and consciences to look from a height to any distance, from a depth up to any
height, from a nook into any expanse. But all these are only preliminary
conditions for his task; this task itself demands something else—it requires
him *to create values*. The philosophical workers, after the excellent pattern
of Kant and Hegel, have to fix and formalise some great existing body of
valuations—that is to say, former *determinations of value*, creations of value,
which have become prevalent, and are for a time called "truths"—whether
in the domain of the *logical*, the *political* (moral), or the *artistic*. It is for
these investigators to make whatever has happened and been esteemed
hitherto, conspicuous, conceivable, intelligible, and manageable, to shorten
everything long, even "time" itself, and to *subjugate* the entire past: an
immense and wonderful task, in the carrying out of which all refined
pride, all tenacious will, can surely find satisfaction. *The real philosophers,
however, are commanders and lawgivers*; they say: "Thus *shall* it be!" They
determine first the Whither and the Why of mankind, and thereby set
aside the previous labour of all philosophical workers, and all subjuga-
tors of the past—they grasp at the future with a creative hand, and
whatever is and was, becomes for them thereby a means, an instrument,
and a hammer. Their "knowing" is *creating*, their creating is a law-giving,
their will to truth is—*Will to Power*. Are there at present such philosophers?
Have there ever been such philosophers? *Must* there not be such philosophers some day? . . .

212

It is always more obvious to me that the philosopher, as a man *indispensable*
for the morrow and the day after the morrow, has ever found himself, and
has been obliged to find himself, in contradiction to the day in which he
lives; his enemy has always been the ideal of his day. Hitherto all those
extraordinary furtherers of humanity whom one calls philosophers—who
rarely regarded themselves as lovers of wisdom, but rather as disagreeable fools and dangerous interrogators—have found their mission, their

hard, involuntary, imperative mission (in the end however the greatness of their mission), in being the bad conscience of their age. In putting the vivisector's knife to the breast of the very *virtues of their age*, they have betrayed their own secret; it has been for the sake of a *new* greatness of man, a new untrodden path to his aggrandisement. They have always disclosed how much hypocrisy, indolence, self-indulgence, and self-neglect, how much falsehood was concealed under the most venerated types of contemporary morality, how much virtue was *outlived*; they have always said: "We must remove hence to where *you* are least at home." In face of a world of "modern ideas," which would like to confine everyone in a corner, in a "specialty," a philosopher, if there could be philosophers nowadays, would be compelled to place the greatness of man, the conception of "greatness," precisely in his comprehensiveness and multifariousness, in his all-roundness; he would even determine worth and rank according to the amount and variety of that which a man could bear and take upon himself, according to the *extent* to which a man could stretch his responsibility. Nowadays the taste and virtue of the age weaken and attenuate the will; nothing is so adapted to the spirit of the age as weakness of will: consequently, in the ideal of the philosopher, strength of will, sternness and capacity for prolonged resolution, must specially be included in the conception of "greatness"; with as good a right as the opposite doctrine, with its ideal of a silly, renouncing, humble, selfless humanity, was suited to an opposite age—such as the sixteenth century, which suffered from its accumulated energy of will, and from the wildest torrents and floods of selfishness. In the time of Socrates, among men only of worn-out instincts, old conservative Athenians who let themselves go—"for the sake of happiness," as they said; for the sake of pleasure, as their conduct indicated—and who had continually on their lips the old pompous words to which they had long forfeited the right by the life they led, *irony* was perhaps necessary for greatness of soul, the wicked Socratic assurance of the old physician and plebeian, who cut ruthlessly into his own flesh, as into the flesh and heart of the "noble," with a look that said plainly enough: "Do not dissemble before me! Here—we are equal!" At present, on the contrary, when throughout Europe the herding animal alone attains to honours, and dispenses honours, when "equality of right" can too readily be transformed into equality in wrong: I mean to say into general war against everything rare, strange, and privileged, against the higher man, the higher soul, the higher duty, the higher responsibility, the creative plenipotence and lordliness—at present it belongs to the conception of "greatness" to be noble, to wish to be apart, to be capable of being different, to stand alone, to have to live by personal initiative; and the philosopher will betray something of his own ideal when he asserts: "He shall be the greatest who can be the most solitary, the most concealed, the most divergent, the man beyond good and evil, the master of his virtues, and of superabundance of will; precisely this shall be called *greatness*: as diversified as can be entire, as ample as can be full." And to ask once more the question: Is greatness *possible*—nowadays?

213

It is difficult to learn what a philosopher is, because it cannot be taught: one must "know" it by experience—or one should have the pride *not* to know it. The fact that at present people all talk of things of which they *cannot* have any experience, is true more especially and unfortunately as concerns the philosopher and philosophical matters: the very few know them, are permitted to know them, and all popular ideas about them are false. Thus, for instance, the truly philosophical combination of a bold, exuberant spirituality which runs at *presto* pace, and a dialectic rigour and necessity which makes no false step, is unknown to most thinkers and scholars from their own experience, and therefore, should anyone speak of it in their presence, it is incredible to them. They conceive of every necessity as troublesome, as a painful compulsory obedience and state of constraint; thinking itself is regarded by them as something slow and hesitating, almost as a trouble, and often enough as "worthy of the *sweat* of the noble"—but not at all as something easy and divine, closely related to dancing and exuberance! "To think" and to take a matter "seriously," "arduously"—that is one and the same thing to them; such only has been their "experience." Artists have here perhaps a finer intuition; they who know only too well that precisely when they no longer do anything "arbitrarily," and everything of necessity, their feeling of freedom, of subtlety, of power, of creatively fixing, disposing, and shaping, reaches its climax— in short, that necessity and "freedom of will" are then the same thing with them. There is, in fine, a gradation of rank in psychical states, to which the gradation of rank in the problems corresponds; and the highest problems repel ruthlessly everyone who ventures too near them, without being predestined for their solution by the loftiness and power of his spirituality. Of what use is it for nimble, everyday intellects, or clumsy, honest mechanics and empiricists to press, in their plebeian ambition, close to such problems, and as it were into this "holy of holies"—as so often happens nowadays! But coarse feet must never tread upon such carpets: this is provided for in the primary law of things; the doors remain closed to those intruders, though they may dash and break their heads thereon! People have always to be born to a high station, or, more definitely, they have to be *bred* for it: a person has only a right to philosophy—taking the word in its higher significance—in virtue of his descent; the ancestors, the "blood," decide here also. Many generations must have prepared the way for the coming of the philosopher; each of his virtues must have been separately acquired, nurtured, transmitted, and embodied; not only the bold, easy, delicate course and current of his thoughts, but above all the readiness for great responsibilities, the majesty of ruling glance and contemning look, the feeling of separation from the multitude with their duties and virtues, the kindly patronage and defence of whatever is misunderstood and calumniated, be it God or devil, the delight and practise of supreme justice, the art of commanding, the amplitude of will, the lingering eye which rarely admires, rarely looks up, rarely loves. . . .

CHAPTER SEVEN

OUR VIRTUES

214

OUR VIRTUES? IT IS PROBABLE THAT WE TOO HAVE STILL OUR VIRTUES, although naturally they are not those sincere and massive virtues on account of which we hold our grandfathers in esteem and also at a little distance from us. We Europeans of the day after tomorrow, we firstlings of the twentieth century—with all our dangerous curiosity, our multifariousness and art of disguising, our mellow and seemingly sweetened cruelty in sense and spirit—we shall presumably, *if* we must have virtues, have those only which have come to agreement with our most secret and heartfelt inclinations, with our most ardent requirements: well, then, let us look for them in our labyrinths! Where, as we know, so many things lose themselves, so many things get quite lost! And is there anything finer than to *search* for one's own virtues? Is it not almost to *believe* in one's own virtues? But this "believing in one's own virtues"—is it not practically the same as what was formerly called one's "good conscience," that long, respectable pigtail of an idea, which our grandfathers used to hang behind their heads, and often enough also behind their understandings? It seems, therefore, that however little we may imagine ourselves to be old-fashioned and grandfatherly respectable in other respects, in one thing we are nevertheless the worthy grandchildren of our grandfathers, we last Europeans with good consciences: we also still wear their pigtail. Ah! If you only knew how soon, so very soon—it will be different!

215

As in the stellar firmament there are sometimes two suns which determine the path of one planet, and in certain cases suns of different colours shine around a single planet, now with red light, now with green, and then simultaneously illumine and flood it with motley colours: so we modern men, owing to the complicated mechanism of our "firmament," are determined by *different* moralities; our actions shine alternately in different colours, and are seldom unequivocal—and there are often cases, also, in which our actions are *motley-coloured*.

216
To love one's enemies? I think that has been well learnt: it takes place thousands of times at present on a large and small scale; indeed, at times the higher and sublimer thing takes place: we learn to *despise* when we love, and precisely when we love best; all of it, however, unconsciously, without noise, without ostentation, with the shame: and secrecy of goodness, which forbids the utterance of the pompous word and the formula of virtue. Morality as attitude—is opposed to our taste nowadays. This is *also* an advance, as it was an advance in our fathers that religion as an attitude finally became opposed to their taste, including the enmity and Voltairean bitterness against religion (and all that formerly belonged to freethinker-pantomime). It is the music in our conscience, the dance in our spirit, to which Puritan litanies, moral sermons, and goody-goodness won't chime.

217
Let us be careful in dealing with those who attach great importance to being credited with moral tact and subtlety in moral discernment! They never forgive us if they have once made a mistake *before* us (or even *with regard to* us)—they inevitably become our instinctive calumniators and detractors, even when they still remain our "friends." Blessed are the forgetful: for they "get the better" even of their blunders.

218
The psychologists of France—and where else are there still psychologists nowadays? Tave never yet exhausted their bitter and manifold enjoyment of the *bêtise bourgeoise*, just as though . . . in short, they betray something thereby. Flaubert, for instance, the honest citizen of Rouen, neither saw, heard, nor tasted anything else in the end; it was his mode of self-torment and refined cruelty. As this is growing wearisome, I would now recommend for a change something else for a pleasure—namely, the unconscious astuteness with which good, fat, honest mediocrity

always behaves towards loftier spirits and the tasks they have to perform, the subtle, barbed, Jesuitical astuteness, which is a thousand times subtler than the taste and understanding of the middle-class in its best moments—subtler even than the understanding of its victims: a repeated proof that "instinct" is the most intelligent of all kinds of intelligence which have hitherto been discovered. In short, you psychologists, study the philosophy of the "rule" in its struggle with the "exception": there you have a spectacle fit for gods and godlike malignity! Or, in plainer words, practise vivisection on "good people," on the "*homo bonae voluntatis*," on *yourselves*!

219

The practise of judging and condemning morally, is the favourite revenge of the intellectually shallow on those who are less so; it is also a kind of indemnity for them being badly endowed by nature; and finally, it is an opportunity for acquiring spirit and *becoming* subtle: malice spiritualises. They are glad in their inmost heart that there is a standard according to which those who are over-endowed with intellectual goods and privileges, are equal to them; they contend for the "equality of all before God," and almost *need* the belief in God for this purpose. It is among them that the most powerful antagonists of atheism are found. If anyone were to say to them: "a lofty spirituality is beyond all comparison with the honesty and respectability of a merely moral man"—it would make them furious; I shall take care not to say so. I would rather flatter them with my theory that lofty spirituality itself exists only as the ultimate product of moral qualities; that it is a synthesis of all qualities attributed to the "merely moral" man, after they have been acquired singly through long training and practise, perhaps during a whole series of generations; that lofty spirituality is precisely the spiritualising of justice, and the beneficent severity which knows that it is authorised to maintain *gradations of rank* in the world, even among things—and not only among men.

220

Now that the praise of the "disinterested person" is so popular, one must—probably not without some danger—get an idea of *what* people actually take an interest in, and what are the things generally which fundamentally and profoundly concern ordinary men—including the cultured, even the learned, and perhaps philosophers also, if appearances do not deceive. The fact thereby becomes obvious that the greater part of what interests and charms higher natures, and more refined and fastidious tastes, seems absolutely "uninteresting" to the average man: if, notwithstanding, he perceive devotion to these interests, he calls it *désintéressé*, and wonders how it is possible to act "disinterestedly." There have been philosophers who could give this popular astonishment a seductive and mystical, other-world expression (perhaps because they did not know the higher nature by experience?) instead of stating the naked and candidly reasonable truth that "disinterested" action is very interesting and "interested" action, provided that.... "And love?" What! Even an action for love's sake shall be "unegoistic?" But you fools! "And the praise of the self-sacrificer?" But whoever has really offered sacrifice knows that he wanted and obtained something for it—perhaps something from himself for something from himself; that he relinquished here in order to have more there, perhaps in general to be more, or even feel himself "more." But this is a realm of questions and answers in which a more fastidious spirit does not like to stay: for here truth has to stifle her yawns so much when she is obliged to answer. And after all, truth is a woman; one must not use force with her.

221

"It sometimes happens," said a moralistic pedant and trifle-retailer, "that I honour and respect an unselfish man: not, however, because he is unselfish, but because I think he has a right to be useful to another man at his own expense." In short, the question is always who *he* is, and who *the other* is. For instance, in a person created and destined for command, self-denial and modest retirement, instead of being virtues would be the waste of virtues: so it seems to me. Every system of unegoistic morality which takes itself unconditionally and appeals to everyone, not only sins against good taste, but is also an incentive to sins of omission, an *additional* seduction under the mask of philanthropy—and precisely a seduction and injury to the higher, rarer, and more privileged types of men. Moral systems must be compelled first of all to bow before the *gradations of rank*; their presumption must be driven home to their conscience—until they thoroughly understand at last that it is *unmoral* to say that "what is right for one is proper for another." So said my moralistic pedant and *bonhomme*. Did he perhaps deserve to be laughed at when he thus exhorted systems of morals to practise morality? But one should not be too much in the right if one wishes to have the laughers on *one's own* side; a grain of wrong pertains even to good taste.

222

Wherever sympathy (fellow-suffering) is preached nowadays—and, if I gather rightly, no other religion is any longer preached—let the psychologist have his ears open: through all the vanity, through all the noise which is natural to these preachers (as to all preachers), he will hear a hoarse, groaning, genuine note of *self-contempt*. It belongs to the overshadowing and uglifying of Europe, which has been on the increase for a century (the first symptoms of which are already specified documentarily in a thoughtful letter of Galiani to Madame d'Epinay)—*if it is not really the cause thereof!* The man of "modern ideas," the conceited ape, is excessively dissatisfied with himself—this is perfectly certain. He suffers, and his vanity wants him only "to suffer with his fellows."

223

The hybrid European—a tolerably ugly plebeian, taken all in all—absolutely requires a costume: he needs history as a storeroom of costumes. To be sure, he notices that none of the costumes fit him properly—he changes and changes. Let us look at the nineteenth century with respect to these hasty preferences and changes in its masquerades of style, and also with respect to its moments of desperation on account of "nothing suiting" us. It is in vain to get ourselves up as romantic, or classical, or Christian, or Florentine, or *barocco*, or "national," *in moribus et artibus*: it does not "clothe us!" But the "spirit," especially the "historical spirit," profits even by this desperation: once and again a new sample of the past or of the foreign is tested, put on, taken off, packed up, and above all *studied*—we are the first studious age *in puncto* of "costumes," I mean as concerns morals, articles of belief, artistic tastes, and religions; we are prepared as no other age has ever been for a carnival in the grand style, for the most spiritual festival-laughter and -arrogance, for the transcendental height of supreme folly and Aristophanic ridicule of the world. Perhaps we are still discovering the domain of our *invention* just here, the domain where even we can still be original, probably as parodists of the world's history and as God's Merry-Andrews—perhaps, though nothing else of the present have a future, our *laughter* itself may have a future!

224

The *historical sense* (or the capacity for divining quickly the order of rank of the valuations according to which a people, a community, or an individual has lived, the "divining instinct" for the relationships of these valuations, for the relation of the authority of the valuations to the authority of the operating forces)—this historical sense, which we Europeans claim as our speciality, has come to us in the train of the enchanting and mad *semi-barbarity* into which Europe has been plunged by the democratic mingling of classes and races—it is only the nineteenth century that has recognised this faculty as its sixth sense. Owing to this mingling, the past of every form and mode of life, and of cultures which were formerly closely contiguous and superimposed on one another, flows forth into us "modern souls"; our instincts now run back in all directions, we ourselves are a kind of chaos: in the end, as we have said, the spirit perceives its advantage therein. By means of our semi-barbarity in body and in desire, we have secret access everywhere, such as a noble age never had; we have access above all to the labyrinth of imperfect civilisations, and to every form of semi-barbarity that has at anytime existed on earth; and insofar as the most considerable part of human civilisation hitherto has just been semi-barbarity, the "historical sense" implies almost the sense and instinct for everything, the taste and tongue for everything: whereby it immediately proves itself to be an *ignoble* sense. For instance, we enjoy Homer once more: it is perhaps our happiest acquisition that we know how to appreciate Homer, whom men of distinguished culture (as the French of the seventeenth century, like Saint-Evremond, who reproached him for his *esprit vaste*, and even Voltaire, the last echo of the century) cannot and could not so easily appropriate—whom they scarcely permitted themselves to enjoy. The very decided Yea and Nay of their palate, their promptly ready disgust, their hesitating reluctance with regard to everything strange, their horror of the bad taste even of lively curiosity, and in general the averseness of every distinguished and self-sufficing culture to avow a new desire, a dissatisfaction with its own condition, or an admiration of what is strange: all this determines and disposes them unfavourably even towards the best things of the world which are not their property or *could not* become their prey—and no faculty is more unintelligible to such men than just this historical sense, with its truckling, plebeian curiosity. The case is not different with Shakespeare, that marvellous Spanish-Moorish-Saxon synthesis of taste, over whom an ancient Athenian of the circle of Aeschylus would have half-killed himself with laughter or irritation: but we—accept precisely this wild motleyness, this medley of the most delicate, the most coarse, and the most artificial, with a secret confidence and cordiality; we enjoy it as a refinement of art reserved expressly for us, and allow ourselves to be as little disturbed by the repulsive fumes and the proximity of the English populace in which Shakespeare's art and taste lives, as perhaps on the Chiaja of Naples, where, with all our senses awake, we go our way, enchanted and voluntarily, in spite of the drain-odour of the lower quarters of the town. That as men of the "historical sense" we have our virtues, is not to be disputed: we are unpretentious, unselfish, modest, brave, habituated to self-control and self-renunciation, very grateful, very patient, very complaisant—but with all this we are perhaps not very "tasteful." Let us finally confess it, that what is most difficult for us men of the "historical sense" to grasp, feel, taste, and love, what finds us fundamentally prejudiced and almost hostile, is precisely the perfection and ultimate maturity in every culture and art, the essentially noble in works and men, their moment of smooth sea and halcyon self-sufficiency, the goldenness and coldness which all things show that have perfected themselves. Perhaps our great virtue of the historical sense is in necessary contrast to *good* taste, at least to the very best taste; and we can only evoke in ourselves imperfectly, hesitatingly, and with compulsion the small, short, and happy godsends and glorifications of human life as they shine here and there: those moments and marvellous experiences, when a great power has voluntarily come to a halt before the boundless and infinite—when a superabundance of refined delight has been enjoyed by a sudden checking and petrifying, by standing firmly and planting oneself fixedly on still trembling ground. *Proportionateness* is strange to us, let us confess it to ourselves; our itching is really the itching for the infinite, the immeasurable. Like the rider on his forward panting horse, we let the reins fall before the infinite, we modern men, we semi-barbarians—and are only in *our* highest bliss when we—*are in most danger.*

225

Whether it be hedonism, pessimism, utilitarianism, or eudaemonism, all those modes of thinking which measure the worth of things according to *pleasure* and *pain*, that is, according to accompanying circumstances and secondary considerations, are plausible modes of thought and naïvetés, which everyone conscious of *creative* powers and an artist's conscience will look down upon with scorn, though not without sympathy. Sympathy for *you!* To be sure, that is not sympathy as you understand it: it is not sympathy for social "distress," for "society" with its sick and misfortuned, for the hereditarily vicious and defective who lie on the ground around us; still less is it sympathy for the grumbling, vexed, revolutionary slave-classes who strive after power—they call it "freedom." *Our* sympathy is a loftier and further-sighted sympathy: we see how *man* dwarfs himself, how *you* dwarf him! And there are moments when we view *your* sympathy with an indescribable anguish, when we resist it—when we regard your seriousness as more dangerous than any kind of levity. You want, if possible—and there is not a more foolish "if possible"—*to do away with suffering*; and we? It really seems that *we* would rather have it increased and made worse than it has ever been! Well-being, as you understand it—is certainly not a goal; it seems to us an *end*; a condition which at once renders man ludicrous and contemptible—and makes his destruction *desirable!* The discipline of suffering, of *great* suffering—know ye not that it is only *this* discipline that has produced all the elevations of humanity hitherto? The tension of soul in misfortune which communicates to it its energy, its shuddering in view of rack and ruin, its inventiveness and bravery in undergoing, enduring, interpreting, and exploiting misfortune, and whatever depth, mystery, disguise, spirit, artifice, or greatness has been bestowed upon the soul— has it not been bestowed through suffering, through the discipline of great suffering? In man *creature* and *creator* are united: in man there is not only matter, shred, excess, clay, mire, folly, chaos; but there is also the creator, the sculptor, the hardness of the hammer, the divinity of the spectator, and the seventh day—do ye understand this contrast? And that *your* sympathy for the "creature in man" applies to that which has to be fashioned, bruised, forged, stretched, roasted, annealed, refined—to that which must necessarily *suffer*, and *is meant* to suffer? And *our* sympathy—do ye not understand what our *reverse* sympathy applies to, when it resists your sympathy as the worst of all pampering and enervation? So it is sympathy *against* sympathy! But to repeat it once more, there are higher problems than the problems of pleasure and pain and sympathy; and all systems of philosophy which deal only with these are naïvetés.

226

We Immoralists. This world with which *we* are concerned, in which *we* have to fear and love, this almost invisible, inaudible world of delicate command and delicate obedience, a world of "almost" in every respect, captious, insidious, sharp, and tender—yes, it is well protected from clumsy spectators and familiar curiosity! We are woven into a strong net and garment of duties, and *cannot* disengage ourselves—precisely here, we are "men of duty," even we! Occasionally it is true we dance in our "chains" and betwixt our "swords"; it is nonetheless true that more often we gnash our teeth under the circumstances, and are impatient at the secret hardship of our lot. But do what we will, fools and appearances say of us: "these are men *without* duty"—we have always fools and appearances against us!

227

Honesty, granting that it is the virtue from which we cannot rid ourselves, we free spirits—well, we will labour at it with all our perversity and love, and not tire of "perfecting" ourselves in *our* virtue, which alone remains: may its glance someday overspread like a gilded, blue, mocking twilight this aging civilisation with its dull gloomy seriousness! And if, nevertheless, our honesty should one day grow weary, and sigh, and stretch its limbs, and find us too hard, and would fain have it pleasanter, easier, and gentler, like an agreeable vice, let us remain *hard*, we latest Stoics, and let us send to its help whatever devilry we have in us: our disgust at the clumsy and undefined, our *"nitimur in vetitum,"* our love of adventure, our sharpened and fastidious curiosity, our most subtle, disguised, intellectual Will to Power and universal conquest, which rambles and roves avidiously around all the realms of the future—let us go with all our "devils" to the help of our "God!" It is probable that people will misunderstand and mistake us on that account: what does it matter! They will say: "Their 'honesty'—that is their devilry, and nothing else!" What does it matter! And even if they were right—have not all Gods hitherto been such sanctified, re-baptised devils? And after all, what do we know of ourselves? And what the spirit that leads us wants *to be called?* (It is a question of names.) And how many spirits we harbour? Our honesty, we free spirits—let us be careful lest it become our vanity, our ornament and ostentation, our limitation, our stupidity! Every virtue inclines to stupidity, every stupidity to virtue; "stupid to the point of sanctity," they say in Russia—let us be careful lest out of pure honesty we do not eventually become saints and bores! Is not life a hundred times too short for us—to bore ourselves? One would have to believe in eternal life in order to. . . .

228

I hope to be forgiven for discovering that all moral philosophy hitherto has been tedious and has belonged to the soporific appliances—and that "virtue," in my opinion, has been *more* injured by the *tediousness* of its advocates than by anything else; at the same time, however, I would not wish to overlook their general usefulness. It is desirable that as few people as possible should reflect upon morals, and consequently it is *very* desirable that morals should not someday become interesting! But let us not be afraid! Things still remain today as they have always been: I see no one in Europe who has (or *discloses*) an idea of the fact that philosophising concerning morals might be conducted in a dangerous, captious, and ensnaring manner—that *calamity* might be involved therein.

Observe, for example, the indefatigable, inevitable English utilitarians: how ponderously and respectably they stalk on, stalk along (a Homeric metaphor expresses it better) in the footsteps of Bentham, just as he had already stalked in the footsteps of the respectable Helvétius! (no, he was not a dangerous man, Helvétius, *ce sénateur Pococurante*, to use an expression of Galiani). No new thought, nothing of the nature of a finer turning or better expression of an old thought, not even a proper history of what has been previously thought on the subject: an *impossible* literature, taking it all in all, unless one knows how to leaven it with some mischief. In effect, the old English vice called *cant*, which is *moral Tartuffism*, has insinuated itself also into these moralists (whom one must certainly read with an eye to their motives if one *must* read them), concealed this time under the new form of the scientific spirit; moreover, there is not absent from them a secret struggle with the pangs of conscience, from which a race of former Puritans must naturally suffer, in all their scientific tinkering with morals. (Is not a moralist the opposite of a Puritan? That is to say, as thinker who regards morality as questionable, as worthy of interrogation, in short, as a problem? Is moralising not—immoral?) In the end, they all want *English* morality to be recognised as authoritative, inasmuch as mankind, or the "general utility," or "the happiness of the greatest number"—no! The happiness of *England*, will be best served thereby. They would like, by all means, to convince themselves that the striving after *English* happiness, I mean after *comfort* and *fashion* (and in the highest instance, a seat in Parliament), is at the same time the true path of virtue; in fact, that insofar as there has been virtue in the world hitherto, it has just consisted in such striving. Not one of those ponderous, conscience-stricken herding-animals (who undertake to advocate the cause of egoism as conducive to the general welfare) wants to have any knowledge or inkling of the facts that the "general welfare" is no ideal, no goal, no notion that can be at all grasped, but is only a nostrum—that what is fair to one *may not* at all be fair to another, that the requirement of one morality for all is really a detriment to higher men, in short, that there is a *distinction of rank* between man and man, and consequently between morality and morality. They are an unassuming and fundamentally mediocre species of men, these utilitarian Englishmen, and, as already remarked, insofar as they are tedious, one cannot think highly enough of their utility. One ought even to *encourage* them, as has been partially attempted in the following rhymes:

> Hail, ye worthies, barrow-wheeling,
> "Longer—better," aye revealing,
> Stiffer aye in head and knee;
> Unenraptured, never jesting,
> Mediocre everlasting,
> *Sans genie et sans esprit!*

229

In these later ages, which may be proud of their humanity, there still remains so much fear, so much *superstition* of the fear, of the "cruel wild beast," the mastering of which constitutes the very pride of these humaner ages—that even obvious truths, as if by the agreement of centuries, have long remained unuttered, because they have the appearance of helping the finally slain wild beast back to life again. I perhaps risk something when I allow such a truth to escape; let others capture it again and give it so much "milk of pious sentiment"[1] to drink, that it will lie down quiet and forgotten, in its old corner. One ought to learn anew about cruelty, and open one's eyes; one ought at last to learn impatience, in order that such immodest gross errors—as, for instance, have been fostered by ancient and modern philosophers with regard to tragedy—may no longer wander about virtuously and boldly. Almost everything that we call "higher culture" is based upon the spiritualising and intensifying of *cruelty*—this is my thesis; the "wild beast" has not been slain at all, it lives, it flourishes, it has only been—transfigured. That which constitutes the painful delight of tragedy is cruelty; that which operates agreeably in so-called tragic sympathy, and at the basis even of everything sublime, up to the highest and most delicate thrills of metaphysics, obtains its sweetness solely from the intermingled ingredient of cruelty. What the Roman enjoys in the arena, the Christian in the ecstasies of the cross, the Spaniard at the sight of the faggot and stake, or of the bullfight, the present-day Japanese who presses his way to the tragedy, the workman of the Parisian suburbs who has a homesickness for bloody revolutions, the Wagnerienne who, with unhinged will, "undergoes" the performance of "Tristan and Isolde"—what all these enjoy, and strive with mysterious ardour to drink in, is the philtre of the great Circe "cruelty." Here, to be sure, we must put aside entirely the blundering psychology of former times, which could only teach with regard to cruelty that it originated at the sight of the suffering of *others*: there is an abundant, superabundant enjoyment even in one's own suffering, in causing one's own suffering—and wherever man has allowed himself to be persuaded to self-denial in the *religious* sense, or to self-mutilation, as among the Phoenicians and ascetics, or in general, to desensualisation, decarnalisation, and contrition, to Puritanical repentance-spasms, to vivisection of conscience and to Pascal-like *sacrifizio dell' intelletto*, he is secretly allured and impelled forwards by his cruelty, by the dangerous thrill of cruelty *towards himself*. Finally, let us consider that even the seeker of knowledge operates as an artist and glorifier of cruelty, in that he compels his spirit to perceive *against* its own inclination, and often enough against the wishes of his heart: he forces it to say Nay, where he would like to affirm, love, and adore; indeed, every instance of taking a thing profoundly and fundamentally, is a violation, an intentional injuring of the fundamental will of the spirit, which instinctively aims at appearance and superficiality—even in every desire for knowledge there is a drop of cruelty.

230

Perhaps what I have here said about a "fundamental will of the spirit" may not be understood without further details; I may be allowed a word of explanation. That imperious something which is popularly called "the spirit," wishes to be master internally and externally, and to feel itself master: it has the will of a multiplicity for a simplicity, a binding, taming, imperious, and essentially ruling will. Its requirements and capacities here, are the same as those assigned by physiologists to everything that lives, grows, and multiplies. The power of the spirit to appropriate foreign elements reveals itself in a strong tendency to assimilate the new to the old, to simplify the manifold, to overlook or repudiate the absolutely contradictory; just as it arbitrarily re-underlines, makes prominent, and falsifies for itself certain traits and lines in the foreign elements, in every portion of the "outside world." Its object thereby is the incorporation of new "experiences," the assortment of new things in the old arrangements —in short, growth; or more properly, the *feeling* of growth, the feeling of increased power—is its object. This same will has at its service an apparently opposed impulse of the spirit, a suddenly adopted preference of ignorance, of arbitrary shutting out, a closing of windows, an inner denial of this or that, a prohibition to approach, a sort of defensive attitude against much that is knowable, a contentment with obscurity, with the shutting-in horizon, an acceptance and approval of ignorance: as that which is all necessary according to the degree of its appropriating power, its "digestive power," to speak figuratively (and in fact "the spirit" resembles a stomach more than anything else). Here also belong an occasional propensity of the spirit to let itself be deceived (perhaps with a waggish suspicion that it is *not* so and so, but is only allowed to pass as such), a delight in uncertainty and ambiguity, an exulting enjoyment of arbitrary, out-of-the-way narrowness and mystery, of the too-near, of the foreground, of the magnified, the diminished, the misshapen, the beautified—an enjoyment of the arbitrariness of all these manifestations of power. Finally, in this connexion, there is the not unscrupulous readiness of the spirit to deceive other spirits and dissemble before them—the constant pressing and straining of a creating, shaping, changeable power: the spirit enjoys therein its craftiness and its variety of disguises, it enjoys also its feeling of security therein—it is precisely by its Protean arts that it is best protected and concealed! *Counter to this* propensity for appearance, for simplification, for a disguise, for a cloak, in short, for an outside—for every outside is a cloak—there operates the sublime tendency of the man of knowledge, which takes, and *insists* on taking things profoundly, variously, and thoroughly; as a kind of cruelty of the intellectual conscience and taste, which every courageous thinker will acknowledge in himself, provided, as it ought to be, that he has sharpened and hardened his eye sufficiently long for introspection, and is accustomed to severe discipline and even severe words. He will say: "There is something cruel in the tendency of my spirit": let the virtuous and amiable try to convince him that it is not so! In fact, it would sound nicer, if, instead of our cruelty, perhaps our "extravagant honesty" were talked about, whispered about and glorified—we free, *very* free spirits—and someday perhaps *such* will actually be our—posthumous glory! Meanwhile—for there is plenty of time until then—we should be least inclined to deck ourselves out in such florid and fringed moral verbiage; our whole former work has just made us sick of this taste and its sprightly exuberance. They are beautiful, glistening, jingling, festive words: honesty, love of truth, love of wisdom, sacrifice for knowledge, heroism of the truthful—there is something in them that makes one's heart swell with pride. But we anchorites and marmots have long-ago persuaded ourselves in all the secrecy of an anchorite's conscience, that this worthy parade of verbiage also belongs to the old false adornment, frippery, and gold-dust of unconscious human vanity, and that even under such flattering colour and repainting, the terrible original text *homo natura* must again be recognised. In effect, to translate man back again into nature; to master the many vain and visionary interpretations and subordinate meanings which have hitherto been scratched and daubed over the eternal original text, *homo natura*; to bring it about that man shall henceforth stand before man as he now, hardened by the discipline of science, stands before the *other* forms of nature, with fearless Œdipus-eyes, and stopped Ulysses-ears, deaf to the enticements of old metaphysical bird-catchers, who have piped to him far too long: "Thou art more! Thou art higher! Thou hast a different origin!" This may be a strange and foolish task, but that it is a *task*, who can deny! Why did we choose it, this foolish task? Or, to put the question differently: "Why knowledge at all?" Everyone will ask us about this. And thus pressed, we, who have asked ourselves the question a hundred times, have not found, and cannot find any better answer. . . .

231

Learning alters us, it does what all nourishment does that does not merely "conserve"—as the physiologist knows. But at the bottom of our souls, quite "down below," there is certainly something unteachable, a granite of spiritual fate, of predetermined decision and answer to predetermined, chosen questions. In each cardinal problem there speaks an unchangeable "I am this"; a thinker cannot learn anew about man and woman, for instance, but can only learn fully—he can only follow to the end what is "fixed" about them in himself. Occasionally we find certain solutions of problems which make strong beliefs for *us*; perhaps they are henceforth called "convictions." Later on—one sees in them only footsteps to self-knowledge, guideposts to the problem which we ourselves *are*—or more correctly to the great stupidity which we embody, our spiritual fate, the *unteachable* in us, quite "down below." In view of this liberal compliment which I have just paid myself, permission will perhaps be more readily allowed me to utter some truths about "woman as she is," provided that it is known at the outset how literally they are merely—*my* truths.

232

Woman wishes to be independent, and therefore she begins to enlighten men about "woman as she is"—*this* is one of the worst developments of the general *uglifying* of Europe. For what must these clumsy attempts of feminine scientificality and self-exposure bring to light! Woman has so much cause for shame; in woman there is so much pedantry, superficiality, schoolmasterliness, petty presumption, unbridledness, and indiscretion concealed—study only woman's behaviour towards children! Which has really been best restrained and dominated hitherto by the *fear* of man. Alas, if ever the "eternally tedious in woman"—she has plenty of it! Is allowed to venture forth! If she begins radically and on principle to unlearn her wisdom and art—of charming, of playing, of frightening-away-sorrow, of alleviating and taking-easily; if she forgets her delicate aptitude for agreeable desires! Female voices are already raised, which, by Saint Aristophanes! Make one afraid: with medical explicitness it is stated in a threatening manner what woman first and last *requires* from man. Is it not in the very worst taste that woman thus sets herself up to be scientific? Enlightenment hitherto has fortunately been men's affair, men's gift—we remained therewith "among ourselves"; and in the end, in view of all that women write about "woman," we may well have considerable doubt as to whether woman really *desires* enlightenment about herself—and *can* desire it. If woman does not thereby seek a new *ornament* for herself—I believe ornamentation belongs to the eternally feminine? Why, then, she wishes to make herself feared: perhaps she thereby wishes to get the mastery. But she does not *want* truth—what does woman care for truth! From the very first nothing is more foreign, more repugnant, or more hostile to woman than truth—her great art is falsehood, her chief concern is appearance and beauty. Let us confess it, we men: we honour and love *this* very art and *this* very instinct in woman: we who have the hard task, and for our recreation gladly seek the company of beings under whose hands, glances, and delicate follies, our seriousness, our gravity, and profundity appear almost like follies to us. Finally, I ask the question: Did a woman herself ever acknowledge profundity in a woman's mind, or justice in a woman's heart? And is it not true that on the whole "woman" has hitherto been most despised by woman herself, and not at all by us? We men desire that woman should not continue to compromise herself by enlightening us; just as it was man's care and the consideration for woman, when the church decreed: *mulier taceat in ecclesia.* It was to the benefit of woman when Napoleon gave the too eloquent Madame de Staël to understand: *mulier taceat in politicis!* And in my opinion, he is a true friend of woman who calls out to women today: *mulier taceat de muliere!*

233

It betrays corruption of the instincts—apart from the fact that it betrays bad taste—when a woman refers to Madame Roland, or Madame de Staël, or Monsieur George Sand, as though something were proved thereby in *favour* of "woman as she is." Among men, these are the three *comical* women as they are—nothing more! And just the best involuntary *counter-arguments* against feminine emancipation and autonomy.

234

Stupidity in the kitchen; woman as cook; the terrible thoughtlessness with which the feeding of the family and the master of the house is managed! Woman does not understand what food *means*, and she insists on being cook! If woman had been a thinking creature, she should certainly, as cook for thousands of years, have discovered the most important physiological facts, and should likewise have got possession of the healing art! Through bad female cooks—through the entire lack of reason in the kitchen—the development of mankind has been longest retarded and most interfered with; even today matters are very little better. A word to High School girls.

235

There are turns and casts of fancy, there are sentences, little handfuls of words, in which a whole culture, a whole society suddenly crystallises itself. Among these is the incidental remark of Madame de Lambert to her son: "*Mon ami, ne vous permettez jamais que des folies, qui vous feront grand plaisir*"—the motherliest and wisest remark, by the way, that was ever addressed to a son.

236

I have no doubt that every noble woman will oppose what Dante and Goethe believed about woman—the former when he sang, "*ella guardava suso, ed io in lei*" and the latter when he interpreted it, "the eternally feminine draws us *aloft*"; for *this* is just what she believes of the eternally masculine.

237

Seven Apophthegms for Women

How the longest ennui flees,
When a man comes to our knees!

Age, alas! And science staid,
Furnish even weak virtue aid.

Sombre garb and silence meet;
Dress for every dame—discreet.

Whom I thank when in my bliss?
God! And my good tailoress!

Young, a flower-decked cavern home;
Old, a dragon thence doth roam.

Noble title, leg that's fine,
Man as well: Oh, were *he* mine!

Speech in brief and sense in mass—
Slippery for the jenny-ass!

237a

Woman has hitherto been treated by men like birds, which, losing their way, have come down among them from an elevation: as something delicate, fragile, wild, strange, sweet, and animating—but as something also which must be cooped up to prevent it flying away.

238

To be mistaken in the fundamental problem of "man and woman," to deny here the profoundest antagonism and the necessity for an eternally hostile tension, to dream here perhaps of equal rights, equal training, equal claims and obligations: that is a *typical* sign of shallow-mindedness; and a thinker who has proved himself shallow at this dangerous spot— shallow in instinct! May generally be regarded as suspicious, nay more, as betrayed, as discovered; he will probably prove too "short" for all fundamental questions of life, future as well as present, and will be unable to descend into *any* of the depths. On the other hand, a man who has depth of spirit as well as of desires, and has also the depth of benevolence which is capable of severity and harshness, and easily confounded with them, can only think of woman as *Orientals* do: he must conceive of her as a possession, as confinable property, as a being predestined for service and accomplishing her mission therein—he must take his stand in this matter upon the immense rationality of Asia, upon the superiority of the instinct of Asia, as the Greeks did formerly; those best heirs and scholars of Asia —who, as is well known, with their *increasing* culture and amplitude of power, from Homer to the time of Pericles, became gradually *stricter* towards woman, in short, more oriental. *How* necessary, *how* logical, even *how* humanely desirable this was, let us consider for ourselves!

239

The weaker sex has in no previous age been treated with so much respect by men as at present—this belongs to the tendency and fundamental taste of democracy, in the same way as disrespectfulness to old age—what wonder is it that abuse should be immediately made of this respect? They want more, they learn to make claims, the tribute of respect is at last felt to be well-nigh galling; rivalry for rights, indeed actual strife itself, would be preferred: in a word, woman is losing modesty. And let us immediately add that she is also losing taste. She is unlearning to *fear* man: but the woman who "unlearns to fear" sacrifices her most womanly instincts. That woman should venture forward when the fear-inspiring quality in man—or more definitely, the *man* in man—is no longer either desired or fully developed, is reasonable enough and also intelligible enough; what is more difficult to understand is that precisely thereby—woman deteriorates. This is what is happening nowadays: let us not deceive ourselves about it! Wherever the industrial spirit has triumphed over the military and aristocratic spirit, woman strives for the economic and legal independence of a clerk: "woman as clerkess" is inscribed on the portal of the modern society which is in course of formation. While she thus appropriates new rights, aspires to be "master," and inscribes "progress" of woman on her flags and banners, the very opposite realises itself with terrible obviousness: *woman retrogrades*. Since the French Revolution the influence of woman in Europe has *declined* in proportion as she has increased her rights and claims; and the "emancipation of woman," insofar as it is desired and demanded by women themselves (and not only by masculine shallow-pates), thus proves to be a remarkable symptom of the increased weakening and deadening of the most womanly instincts. There is *stupidity* in this movement, an almost masculine stupidity, of which a well-reared woman—who is always a sensible woman—might be heartily ashamed. To lose the intuition as to the ground upon which she can most surely achieve victory; to neglect exercise in the use of her proper weapons; to let-herself-go before man, perhaps even "to the book," where formerly she kept herself in control and in refined, artful humility; to neutralise with her virtuous audacity man's faith in a *veiled*, fundamentally different ideal in woman, something eternally, necessarily feminine; to emphatically and loquaciously dissuade man from the idea that woman must be preserved, cared for, protected, and indulged, like some delicate, strangely wild, and often pleasant domestic animal; the clumsy and indignant collection of everything of the nature of servitude and bondage which the position of woman in the hitherto existing order of society has entailed and still entails (as though slavery were a counterargument, and not rather a condition of every higher culture, of every elevation of culture): what does all this betoken, if not a disintegration of womanly instincts, a de-feminising? Certainly, there are enough of idiotic friends and corrupters of woman amongst the learned asses of the masculine sex, who advise woman to de-feminise herself in this manner, and to imitate all the stupidities from which "man" in Europe, European "manliness," suffers—who would like to lower woman to "general culture," indeed even to newspaper reading and meddling with politics. Here and there they wish even to make women into free spirits and literary workers: as though a woman without piety would not be something perfectly obnoxious or ludicrous to a profound and godless man; almost everywhere her nerves are being ruined by the most morbid and dangerous kind of music (our latest German music), and she is daily being made more hysterical and more incapable of fulfiling her first and last function, that of bearing robust children. They wish to "cultivate" her in general still more, and intend, as they say, to make the "weaker sex" *strong* by culture: as if history did not teach in the most emphatic manner that the "cultivating" of mankind and his weakening— that is to say, the weakening, dissipating, and languishing of his *force of will*—have always kept pace with one another, and that the most powerful and influential women in the world (and lastly, the mother of Napoleon) had just to thank their force of will—and not their schoolmasters! For their power and ascendency over men. That which inspires respect in woman, and often enough fear also, is her *nature*, which is more "natural" than that of man, her genuine, carnivora-like, cunning flexibility, her tiger-claws beneath the glove, her *naïveté* in egoism, her untrainableness and innate wildness, the incomprehensibleness, extent, and deviation of her desires and virtues. . . . That which, in spite of fear, excites one's sympathy for the dangerous and beautiful cat, "woman," is that she seems more afflicted, more vulnerable, more necessitous of love and more condemned to disillusionment than any other creature. Fear and sympathy:

it is with these feelings that man has hitherto stood in presence of woman, always with one foot already in tragedy, which rends while it delights. What? And all that is now to be at an end? And the *disenchantment* of woman is in progress? The tediousness of woman is slowly evolving? Oh Europe! Europe! We know the horned animal which was always most attractive to thee, from which danger is ever again threatening thee! Thy old fable might once more become "history"—an immense stupidity might once again overmaster thee and carry thee away! And no God concealed beneath it—no! Only an "idea," a "modern idea!" . . .

→ CHAPTER EIGHT ←

PEOPLES AND COUNTRIES

240

I HEARD, ONCE AGAIN FOR THE FIRST TIME, RICHARD WAGNER'S OVERTURE to the *Mastersingers*: it is a piece of magnificent, gorgeous, heavy, latter-day art, which has the pride to presuppose two centuries of music as still living, in order that it may be understood: it is an honour to Germans that such a pride did not miscalculate! What flavours and forces, what seasons and climes do we not find mingled in it! It impresses us at one time as ancient, at another time as foreign, bitter, and too modern, it is as arbitrary as it is pompously traditional, it is not infrequently roguish, still oftener rough and coarse—it has fire and courage, and at the same time the loose, dun-coloured skin of fruits which ripen too late. It flows broad and full: and suddenly there is a moment of inexplicable hesitation, like a gap that opens between cause and effect, an oppression that makes us dream, almost a nightmare; but already it broadens and widens anew, the old stream of delight—the most manifold delight—of old and new happiness; including *especially* the joy of the artist in himself, which he refuses to conceal, his astonished, happy cognisance of his mastery of the expedients here employed, the new, newly acquired, imperfectly tested expedients of art which he apparently betrays to us. All in all, however, no beauty, no South, nothing of the delicate southern clearness of the sky, nothing of grace, no dance, hardly a will to logic; a certain clumsiness even, which is also emphasised, as though the artist wished to say to us: "It is part of my intention"; a cumbersome drapery, something arbitrarily barbaric and ceremonious, a flirring of learned and venerable conceits and witticisms; something German in the best and worst sense of the word, something in the German style, manifold, formless, and inexhaustible; a certain German

126

potency and super-plenitude of soul, which is not afraid to hide itself under the *raffinements* of decadence—which, perhaps, feels itself most at ease there; a real, genuine token of the German soul, which is at the same time young and aged, too ripe and yet still too rich in futurity. This kind of music expresses best what I think of the Germans: they belong to the day before yesterday and the day after tomorrow—*they have as yet no today.*

241

We "good Europeans," we also have hours when we allow ourselves a warm-hearted patriotism, a plunge and relapse into old loves and narrow views—I have just given an example of it—hours of national excitement, of patriotic anguish, and all other sorts of old-fashioned floods of sentiment. Duller spirits may perhaps only get done with what confines its operations in us to hours and plays itself out in hours—in a considerable time: some in half a year, others in half a lifetime, according to the speed and strength with which they digest and "change their material." Indeed, I could think of sluggish, hesitating races, which, even in our rapidly moving Europe, would require half a century ere they could surmount such atavistic attacks of patriotism and soil-attachment, and return once more to reason, that is to say, to "good Europeanism." And while digressing on this possibility, I happen to become an ear-witness of a conversation between two old patriots—they were evidently both hard of hearing and consequently spoke all the louder. "*He* has as much, and knows as much, philosophy as a peasant or a corps-student," said the one—

... he is still innocent. But what does that matter nowadays! It is the age of the masses: they lie on their belly before everything that is massive. And so also *in politicis*. A statesman who rears up for them a new Tower of Babel, some monstrosity of empire and power, they call "great"—what does it matter that we more prudent and conservative ones do not meanwhile give up the old belief that it is only the great thought that gives greatness to an action or affair. Supposing a statesman were to bring his people into the position of being obliged henceforth to practise "high politics," for which they were by nature badly endowed and prepared, so that they would have to sacrifice their old and reliable virtues, out of love to a new and doubtful mediocrity; supposing a statesman were to condemn his people generally to "practise politics," when they have hitherto had something better to do and think about, and when in the depths of their souls they have been unable to free themselves from a prudent loathing of the restlessness, emptiness, and noisy wranglings of the essentially politics-practising nations; supposing such a statesman were to stimulate the slumbering passions and avidities of his people, were to make a stigma out of their former diffidence and delight in aloofness, an offence out of their exoticism and hidden permanency, were to depreciate their most radical proclivities, subvert their consciences, make their minds narrow, and their tastes "national"—what! A statesman who should do all this, which his people would have to do penance for throughout their whole future, if they had a future, such a statesman would be *great*, would he?

"Undoubtedly!" replied the other old patriot vehemently. "Otherwise he *could not* have done it! It was mad perhaps to wish such a thing! But perhaps everything great has just been mad at its commencement!" "Misuse of words!" cried his interlocutor, contradictorily—"strong! Strong! Strong and mad! *Not* great!" The old men had obviously become heated as they thus shouted their "truths" in each other's faces; but I, in my happiness and apartness, considered how soon a stronger one may become master of the strong; and also that there is a compensation for the intellectual superficialising of a nation—namely, in the deepening of another.

242

Whether we call it "civilisation," or "humanising," or "progress," which now distinguishes the European; whether we call it simply, without praise or blame, by the political formula: the *democratic* movement in Europe— behind all the moral and political foregrounds pointed to by such formulas, an immense *physiological* process goes on, which is ever extending: the process of the assimilation of Europeans; their increasing detachment from the conditions under which, climatically and hereditarily, united races originate; their increasing independence of every definite *milieu*, that for centuries would fain inscribe itself with equal demands on soul and body; that is to say, the slow emergence of an essentially *super-national* and nomadic species of man, who possesses, physiologically speaking, a maximum of the art and power of adaptation as his typical distinction. This process of the *evolving European*, which can be retarded in its *tempo* by great relapses, but will perhaps just gain and grow thereby in vehemence and depth—the still raging storm and stress of "national sentiment" pertains to it, and also the anarchism which is appearing at present—this process will probably arrive at results on which its naïve propagators and panegyrists, the apostles of "modern ideas," would least care to reckon. The same new conditions under which on an average a levelling and mediocrising of man will take place—a useful, industrious, variously serviceable and clever gregarious man—are in the highest degree suitable to give rise to exceptional men of the most dangerous and attractive qualities. For, while the capacity for adaptation, which is ever trying changing conditions, and begins a new work with every generation, almost with every decade, makes the *powerfulness* of the type impossible; while the collective impression of such future Europeans will probably be that of numerous, talkative, weak-willed, and very handy workmen who *require* a master, a commander, as they require their daily bread; while, therefore, the democratising of Europe will tend to the production of a type prepared for *slavery* in the most subtle sense of the term: the *strong* man will necessarily in individual and exceptional cases, become stronger and richer than he has perhaps ever been before—owing to the unprejudicedness of his schooling, owing to the immense variety of practise, art, and disguise. I meant to say that the democratising of Europe is at the same time an involuntary arrangement for the rearing of *tyrants*—taking the word in all its meanings, even in its most spiritual sense.

243

I hear with pleasure that our sun is moving rapidly towards the constellation *Hercules*: and I hope that the men on this earth will do like the sun. And we foremost, we good Europeans!

244

There was a time when it was customary to call Germans "deep," by way of distinction; but now that the most successful type of new Germanism is covetous of quite other honours, and perhaps misses "smartness" in all that has depth, it is almost opportune and patriotic to doubt whether we did not formerly deceive ourselves with that commendation: in short, whether German depth is not at bottom something different and worse—and something from which, thank God, we are on the point of successfully ridding ourselves. Let us try, then, to relearn with regard to German depth; the only thing necessary for the purpose is a little vivisection of the German soul. The German soul is above all manifold, varied in its source, aggregated and superimposed, rather than actually built: this is owing to its origin. A German who would embolden himself to assert: "Two souls, alas, dwell in my breast," would make a bad guess at the truth, or, more correctly, he would come far short of the truth about the number of souls. As a people made up of the most extraordinary mixing and mingling of races, perhaps even with a preponderance of the pre-Aryan element, as the "people of the centre" in every sense of the term, the Germans are more intangible, more ample, more contradictory, more unknown, more incalculable, more surprising, and even more terrifying than other peoples are to themselves: they escape *definition*, and are thereby alone the despair of the French. It is characteristic of the Germans that the question: "What is German?" never dies out among them. Kotzebue certainly knew his Germans well enough: "we are known," they cried jubilantly to him—but Sand also thought he knew them. Jean Paul knew what he was doing when he declared himself incensed at Fichte's lying but patriotic flatteries and exaggerations—but it is probable that Goethe thought differently about Germans from Jean Paul, even though he acknowledged him to be right with regard to Fichte. It is a question what Goethe really thought about the Germans? But about many things around him he never spoke explicitly, and all his life he knew how to keep an astute silence—probably he had good reason for it. It is certain that it was not the "Wars of Independence" that made him look up more joyfully, anymore than it was the French Revolution—the event on account of which he *reconstructed* his *Faust*, and indeed the whole problem of "man," was the appearance of Napoleon. There are words of Goethe in which he condemns with impatient severity, as from a foreign land, that which Germans take a pride in: he once defined the famous German turn of mind as "Indulgence towards its own and others' weaknesses." Was he wrong? It is characteristic of Germans that one is seldom entirely wrong about them. The German soul has passages and galleries in it, there are caves, hiding places, and dungeons therein; its disorder has much of the charm of the mysterious; the German is well acquainted with the bypaths to chaos. And as everything loves its symbol, so the German loves the clouds and all that is obscure, evolving, crepuscular, damp, and shrouded: it seems to him that everything uncertain, undeveloped, self-displacing, and growing is "deep." The German himself does not *exist*: he is *becoming*, he is "developing himself." "Development" is therefore the essentially German discovery and hit in the great domain of philosophical formulas—a ruling idea, which, together with German beer and German music, is labouring to Germanise all Europe. Foreigners are astonished and attracted by the riddles which the conflicting nature at the basis of the German soul propounds to them (riddles which Hegel systematised and Richard Wagner has in the end set to music). "Good-natured and spiteful"—such a juxtaposition, preposterous in the case of every other people, is unfortunately only too often justified in Germany: one has only to live for a while among Swabians to know this! The clumsiness of the German scholar and his social distastefulness agree alarmingly well with his psychical rope-dancing and nimble boldness, of which all the Gods have learnt to be afraid. If anyone wishes to see the "German soul" demonstrated *ad oculos*, let him only look at German taste, at German arts and manner: what boorish indifference to "taste!" How the noblest and the commonest stand there in juxtaposition! How disorderly and how rich is the whole constitution of this soul! The German *drags* at his soul, he drags at everything he experiences. He digests his events badly; he never gets "done" with them; and German depth is often only a difficult, hesitating "digestion." And just as all chronic invalids, all dyspeptics, like what is convenient, so the German loves "frankness" and "honesty"; it is so *convenient* to be frank and honest! This confidingness, this complaisance, this showing-the-cards of German *honesty*, is probably the most dangerous and most successful disguise which the German is up to nowadays: it is his proper Mephistophelean art; with this he can "still achieve much!" The German lets himself go, and thereby gazes with faithful, blue, empty German eyes—and other countries immediately confound him with his dressing gown! I meant to say that, let "German depth" be what it will—among ourselves alone we perhaps take the liberty to laugh at it—we shall do well to continue henceforth to honour its appearance and good name, and not barter away too cheaply our old reputation as a people of depth for Prussian "smartness," and Berlin wit and sand. It is wise for a people to pose, and *let* itself be regarded, as profound, clumsy, good-natured, honest, and foolish: it might even be —profound to do so! Finally, we should do honour to our name—we are not called the "*tiusche Volk*" (deceptive people) for nothing. . . .

245

The "good old" time is past, it sang itself out in Mozart—how happy are *we* that his *rococo* still speaks to us, that his "good company," his tender enthusiasm, his childish delight in the Chinese and in flourishes, his courtesy of heart, his longing for the elegant, the amorous, the tripping, the tearful, and his belief in the South, can still appeal to *something left* in us! Ah, some time or other it will be over with it! But who can doubt that it will be over still sooner with the intelligence and taste for Beethoven!

For he was only the last echo of a break and transition in style, and *not*, like Mozart, the last echo of a great European taste which had existed for centuries. Beethoven is the intermediate event between an old mellow soul that is constantly breaking down, and a future over-young soul that is always *coming*; there is spread over his music the twilight of eternal loss and eternal extravagant hope—the same light in which Europe was bathed when it dreamed with Rousseau, when it danced round the Tree of Liberty of the Revolution, and finally almost fell down in adoration before Napoleon. But how rapidly does *this* very sentiment now pale, how difficult nowadays is even the *apprehension* of this sentiment, how strangely does the language of Rousseau, Schiller, Shelley, and Byron sound to our ear, in whom *collectively* the same fate of Europe was able to *speak*, which knew how to *sing* in Beethoven! Whatever German music came afterwards, belongs to Romanticism, that is to say, to a movement which, historically considered, was still shorter, more fleeting, and more superficial than that great interlude, the transition of Europe from Rousseau to Napoleon, and to the rise of democracy. Weber—but what do *we* care nowadays for *Freischutz* and *Oberon!* Or Marschner's *Hans Heiling* and *Vampyre!* Or even Wagner's *Tannhäuser!* That is extinct, although not yet forgotten music. This whole music of Romanticism, besides, was not noble enough, was not musical enough, to maintain its position anywhere but in the theatre and before the masses; from the beginning it was second-rate music, which was little thought of by genuine musicians. It was different with Felix Mendelssohn, that halcyon master, who, on account of his lighter, purer, happier soul, quickly acquired admiration, and was equally quickly forgotten: as the beautiful *episode* of German music. But with regard to Robert Schumann, who took things seriously, and has been taken seriously from the first—he was the last that founded a school—do we not now regard it as a satisfaction, a relief, a deliverance, that this very Romanticism of Schumann's has been surmounted? Schumann, fleeing into the "Saxon Switzerland" of his soul, with a half Weather-like, half Jean-Paul-like nature (Assuredly not like Beethoven! Assuredly not like Byron!) his *Manfred* music is a mistake and a misunderstanding to the extent of injustice; Schumann, with his taste, which was fundamentally a *petty* taste (that is to say, a dangerous propensity—doubly dangerous among Germans—for quiet lyricism and intoxication of the feelings), going constantly apart, timidly withdrawing and retiring, a noble weakling who revelled in nothing but anonymous joy and sorrow, from the beginning a sort of girl and *noli me tangere*—this Schumann was already merely a *German* event in music, and no longer a European event, as Beethoven had been, as in a still greater degree Mozart had been; with Schumann German music was threatened with its greatest danger, that of *losing the voice for the soul of Europe* and sinking into a merely national affair.

246

What a torture are books written in German to a reader who has a *third* ear! How indignantly he stands beside the slowly turning swamp of sounds without tune and rhythms without dance, which Germans call a "book"! And even the German who *reads* books! How lazily, how reluctantly, how badly he reads! How many Germans know, and consider it obligatory to know, that there is *art* in every good sentence—art which must be divined, if the sentence is to be understood! If there is a misunderstanding about its *tempo*, for instance, the sentence itself is misunderstood! That one must not be doubtful about the rhythm-determining syllables, that one should feel the breaking of the too-rigid symmetry as intentional and as a charm, that one should lend a fine and patient ear to every *staccato* and every *rubato*, that one should divine the sense in the sequence of the vowels and diphthongs, and how delicately and richly they can be tinted and retinted in the order of their arrangement—who among book-reading Germans is complaisant enough to recognise such duties and requirements, and to listen to so much art and intention in language? After all, one just "has no ear for it"; and so the most marked contrasts of style are not heard, and the most delicate artistry is as it were *squandered* on the deaf. These were my thoughts when I noticed how clumsily and unintuitively two masters in the art of prose-writing have been confounded: one, whose words drop down hesitatingly and coldly, as from the roof of a damp cave—he counts on their dull sound and echo; and another who manipulates his language like a flexible sword, and from his arm down into his toes feels the dangerous bliss of the quivering, over-sharp blade, which wishes to bite, hiss, and cut.

247

How little the German style has to do with harmony and with the ear, is shown by the fact that precisely our good musicians themselves write badly. The German does not read aloud, he does not read for the ear, but only with his eyes; he has put his ears away in the drawer for the time. In antiquity when a man read—which was seldom enough—he read something to himself, and in a loud voice; they were surprised when anyone read silently, and sought secretly the reason of it. In a loud voice: that is to say,

with all the swellings, inflections, and variations of key and changes of
tempo, in which the ancient *public* world took delight. The laws of the written style were then the same as those of the spoken style; and these laws
depended partly on the surprising development and refined requirements of the ear and larynx; partly on the strength, endurance, and power
of the ancient lungs. In the ancient sense, a period is above all a physiological whole, inasmuch as it is comprised in one breath. Such periods as
occur in Demosthenes and Cicero, swelling twice and sinking twice, and
all in one breath, were pleasures to the men of *antiquity,* who knew by their
own schooling how to appreciate the virtue therein, the rareness and the
difficulty in the deliverance of such a period; *we* have really no right to
the *big* period, we modern men, who are short of breath in every sense!
Those ancients, indeed, were all of them dilettanti in speaking, consequently connoisseurs, consequently critics—they thus brought their orators
to the highest pitch; in the same manner as in the last century, when all
Italian ladies and gentlemen knew how to sing, the virtuosoship of song
(and with it also the art of melody) reached its elevation. In Germany,
however (until quite recently when a kind of platform eloquence began
shyly and awkwardly enough to flutter its young wings), there was properly
speaking only one kind of public and *approximately* artistical discourse—
that delivered from the pulpit. The preacher was the only one in Germany
who knew the weight of a syllable or a word, in what manner a sentence
strikes, springs, rushes, flows, and comes to a close; he alone had a conscience in his ears, often enough a bad conscience: for reasons are not
lacking why proficiency in oratory should be especially seldom attained
by a German, or almost always too late. The masterpiece of German prose
is therefore with good reason the masterpiece of its greatest preacher:
the *Bible* has hitherto been the best German book. Compared with Luther's
Bible, almost everything else is merely "literature"—something which has
not grown in Germany, and therefore has not taken and does not take
root in German hearts, as the Bible has done.

248

There are two kinds of geniuses: one which above all engenders and seeks
to engender, and another which willingly lets itself be fructified and
brings forth. And similarly, among the gifted nations, there are those on
whom the woman's problem of pregnancy has devolved, and the secret
task of forming, maturing, and perfecting—the Greeks, for instance, were
a nation of this kind, and so are the French; and others which have to

fructify and become the cause of new modes of life—like the Jews, the Romans, and, in all modesty-be it asked: like the Germans? Nations tortured and enraptured by unknown fevers and irresistibly forced out of themselves, amorous and longing for foreign races (for such as "let themselves be fructified"), and withal imperious, like everything conscious of being full of generative force, and consequently empowered "by the grace of God." These two kinds of geniuses seek each other like man and woman; but they also misunderstand each other—like man and woman.

249

Every nation has its own "Tartuffery," and calls that its virtue. One does not know—cannot know, the best that is in one.

250

What Europe owes to the Jews? Many things, good and bad, and above all one thing of the nature both of the best and the worst: the grand style in morality, the fearfulness and majesty of infinite demands, of infinite significations, the whole Romanticism and sublimity of moral questionableness —and consequently just the most attractive, ensnaring, and exquisite element in those iridescences and allurements to life, in the aftersheen of which the sky of our European culture, its evening sky, now glows—perhaps glows out. For this, we artists among the spectators and philosophers, are—grateful to the Jews.

251

It must be taken into the bargain, if various clouds and disturbances—in short, slight attacks of stupidity—pass over the spirit of a people that suffers and *wants* to suffer from national nervous fever and political ambition: for instance, among present-day Germans there is alternately the anti-French folly, the anti-Semitic folly, the anti-Polish folly, the Christian-romantic folly, the Wagnerian folly, the Teutonic folly, the Prussian folly (just look at those poor historians, the Sybels and Treitschkes, and their closely bandaged heads), and whatever else these little obscurations of the German spirit and conscience may be called. May it be forgiven me that I, too, when on a short daring sojourn on very infected ground, did not remain wholly exempt from the disease, but like everyone else, began to entertain thoughts about matters which did not concern me—the first symptom of political infection. About the Jews, for instance, listen to the following: I have never yet met a German who was favourably inclined to the Jews; and however decided the repudiation of actual anti-Semitism may be on the part of all prudent and political men, this prudence and policy is not perhaps directed against the nature of the sentiment itself, but only against its dangerous excess, and especially against the distasteful and infamous expression of this excess of sentiment; on this point we must not deceive ourselves. That Germany has amply *sufficient* Jews, that the German stomach, the German blood, has difficulty (and will long have difficulty) in disposing only of this quantity of "Jew"—as the Italian, the Frenchman, and the Englishman have done by means of a stronger digestion: that is the unmistakable declaration and language of a general instinct, to which one must listen and according to which one must act. "Let no more Jews come in! And shut the doors, especially towards the East (also towards Austria)!" thus commands the instinct of a people whose nature is still feeble and uncertain, so that it could be easily wiped out, easily extinguished, by a stronger race. The Jews, however, are beyond all doubt the strongest, toughest, and purest race at present living in Europe; they know how to succeed even under the worst conditions (in fact better than under favourable ones), by means of virtues of some sort, which one would like nowadays to label as vices—owing above all to a resolute faith which does not need to be ashamed before "modern ideas"; they alter only, *when* they do alter, in the same way that the Russian Empire makes its conquest—as an empire that has plenty of time and is not of yesterday—namely, according to the principle, "as slowly as possible!" A thinker who has the future of Europe at heart, will, in all his perspectives concerning the future, calculate upon the Jews, as he will calculate upon the Russians, as above all the surest and likeliest factors in the great play and battle of forces. That which is at present called a "nation" in Europe, and is really rather a *res facta* than *nata* (indeed, sometimes confusingly similar to a *res ficta et picta*), is in every case something evolving, young, easily displaced, and not yet a race, much less such a race *aere perennius*, as the Jews are: such "nations" should most carefully avoid all hot-headed rivalry and hostility! It is certain that the Jews, if they desired—or if they were driven to it, as the anti-Semites seem to wish—*could* now have the ascendency, nay, literally the supremacy, over Europe; that they are *not* working and planning for that end is equally certain. Meanwhile, they rather wish and desire, even somewhat importunately, to be insorbed and absorbed by Europe; they long to be finally settled, authorised, and respected somewhere, and wish to put an end to the nomadic life, to the "wandering Jew"; and one should certainly take account of this impulse and tendency, and *make advances* to it (it possibly betokens a mitigation of the Jewish instincts): for which purpose it would perhaps be useful and fair to banish the anti-Semitic bawlers out of the country. One should make advances with all prudence, and with selection; pretty much as the English nobility do. It stands to reason that the more powerful and strongly marked types of new Germanism could enter into relation with the Jews with the least hesitation, for instance, the nobleman officer from the Prussian border: it would be interesting in many ways to see whether the genius for money and patience (and especially some intellect and intellectuality—sadly lacking in the place referred to) could not in addition be annexed and trained to the hereditary art of commanding and obeying—for both of which the country in question has now a classic reputation. But here it is expedient to break off my festal discourse and my sprightly Teutonomania: for I have already reached my *serious topic*, the "European problem," as I understand it, the rearing of a new ruling caste for Europe.

252

They are not a philosophical race—the English: Bacon represents an *attack* on the philosophical spirit generally, Hobbes, Hume, and Locke, an abasement, and a depreciation of the idea of a "philosopher" for more than a century. It was *against* Hume that Kant uprose and raised himself; it was Locke of whom Schelling *rightly* said, "*Je méprise Locke*"; in the struggle against the English mechanical stultification of the world, Hegel and Schopenhauer (along with Goethe) were of one accord; the two hostile brother-geniuses in philosophy, who pushed in different directions towards the opposite poles of German thought, and thereby wronged each other as only brothers will do. What is lacking in England, and has always been lacking, that half-actor and rhetorician knew well enough, the absurd muddle-head, Carlyle, who sought to conceal under passionate grimaces what he knew about himself: namely, what was *lacking* in Carlyle—real *power* of intellect, real *depth* of intellectual perception, in short, philosophy. It is characteristic of such an unphilosophical race to hold on firmly to Christianity—they *need* its discipline for "moralising" and humanising. The Englishman, more gloomy, sensual, headstrong, and brutal than the German—is for that very reason, as the baser of the two, also the most pious: he has all the *more need* of Christianity. To finer nostrils, this English Christianity itself has still a characteristic English taint of spleen and alcoholic excess, for which, owing to good reasons, it is used as an antidote—the finer poison to neutralise the coarser: a finer form of poisoning is in fact a step in advance with coarse-mannered people, a step towards spiritualisation. The English coarseness and rustic demureness is still most satisfactorily disguised by Christian pantomime, and by praying and psalm-singing (or, more correctly, it is thereby explained and differently expressed); and for the herd of drunkards and rakes who formerly learned moral grunting under the influence of Methodism (and more recently as the "Salvation Army"), a penitential fit may really be the relatively highest manifestation of "humanity" to which they can be elevated: so much may reasonably be admitted. That, however, which offends even in the humanest Englishman is his lack of music, to speak figuratively (and also literally): he has neither rhythm nor dance in the movements of his soul and body; indeed, not even the desire for rhythm and dance, for "music." Listen to him speaking; look at the most beautiful Englishwomen *walking*—in no country on earth are there more beautiful doves and swans; finally, listen to them singing! But I ask too much. . . .

253

There are truths which are best recognised by mediocre minds, because they are best adapted for them, there are truths which only possess charms and seductive power for mediocre spirits: one is pushed to this probably unpleasant conclusion, now that the influence of respectable but mediocre Englishmen—I may mention Darwin, John Stuart Mill, and Herbert Spencer—begins to gain the ascendency in the middle-class region of European taste. Indeed, who could doubt that it is a useful thing for *such* minds to have the ascendency for a time? It would be an error to consider the highly developed and independently soaring minds as specially qualified for determining and collecting many little common facts, and deducing conclusions from them; as exceptions, they are rather from the first in no very favourable position towards those who are "the rules." After all, they have more to do than merely to perceive: in effect, they have to *be* something new, they have to *signify* something new, they have to *represent* new values! The gulf between knowledge and capacity is perhaps greater, and also more mysterious, than one thinks: the capable man in the grand style, the creator, will possibly have to be an ignorant person; while on the other hand, for scientific discoveries like those of Darwin, a certain narrowness, aridity, and industrious carefulness (in short something English) may not be unfavourable for arriving at them. Finally, let it not be forgotten that the English, with their profound mediocrity, brought about once before a general depression of European intelligence. What is called "modern ideas," or "the ideas of the eighteenth century," or "French ideas"—that, consequently, against which the *German* mind rose up with profound disgust—is of English origin, there is no doubt about it. The French were only the apes and actors of these ideas, their best soldiers, and likewise, alas! Their first and profoundest *victims*; for owing to the diabolical Anglomania of "modern ideas," the *âme français* has in the end become so thin and emaciated, that at present one recalls its sixteenth and seventeenth centuries, its profound, passionate strength, its inventive excellency, almost with disbelief. One must, however, maintain this verdict of historical justice in a determined manner, and defend it against present prejudices and appearances: the European *noblesse*—of sentiment, taste, and manners, taking the word in every high sense—is the work and invention of *France*; the European ignobleness, the plebeianism of modern ideas—is *England's* work and invention.

254

Even at present France is still the seat of the most intellectual and refined culture of Europe, it is still the high school of taste; but one must know how to find this "France of taste." He who belongs to it keeps himself well concealed: they may be a small number in whom it lives and is embodied, besides perhaps being men who do not stand upon the strongest legs, in part fatalists, hypochondriacs, invalids, in part persons over-indulged, over-refined such as have the *ambition* to conceal themselves. They have all something in common: they keep their ears closed in presence of the delirious folly and noisy spouting of the democratic *bourgeois*. In fact, a besotted and brutalised France at present sprawls in the foreground—it recently celebrated a veritable orgy of bad taste, and at the same time of self-admiration, at the funeral of Victor Hugo. There is also something else common to them: a predilection to resist intellectual Germanising—and a still greater inability to do so! In this France of intellect, which is also a France of pessimism, Schopenhauer has perhaps become more at home, and more indigenous than he has ever been in Germany; not to speak of Heinrich Heine, who has long ago been reincarnated in the more refined and fastidious lyrists of Paris; or of Hegel, who at present, in the form of Taine—the *first* of living historians—exercises an almost tyrannical influence. As regards Richard Wagner, however, the more French music learns to adapt itself to the actual needs of the *âme moderne*, the more will it "Wagnerise"; one can safely predict that beforehand—it is already taking place sufficiently! There are, however, three things which the French can still boast of with pride as their heritage and possession, and as indelible tokens of their ancient intellectual superiority in Europe, in spite of all voluntary or involuntary Germanising and vulgarising of taste. *Firstly,* the capacity for artistic emotion, for devotion to "form," for which the expression, *l'art pour l'art,* along with numerous others, has been invented: such capacity has not been lacking in France for three centuries; and owing to its reverence for the "small number," it has again and again made a sort of chamber music of literature possible, which is sought for in vain elsewhere in Europe. The *second* thing whereby the French can lay claim to a superiority over Europe is their ancient, many-sided, *moralistic* culture, owing to which one finds on an average, even in the petty *romanciers* of the newspapers and chance *boulevardiers de Paris,* a psychological sensitiveness and curiosity, of which, for example, one has no conception (to say nothing of the thing itself!) in Germany. The Germans lack a couple of centuries of the moralistic work requisite thereto, which, as we have said, France has not grudged: those who call the Germans "naïve" on that account give them commendation for a defect. (As the opposite of the German inexperience and innocence *in voluptate psychologica,* which is not too remotely associated with the tediousness of German intercourse—and as the most successful expression of genuine French curiosity and inventive talent in this domain of delicate thrills, Henri Beyle may be noted; that remarkable anticipatory and forerunning man, who, with a Napoleonic *tempo,* traversed *his* Europe, in fact, several centuries of the European soul, as a surveyor and discoverer thereof: it has required two generations to *overtake* him one way or other, to divine long afterwards some of the riddles that perplexed and enraptured him—this strange Epicurean and man of interrogation, the last great psychologist of France.) There is yet a *third* claim to superiority: in the French character there is a successful halfway synthesis of the North and South, which makes them comprehend many things, and enjoins upon them other things, which an Englishman can never comprehend. Their temperament, turned alternately to and from the South, in which from time to time the Provençal and Ligurian blood froths over, preserves them from the dreadful, northern gray-in-gray, from sunless conceptual-spectrism and from poverty of blood—our *German* infirmity of taste, for the excessive prevalence of which at the present moment, blood and iron, that is to say "high politics," has with great resolution been prescribed (according to a dangerous healing art, which bids me wait and wait, but not yet hope). There is also still in France a pre-understanding and ready welcome for those rarer and rarely gratified men, who are too comprehensive to find satisfaction in any kind of fatherlandism, and know how to love the South when in the North and the

North when in the South—the born Midlanders, the "good Europeans."
For them *Bizet* has made music, this latest genius, who has seen a new
beauty and seduction—who has discovered a piece of the *South in music.*

255

I hold that many precautions should be taken against German music.
Suppose a person loves the South as I love it—as a great school of recovery
for the most spiritual and the most sensuous ills, as a boundless solar profusion and effulgence which o'erspreads a sovereign existence believing
in itself—well, such a person will learn to be somewhat on his guard
against German music, because, in injuring his taste anew, it will also
injure his health anew. Such a Southerner, a Southerner not by origin but
by *belief,* if he should dream of the future of music, must also dream of it
being freed from the influence of the North; and must have in his ears the
prelude to a deeper, mightier, and perhaps more perverse and mysterious
music, a super-German music, which does not fade, pale, and die away, as
all German music does, at the sight of the blue, wanton sea and the
Mediterranean clearness of sky—a super-European music, which holds its
own even in presence of the brown sunsets of the desert, whose soul is
akin to the palm-tree, and can be at home and can roam with big, beautiful, lonely beasts of prey. . . . I could imagine a music of which the rarest
charm would be that it knew nothing more of good and evil; only that
here and there perhaps some sailor's homesickness, some golden shadows
and tender weaknesses might sweep lightly over it; an art which, from the
far distance, would see the colours of a sinking and almost incomprehensible *moral* world fleeing towards it, and would be hospitable enough and
profound enough to receive such belated fugitives.

256

Owing to the morbid estrangement which the nationality-craze has
induced and still induces among the nations of Europe, owing also to the
short-sighted and hasty-handed politicians, who with the help of this craze,
are at present in power, and do not suspect to what extent the disintegrat-
ing policy they pursue must necessarily be only an interlude policy—owing
to all this, and much else that is altogether unmentionable at present, the
most unmistakable signs that *Europe wishes to be one,* are now overlooked, or
arbitrarily and falsely misinterpreted. With all the more profound and
large-minded men of this century, the real general tendency of the mysterious labour of their souls was to prepare the way for that new *synthesis,* and

tentatively to anticipate the European of the future; only in their simulations, or in their weaker moments, in old age perhaps, did they belong to the "fatherlands"—they only rested from themselves when they became "patriots." I think of such men as Napoleon, Goethe, Beethoven, Stendhal, Heinrich Heine, Schopenhauer: it must not be taken amiss if I also count Richard Wagner among them, about whom one must not let oneself be deceived by his own misunderstandings (geniuses like him have seldom the right to understand themselves), still less, of course, by the unseemly noise with which he is now resisted and opposed in France: the fact remains, nevertheless, that Richard Wagner and the *later French Romanticism* of the forties, are most closely and intimately related to one another. They are akin, fundamentally akin, in all the heights and depths of their requirements; it is Europe, the *one* Europe, whose soul presses urgently and longingly, outwards and upwards, in their multifarious and boisterous art—whither? Into a new light? Towards a new sun? But who would attempt to express accurately what all these masters of new modes of speech could not express distinctly? It is certain that the same storm and stress tormented them, that they *sought* in the same manner, these last great seekers! All of them steeped in literature to their eyes and ears—the first artists of universal literary culture—for the most part even themselves writers, poets, intermediaries and blenders of the arts and the senses (Wagner, as musician is reckoned among painters, as poet among musicians, as artist generally among actors); all of them fanatics for *expression* "at any cost"—I specially mention Delacroix, the nearest related to Wagner; all of them great discoverers in the realm of the sublime, also of the loathsome and dreadful, still greater discoverers in effect, in display, in the art of the show-shop; all of them talented far beyond their genius, out and out *virtuosi*, with mysterious accesses to all that seduces, allures, constrains, and upsets; born enemies of logic and of the straight line, hankering after the strange, the exotic, the monstrous, the crooked, and the self-contradictory; as men, Tantaluses of the will, plebeian parvenus, who knew themselves to be incapable of a noble *tempo* or of a *lento* in life and action—think of Balzac, for instance—unrestrained workers, almost destroying themselves by work; antinomians and rebels in manners, ambitious and insatiable, without equilibrium and enjoyment; all of them finally shattering and sinking down at the Christian cross (and with right and reason, for who of them would have been sufficiently profound and sufficiently original for an *Antichristian* philosophy?); on the whole, a boldly daring, splendidly overbearing, high-flying, and aloft-up-dragging class of higher men, who had first to teach their century—and it is the century of the *masses*—the conception "higher man. . . ." Let the German friends of Richard Wagner advise together as to whether there is anything purely German in the Wagnerian art, or whether its distinction does not consist precisely in coming from *super-German* sources and impulses: in which connexion it may not be underrated how indispensable Paris was to the development of his type, which the strength of his instincts made him long to visit at the most decisive time—and how the whole style of his proceedings, of his self-apostolate, could only perfect itself in sight of the French socialistic original. On a more subtle comparison it will perhaps be found, to the honour of Richard Wagner's German nature, that he has acted in everything with more strength, daring, severity, and elevation than a nineteenth-century Frenchman could have done—owing to the circumstance that we Germans are as yet nearer to barbarism than the French; perhaps even the most remarkable creation of Richard Wagner is not only at present, but forever inaccessible, incomprehensible, and inimitable to the whole latter-day Latin race: the figure of Siegfried, that *very free* man, who is probably far too free, too hard, too cheerful, too healthy, too *anti-Catholic* for the taste of old and mellow civilised nations. He may even have been a sin against Romanticism, this anti-Latin Siegfried: well, Wagner atoned amply for this sin in his old sad days, when—anticipating a taste which has meanwhile passed into politics—he began, with the religious vehemence peculiar to him, to preach, at least, *the way to Rome*, if not to walk therein. That these last words may not be misunderstood, I will call to my aid a few powerful rhymes, which will even betray to less delicate ears what I mean—what I mean *counter to* the "last Wagner" and his Parsifal music:

—Is this our mode?
From German heart came this vexed ululating?
From German body, this self-lacerating?
Is ours this priestly hand-dilation,
This incense-fuming exaltation?
Is ours this faltering, falling, shambling,
This quite uncertain ding-dong-dangling?
This sly nun-ogling, Ave-hour-bell ringing,
This wholly false enraptured heaven-o'erspringing?
—Is this our mode?
Think well! Ye still wait for admission—
For what ye hear is *Rome—Rome's faith by intuition!*

CHAPTER NINE

WHAT IS NOBLE?

257

EVERY ELEVATION OF THE TYPE "MAN," HAS HITHERTO BEEN THE WORK OF an aristocratic society—and so will it always be—a society believing in a long scale of gradations of rank and differences of worth among human beings, and requiring slavery in some form or other. Without the *pathos of distance*, such as grows out of the incarnated difference of classes, out of the constant outlooking and down-looking of the ruling caste on subordinates and instruments, and out of their equally constant practise of obeying and commanding, of keeping down and keeping at a distance—that other more mysterious pathos could never have arisen, the longing for an ever new widening of distance within the soul itself, the formation of ever higher, rarer, further, more extended, more comprehensive states, in short, just the elevation of the type "man," the continued "self-surmounting of man," to use a moral formula in a supermoral sense. To be sure, one must not resign oneself to any humanitarian illusions about the history of the origin of an aristocratic society (that is to say, of the preliminary condition for the elevation of the type "man"): the truth is hard. Let us acknowledge unprejudicedly how every higher civilisation hitherto has *originated*! Men with a still natural nature, barbarians in every terrible sense of the word, men of prey, still in possession of unbroken strength of will and desire for power, threw themselves upon weaker, more moral, more peaceful races (perhaps trading or cattle-rearing communities), or upon old mellow civilisations in which the final vital force was flickering out in brilliant fireworks of wit and depravity. At the commencement, the noble caste was always the barbarian caste: their superiority did not consist first of all in their physical, but in their psychical power—they were more *complete* men (which at every point also implies the same as "more complete beasts").

258

Corruption—as the indication that anarchy threatens to break out among the instincts, and that the foundation of the emotions, called "life," is convulsed—is something radically different according to the organisation in which it manifests itself. When, for instance, an aristocracy like that of France at the beginning of the Revolution, flung away its privileges with sublime disgust and sacrificed itself to an excess of its moral sentiments, it was corruption: it was really only the closing act of the corruption which had existed for centuries, by virtue of which that aristocracy had abdicated step by step its lordly prerogatives and lowered itself to a *function* of royalty (in the end even to its decoration and parade-dress). The essential thing, however, in a good and healthy aristocracy is that it should *not* regard itself as a function either of the kingship or the commonwealth, but as the *significance* and highest justification thereof—that it should therefore accept with a good conscience the sacrifice of a legion of individuals, who, *for its sake*, must be suppressed and reduced to imperfect men, to slaves and instruments. Its fundamental belief must be precisely that society is *not* allowed to exist for its own sake, but only as a foundation and scaffolding, by means of which a select class of beings may be able to elevate themselves to their higher duties, and in general to a higher *existence*: like those sun-seeking climbing plants in Java—they are called *Sipo Matador*—which encircle an oak so long and so often with their arms, until at last, high above it, but supported by it, they can unfold their tops in the open light, and exhibit their happiness.

259

To refrain mutually from injury, from violence, from exploitation, and put one's will on a par with that of others: this may result in a certain rough sense in good conduct among individuals when the necessary conditions are given (namely, the actual similarity of the individuals in amount of force and degree of worth, and their co-relation within one organisation). As soon, however, as one wished to take this principle more generally, and if possible even as *the fundamental principle of society*, it would immediately disclose what it really is—namely, a Will to the *denial* of life, a principle of dissolution and decay. Here one must think profoundly to the very basis and resist all sentimental weakness: life itself is *essentially* appropriation, injury, conquest of the strange and weak, suppression, severity, obtrusion of peculiar forms, incorporation, and at the least, putting it mildest, exploitation; but why should one forever use precisely these words on which for ages a disparaging purpose has been stamped? Even the organisation within which, as was previously supposed, the individuals treat each other as equal—it takes place in every healthy aristocracy—must itself, if it be a living and not a dying organisation, do all that towards other bodies, which the individuals within it refrain from doing to each other: it will have to be the incarnated Will to Power, it will endeavour to grow, to gain ground, attract to itself and acquire ascendency—not owing to any morality or immorality, but because it *lives*, and because life *is* precisely Will to Power. On no point, however, is the ordinary consciousness of Europeans more unwilling to be corrected than on this matter; people now rave everywhere, even under the guise of science, about coming conditions of society in which "the exploiting character" is to be absent: that sounds to my ears as if they promised to invent a mode of life which should refrain from all organic functions. "Exploitation" does not belong to a depraved, or imperfect and primitive society: it belongs to the *nature* of the living being as a primary organic function; it is a consequence of the intrinsic Will to Power, which is precisely the Will to Life. Granting that as a theory this is a novelty—as a reality it is the *fundamental fact* of all history: let us be so far honest towards ourselves!

260

In a tour through the many finer and coarser moralities which have hitherto prevailed or still prevail on the earth, I found certain traits recurring regularly together, and connected with one another, until finally two primary types revealed themselves to me, and a radical distinction was brought to light. There is *master-morality* and *slave-morality*; I would at once add, however, that in all higher and mixed civilisations, there are also attempts at the reconciliation of the two moralities; but one finds still oftener the confusion and mutual misunderstanding of them, indeed, sometimes their close juxtaposition—even in the same man, within one soul. The distinctions of moral values have either originated in a ruling caste, pleasantly conscious of being different from the ruled—or among the ruled class, the slaves and dependents of all sorts. In the first case, when it is the rulers who determine the conception "good," it is the exalted, proud disposition which is regarded as the distinguishing feature, and that which determines the order of rank. The noble type of man separates from himself the beings in whom the opposite of this exalted, proud disposition displays itself: he despises them. Let it at once be noted that in this first kind of morality the antithesis "good" and "bad" means practically the same as "noble" and "despicable"; the antithesis "good" and "*evil*" is of a different origin. The cowardly, the timid, the insignificant, and those thinking merely of narrow utility are despised; moreover, also, the distrustful, with their constrained glances, the self-abasing, the dog-like kind of men who let themselves be abused, the mendicant flatterers, and above all the liars: it is a fundamental belief of all aristocrats that the common people are untruthful. "We truthful ones"—the nobility in ancient Greece called themselves. It is obvious that everywhere the designations of moral value were at first applied to *men*, and were only derivatively and at a later period applied to *actions*; it is a gross mistake, therefore, when historians of morals start with questions like, "Why have sympathetic actions been praised?" The noble type of man regards *himself* as a determiner of values; he does not require to be approved of; he passes the judgement: "What is injurious to me is injurious in itself"; he knows that it is he himself only who confers honour on things; he is a *creator of values*. He honours whatever he recognises in himself: such morality is self-glorification. In the foreground there is the feeling of plenitude, of power, which seeks to overflow, the happiness of high tension, the consciousness of a wealth which would fain give and bestow: the noble man also helps the unfortunate, but not—or scarcely—out of pity, but rather from an impulse generated by the superabundance of power. The noble man honours in himself the powerful one, him also who has power over himself, who knows how to speak and how to keep silence, who takes pleasure in subjecting himself to severity and hardness, and has reverence for all that is severe and hard. "Wotan placed a hard heart in my breast," says an old Scandinavian Saga: it is thus rightly expressed from the soul of a proud Viking. Such a type of man is even proud of *not* being made for sympathy; the hero of the Saga therefore adds warningly: "He who has not a hard heart when young, will never have one." The noble and brave who think thus are the furthest removed from the morality which sees precisely in sympathy, or in acting for the good of others, or in *désintéressement*, the characteristic of the moral; faith in oneself, pride in oneself, a radical enmity and irony towards "selflessness," belong as definitely to noble morality, as do a careless scorn and precaution in presence of sympathy and the "warm heart." It is the powerful who *know* how to honour, it is their art, their domain for invention. The profound reverence for age and for tradition—all law rests on this double reverence—the belief and prejudice in favour of ancestors and unfavourable to newcomers, is typical in the morality of the powerful; and if, reversely, men of "modern ideas" believe almost instinctively in "progress" and the "future," and are more and more lacking in respect for old age, the ignoble origin of these "ideas" has complacently betrayed itself thereby. A morality of the ruling class, however, is more especially foreign and irritating to present-day taste in the sternness of its principle that one has duties only to one's equals; that one may act towards beings of a lower rank, towards all that is foreign, just as seems good to one, or "as the heart desires," and in any case "beyond good and evil": it is here that sympathy and similar sentiments can have a place. The ability and obligation to exercise prolonged gratitude and prolonged revenge—both only within the circle of equals—artfulness in retaliation, *raffinement* of the idea in friendship, a certain necessity to have enemies (as outlets for the emotions of envy, quarrelsomeness, arrogance—in fact, in order to be a good *friend*): all these are typical characteristics of the noble morality, which, as has been pointed out, is not the morality of "modern ideas," and is therefore at present difficult to realise, and also to unearth and disclose. It is otherwise with the second type of morality, *slave-morality*. Supposing that the abused, the oppressed, the suffering, the unemancipated, the weary, and those uncertain of themselves, should moralise, what will be the common element in their moral estimates? Probably a pessimistic suspicion with regard to the entire situation of man will find expression, perhaps a condemnation of man, together with his situation. The slave has an unfavourable eye for the virtues of the powerful; he has a scepticism and distrust, a *refinement* of distrust of everything "good" that is there honoured —he would fain persuade himself that the very happiness there is not genuine. On the other hand, *those* qualities which serve to alleviate the existence of sufferers are brought into prominence and flooded with light; it is here that sympathy, the kind, helping hand, the warm heart, patience, diligence, humility, and friendliness attain to honour; for here these are the most useful qualities, and almost the only means of supporting the burden of existence. Slave-morality is essentially the morality of utility. Here is the seat of the origin of the famous antithesis "good" and "*evil*": power and dangerousness are assumed to reside in the evil, a certain dreadfulness, subtlety, and strength, which do not admit of being despised. According to slave-morality, therefore, the "evil" man arouses fear; according to master-morality, it is precisely the "good" man who arouses fear and seeks to arouse it, while the bad man is regarded as the despicable being. The contrast attains its maximum when, in accordance with the logical consequences of slave-morality, a shade of depreciation—it may be slight and well-intentioned—at last attaches itself even to the "good" man of this morality; because, according to the servile mode of thought, the good man must in any case be the *safe* man: he is good-natured, easily deceived, perhaps a little stupid, *un bonhomme.* Everywhere that slave-morality gains the ascendency, language shows a tendency to approximate the significations of the words "good" and "stupid." A last fundamental difference: the desire for *freedom,* the instinct for happiness and the refinements of the feeling of liberty belong as necessarily to slave-morals and morality, as artifice and enthusiasm in reverence and devotion are the regular symptoms of an aristocratic mode of thinking and esti-mating. Hence we can understand without further detail why love *as a passion*—it is our European speciality—must absolutely be of noble origin; as is well known, its invention is due to the Provençal poet-cavaliers, those brilliant ingenious men of the "*gai saber,*" to whom Europe owes so much, and almost owes itself.

261

Vanity is one of the things which are perhaps most difficult for a noble man to understand: he will be tempted to deny it, where another kind of man thinks he sees it self-evidently. The problem for him is to represent to his mind beings who seek to arouse a good opinion of themselves which they themselves do not possess—and consequently also do not "deserve"—and who yet *believe* in this good opinion afterwards. This seems to him on the one hand such bad taste and so self-disrespectful, and on the other hand so grotesquely unreasonable, that he would like to consider vanity an exception, and is doubtful about it in most cases when it is spoken of. He will say, for instance: "I may be mistaken about my value, and on the other hand may nevertheless demand that my value should be acknowl-edged by others precisely as I rate it: that, however, is not vanity (but self-conceit, or, in most cases, that which is called 'humility,' and also 'modesty')." Or he will even say: "For many reasons I can delight in the good opinion of others, perhaps because I love and honour them, and rejoice in all their joys, perhaps also because their good opinion endorses and strengthens my belief in my own good opinion, perhaps because the good opinion of others, even in cases where I do not share it, is useful to me, or gives promise of usefulness: all this, however, is not vanity." The man of noble character must first bring it home forcibly to his mind, especially with the aid of history, that, from time immemorial, in all social strata in any way dependent, the ordinary man *was* only that which he *passed for*: not being at all accustomed to fix values, he did not assign even to himself any other value than that which his master assigned to him (it is the peculiar *right of masters* to create values). It may be looked upon as the result of an extraordinary atavism, that the ordinary man, even at present, is still always *waiting* for an opinion about himself, and then instinctively submitting himself to it; yet by no means only to a "good" opinion, but also to a bad and unjust one (think, for instance, of the greater part of the self-appreciations and self-depreciations which believing women learn from their confessors, and which in general the believing Christian learns from his Church). In fact, conformably to the slow rise of the democratic social order (and its cause, the blending of the blood of masters and slaves), the originally noble and rare impulse of the masters to assign a value to themselves and to "think well" of themselves, will now be more and more encouraged and extended; but it has at all times an older, ampler, and more radically ingrained propensity opposed to it— and in the phenomenon of "vanity" this older propensity overmasters the younger. The vain person rejoices over *every* good opinion which he hears about himself (quite apart from the point of view of its usefulness, and equally regardless of its truth or falsehood), just as he suffers from every bad opinion: for he subjects himself to both, he *feels* himself subjected to both, by that oldest instinct of subjection which breaks forth in him. It is "the slave" in the vain man's blood, the remains of the slave's craftiness— and how much of the "slave" is still left in woman, for instance! Which seeks to *seduce* to good opinions of itself; it is the slave, too, who immediately afterwards falls prostrate himself before these opinions, as though he had not called them forth. And to repeat it again: vanity is an atavism.

262

A *species* originates, and a typé becomes established and strong in the long struggle with essentially constant *unfavourable* conditions. On the other hand, it is known by the experience of breeders that species which receive superabundant nourishment, and in general a surplus of protection and care, immediately tend in the most marked way to develop variations, and are fertile in prodigies and monstrosities (also in monstrous vices). Now look at an aristocratic commonwealth, say an ancient Greek *polis*, or Venice, as a voluntary or involuntary contrivance for the purpose of *rearing* human beings; there are there men beside one another, thrown upon their own resources, who want to make their species prevail, chiefly because they *must* prevail, or else run the terrible danger of being exterminated. The favour, the superabundance, the protection are there lacking under which variations are fostered; the species needs itself as species, as something which, precisely by virtue of its hardness, its uniformity, and simplicity of structure, can in general prevail and make itself permanent in constant struggle with its neighbours, or with rebellious or rebellion-threatening vassals. The most varied experience teaches it what are the qualities to which it principally owes the fact that it still exists, in spite of all Gods and men, and has hitherto been victorious: these qualities it calls virtues, and these virtues alone it develops to maturity. It does so with severity, indeed it desires severity; every aristocratic morality is intolerant in the education of youth, in the control of women, in the marriage customs, in the relations of old and young, in the penal laws (which have an eye only for the degenerating): it counts intolerance itself among the virtues, under the name of "justice." A type with few, but very marked features, a species of severe, warlike, wisely silent, reserved and reticent men (and as such, with the most delicate sensibility for the charm and nuances of society) is thus established, unaffected by the vicissitudes of generations; the constant struggle with uniform *unfavourable* conditions is, as already remarked, the cause of a type becoming stable and hard. Finally, however, a happy state of things results, the enormous tension is relaxed; there are perhaps no more enemies among the neighbouring peoples, and the means of life, even of the enjoyment of life, are present in superabundance. With one stroke the bond and constraint of the old discipline severs: it is no longer regarded as necessary, as a condition of existence—if it would continue, it can only do so as a form of *luxury*, as an archaïsing *taste*. Variations, whether they be deviations (into the higher, finer, and rarer), or deteriorations and monstrosities, appear suddenly on the scene in the greatest exuberance and splendour; the individual dares to be individual and detach himself. At this turning point of history there manifest themselves, side by side, and often mixed and entangled together, a magnificent, manifold, virgin–forest-like upgrowth and up-striving, a kind of *tropical tempo* in the rivalry of growth, and an extraordinary decay and self-destruction, owing to the savagely opposing and seemingly exploding egoisms, which strive with one another "for sun and light," and can no longer assign any limit, restraint, or forbearance for themselves by means of the hitherto existing morality. It was this morality itself which piled up the strength so enormously, which bent the bow in so threatening a manner: it is now "out of date," it is getting "out of date." The dangerous and disquieting point has been reached when the greater, more manifold, more comprehensive life *is lived beyond* the old morality; the "individual" stands out, and is obliged to have recourse to his own law-giving, his own arts and artifices for self-preservation, self-elevation, and self-deliverance. Nothing but new "Whys," nothing but new "Hows," no common formulas any longer, misunderstanding and disregard in league with each other, decay, deterioration, and the loftiest desires frightfully entangled, the genius of the race overflowing from all the cornucopias of good and bad, a portentous simultaneousness of Spring and Autumn, full of new charms and mysteries peculiar to the fresh, still inexhausted, still unwearied corruption. Danger is again present, the mother of morality, great danger; this time shifted into the individual, into the neighbour and friend, into the street, into their own child, into their own heart, into all the most personal and secret recesses of their desires and volitions. What will the moral philosophers who appear at this time have to preach? They discover, these sharp onlookers and loafers, that the end is quickly approaching, that everything around them decays and produces decay, that nothing will endure until the day after tomorrow, except one species of man, the incurably *mediocre*. The mediocre alone have a prospect of continuing and propagating themselves—they will be the men of the future, the sole survivors; "Be like them! Become mediocre!" is now the only morality which has still a significance, which still obtains a hearing. But it is difficult to preach this morality of mediocrity! It can never avow what it is and what it desires! It has to talk of moderation and dignity and duty and brotherly love—it will have difficulty *in concealing its irony*!

263

There is an *instinct for rank*, which more than anything else is already the sign of a *high* rank; there is a *delight* in the nuances of reverence which leads one to infer noble origin and habits. The refinement, goodness, and loftiness of a soul are put to a perilous test when something passes by that is of the highest rank, but is not yet protected by the awe of authority from obtrusive touches and incivilities: something that goes its way like a living touchstone, undistinguished, undiscovered, and tentative, perhaps voluntarily veiled and disguised. He whose task and practise it is to investigate souls, will avail himself of many varieties of this very art to determine the ultimate value of a soul, the unalterable, innate order of rank to which it belongs: he will test it by its *instinct for reverence. Différence engendre haine:*

the vulgarity of many a nature spurts up suddenly like dirty water, when any holy vessel, any jewel from closed shrines, any book bearing the marks of great destiny, is brought before it; while on the other hand, there is an involuntary silence, a hesitation of the eye, a cessation of all gestures, by which it is indicated that a soul *feels* the nearness of what is worthiest of respect. The way in which, on the whole, the reverence for the *Bible* has hitherto been maintained in Europe, is perhaps the best example of discipline and refinement of manners which Europe owes to Christianity: books of such profoundness and supreme significance require for their protection an external tyranny of authority, in order to acquire the *period* of thousands of years which is necessary to exhaust and unriddle them. Much has been achieved when the sentiment has been at last instilled into the masses (the shallow-pates and the boobies of every kind) that they are not allowed to touch everything, that there are holy experiences before which they must take off their shoes and keep away the unclean hand—it is almost their highest advance towards humanity. On the contrary, in the so-called cultured classes, the believers in "modern ideas," nothing is perhaps so repulsive as their lack of shame, the easy insolence of eye and hand with which they touch, taste, and finger everything; and it is possible that even yet there is more *relative* nobility of taste, and more tact for reverence among the people, among the lower classes of the people, especially among peasants, than among the newspaper-reading *demimonde* of intellect, the cultured class.

264

It cannot be effaced from a man's soul what his ancestors have preferably and most constantly done: whether they were perhaps diligent economisers attached to a desk and a cashbox, modest and citizen-like in their desires, modest also in their virtues; or whether they were accustomed to commanding from morning till night, fond of rude pleasures and probably of still ruder duties and responsibilities; or whether, finally, at one time or another, they have sacrificed old privileges of birth and possession, in order to live wholly for their faith—for their "God"—as men of an inexorable and sensitive conscience, which blushes at every compromise. It is quite impossible for a man *not* to have the qualities and predilections of his parents and ancestors in his constitution, whatever appearances may suggest to the contrary. This is the problem of race. Granted that one knows something of the parents, it is admissible to draw a conclusion about the child: any kind of offensive incontinence, any kind of sordid envy, or of clumsy self-vaunting—the three things which together have constituted the genuine plebeian type in all times—such must pass over to the child, as surely as bad blood; and with the help of the best education and culture one will only succeed in *deceiving* with regard to such heredity. And what else does education and culture try to do nowadays! In our very democratic, or rather, very plebeian age, "education" and "culture" *must* be essentially the art of deceiving—deceiving with regard to origin, with regard to the inherited plebeianism in body and soul. An educator who nowadays preached truthfulness above everything else, and called out constantly to his pupils: "Be true! Be natural! Show yourselves as you are!" even such a virtuous and sincere ass would learn in a short time to have recourse to the *furca* of Horace, *naturam expellere*: with what results? "Plebeianism" *usque recurret.*[1]

265

At the risk of displeasing innocent ears, I submit that egoism belongs to the essence of a noble soul, I mean the unalterable belief that to a being such as "we," other beings must naturally be in subjection, and have to sacrifice themselves. The noble soul accepts the fact of his egoism without question, and also without consciousness of harshness, constraint, or arbitrariness therein, but rather as something that may have its basis in the primary law of things: if he sought a designation for it he would say: "It is justice itself." He acknowledges under certain circumstances, which made him hesitate at first, that there are other equally privileged ones; as soon as he has settled this question of rank, he moves among those equals and equally privileged ones with the same assurance, as regards modesty and delicate respect, which he enjoys in intercourse with himself —in accordance with an innate heavenly mechanism which all the stars understand. It is an *additional* instance of his egoism, this artfulness and self-limitation in intercourse with his equals—every star is a similar egoist; he honours *himself* in them, and in the rights which he concedes to them, he has no doubt that the exchange of honours and rights, as the *essence* of all intercourse, belongs also to the natural condition of things. The noble soul gives as he takes, prompted by the passionate and sensitive instinct of requital, which is at the root of his nature. The notion of "favour" has, *inter pares*, neither significance nor good repute; there may be a sublime way of letting gifts as it were light upon one from above, and of drinking them thirstily like dewdrops; but for those arts and displays the noble soul has no aptitude. His egoism hinders him here: in general, he looks "aloft" unwillingly—he looks either *forward*, horizontally and deliberately, or downwards—*he knows that he is on a height*.

266

"One can only truly esteem him who does not *look out for* himself." Goethe to Rath Schlosser.

267

The Chinese have a proverb which mothers even teach their children: "*Siao-sin*" ("make thy heart *small*"). This is the essentially fundamental tendency in latter-day civilisations. I have no doubt that an ancient Greek, also, would first of all remark the self-dwarfing in us Europeans of today—in this respect alone we should immediately be "distasteful" to him.

268

What, after all, is ignobleness? Words are vocal symbols for ideas; ideas, however, are more or less definite mental symbols for frequently returning and concurring sensations, for groups of sensations. It is not sufficient to use the same words in order to understand one another: we must also employ the same words for the same kind of internal experiences, we must in the end have experiences *in common*. On this account the people of one nation understand one another better than those belonging to different nations, even when they use the same language; or rather, when people have lived long together under similar conditions (of climate, soil, danger, requirement, toil) there *originates* therefrom an entity that "understands itself"—namely, a nation. In all souls a like number of frequently recurring experiences have gained the upper hand over those occurring more rarely: about these matters people understand one another rapidly and always more rapidly—the history of language is the history of a process of abbreviation; on the basis of this quick comprehension people always unite closer and closer. The greater the danger, the greater is the need of agreeing quickly and readily about what is necessary; not to misunderstand one another in danger—that is what cannot at all be dispensed with in intercourse. Also in all loves and friendships one has the experience that nothing of the kind continues when the discovery has been made that in using the same words, one of the two parties has feelings, thoughts, intuitions, wishes, or fears different from those of the other. (The fear of the "eternal misunderstanding": that is the good genius which so often keeps persons of different sexes from too hasty attachments, to which sense and heart prompt them—and *not* some Schopenhauerian "genius of the species.") Whichever groups of sensations within a soul awaken most readily, begin to speak, and give the word of command—these decide as to the general order of rank of its values, and determine ultimately its list of desirable things. A man's estimates of value betray something of the *structure* of his soul, and wherein it sees its conditions of life, its intrinsic needs. Supposing now that necessity has from all time drawn together only such men as could express similar requirements and similar experiences by similar symbols, it results on the whole that the easy *communicability* of need, which implies ultimately the undergoing only of average and *common* experiences, must have been the most potent of all the forces which have hitherto operated upon mankind. The more similar, the more ordinary people, have always had and are still having the advantage; the more select, more refined, more unique, and difficultly comprehensible, are liable to stand alone; they succumb to accidents in their isolation, and seldom propagate themselves. One must appeal to immense opposing forces, in order to thwart this natural, all-too-natural *progressus in simile*, the evolution of man to the similar, the ordinary, the average, the gregarious—to the *ignoble!*

269

The more a psychologist—a born, an unavoidable psychologist and soul-diviner—turns his attention to the more select cases and individuals, the greater is his danger of being suffocated by sympathy: he *needs* sternness and cheerfulness more than any other man. For the corruption, the ruination of higher men, of the more unusually constituted souls, is in fact, the rule: it is dreadful to have such a rule always before one's eyes. The manifold torment of the psychologist who has discovered this ruination, who discovers once, and then discovers *almost* repeatedly throughout all history, this universal inner "desperateness" of higher men, this eternal "too late!" in every sense—may perhaps one day be the cause of his turning with bitterness against his own lot, and of his making an attempt at self-destruction—of his "going to ruin" himself. One may perceive in almost every psychologist a telltale inclination for delightful intercourse with commonplace and well-ordered men: the fact is thereby disclosed that he always requires healing, that he needs a sort of flight and forgetfulness, away from what his insight and incisiveness—from what his "business"—has laid upon his conscience. The fear of his memory is peculiar to him. He is easily silenced by the judgement of others; he hears with unmoved countenance how people honour, admire, love, and glorify, where he has *perceived*—or he even conceals his silence by expressly assenting to some plausible opinion. Perhaps the paradox of his situation becomes so dreadful that, precisely where he has learnt *great sympathy*, together with *great contempt*, the multitude, the educated, and the visionaries, have on their part learnt great reverence—reverence for "great men" and marvellous animals, for the sake of whom one blesses and honours the fatherland, the earth, the dignity of mankind, and one's own self, to whom one points the young, and in view of whom one educates them. And who knows but in all great instances hitherto just the same happened: that the multitude worshipped a God, and that the "God" was only a poor sacrificial animal! *Success* has always been the greatest liar—and the "work" itself is a success; the great statesman, the conqueror, the discoverer, are disguised in their creations until they are unrecognisable; the "work" of the artist, of the philosopher, only invents him who has created it, is *reputed* to have created it; the "great men," as they are reverenced, are poor little fictions composed afterwards; in the world of historical values spurious coinage *prevails.* Those great poets, for example, such as Byron, Musset, Poc, Leopardi, Kleist, Gogol (I do not venture to mention much greater names, but I have them in my mind), as they now appear, and were perhaps obliged to be: men of the moment, enthusiastic, sensuous, and childish, light-minded and impulsive in their trust and distrust; with souls in which usually some flaw has to be concealed; often taking revenge with their works for an internal defilement, often seeking forgetfulness in their soaring from a too true memory, often lost in the mud and almost in love with it, until they become like the Will-o'-the-Wisps around the swamps, and *pretend to be* stars—the people then call them idealists—often struggling with protracted disgust, with an ever-reappearing phantom of disbelief, which makes them cold, and obliges them to languish for *gloria* and devour "faith as it is" out of the hands of intoxicated adulators: what a *torment* these great artists are and the so-called higher men in general, to him who has once found them out! It is thus conceivable that it is just from woman—who is clairvoyant in the world of suffering, and also unfortunately eager to help and save to an extent far beyond her powers—that *they* have learnt so readily those outbreaks of boundless devoted *sympathy*, which the multitude, above all the reverent multitude, do not understand, and overwhelm with prying and self-gratifying interpretations. This sympathising invariably deceives itself as to its power; woman would like to believe that love can do *everything*—it is the *superstition* peculiar to her.

Alas, he who knows the heart finds out how poor, helpless, pretentious, and blundering even the best and deepest love is—he finds that it rather *destroys* than saves! It is possible that under the holy fable and travesty of the life of Jesus there is hidden one of the most painful cases of the martyrdom of *knowledge about love*: the martyrdom of the most innocent and most craving heart, that never had enough of any human love, that *demanded* love, that demanded inexorably and frantically to be loved and nothing else, with terrible outbursts against those who refused him their love; the story of a poor soul insatiated and insatiable in love, that had to invent hell to send thither those who *would not* love him—and that at last, enlightened about human love, had to invent a God who is entire love, entire *capacity* for love—who takes pity on human love, because it is so paltry, so ignorant! He who has such sentiments, he who has such *knowledge* about love—*seeks* for death! But why should one deal with such painful matters? Provided, of course, that one is not obliged to do so.

270

The intellectual haughtiness and loathing of every man who has suffered deeply—it almost determines the order of rank *how* deeply men can suffer—the chilling certainty, with which he is thoroughly imbued and coloured, that by virtue of his suffering he *knows more* than the shrewdest and wisest can ever know, that he has been familiar with, and "at home" in, many distant, dreadful worlds of which "*you* know nothing!" this silent intellectual haughtiness of the sufferer, this pride of the elect of knowledge, of the "initiated," of the almost sacrificed, finds all forms of disguise necessary to protect itself from contact with officious and sympathising hands, and in general from all that is not its equal in suffering. Profound suffering makes noble; it separates. One of the most refined forms of disguise is Epicurism, along with a certain ostentatious boldness of taste, which takes suffering lightly, and puts itself on the defensive against all that is sorrowful and profound. There are "gay men" who make use of gaiety, because they are misunderstood on account of it—they *wish* to be misunderstood. There are "scientific minds" who make use of science, because it gives a gay appearance, and because scientificalness leads to the conclusion that a person is superficial—they *wish* to mislead to a false conclusion. There are free insolent minds which would fain conceal and deny that they are broken, proud, incurable hearts (the cynicism of Hamlet—the case of Galiani); and occasionally folly itself is the mask of an unfortunate *over-assured* knowledge. From which it follows that it is the part of a more refined humanity to have reverence "for the mask," and not to make use of psychology and curiosity in the wrong place.

271

That which separates two men most profoundly is a different sense and grade of purity. What does it matter about all their honesty and reciprocal usefulness, what does it matter about all their mutual goodwill: the fact still remains—they "cannot smell each other!" The highest instinct for purity places him who is affected with it in the most extraordinary and dangerous isolation, as a saint: for it is just holiness—the highest spiritualisation of the instinct in question. Any kind of cognisance of an indescribable excess in the joy of the bath, any kind of ardour or thirst which perpetually impels the soul out of night into the morning, and out of gloom, out of "affliction" into clearness, brightness, depth, and refinement: just as much as such a tendency *distinguishes*—it is a noble tendency —it also *separates*. The pity of the saint is pity for the *filth* of the human, all-too-human. And there are grades and heights where pity itself is regarded by him as impurity, as filth.

272

Signs of nobility: never to think of lowering our duties to the rank of duties for everybody; to be unwilling to renounce or to share our responsibilities; to count our prerogatives, and the exercise of them, among our *duties*.

273

A man who strives after great things, looks upon everyone whom he encounters on his way either as a means of advance, or a delay and hindrance—or as a temporary resting-place. His peculiar lofty *bounty* to his fellow-men is only possible when he attains his elevation and dominates. Impatience, and the consciousness of being always condemned to comedy up to that time—for even strife is a comedy, and conceals the end, as every means does—spoil all intercourse for him; this kind of man is acquainted with solitude, and what is most poisonous in it.

274

The Problem of those who Wait. Happy chances are necessary, and many incalculable elements, in order that a higher man in whom the solution of a problem is dormant, may yet take action, or "break forth," as one might say—at the right moment. On an average it *does not* happen; and in all corners of the earth there are waiting ones sitting who hardly know to what extent they are waiting, and still less that they wait in vain. Occasionally, too, the waking call comes too late—the chance which gives "permission" to take action—when their best youth, and strength for action have been used up in sitting still; and how many a one, just as he "sprang up," has found with horror that his limbs are benumbed and his spirits are now too heavy! "It is too late," he has said to himself—and has become self-distrustful and henceforth forever useless. In the domain of genius, may not the "Raphael without hands" (taking the expression in its widest sense) perhaps not be the exception, but the rule? Perhaps genius is by no means so rare: but rather the five hundred *hands* which it requires in order to tyrannise over the καιρός, "the right time"—in order to take chance by the forelock!

275

He who does not *wish* to see the height of a man, looks all the more sharply at what is low in him, and in the foreground—and thereby betrays himself.

276

In all kinds of injury and loss the lower and coarser soul is better off than the nobler soul: the dangers of the latter must be greater, the probability that it will come to grief and perish is in fact immense, considering the multiplicity of the conditions of its existence. In a lizard a finger grows again which has been lost; not so in man.

277

It is too bad! Always the old story! When a man has finished building his house, he finds that he has learnt unawares something which he *ought* absolutely to have known before he—began to build. The eternal, fatal "Too late!" The melancholia of everything *completed*!

278

—Wanderer, who art thou? I see thee follow thy path without scorn, without love, with unfathomable eyes, wet and sad as a plummet which has returned to the light insatiated out of every depth—what did it seek down there? With a bosom that never sighs, with lips that conceal their loathing, with a hand which only slowly grasps: who art thou? What hast

thou done? Rest thee here: this place has hospitality for everyone—
refresh thyself! And whoever thou art, what is it that now pleases thee?
What will serve to refresh thee? Only name it, whatever I have I offer
thee! "To refresh me? To refresh me? Oh, thou prying one, what sayest
thou! But give me, I pray thee——" What? What? Speak out! "Another
mask! A second mask!"

279

Men of profound sadness betray themselves when they are happy: they
have a mode of seizing upon happiness as though they would choke and
strangle it, out of jealousy—ah, they know only too well that it will flee
from them!

280

"Bad! Bad! What? Does he not—go back?" Yes! But you misunderstand
him when you complain about it. He goes back like everyone who is about
to make a great spring.

281

—"Will people believe it of me? But I insist that they believe it of me: I
have always thought very unsatisfactorily of myself and about myself, only
in very rare cases, only compulsorily, always without delight in 'the subject,' ready to digress from 'myself,' and always without faith in the result,
owing to an unconquerable distrust of the *possibility* of self-knowledge,
which has led me so far as to feel a *contradictio in adjecto* even in the idea
of 'direct knowledge' which theorists allow themselves: this matter of fact
is almost the most certain thing I know about myself. There must be a sort
of repugnance in me to *believe* anything definite about myself. Is there
perhaps some enigma therein? Probably; but fortunately nothing for my
own teeth. Perhaps it betrays the species to which I belong? But not to
myself, as is sufficiently agreeable to me."

282

—"But what has happened to you?" "I do not know," he said, hesitatingly;
"perhaps the Harpies have flown over my table." It sometimes happens
nowadays that a gentle, sober, retiring man becomes suddenly mad,
breaks the plates, upsets the table, shrieks, raves, and shocks everybody—
and finally withdraws, ashamed, and raging at himself—whither? For

what purpose? To famish apart? To suffocate with his memories? To him who has the desires of a lofty and dainty soul, and only seldom finds his table laid and his food prepared, the danger will always be great—nowadays, however, it is extraordinarily so. Thrown into the midst of a noisy and plebeian age, with which he does not like to eat out of the same dish, he may readily perish of hunger and thirst—or, should he nevertheless finally "fall to," of sudden nausea. We have probably all sat at tables to which we did not belong; and precisely the most spiritual of us, who are most difficult to nourish, know the dangerous *dyspepsia* which originates from a sudden insight and disillusionment about our food and our messmates— the *after-dinner nausea*.

283

If one wishes to praise at all, it is a delicate and at the same time a noble self-control, to praise only where one *does not* agree—otherwise in fact one would praise oneself, which is contrary to good taste: a self-control, to be sure, which offers excellent opportunity and provocation to constant *misunderstanding*. To be able to allow oneself this veritable luxury of taste and morality, one must not live among intellectual imbeciles, but rather among men whose misunderstandings and mistakes amuse by their refinement—or one will have to pay dearly for it! "He praises me, *therefore* he acknowledges me to be right"—this asinine method of inference spoils half of the life of us recluses, for it brings the asses into our neighbour-hood and friendship.

284

To live in a vast and proud tranquillity; always beyond. . . . To have, or not to have, one's emotions, one's For and Against, according to choice; to lower oneself to them for hours; to *seat* oneself on them as upon horses, and often as upon asses: for one must know how to make use of their stupidity as well as of their fire. To conserve one's three hundred fore-grounds; also one's black spectacles: for there are circumstances when nobody must look into our eyes, still less into our "motives." And to choose for company that roguish and cheerful vice, politeness. And to remain master of one's four virtues, courage, insight, sympathy, and solitude. For solitude is a virtue with us, as a sublime bent and bias to purity, which divines that in the contact of man and man—"in society"—it must be unavoidably impure. All society makes one somehow, somewhere, or sometime—"commonplace."

285

The greatest events and thoughts—the greatest thoughts, however, are the greatest events—are longest in being comprehended: the generations which are contemporary with them do not *experience* such events—they live past them. Something happens there as in the realm of the stars. The light of the furthest stars is longest in reaching man; and before it has arrived man *denies*—that there are stars there. "How many centuries does a mind require to be understood?" that is also a standard, one also makes a gradation of rank and an etiquette therewith, such as is necessary for mind and for star.

286

"Here is the prospect free, the mind exalted."[2] But there is a reverse kind of man, who is also upon a height, and has also a free prospect—but looks *downwards*.

287

—What is noble? What does the word "noble" still mean for us nowadays? How does the noble man betray himself, how is he recognised under this heavy overcast sky of the commencing plebeianism, by which everything is rendered opaque and leaden? It is not his actions which establish his claim—actions are always ambiguous, always inscrutable; neither is it his "works." One finds nowadays among artists and scholars plenty of those who betray by their works that a profound longing for nobleness impels them; but this very *need of* nobleness is radically different from the needs of the noble soul itself, and is in fact the eloquent and dangerous sign of the lack thereof. It is not the works, but the *belief* which is here decisive and determines the order of rank—to employ once more an old religious formula with a new and deeper meaning—it is some fundamental certainty which a noble soul has about itself, something which is not to be sought, is not to be found, and perhaps, also, is not to be lost. *The noble soul has reverence for itself.*

288

There are men who are unavoidably intellectual, let them turn and twist themselves as they will, and hold their hands before their treacherous eyes—as though the hand were not a betrayer; it always comes out at last that they have something which they hide—namely, intellect. One of the subtlest means of deceiving, at least as long as possible, and of successfully

representing oneself to be stupider than one really is—which in everyday
life is often as desirable as an umbrella—is called *enthusiasm*, including
what belongs to it, for instance, virtue. For as Galiani said, who was obliged
to know it: *vertu est enthousiasme*.

289

In the writings of a recluse one always hears something of the echo of
the wilderness, something of the murmuring tones and timid vigilance
of solitude; in his strongest words, even in his cry itself, there sounds a
new and more dangerous kind of silence, of concealment. He who has
sat day and night, from year's end to year's end, alone with his soul in
familiar discord and discourse, he who has become a cave-bear, or a
treasure-seeker, or a treasure-guardian and dragon in his cave—it may
be a labyrinth, but can also be a goldmine—his ideas themselves eventually acquire a twilight-colour of their own, and an odour, as much of the
depth as of the mould, something uncommunicative and repulsive,
which blows chilly upon every passerby. The recluse does not believe
that a philosopher—supposing that a philosopher has always in the first
place been a recluse—ever expressed his actual and ultimate opinions in
books: are not books written precisely to hide what is in us? Indeed, he
will doubt whether a philosopher *can* have "ultimate and actual" opinions at all; whether behind every cave in him there is not, and must
necessarily be, a still deeper cave: an ampler, stranger, richer world
beyond the surface, an abyss behind every bottom, beneath every "foundation." Every philosophy is a foreground philosophy—this is a recluse's
verdict: "There is something arbitrary in the fact that the *philosopher*
came to a stand here, took a retrospect and looked around; that he *here*
laid his spade aside and did not dig any deeper—there is also something
suspicious in it." Every philosophy also *conceals* a philosophy; every opinion is also a *lurking-place*, every word is also a *mask*.

290

Every deep thinker is more afraid of being understood than of being misunderstood. The latter perhaps wounds his vanity; but the former wounds
his heart, his sympathy, which always says: "Ah, why would *you* also have as
hard a time of it as I have?"

291

Man, a *complex*, mendacious, artful, and inscrutable animal, uncanny to
the other animals by his artifice and sagacity, rather than by his strength,

has invented the good conscience in order finally to enjoy his soul as something *simple*; and the whole of morality is a long, audacious falsification, by virtue of which generally enjoyment at the sight of the soul becomes possible. From this point of view there is perhaps much more in the conception of "art" than is generally believed.

292

A philosopher: that is a man who constantly experiences, sees, hears, suspects, hopes, and dreams extraordinary things; who is struck by his own thoughts as if they came from the outside, from above and below, as a species of events and lightning-flashes *peculiar to him*; who is perhaps himself a storm pregnant with new lightnings; a portentous man, around whom there is always rumbling and mumbling and gaping and something uncanny going on. A philosopher: alas, a being who often runs away from himself, is often afraid of himself—but whose curiosity always makes him "come to himself" again.

293

A man who says: "I like that, I take it for my own, and mean to guard and protect it from everyone"; a man who can conduct a case, carry out a resolution, remain true to an opinion, keep hold of a woman, punish and overthrow insolence; a man who has his indignation and his sword, and to whom the weak, the suffering, the oppressed, and even the animals willingly submit and naturally belong; in short, a man who is a *master* by nature—when such a man has sympathy, well! *That* sympathy has value! But of what account is the sympathy of those who suffer! Or of those even who preach sympathy! There is nowadays, throughout almost the whole of Europe, a sickly irritability and sensitiveness towards pain, and also a repulsive irrestrainableness in complaining, an effeminising, which, with the aid of religion and philosophical nonsense, seeks to deck itself out as something superior—there is a regular cult of suffering. The *unmanliness* of that which is called "sympathy" by such groups of visionaries, is always, I believe, the first thing that strikes the eye. One must resolutely and radically taboo this latest form of bad taste; and finally I wish people to put the good amulet, "*gai saber*" ("gay science," in ordinary language), on heart and neck, as a protection against it.

294

The Olympian Vice. Despite the philosopher who, as a genuine Englishman, tried to bring laughter into bad repute in all thinking minds—"Laughing

is a bad infirmity of human nature, which every thinking mind will strive
to overcome" (Hobbes)—I would even allow myself to rank philosophers according to the quality of their laughing—up to those who are
capable of *golden* laughter. And supposing that Gods also philosophise,
which I am strongly inclined to believe, owing to many reasons—I have
no doubt that they also know how to laugh thereby in an overman-like
and new fashion—and at the expense of all serious things! Gods are
fond of ridicule: it seems that they cannot refrain from laughter even in
holy matters.

295

The genius of the heart, as that great mysterious one possesses it, the
tempter-god and born rat-catcher of consciences, whose voice can descend
into the nether-world of every soul, who neither speaks a word nor casts
a glance in which there may not be some motive or touch of allurement,
to whose perfection it pertains that he knows how to appear—not as he
is, but in a guise which acts as an *additional* constraint on his followers to
press ever closer to him, to follow him more cordially and thoroughly;
the genius of the heart, which imposes silence and attention on everything
loud and self-conceited, which smooths rough souls and makes them
taste a new longing—to lie placid as a mirror, that the deep heavens may
be reflected in them; the genius of the heart, which teaches the clumsy
and too hasty hand to hesitate, and to grasp more delicately; which scents
the hidden and forgotten treasure, the drop of goodness and sweet spirituality under thick dark ice, and is a divining-rod for every grain of gold,
long buried and imprisoned in mud and sand; the genius of the heart,
from contact with which everyone goes away richer; not favoured or surprised, not as though gratified and oppressed by the good things of
others; but richer in himself, newer than before, broken up, blown upon,
and sounded by a thawing wind; more uncertain perhaps, more delicate,
more fragile, more bruised, but full of hopes which as yet lack names, full
of a new will and current, full of a new ill-will and counter-current . . .
but what am I doing, my friends? Of whom am I talking to you? Have I
forgotten myself so far that I have not even told you his name? Unless it
be that you have already divined of your own accord who this questionable God and spirit is, that wishes to be *praised* in such a manner? For, as
it happens to everyone who from childhood onward has always been on
his legs, and in foreign lands, I have also encountered on my path many
strange and dangerous spirits; above all, however, and again and again, the

one of whom I have just spoken: in fact, no less a personage than the God *Dionysus*, the great equivocator and tempter, to whom, as you know, I once offered in all secrecy and reverence my first-fruits—the last, as it seems to me, who has offered a *sacrifice* to him, for I have found no one who could understand what I was then doing. In the meantime, however, I have learned much, far too much, about the philosophy of this God, and, as I said, from mouth to mouth—I, the last disciple and initiate of the God Dionysus: and perhaps I might at last begin to give you, my friends, as far as I am allowed, a little taste of this philosophy? In a hushed voice, as is but seemly: for it has to do with much that is secret, new, strange, wonderful, and uncanny. The very fact that Dionysus is a philosopher, and that therefore Gods also philosophise, seems to me a novelty which is not unensnaring, and might perhaps arouse suspicion precisely amongst philosophers; amongst you, my friends, there is less to be said against it, except that it comes too late and not at the right time; for, as it has been disclosed to me, you are loth nowadays to believe in God and gods. It may happen, too, that in the frankness of my story I must go further than is agreeable to the strict usages of your ears? Certainly the God in question went further, very much further, in such dialogues, and was always many paces ahead of me. . . . Indeed, if it were allowed, I should have to give him, according to human usage, fine ceremonious titles of lustre and merit, I should have to extol his courage as investigator and discoverer, his fearless honesty, truthfulness, and love of wisdom. But such a God does not know what to do with all that respectable trumpery and pomp. "Keep that," he would say, "for thyself and those like thee, and whoever else require it! I—have no reason to cover my nakedness!" One suspects that this kind of divinity and philosopher perhaps lacks shame? He once said: "Under certain circumstances I love mankind"—and referred thereby to Ariadne, who was present; "in my opinion man is an agreeable, brave, inventive animal, that has not his equal upon earth, he makes his way even through all labyrinths. I like man, and often think how I can still further advance him, and make him stronger, more evil, and more profound." "Stronger, more evil, and more profound?" I asked in horror. "Yes," he said again, "stronger, more evil, and more profound; also more beautiful"—and thereby the tempter-god smiled with his halcyon smile, as though he had just paid some charming compliment. One here sees at once that it is not only shame that this divinity lacks; and in general there are good grounds for supposing that in some things the Gods could all of them come to us men for instruction. We men are—more human.

296

Alas! What are you, after all, my written and painted thoughts! Not long ago you were so variegated, young, and malicious, so full of thorns and secret spices, that you made me sneeze and laugh—and now? You have already doffed your novelty, and some of you, I fear, are ready to become truths, so immortal do they look, so pathetically honest, so tedious! And was it ever otherwise? What then do we write and paint, we mandarins with Chinese brush, we immortalisers of things which *lend* themselves to writing, what are we alone capable of painting? Alas, only that which is just about to fade and begins to lose its odour! Alas, only exhausted and departing storms and belated yellow sentiments! Alas, only birds strayed and fatigued by flight, which now let themselves be captured with the hand—with *our* hand! We immortalise what cannot live and fly much longer, things only which are exhausted and mellow! And it is only for your *afternoon*, you, my written and painted thoughts, for which alone I have colours, many colours perhaps, many variegated softenings, and fifty yellows and browns and greens and reds; but nobody will divine thereby how ye looked in your morning, you sudden sparks and marvels of my solitude, you, my old, beloved—*evil* thoughts!

FROM THE HEIGHTS

BY F. W. NIETZSCHE

TRANSLATED BY L. A. MAGNUS

1

MIDDAY OF LIFE! OH, SEASON OF DELIGHT!
My summer's park!
Uneaseful joy to look, to lurk, to hark:
I peer for friends, am ready day and night—
Where linger ye, my friends? The time is right!

2

Is not the glacier's grey today for you
Rose-garlanded?
The brooklet seeks you; wind, cloud, with longing thread
And thrust themselves yet higher to the blue,
To spy for you from farthest eagle's view.

3

My table was spread out for you on high:
Who dwelleth so
Star-near, so near the grisly pit below?
My realm—what realm hath wider boundary?
My honey—who hath sipped its fragrancy?

4

Friends, ye are there! Woe me—yet I am not
He whom ye seek?
Ye stare and stop—better your wrath could speak!
I am not I? Hand, gait, face, changed? And what
I am, to you my friends, now am I not?

5

Am I an other? Strange am I to Me?
Yet from Me sprung?

A wrestler, by himself too oft self-wrung?
Hindering too oft my own self's potency,
Wounded and hampered by self-victory?

6

I sought where-so the wind blow keenest. There
                    I learned to dwell
Where no man dwells, on lonesome ice-lorn fell,
And unlearned Man and God and curse and prayer?
Became a ghost haunting the glaciers bare?

7

Ye, my old friends! Look! Ye turn pale, filled o'er
                    With love and fear!
Go! Yet not in wrath. Ye could ne'er live here.
Here in the farthest realm of ice and scaur,
A huntsman must one be, like chamois soar.

8

An evil huntsman was I? See how taut
                    My bow was bent!
Strongest was he by whom such bolt were sent—
Woe now! That arrow is with peril fraught,
Perilous as none. Have yon safe home ye sought!

9

Ye go! Thou didst endure enough, oh, heart;
                    Strong was thy hope;
Unto new friends thy portals widely ope,
Let old ones be. Bid memory depart!
Wast thou young then, now—better young thou art!

10

What linked us once together, one hope's tie—
                    (Who now doth con
Those lines, now fading, Love once wrote thereon?)
Is like a parchment, which the hand is shy
To touch—like crackling leaves, all seared, all dry.

11

Oh! Friends no more! They are—what name for those?
Friends' phantom-flight
Knocking at my heart's windowpane at night,
Gazing on me, that speaks "We were" and goes—
Oh, withered words, once fragrant as the rose!

12

Pinings of youth that might not understand!
For which I pined,
Which I deemed changed with me, kin of my kind:
But they grew old, and thus were doomed and banned:
None but new kith are native of my land!

13

Midday of life! My second youth's delight I
My summer's park!
Unrestful joy to long, to lurk, to hark!
I peer for friends! Am ready day and night,
For my new friends. Come! Come! The time is right!

*   *   *   *   *   *

14

This song is done—the sweet sad cry of rue
Sang out its end;
A wizard wrought it, he the timely friend,
The midday-friend—no, do not ask me who;
At midday 'twas, when one became as two.

15

We keep our Feast of Feasts, sure of our bourne,
Our aims self-same:
The Guest of Guests, friend Zarathustra, came!
The world now laughs, the grisly veil was torn,
And Light and Dark were one that wedding-morn.

ON THE GENEALOGY
OF MORALS

TRANSLATED BY

HORACE B. SAMUEL

CONTENTS

ON THE GENEALOGY OF MORALS

PREFACE

1

WE ARE UNKNOWN, WE KNOWERS, OURSELVES TO OURSELVES: THIS HAS ITS own good reason. We have never searched for ourselves—how should it then come to pass, that we should ever *find* ourselves? Rightly has it been said: "Where your treasure is, there will your heart be also." *Our* treasure is there, where stand the hives of our knowledge. It is to those hives that we are always striving; as born creatures of flight, and as the honey-gatherers of the spirit, we care really in our hearts only for one thing—to bring something "home to the hive!"

As far as the rest of life with its so-called "experiences" is concerned, which of us has even sufficient serious interest? Or sufficient time? In our dealings with such points of life, we are, I fear, never properly to the point; to be precise, our heart is not there, and certainly not our ear. Rather like one who, delighting in a divine distraction, or sunken in the seas of his own soul, in whose ear the clock has just thundered with all its force its twelve strokes of noon, suddenly wakes up, and asks himself, "What has in point of fact just struck?" so do we at times rub afterwards, as it were, our puzzled ears, and ask in complete astonishment and complete embarrassment, "Through what have we in point of fact just lived?" further, "Who are we in point of fact?" and count, *after they have struck*, as I have explained, all the twelve throbbing beats of the clock of our experience, of our life, of our being—ah! And count wrong in the endeavour. Of necessity we remain strangers to ourselves, we understand ourselves not, in ourselves we are bound to be mistaken, for of us holds good to all eternity the motto, "Each one is the farthest away from himself"—as far as ourselves are concerned we are not "knowers."

2

My thoughts concerning the *genealogy* of our moral prejudices—for they constitute the issue in this polemic—have their first, bald, and provisional expression in that collection of aphorisms entitled *Human, All-Too-Human, a Book for Free Minds*, the writing of which was begun in Sorrento, during a winter which allowed me to gaze over the broad and dangerous territory through which my mind had up to that time wandered. This took place in the winter of 1876–77; the thoughts themselves are older.

They were in their substance already the same thoughts which I take up again in the following treatises: we hope that they have derived benefit from the long interval, that they have grown riper, clearer, stronger, more complete. The fact, however, that I still cling to them even now, that in the meanwhile they have always held faster by each other, have, in fact, grown out of their original shape and into each other, all this strengthens in my mind the joyous confidence that they must have been originally neither separate disconnected capricious nor sporadic phenomena, but have sprung from a common root, from a fundamental "*fiat*" of knowledge, whose empire reached to the soul's depth, and that ever grew more definite in its voice, and more definite in its demands. That is the only state of affairs that is proper in the case of a philosopher.

We have no right to be "*disconnected*"; we must neither err "disconnectedly" nor strike the truth "disconnectedly." Rather with the necessity with which a tree bears its fruit, so do our thoughts, our values, our Yes' and No's and If's and Whether's, grow connected and interrelated, mutual witnesses of *one* will, *one* health, *one* kingdom, *one* sun—as to whether they are to your taste, these fruits of ours? But what matters that to the trees? What matters that to us, us the philosophers?

3

Owing to a scrupulosity peculiar to myself, which I confess reluctantly—it concerns indeed *morality*—a scrupulosity, which manifests itself in my life at such an early period, with so much spontaneity, with so chronic a persistence and so keen an opposition to environment, epoch, precedent, and ancestry that I should have been almost entitled to style it my "a priori" —my curiosity and my suspicion felt themselves betimes bound to halt at the question, of what in point of actual fact was the *origin* of our "Good" and of our "Evil." Indeed, at the boyish age of thirteen the problem of the origin of Evil already haunted me: at an age "when games and God divide one's heart," I devoted to that problem my first childish attempt at the literary game, my first philosophic essay—and as regards my infantile solution of the problem, well, I gave quite properly the honour to God, and made him the *father* of evil. Did my own "a priori" demand that precise solution from me? That new, immoral, or at least "amoral" "a priori" and that "categorical imperative" which was its voice (but oh! How hostile to the Kantian article, and how pregnant with problems!), to which since then I have given more and more attention, and indeed what is more than attention. Fortunately I soon learned to separate theological from moral prejudices, and I gave up looking for a supernatural origin of evil. A certain amount of historical and philological education, to say nothing of an innate faculty of psychological discrimination par excellence succeeded in transforming almost immediately my original problem into the following one: Under what conditions did Man invent for himself those judgements of values, "Good" and "Evil?" *And what intrinsic value do they possess in themselves?* Have they up to the present hindered or advanced human well-being? Are they a symptom of the distress, impoverishment, and degeneration of Human Life? Or, conversely, is it in them that is manifested the fullness, the strength, and the will of Life, its courage, its self-confidence, its future? On this point I found and hazarded in my mind the most diverse answers, I established distinctions in periods, peoples, and castes, I became a specialist in my problem, and from my answers grew new questions, new investigations, new conjectures, new probabilities; until at last I had a land of my own and a soil of my own, a whole secret world growing and flowering, like hidden gardens of whose existence no one could have an inkling—oh, how happy are we, we finders of knowledge, provided that we know how to keep silent sufficiently long.

4

My first impulse to publish some of my hypotheses concerning the origin of morality I owe to a clear, well-written, and even precocious little book, in which a perverse and vicious kind of moral philosophy (your real *English* kind) was definitely presented to me for the first time; and this attracted me—with that magnetic attraction, inherent in that which is diametrically opposed and antithetical to one's own ideas. The title of the book was *The Origin of the Moral Emotions*; its author, Dr. Paul Rée; the year of its appearance, 1877. I may almost say that I have never read anything in which every single dogma and conclusion has called forth from me so emphatic a negation as did that book; albeit a negation untainted by either pique or intolerance. I referred accordingly both in

season and out of season in the previous works, at which I was then working, to the arguments of that book, not to refute them—for what have I
got to do with mere refutations—but substituting, as is natural to a positive
mind, for an improbable theory one which is more probable, and occasionally no doubt for one philosophic error another. In that early period
I gave, as I have said, the first public expression to those theories of origin
to which these essays are devoted, but with a clumsiness which I was the
last to conceal from myself, for I was as yet cramped, being still without a
special language for these special subjects, still frequently liable to relapse
and to vacillation. To go into details, compare what I say in *Human, All-
Too-Human*, part 1, about the parallel early history of Good and Evil, Aph. 45
(namely, their origin from the castes of the aristocrats and the slaves);
similarly, Aph. 136 et seq., concerning the birth and value of ascetic
morality; similarly, Aphs. 96, 99, vol. 2., Aph. 89, concerning the Morality
of Custom, that far older and more original kind of morality which is *toto
caelo* different from the altruistic ethics (in which Dr. Rée, like all the
English moral philosophers, sees the ethical "Thing-in-itself"); finally,
Aph. 92. Similarly, Aph. 26 in *Human, All-Too-Human*, part 2, and Aph. 112,
the *Dawn of Day*, concerning the origin of Justice as a balance between
persons of approximately equal power (equilibrium as the hypothesis
of all contract, consequently of all law); similarly, concerning the origin of
Punishment, *Human, All-Too-Human*, part 2, Aphs. 22, 23, in regard to
which the deterrent object is neither essential nor original (as Dr. Rée
thinks: rather is it that this object is only imported, under certain definite
conditions, and always as something extra and additional).

5

In reality I had set my heart at that time on something much more important than the nature of the theories of myself or others concerning the
origin of morality (or, more precisely, the real function from my view of
these theories was to point an end to which they were one among many
means). The issue for me was the value of morality, and on that subject I
had to place myself in a state of abstraction, in which I was almost alone
with my great teacher Schopenhauer, to whom that book, with all its passion and inherent contradiction (for that book also was a polemic), turned
for present help as though he were still alive. The issue was, strangely
enough, the value of the "unegoistic" instincts, the instincts of pity, self-
denial, and self-sacrifice which Schopenhauer had so persistently painted
in golden colours, deified and etherealised, that eventually they appeared

to him, as it were, high and dry, as "intrinsic values in themselves," on the strength of which he uttered both to Life and to himself his own negation.

But against *these very* instincts there voiced itself in my soul a more and more fundamental mistrust, a scepticism that dug ever deeper and deeper: and in this very instinct I saw the great danger of mankind, its most sublime temptation and seduction—seduction to what? To nothingness? In these very instincts I saw the beginning of the end, stability, the exhaustion that gazes backwards, the will turning *against* Life, the last illness announcing itself with its own mincing melancholy: I realised that the morality of pity which spread wider and wider, and whose grip infected even philosophers with its disease, was the most sinister symptom of our modern European civilisation; I realised that it was the route along which that civilisation slid on its way to—a new Buddhism? A European Buddhism? *Nihilism?* This exaggerated estimation in which modern philosophers have held pity, is quite a new phenomenon: up to that time philosophers were absolutely unanimous as to the worthlessness of pity. I need only mention Plato, Spinoza, La Rochefoucauld, and Kant—four minds as mutually different as is possible, but united on one point; their contempt of pity.

6

This problem of the value of pity and of the pity-morality (I am an opponent of the modern infamous emasculation of our emotions) seems at the first blush a mere isolated problem, a note of interrogation for itself; he, however, who once halts at this problem, and learns how to put questions, will experience what I experienced: a new and immense vista unfolds itself before him, a sense of potentiality seizes him like a vertigo, every species of doubt, mistrust, and fear springs up, the belief in morality, nay, in all morality, totters—finally a new demand voices itself. Let us speak out this *new demand*: we need a *critique* of moral values, *the value of these values* is for the first time to be called into question—and for this purpose a knowledge is necessary of the conditions and circumstances out of which these values grew, and under which they experienced their evolution and their distortion (morality as a result, as a symptom, as a mask, as Tartuffism, as disease, as a misunderstanding; but also morality as a cause, as a remedy, as a stimulant, as a fetter, as a drug), especially as such a knowledge has neither existed up to the present time nor is even now generally desired. The value of these "values" was taken for granted as an indisputable fact, which was beyond all question. No one has, up to the present, exhibited the faintest doubt or hesitation in judging the "good man" to be of a higher value than the "evil man," of a higher value with regard specifically to human progress, utility, and prosperity generally, not forgetting the future. What? Suppose the converse were the truth! What? Suppose there lurked in the "good man" a symptom of retrogression, such as a danger, a temptation, a poison, a *narcotic*, by means of which the present *battened on the future!* More comfortable and less risky perhaps than its opposite, but also pettier, meaner! So that morality would really be saddled with the guilt, if the *maximum potentiality of the power and splendour* of the human species were never to be attained? So that really morality would be the danger of dangers?

7

Enough, that after this vista had disclosed itself to me, I myself had reason to search for learned, bold, and industrious colleagues (I am doing it even to this very day). It means traversing with new clamorous questions, and at the same time with new eyes, the immense, distant, and completely unexplored land of morality—of a morality which has actually existed and been actually lived! And is this not practically equivalent to first *discovering* that land? If, in this context, I thought, amongst others, of the aforesaid Dr. Rée, I did so because I had no doubt that from the very nature of his questions he would be compelled to have recourse to a truer method, in order to obtain his answers. Have I deceived myself on that score? I wished at all events to give a better direction of vision to an eye of such keenness, and such impartiality. I wished to direct him to the real *history of morality*, and to warn him, while there was yet time, against a world of English theories that culminated *in the blue vacuum of heaven.* Other colours, of course, rise immediately to one's mind as being a hundred times more potent than blue for a genealogy of morals: for instance, *grey*, by which I mean authentic facts capable of definite proof and having actually existed, or, to put it shortly, the whole of that long hieroglyphic script (which is so hard to decipher) about the past history of human morals. This script was unknown to Dr. Rée; but he had read Darwin: and so in his philosophy the Darwinian beast and that pink of modernity, the demure weakling and dilettante, who "bites no longer," shake hands politely in a fashion that is at least instructive, the latter exhibiting a certain facial expression of refined and good-humoured indolence, tinged with a touch of pessimism and exhaustion; as if it really did not pay to take all these things—I mean moral problems—so seriously. I, on the other hand, think that there are no subjects which pay better for being taken seriously; part of this payment is, that perhaps eventually they admit of being taken *gaily*. This gaiety indeed, or, to use my own language, this *joyful wisdom*, is a payment; a payment for a protracted, brave, laborious, and burrowing seriousness, which, it goes without saying, is the attribute of but a few. But on that day on which we say from the fullness of our hearts, "Forward! Our old morality too is fit material *for Comedy*," we shall have discovered a new plot, and a new possibility for the Dionysian drama entitled *The Soul's Fate*—and he will speedily utilise it, one can wager safely, he, the great ancient eternal dramatist of the comedy of our existence.

8

If this writing be obscure to any individual, and jar on his ears, I do not think that it is necessarily I who am to blame. It is clear enough, on the hypothesis which I presuppose, namely, that the reader has first read my previous writings and has not grudged them a certain amount of trouble: it is not, indeed, a simple matter to get really at their essence. Take, for instance, my *Zarathustra*; I allow no one to pass muster as knowing that book, unless every single word therein has at sometime wrought in him a profound wound, and at sometime exercised on him a profound enchantment: then and not till then can he enjoy the privilege of participating reverently in the halcyon element, from which that work is born, in its sunny brilliance, its distance, its spaciousness, its certainty. In other cases the aphoristic form produces difficulty, but this is only because this form is treated *too casually*. An aphorism properly coined and cast into its final mould is far from being "deciphered" as soon as it has been read; on the contrary, it is then that it first requires *to be expounded*—of course for that purpose an art of exposition is necessary. The third essay in this book provides an example of what is offered, of what in such cases I call exposition: an aphorism is prefixed to that essay, the essay itself is its commentary. Certainly one *quality* which nowadays has been best forgotten—and that is why it will take sometime yet for my writings to become readable—is essential in order to practise reading as an art—a quality for the exercise of which it is necessary to be a cow, and under *no circumstances* a modern man! *Rumination*.

SILS-MARIA, UPPER ENGADINE,
July 1887

"GOOD AND EVIL,"
"GOOD AND BAD"

1

THOSE ENGLISH PSYCHOLOGISTS, WHO UP TO THE PRESENT ARE THE ONLY philosophers who are to be thanked for any endeavour to get as far as a history of the origin of morality—these men, I say, offer us in their own personalities no paltry problem; they even have, if I am to be quite frank about it, in their capacity of living riddles, an advantage over their books— *they themselves are interesting!* These English psychologists—what do they really mean? We always find them voluntarily or involuntarily at the same task of pushing to the front the partie honteuse of our inner world, and looking for the efficient, governing, and decisive principle in that precise quarter where the intellectual self-respect of the race would be the most reluctant to find it (for example, in the *vis inertiae* of habit, or in forgetfulness, or in a blind and fortuitous mechanism and association of ideas, or in some factor that is purely passive, reflex, molecular, or fundamentally stupid)—what is the real motive power which always impels these psychologists in precisely *this* direction? Is it an instinct for human disparagement somewhat sinister, vulgar, and malignant, or perhaps incomprehensible even to itself? Or perhaps a touch of pessimistic jealousy, the mistrust of disillusioned idealists who have become gloomy, poisoned, and bitter? Or a petty subconscious enmity and rancour against Christianity (and Plato), that has conceivably never crossed the threshold of consciousness? Or just a vicious taste for those elements of life which are bizarre, painfully paradoxical, mystical, and illogical? Or, as a final alternative, a dash of each of these motives—a little vulgarity, a little gloominess, a little anti-Christianity, a little craving for the necessary piquancy?

But I am told that it is simply a case of old frigid and tedious frogs crawling and hopping around men and inside men, as if they were as thoroughly at home there, as they would be in a *swamp.* I am opposed to this statement, nay, I do not believe it; and if, in the impossibility of knowledge, one is permitted to wish, so do I wish from my heart that just the converse metaphor should apply, and that these analysts with their psychological microscopes should be, at bottom, brave, proud, and magnanimous animals who know how to bridle both their hearts and their smarts, and have specifically trained themselves to sacrifice what is desirable to what is true, *any* truth in fact, even the simple, bitter, ugly, repulsive, unchristian, and immoral truths—for there are truths of that description.

2

All honour, then, to the noble spirits who would fain dominate these historians of morality. But it is certainly a pity that they lack the *historical sense* itself, that they themselves are quite deserted by all the beneficent spirits of history. The whole train of their thought runs, as was always the way of old-fashioned philosophers, on *thoroughly* unhistorical lines: there is no doubt on this point. The crass ineptitude of their genealogy of morals is immediately apparent when the question arises of ascertaining the origin of the idea and judgement of "good." "Man had originally," so speaks their decree, "praised and called 'good' altruistic acts from the standpoint of those on whom they were conferred, that is, those to whom they were *useful*; subsequently the origin of this praise was *forgotten*, and altruistic acts, simply because, as a sheer matter of habit, they were praised as good, came also to be felt as good—as though they contained in themselves some intrinsic goodness." The thing is obvious: this initial derivation contains already all the typical and idiosyncratic traits of the English psychologists—we have "utility," "forgetting," "habit," and finally "error," the whole assemblage forming the basis of a system of values, on which the higher man has up to the present prided himself as though it were a kind of privilege of man in general. This pride *must* be brought low, this system of values *must* lose its values: is that attained?

Now the first argument that comes ready to my hand is that the real homestead of the concept "good" is sought and located in the wrong place: the judgement "good" did *not* originate among those to whom goodness was shown. Much rather has it been the good themselves, that is, the aristocratic, the powerful, the high-stationed, the high-minded, who have felt that they themselves were good, and that their actions were good, that is to say of the first order, in contradistinction to all the low, the low-minded, the vulgar, and the plebeian. It was out of this pathos of distance that they first arrogated the right to create values for their own profit, and to coin the names of such values: what had they to do with utility? The standpoint of utility is as alien and as inapplicable as it could possibly be, when we have to deal with so volcanic an effervescence of supreme values, creating and demarcating as they do a hierarchy within themselves: it is at this juncture that one arrives at an appreciation of the contrast to that tepid temperature, which is the presupposition on which every combination of worldly wisdom and every calculation of practical expediency is always based—and not for one occasional, not for one exceptional instance, but chronically. The pathos of nobility and distance, as I have said, the chronic and despotic esprit de corps and fundamental instinct of a higher dominant race coming into association with a meaner race, an "under race," this is the origin of the antithesis of good and bad.

(The masters' right of giving names goes so far that it is permissible to look upon language itself as the expression of the power of the masters: they say "this *is* that, and that," they seal finally every object and every event with a sound, and thereby at the same time take possession of it.) It is because of this origin that the word "good" is far from having any necessary connexion with altruistic acts, in accordance with the superstitious belief of these moral philosophers. On the contrary, it is on the occasion of the *decay* of aristocratic values, that the antithesis between "egoistic" and "altruistic" presses more and more heavily on the human conscience—it is, to use my own language, the *herd instinct* which finds in this antithesis an expression in many ways. And even then it takes a considerable time for this instinct to become sufficiently dominant, for the valuation to be inextricably dependent on this antithesis (as is the case in contemporary Europe); for today that prejudice is predominant, which, acting even now with all the intensity of an obsession and brain disease, holds that "moral," "altruistic," and "*désintéressé*" are concepts of equal value.

3

In the second place, quite apart from the fact that this hypothesis as to the genesis of the value "good" cannot be historically upheld, it suffers from an inherent psychological contradiction. The utility of altruistic conduct has presumably been the origin of its being praised, and this origin has become *forgotten*: But in what conceivable way is this forgetting *possible?* Has perchance the utility of such conduct ceased at some given moment? The contrary is the case. This utility has rather been experienced everyday at all times, and is consequently a feature that obtains a new and regular emphasis with every fresh day; it follows that, so far from vanishing from the consciousness, so far indeed from being forgotten, it must necessarily become impressed on the consciousness with ever-increasing distinctness. How much more logical is that contrary theory (it is not the truer for that) which is represented, for instance, by Herbert Spencer, who places the concept "good" as essentially similar to the concept "useful," "purposive," so that in the judgements "good" and "bad" mankind is simply summarising and investing with a sanction its *unforgotten* and *unforgettable* experiences concerning the "useful-purposive" and the "mischievous-non-purposive." According to this theory, "good" is the attribute of that which has previously shown itself useful; and so is able to claim to be considered "valuable in the highest degree," "valuable in itself." This method of explanation is also, as I have said, wrong, but at any rate the explanation itself is coherent, and psychologically tenable.

4

The guidepost which first put me on the *right* track was this question— what is the true etymological significance of the various symbols for the idea "good" which have been coined in the various languages? I then found that they all led back to *the same evolution of the same idea*—that everywhere "aristocrat," "noble" (in the social sense), is the root idea, out of which have necessarily developed "good" in the sense of "with aristocratic soul," "noble," in the sense of "with a soul of high calibre," "with a privileged soul"—a development which invariably runs parallel with that other evolution by which "vulgar," "plebeian," "low," are made to change finally into "bad." The most eloquent proof of this last contention is the German word "*schlecht*" itself: this word is identical with "*schlicht*"— (compare "*schlechtweg*" and "*schlechterdings*")—which, originally and as yet without any sinister innuendo, simply denoted the plebeian man in contrast to the aristocratic man. It is at the sufficiently late period of the Thirty Years' War that this sense becomes changed to the sense now current. From the standpoint of the *Genealogy of Morals* this discovery seems to be substantial: the lateness of it is to be attributed to the retarding influence exercised in the modern world by democratic prejudice in the sphere of all questions of origin. This extends, as will shortly be shown, even to the province of natural science and physiology, which *prima facie* is the most objective. The extent of the mischief which is caused by this prejudice (once it is free of all trammels except those of its own malice), particularly to Ethics and History, is shown by the notorious case of Buckle: it was in Buckle that that *plebeianism* of the modern spirit, which is of English origin, broke out once again from its malignant soil with all the violence of a slimy volcano, and with that salted, rampant, and vulgar eloquence with which up to the present time all volcanoes have spoken.

5

With regard to our problem, which can justly be called an *intimate* problem, and which elects to appeal to only a limited number of ears: it is of no small interest to ascertain that in those words and roots which denote "good" we catch glimpses of that arch-trait, on the strength of which the aristocrats feel themselves to be beings of a higher order than their fellows. Indeed, they call themselves in perhaps the most frequent instances simply after their superiority in power (e.g., "the powerful," "the lords," "the commanders"), or after the most obvious sign of their superiority, as for example "the rich," "the possessors" (that is the meaning of *arya*; and the Iranian and Slav languages correspond). But they also call themselves after some *characteristic idiosyncrasy*; and this is the case which now concerns us. They name themselves, for instance, "the truthful": this is first done by the Greek nobility whose mouthpiece is found in Theognis, the Megarian poet. The word ἐσθλός, which is coined for the purpose, signifies etymologically "one who is," who has reality, who is real, who is true; and then with a subjective twist, the "true," as the "truthful": at this stage in the evolution of the idea, it becomes the motto and party cry of the nobility, and quite completes the transition to the meaning "noble," so as to place outside the pale the lying, vulgar man, as Theognis conceives and portrays him—till finally the word after the decay of the nobility is left to delineate psychological *noblesse*, and becomes as it were ripe and mellow. In the word κακός as in δειλός (the plebeian in contrast to the ἀγαθός) the cowardice is emphasised. This affords perhaps an inkling on what lines the etymological origin of the very ambiguous ἀγαθός is to be investigated. In the Latin malus (which I place side by side with μέλας) the vulgar man can be distinguished as the dark-coloured, and above all as the black-haired ("*hic niger est*"), as the pre-Aryan inhabitants of the Italian soil, whose complexion formed the clearest feature of distinction from the dominant blondes, namely, the Aryan conquering race: at any rate Gaelic has afforded me the exact analogue—*Fin* (for instance, in the name *Fin-Gal*), the distinctive word of the nobility, finally—good, noble, clean, but originally the blonde-haired man in contrast to the dark black-haired aboriginals. The Celts, if I may make a parenthetic statement, were throughout a blonde race; and it is wrong to connect, as Virchow still connects, those traces of an essentially dark-haired population which are to be seen on the more elaborate ethnographical maps of Germany with any Celtic ancestry or with any admixture of Celtic blood: in this context it is rather the *pre-Aryan* population of Germany which surges up to these districts. (The same is true substantially of the whole of Europe: in point of fact, the subject race has finally again obtained the upper hand, in complexion and the shortness of the skull, and perhaps in the intellectual and social qualities. Who can guarantee that modern democracy, still more modern anarchy, and indeed that tendency to the "Commune," the most primitive form of society, which is now common to all the Socialists in Europe, does not in its real essence signify a monstrous reversion—and that the conquering and *master* race—the Aryan race, is not also becoming inferior physiologically?) I believe that I can explain the Latin *bonus* as the "warrior": my hypothesis is that I am right in deriving *bonus* from an older *duonus* (compare *bellum* = *duellum* = duen-lum, in which the word *duonus* appears to me to be contained). *Bonus* accordingly as the man of discord, of variance, "*entzweiung*" (*duo*), as the warrior: one sees what in ancient Rome "the good" meant for a man. Must not our actual German word *gut* mean "the *godlike*, the man of god-like race?" And be identical with the national name (originally the nobles' name) of the *Goths*?

The grounds for this supposition do not appertain to this work.

6

Above all, there is no exception (though there are opportunities for exceptions) to this rule, that the idea of political superiority always resolves itself into the idea of psychological superiority, in those cases where the highest caste is at the same time the *priestly* caste, and in accordance with its general characteristics confers on itself the privilege of a title which alludes specifically to its priestly function. It is in these cases, for instance, that "clean" and "unclean" confront each other for the first time as badges of class distinction; here again there develops a "good" and a "bad," in a sense which has ceased to be merely social. Moreover, care should be taken not to take these ideas of "clean" and "unclean" too seriously, too broadly, or too symbolically: all the ideas of ancient man have, on the contrary, got to be understood in their initial stages, in a sense which is, to an almost inconceivable extent, crude, coarse, physical, and narrow, and above all essentially *unsymbolical.* The "clean man" is originally only a man who washes himself, who abstains from certain foods which are conducive to skin diseases, who does not sleep with the unclean women of the lower classes, who has a horror of blood—not more, not much more!

On the other hand, the very nature of a priestly aristocracy shows the reasons why just at such an early juncture there should ensue a really dangerous sharpening and intensification of opposed values: it is, in fact, through these opposed values that gulfs are cleft in the social plane, which a veritable Achilles of free thought would shudder to cross. There is from the outset a certain *diseased taint* in such sacerdotal aristocracies, and in the habits which prevail in such societies—habits which, *averse* as they are to action, constitute a compound of introspection and explosive emotionalism, as a result of which there appears that introspective morbidity and neurasthenia, which adheres almost inevitably to all priests at all times: with regard, however, to the remedy which they themselves have invented for this disease—the philosopher has no option but to state, that it has proved itself in its effects a hundred times more dangerous than the disease, from which it should have been the deliverer. Humanity itself is still diseased from the effects of the naïvetés of this priestly cure. Take, for instance, certain kinds of diet (abstention from flesh), fasts, sexual continence, flight into the wilderness (a kind of Weir-Mitchell isolation, though of course without that system of excessive feeding and fattening which is the most efficient antidote to all the hysteria of the ascetic ideal); consider too the whole metaphysic of the priests, with its war on the senses, its enervation, its hair-splitting; consider its self-hypnotism on the fakir and Brahman principles (it uses Brahman as a glass disc and obsession), and that climax which we can understand only too well of an unusual satiety with its panacea of *nothingness* (or God: the demand for a *unio mystica* with God is the demand of the Buddhist for nothingness, Nirvana—and nothing else!). In sacerdotal societies *every* element is on a more dangerous scale, not merely cures and remedies, but also pride, revenge, cunning, exaltation, love, ambition, virtue, morbidity: further, it can fairly be stated that it is on the soil of this *essentially dangerous* form of human society, the sacerdotal form, that man really becomes for the first time an *interesting animal,* that it is in this form that the soul of man has in a higher sense attained *depths* and become *evil*—and those are the two fundamental forms of the superiority which up to the present man has exhibited over every other animal.

7

The reader will have already surmised with what ease the priestly mode of valuation can branch off from the knightly aristocratic mode, and then develop into the very antithesis of the latter: special impetus is given to this opposition, by every occasion when the castes of the priests and warriors confront each other with mutual jealousy and cannot agree over the prize. The knightly aristocratic "values" are based on a careful cult of the physical, on a flowering, rich, and even effervescing healthiness, that goes considerably beyond what is necessary for maintaining life, on war, adventure, the chase, the dance, the tourney—on everything, in fact, which is contained in strong, free, and joyous action. The priestly aristocratic mode of valuation is—we have seen—based on other hypotheses: it is bad enough for this class when it is a question of war! Yet the priests are, as is notorious, *the worst enemies*—why? Because they are the weakest. Their weakness causes their hate to expand into a monstrous and sinister shape, a shape which is most crafty and most poisonous. The really great haters in the history of the world have always been priests, who are also the cleverest haters—in comparison with the cleverness of priestly revenge, every other piece of cleverness is practically negligible. Human history would be too fatuous for anything were it not for the cleverness imported into it by the weak—take at once the most important instance. All the world's efforts against the "aristocrats," the "mighty," the "masters," the "holders of power," are negligible by comparison with what has been accomplished against those classes by *the Jews*—the Jews, that priestly nation which eventually realised that the one method of effecting satisfaction on its enemies and tyrants was by means of a radical transvaluation of values, which was at the same time an act of the *cleverest revenge.* Yet the method was only appropriate to a nation of priests, to a nation of the most jealously nursed priestly revengefulness. It was the Jews who, in opposition to the aristocratic equation (good = aristocratic = beautiful = happy = loved by the gods), dared with a terrifying logic to suggest the contrary equation, and indeed to maintain with the teeth of the most profound hatred (the hatred of weakness) this contrary equation, namely, "the wretched are alone the good; the poor, the weak, the lowly, are alone the good; the suffering, the needy, the sick, the loathsome, are the only ones who are pious, the only ones who are blessed, for them alone is salvation—but you, on the other hand, you aristocrats, you men of power, you are to all eternity the evil, the horrible, the covetous, the insatiate, the godless; eternally also shall you be the unblessed, the cursed, the damned!" We know who it was who reaped the heritage of this Jewish transvaluation. In the context of the monstrous and inordinately fateful initiative which the Jews have exhibited in connexion with this most fundamental of all declarations of war, I remember the passage which came to my pen on another occasion (*Beyond Good and Evil*, Aph. 195)—that it was, in fact, with the Jews that the *revolt of the slaves* begins in the sphere *of morals*; that revolt which has behind it a history of two millennia, and which at the present day has only moved out of our sight, because it—has achieved victory.

8

But you understand this not? You have no eyes for a force which has taken two thousand years to achieve victory? There is nothing wonderful in this: all *lengthy* processes are hard to see and to realise. But *this* is what took place: from the trunk of that tree of revenge and hate, Jewish hate—that most profound and sublime hate, which creates ideals and changes old values to new creations, the like of which has never been on earth—there grew a phenomenon which was equally incomparable, *a new love*, the most profound and sublime of all kinds of love; and from what other trunk could it have grown? But beware of supposing that this love has soared on its upward growth, as in anyway a real negation of that thirst for revenge, as an antithesis to the Jewish hate! No, the contrary is the truth! This love grew out of that hate, as its crown, as its triumphant crown, circling wider and wider amid the clarity and fullness of the sun, and pursuing in the very kingdom of light and height its goal of hatred, its victory, its spoil, its strategy, with the same intensity with which the roots of that tree of hate sank into everything which was deep and evil with increasing stability and increasing desire. This Jesus of Nazareth, the incarnate gospel of love, this "Redeemer" bringing salvation and victory to the poor, the sick, the sinful—was he not really temptation in its most sinister and irresistible form, temptation to take the tortuous path to those very *Jewish* values and those very Jewish ideals? Has not Israel really obtained the final goal of its sublime revenge, by the tortuous paths of this "Redeemer," for all that he might pose as Israel's adversary and Israel's destroyer? Is it not due to the black magic of a really *great* policy of revenge, of a far-seeing, burrowing revenge, both acting and calculating with slowness, that Israel himself must repudiate before all the world the actual instrument of his own revenge and nail it to the cross, so that all the world—that is, all the enemies of Israel—could nibble without suspicion at this very bait? Could, moreover, any human mind with all its elaborate ingenuity invent a bait that was more truly *dangerous?* Anything that was even equivalent in the power of its seductive, intoxicating, defiling, and corrupting influence to that symbol of the holy cross, to that awful paradox of a "god on the cross," to that mystery of the unthinkable, supreme, and utter horror of the self-crucifixion of a god for the *salvation of man?* It is at least certain that *sub hoc signo* Israel, with its revenge and transvaluation of all values, has up to the present always triumphed again over all other ideals, over all more aristocratic ideals.

9

"But why do you talk of nobler ideals? Let us submit to the facts; that the people have triumphed—or the slaves, or the populace, or the herd, or whatever name you care to give them—if this has happened through the Jews, so be it! In that case no nation ever had a greater mission in the world's history. The 'masters' have been done away with; the morality of the vulgar man has triumphed. This triumph may also be called a blood-poisoning (it has mutually fused the races)—I do not dispute it; but there is no doubt but that this intoxication has succeeded. The 'redemption' of the human race (that is, from the masters) is progressing swimmingly; everything is obviously becoming Judaised, or Christian-ised, or vulgarised (what is there in the words?). It seems impossible to stop the course of this poisoning through the whole body politic of mankind—but its *tempo* and pace may from the present time be slower, more delicate, quieter, more discreet—there is time enough. In view of this context has the Church nowadays any necessary purpose? Has it, in fact, a right to live? Or could man get on without it? *Quaeritur.* It seems that it fetters and retards this tendency, instead of accelerating it. Well, even that might be its utility. The Church certainly is a crude and boor-ish institution, that is repugnant to an intelligence with any pretence at delicacy, to a really modern taste. Should it not at any rate learn to be somewhat more subtle? It alienates nowadays, more than it allures. Which of us would, forsooth, be a freethinker if there were no Church? It is the Church which repels us, *not* its poison—apart from the Church we like the poison." This is the epilogue of a freethinker to my discourse, of an honourable animal (as he has given abundant proof), and a democrat to boot; he had up to that time listened to me, and could not endure my silence, but for me, indeed, with regard to this topic there is much on which to be silent.

10

The revolt of the slaves in morals begins in the very principle of *resentment* becoming creative and giving birth to values—a resentment experienced by creatures who, deprived as they are of the proper outlet of action, are forced to find their compensation in an imaginary revenge. While every aristocratic morality springs from a triumphant affirmation of its own demands, the slave morality says "no" from the very outset to what is "outside itself," "different from itself," and "not itself": and this "no" is its creative deed. This volte-face of the valuing standpoint—this *inevitable* gravitation to the objective instead of back to the subjective—is typical of "resentment": the slave-morality requires as the condition of its existence an external and objective world, to employ physiological terminology, it requires objective stimuli to be capable of action at all—its action is fundamentally a reaction. The contrary is the case when we come to the aristocrat's system of values: it acts and grows spontaneously, it merely seeks its antithesis in order to pronounce a more grateful and exultant "yes" to its own self; its negative conception, "low," "vulgar," "bad," is merely a pale late-born foil in comparison with its positive and fundamental conception (saturated as it is with life and passion), of "we aristocrats, we good ones, we beautiful ones, we happy ones."

When the aristocratic morality goes astray and commits sacrilege on reality, this is limited to that particular sphere with which it is *not* sufficiently acquainted—a sphere, in fact, from the real knowledge of which it disdainfully defends itself. It misjudges, in some cases, the sphere which it despises, the sphere of the common vulgar man and the low people: on the other hand, due weight should be given to the consideration that in any case the mood of contempt, of disdain, of superciliousness, even on the supposition that it *falsely* portrays the object of its contempt, will always be far removed from that degree of falsity which will always characterise the attacks—in effigy, of course—of the vindictive hatred and revengefulness of the weak in onslaughts on their enemies. In point of fact, there is in contempt too strong an admixture of nonchalance, of casualness, of boredom, of impatience, even of personal exultation, for it to be capable of distorting its victim into a real caricature or a real monstrosity. Attention again should be paid to the almost benevolent nuances which, for instance, the Greek nobility imports into all the words by which it distinguishes the common people from itself; note how continuously a kind of pity, care, and consideration imparts its honeyed *flavour*, until at last almost all the words which are applied to the vulgar man survive finally as expressions for "unhappy," "worthy of pity" (compare δειλός, δείλαιος, πονηρός, μοχθηρός; the latter two names really denoting the vulgar man as labour-slave and beast of burden)—and how, conversely, "bad," "low," "unhappy" have never ceased to ring in the Greek ear with a tone in which "unhappy" is the predominant note: this is a heritage of the old noble aristocratic morality, which remains true to itself even in contempt (let philologists remember the sense in which ὀϊζυρός, ἄνολβος, τλήμων, δυστυχεῖν, ξυμφορά used to be employed). The "well-born" simply *felt* themselves the "happy"; they did not have to manufacture their happiness artificially through looking at their enemies, or in cases to talk and *lie themselves into* happiness (as is the custom with all resentful men); and similarly, complete men as they were, exuberant with strength, and consequently *necessarily* energetic, they were too wise to dissociate happiness from action—activity becomes in their minds necessarily counted as happiness (that is the etymology of εὖ πράττειν)—all in sharp contrast to the "happiness" of the weak and the oppressed, with their festering venom and malignity, among whom happiness appears essentially as a narcotic, a deadening, a quietude, a peace, a "Sabbath," an enervation of the mind and relaxation of the limbs—in short, a purely *passive* phenomenon. While the aristocratic man lived in confidence and openness with himself (γενναῖος "noble-born," emphasises the nuance "sincere," and perhaps also "naïf"), the resentful man, on the other hand, is neither sincere nor naïf, nor honest and candid with himself. His soul *squints*; his mind loves hidden crannies, tortuous paths and backdoors, everything secret appeals to him as *his* world, *his* safety, *his* balm; he is past master in silence, in not forgetting, in waiting, in provisional self-depreciation and self-abasement. A race of such *resentful* men will of necessity eventually prove more *prudent* than any aristocratic race, it will honour prudence on quite a distinct scale, as, in fact, a paramount condition of existence, while prudence among aristocratic men is apt to be tinged with a delicate flavour of luxury and refinement; so among them it plays nothing like so integral a part as that complete certainty of function of the governing *unconscious* instincts, or as indeed a certain lack of prudence, such as a vehement and valiant charge, whether against danger or the enemy, or as those ecstatic bursts of rage, love, reverence, gratitude, by which at all times noble souls have recognised each other. When the resentment of the aristocratic man manifests itself, it fulfils and exhausts itself in an immediate reaction, and consequently instills no *venom*: on the other hand, it never manifests itself at all in countless instances, when in the case of the feeble and weak it would be inevitable. An inability to take seriously for any length of time their enemies, their disasters, their *misdeeds*—that is the sign of the full strong natures who possess a superfluity of moulding plastic force, that heals completely and produces forgetfulness: a good example of this in the modern world is Mirabeau, who had no memory for any insults and meannesses which were practised on him, and who was only incapable of forgiving because he forgot. Such a man indeed shakes off with a shrug many a worm which would have buried itself in another; it is only in characters like these that we see the possibility (supposing, of course, that there is such a possibility in the world) of the real "*love* of one's enemies." What respect for his enemies is found, forsooth, in an aristocratic man—and such a reverence is already a bridge to love! He insists on having his enemy to himself as his distinction. He tolerates no other enemy but a man in whose character there is nothing to despise and *much* to honour! On the other hand, imagine the "enemy" as the resentful man conceives him—and it is here exactly that we see his work, his creativeness; he has conceived "the evil enemy," the "evil one," and indeed that is the root idea from which he now evolves as a contrasting and corresponding figure a "good one," himself—his very self!

11

The method of this man is quite contrary to that of the aristocratic man, who conceives the root idea "good" spontaneously and straight away, that is to say, out of himself, and from that material then creates for himself a concept of "bad!" This "bad" of aristocratic origin and that "evil" out of the cauldron of unsatisfied hatred—the former an imitation, an "extra," an additional nuance; the latter, on the other hand, the original, the beginning, the essential act in the conception of a slave-morality—these two words "bad" and "evil," how great a difference do they mark, in spite of the fact that they have an identical contrary in the idea "good." But the idea "good" is *not* the same: much rather let the question be asked, "Who is really evil according to the meaning of the morality of resentment?" In all sternness let it be answered thus: *just* the good man of the other morality, just the aristocrat, the powerful one, the one who rules, but who is distorted by the venomous eye of resentfulness, into a new colour, a new signification, a new appearance. This particular point we would be the last to deny: the man who learnt to know those "good" ones only as enemies, learnt at the same time not to know them only as "*evil enemies*," and the same men who *inter pares* were kept so rigorously in bounds through convention, respect, custom, and gratitude, though much more through mutual vigilance and jealousy *inter pares*, these men who in their relations with each other find so many new ways of manifesting consideration, self-control, delicacy, loyalty, pride, and friendship, these men are in reference to what is outside their circle (where the foreign element, a *foreign* country, begins), not much better than beasts of prey, which have been let loose. They enjoy there freedom from all social control, they feel that in the wilderness they can give vent with impunity to that tension which is produced by enclosure and imprisonment in the peace of society, they *revert* to the innocence of the beast-of-prey conscience, like jubilant monsters, who perhaps come from a ghastly bout of murder, arson, rape, and torture, with bravado and a moral equanimity, as though merely some wild student's prank had been played, perfectly convinced that the poets have now an ample theme to sing and celebrate. It is impossible not to recognise at the core of all these aristocratic races the beast of prey; the magnificent *blonde brute*, avidly rampant for spoil and victory; this hidden core needed an outlet from time to time, the beast must get loose again, must return into the wilderness—the Roman, Arabic, German, and Japanese nobility, the Homeric heroes, the Scandinavian Vikings, are all alike in this need. It is the aristocratic races who have left the idea "Barbarian" on all the tracks in which they have marched; nay, a consciousness of this very barbarianism, and even a pride in it, manifests itself even in their highest civilisation (for example, when Pericles says to his Athenians in that celebrated funeral oration, "Our audacity has forced a way over every land and sea, rearing everywhere imperishable memorials of itself for *good* and for *evil*"). This audacity of aristocratic races, mad, absurd, and spasmodic as may be its expression; the incalculable and fantastic nature of their enterprises—Pericles sets in special relief and glory the ῥαθυμία of the Athenians, their nonchalance and contempt for safety, body, life, and comfort, their awful joy and intense delight in all destruction, in all the ecstasies of victory and cruelty—all these features become crystallised, for those who suffered thereby in the picture of the "barbarian," of the "evil enemy," perhaps of the "Goth" and of the "Vandal." The profound, icy mistrust which the German provokes, as soon as he arrives at power—even at the present time—is always still an aftermath of that inextinguishable

horror with which for whole centuries Europe has regarded the wrath
of the blonde Teuton beast (although between the old Germans and
ourselves there exists scarcely a psychological, let alone a physical, relationship). I have once called attention to the embarrassment of Hesiod,
when he conceived the series of social ages, and endeavoured to express
them in gold, silver, and bronze. He could only dispose of the contradiction, with which he was confronted, by the Homeric world, an age
magnificent indeed, but at the same time so awful and so violent, by making two ages out of one, which he henceforth placed one behind each
other—first, the age of the heroes and demigods, as that world had
remained in the memories of the aristocratic families, who found therein
their own ancestors; secondly, the bronze age, as that corresponding age
appeared to the descendants of the oppressed, spoiled, ill-treated, exiled,
enslaved; namely, as an age of bronze, as I have said, hard, cold, terrible,
without feelings and without conscience, crushing everything, and bespat-
tering everything with blood. Granted the truth of the theory now believed
to be true, that the very *essence of all civilisation* is to train out of man, the
beast of prey, a tame and civilised animal, a domesticated animal, it follows indubitably that we must regard as the real *tools of civilisation* all
those instincts of reaction and resentment, by the help of which the
aristocratic races, together with their ideals, were finally degraded and
overpowered; though that has not yet come to be synonymous with saying
that the bearers of those tools also *represented* the civilisation. It is rather
the contrary that is not only probable—nay, it is *palpable* today; these
bearers of vindictive instincts that have to be bottled up, these descendants
of all European and non-European slavery, especially of the pre-Aryan
population—these people, I say, represent the *decline* of humanity! These
"tools of civilisation" are a disgrace to humanity, and constitute in reality
more of an argument against civilisation, more of a reason why civilisation should be suspected. One may be perfectly justified in being always
afraid of the blonde beast that lies at the core of all aristocratic races, and
in being on one's guard: but who would not a hundred times prefer to be
afraid, when one at the same time admires, than to be immune from fear,
at the cost of being perpetually obsessed with the loathsome spectacle of
the distorted, the dwarfed, the stunted, the envenomed? And is that not
our fate? What produces today our repulsion towards "man?" For we *suffer* from "man," there is no doubt about it. It is not fear; it is rather that
we have nothing more to fear from men; it is that the worm "man" is in the
foreground and pullulates; it is that the "tame man," the wretched mediocre

and unedifying creature, has learnt to consider himself a goal and a pinnacle, an inner meaning, an historic principle, a "higher man"; yes, it is
that he has a certain right so to consider himself, insofar as he feels that
in contrast to that excess of deformity, disease, exhaustion, and effeteness
whose odour is beginning to pollute present-day Europe, he at any rate
has achieved a relative success, he at any rate still says "yes" to life.

12

I cannot refrain at this juncture from uttering a sigh and one last hope.
What is it precisely which I find intolerable? That which I alone cannot
get rid of, which makes me choke and faint? Bad air! Bad air! That something misbegotten comes near me; that I must inhale the odour of the
entrails of a misbegotten soul! That excepted, what can one not endure in
the way of need, privation, bad weather, sickness, toil, solitude? In point
of fact, one manages to get over everything, born as one is to a burrowing
and battling existence; one always returns once again to the light, one
always lives again one's golden hour of victory—and then one stands as
one was born, unbreakable, tense, ready for something more difficult, for
something more distant, like a bow stretched but the tauter by every
strain. But from time to time do ye grant me—assuming that "beyond
good and evil" there are goddesses who can grant—one glimpse, grant me
but one glimpse only, of something perfect, fully realised, happy, mighty,
triumphant, of something that still gives cause for fear! A glimpse of a man
that justifies the existence of man, a glimpse of an incarnate human happiness that realises and redeems, for the sake of which one may hold fast
to *the belief in man!* For the position is this: in the dwarfing and levelling
of the European man lurks *our* greatest peril, for it is this outlook which
fatigues—we see today nothing which wishes to be greater, we surmise that
the process is always still backwards, still backwards towards something
more attenuated, more inoffensive, more cunning, more comfortable, more
mediocre, more indifferent, more Chinese, more Christian—man, there is
no doubt about it, grows always "better"—the destiny of Europe lies even
in this—that in losing the fear of man, we have also lost the hope in man,
yea, the will to be man. The sight of man now fatigues. What is present-day
Nihilism if it is not *that?* We are tired of *man.*

13

But let us come back to it; the problem of *another* origin of the *good*—of
the good, as the resentful man has thought it out—demands its solution.

It is not surprising that the lambs should bear a grudge against the great birds of prey, but that is no reason for blaming the great birds of prey for taking the little lambs. And when the lambs say among themselves, "These birds of prey are evil, and he who is as far removed from being a bird of prey, who is rather its opposite, a lamb—is he not good?" then there is nothing to cavil at in the setting up of this ideal, though it may also be that the birds of prey will regard it a little sneeringly, and perchance say to themselves, "We bear no grudge against them, these good lambs, we even like them: nothing is tastier than a tender lamb." To require of strength that it should *not* express itself as strength, that it should not be a wish to overpower, a wish to overthrow, a wish to become master, a thirst for enemies and antagonisms and triumphs, is just as absurd as to require of weakness that it should express itself as strength. A quantum of force is just such a quantum of movement, will, action—rather it is nothing else than just those very phenomena of moving, willing, acting, and can only appear otherwise in the misleading errors of language (and the fundamental fallacies of reason which have become petrified therein), which understands, and understands wrongly, all working as conditioned by a worker, by a "subject." And just exactly as the people separate the lightning from its flash, and interpret the latter as a thing done, as the working of a subject which is called lightning, so also does the popular morality separate strength from the expression of strength, as though behind the strong man there existed some indifferent neutral *substratum*, which enjoyed a *caprice and option* as to whether or not it should express strength. But there is no such *substratum*, there is no "being" behind doing, working, becoming; "the doer" is a mere appanage to the action. The action is everything. In point of fact, the people duplicate the doing, when they make the lightning lighten, that is a "doing-doing": they make the same phenomenon first a cause, and then, secondly, the effect of that cause. The scientists fail to improve matters when they say, "Force moves, force causes," and so on. Our whole science is still, in spite of all its coldness, of all its freedom from passion, a dupe of the tricks of language, and has never succeeded in getting rid of that superstitious changeling "the subject" (the atom, to give another instance, is such a changeling, just as the Kantian "Thing-in-itself"). What wonder, if the suppressed and stealthily simmering passions of revenge and hatred exploit for their own advantage this belief, and indeed hold no belief with a more steadfast enthusiasm than this—"that the strong has the *option* of being weak, and the bird of prey of being a lamb." Thereby do they win for themselves the right of attri-buting to the birds of prey the *responsibility* for being birds of prey: when the oppressed, downtrodden, and overpowered say to themselves with the vindictive guile of weakness, "Let us be otherwise than the evil, namely, good! And good is everyone who does not oppress, who hurts no one, who does not attack, who does not pay back, who hands over revenge to God, who holds himself, as we do, in hiding; who goes out of the way of evil, and demands, in short, little from life; like ourselves the patient, the meek, the just"—yet all this, in its cold and unprejudiced interpretation, means nothing more than "once for all, the weak are weak; it is good to do *nothing for which we are not strong enough*"; but this dismal state of affairs, this prudence of the lowest order, which even insects possess (which in a great danger are fain to sham death so as to avoid doing "too much"), has, thanks to the counterfeiting and self-deception of weakness, come to masquerade in the pomp of an ascetic, mute, and expectant virtue, just as though the *very* weakness of the weak —that is, forsooth, its *being*, its working, its whole unique inevitable inseparable reality—were a voluntary result, something wished, chosen, a deed, an act of *merit*. This kind of man finds the belief in a neutral, free-choosing "subject" *necessary* from an instinct of self-preservation, of self-assertion, in which every lie is fain to sanctify itself. The subject (or, to use popular language, the soul) has perhaps proved itself the best dogma in the world simply because it rendered possible to the horde of mortal, weak, and oppressed individuals of every kind, that most sublime specimen of self-deception, the interpretation of weakness as freedom, of being this, or being that, as *merit*.

14

Will anyone look a little into—right into—the mystery of how *ideals* are *manufactured* in this world? Who has the courage to do it? Come!

Here we have a vista opened into these grimy workshops. Wait just a moment, dear Mr. Inquisitive and Foolhardy; your eye must first grow accustomed to this false changing light—Yes! Enough! Now speak! What is happening below down yonder? Speak out that what you see, man of the most dangerous curiosity—for now *I* am the listener.

"I see nothing, I hear the more. It is a cautious, spiteful, gentle whispering and muttering together in all the corners and crannies. It seems to me that they are lying; a sugary softness adheres to every sound. Weakness is turned to *merit*, there is no doubt about it—it is just as you say."

Further!

"And the impotence which requites not, is turned to 'goodness,' craven baseness to meekness, submission to those whom one hates, to obedience (namely, obedience to one of whom they say that he ordered this submission—they call him God). The inoffensive character of the weak, the very cowardice in which he is rich, his standing at the door, his forced necessity of waiting, gain here fine names, such as 'patience,' which is also called 'virtue'; not being able to avenge one's self, is called not wishing to avenge one's self, perhaps even forgiveness (for *they* know not what they do—we alone know what *they* do). They also talk of the 'love of their enemies' and sweat thereby."

Further!

"They are miserable, there is no doubt about it, all these whisperers and counterfeiters in the corners, although they try to get warm by crouching close to each other, but they tell me that their misery is a favour and distinction given to them by God, just as one beats the dogs one likes best; that perhaps this misery is also a preparation, a probation, a training; that perhaps it is still more something which will one day be compensated and paid back with a tremendous interest in gold, nay in happiness. This they call 'Blessedness.'"

Further!

"They are now giving me to understand, that not only are they better men than the mighty, the lords of the earth, whose spittle they have got to lick (*not* out of fear, not at all out of fear! But because God ordains that one should honour all authority)—not only are they better men, but that they also have a 'better time,' at any rate, will one day have a 'better time.' But enough! Enough! I can endure it no longer. Bad air! Bad air! These workshops *where ideals are manufactured*—verily they reek with the crassest lies."

Nay. Just one minute! You are saying nothing about the masterpieces of these virtuosos of black magic, who can produce whiteness, milk, and innocence out of any black you like: have you not noticed what a pitch of refinement is attained by their *chef d'œuvre*, their most audacious, subtle, ingenious, and lying artist-trick? Take care! These cellar-beasts, full of revenge and hate—what do they make, forsooth, out of their revenge and hate? Do you hear these words? Would you suspect, if you trusted only their words, that you are among men of resentment and nothing else?

"I understand, I prick my ears up again (Ah! Ah! Ah! And I hold my nose). Now do I hear for the first time that which they have said so often:

'We good, *we are the righteous*'—what they demand they call not revenge but 'the triumph of righteousness'; what they hate is not their enemy, no, they hate 'unrighteousness,' 'godlessness'; what they believe in and hope is not the hope of revenge, the intoxication of sweet revenge (—'sweeter than honey,' did Homer call it?), but the victory of God, of the *righteous* God over the 'godless'; what is left for them to love in this world is not their brothers in hate, but their 'brothers in love,' as they say, all the good and righteous on the earth."

And how do they name that which serves them as a solace against all the troubles of life—their phantasmagoria of their anticipated future blessedness?

"How? Do I hear right? They call it 'the last judgement,' the advent of *their* kingdom, 'the kingdom of God'—but *in the meanwhile* they live 'in faith,' 'in love,' 'in hope.'"

Enough! Enough!

15

In the faith in what? In the love for what? In the hope of what? These weaklings! They also, forsooth, wish to be the strong sometime; there is no doubt about it, sometime *their* kingdom also must come—"the kingdom of God" is their name for it, as has been mentioned: they are so meek in everything! Yet in order to experience *that* kingdom it is necessary to live long, to live beyond death—yes, *eternal* life is necessary so that one can make up forever for that earthly life "in faith," "in love," "in hope." Make up for what? Make up by what? Dante, as it seems to me, made a crass mistake when with awe-inspiring ingenuity he placed that inscription over the gate of his hell, "Me too made eternal love": at any rate the following inscription would have a much better right to stand over the gate of the Christian Paradise and its "eternal blessedness"—"Me too made eternal hate"—granted of course that a truth may rightly stand over the gate to a lie! For what is the blessedness of that Paradise? Possibly we could quickly surmise it; but it is better that it should be explicitly attested by an authority who in such matters is not to be disparaged, Thomas of Aquinas, the great teacher and saint. *"Beati in regno celesti,"* says he, as gently as a lamb, *"videbunt paenas damnatorum, ut beatitudo illis magis complaceat."* Or if we wish to hear a stronger tone, a word from the mouth of a triumphant father of the Church, who warned his disciples against the cruel ecstasies of the public spectacles—But why? Faith offers us much more—says he, *de Spectac.*, c. 29 ss. something much stronger; thanks to the redemption,

joys of quite another kind stand at our disposal; instead of athletes we have
our martyrs; we wish for blood, well, we have the blood of Christ—but
what then awaits us on the day of his return, of his triumph. And then does
he proceed, does this enraptured visionary: "*at enim supersunt alia spectac-
ula, ille ultimus et perpetuus judicii dies, ille nationibus insperatus, ille derisus,
cum tanta saeculi vetustas et tot ejus nativitates uno igne haurientur. Quae tunc
spectaculi latitudo! Quid admirer! Quid rideam! Ubigaudeam! Ubi exultem, spec-
tans tot et tantos reges, qui in cœlum recepti nuntiabantur, cum ipso Jove et ipsis
suis testibus in imis tenebris congemescentes! Item praesides*" (the provincial
governors) "*persecutors dominici nominis saevioribus quam ipsi flammis saevierunt insultantibus contra Christianos liquescentes! Quos praeterea sapientes illos
philosophos coram discipulis suis una conflagrantibus erubescentes, quibus nihil
ad deum pertinere suadebant, quibus animas aut nullas aut non in pristina cor-
pora redituras affirmabant! Etiam poetas non ad Rhadamanti nec ad Minois, sed
ad inopinati Christi tribunal palpitantes! Tunc magis tragœdi audiendi, magis
scilicet vocales*" (with louder tones and more violent shrieks) "*in sua propria
calamitate; tunc histriones cognoscendi, solutiores multo per ignem; tunc spectan-
dus auriga in flammea rota totus rubens, tunc xystici contemplandi non in
gymnasiis, sed in igne jaculati, nisi quod ne tunc quidem illos velim vivos, ut qui
malim ad eos potius conspectum insatiabilem conferre, qui in dominum saevierunt.
Hic est ille, dicam fabri aut quaestuariae filius*" (as is shown by the whole of the
following, and in particular by this well-known description of the mother
of Jesus from the Talmud, Tertullian is henceforth referring to the Jews),
"*sabbati destructor, Samarites et daemonium habens. Hic est quem a Juda redemistis,
hic est ille arundine et colaphis diverberatus, sputamentis de decoratus, felle et
aceto potatus. Hic est, quem clam discentes subripuerunt, ut resurrexisse dicatur
vel hortulanus detraxit, ne lactucae suae frequentia commeantium laederentur. Ut
talia spectes, ut talibus exultes, quis tibi praetor aut consul aut sacerdos de sua
liberalitate praestabit? Et tamen haec jam habemus quodammodo per fidem spiritu
imaginante repraesentata. Ceterum qualia illa sunt, quae nec oculus vidit nec
auris audivit nec in cor hominis ascenderunt?*" (1 Cor. ii. 9.) "*Credo circo et
utraque cavea*" (first and fourth row, or, according to others, the comic and
the tragic stage) "*et omni studio gratiora.*" *Per fidem:* so stands it written.

16

Let us come to a conclusion. The two *opposing values,* "good and bad,"
"good and evil," have fought a dreadful, thousand-year fight in the world,
and though indubitably the second value has been for a long time in
the preponderance, there are not wanting places where the fortune of the

fight is still undecisive. It can almost be said that in the meanwhile the fight reaches a higher and higher level, and that in the meanwhile it has become more and more intense, and always more and more psychological; so that nowadays there is perhaps no more decisive mark of the *higher nature*, of the more psychological nature, than to be in that sense self-contradictory, and to be actually still a battleground for those two opposites. The symbol of this fight, written in a writing which has remained worthy of perusal throughout the course of history up to the present time, is called "Rome against Judea, Judea against Rome." Hitherto there has been no greater event than *that* fight, the putting of *that* question, *that* deadly antagonism. Rome found in the Jew the incarnation of the unnatural, as though it were its diametrically opposed monstrosity, and in Rome the Jew was held to be *convicted of hatred* of the whole human race: and rightly so, insofar as it is right to link the well-being and the future of the human race to the unconditional mastery of the aristocratic values, of the Roman values. What, conversely, did the Jews feel against Rome? One can surmise it from a thousand symptoms, but it is sufficient to carry one's mind back to the Johannian Apocalypse, that most obscene of all the written outbursts, which has revenge on its conscience. (One should also appraise at its full value the profound logic of the Christian instinct, when over this very book of hate it wrote the name of the Disciple of Love, that self-same disciple to whom it attributed that impassioned and ecstatic Gospel—therein lurks a portion of truth, however much literary forging may have been necessary for this purpose.) The Romans were the strong and aristocratic; a nation stronger and more aristocratic has never existed in the world, has never even been dreamed of; every relic of them, every inscription enraptures, granted that one can divine *what* it is that writes the inscription. The Jews, conversely, were that priestly nation of resentment *par excellence*, possessed by a unique genius for popular morals: just compare with the Jews the nations with analogous gifts, such as the Chinese or the Germans, so as to realise afterwards what is first rate, and what is fifth rate.

Which of them has been provisionally victorious, Rome or Judea? But there is not a shadow of doubt; just consider to whom in Rome itself nowadays you bow down, as though before the quintessence of all the highest values—and not only in Rome, but almost over half the world, everywhere where man has been tamed or is about to be tamed—to *three Jews*, as we know, and *one Jewess* (to Jesus of Nazareth, to Peter the fisher, to Paul the tent-maker, and to the mother of the aforesaid Jesus, named

Mary). This is very remarkable: Rome is undoubtedly defeated. At any rate there took place in the Renaissance a brilliantly sinister revival of the classical ideal, of the aristocratic valuation of all things: Rome herself, like a man waking up from a trance, stirred beneath the burden of the new Judaised Rome that had been built over her, which presented the appearance of an œcumenical synagogue and was called the "Church": but immediately Judea triumphed again, thanks to that fundamentally popular (German and English) movement of revenge, which is called the Reformation, and taking also into account its inevitable corollary, the restoration of the Church—the restoration also of the ancient graveyard peace of classical Rome. Judea proved yet once more victorious over the classical ideal in the French Revolution, and in a sense which was even more crucial and even more profound: the last political aristocracy that existed in Europe, that of the *French* seventeenth and eighteenth centuries, broke into pieces beneath the instincts of a resentful populace—never had the world heard a greater jubilation, a more uproarious enthusiasm: indeed, there took place in the midst of it the most monstrous and unexpected phenomenon; the ancient ideal *itself* swept before the eyes and conscience of humanity with all its life and with unheard-of splendour, and in opposition to resentment's lying war cry of *the prerogative of the most,* in opposition to the will to lowliness, abasement, and equalisation, the will to a retrogression and twilight of humanity, there rang out once again, stronger, simpler, more penetrating than ever, the terrible and enchanting counter war cry *of the prerogative of the few!* Like a final signpost to other ways, there appeared Napoleon, the most unique and violent anachronism that ever existed, and in him the incarnate problem *of the aristocratic ideal in itself*—consider well what a problem it is: Napoleon, that synthesis of Monster and Superman.

17

Was it therewith over? Was that greatest of all antitheses of ideals thereby relegated *ad acta* for all time? Or only postponed, postponed for a long time? May there not take place at sometime or other a much more awful, much more carefully prepared flaring up of the old conflagration? Further! Should not one wish *that* consummation with all one's strength? Will it one's self? Demand it one's self? He who at this juncture begins, like my readers, to reflect, to think further, will have difficulty in coming quickly to a conclusion—ground enough for me to come myself to a conclusion, taking it for granted that for sometime past what I *mean* has been sufficiently clear, what I exactly mean by that dangerous motto which is inscribed on the body of my last book: *Beyond Good and Evil*—at any rate that is not the same as "Beyond Good and Bad."

NOTE. I avail myself of the opportunity offered by this treatise to express, openly and formally, a wish which up to the present has only been expressed in occasional conversations with scholars, namely, that some Faculty of philosophy should, by means of a series of prize essays, gain the glory of having promoted the further study of the *history of morals*—perhaps this book may serve to give a forcible impetus in such a direction. With regard to a possibility of this character, the following question deserves consideration. It merits quite as much the attention of philologists and historians as of actual professional philosophers.

"*What indication of the history of the evolution of the moral ideas is afforded by philology, and especially by etymological investigation?*"

On the other hand, it is of course equally necessary to induce physiologists and doctors to be interested in these problems (*of the value* of the *valuations* which have prevailed up to the present): in this connexion the professional philosophers may be trusted to act as the spokesmen and intermediaries in these particular instances, after, of course, they have quite succeeded in transforming the relationship between philosophy and physiology and medicine, which is originally one of coldness and suspicion, into the most friendly and fruitful reciprocity. In point of fact, all tables of values, all the "thou shalts" known to history and ethnology, need primarily a *physiological*, at any rate in preference to a psychological, elucidation and interpretation; all equally require a critique from medical science. The question, "What is the *value* of this or that table of 'values' and morality?" will be asked from the most varied standpoints. For instance, the question of "valuable *for what*" can never be analysed with sufficient nicety. That, for instance, which would evidently have value with regard to promoting in a race the greatest possible powers of endurance (or with regard to increasing its adaptability to a specific climate, or with regard to the preservation of the greatest number) would have nothing like the same value, if it were a question of evolving a stronger species. In gauging values, the good of the majority and the good of the minority are opposed standpoints: we leave it to the naïveté of English biologists to regard the former standpoint as *intrinsically* superior. All the sciences have now to pave the way for the future task of the philosopher; this task being understood to mean, that he must solve the problem of *value*, that he has to fix the *hierarchy of values*.

"GUILT," "BAD CONSCIENCE," AND THE LIKE

1

THE BREEDING OF AN ANIMAL THAT *CAN PROMISE*—IS NOT THIS JUST THAT very paradox of a task which nature has set itself in regard to man? Is not this the very problem of man? The fact that this problem has been to a great extent solved, must appear all the more phenomenal to one who can estimate at its full value that force of *forgetfulness* which works in opposition to it. Forgetfulness is no mere *vis inertiae*, as the superficial believe, rather is it a power of obstruction, active and, in the strictest sense of the word, positive—a power responsible for the fact that what we have lived, experienced, taken into ourselves, no more enters into consciousness during the process of digestion (it might be called psychic absorption) than all the whole manifold process by which our physical nutrition, the so-called "incorporation," is carried on. The temporary shutting of the doors and windows of consciousness, the relief from the clamant alarums and excursions, with which our subconscious world of servant organs works in mutual cooperation and antagonism; a little quietude, a little *tabula rasa* of the consciousness, so as to make room again for the new, and above all for the more noble functions and functionaries, room for government, foresight, predetermination (for our organism is on an oligarchic model)—this is the utility, as I have said, of the active forgetfulness, which is a very sentinel and nurse of psychic order, repose, etiquette; and this shows at once why it is that there can exist no happiness, no gladness, no hope, no pride, no real *present*, without forgetfulness. The man in whom this preventative apparatus is damaged and discarded, is to be compared to a dyspeptic, and it is something more than a comparison—he can "get rid of" nothing. But this very animal who finds it necessary to be forgetful, in whom, in fact, forgetfulness represents a force and a form of *robust* health, has reared for himself an opposition-power, a memory, with whose help forgetfulness is, in certain instances, kept in check—in the cases, namely, where promises have to be made; so that it is by no means a mere passive inability to get rid of a once indented impression, not merely the indigestion occasioned by a once pledged word, which one cannot dispose of, but an *active* refusal to get rid of it, a continuing and a wish to continue what has once been willed, an actual *memory of the will*; so that between the original "I will," "I shall do," and the actual discharge of the will, its *act*, we can easily interpose a world of new strange phenomena, circumstances, veritable volitions, without the snapping of this long chain of the will. But what is the underlying hypothesis of all this? How thoroughly, in order to be able to regulate the future in this way, must man have first learnt to distinguish between necessitated and accidental phenomena, to think causally, to see the distant as present and to anticipate it, to fix with certainty what is the end, and what is the means to that end; above all, to reckon, to have power to calculate—how thoroughly must man have first become *calculable, disciplined, necessitated* even for himself and his own conception of himself, that, like a man entering into a promise, he could guarantee himself *as a future*.

2

This is simply the long history of the origin of *responsibility*. That task of breeding an animal which can make promises, includes, as we have already grasped, as its condition and preliminary, the more immediate task of first *making* man to a certain extent, necessitated, uniform, like among his like, regular, and consequently calculable. The immense work of what I have called, "morality of custom"[1] (cp. *Dawn of Day*, Aphs. 9, 14, and 16), the actual work of man on himself during the longest period of the human race, his whole prehistoric work, finds its meaning, its great justification (in spite of all its innate hardness, despotism, stupidity, and idiocy) in this fact: man, with the help of the morality of customs and of social strait-waistcoats, was *made* genuinely calculable. If, however, we place ourselves at the end of this colossal process, at the point where the tree finally matures its fruits, when society and its morality of custom finally bring to light that to which it was only the means, then do we find as the ripest fruit on its tree the *sovereign individual*, that resembles only himself, that has got loose from the morality of custom, the autonomous "super-moral" individual (for "autonomous" and "moral" are mutually exclusive terms)—in short, the man of the personal, long, and independent will, *competent to promise*—and we find in him a proud consciousness (vibrating in every fibre), of *what* has been at last achieved and become vivified in him, a genuine consciousness of power and freedom, a feeling of human perfection in general. And this man who has grown to freedom, who is really competent to promise, this lord of the *free* will, this sovereign—how is it possible for him not to know how great is his superiority over everything incapable of binding itself by promises, or of being its own security, how great is the trust, the awe, the reverence that he awakes—he "deserves" all three—not to know that with this mastery over himself he is necessarily also given the mastery over circumstances, over nature, over all creatures with shorter wills, less reliable characters? The "free" man, the owner of a long unbreakable will, finds in this possession his *standard of value*: looking out from himself upon the others, he honours or he despises, and just as necessarily as he honours his peers, the strong and the reliable (those who can bind themselves by promises)—that is, everyone who promises like a sovereign, with difficulty, rarely and slowly, who is sparing with his trusts but confers *honour* by the very fact of trusting, who gives his word as something that can be relied on, because he knows himself strong enough to keep it even in the teeth of disasters, even in the "teeth of fate"—so with equal necessity will he have the heel of his foot ready for the lean and empty jackasses, who promise when they have no business to do so, and his rod of chastisement ready for the liar, who already breaks his word at the very minute when it is on his lips. The proud knowledge of the extraordinary privilege of *responsibility*, the consciousness of this rare freedom, of this power over himself and over fate, has sunk right down to his innermost depths, and has become an instinct, a dominating instinct—what name will he give to it, to this dominating instinct, if he needs to have a word for it? But there is no doubt about it—the sovereign man calls it his *conscience*.

3

His conscience? One apprehends at once that the idea "conscience," which is here seen in its supreme manifestation, supreme in fact to almost the point of strangeness, should already have behind it a long history and evolution. The ability to guarantee one's self with all due pride, and also at the same time to *say yes* to one's self—that is, as has been said, a ripe fruit, but also a *late* fruit: How long must needs this fruit hang sour and bitter on the tree! And for an even longer period there was not a glimpse of such a fruit to to be had—no one had taken it on himself to promise it, although everything on the tree was quite ready for it, and everything was maturing for that very consummation. "How is a memory to be made for the man-animal? How is an impression to be so deeply fixed upon this ephemeral understanding, half dense, and half silly, upon this incarnate forgetfulness, that it will be permanently present?" As one may imagine, this primeval problem was not solved by exactly gentle answers and gentle means; perhaps there is nothing more awful and more sinister in the early history of man than his *system of mnemonics.* "Something is burnt in so as to remain in his memory: only that which never stops *hurting* remains in his memory." This is an axiom of the oldest (unfortunately also the longest) psychology in the world. It might even be said that wherever solemnity, seriousness, mystery, and gloomy colours are now found in the life of the men and of nations of the world, there is some *survival* of that horror which was once the universal concomitant of all promises, pledges, and obligations. The past, the past with all its length, depth, and hardness, wafts to us its breath, and bubbles up in us again, when we become "serious." When man thinks it necessary to make for himself a memory, he never accomplishes it without blood, tortures, and sacrifice; the most dreadful sacrifices and forfeitures (among them the sacrifice of the first-born), the most loathsome mutilation (for instance, castration), the most cruel rituals of all the religious cults (for all religions are really at bottom systems of cruelty)—all these things originate from that instinct which found in pain its most potent mnemonic. In a certain sense the whole of asceticism is to be ascribed to this: certain ideas have got to be made inextinguishable, omnipresent, "fixed," with the object of hypnotising the whole nervous and intellectual system through these "fixed ideas"—and the ascetic methods and modes of life are the means of freeing those ideas from the competition of all other ideas so as to make them "unforgettable." The worse memory man had, the ghastlier the signs presented by his customs; the severity of the penal laws affords in particular a gauge of the extent of man's difficulty in conquering forgetfulness, and in keeping a few primal postulates of social intercourse ever present to the minds of those who were the slaves of every momentary emotion and every momentary desire. We Germans do certainly not regard ourselves as an especially cruel and hard-hearted nation, still less as an especially casual and happy-go-lucky one; but one has only to look at our old penal ordinances in order to realise what a lot of trouble it takes in the world to evolve a "nation of thinkers" (I mean: *the* European nation which exhibits at this very day the maximum of reliability, seriousness, bad taste, and positiveness, which has on the strength of these qualities a right to train every kind of European mandarin). These Germans employed terrible means to make for themselves a memory, to enable them to master their rooted plebeian instincts and the brutal crudity of those instincts: think of the old German punishments, for instance, stoning (as far back as the legend, the millstone falls on the head of the guilty man), breaking on the wheel (the most original invention and speciality of the German genius in the sphere of punishment), dart-throwing, tearing, or trampling by horses ("quartering"), boiling the criminal in oil or wine (still prevalent in the fourteenth and fifteenth centuries), the highly popular flaying ("slicing into strips"), cutting the flesh out of the breast; think also of the evildoer being besmeared with honey, and then exposed to the flies in a blazing sun. It was by the help of such images and precedents that man eventually kept in his memory five or six "I will nots" with regard to which he had already given his *promise*, so as to be able to enjoy the advantages of society— and verily with the help of this kind of memory man eventually attained "Reason"! Alas! Reason, seriousness, mastery over the emotions, all these gloomy, dismal things which are called reflexion, all these privileges and pageantries of humanity: how dear is the price that they have exacted! How much blood and cruelty is the foundation of all "good things"!

4

But how is it that that other melancholy object, the consciousness of sin, the whole "bad conscience," came into the world? And it is here that we turn back to our genealogists of morals. For the second time I say—or have I not said it yet? That they are worth nothing. Just their own five-spans-long limited modern experience; no knowledge of the past, and no wish to know it; still less a historic instinct, a power of "second sight" (which is what is really required in this case)—and despite this to go in for the history of morals. It stands to reason that this must needs produce results which are removed from the truth by something more than a respectful distance.

Have these current genealogists of morals ever allowed themselves to have even the vaguest notion, for instance, that the cardinal moral idea of "ought"[2] originates from the very material idea of "owe"? Or that punishment developed as a *retaliation* absolutely independently of any preliminary hypothesis of the freedom or determination of the will? And this to such an extent, that a *high* degree of civilisation was always first necessary for the animal man to begin to make those much more primitive distinctions of "intentional," "negligent," "accidental," "responsible," and their contraries, and apply them in the assessing of punishment. That idea—"the wrongdoer deserves punishment *because* he might have acted otherwise," in spite of the fact that it is nowadays so cheap, obvious, natural, and inevitable, and that it has had to serve as an illustration of the way in which the sentiment of justice appeared on earth, is in point of fact an exceedingly late, and even refined form of human judgement and inference; the placing of this idea back at the beginning of the world is simply a clumsy violation of the principles of primitive psychology. Throughout the longest period of human history punishment was *never* based on the responsibility of the evildoer for his action, and was consequently *not* based on the hypothesis that only the guilty should be punished; on the contrary, punishment was inflicted in those days for the same reason that parents punish their children even nowadays, out of anger at an injury that they have suffered, an anger which vents itself mechanically on the author of the injury—but this anger is kept in bounds and modified through the idea that every injury has somewhere or other its *equivalent* price, and can really be paid off, even though it be by means of pain to the author. Whence is it that this ancient deep-rooted and now perhaps ineradicable idea has drawn its strength, this idea of an equivalency between injury and pain? I have already revealed its origin, in the contractual relationship between *creditor* and *ower*, that is as old as the existence of legal rights at all, and in its turn points back to the primary forms of purchase, sale, barter, and trade.

5

The realisation of these contractual relations excites, of course (as would be already expected from our previous observations), a great deal of suspicion and opposition towards the primitive society which made or sanctioned them. In this society promises will be made; in this society the object is to provide the promiser with a memory; in this society, so may we suspect, there will be full scope for hardness, cruelty, and pain: the "ower," in order to induce credit in his promise of repayment, in order to give a guarantee of the earnestness and sanctity of his promise, in order to drill into his own conscience the duty, the solemn duty, of repayment, will, by virtue of a contract with his creditor to meet the contingency of his not paying, pledge something that he still possesses, something that he still has in his power, for instance, his life or his wife, or his freedom or his body (or under certain religious conditions even his salvation, his soul's welfare, even his peace in the grave; so in Egypt, where the corpse of the ower found even in the grave no rest from the creditor—of course, from the Egyptian standpoint, this peace was a matter of particular importance). But especially has the creditor the power of inflicting on the body of the ower all kinds of pain and torture—the power, for instance, of cutting off from it an amount that appeared proportionate to the greatness of the debt; this point of view resulted in the universal prevalence at an early date of precise schemes of valuation, frequently horrible in the minuteness and meticulosity of their application, *legally* sanctioned schemes of valuation for individual limbs and parts of the body. I consider it as already a progress, as a proof of a freer, less petty, and more *Roman* conception of law, when the Roman Code of the Twelve Tables decreed that it was immaterial how much or how little the creditors in such a contingency cut off, "*si plus minusve secuerunt, ne fraude esto.*" Let us make the logic of the whole of this equalisation process clear; it is strange enough. The equivalence consists in this: instead of an advantage directly compensatory of his injury (that is, instead of an equalisation in money, lands, or some kind of chattel), the creditor is granted by way of repayment and compensation a certain *sensation of satisfaction*—the satisfaction of being able to vent, without any trouble, his power on one who is powerless, the delight "*de faire le mal pour le plaisir de le faire,*" the joy in sheer violence: and this joy will be relished in proportion to the lowness and humbleness of the creditor in the social scale, and is quite apt to have the effect of the most delicious dainty, and even seem the foretaste of a higher social position. Thanks to the punishment of the "ower," the creditor participates in the rights of the masters. At last he too, for once in a way, attains the edifying consciousness of being able to despise and ill-treat a creature—as an "inferior"—or at any rate of *seeing* him being despised and ill-treated, in case the actual power of punishment, the administration of punishment, has already become transferred to the "authorities." The compensation consequently consists in a claim on cruelty and a right to draw thereon.

6

It is then in *this* sphere of the law of contract that we find the cradle of the whole moral world of the ideas of "guilt," "conscience," "duty," the "sacredness of duty"—their commencement, like the commencement of all great things in the world, is thoroughly and continuously saturated with blood. And should we not add that this world has never really lost a certain savour of blood and torture (not even in old Kant—the categorical imperative reeks of cruelty). It was in this sphere likewise that there first became formed that sinister and perhaps now indissoluble association of the ideas of "guilt" and "suffering." To put the question yet again, why can suffering be a compensation for "owing?" Because the *infliction* of suffering produces the highest degree of happiness, because the injured party will get in exchange for his loss (including his vexation at his loss) an extraordinary counter-pleasure: the infliction of suffering—a real *feast*, something that, as I have said, was all the more appreciated the greater the paradox created by the rank and social status of the creditor. These observations are purely conjectural; for, apart from the painful nature of the task, it is hard to plumb such profound depths: the clumsy introduction of the idea of "revenge" as a connecting-link simply hides and obscures the view instead of rendering it clearer (revenge itself simply leads back again to the identical problem—"How can the infliction of suffering be a satisfaction?"). In my opinion it is repugnant to the delicacy, and still more to the hypocrisy of tame domestic animals (that is, modern men; that is, ourselves), to realise with all their energy the extent to which *cruelty* constituted the great joy and delight of ancient man, was an ingredient which seasoned nearly all his pleasures, and conversely the extent of the naïveté and innocence with which he manifested his need for cruelty, when he actually made as a matter of principle "disinterested malice" (or, to use Spinoza's expression, the *sympathia malevolent*) into a *normal* characteristic of man—as consequently something to which the conscience says a hearty yes. The more profound observer has perhaps already had sufficient opportunity for noticing this most ancient and radical joy and delight of mankind; in *Beyond Good and Evil*, Aph. 188 (and even earlier, in *The Dawn of Day*, Aphs. 18, 77, 113), I have cautiously indicated the continually growing spiritualisation and "deification" of cruelty, which pervades the whole history of the higher civilisation (and in the larger sense even constitutes it). At any rate the time is not so long past when it was impossible to conceive of royal weddings and national festivals on a grand scale, without executions, tortures, or perhaps an *auto-da-fé*, or similarly to conceive of an aristocratic household, without a creature to serve as a butt for the cruel and malicious baiting of the inmates. (The reader will perhaps remember *Don Quixote* at the court of the Duchess: we read nowadays the whole of Don Quixote with a bitter taste in the mouth, almost with a sensation of torture, a fact which would appear very strange and very incomprehensible to the author and his contemporaries—they read it with the best conscience in the world as the gayest of books; they almost died with laughing at it.) The sight of suffering does one good, the infliction of suffering does one more good—this is a hard maxim, but nonetheless a fundamental maxim, old, powerful, and "human, all-too-human"; one, moreover, to which perhaps even the apes as well would subscribe: for it is said that in inventing bizarre cruelties they are giving abundant proof of their future humanity, to which, as it were, they are playing the prelude. Without cruelty, no feast: so teaches the oldest and longest history of man—and in punishment too is there so much of the *festive*.

7

Entertaining, as I do, these thoughts, I am, let me say in parenthesis, fundamentally opposed to helping our pessimists to new water for the discordant and groaning mills of their disgust with life; on the contrary, it should be shown specifically that, at the time when mankind was not yet ashamed of its cruelty, life in the world was brighter than it is nowadays when there are pessimists. The darkening of the heavens over man has always increased in proportion to the growth of man's shame *before man*. The tired pessimistic outlook, the mistrust of the riddle of life, the icy negation of disgusted ennui, all those are not the signs of the *most evil* age of the human race: much rather do they come first to the light of day, as the swamp-flowers, which they are, when the swamp to which they belong, comes into existence—I mean the diseased refinement and moralisation, thanks to which the "animal man" has at last learnt to be ashamed of all his instincts. On the road to angel-hood (not to use in this context a harder word) man has developed that dyspeptic stomach and coated tongue, which have made not only the joy and innocence of the animal repulsive to him, but also life itself: so that sometimes he stands with stopped nostrils before his own self, and, like Pope Innocent the Third, makes a black list of his own horrors ("unclean generation, loathsome nutrition when in the maternal body, badness of the matter out of which man develops, awful stench, secretion of saliva, urine, and excrement"). Nowadays, when suffering is always trotted out as the first argument *against* existence, as its most sinister query, it is well to remember the times when men judged on converse principles because they could not dispense with the *infliction* of suffering, and saw therein a magic of the first order, a veritable bait of seduction to life.

Perhaps in those days (this is to solace the weaklings) pain did not hurt so much as it does nowadays: any physician who has treated Negroes (granted that these are taken as representative of the prehistoric man) suffering from severe internal inflammations which would bring a European, even though he had the soundest constitution, almost to despair, would be in a position to come to this conclusion. Pain has *not* the same effect with Negroes. (The curve of human sensibilities to pain seems indeed to sink in an extraordinary and almost sudden fashion, as soon as one has passed the upper ten thousand or ten millions of overcivilised humanity, and I personally have no doubt that, by comparison with one painful night passed by one single hysterical chit of a cultured woman, the suffering of all the animals taken together who have been put to the question of the knife, so as to give scientific answers, are simply negligible.) We may perhaps be allowed to admit the possibility of the craving for cruelty not necessarily having become really extinct: it only requires, in view of the fact that pain hurts more nowadays, a certain sublimation and subtilisation, it must especially be translated to the imaginative and psychic plane, and be adorned with such smug euphemisms, that even the most fastidious and hypocritical conscience could never grow suspicious of their real nature ("Tragic pity" is one of these euphemisms: another is "*les nostalgies de la croix*"). What really raises one's indignation against suffering is not suffering intrinsically, but the senselessness of suffering; such a *senselessness*, however, existed neither in Christianity, which interpreted suffering into a whole mysterious salvation-apparatus, nor in the beliefs of the naïve ancient man, who only knew how to find a meaning in suffering from the standpoint of the spectator, or the inflictor of the suffering. In order to get the secret, undiscovered, and unwitnessed suffering out of the world it was almost compulsory to invent gods and a hierarchy of intermediate beings, in short, something which wanders even among secret places, sees even in the dark, and makes a point of never missing an interesting and painful spectacle. It was with the help of such inventions that life got to learn the *tour de force*, which has become part of its stock-in-trade, the *tour de force* of self-justification, of the justification of evil; nowadays this would perhaps require other auxiliary devices (for instance, life as a riddle, life as a problem of knowledge). "Every evil is justified in the sight of which a god finds edification," so rang the logic of primitive sentiment—and, indeed, was it only of primitive? The gods conceived as friends of spectacles of cruelty—oh how far does this primeval conception extend even nowadays into our European civilisation! One would perhaps like in this context to consult Luther and Calvin. It is at any rate certain that even the Greeks knew no more piquant seasoning for the happiness of their gods than the joys of cruelty. What, do you think, was the mood with which Homer makes his gods look down upon the fates of men? What final meaning have at bottom the Trojan War and similar tragic horrors? It is impossible to entertain any doubt on the point: they were intended as festival games for the gods, and, insofar as the poet is of a more godlike breed than other men, as festival games also for the poets. It was in just this spirit and no other, that at a later date the moral philosophers of Greece conceived the eyes of God as still looking down on the moral struggle, the heroism, and the self-torture of the virtuous; the Heracles of duty was on a stage, and was conscious of the fact; virtue without witnesses was something quite unthinkable for this nation of actors. Must not that philosophic invention, so audacious and so fatal, which was then absolutely new to Europe, the invention of "free will," of the absolute spontaneity of man in good and evil, simply have been made for the specific purpose of justifiying the idea, that the interest of the gods in humanity and human virtue was *inexhaustible?*

There would never on the stage of this free will world be a dearth of really new, really novel and exciting situations, plots, catastrophes. A world thought out on completely deterministic lines would be easily guessed by the gods, and would consequently soon bore them—sufficient reason for these *friends of the gods*, the philosophers, not to ascribe to their gods such a deterministic world. The whole of ancient humanity is full of delicate consideration for the spectator, being as it is a world of thorough publicity and theatricality, which could not conceive of happiness without spectacles and festivals. And, as has already been said, even in great *punishment* there is so much which is festive.

8

The feeling of "ought," of personal obligation (to take up again the train of our inquiry), has had, as we saw, its origin in the oldest and most original personal relationship that there is, the relationship between buyer and seller, creditor and ower: here it was that individual confronted individual, and that individual *matched himself against* individual. There has not yet been found a grade of civilisation so low, as not to manifest some trace of this relationship. Making prices, assessing values, thinking out equivalents, exchanging—all this preoccupied the primal thoughts of man to such an extent that in a certain sense it constituted *thinking* itself: it was here that was trained the oldest form of sagacity, it was here in this sphere that we can perhaps trace the first commencement of man's pride, of his feeling of superiority over other animals. Perhaps our word "*Mensch*" (*manas*) still expresses just something of *this* self-pride: man denoted himself as the being who measures values, who values and measures, as the "assessing" animal *par excellence*. Sale and purchase, together with their psychological concomitants, are older than the origins of any form of social organisation and union: it is rather from the most rudimentary form of individual right that the budding consciousness of exchange, commerce, debt, right, obligation, compensation was first transferred to the rudest and most elementary of the social complexes (in their relation to similar complexes), the habit of comparing force with force, together with that of measuring, of calculating. His eye was now focussed to this perspective; and with that ponderous consistency characteristic of ancient thought, which, though set in motion with difficulty, yet proceeds inflexibly along the line on which it has started, man soon arrived at the great generalisation, "everything has its price, *all* can be paid for," the oldest and most naïve moral canon of *justice*, the beginning of all "kindness," of all "equity," of all "goodwill," of all "objectivity" in the world. Justice in this initial phase is the goodwill among people of about equal power to come to terms with each other, to come to an understanding again by means of a settlement, and with regard to the less powerful, to *compel* them to agree among themselves to a settlement.

9

Measured always by the standard of antiquity (this antiquity, moreover, is present or again possible at all periods), the community stands to its members in that important and radical relationship of creditor to his "owers." Man lives in a community, man enjoys the advantages of a community (and what advantages! We occasionally underestimate them nowadays), man lives protected, spared, in peace and trust, secure from certain injuries and enmities, to which the man outside the community, the "peaceless" man, is exposed—a German understands the original meaning of "*Elend*" (*êlend*)—secure because he has entered into pledges and obligations to the community in respect of these very injuries and enmities. What happens *when this is not the case?* The community, the defrauded creditor, will get itself paid, as well as it can, one can reckon on that. In this case the question of the direct damage done by the offender is quite subsidiary: quite apart from this the criminal[3] is above all a breaker, a breaker of word and covenant *to the whole,* as regards all the advantages and amenities of the communal life in which up to that time he had participated. The criminal is an "ower" who not only fails to repay the advances and advantages that have been given to him, but even sets out to attack his creditor: consequently he is in the future not only, as is fair, deprived of all these advantages and amenities—he is in addition reminded of the *importance* of those advantages. The wrath of the injured creditor, of the community, puts him back in the wild and outlawed status from which he was previously protected: the community repudiates him—and now every kind of enmity can vent itself on him. Punishment is in this stage of civilisation simply the copy, the mimic, of the normal treatment of the hated, disdained, and conquered enemy, who is not only deprived of every right and protection but of every mercy; so we have the martial law and triumphant festival of the *vae victis!* In all its mercilessness and cruelty. This shows why war itself (counting the sacrificial cult of war) has produced all the forms under which punishment has manifested itself in history.

10

As it grows more powerful, the community tends to take the offences of the individual less seriously, because they are now regarded as being much less revolutionary and dangerous to the corporate existence: the evildoer is no more outlawed and put outside the pale, the common wrath can no longer vent itself upon him with its old licence—on the contrary, from this very time it is against this wrath, and particularly against the wrath of those directly injured, that the evildoer is carefully shielded and protected by the community. As, in fact, the penal law develops, the following characteristics become more and more clearly marked: compromise with the wrath of those directly affected by the misdeed; a consequent endeavour to localise the matter and to prevent a further, or indeed a general spread of the disturbance; attempts to find equivalents and to settle the whole matter (*compositio*); above all, the will, which manifests itself with increasing definiteness, to treat every offence as in a certain degree capable of *being paid off,* and consequently, at any rate up to a certain point, to *isolate* the offender from his act. As the power and the self-consciousness of a community increases, so proportionately does the penal law become mitigated; conversely every weakening and jeopardising of the community revives the harshest forms of that law. The creditor has always grown more humane proportionately as he has grown more rich; finally the amount of injury he can endure without really suffering becomes the criterion of his wealth. It is possible to conceive of a society blessed with so great a *consciousness of its own power* as to indulge in the most aristocratic luxury of letting its wrongdoers go *scot-free.* "What do my parasites matter to me?" might society say. "Let them live and flourish! I am strong enough for it." The justice which began with the maxim, "Everything can be paid off, everything must be paid off," ends with connivance at the escape of those who cannot pay to escape—it ends, like every good thing on earth, by *destroying itself.* The self-destruction of Justice! We know the pretty name it calls itself—*Grace!* It remains, as is obvious, the privilege of the strongest, better still, their super-law.

11

A deprecatory word here against the attempts, that have lately been made, to find the origin of justice on quite another basis—namely, on that of *resentment.* Let me whisper a word in the ear of the psychologists, if they would fain study revenge itself at close quarters: this plant blooms its prettiest at present among Anarchists and anti-Semites, a hidden flower, as it has ever been, like the violet, though, forsooth, with another perfume. And as like must necessarily emanate from like, it will not be a matter for surprise that it is just in such circles that we see the birth of endeavours (it is their old birthplace—compare above, First Essay, paragraph 14), to sanctify *revenge* under the name of *justice* (as though Justice were at bottom merely a development of the consciousness of injury), and thus with the rehabilitation of revenge to reinstate generally and collectively all the *reactive* emotions. I object to this last point least of all. It even seems *meritorious* when regarded from the standpoint of the whole problem of biology (from which standpoint the value of these emotions has up to the present been underestimated). And that to which I alone call attention, is the circumstance that it is the spirit of revenge itself, from which develops this new nuance of scientific equity (for the benefit of hate, envy, mistrust, jealousy, suspicion, rancour, revenge). This scientific "equity" stops immediately and makes way for the accents of deadly enmity and prejudice, so soon as another group of emotions comes on the scene, which in my opinion are of a much higher biological value than these reactions, and consequently have a paramount claim to the valuation and appreciation of *science:* I mean the really *active* emotions, such as personal and material ambition, and so forth. (E. Dühring,

Value of Life; Course of Philosophy, and passim.) So much against this tendency in general: but as for the particular maxim of Dühring's, that the home of Justice is to be found in the sphere of the reactive feelings, our love of truth compels us drastically to invert his own proposition and to oppose to him this other maxim: the *last* sphere conquered by the spirit of justice is the sphere of the feeling of reaction! When it really comes about that the just man remains just even as regards his injurer (and not merely cold, moderate, reserved, indifferent: being just is always a *positive* state); when, in spite of the strong provocation of personal insult, contempt, and calumny, the lofty and clear objectivity of the just and judging eye (whose glance is as profound as it is gentle) is untroubled, why then we have a piece of perfection, a past master of the world—something, in fact, which it would not be wise to expect, and which should not at any rate be too easily *believed.* Speaking generally, there is no doubt but that even the justest individual only requires a little dose of hostility, malice, or innuendo to drive the blood into his brain and the fairness *from* it. The active man, the attacking, aggressive man is always a hundred degrees nearer to justice than the man who merely reacts; he certainly has no need to adopt the tactics, necessary in the case of the reacting man, of making false and biassed valuations of his object. It is, in point of fact, for this reason that the aggressive man has at all times enjoyed the stronger, bolder, more aristocratic, and also *freer* outlook, the *better* conscience. On the other hand, we already surmise who it really is that has on his conscience the invention of the "bad conscience"—the resentful man! Finally, let man look at himself in history. In what sphere up to the present has the whole administration of law, the actual need of law, found its earthly home? Perchance in the sphere of the reacting man? Not for a minute: rather in that of the active, strong, spontaneous, aggressive man? I deliberately defy the above-mentioned agitator (who himself makes this self-confession, "the creed of revenge has run through all my works and endeavours like the red thread of Justice"), and say, that judged historically law in the world represents the very war *against* the reactive feelings, the very war waged on those feelings by the powers of activity and aggression, which devote some of their strength to damming and keeping within bounds this effervescence of hysterical reactivity, and to forcing it to some compromise. Everywhere where justice is practised and justice is maintained, it is to be observed that the stronger power, when confronted with the weaker powers which are inferior to it (whether they be groups, or individuals), searches for weapons to put an end to the senseless fury of resentment, while it carries on its object, partly by taking the victim of resentment out of the clutches of revenge, partly by substituting for revenge a campaign of its own against the enemies of peace and order, partly by finding, suggesting, and occasionally enforcing settlements, partly by standardising certain equivalents for injuries, to which equivalents the element of resentment is henceforth finally referred. The most drastic measure, however, taken and effectuated by the supreme power, to combat the preponderance of the feelings of spite and vindictiveness—it takes this measure as soon as it is at all strong enough to do so—is the foundation of *law*, the imperative declaration of what in its eyes is to be regarded as just and lawful, and what unjust and unlawful: and while, after the foundation of law, the supreme power treats the aggressive and arbitrary acts of individuals, or of whole groups, as a violation of law, and a revolt against itself, it distracts the feelings of its subjects from the immediate injury inflicted by such a violation, and thus eventually attains the very opposite result to that always desired by revenge, which sees and recognises nothing but the standpoint of the injured party. From henceforth the eye becomes trained to a more and more *impersonal* valuation of the deed, even the eye of the injured party himself (though this is in the final stage of all, as has been previously remarked)—on this principle "right" and "wrong" first manifest themselves after the foundation of law (and *not*, as Dühring maintains, only after the act of violation). To talk of intrinsic right and intrinsic wrong is absolutely nonsensical; intrinsically, an injury, an oppression, an exploitation, an annihilation can be nothing wrong, inasmuch as life is *essentially* (that is, in its cardinal functions) something which functions by injuring, oppressing, exploiting, and annihilating, and is absolutely inconceivable without such a character. It is necessary to make an even more serious confession: viewed from the most advanced biological standpoint, conditions of legality can be only *exceptional conditions*, in that they are partial restrictions of the real life-will, which makes for power, and in that they are subordinated to the life-will's general end as particular means, that is, as means to create *larger* units of strength. A legal organisation, conceived of as sovereign and universal, not as a weapon in a fight of complexes of power, but as a weapon *against* fighting, generally something after the style of Dühring's communistic model of treating every will as equal with every other will, would be a principle *hostile to life*, a destroyer and dissolver of man, an outrage on the future of man, a symptom of fatigue, a secret cut to Nothingness.

12

A word more on the origin and end of punishment—two problems which are or ought to be kept distinct, but which unfortunately are usually lumped into one. And what tactics have our moral genealogists employed up to the present in these cases? Their inveterate naïveté. They find out some "end" in the punishment, for instance, revenge and deterrence, and then in all their innocence set this end at the beginning, as the *causa fiendi* of the punishment, and—they have done the trick. But the patching up of a history of the origin of law is the last use to which the "End in Law"[4] ought to be put. Perhaps there is no more pregnant principle for any kind of history than the following, which, difficult though it is to master, *should* nonetheless be *mastered* in every detail. The origin of the existence of a thing and its final utility, its practical application and incorporation in a system of ends, are *toto caelo* opposed to each other—everything, anything, which exists and which prevails anywhere, will always be put to new purposes by a force superior to itself, will be commandeered afresh, will be turned and transformed to new uses; all "happening" in the organic world consists of *overpowering* and dominating, and again all overpowering and domination is a new interpretation and adjustment, which must necessarily obscure or absolutely extinguish the subsisting "meaning" and "end." The most perfect comprehension of the utility of any physiological organ (or also of a legal institution, social custom, political habit, form in art or in religious worship) does not for a minute imply any simultaneous comprehension of its origin: this may seem uncomfortable and unpalatable to the older men—for it has been the immemorial belief that understanding the final cause or the utility of a thing, a form, an institution, means also understanding the reason for its origin: to give an example of this logic, the eye was made to see, the hand was made to grasp. So even punishment was conceived as invented with a view to punishing. But all ends and all utilities are only *signs* that a Will to Power has mastered a less powerful force, has impressed thereon out of its own self the meaning of a function; and the whole history of a "Thing," an organ, a custom, can on the same principle be regarded as a continuous "sign-chain" of perpetually new interpretations and adjustments, whose causes, so far from needing to have even a mutual connexion, sometimes follow and alternate with each other absolutely haphazard. Similarly, the evolution of a "thing," of a custom, is anything but its *progressus* to an end, still less a logical and direct *progressus* attained with the minimum expenditure of energy and cost: it is rather the succession of processes of subjugation,

more or less profound, more or less mutually independent, which operate
on the thing itself; it is, further, the resistance which in each case invariably displayed this subjugation, the Protean wriggles by way of defence
and reaction, and, further, the results of successful counter-efforts. The
form is fluid, but the meaning is even more so—even inside every individual organism the case is the same: with every genuine growth of the
whole, the "function" of the individual organs becomes shifted—in certain cases a partial perishing of these organs, a diminution of their
numbers (for instance, through annihilation of the connecting members), can be a symptom of growing strength and perfection. What I mean
is this: even partial *loss of utility*, decay, and degeneration, loss of function
and purpose, in a word, death, appertain to the conditions of the genuine
progressus; which always appears in the shape of a will and way to *greater*
power, and is always realised at the expense of innumerable smaller powers. The magnitude of a "progress" is gauged by the greatness of the
sacrifice that it requires: humanity as a mass sacrificed to the prosperity
of the one *stronger* species of Man—that *would* be a progress. I emphasise
all the more this cardinal characteristic of the historic method, for the
reason that in its essence it runs counter to predominant instincts and
prevailing taste, which much prefer to put up with absolute casualness,
even with the mechanical senselessness of all phenomena, than with the
theory of a power-will, in exhaustive play throughout all phenomena.
The democratic idiosyncrasy against everything which rules and wishes to
rule, the modern *misarchism* (to coin a bad word for a bad thing), has
gradually but so thoroughly transformed itself into the guise of intellectualism, the most abstract intellectualism, that even nowadays it penetrates
and *has the right* to penetrate step by step into the most exact and apparently the most objective sciences: this tendency has, in fact, in my view
already dominated the whole of physiology and biology, and to their detriment, as is obvious, insofar as it has spirited away a radical idea, the idea
of true *activity*. The tyranny of this idiosyncrasy, however, results in the
theory of "adaptation" being pushed forward into the van of the argument, exploited; adaptation—that means to say, a second-class activity, a
mere capacity for "reacting"; in fact, life itself has been defined (by Herbert Spencer) as an increasingly effective internal adaptation to external
circumstances. This definition, however, fails to realise the real essence of
life, its will to power. It fails to appreciate the paramount superiority
enjoyed by those plastic forces of spontaneity, aggression, and encroach-
ment with their new interpretations and tendencies, to the operation of

which adaptation is only a natural corollary: consequently the sovereign office of the highest functionaries in the organism itself (among which the life-will appears as an active and formative principle) is repudiated. One remembers Huxley's reproach to Spencer of his "administrative Nihilism": but it is a case of something much *more* than "administration."

13

To return to our subject, namely *punishment*, we must make consequently a double distinction: first, the relatively permanent *element*, the custom, the act, the "drama," a certain rigid sequence of methods of procedure; on the other hand, the fluid element, the meaning, the end, the expectation which is attached to the operation of such procedure. At this point we immediately assume, *per analogiam* (in accordance with the theory of the historic method, which we have elaborated above), that the procedure itself is something older and earlier than its utilisation in punishment, that this utilisation was *introduced* and interpreted into the procedure (which had existed for a long time, but whose employment had another meaning), in short, that the case is *different* from that hitherto supposed by our *naïf* genealogists of morals and of law, who thought that the procedure was *invented* for the purpose of punishment, in the same way that the hand had been previously thought to have been invented for the purpose of grasping. With regard to the other element in *punishment*, its fluid element, its meaning, the idea of punishment in a very late stage of civilisation (for instance, contemporary Europe) is not content with manifesting merely one meaning, but manifests a whole synthesis "of meanings." The past general history of punishment, the history of its employment for the most diverse ends, crystallises eventually into a kind of unity, which is difficult to analyse into its parts, and which, it is necessary to emphasise, absolutely defies definition. (It is nowadays impossible to say definitely *the precise reason* for punishment: all ideas, in which a whole process is promiscuously comprehended, elude definition; it is only that which has no history, which can be defined.) At an earlier stage, on the contrary, that synthesis of meanings appears much less rigid and much more elastic; we can realise how in each individual case the elements of the synthesis change their value and their position, so that now one element and now another stands out and predominates over the others, nay, in certain cases one element (perhaps the end of deterrence) seems to eliminate all the rest. At any rate, so as to give some idea of the uncertain, supplementary, and accidental nature of the meaning of punishment and of the manner in which one identical procedure can be employed and adapted for the most diametrically opposed objects, I will at this point give a scheme that has suggested itself to me, a scheme itself based on comparatively small and accidental material. Punishment, as rendering the criminal harmless and incapable of further injury. Punishment, as compensation for the injury sustained by the injured party, in any form whatsoever (including the form of sentimental compensation). Punishment, as an isolation of that which disturbs the equilibrium, so as to prevent the further spreading of the disturbance. Punishment as a means of inspiring fear of those who determine and execute the punishment. Punishment as a kind of compensation for advantages which the wrongdoer has up to that time enjoyed (for example, when he is utilised as a slave in the mines). Punishment, as the elimination of an element of decay (sometimes of a whole branch, as according to the Chinese laws, consequently as a means to the purification of the race, or the preservation of a social type). Punishment as a festival, as the violent oppression and humiliation of an enemy that has at last been subdued. Punishment as a mnemonic, whether for him who suffers the punishment—the so-called "correction," or for the witnesses of its administration. Punishment, as the payment of a fee stipulated for by the power which protects the evildoer from the excesses of revenge. Punishment, as a compromise with the natural phenomenon of revenge, insofar as revenge is still maintained and claimed as a privilege by the stronger races. Punishment as a declaration and measure of war against an enemy of peace, of law, of order, of authority, who is fought by society with the weapons which war provides, as a spirit dangerous to the community, as a breaker of the contract on which the community is based, as a rebel, a traitor, and a breaker of the peace.

14

This list is certainly not complete; it is obvious that punishment is overloaded with utilities of all kinds. This makes it all the more permissible to eliminate one *supposed* utility, which passes, at any rate in the popular mind, for its most essential utility, and which is just what even now provides the strongest support for that faith in punishment which is nowadays for many reasons tottering. Punishment is supposed to have the value of exciting in the guilty the consciousness of guilt; in punishment is sought the proper *instrumentum* of that psychic reaction which becomes known as a "bad conscience," "remorse." But this theory is even, from the point of view of the present, a violation of reality and psychology: and how much more so is the case when we have to deal with the longest period of man's history, his primitive history! Genuine remorse is certainly extremely rare among wrongdoers and the victims of punishment; prisons and houses of correction are not *the* soil on which this worm of remorse pullulates for choice—this is the unanimous opinion of all conscientious observers, who in many cases arrive at such a judgement with enough reluctance and against their own personal wishes. Speaking generally, punishment hardens and numbs, it produces concentration, it sharpens the consciousness of alienation, it strengthens the power of resistance. When it happens that it breaks the man's energy and brings about a piteous prostration and abjectness, such a result is certainly even less salutary than the average effect of punishment, which is characterised by a harsh and sinister doggedness. The thought of those *prehistoric* millennia brings us to the unhesitating conclusion, that it was simply through punishment that the evolution of the consciousness of guilt was most forcibly retarded—at any rate in the victims of the punishing power. In particular, let us not underestimate the extent to which, by the very sight of the judicial and executive procedure, the wrongdoer is himself prevented from feeling that his deed, the character of his act, is *intrinsically* reprehensible: for he sees clearly the same kind of acts practised in the service of justice, and then called good, and practised with a good conscience; acts such as espionage, trickery, bribery, trapping, the whole intriguing and insidious art of the policeman and the informer—the whole system, in fact, manifested in the different kinds of punishment (a system not excused by passion, but based on principle), of robbing, oppressing, insulting, imprisoning, racking, murdering. All this he sees treated by his judges, not as acts meriting censure and condemnation *in themselves*, but only in a particular context and application. It was *not* on this soil that grew the "bad conscience," that most sinister and interesting plant of our earthly vegetation—in point of fact, throughout a most lengthy period, no suggestion of having to do with a "guilty man" manifested itself in the consciousness of the man who judged and punished. One had merely to deal with an author of an injury, an irresponsible piece of fate. And the man himself, on whom the punishment subsequently fell like a piece of fate, was occasioned no more of an "inner pain" than would be occasioned by the sudden approach of some uncalculated event, some terrible natural catastrophe, a rushing, crushing avalanche against which there is no resistance.

15

This truth came insidiously enough to the consciousness of Spinoza (to the disgust of his commentators, who (like Kuno Fischer, for instance) give themselves no end of *trouble* to misunderstand him on this point), when one afternoon (as he sat raking up who knows what memory) he indulged in the question of what was really left for him personally of the celebrated *morsus conscientiae*—Spinoza, who had relegated "good and evil" to the sphere of human imagination, and indignantly defended the honour of his "free" God against those blasphemers who affirmed that God did everything *sub ratione boni* ("but this was tantamount to subordinating God to fate, and would really be the greatest of all absurdities"). For Spinoza the world had returned again to that innocence in which it lay before the discovery of the bad conscience: what, then, had happened to the *morsus conscientiae*? "The antithesis of *gaudium*," said he at last to himself—"A sadness accompanied by the recollection of a past event which has turned out contrary to all expectation" (*Eth.* III, Propos. XVIII Schol. i. ii.). Evildoers have throughout thousands of years felt when overtaken by punishment *exactly like Spinoza*, on the subject of their "offence": "here is something which went wrong contrary to my anticipation," *not* "I ought not to have done this." They submitted themselves to punishment, just as one submits one's self to a disease, to a misfortune, or to death, with that stubborn and resigned fatalism which gives the Russians, for instance, even nowadays, the advantage over us Westerners, in the handling of life. If at that period there was a critique of action, the criterion was prudence: the real *effect* of punishment is unquestionably chiefly to be found in a sharpening of the sense of prudence, in a lengthening of the memory, in a will to adopt more of a policy of caution, suspicion, and secrecy; in the recognition that there are many things which are unquestionably beyond one's capacity; in a kind of improvement in self-criticism. The broad effects which can be obtained by punishment in man and beast, are the increase of fear, the sharpening of the sense of cunning, the mastery of the desires: so it is that punishment *tames* man, but does not make him "better"—it would be more correct even to go so far as to assert the contrary ("Injury makes a man cunning," says a popular proverb: so far as it makes him cunning, it makes him also bad. Fortunately, it often enough makes him stupid).

16

At this juncture I cannot avoid trying to give a tentative and provisional expression to my own hypothesis concerning the origin of the bad conscience: it is difficult to make it fully appreciated, and it requires continuous meditation, attention, and digestion. I regard the bad conscience as the serious illness which man was bound to contract under the stress of the most radical change which he has ever experienced—that change, when he found himself finally imprisoned within the pale of society and of peace.

Just like the plight of the water-animals, when they were compelled either to become land-animals or to perish, so was the plight of these half-animals, perfectly adapted as they were to the savage life of war, prowling, and adventure—suddenly all their instincts were rendered worthless and "switched off." Henceforward they had to walk on their feet—"carry themselves," whereas heretofore they had been carried by the water: a terrible heaviness oppressed them. They found themselves clumsy in obeying the simplest directions, confronted with this new and unknown world they had no longer their old guides—the regulative instincts that had led them unconsciously to safety—they were reduced, were those unhappy creatures, to thinking, inferring, calculating, putting together causes and results, reduced to that poorest and most erratic organ of theirs, their "consciousness." I do not believe there was ever in the world such a feeling of misery, such a leaden discomfort—further, those old instincts had not immediately ceased their demands! Only it was difficult and rarely possible to gratify them: speaking broadly, they were compelled to satisfy themselves by new and, as it were, hole-and-corner methods. All instincts which do not find a vent without, *turn inwards*—this is what I mean by the growing "internalisation" of man: consequently we have the first growth in man, of what subsequently was called his soul. The whole inner world, originally as thin as if it had been stretched between two layers of skin, burst apart and expanded proportionately, and obtained depth, breadth, and height, when man's external outlet became *obstructed*. These terrible bulwarks, with which the social organisation protected itself against the old instincts of freedom (punishments belong preeminently to these bulwarks), brought it about that all those instincts of wild, free, prowling man became turned backwards *against man himself*. Enmity, cruelty, the delight in persecution, in surprises, change, destruction—the turning all these instincts against their own possessors: this is the origin of the "bad conscience." It was man, who, lacking external enemies and obstacles, and imprisoned as he was in the oppressive narrowness and monotony of custom, in his own impatience lacerated, persecuted, gnawed, frightened, and ill-treated himself; it was this animal in the hands of the tamer, which beat itself against the bars of its cage; it was this being who, pining and yearning for that desert home of which it had been deprived, was compelled to create out of its own self, an adventure, a torture-chamber, a hazardous and perilous desert—it was this fool, this homesick and desperate prisoner—who invented the "bad conscience." But thereby he introduced that most grave and sinister illness, from which mankind has not yet recovered, the suffering of man from the disease called man, as the result of a violent breaking from his animal past, the result, as it were, of a spasmodic plunge into a new environment and new conditions of existence, the result of a declaration of war against the old instincts, which up to that time had been the staple of his power, his joy, his formidableness. Let us immediately add that this fact of an animal ego turning against itself, taking part against itself, produced in the world so novel, profound, unheard-of, problematic, inconsistent, and *pregnant* a phenomenon, that the aspect of the world was radically altered thereby. In sooth, only divine spectators could have appreciated the drama that then began, and whose end baffles conjecture as yet—a drama too subtle, too wonderful, too paradoxical to warrant its undergoing a nonsensical and unheeded performance on some random grotesque planet! Henceforth man is to be counted as one of the most unexpected and sensational lucky shots in the game of the "big baby" of Heracleitus, whether he be called Zeus or Chance—he awakens on his behalf the interest, excitement, hope, almost the confidence, of his being the harbinger and forerunner of something, of man being no end, but only a stage, an interlude, a bridge, a great promise.

<h2 style="text-align:center">17</h2>

It is primarily involved in this hypothesis of the origin of the bad conscience, that that alteration was no gradual and no voluntary alteration, and that it did not manifest itself as an organic adaptation to new conditions, but as a break, a jump, a necessity, an inevitable fate, against which there was no resistance and never a spark of resentment. And secondarily, that the fitting of a hitherto unchecked and amorphous population into a fixed form, starting as it had done in an act of violence, could only be accomplished by acts of violence and nothing else—that the oldest "State" appeared consequently as a ghastly tyranny, a grinding ruthless piece of machinery, which went on working, till this raw material of a semi-animal populace was not only thoroughly kneaded and elastic, but also *moulded*. I used the word "State": my meaning is self-evident, namely, a herd of blonde beasts of prey, a race of conquerors and masters, which with all its warlike organisation and all its organising power pounces with its terrible claws on a population, in numbers possibly tremendously superior, but as yet formless, as yet nomad. Such is the origin of the "State." That fantastic theory that makes it begin with a contract is, I think, disposed of. He who can command, he who is a master by "nature," he who comes on the scene forceful in deed and gesture—what has he to do with contracts? Such beings defy calculation, they come like fate, without cause, reason, notice, excuse, they are there like the lightning is there, too terrible, too sudden, too convincing, too "different," to be personally even hated. Their work is an instinctive creating and impressing of forms, they are the most involuntary, unconscious artists that there are: their appearance produces instantaneously a scheme of sovereignty which is *live*, in which the functions are partitioned and apportioned, in which above all no part is received or finds a place, until pregnant with a "meaning" in regard to the whole. They are ignorant of the meaning of guilt, responsibiltiy, consideration, are these born organisers; in them predominates that terrible artist-egoism, that gleams like brass, and that knows itself justified to all eternity, in its work, even as a mother in her child. It is not in *them* that there grew the bad conscience, that is elementary—but it would not have grown *without them*, repulsive growth as it was, it would be missing, had not a tremendous quantity of freedom been expelled from the world by the stress of their hammer-strokes, their artist violence, or been at any rate made invisible and, as it were, *latent*. This *instinct of freedom* forced into being latent—it is already clear—this instinct of freedom forced back, trodden back, imprisoned within itself, and finally only able to find vent and relief in itself; this, only this, is the beginning of the "bad conscience."

18

Beware of thinking lightly of this phenomenon, by reason of its initial painful ugliness. At bottom it is the same active force which is at work on a more grandiose scale in those potent artists and organisers, and builds states, which here, internally, on a smaller and pettier scale and with a retrogressive tendency, makes itself a bad conscience in the "labyrinth of the breast," to use Goethe's phrase, and which builds negative ideals; it is, I repeat, that identical *instinct of freedom* (to use my own language, the will to power): only the material, on which this force with all its constructive and tyrannous nature is let loose, is here man himself, his whole old animal self—and *not* as in the case of that more grandiose and sensational phenomenon, the *other* man, *other* men. This secret self-tyranny, this cruelty of the artist, this delight in giving a form to one's self as a piece of difficult, refractory, and suffering material, in burning in a will, a critique, a contradiction, a contempt, a negation; this sinister and ghastly labour of love on the part of a soul, whose will is cloven in two within itself, which makes itself suffer from delight in the infliction of suffering; this wholly *active* bad conscience has finally (as one already anticipates)—true fountainhead as it is of idealism and imagination—produced an abundance of novel and amazing beauty and affirmation, and perhaps has really been the first to give birth to beauty at all. What would beauty be, forsooth, if its contradiction had not first been presented to consciousness, if the ugly had not first said to itself, "I am ugly"? At any rate, after this hint the problem of how far idealism and beauty can be traced in such opposite ideas as "*selflessness*," *self-denial*, *self-sacrifice*, becomes less problematical; and indubitably in future we shall certainly know the real and original character of the *delight* experienced by the self-less, the self-denying, the self-sacrificing: this delight is a phase of cruelty. So much provisionally for the origin of "altruism" as a *moral* value, and the marking out the ground from which this value has grown: it is only the bad conscience, only the will for self-abuse, that provides the necessary conditions for the existence of altruism as a *value*.

19

Undoubtedly the bad conscience is an illness, but an illness like pregnancy is an illness. If we search out the conditions under which this illness reaches its most terrible and sublime zenith, we shall see what really first brought about its entry into the world. But to do this we must take a long breath, and we must first of all go back once again to an earlier point of view. The relation at civil law of the ower to his creditor (which has already been discussed in detail), has been interpreted once again (and indeed in a manner which historically is exceedingly remarkable and suspicious) into a relationship, which is perhaps more incomprehensible to us moderns than to any other era; that is, into the relationship of the *existing* generation to its *ancestors*. Within the original tribal association —we are talking of primitive times—each living generation recognises a legal obligation towards the earlier generation, and particularly towards the earliest, which founded the family (and this is something much more than a mere sentimental obligation, the existence of which, during the longest period of man's history, is by no means indisputable). There prevails in them the conviction that it is only thanks to sacrifices and efforts of their ancestors, that the race *persists* at all—and that this has to be *paid back* to them by sacrifices and services. Thus is recognised the *owing* of a debt, which accumulates continually by reason of these ancestors never ceasing in their subsequent life as potent spirits to secure by their power new privileges and advantages to the race. Gratis, perchance? But there is no gratis for that raw and "mean-souled" age. What return can be made? Sacrifice (at first, nourishment, in its crudest sense), festivals, temples, tributes of veneration, above all, obedience—since all customs are, *quâ* works of the ancestors, equally their precepts and commands—are the ancestors ever given enough? This suspicion remains and grows: from time to time it extorts a great wholesale ransom, something monstrous in the way of repayment of the creditor (the notorious sacrifice of the firstborn, for example, blood, human blood in any case). The *fear* of ancestors and their power, the consciousness of owing debts to them, necessarily increases, according to this kind of logic, in the exact proportion that the race itself increases, that the race itself becomes more victorious, more independent, more honoured, more feared. This, and not the contrary, is the fact. Each step towards race decay, all disastrous events, all symptoms of degeneration, of approaching disintegration, always *diminish* the fear of the founders' spirit, and whittle away the idea of his sagacity, providence, and potent presence. Conceive this crude kind of logic carried to its climax: it follows that the ancestors of the *most powerful* races must, through the growing fear that they exercise on the imaginations, grow themselves into monstrous dimensions, and become relegated to the gloom of a divine mystery that transcends imagination— the ancestor becomes at last necessarily transfigured into a *god.* Perhaps this is the very origin of the gods, that is, an origin from *fear!* And those who feel bound to add, "but from piety also," will have difficulty in maintaining this theory, with regard to the primeval and longest period of the human race. And of course this is even more the case as regards the *middle* period, the formative period of the aristocratic races—the aristocratic races which have given back with interest to their founders, the ancestors (heroes, gods), all those qualities which in the meanwhile have appeared in themselves, that is, the aristocratic qualities. We will later on glance again at the ennobling and promotion of the gods (which of course is totally distinct from their "sanctification"): let us now provisionally follow to its end the course of the whole of this development of the consciousness of "owing."

20

According to the teaching of history, the consciousness of owing debts
to the deity by no means came to an end with the decay of the clan organisation of society; just as mankind has inherited the ideas of "good" and
"bad" from the race-nobility (together with its fundamental tendency
towards establishing social distinctions), so with the heritage of the racial
and tribal gods it has also inherited the incubus of debts as yet unpaid and
the desire to discharge them. The transition is effected by those large
populations of slaves and bondsmen, who, whether through compulsion
or through submission and "*mimicry*," have accommodated themselves
to the religion of their masters; through this channel these inherited
tendencies inundate the world. The feeling of owing a debt to the deity
has grown continuously for several centuries, always in the same proportion in which the idea of God and the consciousness of God have
grown and become exalted among mankind. (The whole history of eth-
nic fights, victories, reconciliations, amalgamations, everything, in fact,
which precedes the eventual classing of all the social elements in each
great race-synthesis, are mirrored in the hotch-potch genealogy of
their gods, in the legends of their fights, victories, and reconciliations.
Progress towards universal empires invariably means progress towards
universal deities; despotism, with its subjugation of the independent nobility, always paves the way for some system or other of monotheism.) The
appearance of the Christian god, as the record god up to this time, has
for that very reason brought equally into the world the record amount
of guilt consciousness. Granted that we have gradually started on the
reverse movement, there is no little probability in the deduction, based
on the continuous decay in the belief in the Christian god, to the effect
that there also already exists a considerable decay in the human consciousness of owing (ought); in fact, we cannot shut our eyes to the
prospect of the complete and eventual triumph of atheism freeing mankind from all this feeling of obligation to their origin, their *causa prima*.
Atheism and a kind of second innocence complement and supplement
each other.

21

So much for my rough and preliminary sketch of the interrelation of
the ideas "ought" (owe) and "duty" with the postulates of religion. I have
intentionally shelved up to the present the actual moralisation of these
ideas (their being pushed back into the conscience, or more precisely

the interweaving of the *bad* conscience with the idea of God), and at the end of the last paragraph used language to the effect that this moralisation did not exist, and that consequently these ideas had necessarily come to an end, by reason of what had happened to their hypothesis, the credence in our "creditor," in God. The actual facts differ terribly from this theory. It is with the moralisation of the ideas "ought" and "duty," and with their being pushed back into the *bad* conscience, that comes the first actual attempt to *reverse* the direction of the development we have just described, or at any rate to arrest its evolution; it is just at this juncture that the very hope of an eventual redemption *has* to put itself once for all into the prison of pessimism, it is at this juncture that the eye has to recoil and rebound in despair from off an adamantine impossibility, it is at this juncture that the ideas "guilt" and "duty" have to turn backwards—turn backwards against *whom*? There is no doubt about it; primarily against the "ower," in whom the bad conscience now establishes itself, eats, extends, and grows like a polypus throughout its length and breadth, all with such virulence, that at last, with the impossibility of paying the debt, there becomes conceived the idea of the impossibility of paying the penalty, the thought of its inexpiability (the idea of "eternal punishment")—finally, too, it turns against the "creditor," whether found in the *causa prima* of man, the origin of the human race, its sire, who henceforth becomes burdened with a curse ("Adam," "original sin," "determination of the will"), or in Nature from whose womb man springs, and on whom the responsibility for the principle of evil is now cast ("Diabolisation of Nature"), or in existence generally, on this logic an absolute *white elephant*, with which mankind is landed (the Nihilistic flight from life, the demand for Nothingness, or for the opposite of existence, for some other existence, Buddhism and the like)—till suddenly we stand before that paradoxical and awful expedient, through which a tortured humanity has found a temporary alleviation, that stroke of genius called Christianity: God personally immolating himself for the debt of man, God paying himself personally out of a pound of his own flesh, God as the one being who can deliver man from what man had become unable to deliver himself—the creditor playing scapegoat for his debtor, from *love* (can you believe it?), from love of his debtor! . . .

22

The reader will already have conjectured what took place on the stage and *behind the scenes* of this drama. That will for self-torture, that inverted

cruelty of the animal man, who, turned subjective and scared into introspection (encaged as he was in "the State," as part of his taming process),
invented the bad conscience so as to hurt himself, after the *natural* outlet for this will to hurt, became blocked—in other words, this man of the
bad conscience exploited the religious hypothesis so as to carry his martyrdom to the ghastliest pitch of agonised intensity. Owing something
to *God*: this thought becomes his instrument of torture. He apprehends in
God the most extreme antitheses that he can find to his own characteristic
and ineradicable animal instincts, he himself gives a new interpretation
to these animal instincts as being against what he "owes" to God (as
enmity, rebellion, and revolt against the "Lord," the "Father," the "Sire,"
the "Beginning of the world"), he places himself between the horns
of the dilemma, "God" and "Devil." Every negation which he is inclined to
utter to himself, to the nature, naturalness, and reality of his being, he
whips into an ejaculation of "yes," uttering it as something existing, living,
efficient, as being God, as the holiness of God, the judgement of God, as
the hangmanship of God, as transcendence, as eternity, as unending torment, as hell, as infinity of punishment and guilt. This is a kind of
madness of the will in the sphere of psychological cruelty which is absolutely unparalleled: man's *will* to find himself guilty and blameworthy to
the point of inexpiability, his *will* to think of himself as punished, without the punishment ever being able to balance the guilt, his *will* to infect
and to poison the fundamental basis of the universe with the problem of
punishment and guilt, in order to cut off once and for all any escape out
of this labyrinth of "fixed ideas," his will for rearing an ideal—that of the
"holy God"—face to face with which he can have tangible proof of his
own unworthiness. Alas for this mad melancholy beast man! What phan-
tasies invade it, what paroxysms of perversity, hysterical senselessness, and
mental bestiality break out immediately, at the very slightest check on its
being the beast of action. All this is excessively interesting, but at the
same time tainted with a black, gloomy, enervating melancholy, so that
a forcible veto must be invoked against looking too long into these
abysses. Here is *disease*, undubitably, the most ghastly disease that has as
yet played havoc among men: and he who can still hear (but man turns
now deaf ears to such sounds), how in this night of torment and nonsense there has rung out the cry of *love*, the cry of the most passionate
ecstasy, of redemption in *love*, he turns away gripped by an invincible
horror—in man there is so much that is ghastly—too long has the world
been a madhouse.

23

Let this suffice once for all concerning the origin of the "holy God." The fact that *in itself* the conception of gods is not bound to lead necessarily to this degradation of the imagination (a temporary representation of whose vagaries we felt bound to give), the fact that there exist *nobler* methods of utilising the invention of gods than in this self-crucifixion and self-degradation of man, in which the last two thousand years of Europe have been past masters—these facts can fortunately be still perceived from every glance that we cast at the Grecian gods, these mirrors of noble and grandiose men, in which the *animal* in man felt itself deified, and did *not* devour itself in subjective frenzy. These Greeks long utilised their gods as simple buffers against the "bad conscience"—so that they could continue to enjoy their freedom of soul: this, of course, is diametrically opposed to Christianity's theory of its god. They went *very far* on this principle, did these splendid and lion-hearted children; and there is no lesser authority than that of the Homeric Zeus for making them realise occasionally that they are taking life too casually. "Wonderful," says he on one occasion —it has to do with the case of Aegistheus, a *very* bad case indeed—

Wonderful how they grumble, the mortals against the immortals,
Only from us, they presume, *comes evil*, but in their folly,
Fashion they, spite of fate, the doom of their own disaster.

Yet the reader will note and observe that this Olympian spectator and judge is far from being angry with them and thinking evil of them on this score. "How *foolish* they are," so thinks he of the misdeeds of mortals— and "folly," "imprudence," "a little brain disturbance," and nothing more, are what the Greeks, even of the strongest, bravest period, have admitted to be the ground of much that is evil and fatal. Folly, *not* sin, do you understand? . . . But even this brain disturbance was a problem—"Come, how is it even possible? How could it have really got in brains like ours, the brains of men of aristocratic ancestry, of men of fortune, of men of good natural endowments, of men of the best society, of men of nobility and virtue?" This was the question that for century on century the aristocratic Greek put to himself when confronted with every (to him incomprehensible) outrage and sacrilege with which one of his peers had polluted himself. "It must be that a *god* had infatuated him," he would say at last, nodding his head. This solution is *typical* of the Greeks, . . . accordingly the gods in those times subserved the functions of justifying man to a certain extent even in evil—in those days they took upon themselves not the punishment, but, what is *more noble*, the guilt.

24

I conclude with three queries, as you will see. "Is an ideal actually set up here, or is one pulled down?" I am perhaps asked. . . . But have ye sufficiently asked yourselves how dear a payment has the setting up of *every* ideal in the world exacted? To achieve that consummation how much truth must always be traduced and misunderstood, how many lies must be sanctified, how much conscience has got to be disturbed, how many pounds of "God" have got to be sacrificed everytime? To enable a sanctuary to be set up a *sanctuary has got to be destroyed*: that is a law—show me an instance where it has not been fulfilled! . . . We modern men, we inherit the immemorial tradition of vivisecting the conscience, and practising cruelty to our animal selves. That is the sphere of our most protracted training, perhaps of our artistic prowess, at any rate of our dilettantism and our perverted taste. Man has for too long regarded his natural proclivities with an "evil eye," so that eventually they have become in his system affiliated to a bad conscience. A converse endeavour would be intrinsically feasible—but who is strong enough to attempt it? Namely, to affiliate to the "bad conscience" all those *unnatural* proclivities, all those transcendental aspirations, contrary to sense, instinct, nature, and animalism—in short, all past and present ideals, which are all ideals opposed to life, and traducing the world. To whom is one to turn nowadays with *such* hopes and pretensions? It is just the *good* men that we should thus bring about our ears; and in addition, as stands to reason, the indolent, the hedgers, the vain, the hysterical, the tired. . . . What is more offensive or more thoroughly calculated to alienate, than giving any hint of the exalted severity with which we treat ourselves? And again how conciliatory, how full of love does all the world show itself towards us so soon as we do as all the world does, and "let ourselves go" like all the world. For such a consummation we need spirits of *different* calibre than seems really feasible in this age; spirits rendered potent through wars and victories, to whom conquest, adventure, danger, even pain, have become a need; for such a consummation we need habituation to sharp, rare air, to winter wanderings, to literal and metaphorical ice and mountains; we even need a kind of sublime malice, a supreme and most self-conscious insolence of knowledge, which is the appanage of great health; we need (to summarise the awful truth) just this *great health*!

Is this even feasible today? . . . But someday, in a stronger age than this rotting and introspective present, must he in sooth come to us, even the *redeemer* of great love and scorn, the creative spirit, rebounding by the impetus of his own force back again away from every transcendental plane and dimension, he whose solitude is misunderstanded of the people, as though it were a flight *from* reality; while actually it is only his diving, burrowing, and penetrating *into* reality, so that when he comes again to the light he can at once bring about by these means the *redemption* of this reality; its redemption from the curse which the old ideal has laid upon it. This man of the future, who in this wise will redeem us from the old ideal, as he will from that ideal's necessary corollary of great nausea, will to nothingness, and Nihilism; this tocsin of noon and of the great verdict, which renders the will again free, who gives back to the world its goal and to man his hope, this Antichrist and Antinihilist, this conqueror of God and of Nothingness—*he must one day come.*

25

But what am I talking of? Enough! Enough? At this juncture I have only one proper course, silence: otherwise I trespass on a domain open alone to one who is younger than I, one stronger, more "*future*" than I—open alone to *Zarathustra, Zarathustra the godless.*

WHAT IS THE MEANING OF ASCETIC IDEALS?

Careless, mocking, forceful—so does wisdom wish us:
she is a woman, and never loves anyone but a warrior.

—Thus Spake Zarathustra

1

WHAT IS THE MEANING OF ASCETIC IDEALS? IN ARTISTS, NOTHING, OR TOO much; in philosophers and scholars, a kind of "flair" and instinct for the conditions most favourable to advanced intellectualism; in women, at best an *additional* seductive fascination, a little *morbidezza* on a fine piece of flesh, the angelhood of a fat, pretty animal; in physiological failures and whiners (in the *majority* of mortals), an attempt to pose as "too good" for this world, a holy form of debauchery, their chief weapon in the battle with lingering pain and ennui; in priests, the actual priestly faith, their best engine of power, and also the supreme authority for power; in saints, finally a pretext for hibernation, their *novissima gloriae cupido,* their peace in nothingness ("God"), their form of madness.

But in the very fact that the ascetic ideal has meant so much to man, lies expressed the fundamental feature of man's will, his *horror vacui: he needs a goal*—and he will sooner will nothingness than not will at all. Am I not understood? Have I not been understood? "Certainly not, sir?" Well, let us begin at the beginning.

2

What is the meaning of ascetic ideals? Or, to take an individual case in regard to which I have often been consulted, what is the meaning, for example, of an artist like Richard Wagner paying homage to chastity in his old age? He had always done so, of course, in a certain sense, but it was not till quite the end, that he did so in an ascetic sense. What is the meaning of this "change of attitude," this radical revolution in his attitude—for that was what it was? Wagner veered thereby straight round into his own opposite. What is the meaning of an artist veering round into his own opposite? At this point (granted that we do not mind stopping a little over this question), we immediately call to mind the best, strongest, gayest, and boldest period, that there perhaps ever was in Wagner's life: that was the period when he was genuinely and deeply occupied with the idea of "Luther's Wedding." Who knows what chance is responsible for our now having the *Meistersingers* instead of this wedding music? And how much in the latter is perhaps just an echo of the former? But there is no doubt but that the theme would have dealt with the praise of chastity. And certainly it would also have dealt with the praise of sensuality, and even so, it would seem quite in order, and even so, it would have been equally Wagnerian. For there is no necessary antithesis between chastity and sensuality: every good marriage, every authentic heartfelt love transcends this antithesis. Wagner would, it seems to me, have done well to have brought this *pleasing* reality home once again to his Germans, by means of a bold and graceful "Luther Comedy," for there were and are among the Germans many revilers of sensuality; and perhaps Luther's greatest merit lies just in the fact of his having had the courage of his *sensuality* (it used to be called, prettily enough, "evangelistic freedom"). But even in those cases where that antithesis between chastity and sensuality does exist, there has fortunately been for sometime no necessity for it to be in anyway a tragic antithesis. This should, at any rate, be the case with all beings who are sound in mind and body, who are far from reckoning their delicate balance between "animal" and "angel," as being on the face of it one of the principles opposed to existence—the most subtle and brilliant spirits, such as Goethe, such as Hafiz, have even seen in this a *further* charm of life. Such "conflicts" actually allure one to life. On the other hand, it is only too clear that when once these ruined swine are reduced to worshipping chastity—and there are such swine—they only see and worship in it the antithesis to themselves, the antithesis to ruined swine. Oh what a tragic grunting and eagerness! You can just think of it—they worship that painful and superfluous contrast, which Richard Wagner in his latter days undoubtedly wished to set to music, and to place on the stage! "*For what purpose, forsooth?*" as we may reasonably ask. What did the swine matter to him; what do they matter to us?

246 → ON THE GENEALOGY OF MORALS

3

At this point it is impossible to beg the further question of what he really had to do with that manly (ah, so unmanly) country bumpkin, that poor devil and natural, *Parsifal*, whom he eventually made a Catholic by such fraudulent devices. What? Was this *Parsifal* really meant *seriously*? One might be tempted to suppose the contrary, even to wish it—that the Wagnerian *Parsifal* was meant joyously, like a concluding play of a trilogy or satyric drama, in which Wagner the tragedian wished to take farewell of us, of himself, above all of *tragedy*, and to do so in a manner that should be quite fitting and worthy, that is, with an excess of the most extreme and flippant parody of the tragic itself, of the ghastly earthly seriousness and earthly woe of old—a parody of that *most crude phase* in the unnaturalness of the ascetic ideal, that had at length been overcome. That, as I have said, would have been quite worthy of a great tragedian; who like every artist first attains the supreme pinnacle of his greatness when he can look *down into* himself and his art, when he can *laugh* at himself. Is Wagner's *Parsifal* his secret laugh of superiority over himself, the triumph of that supreme artistic freedom and artistic transcendency which he has at length attained. We might, I repeat, wish it were so, for what can *Parsifal*, *taken seriously*, amount to? Is it really necessary to see in it (according to an expression once used against me) the product of an insane hate of knowledge, mind, and flesh? A curse on flesh and spirit in one breath of hate? An apostasy and reversion to the morbid Christian and obscurantist ideals? And finally a self-negation and self-elimination on the part of an artist, who till then had devoted all the strength of his will to the contrary, namely, the *highest* artistic expression of soul and body. And not only of his art; of his life as well. Just remember with what enthusiasm Wagner followed in the footsteps of Feuerbach. Feuerbach's motto of "healthy sensuality" rang in the ears of Wagner during the thirties and forties of the century, as it did in the ears of many Germans (they dubbed themselves "*Young* Germans"), like the word of redemption. Did he eventually *change his mind* on the subject? For it seems at any rate that he eventually wished to *change his teaching* on that subject . . . and not only is that the case with the *Parsifal* trumpets on the stage: in the melancholy, cramped, and embarrassed lucubrations of his later years, there are a hundred places in which there are manifestations of a secret wish and will, a despondent, uncertain, unavowed will to preach actual retrogression, conversion, Christianity, mediaevalism, and to say to his disciples, "All is vanity! Seek salvation elsewhere!" Even the "blood of the Redeemer" is once invoked.

4

Let me speak out my mind in a case like this, which has many painful elements—and it is a typical case: it is certainly best to separate an artist from his work so completely that he cannot be taken as seriously as his work. He is after all merely the presupposition of his work—the womb, the soil, in certain cases the dung and manure, on which and out of which it grows—and consequently, in most cases, something that must be forgotten if the work itself is to be enjoyed. The insight into the *origin* of a work is a matter for psychologists and vivisectors, but never either in the present or the future for the aesthetes, the artists. The author and creator of *Parsifal* was as little spared the necessity of sinking and living himself into the terrible depths and foundations of mediaeval soul-contrasts, the necessity of a malignant abstraction from all intellectual elevation, severity, and discipline, the necessity of a kind of mental *perversity* (if the reader will pardon me such a word), as little as a pregnant woman is spared the horrors and marvels of pregnancy, which, as I have said, must be forgotten if the child is to be enjoyed. We must guard ourselves against the confusion, into which an artist himself would fall only too easily (to employ the English terminology) out of psychological "contiguity"; as though the artist himself actually *were* the object which he is able to represent, imagine, and express. In point of fact, the position is that even if he conceived he were such an object, he would certainly not represent, conceive, express it. Homer would not have created an Achilles, nor Goethe a Faust, if Homer had been an Achilles or if Goethe had been a Faust. A complete and perfect artist is to all eternity separated from the "real," from the actual; on the other hand, it will be appreciated that he can at times get tired to the point of despair of this eternal "unreality" and falseness of his innermost being—and that he then sometimes attempts to trespass on to the most forbidden ground, on reality, and attempts to have real *existence*. With what success? The success will be guessed—it is the *typical velleity* of the artist; the same velleity to which Wagner fell a victim in his old age, and for which he had to pay so dearly and so fatally (he lost thereby his most valuable friends). But after all, quite apart from this velleity, who would not wish emphatically for Wagner's own sake that he had taken farewell of us and of his art in a *different* manner, not with a Parsifal, but in more victorious, more self-confident, more Wagnerian style—a style less misleading, a style less ambiguous with regard to his whole meaning, less Schopenhauerian, less Nihilistic? . . .

5

What, then, is the meaning of ascetic ideals? In the case of an artist we
are getting to understand their meaning: *Nothing at all . . .* or so much
that it is as good as nothing at all. Indeed, what is the use of them? Our
artists have for a long time past not taken up a sufficiently independent
attitude, either in the world or against it, to warrant their valuations and
the changes in these valuations exciting interest. At all times they have
played the valet of some morality, philosophy, or religion, quite apart
from the fact that unfortunately they have often enough been the inordinately supple courtiers of their clients and patrons, and the inquisitive
toadies of the powers that are existing, or even of the new powers to come.
To put it at the lowest, they always need a rampart, a support, an already
constituted authority: artists never stand by themselves, standing alone is
opposed to their deepest instincts. So, for example, did *Richard Wagner*
take, "when the time had come," the philosopher Schopenhauer for his
covering man in front, for his rampart. Who would consider it even think-
able, that he would have had the courage for an ascetic ideal, without
the support afforded him by the philosophy of Schopenhauer, without the
authority of Schopenhauer, which *dominated* Europe in the seventies?
(This is without consideration of the question whether an artist without
the milk[1] of an orthodoxy would have been possible at all.) This brings us
to the more serious question: What is the meaning of a real *philosopher*
paying homage to the ascetic ideal, a really self-dependent intellect like
Schopenhauer, a man and knight with a glance of bronze, who has the
courage to be himself, who knows how to stand alone without first waiting
for men who cover him in front, and the nods of his superiors? Let us now
consider at once the remarkable attitude of Schopenhauer towards *art*, an
attitude which has even a fascination for certain types. For that is obviously
the reason why Richard Wagner *all at once* went over to Schopenhauer
(persuaded thereto, as one knows, by a poet, Herwegh), went over so
completely that there ensued the cleavage of a complete theoretic contradiction between his earlier and his later aesthetic faiths—the earlier, for
example, being expressed in *Opera and Drama*, the later in the writings
which he published from 1870 onwards. In particular, Wagner from that
time onwards (and this is the volte-face which alienates us the most) had
no scruples about changing his judgement concerning the value and position of music itself. What did he care if up to that time he had made of
music a means, a medium, a "woman," that in order to thrive needed an
end, a man—that is, the drama? He suddenly realised that *more* could be

effected by the novelty of the Schopenhauerian theory in *majorem musicae gloriam*—that is to say, by means of the *sovereignty* of music, as Schopenhauer understood it; music abstracted from and opposed to all the other arts, music as the independent art-in-itself, *not* like the other arts, affording reflexions of the phenomenal world, but rather the language of the will itself, speaking straight out of the "abyss" as its most personal, original, and direct manifestation. This extraordinary rise in the value of music (a rise which seemed to grow out of the Schopenhauerian philosophy) was at once accompanied by an unprecedented rise in the estimation in which the *musician* himself was held: he became now an oracle, a priest, nay, more than a priest, a kind of mouthpiece for the "intrinsic essence of things," a telephone from the other world—from henceforward he talked not only music, did this ventriloquist of God, he talked metaphysic; what wonder that one day he eventually talked *ascetic ideals.*

6

Schopenhauer has made use of the Kantian treatment of the aesthetic problem—though he certainly did not regard it with the Kantian eyes. Kant thought that he showed honour to art when he favoured and placed in the foreground those of the predicates of the beautiful, which constitute the honour of knowledge: impersonality and universality. This is not the place to discuss whether this was not a complete mistake; all that I wish to emphasise is that Kant, just like other philosophers, instead of envisaging the aesthetic problem from the standpoint of the experiences of the artist (the creator), has only considered art and beauty from the standpoint of the spectator, and has thereby imperceptibly imported the spectator himself into the idea of the "beautiful!" But if only the philosophers of the beautiful had sufficient knowledge of this "spectator"! Knowledge of him as a great fact of personality, as a great experience, as a wealth of strong and most individual events, desires, surprises, and raptures in the sphere of beauty! But, as I feared, the contrary was always the case. And so we get from our philosophers, from the very beginning, definitions on which the lack of a subtler personal experience squats like a fat worm of crass error, as it does on Kant's famous definition of the beautiful. "That is beautiful," says Kant, "which pleases without interesting." Without interesting! Compare this definition with this other one, made by a real "spectator" and "artist"—by Stendhal, who once called the beautiful *une promesse de bonheur.* Here, at any rate, the one point which Kant makes prominent in the aesthetic position is repudiated and eliminated—*le désinteressement.* Who is right, Kant or Stendhal? When, forsooth, our aesthetes never get tired of throwing into the scales in Kant's favour the fact that under the magic of beauty men can look at even naked female statues "without interest," we can certainly laugh a little at their expense: in regard to this ticklish point the experiences of *artists* are more "interesting," and at any rate Pygmalion was not necessarily an "unaesthetic man." Let us think all the better of the innocence of our aesthetes, reflected as it is in such arguments; let us, for instance, count to Kant's honour the country-parson naïveté of his doctrine concerning the peculiar character of the sense of touch! And here we come back to Schopenhauer, who stood in much closer neighbourhood to the arts than did Kant, and yet never escaped outside the pale of the Kantian definition; how was that? The circumstance is marvellous enough: he interprets the expression, "without interest," in the most personal fashion, out of an experience which must in his case have been part and parcel of his regular routine. On few subjects does Schopenhauer speak with such certainty as on the working of aesthetic contemplation: he says of it that it simply counteracts sexual interest, like lupulin and camphor; he never gets tired of glorifying this escape from the "Life-will" as the great advantage and utility of the aesthetic state. In fact, one is tempted to ask if his fundamental conception of Will and Idea, the thought that there can only exist freedom from the "will" by means of "idea," did not originate in a generalisation from this sexual experience. (In all questions concerning the Schopenhauerian philosophy, one should, by the bye, never lose sight of the consideration that it is the conception of a youth of twenty-six, so that it participates not only in what is peculiar to Schopenhauer's life, but in what is peculiar to that special period of his life.) Let us listen, for instance, to one of the most expressive among the countless passages which he has written in honour of the aesthetic state (*World as Will and Idea*, i. 231); let us listen to the tone, the suffering, the happiness, the gratitude, with which such words are uttered: "This is the painless state which Epicurus praised as the highest good and as the state of the gods; we are during that moment freed from the vile pressure of the will, we celebrate the Sabbath of the will's hard labour, the wheel of Ixion stands still." What vehemence of language! What images of anguish and protracted revulsion! How almost pathological is that temporal antithesis between "that moment" and everything else, the "wheel of Ixion," "the hard labour of the will," "the vile pressure of the will." But granted that Schopenhauer was a hundred times right for himself personally, how does that help our insight into the nature of the beautiful? Schopenhauer has described one effect of the beautiful—the calming of the will—but is this effect really normal? As has been mentioned, Stendhal, an equally sensual but more happily constituted nature than Schopenhauer, gives prominence to another effect of the "beautiful." "The beautiful *promises* happiness." To him it is just the *excitement* of the will (the "interest") by the beauty that seems the essential fact. And does not Schopenhauer ultimately lay himself open to the objection, that he is quite wrong in regarding himself as a Kantian on this point, that he has absolutely failed to understand in a Kantian sense the Kantian definition of the beautiful—that the beautiful pleased him as well by means of an interest, by means, in fact, of the strongest and most personal interest of all, that of the victim of torture who escapes from his torture? And to come back again to our first question, "What is the *meaning* of a philosopher paying homage to ascetic ideals?" We get now, at any rate, a first hint; he wishes to *escape from a torture.*

7

Let us beware of making dismal faces at the word "torture"—there is certainly in this case enough to deduct, enough to discount—there is even something to laugh at. For we must certainly not underestimate the fact that Schopenhauer, who in practise treated sexuality as a personal enemy (including its tool, woman, that "*instrumentum diaboli*"), needed enemies to keep him in a good humour; that he loved grim, bitter, blackish-green words; that he raged for the sake of raging, out of passion; that he would have grown ill, would have become a *pessimist* (for he was not a pessimist, however much he wished to be), without his enemies, without Hegel, woman, sensuality, and the whole "will for existence" "keeping on." Without them Schopenhauer would not have "kept on," that is a safe wager; he would have run away: but his enemies held him fast, his enemies always enticed him back again to existence, his wrath was just as theirs' was to the ancient Cynics, his balm, his recreation, his recompense, his *remedium* against disgust, his *happiness.* So much with regard to what is most personal in the case of Schopenhauer; on the other hand, there is still much which is typical in him—and only now we come back to our problem. It is an accepted and indisputable fact, so long as there are philosophers in the world, and wherever philosophers have existed (from India to England, to take the opposite poles of philosophic ability), that there exists a real irritation and rancour on the part of philosophers towards sensuality. Schopenhauer is merely the most eloquent, and if one has the ear for it, also the most fascinating and enchanting outburst. There similarly exists a real philosophic bias and affection for the whole ascetic ideal; there should be no illusions on this score. Both these feelings, as has been said, belong to the type; if a philosopher lacks both of them, then he is—you may be certain of it—never anything but a "pseudo." What does this *mean?* For this state of affairs must first be interpreted: in itself it stands there stupid to all eternity, like any "Thing-in-itself." Every animal, including *la bête philosophe*, strives instinctively after an *optimum* of favourable conditions, under which he can let his whole strength have play, and achieves his maximum consciousness of power; with equal instinctiveness, and with a fine perceptive flair which is superior to any reason, every animal shudders mortally at every kind of disturbance and hindrance which obstructs or could obstruct his way to that *optimum* (it is not his way to happiness of which I am talking, but his way to power, to action, the most powerful action, and in point of fact in many cases his way to unhappiness). Similarly, the philosopher shudders mortally at *marriage*, together with all that could persuade him to it—marriage as a fatal hindrance on the way to the *optimum*. Up to the present what great philosophers have been married? Heracleitus, Plato, Descartes, Spinoza, Leibnitz, Kant, Schopenhauer— they were not married, and, further, one cannot *imagine* them as married. A married philosopher belongs to *comedy*, that is my rule; as for that exception of a Socrates—the malicious Socrates married himself, it seems, *ironice*, just to prove this *very* rule. Every philosopher would say, as Buddha said, when the birth of a son was announced to him: "Râhoula has been born to me, a fetter has been forged for me" (Râhoula means here "a little demon"); there must come an hour of reflexion to every "free spirit" (granted that he has had previously an hour of thoughtlessness), just as one came once to the same Buddha: "Narrowly cramped," he reflected, "is life in the house; it is a place of uncleanness; freedom is found in leaving the house." Because he thought like this, he left the house. So many bridges to *independence* are shown in the ascetic ideal, that the philosopher cannot refrain from exultation and clapping of hands when he hears the history of all those resolute ones, who on one day uttered a nay to all servitude and went into some *desert*; even granting that they were only strong asses, and the absolute opposite of strong minds. What, then, does the ascetic ideal mean in a philosopher? This is my answer—it will have been guessed long ago: when he sees this ideal the philosopher smiles because he sees therein an *optimum* of the conditions of the highest and boldest intellectuality; he does not thereby deny "existence," he rather affirms thereby *his* existence and *only* his existence, and this perhaps to the point of not being far off the blasphemous wish, *pereat mundus, fiat philosophia, fiat philosophus, fiam!* . . .

8

These philosophers, you see, are by no means uncorrupted witnesses and judges of the *value* of the ascetic ideal. They think *of themselves*—what is the "saint" to them? They think of that which to them personally is most indispensable; of freedom from compulsion, disturbance, noise; freedom from business, duties, cares; of a clear head; of the dance, spring, and flight of thoughts; of good air—rare, clear, free, dry, as is the air on the heights, in which every animal creature becomes more intellectual and gains wings; they think of peace in every cellar; all the hounds neatly chained; no baying of enmity and uncouth rancour; no remorse of wounded ambition; quiet and submissive internal organs, busy as mills, but unnoticed; the heart alien, transcendent, future, posthumous—to summarise, they mean by the ascetic ideal the joyous asceticism of a deified and newly fledged animal, sweeping over life rather than resting. We know what are the three great catchwords of the ascetic ideal: poverty, humility, chastity; and now just look closely at the life of all the great fruitful inventive spirits—you will always find again and again these three qualities up to a certain extent. *Not* for a minute, as is self-evident, as though, perchance, they were part of their virtues—what has this type of man to do with virtues? But as the most essential and natural conditions of their *best* existence, their *finest* fruitfulness. In this connexion it is quite possible that their predominant intellectualism had first to curb an unruly and irritable pride, or an insolent sensualism, or that it had all its work cut out to maintain its wish for the "desert" against perhaps an inclination to luxury and dilettantism, or similarly against an extravagant liberality of heart and hand. But their intellect did effect all this, simply because it was the *dominant* instinct, which carried through its orders in the case of all the other instincts. It effects it still; if it ceased to do so, it would simply not be dominant. But there is not one iota of "virtue" in all this. Further, the *desert*, of which I just spoke, in which the strong, independent, and well-equipped spirits retreat into their hermitage—oh, how different is it from the cultured classes' dream of a desert! In certain cases, in fact, the cultured classes themselves are the desert. And it is certain that all the actors of the intellect would not endure this desert for a minute. It is nothing like romantic and Syrian enough for them, nothing like enough

of a stage desert! Here as well there are plenty of asses, but at this point
the resemblance ceases. But a desert nowadays is something like this—
perhaps a deliberate obscurity; a getting-out-of the way of one's self; a fear
of noise, admiration, papers, influence; a little office, a daily task, something that hides rather than brings to light; sometimes associating with
harmless, cheerful beasts and fowls, the sight of which refreshes; a mountain for company, but not a dead one, one with *eyes* (that is, with lakes); in
certain cases even a room in a crowded hotel where one can reckon on
not being recognised, and on being able to talk with impunity to everyone:
here is the desert—oh, it is lonely enough, believe me! I grant that when
Heracleitus retreated to the courts and cloisters of the colossal temple of
Artemis, that "wilderness" was worthier; why do we *lack* such temples?
(perchance we do not lack them: I just think of my splendid study in the
Piazza di San Marco, in spring, of course, and in the morning, between ten
and twelve). But that which Heracleitus shunned is still just what we too
avoid nowadays: the noise and democratic babble of the Ephesians,
their politics, their news from the "empire" (I mean, of course, Persia), their
market-trade in "the things of today"—for there is one thing from which
we philosophers especially need a rest—from the things of "today." We
honour the silent, the cold, the noble, the far, the past, everything, in fact,
at the sight of which the soul is not bound to brace itself up and defend
itself—something with which one can speak without *speaking aloud*. Just
listen now to the tone a spirit has when it speaks; every spirit has its own
tone and loves its own tone. That thing yonder, for instance, is bound to be
an agitator, that is, a hollow head, a hollow mug: whatever may go into
him, everything comes back from him dull and thick, heavy with the echo
of the great void. That spirit yonder nearly always speaks hoarse: has he,
perchance, *thought* himself hoarse? It may be so—ask the physiologists—
but he who thinks in *words*, thinks as a speaker and not as a thinker (it
shows that he does not think of objects or think objectively, but only of his
relations with objects—that, in point of fact, he only thinks of himself and
his audience). This third one speaks aggressively, he comes too near our
body, his breath blows on us—we shut our mouth involuntarily, although
he speaks to us through a book: the tone of his style supplies the reason
—he has no time, he has small faith in himself, he finds expression now
or never. But a spirit who is sure of himself speaks softly; he seeks
secrecy, he lets himself be awaited. A philosopher is recognised by the fact
that he shuns three brilliant and noisy things—fame, princes, and women:
which is not to say that they do not come to him. He shuns every glaring

light: therefore he shuns his time and its "daylight." Therein he is as a shadow; the deeper sinks the sun, the greater grows the shadow. As for his humility, he endures, as he endures darkness, a certain dependence and obscurity: further, he is afraid of the shock of lightning, he shudders at the insecurity of a tree which is too isolated and too exposed, on which every storm vents its temper, every temper its storm. His "maternal" instinct, his secret love for that which grows in him, guides him into states where he is relieved from the necessity of taking care of *himself*, in the same way in which the "*mother*" instinct in woman has thoroughly maintained up to the present woman's dependent position. After all, they demand little enough, do these philosophers, their favourite motto is, "He who possesses is possessed." All this is *not*, as I must say again and again, to be attributed to a virtue, to a meritorious wish for moderation and simplicity; but because their supreme lord so demands of them, demands wisely and inexorably; their lord who is eager only for one thing, for which alone he musters, and for which alone he hoards everything—time, strength, love, interest. This kind of man likes not to be disturbed by enmity, he likes not to be disturbed by friendship, it is a type which forgets or despises easily. It strikes him as bad form to play the martyr, "to *suffer* for truth"—he leaves all that to the ambitious and to the stage-heroes of the intellect, and to all those, in fact, who have time enough for such luxuries (they themselves, the philosophers, have something *to do* for truth). They make a sparing use of big words; they are said to be adverse to the word "truth" itself: it has a "high falutin'" ring. Finally, as far as the chastity of philosophers is concerned, the fruitfulness of this type of mind is manifestly in another sphere than that of children; perchance in some other sphere, too, they have the survival of their name, their little immortality (philosophers in ancient India would express themselves with still greater boldness: "Of what use is posterity to him whose soul is the world?"). In this attitude there is not a trace of chastity, by reason of any ascetic scruple or hatred of the flesh, anymore than it is chastity for an athlete or a jockey to abstain from women; it is rather the will of the dominant instinct, at any rate, during the period of their advanced philosophic pregnancy. Every artist knows the harm done by sexual intercourse on occasions of great mental strain and preparation; as far as the strongest artists and those with the surest instincts are concerned, this is not necessarily a case of experience—hard experience—but it is simply their "maternal" instinct which, in order to benefit the growing work, disposes recklessly (beyond all its normal stocks and supplies) of the *vigour* of its *animal* life; the greater power then *absorbs* the lesser. Let us now apply this interpretation to gauge correctly the case of Schopenhauer, which we have already mentioned: in his case, the sight of the beautiful acted manifestly like a resolving irritant on the chief power of his nature (the power of contemplation and of intense penetration); so that this strength exploded and became suddenly master of his consciousness. But this by no means excludes the possibility of that particular sweetness and fullness, which is peculiar to the aesthetic state, springing directly from the ingredient of sensuality (just as that "idealism" which is peculiar to girls at puberty originates in the same source)—it may be, consequently, that sensuality is not removed by the approach of the aesthetic state, as Schopenhauer believed, but merely becomes transfigured, and ceases to enter into the consciousness as sexual excitement. (I shall return once again to this point in connexion with the more delicate problems of the physiology of the aesthetic, a subject which up to the present has been singularly untouched and unelucidated.)

9

A certain asceticism, a grimly gay whole-hearted renunciation, is, as we have seen, one of the most favourable conditions for the highest intellectualism, and, consequently, for the most natural corollaries of such intellectualism: we shall therefore be proof against any surprise at the philosophers in particular always treating the ascetic ideal with a certain amount of predilection. A serious historical investigation shows the bond between the ascetic ideal and philosophy to be still much tighter and still much stronger. It may be said that it was only in the *leading strings* of this ideal that philosophy really learnt to make its first steps and baby paces— alas how clumsily, alas how crossly, alas how ready to tumble down and lie on its stomach was this shy little darling of a brat with its bandy legs! The early history of philosophy is like that of all good things; for a long time they had not the courage to be themselves, they kept always looking round to see if no one would come to their help; further, they were afraid of all who looked at them. Just enumerate in order the particular tendencies and virtues of the philosopher—his tendency to doubt, his tendency to deny, his tendency to wait (to be "ephectic"), his tendency to analyse, search, explore, dare, his tendency to compare and to equalise, his will to be neutral and objective, his will for everything which is *"sine ira et studio"*: has it yet been realised that for quite a lengthy period these tendencies went counter to the first claims of morality and conscience? (To say nothing at all of *Reason*, which even Luther chose to call *Frau Klüglin*,[2] *the sly whore.*) Has it been yet appreciated that a philosopher, in the event of his *arriving* at self-consciousness, must needs feel himself an incarnate "*nitimur in vetitum*"—and consequently *guard* himself against "his own sensations," against self-consciousness? It is, I repeat, just the same with all good things, on which we now pride ourselves; even judged by the standard of the ancient Greeks, our whole modern life, insofar as it is not weakness, but power and the consciousness of power, appears pure "Hybris" and godlessness: for the things which are the very reverse of those which we honour today, have had for a long time conscience on their side, and God as their guardian. "Hybris" is our whole attitude to nature nowadays, our violation of nature with the help of machinery, and all the unscrupulous ingenuity of our scientists and engineers. "Hybris" is our attitude to God, that is, to some alleged teleological and ethical spider behind the meshes of the great trap of the causal web. Like Charles the Bold in his war with Louis the Eleventh, we may say, "*je combats l'universelle araignée*"; "Hybris" is our attitude to ourselves—for we experiment with ourselves in a way that we would not allow with any animal, and with pleasure and curiosity open our soul in our living body: what matters now to us the "salvation" of the soul? We heal ourselves afterwards: being ill is instructive, we doubt it not, even more instructive than being well—inoculators of disease seem to us today even more necessary than any medicine men and "saviours." There is no doubt we do violence to ourselves nowadays, we crackers of the soul's kernel, we incarnate riddles, who are ever asking riddles, as though life were naught else than the cracking of a nut; and even thereby must we necessarily become day by day more and more worthy to be asked questions and *worthy* to ask them, even thereby do we perchance also become worthier to—live?

. . . All good things were once bad things; from every original sin has grown an original virtue. Marriage, for example, seemed for a long time a sin against the rights of the community; a man formerly paid a fine for the insolence of claiming one woman to himself (to this phase belongs, for instance, the *jus primae noctis*, today still in Cambodia the privilege of the priest, that guardian of the "good old customs").

The soft, benevolent, yielding, sympathetic feelings—eventually valued so highly that they almost became "intrinsic values," were for a very long time actually despised by their possessors: gentleness was then a subject for shame, just as hardness is now (compare *Beyond Good and Evil*, Aph. 260). The submission to *law*: oh, with what qualms of conscience was it that the noble races throughout the world renounced the *vendetta* and gave the law power over themselves! Law was long a *vetitum*, a blasphemy, an innovation; it was introduced with force, *like* a force, to which men only submitted with a sense of personal shame. Every tiny step forward in the world was formerly made at the cost of mental and physical torture. Nowadays the whole of this point of view—"that not only stepping forward, nay, stepping at all, movement, change, all needed their countless martyrs," rings in our ears quite strangely. I have put it forward in the *Dawn of Day*, Aph. 18. "Nothing is purchased more dearly," says the same book a little later,

> . . . than the modicum of human reason and freedom which is now our pride. But that pride is the reason why it is now almost impossible for us to feel in sympathy with those immense periods of the "Morality of Custom," which lie at the beginning of the "world's history," constituting as they do the real decisive historical principle which has fixed the character of humanity; those periods, I repeat, when throughout the world suffering passed for virtue, cruelty for virtue, deceit for virtue, revenge for virtue, repudiation of the reason for virtue; and when, conversely, well-being passed current for danger, the desire for knowledge for danger, pity for danger, peace for danger, being pitied for shame, work for shame, madness for divinity, and *change* for immorality and incarnate corruption!

10

There is in the same book, Aph. 12, an explanation of the *burden* of unpopularity under which the earliest race of contemplative men had to live—despised almost as widely as they were first feared! Contemplation first appeared on earth in a disguised shape, in an ambiguous form, with an evil heart and often with an uneasy head: there is no doubt about it. The inactive, brooding, unwarlike element in the instincts of contemplative men long invested them with a cloud of suspicion: the only way to combat this was to excite a definite *fear*. And the old Brahmans, for example, knew to a nicety how to do this! The oldest philosophers were well versed in giving to their very existence and appearance, meaning, firmness, background, by reason whereof men learnt to *fear* them; considered more precisely, they did this from an even more fundamental need, the need of inspiring in themselves fear and self-reverence. For they found even in their own souls all the valuations turned *against* themselves; they had to fight down every kind of suspicion and antagonism against "the philosophic element in themselves." Being men of a terrible age, they did this with terrible means: cruelty to themselves, ingenious self-mortification —this was the chief method of these ambitious hermits and intellectual revolutionaries, who were obliged to force down the gods and the traditions of their own soul, so as to enable themselves to *believe* in their own revolution. I remember the famous story of the King Vicvamitra, who, as the result of a thousand years of self-martyrdom, reached such a consciousness of power and such a confidence in himself that he undertook to build a *new heaven*: the sinister symbol of the oldest and newest history of philosophy in the whole world. Everyone who has ever built anywhere a *"new heaven"* first found the power thereto in his *own hell*. . . . Let us compress the facts into a short formula. The philosophic spirit had, in order to be *possible* to any extent at all, to masquerade and disguise itself as one of the *previously fixed* types of the contemplative man, to disguise itself as priest, wizard, soothsayer, as a religious man generally: the *ascetic ideal* has for a long time served the philosopher as a superficial form, as a condition which enabled him to exist. . . . To be able to be a philosopher he had to exemplify the ideal; to exemplify it, he was bound to *believe* in it. The peculiarly etherealised abstraction of philosophers, with their negation of the world, their enmity to life, their disbelief in the senses, which has been maintained up to the most recent time, and has almost thereby come to be accepted as the ideal *philosophic attitude*—this abstraction is the result of those enforced conditions under which philosophy came into existence, and continued to exist; inasmuch as for quite a very long time philosophy would have been *absolutely impossible* in the world without an ascetic cloak and dress, without an ascetic self-misunderstanding. Expressed plainly and palpably, the *ascetic priest* has taken the repulsive and sinister form of the caterpillar, beneath which and behind which alone philosophy could live and slink about. . . .

Has all that really changed? Has that flamboyant and dangerous winged creature, that "spirit" which that caterpillar concealed within itself, has it, I say, thanks to a sunnier, warmer, lighter world, really and finally flung off its hood and escaped into the light? Can we today point to enough pride, enough daring, enough courage, enough self-confidence, enough mental will, enough will for responsibility, enough freedom of the will, to enable the philosopher to *be* now in the world really—*possible?*

11

And now, after we have caught sight of the *ascetic priest*, let us tackle our problem. What is the meaning of the ascetic ideal? It now first becomes serious—vitally serious. We are now confronted with the *real representatives of the serious.* "What is the meaning of all seriousness?" This even more radical question is perchance already on the tip of our tongue: a question, fairly, for physiologists, but which we for the time being skip. In that ideal the ascetic priest finds not only his faith, but also his will, his power, his interest. His *right* to existence stands and falls with that ideal. What wonder that we here run up against a terrible opponent (on the supposition, of course, that we are the opponents of that ideal), an opponent fighting for his life against those who repudiate that ideal! . . . On the other hand, it is from the outset improbable that such a biased attitude towards our problem will do him any particular good; the ascetic priest himself will scarcely prove the happiest champion of his own ideal (on the same principle on which a woman usually fails when she wishes to champion "woman")—let alone proving the most objective critic and judge of the controversy now raised. We shall therefore—so much is already obvious —rather have actually to help him to defend himself properly against ourselves, than we shall have to fear being too well beaten by him. The idea, which is the subject of this dispute, is the *value* of our life from the standpoint of the ascetic priests: this life, then (together with the whole of which it is a part, "Nature," "the world," the whole sphere of becoming and passing away), is placed by them in relation to an existence of quite another character, which it excludes and to which it is opposed, unless it *deny* its own self: in this case, the case of an ascetic life, life is taken as a bridge to another existence. The ascetic treats life as a maze, in which one must walk backwards till one comes to the place where it starts; or he treats it as an error which one may, nay *must*, refute by action: for he *demands* that he should be followed; he enforces, where he can, *his* valuation of existence. What does this mean? Such a monstrous valuation is not an exceptional case, or a curiosity recorded in human history: it is one of the most general and persistent facts that there are. The reading from the vantage of a distant star of the capital letters of our earthly life, would perchance lead to the conclusion that the earth was the especially *ascetic planet,* a den of discontented, arrogant, and repulsive creatures, who never got rid of a deep disgust of themselves, of the world, of all life, and did themselves as much hurt as possible out of pleasure in hurting— presumably their one and only pleasure. Let us consider how regularly, how universally, how practically at every single period the ascetic priest puts in his appearance: he belongs to no particular race; he thrives everywhere; he grows out of all classes. Not that he perhaps bred this valuation by heredity and propagated it—the contrary is the case. It must be a necessity of the first order which makes this species, *hostile*, as it is, to *life*, always grow again and always thrive again. *Life* itself must certainly *have an interest* in the continuance of such a type of self-contradiction. For an ascetic life is a self-contradiction: here rules resentment without parallel, the resentment of an insatiate instinct and ambition, that would be master, not over some element in life, but over life itself, over life's deepest, strongest, innermost conditions; here is an attempt made to utilise power to dam the sources of power; here does the green eye of jealousy turn even against physiological well-being, especially against the expression of such well-being, beauty, joy; while a sense of pleasure is experienced and *sought* in abortion, in decay, in pain, in misfortune, in ugliness, in voluntary punishment, in the exercising, flagellation, and sacrifice of the self. All this is in the highest degree paradoxical: we are here confronted with a rift that *wills* itself to be a rift, which *enjoys* itself in this very *suffering*, and even becomes more and more certain of itself, more and more triumphant, in proportion as its own presupposition, physiological vitality, *decreases*. "The triumph just in the supreme agony": under this extravagant emblem did the ascetic ideal fight from of old; in this mystery of seduction, in this picture of rapture and torture, it recognised its brightest light, its salvation, its final victory. *Crux, nux, lux*—it has all these three in one.

12

Granted that such an incarnate will for contradiction and unnaturalness is induced to *philosophise*; on what will it vent its pet caprice? On that which has been felt with the greatest certainty to be true, to be real; it will look for *error* in those very places where the life instinct fixes truth with the greatest positiveness. It will, for instance, after the example of the ascetics of the Vedanta Philosophy, reduce matter to an illusion, and similarly treat pain, multiplicity, the whole logical contrast of "*Subject*" and "*Object*"—errors, nothing but errors! To renounce the belief in one's own ego, to deny to one's self one's own "reality"—what a triumph! And here already we have a much higher kind of triumph, which is not merely a triumph over the senses, over the palpable, but an infliction of violence and cruelty on *reason*; and this ecstasy culminates in the ascetic self-contempt, the ascetic scorn of one's own reason making this decree: *there is* a domain of truth and of life, but reason is specially *excluded* therefrom. . . . By the bye, even in the Kantian idea of "the intellegible character of things" there remains a trace of that schism, so dear to the heart of the ascetic, that schism which likes to turn reason against reason; in fact, "intelligible character" means in Kant a kind of quality in things of which the intellect comprehends this much, that for it, the intellect, it is *absolutely incomprehensible.* After all, let us, in our character of knowers, not be ungrateful towards such determined reversals of the ordinary perspectives and values, with which the mind had for too long raged against itself with an apparently futile sacrilege! In the same way the very seeing of another vista, the very *wishing* to see another vista, is no little training and preparation of the intellect for its eternal "*Objectivity*"—objectivity being understood not as "contemplation without interest" (for that is inconceivable and nonsensical), but as the ability to have the pros and cons in *one's power* and to switch them on and off, so as to get to know how to utilise, for the advancement of knowledge, the *difference* in the perspective and in the emotional interpretations. But let us, forsooth, my philosophic colleagues, henceforward guard ourselves more carefully against this mythology of dangerous ancient ideas, which has set up a "pure, will-less, painless, timeless subject of knowledge"; let us guard ourselves from the tentacles of such contradictory ideas as "pure reason," "absolute spirituality," "knowledge-in-itself": in these theories an eye that cannot be thought of is required to think, an eye which *ex hypothesi* has no direction at all, an eye in which the active and interpreting functions are cramped, are absent; those functions, I say, by means of which "abstract" seeing first became seeing something; in these theories consequently the absurd and the nonsensical is always demanded of the eye. There is only a seeing from a perspective, only a "knowing" from a perspective, and the *more* emotions we express over a thing, the *more* eyes, different eyes, we train on the same thing, the more complete will be our "idea" of that thing, our "objectivity." But the elimination of the will altogether, the switching off of the emotions all and sundry, granted that we could do so, what! Would not that be called intellectual *castration?*

13

But let us turn back. Such a self-contradiction, as apparently manifests itself among the ascetics, "Life turned against Life," is—this much is absolutely obvious—from the physiological and not now from the psychological standpoint, simply nonsense. It can only be an *apparent* contradiction; it must be a kind of provisional expression, an explanation, a formula, an adjustment, a psychological misunderstanding of something, whose real nature could not be understood for a long time, and whose *real essence* could not be described; a mere word jammed into an old *gap* of human knowledge. To put briefly the facts against its being real: *the ascetic ideal springs from the prophylactic and self-preservative instincts which mark a decadent life*, which seeks by every means in its power to maintain its position and fight for its existence; it points to a partial physiological depression and exhaustion, against which the most profound and intact life-instincts fight ceaselessly with new weapons and discoveries. The ascetic ideal is such a weapon: its position is consequently exactly the reverse of that which the worshippers of the ideal imagine—life struggles in it and through it with death and *against* death; the ascetic ideal is a dodge for the *preservation* of life. An important fact is brought out in the extent to which, as history teaches, this ideal could rule and exercise power over man, especially in all those places where the civilisation and taming of man was completed: that fact is, the diseased state of man up to the present, at any rate, of the man who has been tamed, the physiological struggle of man with death (more precisely, with the disgust with life, with exhaustion, with the wish for the "end"). The ascetic priest is the incarnate wish for an existence of another kind, an existence on another plane—he is, in fact, the highest point of this wish, its official ecstasy and passion: but it is the very *power* of this wish which is the fetter that binds him here; it is just that which makes him into a tool that must labour to create more favourable conditions for earthly existence, for existence on the human plane—it is with this very *power* that he keeps the whole herd of failures, distortions, abortions, unfortunates, *sufferers from themselves* of every kind, fast to existence, while he as the herdsman goes instinctively on in front. You understand me already: this ascetic priest, this apparent enemy of life, this denier—he actually belongs to the really great *conservative* and *affirmative* forces of life. . . . What does it come from, this diseased state? For man is more diseased, more uncertain, more changeable, more unstable than any other animal, there is no doubt of it—he is *the* diseased animal: what does it spring from? Certainly he has also dared, innovated, braved more, challenged fate more than all the other animals put together; he, the great experimenter with himself, the unsatisfied, the insatiate, who struggles for the supreme mastery with beast, Nature, and gods, he, the as yet ever uncompelled, the ever future, who finds no more any rest from his own aggressive strength, goaded inexorably on by the spur of the future dug into the flesh of the present: how should not so brave and rich an animal also be the most endangered, the animal with the longest and deepest sickness among all sick animals? . . . Man is sick of it, oft enough there are whole epidemics of this satiety (as about 1348, the time of the Dance of Death): but even this very nausea, this tiredness, this disgust with himself, all this is discharged from him with such force that it is immediately made into a new fetter. His "nay," which he utters to life, brings to light as though by magic an abundance of graceful "yeas"; even when he *wounds* himself, this master of destruction, of self-destruction, it is subsequently the wound itself that forces him to live.

14

The more normal is this sickliness in man—and we cannot dispute this normality—the higher honour should be paid to the rare cases of psychical and physical powerfulness, the *windfalls* of humanity, and the more strictly should the sound be guarded from that worst of air, the air of the sickroom. Is that done? The sick are the greatest danger for the healthy; it is not from the strongest that harm comes to the strong, but from the weakest. Is that known? Broadly considered, it is not for a minute the fear of man, whose diminution should be wished for; for this fear forces the strong to be strong, to be at times terrible—it preserves in its integrity the sound type of man. What is to be feared, what does work with a fatality found in no other fate, is not the great fear of, but the great *nausea* with, man; and equally so the great pity for man. Supposing that both these things were one day to espouse each other, then inevitably the maximum of monstrousness would immediately come into the world— the "last will" of man, his will for nothingness, Nihilism. And, in sooth, the way is well paved thereto. He who not only has his nose to smell with, but also has eyes and ears, he sniffs almost wherever he goes today an air something like that of a mad-house, the air of a hospital—I am speaking, as stands to reason, of the cultured areas of mankind, of every kind of "Europe" that there is in fact in the world. The *sick* are the great danger of man, *not* the evil, *not* the "beasts of prey." They who are from the outset botched, oppressed, broken, those are they, the weakest are they, who most undermine the life beneath the feet of man, who instil the most dangerous venom and scepticism into our trust in life, in man, in ourselves. Where shall we escape from it, from that covert look (from which we carry away a deep sadness), from that averted look of him who is misborn from the beginning, that look which betrays what such a man says to himself—that look which is a groan? "Would that I were something else," so groans this look, "but there is no hope. I am what I am: how could I get away from myself? And, verily—*I am sick of myself!*" On such a soil of self-contempt, a veritable swamp soil, grows that weed, that poisonous growth, and all so tiny, so hidden, so ignoble, so sugary. Here teem the worms of revenge and vindictiveness; here the air reeks of things secret and unmentionable; here is ever spun the net of the most malignant conspiracy—the conspiracy of the sufferers against the sound and the victorious; here is the sight of the victorious *hated.* And what lying so as not to acknowledge this hate as hate! What a show of big words and attitudes, what an art of "righteous" calumniation! These abortions! What a noble eloquence gushes from their lips! What an amount of sugary, slimy, humble submission oozes in their eyes! What do they really want? At any rate to *represent* righteousness, love, wisdom, superiority, that is the ambition of these "lowest ones," these sick ones! And how clever does such an ambition make them! You cannot, in fact, but admire the counterfeiter dexterity with which the stamp of virtue, even the ring, the golden ring of virtue, is here imitated. They have taken a lease of virtue absolutely for themselves, have these weaklings and wretched invalids, there is no doubt of it; "We alone are the good, the righteous," so do they speak, "we alone are the *homines bonae voluntatis.*" They stalk about in our midst as living reproaches, as warnings to us—as though health, fitness, strength, pride, the sensation of power, were really vicious things in themselves, for which one would have someday to do penance, bitter penance. Oh, how they themselves are ready in their hearts to *exact* penance, how they thirst after being *hangmen!*

Among them is an abundance of revengeful ones disguised as judges, who ever mouth the word righteousness like a venomous spittle—with mouth, I say, always pursed, always ready to spit at everything, which does not wear a discontented look, but is of good cheer as it goes on its way. Among them, again, is that most loathsome species of the vain, the lying abortions, who make a point of representing "beautiful souls," and perchance of bringing to the market as "purity of heart" their distorted sensualism swathed in verses and other bandages; the species of "self-comforters" and masturbators of their own souls. The sick man's will to represent *some* form or other of superiority, his instinct for crooked paths, which lead to a tyranny over the healthy—where can it not be found, this will to power of the very weakest? The sick woman especially: no one surpasses her in refinements for ruling, oppressing, tyrannising. The sick woman, moreover, spares nothing living, nothing dead; she grubs up again the most buried things (the Bogos say, "Woman is a hyena"). Look into the background of every family, of everybody, of every community: everywhere the fight of the sick against the healthy—a silent fight for the most part with minute poisoned powders, with pin-pricks, with spiteful grimaces of patience, but also at times with that diseased pharisaism of *pure* pantomime, which plays for choice the role of "righteous indignation." Right into the hallowed chambers of knowledge can it make itself heard, can this hoarse yelping of sick hounds, this rabid lying and frenzy of such "noble" Pharisees (I remind readers, who have ears, once more of that Berlin apostle of revenge, Eugen Dühring, who makes the most disreputable and revolting use in all present-day Germany of moral refuse; Dühring, the paramount moral blusterer that there is today, even among his own kidney, the Anti-Semites). They are all men of resentment, are these physiological distortions and worm-riddled objects, a whole quivering kingdom of burrowing revenge, indefatigable and insatiable in its outbursts against the happy, and equally so in disguises for revenge, in pretexts for revenge: when will they really reach their final, fondest, most sublime triumph of revenge? At that time, doubtless, when they succeed in pushing their own misery, in fact, all misery, *into the consciousness* of the happy; so that the latter begin one day to be ashamed of their happiness, and perchance say to themselves when they meet, "It is a shame to be happy! *There is too much misery!*" . . . But there could not possibly be a greater and more fatal misunderstanding than that of the happy, the fit, the strong in body and soul, beginning in this way to doubt their right to happiness. Away with this "perverse world"! Away with this shameful soddenness of sentiment! Preventing the sick making the healthy sick—for that is what such a soddenness comes to—this ought to be our supreme object in the world—but for this it is above all essential that the healthy should remain *separated* from the sick, that they should even guard themselves from the look of the sick, that they should not even associate with the sick. Or may it, perchance, be their mission to be nurses or doctors? But they could not mistake and disown *their* mission more grossly—the higher *must* not degrade itself to be the tool of the lower, the pathos of distance must to all eternity keep their missions also separate. The right of the happy to existence, the right of bells with a full tone over the discordant cracked bells, is verily a thousand times greater: they alone are the *sureties* of the future, they alone are *bound* to man's future. What they can, what they must do, that can the sick never do, should never do! But if *they are to* be enabled to do what *only* they must do, how can they possibly be free to play the doctor, the comforter, the "Saviour" of the sick? . . . And therefore good air! Good air! And away, at any rate, from the neighbourhood of all the madhouses and hospitals of civilisation! And therefore good company, our own company, or solitude, if it must be so! But away, at any rate, from the evil fumes of internal corruption and the secret worm-eaten state of the sick! That, forsooth, my friends, we may defend ourselves, at any rate for still a time, against the two worst plagues that could have been reserved for us—against the *great nausea with man!* Against the *great pity for man!*

15

If you have understood in all their depths—and I demand that you should *grasp them profoundly* and understand them profoundly—the reasons for the impossibility of its being the business of the healthy to nurse the sick, to make the sick healthy, it follows that you have grasped this further necessity—the necessity of doctors and nurses *who themselves are sick.* And now we have and hold with both our hands the essence of the ascetic priest. The ascetic priest must be accepted by us as the predestined saviour, herdsman, and champion of the sick herd: thereby do we first understand his awful historic mission. The *lordship over sufferers* is his kingdom, to that points his instinct, in that he finds his own special art, his master-skill, his kind of happiness. He must himself be sick, he must be kith and kin to the sick and the abortions so as to understand them, so as to arrive at an understanding with them; but he must also be strong, even more master of himself than of others, impregnable, forsooth, in his will for power, so as to acquire the trust and the awe of the weak, so that he can be their hold, bulwark, prop, compulsion, overseer, tyrant, god. He has to protect them, protect his herds—*against* whom? Against the healthy, doubtless also against the envy towards the healthy. He must be the natural adversary and *scorner* of every rough, stormy, reinless, hard, violently-predatory health and power. The priest is the first form of the more delicate animal that scorns more easily than it hates. He will not be spared the waging of war with the beasts of prey, a war of guile (of "spirit") rather than of force, as is self-evident—he will in certain cases find it necessary to conjure up out of himself, or at any rate to represent practically a new type of the beast of prey—a new animal monstrosity in which the polar bear, the supple, cold, crouching panther, and, not least important, the fox, are joined together in a trinity as fascinating as it is fearsome. If necessity exacts it, then will he come on the scene with bearish seriousness, venerable, wise, cold, full of treacherous superiority, as the herald and mouthpiece of mysterious powers, sometimes going among even the other kind of beasts of prey, determined as he is to sow on their soil, wherever he can, suffering, discord, self-contradiction, and only too sure of his art, always to be lord of *sufferers* at all times. He brings with him, doubtless, salve and balsam; but before he can play the physician he must first wound; so, while he soothes the pain which the wound makes, *he at the same time poisons the wound.* Well versed is he in this above all things, is this wizard and wild beast tamer, in whose vicinity everything healthy must needs become ill, and everything ill must needs become tame. He protects, in sooth, his sick herd well enough, does this strange herdsman; he protects them also against themselves, against the sparks (even in the centre of the herd) of wickedness, knavery, malice, and all the other ills that the plaguey and the sick are heir to; he fights with cunning, hardness, and stealth against anarchy and against the ever imminent break-up inside the herd, where *resentment*, that most dangerous blasting-stuff and explosive, ever accumulates and accumulates. Getting rid of this blasting-stuff in such a way that it does not blow up the herd and the herdsman, that is his real feat, his supreme utility; if you wish to comprise in the shortest formula the value of the priestly life, it would be correct to say the priest is the *diverter of the course of resentment.* Every sufferer, in fact, searches instinctively for a cause of his suffering; to put it more exactly, a doer—to put it still more precisely, a sentient *responsible* doer—in brief, something living, on which, either actually or in *effigie*, he can on any pretext vent his emotions. For the venting of emotions is the sufferer's greatest attempt at alleviation, that is to say, *stupefaction*, his mechanically desired narcotic against pain of any kind. It is in this phenomenon alone that is found, according to my judgement, the real physiological cause of resentment, revenge, and their family is to be found—that is, in a demand for the *deadening of pain through emotion*: this cause is generally, but in my view very erroneously, looked for in the defensive parry of a bare protective principle of reaction, of a "reflex movement" in the case of any sudden hurt and danger, after the manner that a decapitated frog still moves in order to get away from a corrosive acid. But the difference is fundamental. In one case the object is to prevent being hurt anymore; in the other case the object is to *deaden* a racking, insidious, nearly unbearable pain by a more violent emotion of any kind whatsoever, and at any rate for the time being to drive it out of the consciousness—for this purpose an emotion is needed, as wild an emotion as possible, and to excite that emotion some excuse or other is needed. "It must be somebody's fault that I feel bad"—

this kind of reasoning is peculiar to all invalids, and is but the more pronounced, the more ignorant they remain of the real cause of their feeling bad, the physiological cause (the cause may lie in a disease of the *nervus sympathicus,* or in an excessive secretion of bile, or in a want of sulphate and phosphate of potash in the blood, or in pressure in the bowels which stops the circulation of the blood, or in degeneration of the ovaries, and so forth).

All sufferers have an awful resourcefulness and ingenuity in finding excuses for painful emotions; they even enjoy their jealousy, their broodings over base actions and apparent injuries, they burrow through the intestines of their past and present in their search for obscure mysteries, wherein they will be at liberty to wallow in a torturing suspicion and get drunk on the venom of their own malice—they tear open the oldest wounds, they make themselves bleed from the scars which have long been healed, they make evildoers out of friends, wife, child, and everything which is nearest to them. "I suffer: it must be somebody's fault"—so thinks every sick sheep. But his herdsman, the ascetic priest, says to him, "Quite so, my sheep, it must be the fault of someone; but thou thyself art that someone, it is all the fault of thyself alone—*it is the fault of thyself alone against thyself*": that is bold enough, false enough, but one thing is at least attained; thereby, as I have said, the course of resentment is—*diverted.*

16

You can see now what the remedial instinct of life has at least *tried* to effect, according to my conception, through the ascetic priest, and the purpose for which he had to employ a temporary tyranny of such paradoxical and anomalous ideas as "guilt," "sin," "sinfulness," "corruption," "damnation." What was done was to make the sick *harmless* up to a certain point, to destroy the incurable by means of themselves, to turn the milder cases severely on to themselves, to give their resentment a backward direction ("man needs but one thing"), and to *exploit* similarly the bad instincts of all sufferers with a view to self-discipline, self-surveillance, self-mastery. It is obvious that there can be no question at all in the case of a "medication" of this kind, a mere emotional medication, of any real *healing* of the sick in the physiological sense; it cannot even for a moment be asserted that in this connexion the instinct of life has taken healing as its goal and purpose. On the one hand, a kind of congestion and organisation of the sick (the word "Church" is the most popular name for it); on the other, a kind of provisional safeguarding of the comparatively healthy, the more perfect specimens, the cleavage of a *rift* between healthy and sick—for a long time that was all! And it was much! It was very much!

I am proceeding, as you see, in this essay, from an hypothesis which, as far as such readers as I want are concerned, does not require to be proved; the hypothesis that "sinfulness" in man is not an actual fact, but rather merely the interpretation of a fact, of a physiological discomfort—a discomfort seen through a moral religious perspective which is no longer binding upon us. The fact, therefore, that anyone feels "guilty," "sinful," is certainly not yet any proof that he is right in feeling so, anymore than anyone is healthy simply because he feels healthy. Remember the celebrated witch-ordeals: in those days the most acute and humane judges had no doubt but that in these cases they were confronted with guilt— the "witches" *themselves had no doubt on the point*—and yet the guilt was lacking. Let me elaborate this hypothesis: I do not for a minute accept the very "pain in the soul" as a real fact, but only as an explanation (a casual explanation) of facts that could not hitherto be precisely formulated; I regard it therefore as something as yet absolutely in the air and devoid of scientific cogency—just a nice fat word in the place of a lean note of interrogation. When anyone fails to get rid of his "pain in the soul," the cause is, speaking crudely, to be found *not* in his "soul" but more probably in his stomach (speaking crudely, I repeat, but by no means wishing thereby that you should listen to me or understand me in a crude spirit). A strong and well-constituted man digests his experiences (deeds and misdeeds all included) just as he digests his meats, even when he has some tough morsels to swallow. If he fails to "relieve himself" of an experience, this kind of indigestion is quite as much physiological as the other indigestion—and indeed, in more ways than one, simply one of the results of the other. You can adopt such a theory, and yet *entre nous* be nevertheless the strongest opponent of all materialism.

17

But is he really a *physician*, this ascetic priest? We already understand why we are scarcely allowed to call him a physician, however much he likes to feel a "saviour" and let himself be worshipped as a saviour.[3] It is only the actual suffering, the discomfort of the sufferer, which he combats, *not* its cause, not the actual state of sickness—this needs must constitute our most radical objection to priestly medication. But just once put yourself into that point of view, of which the priests have a monopoly, you will find it hard to exhaust your amazement, at what from that standpoint he has completely seen, sought, and found. The *mitigation* of suffering, every kind of "consoling"—all this manifests itself as his very genius: with what ingenuity has he interpreted his mission of consoler, with what aplomb and audacity has he chosen weapons necessary for the part. Christianity in particular should be dubbed a great treasure-chamber of ingenious consolations—such a store of refreshing, soothing, deadening drugs has it accumulated within itself; so many of the most dangerous and daring expedients has it hazarded; with such subtlety, refinement, Oriental refinement, has it divined what emotional stimulants can conquer, at any rate for a time, the deep depression, the leaden fatigue, the black melancholy of physiological cripples—for, speaking generally, all religions are mainly concerned with fighting a certain fatigue and heaviness that has infected everything. You can regard it as *prima facie* probable that in certain places in the world there was almost bound to prevail from time to time among large masses of the population a *sense of physiological depression*, which, however, owing to their lack of physiological knowledge, did not appear to their consciousness as such, so that consequently its "cause" and its *cure* can only be sought and essayed in the science of moral psychology (this, in fact, is my most general formula for what is generally called a "*religion*"). Such a feeling of depression can have the most diverse origins; it may be the result of the crossing of too heterogeneous races (or of classes—genealogical and racial differences are also brought out in the classes: the European "Weltschmerz," the "Pessimism" of the nineteenth century, is really the result of an absurd and sudden class-mixture); it may be brought about by a mistaken emigration—a race falling into a climate for which its power of adaptation is insufficient (the case of the Indians in India); it may be the effect of old age and fatigue (the Parisian pessimism from 1850 onwards); it may be a wrong diet (the alcoholism of the Middle Ages, the nonsense of vegetarianism—which, however, have in their favour the authority of Sir Christopher in Shakespeare); it may be blood-deterioration, malaria, syphilis, and the like (German depression after the Thirty Years' War, which infected half Germany with evil diseases, and thereby paved the way for German servility, for German pusillanimity). In such a case there is invariably recourse to a *war* on a grand scale with the feeling of depression; let us inform ourselves briefly on its most important practises and phases (I leave on one side, as stands to reason, the actual *philosophic* war against the feeling of depression which is usually simultaneous—it is interesting enough, but too absurd, too practically negligible, too full of cobwebs, too much of a hole-and-corner affair, especially when pain is proved to be a mistake, on the *naïf* hypothesis that pain must needs *vanish* when the mistake underlying it is recognised—but behold! It does anything but vanish . . .). That dominant depression is *primarily fought* by weapons which reduce the consciousness of life itself to the lowest degree. Wherever possible, no more wishes, no more wants; shun everything which produces emotion, which produces "blood" (eating no salt, the fakir hygiene); no love; no hate; equanimity; no revenge; no getting rich; no work; begging; as far as possible, no woman, or as little woman as possible; as far as the intellect is concerned, Pascal's principle, "*il faut s'abêtir.*" To put the result in ethical and psychological language, "self-annihilation," "sanctification"; to put it in physiological language, "hypnotism"—the attempt to find some approximate human equivalent for what *hibernation* is for certain animals, for what *aestivation* is for many tropical plants, a minimum of assimilation and metabolism in which life just manages to subsist without really coming into the consciousness. An amazing amount of human energy has been devoted to this object—perhaps uselessly? There cannot be the slightest doubt but that such *sportsmen* of "saintliness," in whom at times nearly every nation has abounded, have really found a genuine relief from that which they have combated with such a rigorous *training*—in countless cases they really escaped by the help of their system of hypnotism *away* from deep physiological depression; their method is consequently counted among the most universal ethnological facts. Similarly it is improper to consider such a plan for starving the physical element and the desires, as in itself a symptom of insanity (as a clumsy species of roast-beef-eating "freethinkers" and Sir Christophers are fain to do); all the more certain is it that their method can and does pave the way to all kinds of mental disturbances, for instance, "inner lights" (as far as the case of the Hesychasts of Mount Athos), auditory and visual hallucinations, voluptuous ecstasies and effervescences of sensualism (the history of St. Theresa). The explanation of such events given by the victims is always the acme of fanatical falsehood; this is self-evident. Note well, however, the tone of implicit gratitude that rings in the very *will* for an explanation of such a character. The supreme state, salvation itself, that final goal of universal hypnosis and peace, is always regarded by them as the mystery of mysteries, which even the most supreme symbols are inadequate to express; it is regarded as an entry and homecoming to the essence of things, as a liberation from all illusions, as "knowledge," as "truth," as "being," as an escape from every end, every wish, every action, as something even beyond Good and Evil.

"Good and Evil," quoth the Buddhists, "both are fetters. The perfect man is master of them both."

"The done and the undone," quoth the disciple of the Vedânta, "do him no hurt; the good and the evil he shakes from off him, sage that he is; his kingdom suffers no more from any act; good and evil, he goes beyond them both." An absolutely Indian conception, as much Brahmanist as Buddhist. Neither in the Indian nor in the Christian doctrine is this "Redemption" regarded as attainable by means of virtue and moral improvement, however high they may place the value of the hypnotic efficiency of virtue: keep clear on this point—indeed it simply corresponds with the facts. The fact that they remained *true* on this point is perhaps to be regarded as the best specimen of realism in the three great religions, absolutely soaked as they are with morality, with this one exception. "For those who know, there is no duty." "Redemption is not attained by the acquisition of virtues; for redemption consists in being one with Brahman, who is incapable of acquiring any perfection; and equally little does it consist in the *giving up of* faults, for the Brahman, unity with whom is what constitutes redemption, is eternally pure" (these passages are from the Commentaries of the Cankara, quoted from the first real European *expert* of the Indian philosophy, my friend Paul Deussen). We wish, therefore, to pay honour to the idea of "redemption" in the great religions, but it is somewhat hard to remain serious in view of the appreciation meted out to the *deep sleep* by these exhausted pessimists who are too tired even to dream—to the deep sleep considered, that is, as already a fusing into Brahman, as the attainment of the *unio mystica* with God. "When he has completely gone to sleep," says on this point the oldest and most venerable "script," "and come to perfect rest, so that he sees no more any vision, then, oh dear one, is he united with Being, he has entered into his own self—encircled by the Self with its absolute knowledge, he has no more any consciousness of that which is without or of that which is within. Day and night cross not these bridges, nor age, nor death, nor suffering, nor good deeds, nor evil deeds." "In deep sleep," say similarly the believers in this deepest of the three great religions, "does the soul lift itself from out this body of ours, enters the supreme light and stands out therein in its true shape: therein is it the supreme spirit itself, which travells about, while it jests and plays and enjoys itself, whether with women, or chariots, or friends; there do its thoughts turn no more back to this appanage of a body, to which the 'prâna' (the vital breath) is harnessed like a beast of burden to the cart." Nonetheless we will take care to realise (as we did when discussing "redemption") that in spite of all its pomps of Oriental extravagance this simply expresses the same criticism on life as did the clear, cold, Greekly cold, but yet suffering Epicurus. The hypnotic sensation of nothingness, the peace of deepest sleep, anaesthesia in short—that is what passes with the sufferers and the absolutely depressed for, forsooth, their supreme good, their value of values; that is what *must* be treasured by them as something positive, be felt by them as the essence of *the* Positive (according to the same logic of the feelings, nothingness is in all pessimistic religions called God).

18

Such a hypnotic deadening of sensibility and susceptibility to pain, which presupposes somewhat rare powers, especially courage, contempt of opinion, intellectual stoicism, is less frequent than another and certainly easier *training* which is tried against states of depression. I mean *mechanical activity*. It is indisputable that a suffering existence can be thereby considerably alleviated. This fact is called today by the somewhat ignoble title of the "Blessing of work." The alleviation consists in the attention of the sufferer being absolutely diverted from suffering, in the incessant monopoly of the consciousness by action, so that consequently there is little room left for suffering—for *narrow* is it, this chamber of human consciousness! Mechanical activity and its corollaries, such as absolute regularity, punctilious unreasoning obedience, the chronic routine of life, the complete occupation of time, a certain liberty to be impersonal, nay, a training in "impersonality," self-forgetfulness, "*incuria sui*"—with what thoroughness and expert subtlety have all these methods been exploited by the ascetic priest in his war with pain!

When he has to tackle sufferers of the lower orders, slaves, or prisoners (or women, who for the most part are a compound of labour-slave and prisoner), all he has to do is to juggle a little with the names, and to rechristen, so as to make them see henceforth a benefit, a comparative happiness, in objects which they hated—the slave's discontent with his lot was at any rate *not* invented by the priests. An even more popular means of fighting depression is the ordaining of a *little joy*, which is easily accessible and can be made into a rule; this medication is frequently used in conjunction with the former ones. The most frequent form in which joy is prescribed as a cure is the joy in *producing* joy (such as doing good, giving presents, alleviating, helping, exhorting, comforting, praising, treating with distinction); together with the prescription of "love your neighbour." The ascetic priest prescribes, though in the most cautious doses, what is practically a stimulation of the strongest and most life-assertive impulse—the Will for Power. The happiness involved in the "smallest superiority" which is the concomitant of all benefiting, helping, extolling, making one's self useful, is the most ample consolation, of which, if they are well-advised, physiological distortions avail themselves: in other cases they hurt each other, and naturally in obedience to the same radical instinct. An investigation of the origin of Christianity in the Roman world shows that cooperative unions for poverty, sickness, and burial sprang up in the lowest stratum of contemporary society, amid which the chief antidote against depression, the little joy experienced in mutual benefits, was deliberately fostered. Perchance this was then a novelty, a real discovery? This conjuring up of the will for cooperation, for family organisation, for communal life, for "*Caenacula,*" necessarily brought the Will for Power, which had been already infinitesimally stimulated, to a new and much fuller manifestation. The herd organisation is a genuine advance and triumph in the fight with depression. With the growth of the community there matures even to individuals a new interest, which often enough takes him out of the more personal element in his discontent, his aversion to himself, the "*despectus sui*" of Geulincx. All sick and diseased people strive instinctively after a herd-organisation, out of a desire to shake off their sense of oppressive discomfort and weakness; the ascetic priest divines this instinct and promotes it; wherever a herd exists it is the instinct of weakness which has wished for the herd, and the cleverness of the priests which has organised it, for, mark this: by an equally natural necessity the strong strive as much for *isolation* as the weak for *union*: when the former bind themselves it is only with a view to an aggressive joint action and joint satisfaction of their Will for Power, much against the wishes of their individual consciences; the latter, on the contrary, range themselves together with positive *delight* in such a muster—their instincts are as much gratified thereby as the instincts of the "born master" (that is, the solitary beast-of-prey species of man) are disturbed and wounded to the quick by organisation. There is always lurking beneath every oligarchy —such is the universal lesson of history—the desire for tyranny. Every oligarchy is continually quivering with the tension of the effort required by each individual to keep mastering this desire. (Such, e.g., was the Greek; Plato shows it in a hundred places, Plato, who knew his contemporaries— and *himself.*)

19

The methods employed by the ascetic priest, which we have already learnt to know—stifling of all vitality, mechanical energy, the little joy, and especially the method of "love your neighbour" herd-organisation, the awaking of the communal consciousness of power, to such a pitch that the individual's disgust with himself becomes eclipsed by his delight in the thriving of the community—these are, according to modern standards, the "innocent" methods employed in the fight with depression; let us turn now to the more interesting topic of the "guilty" methods. The guilty methods spell one thing: to produce *emotional excess*—which is used as the most efficacious anaesthetic against their depressing state of protracted pain; this is why priestly ingenuity has proved quite inexhaustible in thinking out this one question: "*By what means* can you produce an emotional excess?" This sounds harsh: it is manifest that it would sound nicer and would grate on one's ears less, if I were to say, forsooth: "The ascetic priest made use at all times of the enthusiasm contained in all strong emotions." But what is the good of still soothing the delicate ears of our modern effeminates? What is the good *on our side* of budging one single inch before their verbal Pecksniffianism. For us psychologists to do that would be at once *practical Pecksniffianism*, apart from the fact of its nauseating us. The *good taste* (others might say, the righteousness) of a psychologist nowadays consists, if at all, in combating the shamefully moralised language with which all modern judgements on men and things are smeared. For, do not deceive yourself: what constitutes the chief characteristic of modern souls and of modern books is not the lying, but the *innocence* which is part and parcel of their intellectual dishonesty. The inevitable running up against this "innocence" everywhere constitutes the most distasteful feature of the somewhat dangerous business which a modern psychologist has to undertake: it is a part of *our* great danger—it is a road which perhaps leads us straight to the great nausea—I know quite well the purpose which all modern books will and can serve (granted that they last, which I am not afraid of, and granted equally that there is to be at some future day a generation with a more rigid, more severe, and *healthier* taste)—the *function* which all modernity generally will serve with posterity: that of an emetic—and this by reason of its moral sugariness and falsity, its ingrained feminism, which it is pleased to call "Idealism," and at any rate believes to be idealism. Our cultured men of today, our "good" men, do not lie—that is true; but it does *not* redound to their honour! The real lie, the genuine, determined, "honest" lie (on whose value you can listen to Plato) would prove too tough and strong an article for them by a long way; it would be asking them to do what people have been forbidden to ask them to do, to open their eyes to their own selves, and to learn to distinguish between "true" and "false" in their own selves. The dishonest lie alone suits them: everything which feels a good man is perfectly incapable of any other attitude to anything than that of a dishonourable liar, an absolute liar, but nonetheless an innocent liar, a blue-eyed liar, a virtuous liar. These "good men," they are all now tainted with morality through and through, and as far as honour is concerned they are disgraced and corrupted for all eternity. Which of them *could stand* a further truth "about man"? Or, put more tangibly, which of them could put up with a true biography? One or two instances: Lord Byron composed a most personal autobiography, but Thomas Moore was "too good" for it; he burnt his friend's papers. Dr. Gwinner, Schopenhauer's executor, is said to have done the same; for Schopenhauer as well wrote much about himself, and perhaps also *against* himself (εἰς ἑαυτόν). The virtuous American Thayer, Beethoven's biographer, suddenly stopped his work: he had come to a certain point in that honourable and simple life, and could stand it no longer. Moral: What sensible man nowadays writes one honest word about himself? He must already belong to the Order of Holy Foolhardiness. We are promised an autobiography of Richard Wagner; who doubts but that it would be a *clever* autobiography? Think, forsooth, of the grotesque horror which the Catholic priest Janssen aroused in Germany with his inconceivably square and harmless pictures of the German Reformation; what wouldn't people do if some real psychologist were to tell us about a genuine Luther, tell us, not with the moralist simplicity of a country priest or the sweet and cautious modesty of a Protestant historian, but say with the fearlessness of a Taine, that springs from force of character and not from a prudent toleration of force. (The Germans, by the bye, have already produced the classic specimen of this toleration—they may well be allowed to reckon him as one of their own, in Leopold Ranke, that born classical advocate of every *causa fortior*, that cleverest of all the clever opportunists.)

20

But you will soon understand me. Putting it shortly, there is reason enough, is there not, for us psychologists nowadays never getting away from a certain mistrust of our *own selves*? Probably even we ourselves are still "too good" for our work; probably, whatever contempt we feel for this popular craze for morality, we ourselves are perhaps nonetheless its victims, prey, and slaves; probably it infects even *us*. Of what was that diplomat warning us, when he said to his colleagues: "Let us especially mistrust our first impulses, gentlemen! *They are almost always good*"? So should nowadays every psychologist talk to his colleagues. And thus we get back to our problem, which in point of fact does require from us a certain severity, a certain mistrust especially against "first impulses." *The ascetic ideal in the service of projected emotional excess*: he who remembers the previous essay will already partially anticipate the essential meaning compressed into these above ten words. The thorough unswitching of the human soul, the plunging of it into terror, frost, ardour, rapture, so as to free it, as through some lightning shock, from all the smallness and pettiness of unhappiness, depression, and discomfort: what ways lead to *this* goal? And which of these ways does so most safely? . . . At bottom all great emotions have this power, provided that they find a sudden outlet —emotions such as rage, fear, lust, revenge, hope, triumph, despair, cruelty; and, in sooth, the ascetic priest has had no scruples in taking into his service the whole pack of hounds that rage in the human kennel, unleashing now these and now those, with the same constant object of waking man out of his protracted melancholy, of chasing away, at any rate for a time, his dull pain, his shrinking misery, but always under the sanction of a religious interpretation and justification. This emotional excess has subsequently to be *paid for*, this is self-evident—it makes the ill more ill—and therefore this kind of remedy for pain is according to modern standards a "guilty" kind.

The dictates of fairness, however, require that we should all the more emphasise the fact that this remedy is applied with a *good conscience*, that the ascetic priest has prescribed it in the most implicit belief in its utility and indispensability; often enough almost collapsing in the presence of the pain which he created; that we should similarly emphasise the fact that the violent physiological revenges of such excesses, even perhaps the mental disturbances, are not absolutely inconsistent with the general tenor of this kind of remedy; this remedy, which, as we have shown previously, is *not* for the purpose of healing diseases, but of fighting the unhappiness of that depression, the alleviation and deadening of which was its object. The object was consequently achieved. The keynote by which the ascetic priest was enabled to get every kind of agonising and ecstatic music to play on the fibres of the human soul—was, as everyone knows, the exploitation of the feeling of "*guilt*." I have already indicated in the previous essay the origin of this feeling—as a piece of animal psychology and nothing else: we were thus confronted with the feeling of "guilt," in its crude state, as it were. It was first in the hands of the priest, real artist that he was in the feeling of guilt, that it took shape—oh, what a shape!

"Sin"—for that is the name of the new priestly version of the animal "bad-conscience" (the inverted cruelty)—has up to the present been the greatest event in the history of the diseased soul: in "sin" we find the most perilous and fatal masterpiece of religious interpretation. Imagine man, suffering from himself, some way or other but at any rate physiologically, perhaps like an animal shut up in a cage, not clear as to the why and the wherefore! Imagine him in his desire for reasons—reasons bring relief— in his desire again for remedies, narcotics at last, consulting one, who knows even the occult—and see, lo and behold, he gets a hint from his wizard, the ascetic priest, his *first* hint on the "cause" of his trouble: he must search for it *in himself*, in his guiltiness, in a piece of the past, he must understand his very suffering as a *state of punishment*. He has heard, he has understood, has the unfortunate: he is now in the plight of a hen round which a line has been drawn. He never gets out of the circle of lines. The sick man has been turned into "the sinner"—and now for a few thousand years we never get away from the sight of this new invalid, of "a sinner"—shall we ever get away from it? Wherever we just look, every- where the hypnotic gaze of the sinner always moving in one direction (in the direction of guilt, the *only* cause of suffering); everywhere the evil conscience, this "*greuliche thier*,"[4] to use Luther's language; everywhere rumination over the past, a distorted view of action, the gaze of the "green-eyed monster" turned on all action; everywhere the wilful misun- derstanding of suffering, its transvaluation into feelings of guilt, fear of retribution; everywhere the scourge, the hairy shirt, the starving body, contrition; everywhere the sinner breaking himself on the ghastly wheel of a restless and morbidly eager conscience; everywhere mute pain, extreme fear, the agony of a tortured heart, the spasms of an unknown happi- ness, the shriek for "redemption." In point of fact, thanks to this system of procedure, the old depression, dulness, and fatigue were absolutely con- quered, life itself became *very* interesting again, awake, eternally awake, sleepless, glowing, burnt away, exhausted and yet not tired—such was the figure cut by man, "the sinner," who was initiated into these mysteries. This grand old wizard of an ascetic priest fighting with depression—he had clearly triumphed, *his* kingdom had come: men no longer grumbled at pain, men *panted* after pain: "*More pain!* More pain!" So for centuries on end shrieked the demand of his acolytes and initiates. Every emotional excess which hurt; everything which broke, overthrew, crushed, transported, ravished; the mystery of torture-chambers, the ingenuity of hell itself—all this was now discovered, divined, exploited, all this was at the service of the wizard, all this served to promote the triumph of his ideal, the ascetic ideal. "*My kingdom is not of this world,*" quoth he, both at the beginning and at the end: had he still the right to talk like that? Goethe has maintained that there are only thirty-six tragic situations: we would infer from that, did we not know otherwise that Goethe was no ascetic priest. He—knows more.

21

So far as all *this* kind of priestly medicine-mongering, the "guilty" kind, is concerned, every word of criticism is superfluous. As for the suggestion that emotional excess of the type, which in these cases the ascetic priest is fain to order to his sick patients (under the most sacred euphemism, as is obvious, and equally impregnated with the sanctity of his purpose), has ever really been of use to any sick man, who, forsooth, would feel inclined to maintain a proposition of that character? At any rate, some understanding should be come to as to the expression "be of use." If you only wish to express that such a system of treatment has *reformed* man, I do not gainsay it: I merely add that "reformed" conveys to my mind as much as "tamed," "weakened," "discouraged," "refined," "daintified," "emasculated" (and thus it means almost as much as injured). But when you have to deal principally with sick, depressed, and oppressed creatures, such a system, even granted that it makes the ill "better," under any circumstances also makes them more *ill*: ask the mad-doctors the invariable result of a methodical application of penance-torture, contrition, and salvation ecstasies. Similarly ask history. In everybody politic where the ascetic priest has established this treatment of the sick, disease has on every occasion spread with sinister speed throughout its length and breadth. What was always the "result"? A shattered nervous system, in addition to the existing malady, and this in the greatest as in the smallest, in the individuals as in masses. We find, in consequence of the penance and redemption-training, awful epileptic epidemics, the greatest known to history, such as the St. Vitus and St. John dances of the Middle Ages; we find, as another phase of its after-effect, frightful mutilations and chronic depressions, by means of which the temperament of a nation or a city (Geneva, Bâle) is turned once for all into its opposite; this *training*, again, is responsible for the witch-hysteria, a phenomenon analogous to somnambulism (eight great epidemic outbursts of this only between 1564 and 1605); we find similarly in its train those delirious death-cravings of large masses, whose awful "shriek," "*evviva la morte!*" was heard over the whole of Europe, now interrupted by voluptuous variations and anon by a rage for destruction, just as the same emotional sequence with the same intermittencies and sudden changes is now universally observed in every case where the ascetic doctrine of sin scores once more a great success (religious neurosis *appears* as a manifestation of the devil, there is no doubt of it. What is it? *Quaeritur*). Speaking generally, the ascetic ideal and its sublime-moral cult, this most ingenious, reckless, and perilous systematisation of all methods of emotional excess, is writ large in a dreadful and unforgettable fashion on the whole history of man, and unfortunately not only on history. I was scarcely able to put forward any other element which attacked the *health* and race efficiency of Europeans with more destructive power than did this ideal; it can be dubbed, without exaggeration, *the real fatality* in the history of the health of the European man. At the most you can merely draw a comparison with the specifically German influence: I mean the alcohol poisoning of Europe, which up to the present has kept pace exactly with the political and racial predominance of the Germans (where they inoculated their blood, there too did they inoculate their vice). Third in the series comes syphilis—*magno sed proximo intervallo.*

22

The ascetic priest has, wherever he has obtained the mastery, corrupted the health of the soul, he has consequently also corrupted *taste in artibus et litteris*—he corrupts it still. "Consequently?" I hope I shall be granted this "consequently"; at any rate, I am not going to prove it first. One solitary indication, it concerns the arch-book of Christian literature, their real model, their "book-in-itself." In the very midst of the Graeco-Roman splendour, which was also a splendour of books, face to face with an ancient world of writings which had not yet fallen into decay and ruin, at a time when certain books were still to be read, to possess which we would give nowadays half our literature in exchange, at that time the simplicity and vanity of Christian agitators (they are generally called Fathers of the Church) dared to declare: "We too have our classical literature, *we do not need that of the Greeks*"—and meanwhile they proudly pointed to their books of legends, their letters of apostles, and their apologetic tractlets, just in the same way that today the English "Salvation Army" wages its fight against Shakespeare and other "heathens" with an analogous literature. You already guess it, I do not like the "New Testament"; it almost upsets me that I stand so isolated in my taste so far as concerns this valued, this over-valued Scripture; the taste of two thousand years is *against* me; but what boots it! "Here I stand! I cannot help myself"⁵—I have the courage of my bad taste. The *Old* Testament—yes, that is something quite different, all honour to the Old Testament! I find therein great men, an heroic landscape, and one of the rarest phenomena in the world, the incomparable naïveté *of the strong heart*; further still, I find a people. In the New, on the contrary, just a hostel of petty sects, pure rococo of the soul, twisting angles and fancy touches, nothing but conventicle air, not to forget an occasional whiff of bucolic sweetness which appertains to the epoch (*and* the Roman province) and is less Jewish than Hellenistic. Meekness and braggadocio cheek by jowl; an emotional garrulousness that almost deafens; passionate hysteria, but no passion; painful pantomime; here manifestly everyone lacked good breeding. How dare anyone make so much fuss about their little failings as do these pious little fellows! No one cares a straw about it—let alone God. Finally they actually wish to have "the crown of eternal life," do all these little provincials! In return for what, in sooth? For what end? It is impossible to carry insolence any further. An immortal Peter! Who could stand *him*! They have an ambition which makes one laugh: the *thing* dishes up cut and dried his most personal life, his melancholies, and common-or-garden troubles, as though the Universe itself were under an obligation to bother itself about them, for it never gets tired of wrapping up God Himself in the petty misery in which its troubles are involved. And how about the atrocious form of this chronic hobnobbing with God? This Jewish, and not merely Jewish, slobbering and clawing importunacy towards God! There exist little despised "heathen nations" in East Asia, from whom these first Christians could have learnt something worth learning, a little tact in worshiping; these nations do not allow themselves to say aloud the name of their God. This seems to me delicate enough, it is certain that it is *too* delicate, and not only for primitive Christians; to take a contrast, just recollect Luther, the most "eloquent" and insolent peasant whom Germany has had, think of the Lutherian tone, in which he felt quite the most in his element during his *tête-à-têtes* with God. Luther's opposition to the mediaeval saints of the Church (in particular, against "that devil's hog, the Pope"), was, there is no doubt, at bottom the opposition of a boor, who was offended at the *good etiquette* of the Church, that worship-etiquette of the sacerdotal code, which only admits to the holy of holies the initiated and the silent, and shuts the door against the boors. These definitely were not to be allowed a hearing in this planet—but Luther the peasant simply wished it otherwise; as it was, it was not German enough for him. He personally wished himself to talk direct, to talk personally, to talk "straight from the shoulder" with his God. Well, he's done it. The ascetic ideal, you will guess, was at no time and in no place, a school of good taste, still less of good manners—at the best it was a school for sacerdotal manners: that is, it contains in itself something which was a deadly enemy to all good manners. Lack of measure, opposition to measure it is itself a *"non plus ultra."*

23

The ascetic ideal has corrupted not only health and taste, there are also third, fourth, fifth, and sixth things which it has corrupted—I shall take care not to go through the catalogue (when should I get to the end?). I have here to expose not what this ideal effected; but rather only what it *means,* on what it is based, what lies lurking behind it and under it, that of which it is the provisional expression, an obscure expression bristling with queries and misunderstandings. And with *this* object only in view I presumed "not to spare" my readers a glance at the awfulness of its results, a glance at its fatal results; I did this to prepare them for the final and most awful aspect presented to me by the question of the significance of that ideal. What is the significance of the *power* of that ideal, the monstrousness of its power? Why is it given such an amount of scope? Why is not a better resistance offered against it? The ascetic ideal expresses one will: where is the opposition will, in which an *opposition ideal* expresses itself? The ascetic ideal has an aim—this goal is, putting it generally, that all the other interests of human life should, measured by its standard, appear petty and narrow; it explains epochs, nations, men, in reference to this one end; it forbids any other interpretation, any other end; it repudiates, denies, affirms, confirms, only in the sense of its own interpretation (and was there ever a more thoroughly elaborated system of interpretation?); it subjects itself to no power, rather does it believe in its own precedence over every power—it believes that nothing powerful exists in the world that has not first got to receive from "it" a meaning, a right to exist, a value, as being an instrument in its work, a way and means to its end, to one end. Where is the *counterpart* of this complete system of will, end, and interpretation? Why is the counterpart lacking? Where is the other "one aim"? But I am told it is not lacking, that not only has it fought a long and fortunate fight with that ideal, but that further it has already won the mastery over that ideal in all essentials: let our whole modern *science* attest this—that modern science, which, like the genuine reality-philosophy which it is, manifestly believes in itself alone, manifestly has the courage to be itself, the will to be itself, and has got on well enough without God, another world, and negative virtues.

With all their noisy agitator-babble, however, they effect nothing with me; these trumpeters of reality are bad musicians, their voices do not come from the deeps with sufficient audibility, they are *not* the mouthpiece for the abyss of scientific knowledge—for today scientific knowledge is an abyss—the word "science," in such trumpeter-mouths, is a prostitution, an abuse, an impertinence. The truth is just the opposite from what is maintained in the ascetic theory. Science has today absolutely *no* belief in itself, let alone in an ideal superior to itself, and wherever science still consists of passion, love, ardour, suffering, it is not the opposition to that ascetic ideal, but rather the *incarnation of its latest and noblest form.* Does that ring strange? There are enough brave and decent working people, even among the learned men of today, who like their little corner, and who, just because they are pleased so to do, become at times indecently loud with their demand, that people today should be quite content, especially in science—for in science there is so much useful work to do. I do not deny it—there is nothing I should like less than to spoil the delight of these honest workers in their handiwork; for I rejoice in their work. But the fact of science requiring hard work, the fact of its having contented workers, is absolutely no proof of science as a whole having today one end, one will, one ideal, one passion for a great faith; the contrary, as I have said, is the case. When science is not the latest manifestation of the ascetic ideal—but these are cases of such rarity, selectness, and exquisiteness, as to preclude the general judgement being affected thereby—science is a *hiding-place* for every kind of cowardice, disbelief, remorse, *despectio sui,* bad conscience—it is the very *anxiety* that springs from having no ideal, the suffering from the *lack* of a great love, the discontent with an enforced moderation. Oh, what does all science not cover today? How much, at any rate, does it not try to cover? The diligence of our best scholars, their senseless industry, their burning the candle of their brain at both ends— their very mastery in their handiwork—how often is the real meaning of all that to prevent themselves continuing to see a certain thing? Science as a self-anaesthetic: *do you know that?* You wound them—everyone who consorts with scholars experiences this—you wound them sometimes to the quick through just a harmless word; when you think you are paying them a compliment you embitter them beyond all bounds, simply because you didn't have the *finesse* to infer the real kind of customers you had to tackle, the *sufferer* kind (who won't own up even to themselves what they really are), the dazed and unconscious kind who have only one fear—*coming to consciousness.*

24

And now look at the other side, at those rare cases, of which I spoke, the most supreme idealists to be found nowadays among philosophers and scholars. Have we, perchance, found in them the sought-for *opponents* of the ascetic ideal, its *anti-idealists?* In fact, they *believe* themselves to be such, these "unbelievers" (for they are all of them that): it seems that this idea is their last remnant of faith, the idea of being opponents of this ideal, so earnest are they on this subject, so passionate in word and gesture; but does it follow that what they believe must necessarily be *true?* We "knowers" have grown by degrees suspicious of all kinds of believers, our suspicion has step by step habituated us to draw just the opposite conclusions to what people have drawn before; that is to say, wherever the strength of a belief is particularly prominent to draw the conclusion of the difficulty of proving what is believed, the conclusion of its actual *improbability.* We do not again deny that "faith produces salvation": *for that very reason* we do deny that faith *proves* anything—a strong faith, which produces happiness, causes suspicion of the object of that faith, it does not establish its "truth," it does establish a certain probability of—*illusion.* What is now the position in these cases? These solitaries and deniers of today; these fanatics in one thing, in their claim to intellectual cleanness; these hard, stern, continent, heroic spirits, who constitute the glory of our time; all these pale atheists, anti-Christians, immoralists, Nihilists; these sceptics, "ephectics," and "hectics" of the intellect (in a certain sense they are the latter, both collectively and individually); these supreme idealists of knowledge, in whom alone nowadays the intellectual conscience dwells and is alive—in point of fact they believe themselves as far away as possible from the ascetic ideal, do these "free, very free spirits": and yet, if I may reveal what they themselves cannot see—for they stand too near themselves: this ideal is simply *their* ideal, they represent it nowadays and perhaps no one else, they themselves are its most spiritualised product, its most advanced picket of skirmishers and scouts, its most insidious delicate and elusive form of seduction. If I am in any way a reader of riddles, then I will be one with this sentence: for sometime past there have been no *free spirits; for they still believe in truth*. When the Christian Crusaders in the East came into collision with that invincible order of assassins, that order of free spirits *par excellence*, whose lowest grade lives in a state of discipline such as no order of monks has ever attained, then in some way or other they managed to get an inkling of that symbol and tally-word, that was reserved for the highest grade alone as their *secretum*, "Nothing is true, everything is allowed"—in sooth, *that* was *freedom* of thought, thereby was *taking leave* of the very belief in truth. Has indeed any European, any Christian freethinker, ever yet wandered into this proposition and its labyrinthine *consequences*? Does he know *from experience* the Minotauros of this den. I doubt it—nay, I know otherwise. Nothing is more really alien to these "mono-fanatics," these *so-called* "free spirits," than freedom and unfettering in that sense; in no respect are they more closely tied, the absolute fanaticism of their belief in truth is unparalleled. I know all this perhaps too much from experience at close quarters—that dignified philosophic abstinence to which a belief like that binds its adherents, that stoicism of the intellect, which eventually vetoes negation as rigidly as it does affirmation, that wish for standing still in front of the actual, the *factum brutum*, that fatalism in "*petits faits*" (*ce petit faitalism*, as I call it), in which French Science now attempts a kind of moral superiority over German, this renunciation of interpretation generally (that is, of forcing, doctoring, abridging, omitting, suppressing, inventing, falsifying, and all the other *essential* attributes of interpretation) —all this, considered broadly, expresses the asceticism of virtue, quite as efficiently as does any repudiation of the senses (it is at bottom only a *modus* of that repudiation). But what forces it into that unqualified will for truth is the faith *in the ascetic ideal itself*, even though it take the form of its unconscious imperatives—make no mistake about it, it is the faith, I repeat, in a *metaphysical* value, an *intrinsic* value of truth, of a character which is only warranted and guaranteed in this ideal (it stands and falls with that ideal). Judged strictly, there does not exist a science without its "hypotheses," the thought of such a science is inconceivable, illogical: a philosophy, a faith, must always exist first to enable science to gain thereby a direction, a meaning, a limit and method, a *right* to existence. (He who holds a contrary opinion on the subject—he, for example, who takes it upon himself to establish philosophy "upon a strictly scientific basis"—has first got to "turn up-side-down" not only philosophy but also truth itself—the gravest insult which could possibly be offered to two such respectable females!) Yes, there is no doubt about it—and here I quote my *Joyful Wisdom*, cp. Book 5. Aph. 344:

The man who is truthful in that daring and extreme fashion, which is the presupposition of the faith in science, asserts *thereby a different world* from that of life, nature, and history; and insofar as he asserts the existence of that different world, come, must he not similarly repudiate its counterpart, this world, *our* world? The belief on which our faith in science is based has remained to this day a metaphysical belief—even we knowers of today, we godless foes of metaphysics, we too take our fire from that conflagration which was kindled by a thousand-year-old faith, from that Christian belief, which was also Plato's belief, the belief that God is truth, that truth is *divine.* . . . But what if this belief becomes more and more incredible, what if nothing proves itself to be divine, unless it be error, blindness, lies—what if God Himself proved Himself to be our *oldest lie?*

It is necessary to stop at this point and to consider the situation carefully. Science itself now *needs* a justification (which is not for a minute to say that there is such a justification). Turn in this context to the most ancient and the most modern philosophers: they all fail to realise the extent of the need of a justification on the part of the Will for Truth—here is a gap in every philosophy—what is it caused by? Because up to the present the ascetic ideal dominated all philosophy, because Truth was fixed as Being, as God, as the Supreme Court of Appeal, because Truth was not allowed to be a problem. Do you understand this "allowed"? From the minute that the belief in the God of the ascetic ideal is repudiated, there exists a *new problem*: the problem of the value of truth. The Will for Truth needed a critique—let us define by these words our own task—the value of truth is tentatively *to be called in question.* . . . (If this seems too laconically expressed, I recommend the reader to peruse again that passage from the *Joyful Wisdom* which bears the title, "How far we also are still pious," Aph. 344, and best of all the whole fifth book of that work, as well as the preface to *The Dawn of Day*.)

25

No! You can't get round me with science, when I search for the natural antagonists of the ascetic ideal, when I put the question: "*Where* is the opposed will in which the *opponent ideal* expresses itself?" Science is not,

by a long way, independent enough to fulfil this function; in every department science needs an ideal value, a power which creates values, and in
whose *service* it *can believe* in itself—science itself never creates values. Its
relation to the ascetic ideal is not in itself antagonistic; speaking roughly,
it rather represents the progressive force in the inner evolution of that
ideal. Tested more exactly, its opposition and antagonism are concerned
not with the ideal itself, but only with that ideal's outworks, its outer garb,
its masquerade, with its temporary hardening, stiffening, and dogmatising
—it makes the life in the ideal free once more, while it repudiates its
superficial elements. These two phenomena, science and the ascetic
ideal, both rest on the same basis—I have already made this clear—the
basis, I say, of the same over-appreciation of truth (more accurately the same
belief in the *impossibility* of valuing and of criticising truth), and consequently they are *necessarily* allies, so that, in the event of their being
attacked, they must always be attacked and called into question together.
A valuation of the ascetic ideal inevitably entails a valuation of science as
well; lose no time in seeing this clearly, and be sharp to catch it! (*Art*, I
am speaking provisionally, for I will treat it on some other occasion in
greater detail—art, I repeat, in which lying is sanctified and the *will for
deception* has good conscience on its side, is much more fundamentally
opposed to the ascetic ideal than is science: Plato's instinct felt this—
Plato, the greatest enemy of art which Europe has produced up to the
present. Plato *versus* Homer, that is the complete, the true antagonism—
on the one side, the whole-hearted "transcendental," the great defamer
of life; on the other, its involuntary panegyrist, the *golden* nature. An
artistic subservience to the service of the ascetic ideal is consequently the
most absolute artistic *corruption* that there can be, though unfortunately
it is one of the most frequent phases, for nothing is more corruptible
than an artist.) Considered physiologically, moreover, science rests on
the same basis as does the ascetic ideal: a certain *impoverishment of life*
is the presupposition of the latter as of the former—add, frigidity of the
emotions, slackening of the *tempo*, the substitution of dialectic for instinct,
seriousness impressed on mien and gesture (seriousness, that most unmistakable sign of strenuous metabolism, of struggling, toiling life). Consider
the periods in a nation in which the learned man comes into prominence; they are the periods of exhaustion, often of sunset, of decay—the
effervescing strength, the confidence in life, the confidence in the future
are no more. The preponderence of the mandarins never signifies any
good, anymore than does the advent of democracy, or arbitration instead

of war, equal rights for women, the religion of pity, and all the other symptoms of declining life. (Science handled as a problem! What is the meaning of science? Upon this point the Preface to the *Birth of Tragedy*.) No! This "modern science"—mark you this well—is at times the *best* ally for the ascetic ideal, and for the very reason that it is the ally which is most unconscious, most automatic, most secret, and most subterranean! They have been playing into each other's hands up to the present, have these "poor in spirit" and the scientific opponents of that ideal (take care, by the bye, not to think that these opponents are the antithesis of this ideal, that they are the *rich* in spirit—that they are *not*; I have called them the *hectic* in spirit). As for these celebrated *victories* of science; there is no doubt that they are victories—but victories over what? There was not for a single minute any victory among their list over the ascetic ideal, rather was it made stronger, that is to say, more elusive, more abstract, more insidious, from the fact that a wall, an outwork, that had got built on to the main fortress and disfigured its appearance, should from time to time be ruthlessly destroyed and broken down by science. Does anyone seriously suggest that the downfall of the theological astronomy signified the downfall of that ideal? Has, perchance, man grown *less in need* of a transcendental solution of his riddle of existence, because since that time this existence has become more random, casual, and superfluous in the *visible* order of the universe? Has there not been since the time of Copernicus an unbroken progress in the self-belittling of man and his *will* for belittling himself? Alas, his belief in his dignity, his uniqueness, his irreplaceableness in the scheme of existence, is gone—he has become animal, literal, unqualified, and unmitigated animal, he who in his earlier belief was almost God ("child of God," "demi-God"). Since Copernicus man seems to have fallen on to a steep plane—he rolls faster and faster away from the centre—whither? Into nothingness? *Into the "thrilling sensation of his own nothingness"?* Well! This would be the straight way—to the *old* ideal? *All* science (and by no means only astronomy, with regard to the humiliating and deteriorating effect of which Kant has made a remarkable confession, "it annihilates my own importance"), all science, natural as much as *unnatural*—by unnatural I mean the self-critique of reason—nowadays sets out to talk man out of his present opinion of himself, as though that opinion had been nothing but a bizarre piece of conceit; you might go so far as to say that science finds its peculiar pride, its peculiar bitter form of stoical ataraxia, in preserving man's *contempt of himself*, that state which it took so much trouble to bring about, as man's final and most serious claim to self-appreciation (rightly so, in point of fact, for he who despises is always "one who has not forgotten how to appreciate"). But does all this involve any real effort to *counteract* the ascetic ideal? Is it really seriously suggested that Kant's *victory* over the theological dogmatism about "God," "Soul," "Freedom," "Immortality," has damaged that ideal in anyway (as the theologians have imagined to be the case for a long time past)? And in this connexion it does not concern us for a single minute, if Kant himself intended any such consummation. It is certain that from the time of Kant every type of transcendentalist is playing a winning game—they are emancipated from the theologians; what luck! He has revealed to them that secret art, by which they can now pursue their "heart's desire" on their own responsibility, and with all the respectability of science. Similarly, who can grumble at the agnostics, reverers, as they are, of the unknown and the absolute mystery, if they now worship *their very query* as God? (Xaver Doudan talks somewhere of the *ravages* which *l'habitude d'admirer l'inintelligible au lieu de rester tout simplement dans l'inconnu* has produced—the ancients, he thinks, must have been exempt from those ravages.) Supposing that everything, "known" to man, fails to satisfy his desires, and on the contrary contradicts and horrifies them, what a divine way out of all this to be able to look for the responsibility, not in the "desiring" but in "knowing"! "There is no knowledge. *Consequently*—there is a God"; what a novel *elegantia syllogismi!* What a triumph for the ascetic ideal!

26

Or, perchance, does the whole of modern history show in its demeanor greater confidence in life, greater confidence in its ideals? Its loftiest pretension is now to be a *mirror*; it repudiates all teleology; it will have no more "proving"; it disdains to play the judge, and thereby shows its good taste—it asserts as little as it denies, it fixes, it "describes." All this is to a high degree ascetic, but at the same time it is to a much greater degree *nihilistic*, make no mistake about this! You see in the historian a gloomy, hard, but determined gaze—an eye that *looks out* as an isolated North Pole explorer looks out (perhaps so as not to look within, so as not to look back?)—there is snow—here is life silenced, the last crows which caw here are called "whither?" "Vanity," "Nada"—here nothing more flourishes and grows, at the most the metapolitics of St. Petersburg and the "pity" of Tolstoi. But as for that other school of historians, a perhaps still more "modern" school, a voluptuous and lascivious school which ogles life and the ascetic ideal with equal fervour, which uses the word "artist" as a glove, and has nowadays established a "corner" for itself, in all the praise given to contemplation; oh, what a thirst do these sweet intellectuals excite even for ascetics and winter landscapes! Nay! The devil take these "contemplative" folk! How much liefer would I wander with those historical Nihilists through the gloomiest, grey, cold mist! Nay, I shall not mind listening (supposing I have to choose) to one who is completely unhistorical and anti-historical (a man, like Dühring for instance, over whose periods a hitherto shy and unavowed species of "beautiful souls" has grown intoxicated in contemporary Germany, the *species anarchistica* within the educated proletariate). The "contemplative" are a hundred times worse—I never knew anything which produced such intense nausea as one of those "objective" *chairs*,[6] one of those scented mannikins-about-town of history, a thing half-priest, half-satyr (Renan *parfum*), which betrays by the high, shrill falsetto of his applause what he lacks and where he lacks it, who betrays where in this case the Fates have plied their ghastly shears, alas! In too surgeon-like a fashion! This is distasteful to me, and irritates my patience; let him keep patient at such sights who has nothing to lose thereby—such a sight enrages me, such spectators embitter me against the "play," even more than does the play itself (history itself, you understand); Anacreontic moods imperceptibly come over me. This Nature, who gave to the steer its horn, to the lion its χάσμ' ὀδόντων, for what purpose did Nature give me my foot? To kick, by St. Anacreon, and not merely to run away! To trample on all the worm-eaten "chairs," the cowardly contemplators, the lascivious eunuchs of history, the flirters with ascetic ideals, the righteous hypocrites of impotence! All reverence on my part to the ascetic ideal, *insofar as it is honourable!* So long as it believes in itself and plays no pranks on us! But I like not all these coquettish bugs who have an insatiate ambition to smell of the infinite, until eventually the infinite smells of bugs; I like not the whited sepulchres with their stagey reproduction of life; I like not the tired and the used up who wrap themselves in wisdom and look "objective"; I like not the agitators dressed up as heroes, who hide their dummy-heads behind the stalking-horse of an ideal; I like not the ambitious artists who would fain play the ascetic and the priest, and are at bottom nothing but tragic clowns; I like not, again, these newest speculators in idealism, the Anti-Semites, who nowadays roll their eyes in the patent Christian-Aryan-man-of-honour fashion, and by an abuse of moralist attitudes and agitation dodges, so cheap as to exhaust any patience, strive to excite all the blockhead elements in the populace (the

invariable success of every *kind* of intellectual charlatanism in present-day
Germany hangs together with the almost indisputable and already quite
palpable desolation of the German mind, whose cause I look for in a too
exclusive diet, of papers, politics, beer, and Wagnerian music, not forgetting the condition precedent of this diet, the national exclusiveness and
vanity, the strong but narrow principle, "Germany, Germany above everything,"[7] and finally the *paralysis agitans* of "modern ideas"). Europe
nowadays is, above all, wealthy and ingenious in means of excitement; it
apparently has no more crying necessity than *stimulantia* and alcohol.
Hence the enormous counterfeiting of ideals, those most fiery spirits
of the mind; hence too the repulsive, evil-smelling, perjured, pseudo-
alcoholic air everywhere. I should like to know how many cargoes of
imitation idealism, of hero-costumes and high falutin' clap-trap, how many
casks of sweetened pity liqueur (Firm: *la religion de la souffrance*), how
many crutches of righteous indignation for the help of these flat-footed
intellects, how many *comedians* of the Christian moral ideal would need
today to be exported from Europe, to enable its air to smell pure again. It
is obvious that, in regard to this over-production, a new *trade* possibility
lies open; it is obvious that there is a new business to be done in little ideal
idols and obedient "idealists"—don't pass over this tip! Who has sufficient
courage? We have *in our hands* the possibility of idealising the whole earth.
But what am I talking about courage? We only need one thing here—a
hand, a free, a very free hand.

27

Enough! Enough! Let us leave these curiosities and complexities of the
modern spirit, which excite as much laughter as disgust. *Our* problem can
certainly do without them, the problem of the *meaning* of the ascetic
ideal—what has it got to do with yesterday or today? Those things shall
be handled by me more thoroughly and severely in another connexion
(under the title "*A Contribution to the History of European Nihilism*," I refer
for this to a work which I am preparing: *The Will to Power, an Attempt at a
Transvaluation of All Values*). The only reason why I come to allude to it
here is this: the ascetic ideal has at times, even in the most intellectual
sphere, only one real kind of enemies and *damagers*: these are the
comedians of this ideal—for they awake mistrust. Everywhere otherwise,
where the mind is at work seriously, powerfully, and without counterfeiting, it dispenses altogether now with an ideal (the popular expression for
this abstinence is "Atheism")—*with the exception of the will for truth*. But this

will, this *remnant* of an ideal, is, if you will believe me, that ideal itself in its severest and cleverest formulation, esoteric through and through, stripped of all outworks, and consequently not so much its remnant as its *kernel.* Unqualified honest atheism (and its air only do we breathe, we, the most intellectual men of this age) is *not* opposed to that ideal, to the extent that it appears to be; it is rather one of the final phases of its evolution, one of its syllogisms and pieces of inherent logic—it is the awe-inspiring *catastrophe* of a two-thousand-year training in truth, which finally forbids itself the *lie of the belief in God.* (The same course of development in India—quite independently, and consequently of some demonstrative value—the same ideal driving to the same conclusion the decisive point reached five hundred years before the European era, or more precisely at the time of Buddha—it started in the Sankhyam philosophy, and then this was popularised through Buddha, and made into a religion.)

What, I put the question with all strictness, has really *triumphed* over the Christian God? The answer stands in my *Joyful Wisdom,* Aph. 357:

. . . the Christian morality itself, the idea of truth, taken as it was with increasing seriousness, the confessor-subtlety of the Christian conscience translated and sublimated into the scientific conscience into intellectual cleanness at any price. Regarding Nature as though it were a proof of the goodness and guardianship of God; interpreting history in honour of a divine reason, as a constant proof of a moral order of the world and a moral teleology; explaining our own personal experiences, as pious men have for long enough explained them, as though every arrangement, every nod, every single thing were invented and sent out of love for the salvation of the soul; all this is now done away with, all this has the conscience *against* it, and is regarded by every subtler conscience as disreputable, dishonourable, as lying, feminism, weakness, cowardice—by means of this severity, if by means of anything at all, are we, in sooth, *good Europeans* and heirs of Europe's longest and bravest self-mastery. . . .

All great things go to ruin by reason of themselves, by reason of an act of self-dissolution: so wills the law of life, the law of *necessary* "self-mastery" even in the essence of life—ever is the lawgiver finally exposed to the cry, "*patere legem quam ipse tulisti*"; in thus wise did Christianity *go to ruin as a dogma*, through its own morality; in thus wise must Christianity go again to ruin today as a morality—we are standing on the threshold of this event. After Christian truthfulness has drawn one conclusion after the other, it finally draws its *strongest conclusion*, its conclusion *against* itself; this, however, happens, when it puts the question, "*what is the meaning of every will for truth?*" And here again do I touch on my problem, on our problem, my *unknown* friends (for as yet *I know* of no friends): what sense has our whole being, if it does not mean that in our own selves that will for truth has come to its own consciousness *as a problem?* By reason of this attainment of self-consciousness on the part of the will for truth, morality from henceforward—there is no doubt about it—goes *to pieces*: this is that great hundred-act play that is reserved for the next two centuries of Europe, the most terrible, the most mysterious, and perhaps also the most hopeful of all plays.

28

If you except the ascetic ideal, man, the *animal* man had no meaning. His existence on earth contained no end; "What is the purpose of man at all?" was a question without an answer; the *will* for man and the world was lacking; behind every great human destiny rang as a refrain a still greater "Vanity!" The ascetic ideal simply means this: that something *was lacking*, that a tremendous *void* encircled man—he did not know how to justify himself, to explain himself, to affirm himself, he *suffered* from the problem of his own meaning. He suffered also in other ways, he was in the main a *diseased* animal; but his problem was not suffering itself, but the lack of an answer to that crying question, "*To what purpose* do we suffer?" Man, the bravest animal and the one most inured to suffering, does *not* repudiate suffering in itself: he *wills* it, he even seeks it out, provided that he is shown a meaning for it, a *purpose* of suffering. *Not* suffering, but the senselessness of suffering was the curse which till then lay spread over humanity—*and the ascetic ideal gave it a meaning!* It was up till then the only meaning; but any meaning is better than no meaning; the ascetic ideal was in that connexion the "*faute de mieux*" *par excellence* that existed at that time. In that ideal suffering *found an explanation*; the tremendous gap seemed filled; the door to all suicidal Nihilism was closed. The explanation—there is no doubt about it—brought in its train new suffering, deeper, more penetrating, more venomous, gnawing more brutally into life: it brought all suffering under the perspective of *guilt*; but in spite of all that—man was *saved* thereby, he had a *meaning*, and from henceforth was no more like a leaf in the wind, a shuttlecock of chance, of nonsense, he could now "will" something—absolutely immaterial to what end, to what purpose, with what means he wished: *the will itself was saved.* It is absolutely impossible to disguise *what* in point of fact is made clear by every complete will that has taken its direction from the ascetic ideal: this hate of the human, and even more of the animal, and more still of the material, this horror of the senses, of reason itself, this fear of happiness and beauty, this desire to get right away from all illusion, change, growth, death, wishing and even desiring—all this means—let us have the courage to grasp it—a will for Nothingness, a will opposed to life, a repudiation of the most fundamental conditions of life, but it is and remains *a will!* And to say at the end that which I said at the beginning—man will wish *Nothingness* rather than not wish *at all.*

TWILIGHT OF THE IDOLS

TRANSLATED BY

ANTHONY M. LUDOVICI

Contents

PREFACE

To MAINTAIN A CHEERFUL ATTITUDE OF MIND IN THE MIDST OF A GLOOMY and exceedingly responsible task, is no slight artistic feat. And yet, what could be more necessary than cheerfulness? Nothing ever succeeds which exuberant spirits have not helped to produce. Surplus power, alone, is the proof of power. A *transvaluation of all values*—this note of interrogation which is so black, so huge, that it casts a shadow even upon him who affixes it—is a task of such fatal import, that he who undertakes it is compelled every now and then to rush out into the sunlight in order to shake himself free from an earnestness that becomes crushing, far too crushing. This end justifies every means, every event on the road to it is a windfall. Above all *war*. War has always been the great policy of all spirits who have penetrated too far into themselves or who have grown too deep; a wound stimulates the recuperative powers. For many years, a maxim, the origin of which I withhold from learned curiosity, has been my motto:

increscunt animi, virescit volnere virtus.

At other times another means of recovery which is even more to my taste, is to cross-examine idols. There are more idols than realities in the world: this constitutes my "evil eye" for this world: it is also my "evil ear." To put questions in this quarter with a hammer, and to hear perchance that well-known hollow sound which tells of blown-out frogs—what a joy this is for one who has ears even behind his ears, for an old psychologist and Pied Piper like myself in whose presence precisely that which would fain be silent, *must betray itself.*

Even this treatise—as its title shows—is above all a recreation, a ray of sunshine, a leap sideways of a psychologist in his leisure moments. Maybe, too, a new war? And are we again cross-examining new idols? This little work is a great declaration of war; and with regard to the cross-examining of idols, this time it is not the idols of the age but eternal idols which are here struck with a hammer as with a tuning fork—there are certainly no idols which are older, more convinced, and more inflated. Neither are there anymore hollow. This does not alter the fact that they are believed in more than any others, besides they are never called idols—at least, not the most exalted among their number.

FRIEDRICH NIETZSCHE

TURIN, the 30th September 1888,
on the day when the first
book of the Transvaluation
of All Values was finished.

MAXIMS AND MISSILES

1

IDLENESS IS THE PARENT OF ALL PSYCHOLOGY. WHAT? IS PSYCHOLOGY then a—vice?

2

Even the pluckiest among us has but seldom the courage of what he really knows.

3

Aristotle says that in order to live alone, a man must be either an animal or a god. The third alternative is lacking: a man must be both—a *philosopher*.

4

"All truth is simple." Is not this a double lie?

5

Once for all I wish to be blind to many things—Wisdom sets bounds even to knowledge.

6

A man recovers best from his exceptional nature—his intellectuality—by giving his animal instincts a chance.

7

Which is it? Is man only a blunder of God? Or is God only a blunder of man?

8

From the military school of life. That which does not kill me, makes me stronger.

9

Help thyself, then everyone will help thee. A principle of neighbour-love.

10

A man should not play the coward to his deeds. He should not repudiate them once he has performed them. Pangs of conscience are indecent.

11

Can a donkey be tragic? To perish beneath a load that one can neither bear nor throw off? This is the case of the Philosopher.

12

If a man knows the wherefore of his existence, then the manner of it can take care of itself. Man does not aspire to happiness; only the Englishman does that.

13

Man created woman—out of what? Out of a rib of his god—of his "ideal."

14

What? Art thou looking for something? Thou wouldst fain multiply thyself tenfold, a hundredfold? Thou seekest followers? Seek ciphers!

15

Posthumous men, like myself, are not so well understood as men who reflect their age, but they are heard with more respect. In plain English: we are never understood—hence our authority.

16

Among women. "Truth? Oh, you do not know truth! Is it not an outrage on all our *pudeurs?*"

17

There is an artist after my own heart, modest in his needs: he really wants only two things, his bread and his art—*panem et Circen.*

18

He who knows not how to plant his will in things at least endows them with some meaning: that is to say, he believes that a will is already present in them. (A principle of faith.)

19

What? Ye chose virtue and the heaving breast, and at the same time ye squint covetously at the advantages of the unscrupulous. But with virtue ye renounce all "advantages" . . . (to be nailed to an Antisemite's door).

20

The perfect woman perpetrates literature as if it were a petty vice: as an experiment, *en passant*, and looking about her all the while to see whether anybody is noticing her, hoping that somebody *is* noticing her.

21

One should adopt only those situations in which one is in no need of sham virtues, but rather, like the tightrope dancer on his tight rope, in which one must either fall or stand—or escape.

22

"Evil men have no songs."[1] How is it that the Russians have songs?

23

"German intellect"; for eighteen years this has been a *contradictio in adjecto*.

24

By seeking the beginnings of things, a man becomes a crab. The historian looks backwards: in the end he also *believes* backwards.

25

Contentment preserves one even from catching cold. Has a woman who knew that she was well-dressed ever caught cold? No, not even when she had scarcely a rag to her back.

26

I distrust all systematisers, and avoid them. The will to a system shows a lack of honesty.

27

Man thinks woman profound—why? Because he can never fathom her depths. Woman is not even shallow.

28

When woman possesses masculine virtues, she is enough to make you run away. When she possesses no masculine virtues, she herself runs away.

29

"How often conscience had to bite in times gone by! What good teeth it must have had! And today, what is amiss?" A dentist's question.

30

Errors of haste are seldom committed singly. The first time a man always does too much. And precisely on that account he commits a second error, and then he does too little.

31

The trodden worm curls up. This testifies to its caution. It thus reduces its chances of being trodden upon again. In the language of morality: Humility.

32

There is such a thing as a hatred of lies and dissimulation, which is the outcome of a delicate sense of humour; there is also the selfsame hatred but as the result of cowardice, insofar as falsehood is forbidden by Divine law. Too cowardly to lie. . . .

33

What trifles constitute happiness! The sound of a bagpipe. Without music life would be a mistake. The German imagines even God as a songster.

34

On ne peut penser et écrire qu'assis (G. Flaubert). Here I have got you, you nihilist! A sedentary life is the real sin against the Holy Spirit. Only those thoughts that come by walking have any value.

35

There are times when we psychologists are like horses, and grow fretful. We see our own shadow rise and fall before us. The psychologist must look away from himself if he wishes to see anything at all.

36

Do we immoralists injure virtue in any way? Just as little as the anarchists injure royalty. Only since they have been shot at do princes sit firmly on their thrones once more. Moral: *morality must be shot at.*

37

Thou runnest *ahead?* Dost thou do so as a shepherd or as an exception? A third alternative would be the fugitive. . . . First question of conscience.

38

Art thou genuine or art thou only an actor? Art thou a representative or the thing represented, itself? Finally, art thou perhaps simply a copy of an actor? . . . Second question of conscience.

39

The disappointed man speaks: I sought for great men, but all I found were the apes of their ideal.

40

Art thou one who looks on, or one who puts his own shoulder to the wheel? Or art thou one who looks away, or who turns aside? . . . Third question of conscience.

41

Wilt thou go in company, or lead, or go by thyself? . . . A man should know what he desires, and that he desires something. Fourth question of conscience.

42

They were but rungs in my ladder, on them I made my ascent: to that end I had to go beyond them. But they imagined that I wanted to lay myself to rest upon them.

43

What matters it whether I am acknowledged to be right! I am much too right. And he who laughs best today, will also laugh last.

44

The formula of my happiness: a Yea, a Nay, a straight line, a *goal.* . . .

THE PROBLEM OF SOCRATES

1

IN ALL AGES THE WISEST HAVE ALWAYS AGREED IN THEIR JUDGEMENT OF life: *it is no good*. At all times and places the same words have been on their lips—words full of doubt, full of melancholy, full of weariness of life, full of hostility to life. Even Socrates' dying words were: "To live—means to be ill a long while: I owe a cock to the god Aesculapius." Even Socrates had had enough of it. What does that prove? What does it point to? Formerly people would have said (oh, it has been said, and loudly enough too; by our Pessimists loudest of all!): "In any case there must be some truth in this! The *consensus sapientium* is a proof of truth." Shall we say the same today? *May* we do so? "In any case there must be some sickness here," we make reply. These great sages of all periods should first be examined more closely! Is it possible that they were, every one of them, a little shaky on their legs, effete, rocky, decadent? Does wisdom perhaps appear on earth after the manner of a crow attracted by a slight smell of carrion?

2

This irreverent belief that the great sages were decadent types, first occurred to me precisely in regard to that case concerning which both learned and vulgar prejudice was most opposed to my view. I recognised Socrates and Plato as symptoms of decline, as instruments in the disintegration of Hellas, as pseudo-Greek, as anti-Greek (*The Birth of Tragedy*, 1872). That *consensus sapientium*, as I perceived ever more and more clearly, did not in the least prove that they were right in the matter on which they agreed. It proved rather that these sages themselves must have been alike in some physiological particular, in order to assume the same negative attitude towards life—in order to be bound to assume that attitude. After all, judgements and valuations of life, whether for or against, cannot be true: their only value lies in the fact that they are symptoms; they can be considered only as symptoms—per se such judgements are nonsense. You must therefore endeavour by all means to reach out and try to grasp this astonishingly subtle axiom, *that the value of life cannot be estimated*. A living man cannot do so, because he is a contending party, or rather the very object in the dispute, and not a judge; nor can a dead man estimate it—for other reasons. For a philosopher to see a problem in the value of life, is almost an objection against him, a note of interrogation set against his wisdom—a lack of wisdom. What? Is it possible that all these great sages were not only decadents, but that they were not even wise? Let me however return to the problem of Socrates.

3

To judge from his origin, Socrates belonged to the lowest of the low: Socrates was mob. You know, and you can still see it for yourself, how ugly he was. But ugliness, which in itself is an objection, was almost a refutation among the Greeks. Was Socrates really a Greek? Ugliness is not infrequently the expression of thwarted development, or of development arrested by crossing. In other cases it appears as a decadent development. The anthropologists among the criminal specialists declare that the typical criminal is ugly: *monstrum in fronte, monstrum in animo*. But the criminal is a decadent.[1] Was Socrates a typical criminal? At all events this would not clash with that famous physiognomist's judgement which was so repugnant to Socrates' friends. While on his way through Athens a certain foreigner who was no fool at judging by looks, told Socrates to his face that he was a monster, that his body harboured all the worst vices and passions. And Socrates replied simply: "You know me, sir!"

4

Not only are the acknowledged wildness and anarchy of Socrates' instincts indicative of decadence, but also that preponderance of the logical faculties and that malignity of the misshapen which was his special characteristic. Neither should we forget those aural delusions which were religiously interpreted as "the demon of Socrates." Everything in him is exaggerated, *buffo*, caricature, his nature is also full of concealment, of ulterior motives, and of underground currents. I try to understand the idiosyncrasy from which the Socratic equation: Reason = Virtue = Happiness, could have arisen: the weirdest equation ever seen, and one which was essentially opposed to all the instincts of the older Hellenes.

5

With Socrates Greek taste veers round in favour of dialectics: what actually occurs? In the first place a noble taste is vanquished: with dialectics the mob comes to the top. Before Socrates' time, dialectical manners were avoided in good society: they were regarded as bad manners, they were compromising. Young men were cautioned against them. All such proffering of one's reasons was looked upon with suspicion. Honest things like honest men do not carry their reasons on their sleeve in such fashion. It is not good form to make a show of everything. That which needs to be proved cannot be worth much. Wherever authority still belongs to good usage, wherever men do not prove but command, the dialectician is regarded as a sort of clown. People laugh at him, they do not take him seriously. Socrates was a clown who succeeded in making men take him seriously: what then was the matter?

6

A man resorts to dialectics only when he has no other means to hand. People know that they excite suspicion with it and that it is not very convincing. Nothing is more easily dispelled than a dialectical effect: this is proved by the experience of every gathering in which discussions are held. It can be only the last defence of those who have no other weapons. One must require to extort one's right, otherwise one makes no use of it. That is why the Jews were dialecticians. Reynard the Fox was a dialectician: what? And was Socrates one as well?

7

Is the Socratic irony an expression of revolt, of mob resentment? Does Socrates, as a creature suffering under oppression, enjoy his innate ferocity in the knife-thrusts of the syllogism? Does he wreak his revenge on the noblemen he fascinates? As a dialectician a man has a merciless instrument to wield; he can play the tyrant with it: he compromises when he conquers with it. The dialectician leaves it to his opponent to prove that he is no idiot: he infuriates, he likewise paralyses. The dialectician cripples the intellect of his opponent. Can it be that dialectics was only a form of revenge in Socrates?

8

I have given you to understand in what way Socrates was able to repel: now it is all the more necessary to explain how he fascinated. One reason is that he discovered a new kind of *Agon*, and that he was the first fencing-master in the best circles in Athens. He fascinated by appealing to the combative instinct of the Greeks—he introduced a variation into the contests between men and youths. Socrates was also a great erotic.

9

But Socrates divined still more. He saw right through his noble Athenians; he perceived that his case, his peculiar case, was no exception even in his time. The same kind of degeneracy was silently preparing itself everywhere: ancient Athens was dying out. And Socrates understood that the whole world needed him—his means, his remedy, his special artifice for self-preservation. Everywhere the instincts were in a state of anarchy; everywhere people were within an ace of excess: the *monstrum in animo* was the general danger. "The instincts would play the tyrant; we must discover a counter-tyrant who is stronger than they." On the occasion when that physiognomist had unmasked Socrates, and had told him what he was—a crater full of evil desires, the great Master of Irony let fall one or two words more, which provide the key to his nature. "This is true," he said, "but I overcame them all." How did Socrates succeed in mastering himself? His case was at bottom only the extreme and most apparent example of a state of distress which was beginning to be general: that state in which no one was able to master himself and in which the instincts turned one against the other. As the extreme example of this state, he fascinated—his terrifying ugliness made him conspicuous to every eye: it is quite obvious that he fascinated still more as a reply, as a solution, as an apparent cure of this case.

10

When a man finds it necessary, as Socrates did, to create a tyrant out of reason, there is no small danger that something else wishes to play the tyrant. Reason was then discovered as a saviour; neither Socrates nor his "patients" were at liberty to be rational or not, as they pleased; at that time it was *de rigueur*, it had become a last shift. The fanaticism with which the whole of Greek thought plunges into reason, betrays a critical condition of things: men were in danger; there were only two alternatives: either perish or else be absurdly rational. The moral bias of Greek philosophy from Plato onward, is the outcome of a pathological condition, as is also its appreciation of dialectics. Reason = Virtue = Happiness, simply means: we must imitate Socrates, and confront the dark passions permanently with the light of day—the light of reason. We must at all costs be clever, precise, clear: all yielding to the instincts, to the unconscious, leads downwards.

11

I have now explained how Socrates fascinated: he seemed to be a doctor, a saviour. Is it necessary to expose the errors which lay in his faith in "reason at any price?" It is a piece of self-deception on the part of philosophers and moralists to suppose that they can extricate themselves from degeneration by merely waging war upon it. They cannot thus extricate themselves: that which they choose as a means, as the road to salvation, is in itself again only an expression of degeneration—they only modify its mode of manifesting itself: they do not abolish it. Socrates was a misunderstanding. *The whole of the morality of amelioration—that of Christianity as well—was a misunderstanding.* The most blinding light of day: reason at any price; life made clear, cold, cautious, conscious, without instincts, opposed to the instincts, was in itself only a disease, another kind of disease—and by no means a return to "virtue," to "health," and to happiness. To be obliged to fight the instincts—this is the formula of degeneration: as long as life is in the ascending line, happiness is the same as instinct.

12

—Did he understand this himself, this most intelligent of self-deceivers? Did he confess this to himself in the end, in the wisdom of his courage before death. Socrates wished to die. Not Athens, but his own hand gave him the draught of hemlock; he drove Athens to the poisoned cup. "Socrates is not a doctor," he whispered to himself, "death alone can be a doctor here. . . . Socrates himself has only been ill a long while."

"Reason" in Philosophy

You ask me what all idiosyncrasy is in philosophers? . . . For instance their lack of the historical sense, their hatred even of the idea of Becoming, their Egyptianism. They imagine that they do honour to a thing by divorcing it from history *sub specie aeterni*—when they make a mummy of it. All the ideas that philosophers have treated for thousands of years have been mummied concepts; nothing real has ever come out of their hands alive. These idolaters of concepts merely kill and stuff things when they worship—they threaten the life of everything they adore. Death, change, age, as well as procreation and growth, are in their opinion objections—even refutations. That which is cannot evolve; that which evolves *is* not. Now all of them believe, and even with desperation, in Being. But, as they cannot lay hold of it, they try to discover reasons why this privilege is withheld from them. "Some merely apparent quality, some deception must be the cause of our not being able to ascertain the nature of Being: where is the deceiver?" "We have him," they cry rejoicing; "it is sensuality!" These senses, *which in other things are so immoral*, cheat us concerning the true world. Moral: we must get rid of the deception of the senses, of Becoming, of history, of falsehood. History is nothing more than the belief in the senses, the belief in falsehood. Moral: we must say "no" to everything in which the senses believe: to all the rest of mankind: all that belongs to the "people." Let us be philosophers, mummies, monotono-theists, gravediggers! And above all, away with the *body*, this wretched *idée fixe* of the senses, infected with all the faults of logic that exist, refuted, even impossible, although it be impudent enough to pose as if it were real!

2

With a feeling of great reverence I except the name of Heraclitus. If the rest of the philosophic gang rejected the evidences of the senses, because the latter revealed a state of multifariousness and change, he rejected the same evidence because it revealed things as if they possessed permanence and unity. Even Heraclitus did an injustice to the senses. The latter lie neither as the Eleatics believed them to lie, nor as he believed them to lie—they do not lie at all. The interpretations we give to their evidence is what first introduces falsehood into it; for instance the lie of unity, the lie of matter, of substance and of permanence. Reason is the cause of our falsifying the evidence of the senses. Insofar as the senses show us a state of Becoming, of transiency, and of change, they do not lie. But in declaring that Being was an empty illusion, Heraclitus will remain eternally right. The "apparent" world is the only world: the "true world" is no more than a false adjunct thereto.

3

And what delicate instruments of observation we have in our senses! This human nose, for instance, of which no philosopher has yet spoken with reverence and gratitude, is, for the present, the most finely adjusted instrument at our disposal: it is able to register even such slight changes of movement as the spectroscope would be unable to record. Our scientific triumphs at the present day extend precisely so far as we have accepted the evidence of our senses—as we have sharpened and armed them, and learned to follow them up to the end. What remains is abortive and not yet science—that is to say, metaphysics, theology, psychology, epistemology, or formal science, or a doctrine of symbols, like logic and its applied form mathematics. In all these things reality does not come into consideration at all, even as a problem; just as little as does the question concerning the general value of such a convention of symbols as logic.

4

The other idiosyncrasy of philosophers is no less dangerous; it consists in confusing the last and the first things. They place that which makes its appearance last—unfortunately! For it ought not to appear at all! The "highest concept," that is to say, the most general, the emptiest, the last cloudy streak of evaporating reality, at the beginning as the beginning. This again is only their manner of expressing their veneration: the highest thing must not have grown out of the lowest, it must not have grown at all. . . . Moral: everything of the first rank must be *causa sui*. To have been derived from something else is as good as an objection; it sets the value of a thing in question. All superior values are of the first rank, all the highest concepts—that of Being, of the Absolute, of Goodness, of Truth, and of Perfection; all these things cannot have been evolved; they must therefore be *causa sui*. All these things cannot however be unlike one another, they cannot be opposed to one another. Thus they attain to their stupendous concept "God." The last, most attenuated and emptiest thing is postulated as the first thing, as the absolute cause, as *ens realissimum*. Fancy humanity having to take the brain diseases of morbid cobweb-spinners seriously! And it has paid dearly for having done so.

5

—Against this let us set the different manner in which we (you observe that I am courteous enough to say "we") conceive the problem of the error and deceptiveness of things. Formerly people regarded change and evolution in general as the proof of appearance, as a sign of the fact that something must be there that leads us astray. Today, on the other hand, we realise that precisely as far as the rational bias forces us to postulate unity, identity, permanence, substance, cause, materiality, and being, we are in a measure involved in error, driven necessarily to error; however certain we may feel, as the result of a strict examination of the matter, that the error lies here. It is just the same here as with the motion of the sun: In its case it was our eyes that were wrong; in the matter of the concepts above-mentioned it is our language itself that pleads most constantly in their favour. In its origin language belongs to an age of the most rudimentary-forms of psychology: if we try to conceive of the first conditions of the metaphysics of language, i.e., in plain English, of reason, we immediately find ourselves in the midst of a system of fetichism. For here, the doer and his deed are seen in all circumstances, will is believed in as a cause in general; the ego is taken for granted, the ego as Being, and as substance, and the faith in the ego as substance is projected into all things—in this way, alone, the concept "thing" is created. Being is thought into and insinuated into everything as cause; from the concept "ego," alone, can the concept "Being" proceed. At the beginning stands the tremendously fatal error of supposing the will to be something that actuates—a faculty. Now we know that it is only a word.[1] Very much later, in a world a thousand times more enlightened, the assurance, the subjective certitude, in the handling of the categories of reason came into the minds of philosophers as a surprise. They concluded that these categories could not be derived from experience—on the contrary, the whole of experience rather contradicts them. *Whence do they come therefore?* In India, as in Greece, the same mistake was made: "we must already once have lived in a higher world (instead of in a much lower one, which would have been the truth!), we must have been divine, for we possess reason!" . . . Nothing indeed has exercised a more simple power of persuasion hitherto than the error of Being, as it was formulated by the Eleatics for instance: in its favour are every word and every sentence that we utter! Even the opponents of the Eleatics succumbed to the seductive powers of their concept of Being. Among others there was Democritus in his discovery of the atom. "Reason" in language! Oh what a deceptive old witch it has been! I fear we shall never be rid of God, so long as we still believe in grammar.

6

People will feel grateful to me if I condense a point of view, which is at once so important and so new, into four theses: by this means I shall facilitate comprehension, and shall likewise challenge contradiction.

Proposition One. The reasons upon which the apparent nature of "this" world have been based, rather tend to prove its reality—any other kind of reality defies demonstration.

Proposition Two. The characteristics with which man has endowed the "true Being" of things are the characteristics of non-Being, of *nonentity*. The "true world" has been erected upon a contradiction of the real world; and it is indeed an apparent world, seeing that it is merely a *moralo-optical* delusion.

Proposition Three. There is no sense in spinning yarns about another world, provided, of course, that we do not possess a mighty instinct which urges us to slander, belittle, and cast suspicion upon this life: in this case we should be avenging ourselves on this life with the phantasmagoria of "another," of a "better" life.

Proposition Four. To divide the world into a "true" and an "apparent" world, whether after the manner of Christianity or of Kant (after all a Christian in disguise), is only a sign of decadence—a symptom of *degenerating* life. The fact that the artist esteems the appearance of a thing higher than reality is no objection to this statement. For "appearance" signifies once more reality here, but in a selected, strengthened and corrected form. The tragic artist is no pessimist—he says *Yea* to everything questionable and terrible, he is Dionysian.

HOW THE "TRUE WORLD" ULTIMATELY BECAME A FABLE

THE HISTORY OF AN ERROR

1. THE TRUE WORLD, ATTAINABLE TO THE SAGE, THE PIOUS MAN AND THE man of virtue—he lives in it, *he is it.*

    (The most ancient form of the idea was relatively clever, simple, convincing. It was a paraphrase of the proposition "I, Plato, am the truth.")

2. The true world which is unattainable for the moment, is promised to the sage, to the pious man and to the man of virtue ("to the sinner who repents").

    (Progress of the idea: it becomes more subtle, more insidious, more evasive—*it becomes a woman*, it becomes Christian.)

3. The true world is unattainable, it cannot be proved, it cannot promise anything; but even as a thought, alone, it is a comfort, an obligation, a command.

    (At bottom this is still the old sun; but seen through mist and scepticism: the idea has become sublime, pale, northern, Königsbergian.[1])

4. The true world—is it unattainable? At all events it is unattained. And as unattained it is also *unknown.* Consequently it no longer comforts, nor saves, nor constrains: what could something unknown constrain us to?

    (The grey of dawn. Reason stretches itself and yawns for the first time. The cock-crow of positivism.)

5. The "true world"—an idea that no longer serves any purpose, that no longer constrains one to anything—a useless idea that has become quite superfluous, consequently an exploded idea: let us abolish it!

    (Bright daylight; breakfast; the return of common sense and of cheerfulness; Plato blushes for shame and all free-spirits kick up a shindy.)

6. We have suppressed the true world: what world survives? The apparent world perhaps? . . . Certainly not! *In abolishing the true world we have also abolished the world of appearance!*

(Noon; the moment of the shortest shadows; the end of the longest error; mankind's zenith; *Incipit Zarathustra.*)

MORALITY AS THE ENEMY
OF NATURE

1

THERE IS A TIME WHEN ALL PASSIONS ARE SIMPLY FATAL IN THEIR ACTION, when they wreck their victims with the weight of their folly—and there is a later period, a very much later period, when they marry with the spirit, when they "spiritualise" themselves. Formerly, owing to the stupidity inherent in passion, men waged war against passion itself: men pledged themselves to annihilate it—all ancient moral-mongers were unanimous on this point, "*il faut tuer les passions.*" The most famous formula for this stands in the New Testament, in that Sermon on the Mount, where, let it be said incidentally, things are by no means regarded *from a height*. It is said there, for instance, with an application to sexuality: "if thy eye offend thee, pluck it out": fortunately no Christian acts in obedience to this precept. To annihilate the passions and desires, simply on account of their stupidity, and to obviate the unpleasant consequences of their stupidity, seems to us today merely an aggravated form of stupidity. We no longer admire those dentists who extract teeth simply in order that they may not ache again. On the other hand, it will be admitted with some reason, that on the soil from which Christianity grew, the idea of the "spiritualisation of passion" could not possibly have been conceived. The early Church, as everyone knows, certainly did wage war against the "intelligent," in favour of the "poor in spirit." In these circumstances how could the passions be combated intelligently? The Church combats passion by means of excision of all kinds: its practise, its "remedy," is *castration*. It never inquires "how can a desire be spiritualised, beautified, deified?" In all ages it has

319

laid the weight of discipline in the process of extirpation (the extirpation of sensuality, pride, lust of dominion, lust of property, and revenge). But to attack the passions at their roots, means attacking life itself at its source: the method of the Church is hostile to life.

2

The same means, castration and extirpation, are instinctively chosen for waging war against a passion, by those who are too weak of will, too degenerate, to impose some sort of moderation upon it; by those natures who, to speak in metaphor (and without metaphor), need *la Trappe*, or some kind of ultimatum of war, a *gulf* set between themselves and a passion. Only degenerates find radical methods indispensable: weakness of will, or more strictly speaking, the inability not to react to a stimulus, is in itself simply another form of degeneracy. Radical and mortal hostility to sensuality, remains a suspicious symptom: it justifies one in being suspicious of the general state of one who goes to such extremes. Moreover, that hostility and hatred reach their height only when such natures no longer possess enough strength of character to adopt the radical remedy, to renounce their inner "Satan." Look at the whole history of the priests, the philosophers, and the artists as well: the most poisonous diatribes against the senses have not been said by the impotent, nor by the ascetics; but by those impossible ascetics, by those who found it necessary to be ascetics.

3

The spiritualisation of sensuality is called *love*: it is a great triumph over Christianity. Another triumph is our spiritualisation of hostility. It consists in the fact that we are beginning to realise very profoundly the value of having enemies: in short that with them we are forced to do and to conclude precisely the reverse of what we previously did and concluded. In all ages the Church wished to annihilate its enemies: we, the immoralists and Antichrists, see our advantage in the survival of the Church. Even in political life, hostility has now become more spiritual—much more cautious, much more thoughtful, and much more moderate. Almost every party sees its self-preservative interests in preventing the Opposition from going to pieces; and the same applies to politics on a grand scale. A new creation, more particularly, like the new Empire, has more need of enemies than friends: only as a contrast does it begin to feel necessary, only as a contrast does it *become* necessary. And we behave in precisely the same way to the "inner enemy": in this quarter too we have spiritualised enmity, in this quarter too we have understood its value. A man is productive only insofar as he is rich in contrasted instincts; he can remain young only on condition that his soul does not begin to take things easy and to yearn for peace. Nothing has grown more alien to us than that old desire—the "peace of the soul," which is the aim of Christianity. Nothing could make us less envious than the moral cow and the plump happiness of a clean conscience. The man who has renounced war has renounced a grand life. In many cases, of course, "peace of the soul" is merely a misunderstanding— it is something *very different* which has failed to find a more honest name for itself. Without either circumlocution or prejudice I will suggest a few cases. "Peace of the soul" may for instance be the sweet effulgence of rich animality in the realm of morality (or religion). Or the first presage of weariness, the first shadow that evening, every kind of evening, is wont to cast. Or a sign that the air is moist, and that winds are blowing up from the south. Or unconscious gratitude for a good digestion (sometimes called "brotherly love"). Or the serenity of the convalescent, on whose lips all things have a new taste, and who bides his time. Or the condition which follows upon a thorough gratification of our strongest passion, the well-being of unaccustomed satiety. Or the senility of our will, of our desires, and of our vices. Or laziness, coaxed by vanity into togging itself out in a moral garb. Or the ending of a state of long suspense and of agonising uncertainty, by a state of certainty, of even terrible certainty. Or the expression of ripeness and mastery in the midst of a task, of a creative work, of a production, of a thing willed, the calm breathing that denotes that "freedom of will" has been attained. Who knows? Maybe *The Twilight of the Idols* is only a sort of "peace of the soul."

4

I will formulate a principle. All naturalism in morality—that is to say, every sound morality is ruled by a life instinct—any one of the laws of life is fulfiled by the definite canon "thou shalt," "thou shalt not," and any sort of obstacle or hostile element in the road of life is thus cleared away. Conversely, the morality which is antagonistic to nature—that is to say, almost every morality that has been taught, honoured and preached hitherto, is directed precisely against the life-instincts—it is a condemnation, now secret, now blatant and impudent, of these very instincts. Inasmuch as it says "God sees into the heart of man," it says Nay to the profoundest and most superior desires of life and takes God as the enemy of life. The saint in whom God is well pleased, is the ideal eunuch. Life terminates where the "Kingdom of God" begins.

5

Admitting that you have understood the villainy of such a mutiny against life as that which has become almost sacrosanct in Christian morality, you have fortunately understood something besides; and that is the futility, the fictitiousness, the absurdity and the falseness of such a mutiny. For the condemnation of life by a living creature is after all but the symptom of a definite kind of life: the question as to whether the condemnation is justified or the reverse is not even raised. In order even to approach the problem of the value of life, a man would need to be placed outside life, and moreover know it as well as one, as many, as all in fact, who have lived it. These are reasons enough to prove to us that this problem is an inaccessible one to us. When we speak of values, we speak under the inspiration, and through the optics of life: life itself urges us to determine values: life itself values through us when we determine values. From which it follows that even that morality which is antagonistic to life, and which conceives God as the opposite and the condemnation of life, is only a valuation of life—of what life? Of what kind of life? But I have already answered this question: it is the valuation of declining, of enfeebled, of exhausted and of condemned life. Morality, as it has been understood hitherto—as it was finally formulated by Schopenhauer in the words "The Denial of the Will to Life," is the instinct of degeneration itself, which converts itself into an imperative: it says: "Perish!" It is the death sentence of men who are already doomed.

6

Let us at last consider how exceedingly simple it is on our part to say: "Man should be thus and thus!" Reality shows us a marvellous wealth of types, and a luxuriant variety of forms and changes: and yet the first wretch of a moral loafer that comes along cries "No! Man should be different!" He even knows what man should be like, does this sanctimonious prig: he draws his own face on the wall and declares: "*ecce homo!*" But even when the moralist addresses himself only to the individual and says "thus and thus shouldst thou be!" he still makes an ass of himself. The individual in his past and future is a piece of fate, one law the more, one necessity the more for all that is to come and is to be. To say to him "change thyself," is tantamount to saying that everything should change, even backwards as well. Truly these have been consistent moralists, they wished man to be different, i.e., virtuous; they wished him to be after their own image—that is to say sanctimonious humbugs. And to this end they denied the world! No slight form of insanity! No modest form of immodesty! Morality, insofar it condemns per se, and *not* out of any aim, consideration or motive of life, is a specific error, for which no one should feel any mercy, a degenerate idiosyncrasy, that has done an unutterable amount of harm. We others, we immoralists, on the contrary, have opened our hearts wide to all kinds of comprehension, understanding and approbation.[1] We do not deny readily, we glory in saying yea to things. Our eyes have opened ever wider and wider to that economy which still employs and knows how to use to its own advantage all that which the sacred craziness of priests and the morbid reason in priests, rejects; to that economy in the law of life which draws its own advantage even out of the repulsive race of bigots, the priests and the virtuous—what advantage? But we ourselves, we immoralists, are the reply to this question.

THE FOUR GREAT ERRORS

1

THE ERROR OF THE CONFUSION OF CAUSE AND EFFECT. THERE IS NO MORE dangerous error than to confound the effect with the cause: I call this error the intrinsic perversion of reason. Nevertheless this error is one of the most ancient and most recent habits of mankind. In one part of the world it has even been canonised; and it bears the name of "Religion" and "Morality." Every postulate formulated by religion and morality contains it. Priests and the promulgators of moral laws are the promoters of this perversion of reason. Let me give you an example. Everybody knows the book of the famous Cornaro, in which he recommends his slender diet as the recipe for a long, happy and also virtuous life. Few books have been so widely read, and to this day many thousand copies of it are still printed annually in England. I do not doubt that there is scarcely a single book (the Bible of course excepted) that has worked more mischief, shortened more lives, than this well-meant curiosity. The reason of this is the confusion of effect and cause. This worthy Italian saw the cause of his long life in his diet: whereas the prerequisites of long life, which are exceptional slowness of molecular change, and a low rate of expenditure in energy, were the cause of his meagre diet. He was not at liberty to eat a small or a great amount. His frugality was not the result of free choice, he would have been ill had he eaten more. He who does not happen to be a carp, however, is not only wise to eat well, but is also compelled to do so. A scholar of the present day, with his rapid consumption of nervous energy, would soon go to the dogs on Cornaro's diet. *Crede experto.*

2

The most general principle lying at the root of every religion and morality, is this: "Do this and that and avoid this and that—and thou wilt be happy. Otherwise——." Every morality and every religion is this Imperative— I call it the great original sin of reason—*immortal unreason*. In my mouth this principle is converted into its opposite—first example of my *Transvaluation of All Values*: a well-constituted man, a man who is one of "Nature's lucky strokes," *must* perform certain actions and instinctively fear other actions; he introduces the element of order, of which he is the physiological manifestation, into his relations with men and things. In a formula: his virtue is the consequence of his good constitution. Longevity and plentiful offspring are not the reward of virtue, virtue itself is on the contrary that retardation of the metabolic process which, among other things, results in a long life and in plentiful offspring, in short in *Cornarism*. The Church and morality say: "A race, a people perish through vice and luxury." My reinstated reason says: when a people are going to the dogs, when they are degenerating physiologically, vice and luxury (that is to say, the need of ever stronger and more frequent stimuli such as all exhausted natures are acquainted with) are bound to result. Such and such a young man grows pale and withered prematurely. His friends say this or that illness is the cause of it. I say: the fact that he became ill, the fact that he did not resist illness, was in itself already the outcome of impoverished life, of hereditary exhaustion. The newspaper reader says: such and such a party by committing such an error will meet its death. My superior politics say: a party that can make such mistakes, is in its last agony—it no longer possesses any certainty of instinct. Every mistake is in every sense the sequel to degeneration of the instincts, to disintegration of the will. This is almost the definition of evil, Everything valuable is instinct—and consequently easy, necessary, free. Exertion is an objection, the god is characteristically different from the hero (in my language: light feet are the first attribute of divinity).

3

The error of false causality. In all ages men have believed that they knew what a cause was: but whence did we derive this knowledge, or more accurately, this faith in the fact that we know? Out of the realm of the famous "inner facts of consciousness," not one of which has yet proved itself to be a fact. We believed ourselves to be causes even in the action of the will; we thought that in this matter at least we caught causality red-handed. No one doubted that all the *antecedentia* of an action were to be sought in consciousness, and could be discovered there—as "motive"—if only they were sought. Otherwise we should not be free to perform them, we should not have been responsible for them. Finally who would have questioned that a thought is caused? That the ego causes the thought? Of these three "facts of inner consciousness" by means of which causality seemed to be guaranteed, the first and most convincing is that of the will as cause; the conception of consciousness ("spirit") as a cause, and subsequently that of the ego (the "subject") as a cause, were merely born afterwards, once the causality of the will stood established as "given," as a fact of experience. Meanwhile we have come to our senses. Today we no longer believe a word of all this. The "inner world" is full of phantoms and will-o'-the-wisps: the will is one of these. The will no longer actuates, consequently it no longer explains anything—all it does is to accompany processes; it may even be absent. The so-called "motive" is another error. It is merely a ripple on the surface of consciousness, a side issue of the action, which is much more likely to conceal than to reveal the *antecedentia* of the latter. And as for the ego! It has become legendary, fictional, a play upon words: it has ceased utterly and completely from thinking, feeling, and willing! What is the result of it all? There are no such things as spiritual causes. The whole of popular experience on this subject went to the devil! That is the result of it all. For we had blissfully abused that experience, we had built the world upon it as a world of causes, as a world of will, as a world of spirit. The most antiquated and most traditional psychology has been at work here, it has done nothing else: all phenomena were deeds in the light of this psychology, and all deeds were the result of will; according to it the world was a complex mechanism of agents, an agent (a "subject") lay at the root of all things. Man projected his three "inner facts of consciousness," the will, the spirit, and the ego in which he believed most firmly, outside himself. He first deduced the concept Being out of the concept Ego, he supposed "things" to exist as he did himself, according to his notion of the ego as cause. Was it to be wondered at that later on he always found in things only that which he had laid in them? The thing itself, I repeat, the concept thing was merely a reflex of the belief in the ego as cause. And even your atom, my dear good Mechanists and Physicists, what an amount of error, of rudimentary psychology still adheres to it! Not to speak of the "thing-in-itself," of the *horrendum pudendum* of the metaphysicians! The error of spirit regarded as a cause, confounded with reality! And made the measure of reality! And called *God*!

4

The Error of imaginary Causes. Starting out from dreamland, we find that to any definite sensation, like that produced by a distant cannon shot for instance, we are wont to ascribe a cause after the fact (very often quite a little romance in which the dreamer himself is, of course, the hero). Meanwhile the sensation becomes protracted like a sort of continuous echo, until, as it were, the instinct of causality allows it to come to the front rank, no longer however as a chance occurrence, but as a thing which has some meaning. The cannon shot presents itself in a *causal* manner, by means of an apparent reversal in the order of time. That which occurs last, the motivation, is experienced first, often with a hundred details which flash past like lightning, and the shot is the *result.* What has happened? The ideas suggested by a particular state of our senses, are misinterpreted as the cause of that state. As a matter of fact we proceed in precisely the same manner when we are awake. The greater number of our general sensations—every kind of obstacle, pressure, tension, explosion in the interplay of the organs, and more particularly the condition of the *nervus sympathicus*—stimulate our instinct of causality: we will have a reason which will account for our feeling thus or thus—for feeling ill or well. We are never satisfied by merely ascertaining the fact that we feel thus or thus: we admit this fact—we become conscious of it—only when we have attributed it to some kind of motivation. Memory, which, in such circumstances unconsciously becomes active, adduces former conditions of a like kind, together with the causal interpretations with which they are associated— but not their real cause. The belief that the ideas, the accompanying processes of consciousness, have been the causes, is certainly produced by the agency of memory. And in this way we become *accustomed* to a particular interpretation of causes which, truth to tell, actually hinders and even utterly prevents the investigation of the proper cause.

5

The Psychological Explanation of the above Fact. To trace something unfamiliar back to something familiar, is at once a relief, a comfort and a satisfaction, while it also produces a feeling of power. The unfamiliar involves danger, anxiety and care—the fundamental instinct is to get rid of these painful circumstances. First principle: any explanation is better than none at all. Since, at bottom, it is only a question of shaking one's self free from certain oppressive ideas, the means employed to this end are not selected with overmuch punctiliousness: the first idea by means of which the unfamiliar is revealed as familiar, produces a feeling of such comfort that it is "held to be true." The proof of happiness ("of power") as the criterion of truth. The instinct of causality is therefore conditioned and stimulated by the feeling of fear. Whenever possible, the question "why?" should not only educe the cause as cause, but rather a certain kind of cause—a comforting, liberating and reassuring cause. The first result of this need is that something known or already experienced, and recorded in the memory, is posited as the cause. The new factor, that which has not been experienced and which is unfamiliar, is excluded from the sphere of causes. Not only do we try to find a certain kind of explanation as the cause, but those kinds of explanations are selected and preferred which dissipate most rapidly the sensation of strangeness, novelty and unfamiliarity—in fact the most ordinary explanations. And the result is that a certain manner of postulating causes tends to predominate ever more and more, becomes concentrated into a system, and finally reigns supreme, to the complete exclusion of all other causes and explanations. The banker thinks immediately of business, the Christian of "sin," and the girl of her love affair.

6

The whole Domain of Morality and Religion may be classified under the Rubric *"Imaginary Causes."* The "explanation" of general unpleasant sensations. These sensations are dependent upon certain creatures who are hostile to us (evil spirits: the most famous example of this—the mistaking of hysterical women for witches). These sensations are dependent upon actions which are reprehensible (the feeling of "sin," "sinfulness" is a manner of accounting for a certain physiological disorder—people always find reasons for being dissatisfied with themselves). These sensations depend upon punishment, upon compensation for something which we ought not to have done, which we ought not to have been (this idea was generalised in a more impudent form by Schopenhauer, into that principle in which morality appears in its real colours—that is to say, as a veritable poisoner and slanderer of life: "all great suffering, whether mental or physical, reveals what we deserve: for it could not visit us if we did not deserve it"—*The World as Will and Idea*, vol. 2, p. 666). These sensations are the outcome of ill-considered actions, having evil consequences, (—the passions, the senses, postulated as causes, as guilty. By means of other calamities distressing physiological conditions are interpreted as "merited"). The "explanation" of pleasant sensations. These sensations are dependent upon a trust in God. They may depend upon our consciousness of having done one or two good actions (a so-called "good conscience" is a physiological condition, which may be the outcome of good digestion). They may depend upon the happy issue of certain undertakings (an ingenuous mistake: the happy issue of an undertaking certainly does not give a hypochondriac or a Pascal any general sensation of pleasure). They may depend upon faith, love and hope—the Christian virtues. As a matter of fact all these pretended explanations are but the results of certain states, and as it were translations of feelings of pleasure and pain into a false dialect: a man is in a condition of hopefulness because the dominant physiological sensation of his being is again one of strength and wealth; he trusts in God because the feeling of abundance and power gives him a peaceful state of mind. Morality and religion are completely and utterly parts of the psychology of error: in every particular case cause and effect are confounded; as truth is confounded with the effect of that which is believed to be true; or a certain state of consciousness is confounded with the chain of causes which brought it about.

7

The Error of Free-Will. At present we no longer have any mercy upon the concept "freewill": we know only too well what it is—the most egregious theological trick that has ever existed for the purpose of making mankind "responsible" in a theological manner—that is to say, to make mankind dependent upon theologians. I will now explain to you only the psychology of the whole process of inculcating the sense of responsibility. Wherever men try to trace responsibility home to anyone, it is the instinct of punishment and of the desire to judge which is active. Becoming is robbed of its innocence when any particular condition of things is traced to a will, to intentions and to responsible actions. The doctrine of the will was invented principally for the purpose of punishment—that is to say, with the intention of tracing guilt. The whole of ancient psychology, or the psychology of the will, is the outcome of the fact that its originators, who were the priests at the head of ancient communities, wanted to create for themselves a right to administer punishments—or the right for God to do so. Men were thought of as "free" in order that they might be judged and punished—in order that they might be held guilty: consequently every action had to be regarded as voluntary, and the origin of every action had to be imagined as lying in consciousness (in this way the most fundamentally fraudulent character of psychology was established as the very principle of psychology itself). Now that we have entered upon the opposite movement, now that we immoralists are trying with all our power to eliminate the concepts of guilt and punishment from the world once more, and to cleanse psychology, history, nature and all social institutions and customs of all signs of those two concepts, we recognise no more radical opponents than the theologians, who with their notion of "a moral order of things," still continue to pollute the innocence of Becoming with punishment and guilt. Christianity is the metaphysics of the hangman.

8

What then, alone, can our teaching be? That no one gives man his qualities, neither God, society his parents, his ancestors, nor himself (this nonsensical idea which is at last refuted here, was taught as "intelligible freedom" by Kant, and perhaps even as early as Plato himself). No one is responsible for the fact that he exists at all, that he is constituted as he is, and that he happens to be in certain circumstances and in a particular environment. The fatality of his being cannot be divorced from the fatality of all that which has been and will be. This is not the result of an individual intention, of a will, of an aim, there is no attempt at attaining to any "ideal man," or "ideal happiness" or "ideal morality" with him—it is absurd to wish him to be careering towards some sort of purpose. *We* invented the concept "purpose"; in reality purpose is altogether lacking. One is necessary, one is a piece of fate, one belongs to the whole, one is in the whole—there is nothing that could judge, measure, compare, and condemn our existence, for that would mean judging, measuring, comparing and condemning the whole. *But there is nothing outside the whole!* The fact that no one shall any longer be made responsible, that the nature of existence may not be traced to a *causa prima*, that the world is an entity neither as a sensorium nor as a spirit—*this alone is the great deliverance*— thus alone is the innocence of Becoming restored. . . . The concept "God" has been the greatest objection to existence hitherto. . . . We deny God, we deny responsibility in God: thus alone do we save the world.

THE "IMPROVERS" OF MANKIND

1

YOU ARE AWARE OF MY DEMAND UPON PHILOSOPHERS, THAT THEY SHOULD take up a stand Beyond Good and Evil—that they should have the illusion of the moral judgement beneath them. This demand is the result of a point of view which I was the first to formulate: *that there are no such things as moral facts*. Moral judgement has this in common with the religious one, that it believes in realities which are not real. Morality is only an interpretation of certain phenomena: or, more strictly speaking, a misinterpretation of them. Moral judgement, like the religious one, belongs to a stage of ignorance in which even the concept of reality, the distinction between real and imagined things, is still lacking: so that truth, at such a stage, is applied to a host of things which today we call "imaginary." That is why the moral judgement must never be taken quite literally: as such it is sheer nonsense. As a sign code, however, it is invaluable: to him at least who knows, it reveals the most valuable facts concerning cultures and inner conditions, which did not know enough to "understand" themselves. Morality is merely a sign-language, simply symptomatology: one must already know what it is all about in order to turn it to any use.

2

Let me give you one example, quite provisionally. In all ages there have been people who wished to "improve" mankind: this above all is what was called morality. But the most different tendencies are concealed beneath the same word. Both the taming of the beast man, and the rearing of a particular type of man, have been called "improvement": these zoological *termini,* alone, represent real things—real things of which the typical "improver," the priest, naturally knows nothing, and will know nothing. To call the taming of an animal "improving" it, sounds to our ears almost like a joke. He who knows what goes on in menageries, doubts very much whether an animal is improved in such places. It is certainly weakened, it is made less dangerous, and by means of the depressing influence of fear, pain, wounds, and hunger, it is converted into a sick animal. And the same holds good of the tamed man whom the priest has "improved." In the early years of the Middle Ages, during which the Church was most distinctly and above all a menagerie, the most beautiful examples of the "blond beast" were hunted down in all directions—the noble Germans, for instance, were "improved." But what did this "improved" German, who had been lured to the monastery look like after the process? He looked like a caricature of man, like an abortion: he had become a "sinner," he was caged up, he had been imprisoned behind a host of appalling notions. He now lay there, sick, wretched, malevolent even toward himself: full of hate for the instincts of life, full of suspicion in regard to all that is still strong and happy. In short a "Christian." In physiological terms: in a fight with an animal, the only way of making it weak may be to make it sick. The Church understood this: it ruined man, it made him weak—but it laid claim to having "improved" him.

3

Now let us consider the other case which is called morality, the case of the rearing of a particular race and species. The most magnificent example of this is offered by Indian morality, and is sanctioned religiously as the *Law of Manu.* In this book the task is set of rearing no less than four races at once: a priestly race, a warrior race, a merchant and agricultural race, and finally a race of servants—the Sudras. It is quite obvious that we are no longer in a circus watching tamers of wild animals in this book. To have conceived even the plan of such a breeding scheme, presupposes the existence of a man who is a hundred times milder and more reasonable than the mere lion-tamer. One breathes more freely, after stepping out of the Christian atmosphere of hospitals and prisons, into this more salubrious, loftier and more spacious world. What a wretched thing the New Testament is beside Manu, what an evil odour hangs around it! But even this organisation found it necessary to be terrible—not this time in a struggle with the animal-man, but with his opposite, the noncaste man, the hotch-potch man, the Chandala. And once again it had no other means of making him weak and harmless, than by making him sick—it was the struggle with the greatest "number." Nothing perhaps is more offensive to our feelings than these measures of security on the part of Indian morality. The third edict, for instance (Avadana-Sastra I), which treats "of impure vegetables," ordains that the only nourishment that the Chandala should be allowed must consist of garlic and onions, as the holy scriptures forbid their being given corn or grain-bearing fruit, water and fire. The same edict declares that the water which they need must be drawn neither out of rivers, wells or ponds, but only out of the ditches leading to swamps and out of the holes left by the footprints of animals. They are likewise forbidden to wash either their linen or themselves, since the water which is graciously granted to them must only be used for quenching their thirst. Finally Sudra women are forbidden to assist Chandala women at their confinements, while Chandala women are also forbidden to assist each other at such times. The results of sanitary regulations of this kind could not fail to make themselves felt; deadly epidemics and the most ghastly venereal diseases soon appeared, and in consequence of these again "the Law of the Knife"—that is to say circumcision, was prescribed for male children and the removal of the small labia from the females. Manu himself says: "the Chandala are the fruit of adultery, incest, and crime (this is the necessary consequence of the idea of breeding). Their clothes shall consist only of the rags torn from corpses, their vessels shall be the fragments of broken pottery, their ornaments shall be made of old iron, and their religion shall be the worship of evil spirits; without rest they shall wander from place to place. They are forbidden to write from left to right or to use their right hand in writing: the use of the right hand and writing from left to right are reserved to people of virtue, to people of race."

4

These regulations are instructive enough: we can see in them the absolutely pure and primeval humanity of the Aryans—we learn that the notion "pure blood," is the reverse of harmless. On the other hand it becomes clear among which people the hatred, the Chandala hatred of this humanity has been immortalised, among which people it has become religion and genius. From this point of view the gospels are documents of the highest value; and the Book of Enoch is still more so. Christianity as sprung from Jewish roots and comprehensible only as grown upon this soil, represents the counter-movement against that morality of breeding, of race and of privilege: it is essentially an anti-Aryan religion: Christianity is the transvaluation of all Aryan values, the triumph of Chandala values, the proclaimed gospel of the poor and of the low, the general insurrection of all the downtrodden, the wretched, the bungled and the botched, against the "race"—the immortal revenge of the Chandala as the *religion of love*.

5

The morality of breeding and the morality of taming, in the means which they adopt in order to prevail, are quite worthy of each other: we may lay down as a leading principle that in order to create morality a man must have the absolute will to immorality. This is the great and strange problem with which I have so long been occupied: the psychology of the "Improvers" of mankind. A small, and at bottom perfectly insignificant fact, known as the "*pia frans*," first gave me access to this problem: the *pia fraus*, the heirloom of all philosophers and priests who "improve" mankind. Neither Manu, nor Plato, nor Confucius, nor the teachers of Judaism and Christianity, have ever doubted their right to falsehood. They have never doubted their right to quite a number of other things. To express oneself in a formula, one might say: all means which have been used heretofore with the object of making man moral, were through and through immoral.

THINGS THE GERMANS LACK

1

AMONG GERMANS AT THE PRESENT DAY IT DOES NOT SUFFICE TO HAVE intellect; one is actually forced to appropriate it, to lay claim to it.

Maybe I know the Germans, perhaps I may tell them a few home-truths. Modern Germany represents such an enormous store of inherited and acquired capacity, that for some time it might spend this accumulated treasure even with some prodigality. It is no superior culture that has ultimately become prevalent with this modern tendency, nor is it by any means delicate taste, or noble beauty of the instincts; but rather a number of virtues more manly than any that other European countries can show. An amount of good spirits and self-respect, plenty of firmness in human relations and in the reciprocity of duties; much industry and much perseverance—and a certain inherited soberness which is much more in need of a spur than of a brake. Let me add that in this country people still obey without feeling that obedience humiliates. And no one despises his opponent.

You observe that it is my desire to be fair to the Germans: and in this respect I should not like to be untrue to myself—I must therefore also state my objections to them. It costs a good deal to attain to a position of power; for power *stultifies*. The Germans—they were once called a people of thinkers: do they really think at all at present? Nowadays the Germans are bored by intellect, they mistrust intellect; politics have swallowed up all earnestness for really intellectual things—"Germany, Germany above all."[1] I fear this was the deathblow to German philosophy. "Are there any German philosophers? Are there any German poets? Are there any good

German books?" people ask me abroad. I blush; but with that pluck which is peculiar to me, even in moments of desperation, I reply: "Yes, Bismarck!" Could I have dared to confess what books *are* read today? Cursed instinct of mediocrity!

2

What might not German intellect have been! Who has not thought sadly upon this question! But this nation has deliberately stultified itself for almost a thousand years: nowhere else have the two great European narcotics, alcohol and Christianity, been so viciously abused as in Germany. Recently a third opiate was added to the list, one which in itself alone would have sufficed to complete the ruin of all subtle and daring intellectual animation, I speak of music, our costive and constipating German music. How much peevish ponderousness, paralysis, dampness, dressing gown languor, and beer is there not in German intelligence!

How is it really possible that young men who consecrate their whole lives to the pursuit of intellectual ends, should not feel within them the first instinct of intellectuality, the *self-preservative instinct of the intellect*—and should drink beer? The alcoholism of learned youths does not incapacitate them for becoming scholars—a man quite devoid of intellect may be a great scholar—but it is a problem in every other respect. Where can that soft degeneracy not be found, which is produced in the intellect by beer! I once laid my finger upon a case of this sort, which became almost famous—the degeneration of our leading German free-spirit, the *clever* David Strauss, into the author of a suburban gospel and New Faith. Not in vain had he sung the praises of "the dear old brown liquor" in verse—true unto death.

3

I have spoken of German intellect. I have said that it is becoming coarser and shallower. Is that enough? In reality something very different frightens me, and that is the ever steady decline of German earnestness, German profundity, and German passion in things intellectual. Not only intellectuality, but also pathos has altered. From time to time I come in touch with German universities; what an extraordinary atmosphere prevails among their scholars! What barrenness! And what self-satisfied and lukewarm intellectuality! For anyone to point to German science as an argument against me would show that he grossly misunderstood my meaning, while it would also prove that he had not read a word of my writings. For seventeen years I have done little else than expose the de-intellectualising influence of our modern scientific studies. The severe slavery to which every individual nowadays is condemned by the enormous range covered by the sciences, is the chief reason why fuller, richer and profounder natures can find no education or educators that are fit for them. Nothing is more deleterious to this age than the superfluity of pretentious loafers and fragmentary human beings; our universities are really the involuntary forcing houses for this kind of withering-up of the instincts of intellectuality. And the whole of Europe is beginning to know this—politics on a large scale deceive no one. Germany is becoming ever more and more the Flat-land of Europe. I am still in search of a German with whom I could be serious after my own fashion. And how much more am I in search of one with whom I could be cheerful—*The Twilight of the Idols*: ah! What man today would be capable of understanding the kind of seriousness from which a philosopher is recovering in this work! It is our cheerfulness that people understand least.

4

Let us examine another aspect of the question: it is not only obvious that German culture is declining, but adequate reasons for this decline are not lacking. After all, nobody can spend more than he has: this is true of individuals, it is also true of nations. If you spend your strength in acquiring power, or in politics on a large scale, or in economy, or in universal commerce, or in parliamentarism, or in military interests—if you dissipate the modicum of reason, of earnestness, of will, and of self-control that constitutes your nature in one particular fashion, you cannot dissipate it in another. Culture and the state—let no one be deceived on this point—are antagonists: A "culture-state"[2] is merely a modern idea. The one lives upon the other, the one flourishes at the expense of the other. All great periods of culture have been periods of political decline; that which is great from the standpoint of culture, was always unpolitical—even anti-political. Goethe's heart opened at the coming of Napoleon—it closed at the thought of the "Wars of Liberation." At the very moment when Germany arose as a great power in the world of politics, France won new importance as a force in the world of culture. Even at this moment a large amount of fresh intellectual earnestness and passion has emigrated to Paris; the question of pessimism, for instance, and the question of Wagner; in France almost all psychological and artistic questions are considered with incomparably more subtlety and thoroughness than they are in Germany—the

Germans are even incapable of this kind of earnestness. In the history of European culture the rise of the Empire signifies, above all, a displacement of the centre of gravity. Everywhere people are already aware of this: in things that really matter—and these after all constitute culture—the Germans are no longer worth considering. I ask you, can you show me one single man of brains who could be mentioned in the same breath with other European thinkers, like your Goethe, your Hegel, your Heinrich Heine, and your Schopenhauer? The fact that there is no longer a single German philosopher worth mentioning is an increasing wonder.

5

Everything that matters has been lost sight of by the whole of the higher educational system of Germany: the end quite as much as the means to that end. People forget that education, the process of cultivation itself, is the end—and not "the Empire"—they forget that the *educator* is required for this end—and not the public school teacher and university scholar. Educators are needed who are themselves educated, superior and noble intellects, who can prove that they are thus qualified, that they are ripe and mellow products of culture at every moment of their lives, in word and in gesture; not the learned louts who, like "superior wet-nurses," are now thrust upon the youth of the land by public schools and universities. With but rare exceptions, that which is lacking in Germany is the first prerequisite of education—that is to say, the educators; hence the decline of German culture. One of those rarest exceptions is my highly respected friend Jacob Burckhardt of Bâle: to him above all is Bâle indebted for its foremost position in human culture What the higher schools of Germany really do accomplish is this, they brutally train a vast crowd of young men, in the smallest amount of time possible, to become useful and exploitable servants of the state. "Higher education" and a vast crowd—these terms contradict each other from the start. All superior education can only concern the exception: a man must be privileged in order to have a right to such a great privilege. All great and beautiful things cannot be a common possession: *pulchrum est paucorum hominum.* What is it that brings about the decline of German culture? The fact that "higher education" is no longer a special privilege—the democracy of a process of cultivation that has become "general," *common.* Nor must it be forgotten that the privileges of the military profession by urging many too many to attend the higher schools, involve the downfall of the latter. In modern Germany nobody is at liberty to give his children a noble education: in regard to their teachers, their curricula, and their educational aims, our higher schools are one and all established upon a fundamentally doubtful mediocre basis. Everywhere, too, a hastiness which is unbecoming rules supreme; just as if something would be forfeited if the young man were not "finished" at the age of twenty-three, or did not know how to reply to the most essential question, "which calling to choose?" The superior kind of man, if you please, does not like "callings," precisely because he knows himself to be called. He has time, he takes time, he cannot possibly think of becoming "finished"—in the matter of higher culture, a man of thirty years is a beginner, a child. Our overcrowded public schools, our accumulation of foolishly manufactured public school masters, are a scandal: maybe there are very serious *motives* for defending this state of affairs, as was shown quite recently by the professors of Heidelberg; but there can be no reasons for doing so.

6

In order to be true to my nature, which is affirmative and which concerns itself with contradictions and criticism only indirectly and with reluctance, let me state at once what the three objects are for which we need educators. People must learn to see; they must learn to think, and they must learn to speak and to write: the object of all three of these pursuits is a noble culture. To learn to see—to accustom the eye to calmness, to patience, and to allow things to come up to it; to defer judgement, and to acquire the habit of approaching and grasping an individual case from all sides. This is the first preparatory schooling of intellectuality. One must not respond immediately to a stimulus; one must acquire a command of the obstructing and isolating instincts. To learn to see, as I understand this matter, amounts almost to that which in popular language is called "strength of will": its essential feature is precisely *not* to *wish* to see, to be able to postpone one's decision. All lack of intellectuality, all vulgarity, arises out of the inability to resist a stimulus: one must respond or react, every impulse is indulged. In many cases such necessary action is already a sign of morbidity, of decline, and a symptom of exhaustion. Almost everything that coarse popular language characterises as vicious, is merely that physiological inability to refrain from reacting. As an instance of what it means to have learnt to see, let me state that a man thus trained will as a learner have become generally slow, suspicious, and refractory. With hostile calm he will first allow every kind of strange and *new* thing to come right up to him—he will draw back his hand at its approach. To stand with all the doors of one's soul wide open, to lie slavishly in the dust before every trivial fact, at all times of the day to be strained ready for the leap, in order to deposit one's self, to plunge one's self, into other souls and other things, in short, the famous "objectivity" of modern times, is bad taste, it is essentially vulgar and cheap.

7

As to learning how to think—our schools no longer have any notion of such a thing. Even at the universities, among the actual scholars in philosophy, logic as a theory, as a practical pursuit, and as a business, is beginning to die out. Turn to any German book: you will not find the remotest trace of a realisation that there is such a thing as a technique, a plan of study, a will to mastery, in the matter of thinking—that thinking insists upon being learnt, just as dancing insists upon being learnt, and that thinking insists upon being learnt as a form of dancing. What single German can still say he knows from experience that delicate shudder which *light footfalls* in matters intellectual cause to pervade his whole body and limbs! Stiff awkwardness in intellectual attitudes, and the clumsy fist in grasping—these things are so essentially German, that outside Germany they are absolutely confounded with the German spirit. The German has no fingers for delicate nuances. The fact that the people of Germany have actually tolerated their philosophers, more particularly that most deformed cripple of ideas that has ever existed—the great Kant, gives one no inadequate notion of their native elegance. For, truth to tell, dancing in all its forms cannot be excluded from the curriculum of all noble education: dancing with the feet, with ideas, with words, and, need I add that one must also be able to dance with the pen—that one must learn how to write? But at this stage I should become utterly enigmatical to German readers.

SKIRMISHES IN A WAR WITH
THE AGE

1

MY IMPOSSIBLE PEOPLE. SENECA, OR THE TOREADOR OF VIRTUE. ROUSSEAU,
or the return to nature, *in impuris naturalibus.* Schiller, or the Moral-
Trumpeter of Säckingen. Dante, or the hyaena that writes poetry in
tombs. Kant, or *cant* as an intelligible character. Victor Hugo, or the light-
house on the sea of nonsense. Liszt, or the school of racing—after women.
George Sand, or *lactea ubertas,* in plain English: the cow with plenty of
beautiful milk. Michelet, or enthusiasm in its shirt sleeves. Carlyle, or
Pessimism after undigested meals. John Stuart Mill, or offensive lucidity.
The brothers Goncourt, or the two Ajaxes fighting with Homer. Music by
Offenbach. Zola, or the love of stinking.

2

Renan. Theology, or the corruption of reason by original sin (Christianity). Proof of this—Renan who, even in those rare cases where he ventures
to say either Yes or No on a general question, invariably misses the point
with painful regularity. For instance, he would fain associate science and
nobility: but surely it must be obvious that science is democratic. He
seems to be actuated by a strong desire to represent an aristocracy of
intellect: but, at the same time he grovels on his knees, and not only on
his knees, before the opposite doctrine, the gospel of the humble. What
is the good of all free-spiritedness, modernity, mockery and acrobatic
suppleness, if in one's belly one is still a Christian, a Catholic, and even a
priest! Renan's forte, precisely like that of a Jesuit and Father Confessor,

lies in his seductiveness. His intellectuality is not devoid of that unctuous complacency of a parson—like all priests, he becomes dangerous only when he loves. He is second to none in the art of skilfully worshipping a dangerous thing. This intellect of Renan's, which in its action is enervating, is one calamity the more, for poor, sick France with her will-power all going to pieces.

3

Sainte-Beuve. There is naught of man in him; he is full of petty spite towards all virile spirits. He wanders erratically; he is subtle, inquisitive, a little bored, forever with his ear to keyholes—at bottom a woman, with all woman's revengefulness and sensuality. As a psychologist he is a genius of slander; inexhaustively rich in means to this end; no one understands better than he how to introduce a little poison into praise. In his fundamental instincts he is plebeian and next of kin to Rousseau's resentful spirit: consequently he is a Romanticist—for beneath all romanticism Rousseau's instinct for revenge grunts and frets. He is a revolutionary, but kept within bounds by "funk." He is embarrassed in the face of everything that is strong (public opinion, the Academy, the court, even Port Royal). He is embittered against everything great in men and things, against everything that believes in itself. Enough of a poet and of a female to be able to feel greatness as power; he is always turning and twisting, because, like the proverbial worm, he constantly feels that he is being trodden upon. As a critic he has no standard of judgement, no guiding principle, no backbone. Although he possesses the tongue of the Cosmopolitan libertine which can chatter about a thousand things, he has not the courage even to acknowledge his *libertinage*. As a historian he has no philosophy, and lacks the power of philosophical vision—hence his refusal to act the part of a judge, and his adoption of the mask of "objectivity" in all important matters. His attitude is better in regard to all those things in which subtle and effete taste is the highest tribunal: in these things he really does have the courage of his own personality—he really does enjoy his own nature— he actually is a *master.* In some respects he is a prototype of Beaudelaire.

4

The Imitation of Christ is one of those books which I cannot even take hold of without physical loathing: it exhales a perfume of the eternally feminine, which to appreciate fully one must be a Frenchman or a Wagnerite. This saint has a way of speaking about love which makes even Parisiennes feel a little curious. I am told that that *most intelligent* of Jesuits, Auguste Comte, who wished to lead his compatriots back to Rome by the circuitous route of science, drew his inspiration from this book. And I believe it: *The religion of the heart.*

5

G. Eliot. They are rid of the Christian God and therefore think it all the more incumbent upon them to hold tight to Christian morality: this is an English way of reasoning; but let us not take it ill in moral females *à la* Eliot. In England, every man who indulges in any trifling emancipation from theology, must retrieve his honour in the most terrifying manner by becoming a moral fanatic. That is how they do penance in that country. As for us, we act differently. When we renounce the Christian faith, we abandon all right to Christian morality. This is not by any means self-evident, and in defiance of English shallow-pates the point must be made ever more and more plain. Christianity is a system, a complete outlook upon the world, conceived as a whole. If its leading concept, the belief in God, is wrenched from it, the whole is destroyed; nothing vital remains in our grasp. Christianity presupposes that man does not and cannot know what is good or bad for him: the Christian believes in God who, alone, can know these things. Christian morality is a command, its origin is transcendental. It is beyond all criticism, all right to criticism; it is true only on condition that God is truth—it stands or falls with the belief in God. If the English really believe that they know intuitively, and of their own accord, what is good and evil; if, therefore, they assert that they no longer need Christianity as a guarantee of morality, this in itself is simply the outcome of the dominion of Christian valuations, and a proof of the strength and profundity of this dominion. It only shows that the origin of English morality has been forgotten, and that its exceedingly relative right to exist is no longer felt. For Englishmen morality is not yet a problem.

6

George Sand. I have been reading the first "*Lettres d'un Voyageur*": like everything that springs from Rousseau's influence it is false, made-up, blown out, and exaggerated! I cannot endure this bright wallpaper style, any more than I can bear the vulgar striving after generous feelings. The worst feature about it is certainly the coquettish adoption of male attributes by this female, after the manner of ill-bred schoolboys. And how cold she must have been inwardly all the while, this insufferable artist! She wound herself up like a clock—and wrote. As cold as Hugo and Balzac, as cold as all Romanticists are as soon as they begin to write! And how self-complacently she must have lain there, this prolific ink-yielding cow. For she had something German in her (German in the bad sense), just as Rousseau, her master, had; something which could only have been possible when French taste was declining! And Renan adores her! . . .

7

A Moral for Psychologists. Do not go in for any notebook psychology! Never observe for the sake of observing! Such things lead to a false point of view, to a squint, to something forced and exaggerated. To experience things on purpose—this is not a bit of good. In the midst of an experience a man should not turn his eyes upon himself; in such cases any eye becomes the "evil eye." A born psychologist instinctively avoids seeing for the sake of seeing. And the same holds good of the born painter. Such a man never works "from nature"—he leaves it to his instinct, to his *camera obscura* to sift and to define the "fact," "nature," the "experience." The general idea, the conclusion, the result, is the only thing that reaches his consciousness. He knows nothing of that wilful process of deducing from particular cases. What is the result when a man sets about this matter differently? When, for instance, after the manner of Parisian novelists, he goes in for notebook psychology on a large and small scale? Such a man is constantly spying on reality, and every evening he bears home a handful of fresh curios. . . . But look at the result! A mass of daubs, at best a piece of mosaic, in any case something heaped together, restless and garish. The Goncourts are the greatest sinners in this respect: they cannot put three sentences together which are not absolutely painful to the eye—the eye of the psychologist. From an artistic standpoint, nature is no model. It exaggerates, distorts, and leaves gaps. Nature is the *accident.* To study "from nature" seems to me a bad sign: it betrays submission, weakness, fatalism—this lying in the dust before trivial facts is unworthy of a thorough artist. To see *what is*—is the function of another order of intellects, the *anti-artistic,* the matter-of-fact. One must know *who* one is.

8

Concerning the psychology of the artist. For art to be possible at all—that is to say, in order that an aesthetic mode of action and of observation may exist, a certain preliminary physiological state is indispensable: *ecstasy.*[1] This state of ecstasy must first have intensified the susceptibility of the whole machine:

otherwise, no art is possible. All kinds of ecstasy, however differently produced, have this power to create art, and above all the state dependent
upon sexual excitement—this most venerable and primitive form of ecstasy.
The same applies to that ecstasy which is the outcome of all great desires,
all strong passions; the ecstasy of the feast, of the arena, of the act of bravery, of victory, of all extreme action; the ecstasy of cruelty; the ecstasy of
destruction; the ecstasy following upon certain meteorological influences,
as for instance that of springtime, or upon the use of narcotics; and finally
the ecstasy of will, that ecstasy which results from accumulated and surging
will-power. The essential feature of ecstasy is the feeling of increased
strength and abundance. Actuated by this feeling a man gives of himself to
things, he *forces* them to partake of his riches, he does violence to them—
this proceeding is called *idealising*. Let us rid ourselves of a prejudice here:
idealising does not consist, as is generally believed, in a suppression or an
elimination of detail or of unessential features. A stupendous *accentuation*
of the principal characteristics is by far the most decisive factor at work, and
in consequence the minor characteristics vanish.

9

In this state a man enriches everything from out his own abundance: what
he sees, what he wills, he sees distended, compressed, strong, overladen
with power. He transfigures things until they reflect his power—until they
are stamped with his perfection. This compulsion to transfigure into the
beautiful is—Art. Everything—even that which he is not—is nevertheless
to such a man a means of rejoicing over himself; in Art man rejoices over
himself as perfection. It is possible to imagine a contrary state, a specifically anti-artistic state of the instincts—a state in which a man impoverishes,
attenuates, and draws the blood from everything. And, truth to tell, history
is full of such anti-artists, of such creatures of low vitality who have no
choice but to appropriate everything they see and to suck its blood and
make it thinner. This is the case with the genuine Christian, Pascal for
instance. There is no such thing as a Christian who is also an artist. . . . Let
no one be so childish as to suggest Raphael or any homeopathic Christian
of the nineteenth century as an objection to this statement: Raphael said
Yea, Raphael *did* Yea—consequently Raphael was no Christian.

10

What is the meaning of the antithetical concepts *Apollonian* and *Dionysian*
which I have introduced into the vocabulary of Aesthetic, as representing

two distinct modes of ecstasy? Apollonian ecstasy acts above all as a force stimulating the eye, so that it acquires the power of vision. The painter, the sculptor, the epic poet are essentially visionaries. In the Dionysian state, on the other hand, the whole system of passions is stimulated and intensified, so that it discharges itself by all the means of expression at once, and vents all its power of representation, of imitation, of transfiguration, of transformation, together with every kind of mimicry and histrionic display at the same time. The essential feature remains the facility in transforming, the inability to refrain from reaction (—a similar state to that of certain hysterical patients, who at the slightest hint assume any role). It is impossible for the Dionysian artist not to understand any suggestion; no outward sign of emotion escapes him, he possesses the instinct of comprehension and of divination in the highest degree, just as he is capable of the most perfect art of communication. He enters into every skin, into every passion: he is continually changing himself. Music as we understand it today is likewise a general excitation and discharge of the emotions; but, notwithstanding this, it is only the remnant of a much richer world of emotional expression, a mere residuum of Dionysian histrionism. For music to be made possible as a special art, quite a number of senses, and particularly the muscular sense, had to be paralysed (at least relatively: for all rhythm still appeals to our muscles to a certain extent): and thus man no longer imitates and represents physically everything he feels, as soon as he feels it. Nevertheless that is the normal Dionysian state, and in any case its primitive state. Music is the slowly attained specialisation of this state at the cost of kindred capacities.

11

The actor, the mime, the dancer, the musician, and the lyricist, are in their instincts fundamentally related; but they have gradually specialised in their particular branch, and become separated—even to the point of contradiction. The lyricist remained united with the musician for the longest period of time; and the actor with the dancer. The architect manifests neither a Dionysian nor an Apollonian state: In his case it is the great act of will, the will that moveth mountains, the ecstasy of the great will which aspires to art. The most powerful men have always inspired architects; the architect has always been under the suggestion of power. In the architectural structure, man's pride, man's triumph over gravitation, man's will to power, assume a visible form. Architecture is a sort of oratory of power by means of forms. Now it is persuasive, even flattering, and at other times merely commanding. The highest sensation of power and security finds expression in grandeur of style. That power which no longer requires to be proved, which scorns to please; which responds only with difficulty; which feels no witnesses around it; which is oblivious of the fact that it is being opposed; which relies on itself fatalistically, and is a law among laws: such power expresses itself quite naturally in grandeur of style.

12

I have been reading the life of Thomas Carlyle, that unconscious and involuntary farce, that heroicomoral interpretation of dyspeptic moods. Carlyle, a man of strong words and attitudes, a rhetorician by necessity, who seems ever to be tormented by the desire of finding some kind of strong faith, and by his inability to do so (—in this respect a typical Romanticist!). To yearn for a strong faith is not the proof of a strong faith, but rather the reverse. If a man have a strong faith he can indulge in the luxury of scepticism; he is strong enough, firm enough, well-knit enough for such a luxury. Carlyle stupefies something in himself by means of the *fortissimo* of his reverence for men of a strong faith, and his rage over those who are less foolish: he is in sore need of noise. An attitude of constant and passionate dishonesty towards himself—this is his *proprium*; by virtue of this he is and remains interesting. Of course, in England he is admired precisely on account of his honesty. Well, that is English; and in view of the fact that the English are the nation of consummate cant, it is not only comprehensible but also very natural. At bottom, Carlyle is an English atheist who makes it a point of honour not to be one.

13

Emerson. He is much more enlightened, much broader, more versatile, and more subtle than Carlyle; but above all, he is happier. He is one who instinctively lives on ambrosia and who leaves the indigestible parts of things on his plate. Compared with Carlyle he is a man of taste. Carlyle, who was very fond of him, nevertheless declared that "he does not give us enough to chew." This is perfectly true but it is not unfavourable to Emerson. Emerson possesses that kindly intellectual cheerfulness which deprecates overmuch seriousness; he has absolutely no idea of how old he is already, and how young he will yet be—he could have said of himself, in Lope de Vega's words: "*yo me sucedo a mi mismo.*" His mind is always finding reasons for being contented and even thankful; and at times he gets preciously near to that serene superiority of the worthy bourgeois who returning from an amorous rendezvous *tamquam re bene gesta,* said gratefully "*Ut desint vires, tainen est laudanda voluptas.*"

14

Anti-Darwin. As to the famous "struggle for existence," it seems to me, for the present, to be more of an assumption than a fact. It does occur, but as an exception. The general condition of life is not one of want or famine, but rather of riches, of lavish luxuriance, and even of absurd prodigality—where there is a struggle, it is a struggle for power. We should not confound Malthus with nature. Supposing, however, that this struggle exists—and it does indeed occur—its result is unfortunately the very reverse of that which the Darwinian school seems to desire, and of that which in agreement with them we also might desire: that is to say, it is always to the disadvantage of the strong, the privileged, and the happy exceptions. Species do not evolve towards perfection: the weak always prevail over the strong—simply because they are the majority, and because they are also the more crafty. Darwin forgot the intellect (that is English!), the weak have more intellect. In order to acquire intellect, one must be in need of it. One loses it when one no longer needs it. He who possesses strength flings intellect to the deuce ("let it go hence!"[2] say the Germans of the present day, "the *Empire* will remain"). As you perceive, intellect to me means caution, patience, craft, dissimulation, great self-control, and everything related to mimicry (what is praised nowadays as virtue is very closely related to the latter).

15

Casuistry of a Psychologist. This man knows mankind: to what purpose does he study his fellows? He wants to derive some small or even great advantages from them—he is a politician! . . . That man yonder is also well versed in human nature: and ye tell me that he wishes to draw no personal profit from his knowledge, that he is a thoroughly disinterested person? Examine him a little more closely! Maybe he wishes to derive a more wicked advantage from his possession; namely, to feel superior to men, to be able to look down upon them, no longer to feel one of them. This "disinterested person" is a despiser of mankind; and the former is of a more humane type, whatever appearances may seem to say to the contrary. At least he considers himself the equal of those about him, at least he classifies himself with them.

16

The psychological tact of Germans seems to me to have been set in doubt by a whole series of cases which my modesty forbids me to enumerate. In one case at least I shall not let the occasion slip for substantiating my contention: I bear the Germans a grudge for having made a mistake about Kant and his "backstairs philosophy," as I call it. Such a man was not the type of intellectual uprightness. Another thing I hate to hear is a certain infamous "and": the Germans say, "Goethe *and* Schiller"—I even fear that they say, "Schiller and Goethe. . . ." Has nobody found Schiller out yet? But there are other "ands" which are even more egregious. With my own ears I have heard—only among University professors, it is true! Men speak of "Schopenhauer *and* Hartmann. . . ."[3]

17

The most intellectual men, provided they are also the most courageous, experience the most excruciating tragedies: but on that very account they honour life, because it confronts them with its most formidable antagonism.

18

Concerning "*the Conscience of the Intellect.*" Nothing seems to me more uncommon today than genuine hypocrisy. I strongly suspect that this growth is unable to flourish in the mild climate of our culture. Hypocrisy belongs to an age of strong faith—one in which one does not lose one's own faith in spite of the fact that one has to make an outward show of holding another faith. Nowadays a man gives it up; or, what is still more common, he acquires a second faith—in any case, however, he remains honest. Without a doubt it is possible to have a much larger number of convictions at present, than it was formerly: *possible*—that is to say, allowable—that is to say, *harmless.* From this there arises an attitude of toleration towards one's self. Toleration towards one's self allows of a greater number of convictions: the latter live comfortably side by side, and they take jolly good care, as all the world does today, not to compromise themselves. How does a man compromise himself today? When he is consistent; when he pursues a straight course; when he has anything less than five faces; when he is genuine. . . . I very greatly fear that modern man is much too fond of comfort for certain vices; and the consequence is that the latter are dying out. Everything evil which is the outcome of strength of will—and maybe there is nothing evil without the strength of will—degenerates, in our muggy atmosphere, into virtue. The few hypocrites I have known only imitated hypocrisy: like almost every tenth man today, they were actors.

19

Beautiful and Ugly: Nothing is more relative, let us say, more restricted, than our sense of the beautiful. He who would try to divorce it from the delight man finds in his fellows, would immediately lose his footing. "Beauty in itself," is simply a word, it is not even a concept. In the beautiful, man postulates himself as the standard of perfection; in exceptional cases he worships himself as that standard. A species has no other alternative than to say "yea" to itself alone, in this way. Its lowest instinct, the instinct of self-preservation and self-expansion, still radiates in such sublimities. Man imagines the world itself to be overflowing with beauty—he forgets that he is the cause of it all. He alone has endowed it with beauty. Alas! And only with human all-too-human beauty! Truth to tell man reflects himself in things, he thinks everything beautiful that throws his own image back at him. The judgement "beautiful" is the "vanity of his species. . . ." A little demon of suspicion may well whisper into the sceptic's ear: is the world really beautified simply because man thinks it beautiful? He has only humanised it—that is all. But nothing, absolutely nothing proves to us that it is precisely man who is the proper model of beauty. Who knows what sort of figure he would cut in the eyes of a higher judge of taste? He might seem a little *outré*? Perhaps even somewhat amusing? Perhaps a trifle arbitrary? "O Dionysus, thou divine one, why dost thou pull mine ears?" Ariadne asks on one occasion of her philosophic lover, during one of those famous conversations on the island of Naxos. "I find a sort of humour in thine ears, Ariadne: why are they not a little longer?"

20

Nothing is beautiful; man alone is beautiful: all aesthetic rests on this piece of ingenuousness, it is the first axiom of this science. And now let us straightway add the second to it: nothing is ugly save the degenerate man—within these two first principles the realm of aesthetic judgements is confined. From the physiological standpoint, everything ugly weakens and depresses man. It reminds him of decay, danger, impotence; he literally loses strength in its presence. The effect of ugliness may be gauged by the dynamometer. Whenever man's spirits are downcast, it is a sign that he scents the proximity of something "ugly." His feeling of power, his will to power, his courage and his pride—these things collapse at the sight of what is ugly, and rise at the sight of what is beautiful. In both cases an inference is drawn; the premises to which are stored with extra ordinary abundance in the instincts. Ugliness is understood to signify a hint and a symptom of degeneration: that which reminds us however remotely of degeneracy, impels us to the judgement "ugly." Every sign of exhaustion, of gravity, of age, of fatigue; every kind of constraint, such as cramp, or paralysis; and above all the smells, colours and forms associated with decomposition and putrefaction, however much they may have been attenuated into symbols—all these things provoke the same reaction which is the judgement "ugly." A certain hatred expresses itself here: what is it that man hates? Without a doubt it is the *decline of his type.* In this regard his hatred springs from the deepest instincts of the race: there is horror, caution, profundity and far-reaching vision in this hatred—it is the most profound hatred that exists. On its account alone Art is profound.

21

Schopenhauer. Schopenhauer, the last German who is to be reckoned with (—who is a European event like Goethe, Hegel, or Heinrich Heine, and who is not merely local, national), is for a psychologist a case of the first rank: I mean as a malicious though masterly attempt to enlist on the side of a general nihilistic depreciation of life, the very forces which are opposed to such a movement—that is to say, the great self-affirming powers of the "will to live," the exuberant forms of life itself. He interpreted Art, heroism, genius, beauty, great sympathy, knowledge, the will to truth, and tragedy, one after the other, as the results of the denial, or of the need of the denial, of the "will"—the greatest forgery, Christianity always excepted, which history has to show. Examined more carefully, he is in this respect simply the heir of the Christian interpretation; except that he knew how to approve in a Christian fashion (i.e., nihilistically) even of the great facts of human culture, which Christianity completely repudiates. (He approved of them as paths to "salvation," as preliminary stages to "salvation," as *appetisers* calculated to arouse the desire for "salvation.")

22

Let me point to one single instance. Schopenhauer speaks of beauty with melancholy ardour—why in sooth does he do this? Because in beauty he sees a bridge on which one can travell further, or which stimulates one's desire to travell further. According to him it constitutes a momentary emancipation from the "will"—it lures to eternal salvation. He values it more particularly as a deliverance from the "burning core of the will" which is sexuality—in beauty he recognises the negation of the procreative instinct. Singular Saint! Someone contradicts thee; I fear it is Nature. Why is there beauty of tone, colour, aroma, and of rhythmic movement in Nature at all? What is it forces beauty to the fore? Fortunately, too, a certain philosopher contradicts him. No less an authority than the divine Plato himself (thus does Schopenhauer call him), upholds another proposition: that all beauty lures to procreation—that this precisely is the chief characteristic of its effect, from the lowest sensuality to the highest spirituality.

23

Plato goes further. With an innocence for which a man must be Greek and not "Christian," he says that there would be no such thing as Platonic philosophy if there were not such beautiful boys in Athens: it was the sight of them alone that set the soul of the philosopher reeling with erotic passion, and allowed it no rest until it had planted the seeds of all lofty things in a soil so beautiful. He was also a singular saint! One scarcely believes one's ears, even supposing one believes Plato. At least one realises that philosophy was pursued differently in Athens; above all, publicly. Nothing is less Greek than the cobweb-spinning with concepts by an anchorite, *amor intellectualis dei* after the fashion of Spinoza. Philosophy according to Plato's style might be defined rather as an erotic competition, as a continuation and a spiritualisation of the old agonal gymnastics and the conditions on which they depend. . . . What was the ultimate outcome of this philosophic eroticism of Plato's? A new art-form of the Greek *Agon*, dialectics. In opposition to Schopenhauer and to the honour of Plato, I would remind you that all the higher culture and literature of classical France, as well, grew up on the soil of sexual interests. In all its manifestations you may look for gallantry, the senses, sexual competition, and "woman," and you will not look in vain.

24

L'Art pour l'Art. The struggle against a purpose in art is always a struggle against the moral tendency in art, against its subordination to morality. *L'art pour l'art* means, "let morality go to the devil!" But even this hostility betrays the preponderating power of the moral prejudice. If art is deprived of the purpose of preaching morality and of improving mankind, it does not by any means follow that art is absolutely pointless, purposeless, senseless, in short *l'art pour l'art*—a snake which bites its own tail. "No purpose at all is better than a moral purpose!" thus does pure passion speak. A psychologist, on the other hand, puts the question: what does all art do? Does it not praise? Does it not glorify? Does it not select? Does it not bring things into prominence? In all this it strengthens or weakens certain valuations. Is this only a secondary matter? An accident? Something in which the artist's instinct has no share? Or is it not rather the very prerequisite which enables the artist to accomplish something? . . . Is his most fundamental instinct concerned with art? Is it not rather concerned with the purpose of art, with life? With a certain desirable kind of life? Art is the great stimulus to life: how can it be regarded as purposeless, as pointless, as *l'art pour l'art?* There still remains one question to be answered: Art also reveals much that is ugly, hard and questionable in life—does it not thus seem to make life intolerable? And, as a matter of fact, there have been philosophers who have ascribed this function to art. According to Schopenhauer's doctrine, the general object of art was to "free one from the Will"; and what he honoured as the great utility of tragedy, was that it "made people more resigned." But this, as I have already shown, is a pessimistic standpoint; it is the "evil eye": the artist himself must be appealed to. What is it that the soul of the tragic artist communicates to others? Is it not precisely his fearless attitude towards that which is terrible and questionable? This attitude is in itself a highly desirable one; he who has once experienced it honours it above everything else. He communicates it. He must communicate, provided he is an artist and a genius in the art of communication. A courageous and free spirit, in the presence of a mighty foe, in the presence of a sublime misfortune, and face to face with a problem that inspires horror—this is the triumphant attitude which the tragic artist selects and which he glorifies. The martial elements in our soul celebrate their Saturnalia in tragedy; he who is used to suffering, he who looks out for suffering, the heroic man, extols his existence by means of tragedy—to him alone does the tragic artist offer this cup of sweetest cruelty.

25

To associate in an amiable fashion with anybody; to keep the house of one's heart open to all, is certainly liberal: but it is nothing else. One can recognise the hearts that are capable of noble hospitality, by their wealth of screened windows and closed shutters: they keep their best rooms empty. Whatever for? Because they are expecting guests who are somebodies.

26

We no longer value ourselves sufficiently highly when we communicate our soul's content. Our real experiences are not at all garrulous. They could not communicate themselves even if they wished to. They are at a loss to find words for such confidences. Those things for which we find words, are things we have already overcome. In all speech there lies an element of contempt. Speech, it would seem, was only invented for average, mediocre and communicable things. Every spoken word proclaims the speaker vulgarised. (Extract from a moral code for deaf-and-dumb people and other philosophers.)

27

"This picture is perfectly beautiful!"[4] The dissatisfied and exasperated literary woman with a desert in her heart and in her belly, listening with agonised curiosity every instant to the imperative which whispers to her from the very depths of her being: *aut liberi, aut libri*: the literary woman, sufficiently educated to understand the voice of nature, even when nature speaks Latin, and moreover enough of a peacock and a goose to speak even French with herself in secret. "*Je me verrai, je me lirai, je m'extasierai et je dirai: Possible, que j'aie eu tant d'esprit?*" . . .

28

The objective ones speak. "Nothing comes more easily to us, than to be wise, patient, superior. We are soaked in the oil of indulgence and of sympathy, we are absurdly just, we forgive everything. Precisely on that account we should be severe with ourselves; for that very reason we ought from time to time to go in for a little emotion, a little emotional vice. It may seem bitter to us; and between ourselves we may even laugh at the figure which it makes us cut. But what does it matter? We have no other kind of self-control left. This is our asceticism, our manner of performing penance." *To become personal*—the virtues of the "impersonal and objective one."

29

Extract from a doctor's examination paper. "What is the task of all higher schooling?" To make man into a machine. "What are the means employed?" He must learn how to be bored. "How is this achieved?" By means of the concept duty. "What example of duty has he before his eyes?" The philologist: it is he who teaches people how to swat. "Who is the perfect man?" The Government official. "Which philosophy furnishes the highest formula for the government official?" Kant's philosophy: the Government official as thing-in-itself made judge over the Government official as appearance.

30

The right to Stupidity. The worn-out worker, whose breath is slow, whose look is good-natured, and who lets things slide just as they please: this typical figure which in this age of labour (and of "Empire!") is to be met with in all classes of society, has now begun to appropriate even Art, including the book, above all the newspaper—and how much more so beautiful nature, Italy! This man of the evening, with his "savage instincts lulled," as Faust has it; needs his summer holiday, his sea baths, his glacier, his Bayreuth. In such ages Art has the right to be *purely foolish*—as a sort of vacation for spirit, wit and sentiment. Wagner understood this. Pure foolishness[5] is a pick-me-up. . . .

31

Yet another problem of diet. The means with which Julius Caesar preserved himself against sickness and headaches: heavy marches, the simplest mode of living, uninterrupted sojourns in the open air, continual hardships —generally speaking these are the self-preservative and self-defensive measures against the extreme vulnerability of those subtle machines working at the highest pressure, which are called geniuses.

32

The Immoralist speaks. Nothing is more distasteful to true philosophers than man when he begins to wish. . . . If they see man only at his deeds; if they see this bravest, craftiest and most enduring of animals even inextricably entangled in disaster, how admirable he then appears to them! They even encourage him. . . . But true philosophers despise the man who wishes, as also the "desirable" man—and all the desiderata and *ideals* of man in general. If a philosopher could be a nihilist, he would be one; for he finds only nonentity behind all human ideals. Or, not even nonentity, but vileness, absurdity, sickness, cowardice, fatigue and all sorts of dregs from out the quaffed goblets of his life. . . . How is it that man, who as a reality is so estimable, ceases from deserving respect the moment he begins to desire? Must he pay for being so perfect as a reality? Must he make up for his deeds, for the tension of spirit and will which underlies all his deeds, by an eclipse of his powers in matters of the imagination and in absurdity? Hitherto the history of his desires has been the *partie honteuse* of mankind: one should take care not to read too deeply in this history. That which justifies man is his reality—it will justify him to all eternity. How much more valuable is a real man than any other man who is merely the phantom of desires, of dreams of stinks and of lies? Than any kind of ideal man? . . . And the ideal man, alone, is what the philosopher cannot abide.

33

The Natural Value of Egoism. Selfishness has as much value as the physiological value of him who practises it: its worth may be great, or it may be worthless and contemptible. Every individual may be classified according to whether he represents the ascending or the descending line of life. When this is decided, a canon is obtained by means of which the value of his selfishness may be determined. If he represent the ascending line of life, his value is of course extraordinary—and for the sake of the collective life which in him makes one step *forward,* the concern about his maintenance, about procuring his *optimum* of conditions may even be extreme. The human unit, the "individual," as the people and the philosopher have always understood him, is certainly an error: he is nothing in himself, no atom, no "link in the chain," no mere heritage from the past—he represents the whole direct line of mankind up to his own life. . . . If he represent declining development, decay, chronic degeneration, sickness (illnesses are on the whole already the outcome of decline, and not the cause thereof), he is of little worth, and the purest equity would have him *take away* as little as possible from those who are lucky strokes of nature. He is then only a parasite upon them. . . .

34

The Christian and the Anarchist. When the anarchist, as the mouthpiece of the decaying strata of society, raises his voice in splendid indignation for "right," "justice," "equal rights," he is only groaning under the burden of his ignorance, which cannot understand *why* he actually suffers—what his poverty consists of—the poverty of life. An instinct of causality is active in him: someone must be responsible for his being so ill at ease. His "splendid indignation" alone relieves him somewhat, it is a pleasure for all poor devils to grumble—it gives them a little intoxicating sensation of power. The very act of complaining, the mere fact that one bewails one's lot, may lend such a charm to life that on that account alone one is ready to endure it. There is a small dose of revenge in every lamentation. One casts one's afflictions, and, under certain circumstances, even one's baseness, in the teeth of those who are different, as if their condition were an injustice, an *iniquitous* privilege. "Since I am *a blackguard* you ought to be one too." It is upon such reasoning that revolutions are based. To bewail one's lot is always despicable: it is always the outcome of weakness. Whether one ascribes one's afflictions to others or to *one's self*, it is all the same. The socialist does the former, the Christian, for instance, does the latter. That which is common to both attitudes, or rather that which is equally ignoble in them both, is the fact that somebody must be to *blame* if one suffers—in short that the sufferer drugs himself with the honey of revenge to allay his anguish. The objects towards which this lust of vengeance, like a lust of pleasure, are directed, are purely accidental causes. In all directions the sufferer finds reasons for cooling his petty passion for revenge. If he is a Christian, I repeat, he finds these reasons in himself. The Christian and the Anarchist—both are decadents. But even when the Christian condemns, slanders, and sullies the world, he is actuated by precisely the same instinct as that which leads the socialistic workman to curse, calumniate and cast dirt at society. The last "Judgement" itself is still the sweetest solace to revenge—revolution, as the socialistic workman expects it, only thought of as a little more remote. . . . The notion of a "Beyond," as well—why a Beyond, if it be not a means of splashing mud over a "Here," over this world? . . .

35

A Criticism of the Morality of Decadence. An "altruistic" morality, a morality under which selfishness withers, is in all circumstances a bad sign. This is true of individuals and above all of nations. The best are lacking when selfishness begins to be lacking. Instinctively to select that which is harmful to one, to be *lured* by "disinterested" motives—these things almost provide the formula for decadence. "Not to have one's own interests at heart"—this is simply a moral fig-leaf concealing a very different fact, a physiological one, to wit: "I no longer know how to find what is to my interest. . . ." Disintegration of the instincts! All is up with man when he becomes altruistic. Instead of saying ingenuously "I am no longer any good," the lie of morality in the decadent's mouth says: "Nothing is any good—life is no good." A judgement of this kind ultimately becomes a great danger; for it is infectious, and it soon flourishes on the polluted soil of society with tropical luxuriance, now as a religion (Christianity), anon as a philosophy (Schopenhauerism). In certain circumstances the mere effluvia of such a venomous vegetation, springing as it does out of the very heart of putrefaction, can poison life for thousands and thousands of years.

36

A moral for doctors. The sick man is a parasite of society. In certain cases it is indecent to go on living. To continue to vegetate in a state of cowardly dependence upon doctors and special treatments, once the meaning of life, the right to life, has been lost, ought to be regarded with the greatest contempt by society. The doctors, for their part, should be the agents for imparting this contempt—they should no longer prepare prescriptions, but should every day administer a fresh dose of *disgust* to their patients. A new responsibility should be created, that of the doctor—the responsibility of ruthlessly suppressing and eliminating *degenerate* life, in all cases in which the highest interests of life itself, of ascending life, demand such a course—for instance in favour of the right of procreation, in favour of the right of being born, in favour of the right to live. One should die proudly when it is no longer possible to live proudly. Death should be chosen freely—death at the right time, faced clearly and joyfully and embraced while one is surrounded by one's children and other witnesses. It should be affected in such a way that a proper farewell is still possible, that he who is about to take leave of us is still *himself,* and really capable not only of valuing what he has achieved and willed in life, but also of *summing-up* the value of life itself. Everything precisely the opposite of the ghastly comedy which Christianity has made of the hour of death. We should never forgive Christianity for having so abused the weakness of the dying man as to do violence to his conscience, or for having used his manner of dying as a means of valuing both man and his past! In spite of all cowardly prejudices, it is our duty, in this respect, above all to reinstate the proper—that is to say, the physiological, aspect of so-called *natural* death, which after all is perfectly "unnatural" and nothing else than suicide. One never perishes through anybody's fault but one's own. The only thing is that the death which takes place in the most contemptible circumstances, the death that is not free, the death which occurs at the wrong time, is the death of a coward. Out of the very love one bears to life, one should wish death to be different from this—that is to say, free, deliberate, and neither a matter of chance nor of surprise. Finally let me whisper a word of advice to our friends the pessimists and all other decadents. We have not the power to prevent ourselves from being born: but this error—for sometimes it is an error—can be rectified if we choose. The man who does away with himself, performs the most estimable of deeds: he almost deserves to live for having done so. Society—nay, life itself, derives more profit from such a deed than from any sort of life spent in renunciation, anaemia and other virtues—at least the suicide frees others from the sight of him, at least he removes one objection against life. Pessimism *pur et vert,* can *be proved only* by the self refutation of the pessimists themselves: one should go a step further in one's consistency; one should not merely deny life with "The World as Will and Idea," as Schopenhauer did; one should in the first place *deny Schopenhauer.* . . . Incidentally, Pessimism, however infectious it may be, does not increase the morbidness of an age or of a whole species; it is rather the expression of that morbidness. One falls a victim to it in the same way as one falls a victim to cholera; one must already be predisposed to the disease. Pessimism in itself does not increase the number of the world's *decadents* by a single unit. Let me remind you of the statistical fact that in those years in which cholera rages, the total number of deaths does not exceed that of other years.

37

Have we become more moral? As might have been expected, the whole *ferocity* of moral stultification, which, as is well known, passes for morality itself in Germany, hurled itself against my concept *Beyond Good and Evil.* I could tell you some nice tales about this. Above all, people tried to make me see the "incontestable superiority" of our age in regard to moral senti- ment, and the *progress* we had made in these matters. Compared with us, a Caesar Borgia was by no means to be represented as "higher man," the sort of *Superman,* which I declared him to be. The editor of the Swiss paper the *Bund* went so far as not only to express his admiration for the courage displayed by my enterprise, but also to pretend to "understand" that the intended purpose of my work was to abolish all decent feeling. Much obliged! In reply, I venture to raise the following question: *have we really become more moral?* The fact that everybody believes that we have is already an objection to the belief. We modern men, so extremely delicate and susceptible, full of consideration one for the other, actually dare to sup- pose that the pampering fellow-feeling which we all display, this unanimity which we have at last acquired in sparing and helping and trusting one another marks a definite step forward, and shows us to be far ahead of the man of the Renaissance. But every age thinks the same, it is *bound* to think the same. This at least is certain, that we should not dare to stand amid the conditions which prevailed at the Renaissance, we should not even dare to imagine ourselves in those conditions: our nerves could not endure that reality, not to speak of our muscles. The inability to do this however does not denote any progress; but simply the different and more senile quality of our particular nature, its greater weakness, delicateness, and susceptibility, out of which a morality *more rich in consideration* was bound to arise. If we imagine our delicateness and senility, our physiological decrepitude as non-existent, our morality of "humanisation" would immediately lose all value—no morality has any value per se—it would even fill us with scorn. On the other hand, do not let us doubt that we moderns, wrapped as we are in the thick cotton wool of our humanitarianism which would shrink even from grazing a stone, would present a comedy to Caesar Borgia's contemporaries which would literally make them die of laughter. We are indeed, without knowing it, exceedingly ridiculous with our modern "virtues. . . ." The decline of the instincts of hostility and of those instincts that arouse suspicion—for this if anything is what constitutes our progress —is only one of the results manifested by the general decline in *vitality*: it requires a hundred times more trouble and caution to live such a dependent and senile existence. In such circumstances everybody gives everybody else a helping hand, and, to a certain extent, everybody is either an invalid or an invalid's attendant. This is then called "virtue": among those men who knew a different life—that is to say, a fuller, more prodigal, more superabundant sort of life, it might have been called by another name— possibly "cowardice," or "vileness," or "old woman's morality. . . ." Our mollification of morals—this is my cry; this if you will is my *innovation*—is the outcome of our decline; conversely hardness and terribleness in morals may be the result of a surplus of life. When the latter state prevails, much is dared, much is challenged, and much is also *squandered.* That which formerly was simply the salt of life, would now be our *poison.* To be indifferent—even this is a form of strength—for that, likewise, we are too senile, too decrepit: our morality of fellow-feeling, against which I was the first to raise a finger of warning, that which might be called *moral impressionism,* is one symptom the more of the excessive physiological irritability which is peculiar to everything decadent. That movement which attempted to introduce itself in a scientific manner on the shoulders of Schopenhauer's morality of pity—a very sad attempt! Is in its essence the movement of decadence in morality, and as such it is intimately related to Christian morality. Strong ages and noble cultures see something contemptible in pity, in the "love of one's neighbour," and in a lack of egoism and of self-esteem. Ages should be measured according to their *positive forces*; valued by this standard that prodigal and fateful age of the Renaissance, appears as the last *great* age, while we moderns with our anxious care of ourselves and love of our neighbours, with all our unassuming virtues of industry, equity, and scientific method—with our lust of collection, of economy and of mechanism—representa *weak* age. . . . Our virtues are necessarily determined, and are even stimulated, by our weakness. "Equality," a certain definite process of making everybody uniform, which only finds its expression in the theory of equal rights, is essentially bound up with a declining culture: the chasm between man and man, class and class, the multiplicity of types, the will to be one's self, and to distinguish one's self—that, in fact, which I call the *pathos of distance* is proper to all *strong* ages. The force of tension—nay, the tension itself, between extremes grows slighter every day—the extremes themselves are tending to become obliterated to the point of becoming identical. All our political theories and state constitutions, not by any means excepting "The German Empire," are the logical consequences, the necessary consequences of decline; the unconscious effect of *decadence* has begun to dominate even the ideals of the various sciences. My objection to the whole of English and French sociology still continues to be this, that it knows only the *decadent form* of society from experience, and with perfectly childlike innocence takes the instincts of decline as the *norm*, the standard, of sociological valuations. *Descending* life, the decay of all organising power—that is to say, of all that power which separates, cleaves gulfs, and establishes rank above and below, formulated itself in modern sociology as *the* ideal. Our socialists are decadents: but Herbert Spencer was also a *decadent*—he saw something to be desired in the triumph of altruism! . . .

38

My Concept of Freedom. Sometimes the value of a thing does not lie in that which it helps us to achieve, but in the amount we have to pay for it—what it *costs* us. For instance, liberal institutions straightway cease from being liberal, the moment they are soundly established: once this is attained no more grievous and more thorough enemies of freedom exist than liberal institutions! One knows, of course, what they bring about: they undermine the Will to Power, they are the levelling of mountain and valley exalted to a morality, they make people small, cowardly and pleasure-loving—by means of them the gregarious animal invariably triumphs. Liberalism, or, in plain English, the *transformation of mankind into cattle*. The same institutions, so long as they are fought for, produce quite other results; then indeed they promote the cause of freedom quite powerfully. Regarded more closely, it is war which produces these results, war in favour of liberal institutions, which, as war, allows the illiberal instincts to subsist. For war trains men to be free. What in sooth is freedom? Freedom is the will to be responsible for ourselves. It is to preserve the distance which separates us from other men. To grow more indifferent to hardship, to severity, to privation, and even to life itself. To be ready to sacrifice men for one's cause, one's self included. Freedom denotes that the virile instincts which rejoice in war and in victory, prevail over other instincts; for instance, over the instincts of "happiness." The man who has won his freedom, and how much more so, therefore, the spirit that has won its freedom, tramples ruthlessly upon that contemptible kind of comfort which tea-grocers, Christians, cows, women, Englishmen and other democrats worship in their dreams. The free man is a *warrior*. How is freedom measured in individuals as well as in nations? According to the resistance which has to be overcome, according to the pains which it costs to remain *uppermost*. The highest type of free man would have to be sought where the greatest resistance has continually to be overcome: five paces away from tyranny, on the very threshold of the danger of thraldom. This is psychologically true if, by the word "Tyrants" we mean inexorable and terrible instincts which challenge the *maximum* amount of authority and discipline to oppose them —the finest example of this is Julius Caesar; it is also true politically: just examine the course of history. The nations which were worth anything, which *got to be* worth anything, never attained to that condition under liberal institutions: *great danger* made out of them something which deserves reverence, that danger which alone can make us aware of our resources, our virtues, our means of defence, our weapons, our *genius*—which *compels* us to be strong. *First* principle: a man must need to be strong, otherwise he will never attain it. Those great forcing-houses of the strong, of the strongest kind of men that have ever existed on earth, the aristocratic communities like those of Rome and Venice, understood freedom precisely as I understand the word: as something that one has and that one has *not*, as something that one *will* have and that one *seizes by force*.

39

A Criticism of Modernity. Our institutions are no longer any good; on this point we are all agreed. But the fault does not lie with them; but with *us*.

Now that we have lost all the instincts out of which institutions grow, the latter on their part are beginning to disappear from our midst because we are no longer fit for them. Democracy has always been the death agony of the power of organisation: already in *Human, All-Too-Human*, Part 1, Aph. 472, I pointed out that modern democracy, together with its half-measures, of which the "German Empire" is an example, was a decaying form of the State. For institutions to be possible there must exist a sort of will, instinct, imperative, which cannot be otherwise than anti-liberal to the point of wickedness: the will to tradition, to authority, to responsibility for centuries to come, to *solidarity* in long family lines forwards and backwards *in infinitum*. If this will is present, something is founded which resembles the *imperium Romanum*: or Russia, the *only* great nation today that has some lasting power and grit in her, that can bide her time, that can still promise something. Russia the opposite of all wretched European petty-statism and neurasthenia, which the foundation of the German Empire has brought to a crisis. The whole of the Occident no longer possesses those instincts from which institutions spring, out of which a *future* grows: maybe nothing is more opposed to its "modern spirit" than these things. People live for the present, they live at top speed—they certainly live without any sense of responsibility; and this is precisely what they call "freedom." Everything in institutions which makes them institutions, is scorned, loathed and repudiated: everybody is in mortal fear of a new slavery, wherever the word "authority" is so much as whispered. The decadence of the valuing instinct, both in our politicians and in our political parties, goes so far, that they instinctively prefer that which acts as a solvent, that which precipitates the final catastrophe. . . . As an example of this behold *modern* marriage. All reason has obviously been divorced from modern marriage: but this is no objection to matrimony itself but to modernity. The rational basis of marriage—it lay in the exclusive legal responsibility of the man: by this means some ballast was laid in the ship of matrimony, whereas nowadays it has a list, now on this side, now on that. The rational basis of marriage—it lay in its absolute indissolubleness: in this way it was given a gravity which knew how to make its influence felt, in the face of the accident of sentiment, passion and momentary impulse: it lay also in the fact that the responsibility of choosing the parties to the contract, lay with the families. By showing ever more and more favour to *love*-marriages, the very foundation of matrimony, that which alone makes it an institution, has been undermined. No institution ever has been nor ever will be built upon an idiosyncrasy; as I say, marriage

364 TWILIGHT OF THE IDOLS

cannot be based upon "love." It can be based upon sexual desire; upon the instinct of property (wife and child as possessions); upon the instinct of dominion, which constantly organises for itself the smallest form of dominion—the family which *requires* children and heirs in order to hold fast, also in the physiological sense, to a certain quantum of acquired power, influence and wealth, so as to prepare for lasting tasks, and for solidarity in the instincts from one century to another. Marriage as an institution presupposes the affirmation of the greatest and most permanent form of organisation; if society cannot as a whole *stand security* for itself into the remotest generations, marriage has no meaning whatsoever. Modern marriage *has lost* its meaning; consequently it is being abolished.

40

The question of the Workingman. The mere fact that there is such a thing as the question of the workingman is due to stupidity, or at bottom to degenerate instincts which are the cause of all the stupidity of modern times. Concerning certain things *no questions ought to be put*: the first imperative principle of instinct. For the life of me I cannot see what people want to do with the workingman of Europe, now that they have made a question of him. He is far too comfortable to cease from questioning ever more and more, and with ever less modesty. After all, he has the majority on his side. There is now not the slightest hope that an unassuming and contented sort of man, after the style of the Chinaman, will come into being in this quarter: and this would have been the reasonable course, it was even a dire necessity. What has been done? Everything has been done with the view of nipping the very prerequisite of this accomplishment in the bud—with the most frivolous thoughtlessness those self-same instincts by means of which a working-class becomes possible, and *tolerable* even to its members themselves, have been destroyed root and branch. The workingman has been declared fit for military service; he has been granted the right of combination, and of voting: can it be wondered at that he already regards his condition as one of distress (expressed morally, as an injustice)? But, again I ask, what do people want? If they desire a certain end, then they should desire the means thereto. If they will have slaves, then it is madness to educate them to be masters.

41

"The kind of freedom I do *not* mean. . . ."[6] In an age like the present, it simply adds to one's perils to be left to one's instincts. The instincts contradict, disturb, and destroy each other; I have already defined modernism as physiological self-contradiction. A reasonable system of education would insist upon at least one of these instinct-systems being *paralysed* beneath an iron pressure, in order to allow others to assert their power, to grow strong, and to dominate. At present, the only conceivable way of making the individual possible would be to *prune* him: of making him possible—that is to say, *whole.* The very reverse occurs. Independence, free development, and *laisser aller* are clamoured for most violently precisely by those for whom no restraint *could be too severe*—this is true *in politics*, it is true in Art. But this is a symptom of decadence: our modern notion of "freedom" is one proof the more of the degeneration of instinct.

42

Where faith is necessary. Nothing is more rare among moralists and saints than uprightness; maybe they say the reverse is true, maybe they even believe it. For, when faith is more useful, more effective, more convincing than *conscious* hypocrisy, by instinct that hypocrisy forthwith becomes *innocent*: first principle towards the understanding of great saints. The same holds good of philosophers, that other order of saints; their whole business compels them to concede only certain truths—that is to say, those by means of which their particular trade receives the *public* sanction—to speak "Kantingly": the truths of *practical* reason. They know what they *must* prove; in this respect they are practical—they recognise each other by the fact that they agree upon "certain truths." "Thou shalt not lie"—in plain English: *Beware*, Mr. Philosopher, of speaking the truth. . . .

43

A quiet hint to Conservatives. That which we did not know formerly, and know now, or might know if we chose—is the fact that a *retrograde formation*, a reversion in any sense or degree, is absolutely impossible. We physiologists, at least, are aware of this. But all priests and moralists have believed in it—they wished to drag and screw man back to a *former* standard of virtue. Morality has always been a Procrustean bed. Even the politicians have imitated the preachers of virtue in this matter. There are parties at the present day whose one aim and dream is to make all things adopt the *crab-march*. But not everyone can be a crab. It cannot be helped: we must go forward—that is to say step by step further and further into decadence (this is my definition of modern "progress"). We can hinder this development, and by so doing dam up and accumulate degeneration itself and render it more convulsive, more *volcanic*: we cannot do more.

44

My concept of Genius. Great men, like great ages, are explosive material, in which a stupendous amount of power is accumulated; the first conditions of their existence are always historical and physiological; they are the outcome of the fact that for long ages energy has been collected, hoarded up, saved up and preserved for their use, and that no explosion has taken place. When the tension in the bulk has become sufficiently excessive, the most fortuitous stimulus suffices in order to call "genius," "great deeds," and momentous fate into the world. What then is the good of all environment, historical periods, "*Zeitgeist*" (Spirit of the age) and "public opinion?" Take the case of Napoleon. France of the Revolution, and still more of the period preceding the Revolution, would have brought forward a type which was the very reverse of Napoleon: it actually *did* produce such a type. And because Napoleon was something different, the heir of a stronger, more lasting and older civilisation than that which in France was being smashed to atoms he became master there, he was the only master there. Great men are necessary, the age in which they appear is a matter of chance; the fact that they almost invariably master their age is accounted for simply by the fact that they are stronger, that they are older, and that power has been stored longer for them. The relation of a genius to his age is that which exists between strength and weakness and between maturity and youth: the age is relatively always very much younger, thinner, less mature, less resolute and more childish. The fact that the general opinion in France at the present day, is utterly different on this very point (in Germany too, but that is of no consequence); the fact that in that country the theory of environment—a regular neuropathic notion—has become sacrosanct and almost scientific, and finds acceptance even among the physiologists, is a very bad, and exceedingly depressing sign. In England too the same belief prevails: but nobody will be surprised at that. The Englishman knows only two ways of understanding the genius and the "great man": either *democratically* in the style of Buckle, or *religiously* after the manner of Carlyle. The danger which great men and great ages represent, is simply extraordinary; every kind of exhaustion and of sterility follows in their wake. The great man is an end; the great age—the Renaissance for instance—is an end. The genius—in work and in deed—is necessarily a squanderer: the fact that he spends himself constitutes his greatness. The instinct of self-preservation is as it were suspended in him; the overpowering pressure of out-flowing energy in him forbids any such protection and prudence. People call this "self-sacrifice," they praise his "heroism," his indifference to his own well-being, his utter devotion to an idea, a great cause, a fatherland: All misunderstandings. . . . He flows out, he flows over, he consumes himself, he does not spare himself—and does all this with fateful necessity, irrevocably, involuntarily, just as a river involuntarily bursts its dams. But, owing to the fact that humanity has been much indebted to such explosives, it has endowed them with many things, for instance, with a kind of *higher morality.* . . . This is indeed the sort of gratitude that humanity is capable of: it *misunderstands* its benefactors.

45

The criminal and his like. The criminal type is the type of the strong man amid unfavourable conditions, a strong man made sick. He lacks the wild and savage state, a form of nature and existence which is freer and more dangerous, in which everything that constitutes the shield and the sword in the instinct of the strong man, takes a place by right. Society puts a ban upon his virtues; the most spirited instincts inherent in him immediately become involved with the depressing passions, with suspicion, fear and dishonour. But this is almost the recipe for physiological degeneration. When a man has to do that which he is best suited to do, which he is most fond of doing, not only clandestinely, but also with long suspense, caution and ruse, he becomes anaemic; and inasmuch as he is always having to pay for his instincts in the form of danger, persecution and fatalities, even his feelings begin to turn against these instincts—he begins to regard them as fatal. It is society, our tame, mediocre, castrated society, in which an untutored son of nature who comes to us from his mountains or from his adventures at sea, must necessarily degenerate into a criminal. Or almost necessarily: for there are cases in which such a man shows himself to be stronger than society: the Corsican Napoleon is the most celebrated case of this. Concerning the problem before us, Dostoiewsky's testimony is of importance—Dostoiewsky who, incidentally, was the only psychologist from whom I had anything to learn: he belongs to the happiest windfalls of my life, happier even than the discovery of Stendhal. This profound man, who was right ten times over in esteeming the superficial Germans low, found the Siberian convicts among whom he lived for many years—those thoroughly hopeless criminals for whom no road back to society stood open—very different from what even he had expected—that is to say carved from about the best, hardest and most valuable material that grows on Russian soil.[7] Let us generalise the case of the criminal; let us imagine creatures who for some reason or other fail to meet with public approval, who know that they are regarded neither as beneficent nor useful—the feeling of the Chandala, who are aware that they are not looked upon as equal, but as proscribed, unworthy, polluted. The thoughts and actions of all such natures are tainted with a subterranean mouldiness; everything in them is of a paler hue than in those on whose existence the sun shines. But almost all those creatures whom, nowadays, we honour and respect, formerly lived in this semi-sepulchral atmosphere: the man of science, the artist, the genius, the free spirit, the actor, the business man, and the great explorer. As long as the *priest* represented the highest type of man, every valuable kind of man was depreciated. . . . The time is coming—this I guarantee—when he will pass as the *lowest* type, as our Chandala, as the falsest and most disreputable kind of man. . . . I call your attention to the fact that even now, under the sway of the mildest customs and usages which have ever ruled on earth or at least in Europe, every form of standing aside, every kind of prolonged, excessively prolonged concealment, every unaccustomed and obscure form of existence tends to approximate to that type which the criminal exemplifies to perfection. All pioneers of the spirit have, for a while, the grey and fatalistic mark of the Chandala on their brows: *not* because they are regarded as Chandala, but because they themselves feel the terrible chasm which separates them from all that is traditional and honourable. Almost every genius knows the "Catilinarian life" as one of the stages in his development, a feeling of hate, revenge and revolt against everything that exists, that has ceased to evolve. . . . Catiline—the early stage of every Caesar.

46

Here the outlook is free. When a philosopher holds his tongue it may be the sign of the loftiness of his soul: when he contradicts himself it may be love; and the very courtesy of a knight of knowledge may force him to lie. It has been said, and not without subtlety: *il est indigne des grands cœurs de répandre le trouble qu'ils ressentent:*[8] but it is necessary to add that there may also be *grandeur de cœur* in not shrinking *from the most undignified* proceeding. A woman who loves sacrifices her honour; a knight of knowledge who "loves," sacrifices perhaps his humanity; a God who loved, became a Jew. . . .

47

Beauty no accident. Even the beauty of a race or of a family, the charm and perfection of all its movements, is attained with pains: like genius it is the final result of the accumulated work of generations. Great sacrifices must have been made on the altar of good taste, for its sake many things must have been done, and much must have been left undone—the seventeenth century in France is admirable for both of these things—in this century there must have been a principle of selection in respect to company, locality, clothing, the gratification of the instinct of sex; beauty must have been preferred to profit, to habit, to opinion and to indolence. The first rule of all: nobody must "let himself go," not even when he is alone. Good things are exceedingly costly: and in all cases the law obtains that he who possesses them is a different person from him who is *acquiring* them. Everything good is an inheritance: that which is not inherited is imperfect, it is simply a beginning. In Athens at the time of Cicero—who expresses his surprise at the fact—the men and youths were by far superior in beauty to the women: but what hard work and exertions the male sex had for centuries imposed upon itself in the service of beauty! We must not be mistaken in regard to the method employed here: the mere discipline of feelings and thoughts is little better than nil (it is in this that the great error of German culture, which is quite illusory, lies): the *body* must be persuaded first. The strict maintenance of a distinguished and tasteful demeanour, the obligation of frequenting only those who do not "let themselves go," is amply sufficient to render one distinguished and tasteful: in two or three generations everything has already *taken deep root.* The fate of a people and of humanity is decided according to whether they begin culture at the *right place*—not at the "soul" (as the fatal superstition of the priests and half-priests would have it): the right place is the body, demeanour, diet, physiology—the rest follows as the night the day. . . . That is why the Greeks remain the *first event in culture*—they knew and they *did* what was needful. Christianity with its contempt of the body is the greatest mishap that has ever befallen mankind.

48

Progress in my sense. I also speak of a "return to nature," although it is not a process of going back but of going up—up into lofty, free and even terrible nature and naturalness; such a nature as can play with great tasks and *may* play with them. . . . To speak in a *parable*, Napoleon was an example of a "return to nature," as I understand it (for instance *in rebus tacticis*, and still more, as military experts know, in strategy). But Rousseau—whither did he want to return? Rousseau this first modern man, idealist and *canaille* in one person; who was in need of moral "dignity," in order even to endure the sight of his own person—ill with unbridled vanity and wanton self-contempt; this abortion, who planted his tent on the threshold of modernity, also wanted a "return to nature"; but, I ask once more, whither did he wish to return? I hate Rousseau, even *in* the Revolution itself: the latter was the historical expression of this hybrid of idealist and *canaille*. The bloody farce which this Revolution ultimately became, its "immorality," concerns me but slightly; what I loathe however is its Rousseauesque *morality*—the so-called "truths" of the Revolution, by means of which it still exercises power and draws all flat and mediocre things over to its side. The doctrine of equality! . . . But there is no more deadly poison than this; for it *seems* to proceed from the very lips of justice, whereas in reality it draws the curtain down on all justice. . . . "To equals equality, to unequals inequality"—that would be the real speech of justice and that which follows from it. "Never make unequal things equal." The fact that so much horror and blood are associated with this doctrine of equality, has lent this "modern idea" *par excellence* such a halo of fire and glory, that the Revolution as a drama has misled even the most noble minds. That after all is no reason for honouring it the more. I can see only one who regarded it as it should be regarded—that is to say, with *loathing*; I speak of Goethe.

49

Goethe. No mere German, but a European event: a magnificent attempt to overcome the eighteenth century by means of a return to nature, by means of an ascent to the naturalness of the Renaissance, a kind of self-overcoming on the part of the century in question. He bore the strongest instincts of this century in his breast: its sentimentality, and idolatry of nature, its anti-historic, idealistic, unreal, and revolutionary spirit (the latter is only a form of the unreal). He enlisted history, natural science, antiquity, as well as Spinoza, and above all practical activity, in his service. He drew a host of very definite horizons around him; far from liberating himself from life, he plunged right into it; he did not give in; he took as much as he could on his own shoulders, and into his heart. That to which he aspired was *totality*; he was opposed to the sundering of reason, sensuality, feeling and will (as preached with most repulsive scholasticism by Kant, the antipodes of Goethe); he disciplined himself into a harmonious

whole, he *created* himself. Goethe in the midst of an age of unreal sentiment, was a convinced realist: he said yea to everything that was like him
in this regard—there was no greater event in his life than that *ens realissimum*, surnamed Napoleon. Goethe conceived a strong, highly cultured
man, skilful in all bodily accomplishments, able to keep himself in check,
having a feeling of reverence for himself, and so constituted as to be able
to risk the full enjoyment of naturalness in all its rich profusion and be
strong enough for this freedom; a man of tolerance, not out of weakness
but out of strength, because he knows how to turn to his own profit that
which would ruin the mediocre nature; a man unto whom nothing is any
longer forbidden, unless it be weakness either as a vice or as a virtue. Such
a spirit, *become free*, appears in the middle of the universe with a feeling of
cheerful and confident fatalism; he believes that only individual things
are bad, and that as a whole the universe justifies and affirms itself—*He no
longer denies*. . . . But such a faith is the highest of all faiths: I christened it
with the name of Dionysus.

50

It might be said that, in a certain sense, the nineteenth century also strove
after all that Goethe himself aspired to: catholicity in understanding,
in approving; a certain reserve towards everything, daring realism, and
a reverence for every fact. How is it that the total result of this is not a
Goethe, but a state of chaos, a nihilistic groan, an inability to discover
where one is, an instinct of fatigue which *in praxi* is persistently driving
Europe *to hark back to the eighteenth century?* (For instance in the form of
maudlin romanticism, altruism, hyper-sentimentality, pessimism in taste,
and socialism in politics). Is not the nineteenth century, at least in its
closing years, merely an accentuated, brutalised eighteenth century—that
is to say a century of decadence? And has not Goethe been—not alone
for Germany, but also for the whole of Europe—merely an episode, a
beautiful "in vain?" But great men are misunderstood when they are
regarded from the wretched standpoint of public utility. The fact that
no advantage can be derived from them—*this in itself may perhaps be peculiar to greatness.*

51

Goethe is the last German whom I respect: he had understood three
things as I understand them. We also agree as to the "cross."[9] People often
ask me why on earth I write in *German:* nowhere am I less read than in the

Fatherland. But who knows whether I even *desire* to be read at present? To create things on which time may try its teeth in vain; to be concerned both in the form and the substance of my writing, about a certain degree of immortality—never have I been modest enough to demand less of myself. The aphorism, the sentence, in both of which I, as the first among Germans, am a master, are the forms of "eternity"; it is my ambition to say in ten sentences what everyone else says in a whole book—what everyone else does *not* say in a whole book.

I have given mankind the deepest book it possesses, my *Zarathustra*; before long I shall give it the most independent one.

Things I Owe to the Ancients

IN CONCLUSION I WILL JUST SAY A WORD CONCERNING THAT WORLD TO which I have sought new means of access, to which I may perhaps have found a new passage—the ancient world. My taste, which is perhaps the reverse of tolerant, is very far from saying yea through and through even to this world: on the whole it is not over eager to say *Yea*, it would prefer to say *Nay*, and better still nothing whatever. . . . This is true of whole cultures; it is true of books—it is also true of places and of landscapes. Truth to tell, the number of ancient books that count for something in my life is but small; and the most famous are not of that number. My sense of style, for the epigram as style, was awakened almost spontaneously upon my acquaintance with Sallust. I have not forgotten the astonishment of my respected teacher Corssen, when he was forced to give his worst Latin pupil the highest marks—at one stroke I had learned all there was to learn. Condensed, severe, with as much substance as possible in the background, and with cold but roguish hostility towards all "beautiful words" and "beautiful feelings"—in these things I found my own particular bent. In my writings up to my "Zarathustra," there will be found a very earnest ambition to attain to the *Roman* style, to the "*aere perennius*" in style. The same thing happened on my first acquaintance with Horace. Up to the present no poet has given me the same artistic raptures as those which from the first I received from an Horatian ode. In certain languages it would be absurd even to aspire to what is accomplished by this poet. This mosaic of words, in which every unit spreads its power to the left and to the right over the whole, by its sound, by its place in the sentence, and by its meaning, this *minimum* in the compass and number of the signs, and the *maximum* of energy in the signs which is thereby achieved—all this is Roman, and, if you will believe me, noble *par excellence*. By the side of this all the rest of poetry becomes something popular—nothing more than senseless sentimental twaddle.

2

I am not indebted to the Greeks for anything like such strong impressions; and, to speak frankly, they cannot be to us what the Romans are. One cannot *learn* from the Greeks—their style is too strange, it is also too fluid, to be imperative or to have the effect of a classic. Who would ever have learnt writing from a Greek! Who would ever have learned it without the Romans! . . . Do not let anyone suggest Plato to me. In regard to Plato I am a thorough sceptic, and have never been able to agree to the admiration of Plato the *artist*, which is traditional among scholars. And after all, in this matter, the most refined judges of taste in antiquity are on my side. In my opinion Plato bundles all the forms of style pell-mell together, in this respect he is one of the first decadents of style: he has something similar on his conscience to that which the Cynics had who invented the *satura Menippea*. For the Platonic dialogue—this revoltingly self-complacent and childish kind of dialectics—to exercise any charm over you, you must never have read any good French authors—Fontenelle for instance. Plato is boring. In reality my distrust of Plato is fundamental. I find him so very much astray from all the deepest instincts of the Hellenes, so steeped in moral prejudices, so pre-existently Christian—the concept "good" is already the highest value with him—that rather than use any other expression I would prefer to designate the whole phenomenon Plato with the hard word "superior bunkum," or, if you would like it better, "idealism." Humanity has had to pay dearly for this Athenian having gone to school among the Egyptians (or among the Jews in Egypt?). In the great fatality of Christianity, Plato is that double-faced fascination called the "ideal," which made it possible for the more noble natures of antiquity to misunderstand themselves and to tread the *bridge* which led to the "cross." And what an amount of Plato is still to be found in the concept "church," and in the construction, the system and the practise of the church! My recreation, my predilection, my cure, after all Platonism, has always been Thucydides. Thucydides and perhaps Machiavelli's *principe* are most closely related to me owing to the absolute determination which they show of refusing to deceive themselves and of seeing reason in *reality*—not in

"rationality," and still less in "morality." There is no more radical cure
than Thucydides for the lamentably rose-coloured idealisation of the
Greeks which the "classically cultured" stripling bears with him into life, as
a reward for his public school training. His writings must be carefully
studied line by line, and his unuttered thoughts must be read as distinctly
as what he actually says. There are few thinkers so rich in unuttered
thoughts. In him the culture "of the Sophists"—that is to say, the culture
of realism, receives its most perfect expression: this inestimable movement
in the midst of the moral and idealistic knavery of the Socratic Schools
which was then breaking out in all directions. Greek philosophy is the
decadence of the Greek instinct: Thucydides is the great summing up,
the final manifestation of that strong, severe positivism which lay in the
instincts of the ancient Hellene. After all, it is courage in the face of reality
that distinguishes such natures as Thucydides from Plato: Plato is a coward
in the face of reality—consequently he takes refuge in the ideal: Thucydides is master of himself—consequently he is able to master life.

3

To rout up cases of "beautiful souls," "golden means" and other perfec-
tions among the Greeks, to admire, say, their calm grandeur, their ideal
attitude of mind, their exalted simplicity—from this "exalted simplicity,"
which after all is a piece of *niaiserie allemande*, I was preserved by the
psychologist within me. I saw their strongest instinct, the Will to Power, I
saw them quivering with the fierce violence of this instinct—I saw all their
institutions grow out of measures of security calculated to preserve each
member of their society from the inner *explosive material* that lay in his
neighbour's breast. This enormous internal tension thus discharged itself
in terrible and reckless hostility outside the state: the various states mutually tore each other to bits, in order that each individual state could
remain at peace with itself. It was then necessary to be strong; for danger
lay close at hand—it lurked in ambush everywhere. The superb suppleness
of their bodies, the daring realism and immorality which is peculiar to the
Hellenes, was a necessity not an inherent quality. It was a result, it had
not been there from the beginning. Even their festivals and their arts were
but means in producing a feeling of superiority, and of showing it: they
are measures of self-glorification; and in certain circumstances of making
one's self terrible. . . . Fancy judging the Greeks in the German style, from
their philosophers; fancy using the suburban respectability of the Socratic
schools as a key to what is fundamentally Hellenic! . . . The philosophers

are of course the decadents of Hellas, the counter-movement directed against the old and noble taste (against the agonal instinct, against the *Polis*, against the value of the race, against the authority of tradition). Socratic virtues were preached to the Greeks, *because* the Greeks had lost virtue: irritable, cowardly, unsteady, and all turned to play-actors, they had more than sufficient reason to submit to having morality preached to them. Not that it helped them in any way; but great words and attitudes are so becoming to decadents.

4

I was the first who, in order to understand the ancient, still rich and even superabundant Hellenic instinct, took that marvellous phenomenon, which bears the name of Dionysus, seriously: it can be explained only as a manifestation of excessive energy. Whoever had studied the Greeks, as that most profound of modern connoisseurs of their culture, Jakob Burckhardt of Bâle, had done, knew at once that something had been achieved by means of this interpretation. And in his "*Cultur der Griechen*," Burckhardt inserted a special chapter on the phenomenon in question. If you would like a glimpse of the other side, you have only to refer to the almost laughable poverty of instinct among German philologists when they approach the Dionysian question. The celebrated Lobeck, especially, who with the venerable assurance of a worm dried up between books, crawled into this world of mysterious states, succeeded in convincing himself that he was scientific, whereas he was simply revoltingly superficial and childish—Lobeck, with all the pomp of profound erudition, gave us to understand that, as a matter of fact, there was nothing at all in all these curiosities. Truth to tell, the priests may well have communicated not a few things of value to the participators in such orgies; for instance, the fact that wine provokes desire, that man in certain circumstances lives on fruit, that plants bloom in the spring and fade in the autumn. As regards the astounding wealth of rites, symbols and myths which take their origin in the orgy, and with which the world of antiquity is literally smothered, Lobeck finds that it prompts him to a feat of even greater ingenuity than the foregoing phenomenon did. "The Greeks," he says, (*Aglaophamus*, I p. 672), "when they had nothing better to do, laughed, sprang and romped about, or, inasmuch as men also like a change at times, they would sit down, weep and bewail their lot. Others then came up who tried to discover some reason for this strange behaviour; and thus, as an explanation of these habits, there arose an incalculable number of festivals, legends, and myths. On the other hand it was believed that the *farcical performances* which then perchance began to take place on festival days, necessarily formed part of the celebrations, and they were retained as an indispensable part of the ritual." This is contemptible nonsense, and no one will take a man like Lobeck seriously for a moment. We are very differently affected when we examine the notion "Hellenic," as Winckelmann and Goethe conceived it, and find it incompatible with that element out of which Dionysian art springs—I speak of orgiasm. In reality I do not doubt that Goethe would have completely excluded any such thing from the potentialities of the Greek soul. *Consequently Goethe did not understand the Greeks.* For it is only in the Dionysian mysteries, in the psychology of the Dionysian state, that the *fundamental fact* of the Hellenic instinct—its "will to life"—is expressed. What did the Hellene secure himself with these mysteries? *Eternal* life, the eternal recurrence of life; the future promised and hallowed in the past; the triumphant Yea to life despite death and change; real life conceived as the collective prolongation of life through procreation, through the mysteries of sexuality. To the Greeks, the symbol of sex was the most venerated of symbols, the really deep significance of all the piety of antiquity. All the details of the act of procreation, pregnancy and birth gave rise to the loftiest and most solemn feelings. In the doctrine of mysteries, *pain* was pronounced holy: the "pains of childbirth" sanctify pain in general—all becoming and all growth, everything that guarantees the future *involves* pain. . . . In order that there may be eternal joy in creating, in order that the will to life may say Yea to itself in all eternity, the "pains of childbirth" must also be eternal. All this is what the word Dionysus signifies: I know of no higher symbolism than this Greek symbolism, this symbolism of the Dionysian phenomenon. In it the profoundest instinct of life, the instinct that guarantees the future of life and life eternal, is understood religiously—the road to life itself, procreation, is pronounced *holy*. . . . It was only Christianity which, with its fundamental resentment against life, made something impure out of sexuality: it flung *filth* at the very basis, the very first condition of our life.

5

The psychology of orgiasm conceived as the feeling of a superabundance of vitality and strength, within the scope of which even pain acts as a *stimulus*, gave me the key to the concept *tragic* feeling, which has been misunderstood not only by Aristotle, but also even more by our pessimists. Tragedy is so far from proving anything in regard to the pessimism of the Greeks, as Schopenhauer maintains, that it ought rather to be considered as the categorical repudiation and *condemnation* thereof. The saying of Yea to life, including even its most strange and most terrible problems, the will to life rejoicing over its own inexhaustibleness in the *sacrifice* of its highest types—this is what I called Dionysian, this is what I divined as the bridge leading to the psychology of the *tragic* poet. Not in order to escape from terror and pity, not to purify one's self of a dangerous passion by discharging it with vehemence—this is how Aristotle understood it—but to be far beyond terror and pity and to be the eternal lust of Becoming itself—that lust which also involves the *lust of destruction*. And with this I once more come into touch with the spot from which I once set out—the *Birth of Tragedy* was my first transvaluation of all values: with this I again take my stand upon the soil from out of which my will and my capacity spring—I, the last disciple of the philosopher Dionysus—I, the prophet of eternal recurrence.

THE ANTICHRIST

TRANSLATED BY

ANTHONY M. LUDOVICI

CONTENTS

THE ANTICHRIST

PREFACE

THIS BOOK BELONGS TO THE VERY FEW. MAYBE NOT ONE OF THEM IS YET alive; unless he be of those who understand my Zarathustra. How *can* I confound myself with those who today already find a hearing? Only the day after tomorrow belongs to me. Some are born posthumously.

I am only too well aware of the conditions under which a man understands me, and then *necessarily* understands. He must be intellectually upright to the point of hardness, in order even to endure my seriousness and my passion. He must be used to living on mountain-tops, and to feeling the wretched gabble of politics and national egotism *beneath* him. He must have become indifferent; he must never inquire whether truth is profitable or whether it may prove fatal. . . . Possessing from strength a predilection for questions for which no one has enough courage nowadays; the courage for the *forbidden*; his predestination must be the labyrinth. The experience of seven solitudes. New ears for new music. New eyes for the most remote things. A new conscience for truths which hitherto have remained dumb. And the will to economy on a large scale: to husband his strength and his enthusiasm. . . . He must honour himself, he must love himself; he must be absolutely free with regard to himself. . . . Very well then! Such men alone are my readers, my proper readers, my preordained readers: of what account are the rest? The rest are simply— humanity. One must be superior to humanity in power, in loftiness of soul, in contempt.

FRIEDRICH NIETZSCHE

THE ANTICHRIST

1

LET US LOOK EACH OTHER IN THE FACE. WE ARE HYPERBOREANS, WE KNOW well enough how far outside the crowd we stand. "Thou wilt find the way to the Hyperboreans neither by land nor by water": Pindar already knew this much about us. Beyond the north, the ice, and death—*our life, our happiness*. . . . We discovered happiness; we know the way; we found the way out of thousands of years of labyrinth. Who *else* would have found it? Not the modern man, surely? "I do not know where I am or what I am to do; I am everything that knows not where it is or what to do"—sighs the modern man. We were made quite ill by *this* modernity, with its indolent peace, its cowardly compromise, and the whole of the virtuous filth of its Yea and Nay. This tolerance and *largeur de cœur* which "forgives" everything because it "understands" everything, is a Sirocco for us. We prefer to live amid ice than to be breathed upon by modern virtues and other southerly winds! . . . We were brave enough; we spared neither ourselves nor others: but we were very far from knowing whither to direct our bravery. We were becoming gloomy; people called us fatalists. *Our* fate—it was the abundance, the tension and the storing up of power. We thirsted for thunderbolts and great deeds; we kept at the most respectful distance from the joy of the weakling, from "resignation. . . ." Thunder was in our air, that part of nature which we are, became overcast—*for we had no direction*. The formula of our happiness: a Yea, a Nay, a straight line, a goal.

2

What is good? All that enhances the feeling of power, the Will to Power, and power itself in man. What is bad? All that proceeds from weakness.

What is happiness? The feeling that power is *increasing*, that resistance has been overcome.

Not contentment, but more power; not peace at any price, but war; not virtue, but efficiency[1] (virtue in the Renaissance sense, *virtù*, free from all moralic acid). The weak and the botched shall perish: first principle of our humanity. And they ought even to be helped to perish.

What is more harmful than any vice? Practical sympathy with all the botched and the weak Christianity.

3

The problem I set in this work is not what will replace mankind in the order of living beings (Man is an *end*); but, what type of man must be *reared*, must be *willed*, as having the highest value, as being the most worthy of life and the surest guarantee of the future.

This more valuable type has appeared often enough already: but as a happy accident, as an exception, never as *willed*. He has rather been precisely the most feared; hitherto he has been almost the terrible in itself; and from out the very fear he provoked there arose the will to rear the type which has now been reared, *attained*: the domestic animal, the gregarious animal, the sick animal man, the Christian.

4

Mankind does *not* represent a development towards a better, stronger or higher type, in the sense in which this is supposed to occur today. "Progress" is merely a modern idea—that is to say, a false idea.[2] The modern European is still far below the European of the Renaissance in value. The process of evolution does not by any means imply elevation, enhancement and increasing strength.

On the other hand isolated and individual cases are continually succeeding in different places on earth, as the outcome of the most different cultures, and in these a *higher type* certainly manifests itself: something which by the side of mankind in general, represents a kind of superman. Such lucky strokes of great success have always been possible and will perhaps always be possible. And even whole races, tribes and nations may in certain circumstances represent such *lucky strokes*.

5

We must not deck out and adorn Christianity: it has waged a deadly war upon this *higher* type of man, it has set a ban upon all the fundamental instincts of this type, and has distilled evil and the devil himself out of these instincts: the strong man as the typical pariah, the villain. Christianity has sided with everything weak, low, and botched; it has made an ideal out of *antagonism* towards all the self-preservative instincts of strong life: it has corrupted even the reason of the strongest intellects, by teaching that the highest values of intellectuality are sinful, misleading and full of temptations. The most lamentable example of this was the corruption of Pascal, who believed in the perversion of his reason through original sin, whereas it had only been perverted by his Christianity.

6

A painful and ghastly spectacle has just risen before my eyes. I tore down the curtain which concealed mankind's *corruption.* This word in my mouth is at least secure from the suspicion that it contains a moral charge against mankind. It is—I would fain emphasise this again—free from moralic acid: to such an extent is this so, that I am most thoroughly conscious of the corruption in question precisely in those quarters in which hitherto people have aspired with most determination to "virtue" and to "godliness." As you have already surmised, I understand corruption in the sense of *decadence.* What I maintain is this, that all the values upon which mankind builds its highest hopes and desires are *decadent* values.

I call an animal, a species, an individual corrupt, when it loses its instincts, when it selects and *prefers* that which is detrimental to it. A history of the "higher feelings," of "human ideals"—and it is not impossible that I shall have to write it—would almost explain why man is so corrupt. Life itself, to my mind, is nothing more nor less than the instinct of growth, of permanence, of accumulating forces, of power: where the will to power is lacking, degeneration sets in. My contention is that all the highest values of mankind *lack* this will, that the values of decline and of *nihilism* are exercising the sovereign power under the cover of the holiest names.

7

Christianity is called the religion of *pity.* Pity is opposed to the tonic passions which enhance the energy of the feeling of life: its action is depressing. A man loses power when he pities. By means of pity the drain on strength which suffering itself already introduces into the world is multiplied a thousandfold. Through pity, suffering itself becomes infectious; in certain circumstances it may lead to a total loss of life and vital energy, which is absurdly out of proportion to the magnitude of the cause (the case of the death of the Nazarene). This is the first standpoint; but there is a still more important one. Supposing one measures pity according to the value of the reactions it usually stimulates, its danger to life appears in a much more telling light. On the whole, pity thwarts the law of development which is the law of selection. It preserves that which is ripe for death, it fights in favour of the disinherited and the condemned of life; thanks to the multitude of abortions of all kinds which it maintains in life, it lends life itself a sombre and questionable aspect. People have dared to call pity a virtue (in every *noble* culture it is considered as a weakness); people went still further, they exalted it to *the* virtue, the root and origin of all virtues, but, of course, what must never be forgotten is the fact that this was done from the standpoint of a philosophy which was nihilistic, and on whose shield the device *The Denial of Life* was inscribed. Schopenhauer was right in this respect: by means of pity, life is denied and made *more worthy of denial*, pity is the *praxis* of Nihilism. I repeat, this depressing and infectious instinct thwarts those instincts which aim at the preservation and enhancement of the value life: by *multiplying* misery quite as much as by preserving all that is miserable, it is the principal agent in promoting decadence, pity exhorts people to nothing, to *nonentity*! But they do not say "*nonentity*," they say "Beyond," or "God," or "the true life"; or Nirvana, or Salvation, or Blessedness, instead. This innocent rhetoric, which belongs to the realm of the religio-moral idiosyncrasy, immediately appears to be *very much less innocent* if one realises what the tendency is which here tries to drape itself in the mantle of sublime expressions—the tendency of hostility to life. Schopenhauer was hostile to life: that is why he elevated pity to a virtue. . . . Aristotle, as you know, recognised in pity a morbid and dangerous state, of which it was wise to rid one's self from time to time by a purgative: he regarded tragedy as a purgative. For the sake of the instinct of life, it would certainly seem necessary to find some means of lancing any such morbid and dangerous accumulation of pity, as that which possessed Schopenhauer (and unfortunately the whole of our literary and artistic decadence as well, from St. Petersburg to Paris, from Tolstoy to Wagner), if only to make it *burst*. . . . Nothing is more unhealthy in the midst of our unhealthy modernity, than Christian pity. To be doctors *here*, to be inexorable *here*, to wield the knife effectively *here*, all this is our business, all this is *our* kind of love to our fellows, this is what makes *us* philosophers, us hyperboreans!

8

It is necessary to state whom we regard as our antithesis: the theologians, and all those who have the blood of theologians in their veins—the whole of our philosophy. . . . A man must have had his very nose upon this fatality, or better still he must have experienced it in his own soul; he must almost have perished through it, in order to be unable to treat this matter lightly (the free-spiritedness of our friends the naturalists and physiologists is, in my opinion, a *joke*, what they lack in these questions is passion, what they lack is having suffered from these questions). This poisoning extends much further than people think: I unearthed the "arrogant" instinct of the theologian, wherever nowadays people feel themselves idealists, wherever, thanks to superior antecedents, they claim the right to rise above reality and to regard it with suspicion. . . . Like the priest the idealist has every grandiloquent concept in his hand (and not only in his hand!), he wields them all with kindly contempt against the "understanding," the "senses," "honours," "decent living," "science"; he regards such things as *beneath* him, as detrimental and seductive forces, upon the face of which, "the Spirit" moves in pure absoluteness: as if humility, chastity, poverty, in a word *holiness*, had not done incalculably more harm to life hitherto, than any sort of horror and vice. . . . Pure spirit is pure falsehood. . . . As long as the priest, the *professional* denier, calumniator and poisoner of life, is considered as the *highest* kind of man, there can be no answer to the question, what *is* truth? Truth has already been turned topsy-turvy, when the conscious advocate of nonentity and of denial passes as the representative of "truth."

9

It is upon this theological instinct that I wage war. I find traces of it everywhere. Whoever has the blood of theologians in his veins, stands from the start in a false and dishonest position to all things. The pathos which grows out of this state, is called *Faith*: that is to say, to shut one's eyes once and for all, in order not to suffer at the sight of incurable falsity. People convert this faulty view of all things into a moral, a virtue, a thing of holiness. They endow their distorted vision with a good conscience, they claim that no *other* point of view is any longer of value, once theirs has been made sacrosanct with the names "God," "Salvation," "Eternity." I unearthed the instinct of the theologian everywhere: it is the most universal, and actually the most subterranean form of falsity on earth. That which a theologian considers true, *must* of necessity be false: this furnishes almost the

390 of FRIEDRICH NIETZSCHE

criterion of truth. It is his most profound self-preservative instinct which forbids reality ever to attain to honour in anyway, or even to raise its voice. Whithersoever the influence of the theologian extends, *valuations* are topsy-turvy, and the concepts "true" and "false" have necessarily changed places: that which is most deleterious to life, is here called "true," that which enhances it, elevates it, says Yea to it, justifies it and renders it triumphant, is called "false. . . ." If it should happen that theologians, *via* the "conscience" either of princes or of the people, stretch out their hand for power, let us not be in any doubt as to what results therefrom each time, namely: the will to the end, the *nihilistic* will to power. . . .

10

Among Germans I am immediately understood when I say, that philosophy is ruined by the blood of theologians. The Protestant minister is the grandfather of German philosophy, Protestantism itself is the latter's *peccatum originale.* Definition of Protestantism: the partial paralysis of Christianity—and of reason. . . . One needs only to pronounce the words "Tübingen Seminary," in order to understand what German philosophy really is at bottom, i.e.,: theology *in disguise.* . . . The Swabians are the best liars in Germany, they lie innocently. . . . Whence came all the rejoicing with which the appearance of Kant was greeted by the scholastic world of Germany, three-quarters of which consist of clergymen's and schoolmasters' sons? Whence came the German conviction, which finds an echo even now, that Kant inaugurated a change for the *better?* The theologian's instinct in the German scholar divined what had once again been made possible. . . . A back staircase leading into the old ideal was discovered, the concept "true world," the concept morality as the *essence* of the world (those two most vicious errors that have ever existed!), were, thanks to a subtle and wily scepticism, once again, if not demonstrable, at least no longer *refutable.* . . . Reason, the *prerogative* of reason, does not extend so far. . . . Out of reality they had made "appearance"; and an absolutely false world—that of being—had been declared to be reality. Kant's success is merely a theologian's success. Like Luther, and like Leibniz, Kant was one brake the more upon the already squeaky wheel of German uprightness.

11

One word more against Kant as a *moralist.* A virtue *must* be *our* invention, our most personal defence and need: in every other sense it is merely a danger. That which does not constitute a condition of our life, is merely harmful to it: to possess a virtue merely because one happens to respect the concept "virtue," as Kant would have us do, is pernicious. "Virtue," "Duty," "Goodness in itself," goodness stamped with the character of impersonality and universal validity—these things are mere mental hallucinations, in which decline the final devitalisation of life and Kœnigsbergian Chinadom find expression. The most fundamental laws of preservation and growth demand precisely the reverse, namely: that each should discover *his* own virtue, his own Categorical Imperative. A nation goes to the dogs when it confounds its concept of duty with the general concept of duty. Nothing is more profoundly, more thoroughly pernicious, than every impersonal feeling of duty, than every sacrifice to the Moloch of abstraction. Fancy no one's having thought Kant's Categorical Imperative *dangerous to life*! . . . The instinct of the theologist alone took it under its wing! An action stimulated by the instinct of life, is proved to be a proper action by the happiness that accompanies it: and that nihilist with the bowels of a Christian dogmatist regarded happiness as an *objection*. . . . What is there that destroys a man more speedily than to work, think, feel, as an automaton of "duty," without internal promptings, without a profound personal predilection, without joy? This is the recipe *par excellence* of decadence and even of idiocy. . . . Kant became an idiot. And he was the contemporary of Goethe! This fatal spider was regarded as *the* German philosopher, is still regarded as such! . . . I refrain from saying what I think of the Germans. . . . Did Kant not see in the French Revolution the transition of the State from the inorganic to the *organic* form? Did he not ask himself whether there was a single event on record which could be explained otherwise than as a moral faculty of mankind; so that by means of it, "mankind's tendency towards good," might be *proved* once and for all? Kant's reply: "that is the Revolution." Instinct at fault in anything and everything, hostility to nature as an instinct, German decadence made into philosophy *that is Kant*!

12

Except for a few sceptics, the respectable type in the history of philosophy, the rest do not know the very first pre-requisite of intellectual uprightness. They all behave like females, do these great enthusiasts and animal prodigies, they regard "beautiful feelings" themselves as arguments, the "heaving breast" as the bellows of divinity, and conviction as the *criterion* of truth. In the end, even Kant, with "Teutonic" innocence, tried to dress this lack of intellectual conscience up in a scientific garb by means of the concept "practical reason." He deliberately invented a kind of reason which at times would allow one to dispense with reason, that is to say when "morality," when the sublime command "thou shalt," makes itself heard. When one remembers that in almost all nations the philosopher is only a further development of the priestly type, this heirloom of priesthood, *this fraud towards one's self*, no longer surprises one. When a man has a holy life-task, as for instance to improve, save, or deliver mankind, when a man bears God in his breast, and is the mouthpiece of imperatives from another world, with such a mission he stands beyond the pale of all merely reasonable valuations. He is even sanctified by such a taste, and is already the type of a higher order! What does a priest care about science! He stands too high for that! And until now the priest has *ruled!* He it was who determined the concept "true and false."

13

Do not let us undervalue the fact that we *ourselves*, we free spirits, are already a "transvaluation of all values," an incarnate declaration of war against all the old concepts "true" and "untrue" and of a triumph over them. The most valuable standpoints are always the last to be found: but the most valuable standpoints are the methods. All the methods and the first principles of our modern scientific procedure, had for years to encounter the profoundest contempt: association with them meant exclusion from the society of decent people—one was regarded as an "enemy of God," as a scoffer at truth and as "one possessed." With one's scientific nature, one belonged to the Chandala. We have had the whole feeling of mankind against us; hitherto their notion of that which ought to be truth, of that which ought to serve the purpose of truth: every "thou shalt," has been directed against us. . . . Our objects, our practises, our calm, cautious distrustful manner—everything about us seemed to them absolutely despicable and beneath contempt. After all, it might be asked with some justice, whether the thing which kept mankind blindfold so long, were not an aesthetic taste: what they demanded of truth was a *picturesque* effect, and from the man of science what they expected was that he should make a forcible appeal to their senses. It was our *modesty* which ran counter to their taste so long. . . . And oh! How well they guessed this, did these divine turkey-cocks!

14

We have altered our standpoint. In every respect we have become more modest. We no longer derive man from the "spirit," and from the "godhead";

we have thrust him back among the beasts. We regard him as the strongest animal, because he is the craftiest: one of the results thereof is his intellectuality. On the other hand we guard against the vain pretension, which even here would fain assert itself: that man is the great *arrière pensée* of organic evolution! He is by no means the crown of creation, beside him, every other creature stands at the same stage of perfection. . . . And even in asserting this we go a little too far; for, relatively speaking, man is the most botched and diseased of animals, and he has wandered furthest from his instincts. Be all this as it may, he is certainly the most *interesting*! As regards animals, Descartes was the first, with really admirable daring, to venture the thought that the beast was *machina,* and the whole of our physiology is endeavouring to prove this proposition. Moreover, logically we do not set man apart, as Descartes did: the extent to which man is understood today goes only so far as he has been understood mechanistically. Formerly man was given "free will," as his dowry from a higher sphere; nowadays we have robbed him even of will, in view of the fact that no such faculty is any longer known. The only purpose served by the old word "will," is to designate a result, a sort of individual reaction which necessarily follows upon a host of partly discordant and partly harmonious stimuli: the will no longer "effects" or "moves" anything. . . . Formerly people thought that man's consciousness, his "spirit," was a proof of his lofty origin, of his divinity. With the idea of perfecting man, he was conjured to draw his senses inside himself, after the manner of the tortoise, to cut off all relations with terrestrial things, and to divest himself of his mortal shell. Then the most important thing about him, the "pure spirit," would remain over. Even concerning these things we have improved our standpoint. Consciousness, "spirit," now seems to us rather a symptom of relative imperfection in the organism, as an experiment, a groping, a misapprehension, an affliction which absorbs an unnecessary quantity of nervous energy. We deny that anything can be done perfectly so long as it is done consciously. "Pure spirit" is a piece of "pure stupidity": if we discount the nervous system, the senses and the "mortal shell," we have miscalculated—that it is all! . . .

15

In Christianity, neither morality nor religion comes in touch at all with reality. Nothing but imaginary *causes* (God, the soul, the ego, spirit, free will—or even non-free will); nothing but imaginary *effects* (sin, salvation, grace, punishment, forgiveness of sins). Imaginary beings are supposed to have intercourse (God, spirits, souls); imaginary Natural History (anthropocentric: total lack of the notion "natural causes"); an imaginary *psychology* (nothing but misunderstandings of self, interpretations of pleasant or unpleasant general feelings; for instance of the states of the *nervus sympathicus*, with the help of the sign language of a religio-moral idiosyncrasy, repentance, pangs of conscience, the temptation of the devil, the presence of God); an imaginary teleology (the Kingdom of God, the Last Judgement, Everlasting Life). This purely fictitious world distinguishes itself very unfavourably from the world of dreams: the latter *reflects* reality, whereas the former falsifies, depreciates and denies it. Once the concept "nature" was taken to mean the opposite of the concept God, the word "natural" had to acquire the meaning of abominable, the whole of that fictitious world takes its root in the hatred of nature (reality!), it is the expression of profound discomfiture in the presence of reality. . . . *But this explains everything.* What is the only kind of man who has reasons for wriggling out of reality by lies? The man who suffers from reality. But in order to suffer from reality one must be a bungled portion of it. The preponderance of pain over pleasure is the *cause* of that fictitious morality and religion: but any such preponderance furnishes the formula for decadence.

16

A criticism of the Christian concept of God inevitably leads to the same conclusion. A nation that still believes in itself, also has its own God. In him it honours the conditions which enable it to remain uppermost, that is to say, its virtues. It projects its joy over itself, its feeling of power, into a being, to whom it can be thankful for such things. He who is rich, will give of his riches: a proud people requires a God, unto whom it can *sacrifice* things. . . . Religion, when restricted to these principles, is a form of gratitude. A man is grateful for his own existence; for this he must have a God. Such a God must be able to benefit and to injure him, he must be able to act the friend and the foe. He must be esteemed for his good as well as for his evil qualities. The monstrous castration of a God by making him a God only of goodness, would lie beyond the pale of the desires of such a community. The evil God is just as urgently needed as the good God: for a people in such a form of society certainly does not owe its existence to toleration and humaneness. . . . What would be the good of a God who knew nothing of anger, revenge, envy, scorn, craft, and violence? Who had perhaps never experienced the rapturous *ardeurs* of victory and of

annihilation? No one would understand such a God: why should one possess him? Of course, when a people is on the road to ruin; when it feels its
belief in a future, its hope of freedom vanishing for ever; when it becomes
conscious of submission as the most useful quality, and of the virtues of
the submissive as self-preservative measures, then its God must also modify
himself. He then becomes a tremulous and unassuming sneak; he coun-
sels "peace of the soul," the cessation of all hatred, leniency and "love"
even towards friend and foe. He is forever moralising, he crawls into the
heart of every private virtue, becomes a God for everybody, he retires from
active service and becomes a Cosmopolitan. . . . Formerly he represented
a people, the strength of a people, everything aggressive and desirous of
power lying concealed in the heart of a nation: now he is merely the good
God. . . . In very truth Gods have no other alternative, they are *either* the
Will to Power—in which case they are always the Gods of whole nations,
or, on the other hand, the incapacity for power—in which case they necessarily become good.

17

Wherever the Will to Power, no matter in what form, begins to decline,
a physiological retrogression, decadence, always supervenes. The godhead of *decadence*, shorn of its masculine virtues and passions is perforce
converted into the God of the physiologically degraded, of the weak. Of
course they do not call themselves the weak, they call themselves "the
good. . . ." No hint will be necessary to help you to understand at what
moment in history the dualistic fiction of a good and an evil God first
became possible. With the same instinct by which the subjugated reduce
their God to "Goodness in itself," they also cancel the good qualities
from their conquerer's God; they avenge themselves on their masters by
diabolising the latter's God. The *good God* and the devil as well: both the
abortions of decadence. How is it possible that we are still so indulgent
towards the simplicity of Christian theologians today, as to declare with
them that the evolution of the concept God, from the "God of Israel,"
the God of a people, to the Christian God, the quintessence of all goodness, marks a *step forward*? But even Renan does this. As if Renan had a
right to simplicity! Why the very contrary stares one in the face. When
the pre-requisites of *ascending* life, when everything strong, plucky, mas-
terful and proud has been eliminated from the concept of God, and step
by step he has sunk down to the symbol of a staff for the weary, of a last
straw for all those who are drowning; when he becomes the pauper's

God, the sinner's God, the sick man's God *par excellence,* and the attribute "Saviour," "Redeemer," remains *over* as the one essential attribute of divinity: what does such a metamorphosis, such an abasement of the godhead imply? Undoubtedly, "the kingdom of God" has thus become larger. Formerly all he had was his people, his "chosen" people. Since then he has gone travelling over foreign lands, just as his people have done; since then he has never rested anywhere: until one day he felt at home everywhere, the Great Cosmopolitan, until he got the "greatest number," and half the world on his side. But the God of the "greatest number," the democrat among gods, did not become a proud heathen god notwithstanding: he remained a Jew, he remained the God of the back streets, the God of all dark corners and hovels, of all the unwholesome quarters of the world! . . . His universal empire is now as ever a netherworld empire, an infirmary, a subterranean empire, a ghetto-empire. . . . And he himself is so pale, so weak, so decadent. . . . Even the palest of the pale were able to master him—our friends the metaphysicians, those albinos of thought. They spun their webs around him so long that ultimately he was hypnotised by their movements and himself became a spider, a metaphysician. Thenceforward he once more began spinning the world out of his inner being—*sub specie Spinozae,* thenceforward he transfigured himself into something ever thinner and ever more anaemic, became "ideal," became "pure spirit," became "*absolutum*" and "thing-in-itself. . . ." *The decline and fall of a god*: God became the "thing-in-itself."

18

The Christian concept of God—God as the deity of the sick, God as a spider, God as spirit—is one of the most corrupt concepts of God that has ever been attained on earth. Maybe it represents the low-water mark in the evolutionary ebb of the godlike type. God degenerated into the *contradiction of life*, instead of being its transfiguration and eternal Yea! With God war is declared on life, nature, and the will to life! God is the formula for every calumny of this world and for every lie concerning a beyond! In God, nonentity is deified, and the will to nonentity is declared holy!

19

The fact that the strong races of Northern Europe did not repudiate the Christian God, certainly does not do any credit to their religious power, not to speak of their taste. They ought to have been able successfully to cope with such a morbid and decrepit offshoot of decadence. And a curse lies on their heads; because they were unable to cope with him: they made illness, decrepitude and contradiction a part of all their instincts, since then they have not *created* any other God! Two thousand years have passed and not a single new God! But still there exists, and as if by right, like an *ultimum* and *maximum* of god-creating power, the *creator spiritus* in man, this miserable God of Christian monotono-theism! This hybrid creature of decay, nonentity, concept and contradiction, in which all the instincts of decadence, all the cowardices and languors of the soul find their sanction!

20

With my condemnation of Christianity I should not like to have done an injustice to a religion which is related to it and the number of whose followers is even greater; I refer to Buddhism. As nihilistic religions, they are akin, they are religions of decadence, while each is separated from the other in the most extraordinary fashion. For being able to compare them at all, the critic of Christianity is profoundly grateful to Indian scholars. Buddhism is a hundred times more realistic than Christianity, it is part of its constitutional heritage to be able to face problems objectively and coolly, it is the outcome of centuries of lasting philosophical activity. The concept "God" was already exploded when it appeared. Buddhism is the only really *positive* religion to be found in history, even in its epistemology (which is strict phenomenalism)—it no longer speaks of the "struggle with *sin*" but fully recognising the true nature of reality it speaks of the "struggle with *pain*." It already has—and this distinguishes it fundamentally from Christianity, the self-deception of moral concepts beneath it, to use my own phraseology, it stands *Beyond Good and Evil.* The two physiological facts upon which it rests and upon which it bestows its attention are: in the first place excessive irritability of feeling, which manifests itself as a refined susceptibility to pain, *and also* as super-spiritualisation, an all-too-lengthy sojourn amid concepts and logical procedures, under the influence of which the personal instinct has suffered in favour of the "impersonal." (Both of these states will be known to a few of my readers, the objective ones, who, like myself, will know them from experience.) Thanks to these physiological conditions, a state of depression set in, which Buddha sought to combat by means of hygiene. Against it, he prescribes life in the open, a life of travell; moderation and careful choice in food; caution in regard to all intoxicating liquor, as also in regard to all the passions which tend to create bile and to heat the blood; and he deprecates care either on one's own or on other people's account. He recommends ideas that bring one either peace or good cheer, he invents means whereby the habit of contrary ideas may be lost. He understands goodness—being good—as promoting health. *Prayer* is out of the question, as is also *asceticism*; there is neither a Categorical Imperative nor any discipline whatsoever, even within the walls of a monastery (it is always possible to leave it if one wants to). All these things would have been only a means of accentuating the excessive irritability already referred to. Precisely on this account he does not exhort his followers to wage war upon those who do not share their views; nothing is more abhorred in his doctrine than the feeling of revenge, of aversion, and of resentment ("not through hostility doth hostility end": the touching refrain of the whole of Buddhism . . .). And in this he was right; for it is precisely these passions which are thoroughly unhealthy in view of the principal dietetic object. The mental fatigue which he finds already existent and which expresses itself in excessive "objectivity" (i.e., the enfeeblement of the individual's interest—loss of ballast and of "egoism"), he combats by leading the spiritual interests as well imperatively back to the individual. In Buddha's doctrine egoism is a duty: the thing which is above all necessary, i.e., "how canst thou be rid of suffering" regulates and defines the whole of the spiritual diet (let anyone but think of that Athenian who also declared war upon pure "scientificality," Socrates, who made a morality out of personal egoism even in the realm of problems).

21

The pre-requisites for Buddhism are a very mild climate, great gentleness and liberality in the customs of a people and *no* militarism. The movement must also originate among the higher and even learned classes. Cheerfulness, peace and absence of desire, are the highest of inspirations, and they are *realised*. Buddhism is not a religion in which perfection is merely aspired to: perfection is the normal case. In Christianity all the instincts of the subjugated and oppressed come to the fore: it is the lowest classes who seek their salvation in this religion. Here the pastime, the manner of killing time is to practise the casuistry of sin, self-criticism, and conscience inquisition. Here the ecstasy in the presence of a *powerful being*, called "god," is constantly maintained by means of prayer; while the highest thing is regarded as unattainable, as a gift, as an act of "grace." Here plain dealing is also entirely lacking: concealment and the darkened room are Christian. Here the body is despised, hygiene is repudiated as sensual; the church repudiates even cleanliness (the first Christian measure after the banishment of the Moors was the closing of the public baths, of which Cordova alone possessed 270). A certain spirit of cruelty towards one's self and others is also Christian: hatred of all those who do not share one's views; the will to persecute. Sombre and exciting ideas are in the foreground; the most coveted states and those which are endowed with the finest names, are really epileptic in their nature; diet is selected in such a way as to favour morbid symptoms and to over-excite the nerves. Christian, too, is the mortal hatred of the earth's rulers, the "noble"—and at the same time a sort of concealed and secret competition with them (the subjugated leave the "body" to their master—all they want is the "soul"). Christian is the hatred of the intellect, of pride, of courage, freedom, intellectual *libertinage*; Christian is the hatred of the *senses*, of the joys of the senses, of joy in general.

22

When Christianity departed from its native soil, which consisted of the lowest classes, the *submerged masses* of the ancient world, and set forth in quest of power among barbaric nations, it no longer met with exhausted men but inwardly savage and self-lacerating men—the strong but bungled men. Here, dissatisfaction with one's self, suffering through one's self, is not as in the case of Buddhism, excessive irritability and susceptibility to pain, but rather, conversely, it is an inordinate desire for inflicting pain, for a discharge of the inner tension in hostile deeds and ideas. Christianity was in need of *barbaric* ideas and values, in order to be able to master barbarians: such are for instance, the sacrifice of the first-born, the drinking of blood at communion, the contempt of the intellect and of culture; torture in all its forms, sensual and non-sensual; the great pomp of the cult. Buddhism is a religion for *senile* men, for races which have become kind, gentle, and over-spiritual, and which feel pain too easily (Europe is not nearly ripe for it yet); it calls them back to peace and cheerfulness, to a regimen for the intellect, to a certain hardening of the body. Christianity aims at mastering *beasts of prey*; its expedient is to make them *ill*, to render feeble is the Christian recipe for taming, for "civilisation." Buddhism is a religion for the close and exhaustion of civilisation; Christianity does not even find civilisation at hand when it appears, in certain circumstances it lays the foundation of civilisation.

23

Buddhism, I repeat, is a hundred times colder, more truthful, more objective. It no longer requires to justify pain and its susceptibility to suffering by the interpretation of sin, it simply says what it thinks, "I suffer." To the barbarian, on the other hand, suffering in itself is not a respectable thing: in order to acknowledge to himself that he suffers, what he requires, in the first place, is an explanation (his instinct directs him more readily to deny his suffering, or to endure it in silence). In his case, the word "devil" was a blessing: man had an almighty and terrible enemy, he had no reason to be ashamed of suffering at the hands of such an enemy.

At bottom there are in Christianity one or two subtleties which belong to the Orient. In the first place it knows that it is a matter of indifference whether a thing be true or not; but that it is of the highest importance that it should be believed to be true. Truth and the belief that something is true: two totally separate worlds of interest, almost *opposite worlds*, the road to the one and the road to the other lie absolutely apart. To be initiated into this fact almost constitutes one a sage in the Orient: the Brahmins understood it thus, so did Plato, and so does every disciple of esoteric wisdom. If for example it give anyone pleasure to believe himself delivered from sin, it is *not* a necessary prerequisite thereto that he should be sinful, but only that he should *feel* sinful. If, however, *faith* is above all necessary, then reason, knowledge, and scientific research must be brought into evil repute: the road to truth becomes the *forbidden* road. Strong *hope* is a much greater stimulant of life than any single realised joy could be. Sufferers must be sustained by a hope which no actuality can contradict, and which cannot ever be realised: the hope of another world. (Precisely on account of this power that hope has of making the unhappy linger on, the Greeks regarded it as the evil of evils, as the most *mischievous* evil: it remained behind in Pandora's box.) In order that *love* may be possible, God must be a person. In order that the lowest instincts may also make their voices heard God must be young. For the ardour of the women a beautiful saint, and for the ardour of the men a Virgin Mary has to be pressed into the foreground. All this on condition that Christianity wishes to rule over a certain soil, on which Aphrodisiac or Adonis cults had already determined the *notion* of a cult. To insist upon *chastity* only intensifies the vehemence and profundity of the religious instinct—it makes the cult warmer, more enthusiastic, more soulful. Love is the state in which man sees things most widely different from what they are. The force of illusion reaches its zenith here, as likewise the sweetening and transfiguring power. When a man is in love he endures more than at other times; he submits to everything. The thing was to discover a religion in which it was possible to love: by this means the worst in life is overcome—it is no longer even seen. So much for three Christian virtues Faith, Hope, and Charity: I call them the three Christian *precautionary measures*. Buddhism is too full of aged wisdom, too positivistic to be shrewd in this way.

24

Here I only touch upon the problem of the origin of Christianity. The first principle of its solution reads: Christianity can be understood only in relation to the soil out of which it grew, it is not a counter-movement against the Jewish instinct, it is the rational outcome of the latter, one step further in its appalling logic. In the formula of the Saviour: "for Salvation is of the Jews." The second principle is: the psychological type of the Galilean is still recognisable, but it was only in a state of utter degeneration (which is at once a distortion and an overloading with foreign features) that he was able to serve the purpose for which he has been used, namely, as the type of a Redeemer of mankind.

The Jews are the most remarkable people in the history of the world, because when they were confronted with the question of Being or non-Being, with simply uncanny deliberateness, they preferred Being *at any price*: this price was the fundamental *falsification* of all Nature, all the naturalness and all the reality, of the inner quite as much as of the outer world. They hedged themselves in behind all those conditions under which hitherto a people has been able to live, has been allowed to live; of themselves they created an idea which was the reverse of *natural* conditions, each in turn, they twisted first religion, then the cult, then morality, history and psychology, about in a manner so perfectly hopeless that they were made *to contradict their natural value*. We meet with the same phenomena again, and exaggerated to an incalculable degree, although only as a copy: the Christian Church as compared with the "chosen people," lacks all claim to originality. Precisely on this account the Jews are the most *fatal* people in the history of the world: their ultimate influence has falsified mankind to such an extent, that even to this day the Christian can be anti-Semitic in spirit, without comprehending that he himself is the *final consequence of Judaism*.

It was in my *Genealogy of Morals* that I first gave a psychological exposition of the idea of the antithesis noble- and *resentment*-morality, the latter having arisen out of an attitude of negation to the former: but this is

Judaeo-Christian morality heart and soul. In order to be able to say Nay to everything that represents the ascending movement of life, prosperity, power, beauty, and self-affirmation on earth, the instinct of resentment, become genius, had to invent *another* world, from the standpoint of which that *Yea-saying* to life appeared as *the* most evil and most abominable thing. From the psychological standpoint the Jewish people are possessed of the toughest vitality. Transplanted amid impossible conditions, with profound self-preservative intelligence, it voluntarily took the side of all the instincts of decadence, *not* as though dominated by them, but because it detected a power in them by means of which it could assert itself *against* "the world." The Jews are the opposite of all *decadents*: they have been forced to represent them to the point of illusion, and with a *non plus ultra* of histrionic genius, they have known how to set themselves at the head of all decadent movements (St. Paul and Christianity for instance), in order to create something from them which is stronger than every party *saying Yea to life*. For the category of men which aspires to power in Judaism and Christianity, that is to say, for the sacerdotal class, decadence is but a *means*: this category of men has a vital interest in making men sick, and in turning the notions "good" and "bad," "true" and "false," upside down in a manner which is not only dangerous to life, but also slanders it.

25

The history of Israel is invaluable as the typical history of every *denaturalisation* of natural values: let me point to five facts which relate thereto. Originally, and above all in the period of the kings, even Israel's attitude to all things was the *right* one—that is to say, the natural one. Its Jehovah was the expression of its consciousness of power, of its joy over itself, of its hope for itself: victory and salvation were expected from him, through him it was confident that Nature would give what a people requires—above all rain. Jehovah is the God of Israel, and *consequently* the God of justice: this is the reasoning of every people which is in the position of power, and which has a good conscience in that position. In the solemn cult both sides of this self-affirmation of a people find expression: it is grateful for the great strokes of fate by means of which it became uppermost; it is grateful for the regularity in the succession of the seasons and for all good fortune in the rearing of cattle and in the tilling of the soil. This state of affairs remained the ideal for some considerable time, even after it had been swept away in a deplorable manner by anarchy from within and the Assyrians from without. But the people still retained, as their highest desideratum, that vision of a king who was a good soldier and a severe judge; and he who retained it most of all was that typical prophet (that is to say, critic and satirist of the age), Isaiah. But all hopes remained unrealised. The old God was no longer able to do what he had done formerly. He ought to have been dropped. What happened? The idea of him was changed, the idea of him was denaturalised: this was the price they paid for retaining him. Jehovah, the God of "Justice," is no longer one with Israel, no longer the expression of a people's sense of dignity: he is only a god on certain conditions. . . . The idea of him becomes a weapon in the hands of priestly agitators who henceforth interpret all happiness as a reward, all unhappiness as a punishment for disobedience to God, for "sin": that most fraudulent method of interpretation which arrives at a so-called "moral order of the Universe," by means of which the concept "cause" and "effect" is turned upside down. Once natural causation has been swept out of the world by reward and punishment, a causation *hostile to nature* becomes necessary; whereupon all the forms of unnaturalness follow. A God who *demands*, in the place of a God who helps, who advises, who is at bottom only a name for every happy inspiration of courage and of self-reliance. . . . Morality is no longer the expression of the conditions of life and growth, no longer the most fundamental instinct of life, but it has become abstract, it has become the opposite of life, Morality as the fundamental perversion of the imagination, as the "evil eye" for all things. What is Jewish morality, what is Christian morality? Chance robbed of its innocence; unhappiness polluted with the idea of "sin"; well-being interpreted as a danger, as a "temptation"; physiological indisposition poisoned by means of the canker-worm of conscience. . . .

26

The concept of God falsified; the concept of morality falsified: but the Jewish priesthood did not stop at this. No use could be made of the whole *history* of Israel, therefore it must go! These priests accomplished that miracle of falsification, of which the greater part of the Bible is the document: with unparalleled contempt and in the teeth of all tradition and historical facts, they interpreted their own people's past in a religious manner, that is to say, they converted it into a ridiculous mechanical process of salvation, on the principle that all sin against Jehovah led to punishment, and that all pious worship of Jehovah led to reward. We would feel this shameful act of historical falsification far more poignantly if the ecclesiastical interpretation of history through millenniums had not blunted almost all our sense for the demands of uprightness *in historicis*. And the church is seconded by the philosophers: *the lie* of "a moral order of the universe" permeates the whole development even of more modern philosophy. What does a "moral order of the universe" mean? That once and for all there is such a thing as a will of God which determines what man has to do and what he has to leave undone; that the value of a people or of an individual is measured according to how much or how little the one or the other obeys the will of God; that in the destinies of a people or of an individual, the will of God shows itself dominant, that is to say it punishes or rewards according to the degree of obedience. In the place of this miserable falsehood, *reality* says: a parasitical type of man, who can flourish only at the cost of all the healthy elements of life, the priest abuses the name of God: he calls that state of affairs in which the priest determines the value of things "the Kingdom of God"; he calls the means whereby such a state of affairs is attained or maintained, "the Will of God"; with cold-blooded cynicism he measures peoples, ages and individuals according to whether they favour or oppose the ascendancy of the priesthood. Watch him at work: in the hands of the Jewish priesthood the Augustan Age in the history of Israel became an age of decline; the exile, the protracted misfortune transformed itself into eternal *punishment* for the Augustan Age—that age in which the priest did not yet exist. Out of the mighty and thoroughly freeborn figures of the history of Israel, they made, according to their requirements, either wretched bigots and hypocrites, or "godless ones": they simplified the psychology of every great event to the idiotic formula "obedient or disobedient to God." A step further: the "Will of God," that is to say the self-preservative measures of the priesthood, must be known—to this end a "revelation" is necessary. In plain English: a stupendous literary fraud becomes necessary, "holy scriptures" are discovered, and they are published abroad with all hieratic pomp, with days of penance and lamentations over the long state of "sin." The "Will of God" has long stood firm: the whole of the trouble lies in the fact that the "Holy Scriptures" have been discarded. . . . Moses was already the "Will of God" revealed. . . . What had happened? With severity and pedantry, the priest had formulated once and for all—even to the largest and smallest contributions that were to be paid to him (—not forgetting the daintiest portions of meat; for the priest is a consumer of beef-steaks)—*what he wanted,* "what the Will of God was. . . ." Henceforward everything became so arranged that the priests were *indispensable everywhere.* At all the natural events of life, at birth, at marriage, at the sick bed, at death, not to speak of the sacrifice ("the meal"), the holy parasite appears in order to denaturalise, or in his language, to "sanctify," everything. . . . For this should be understood: every natural custom, every natural institution (the State, the administration of justice, marriage, the care of the sick and the poor), every demand inspired by the instinct of life, in short everything that has a value in itself, is rendered absolutely worthless and even dangerous through the parasitism of the priest (or of the "moral order of the universe"): a sanction after the fact is required, a *power which imparts value* is necessary, which in so doing says, Nay to nature, and which by this means alone *creates* a valuation. . . . The priest depreciates and desecrates nature: it is only at this price that he exists at all. Disobedience to God, that is to say, to the priest, to the "law," now receives the name of "sin"; the means of "reconciling one's self with God" are of course of a nature which render subordination to the priesthood all the more fundamental: the priest alone is able to "save. . . ." From the psychological standpoint, in every society organised upon a hieratic basis, "sins" are indispensable: they are the actual weapons of power, the priest *lives* upon sins, it is necessary for him that people should "sin. . . ." Supreme axiom: "God forgiveth him that repenteth"— in plain English: *him that submitteth himself to the priest.*

27

Christianity grew out of an utterly *false* soil, in which all nature, every natural value, every *reality* had the deepest instincts of the ruling class against it; it was a form of deadly hostility to reality which has never been surpassed. The "holy people" which had retained only priestly values and priestly names for all things, and which, with a logical consistency that is terrifying, had divorced itself from everything still powerful on earth as if it were "unholy," "worldly," "sinful"—this people created a final formula for its instinct which was consistent to the point of self-suppression; as *Christianity* it denied even the last form of reality, the "holy people," the "chosen people," *Jewish* reality itself. The case is of supreme interest: the small insurrectionary movement christened with the name of Jesus of Nazareth, is the Jewish instinct *over again*, in other words, it is the sacerdotal instinct which can no longer endure the priest as a fact; it is the discovery of a kind of life even more fantastic than the one previously conceived, a vision of life which is even more unreal than that which the organisation of a church stipulates. Christianity denies the church.[3]

I fail to see against whom was directed the insurrection of which rightly or *wrongly* Jesus is understood to have been the promoter, if it were not directed against the Jewish church, the word "church" being used here in precisely the same sense in which it is used today. It was an insurrection against the "good and the just," against the "prophets of Israel," against the hierarchy of society—not against the latter's corruption, but against caste, privilege, order, formality. It was the lack of faith in "higher men," it was a "Nay" uttered against everything that was tinctured with the blood of priests and theologians. But the hierarchy which was set in question if only temporarily by this movement, formed the construction of piles upon which, alone, the Jewish people was able to subsist in the midst of the "waters"; it was that people's *last* chance of survival wrested from the world at enormous pains, the *residuum* of its political autonomy: to attack this construction was tantamount to attacking the most profound popular instinct, the most tenacious national will to live that has ever existed on earth. This saintly anarchist who called the lowest of the low, the outcasts and "sinners," the Chandala of Judaism, to revolt against the established order of things (and in language which, if the gospels are to be trusted, would get one sent to Siberia even today)—this man was a political criminal insofar as political criminals were possible in a community so absurdly non-political. This brought him to the cross: the proof of this is the inscription found thereon. He died for *his* sins—and no matter how often the contrary has been asserted there is absolutely nothing to show that he died for the sins of others.

28

As to whether he was conscious of this contrast, or whether he was merely *regarded* as such, is quite another question. And here, alone, do I touch upon the problem of the psychology of the Saviour. I confess there are few books which I have as much difficulty in reading as the gospels. These difficulties are quite different from those which allowed the learned curiosity of the German mind to celebrate one of its most memorable triumphs. Many years have now elapsed since I, like every young scholar, with the sage conscientiousness of a refined philologist, relished the work of the incomparable Strauss. I was then twenty years of age; now I am too serious for that sort of thing. What do I care about the contradictions of "tradition"? How can saintly legends be called "tradition" at all! The stories of saints constitute the most ambiguous literature on earth: to apply the scientific method to them, *when there are no other documents to hand*, seems to me to be a fatal procedure from the start—simply learned fooling.

29

The point that concerns me is the psychological type of the Saviour. This type might be contained in the gospels, in spite of the gospels, and however much it may have been mutilated, or overladen with foreign features: just as that of Francis of Assisi is contained in his legends in spite of his legends. It is *not* a question of the truth concerning what he has done, what he has said, and how he actually died; but whether his type may still be conceived in anyway, whether it has been handed down to us at all? The attempts which to my knowledge have been made to read the *history* of a "soul" out of the gospels, seem to me to point only to disreputable levity in psychological matters. M. Renan, that buffoon *in psychologicis*, has contributed the two most monstrous ideas imaginable to the explanation of the type of Jesus: the idea of the *genius* and the idea of the *hero* ("*héros*"). But if there is anything thoroughly unevangelical surely it is the idea of the hero. It is precisely the reverse of all struggle, of all consciousness of taking part in the fight, that has become instinctive here: the inability to resist is here converted into a morality ("resist not evil," the profoundest sentence in the whole of the gospels, their key in a certain sense), the blessedness of peace, of gentleness, of not *being able* to be an enemy. What is the meaning of "glad tidings"? True life, eternal life has been found—it is not promised, it is actually here, it is in *you*; it is life in love, in love free from all selection or exclusion, free from all distance. Everybody is the child of God—Jesus does not by any means claim anything for himself alone, as the child of God everybody is equal to everybody else. . . . Fancy making Jesus a *hero!* And what a tremendous misunderstanding the word "genius" is! Our whole idea of "spirit," which is a civilised idea, could have had no meaning whatever in the world in which Jesus lived. In the strict terms of the physiologist, a very different word ought to be used here. . . . We know of a condition of morbid irritability of the sense of *touch*, which recoils shuddering from every kind of contact, and from every attempt at grasping a solid object. Any such physiological *habitus* reduced to its ultimate logical conclusion, becomes an instinctive hatred of all reality, a flight into the "intangible," into the "incomprehensible"; a repugnance to all formulae, to every notion of time and space, to everything that is established such as customs, institutions, the church; a feeling at one's ease in a world in which no sign of reality is any longer visible, a merely "inner" world, a "true" world, an "eternal" world. . . . "The Kingdom of God is within you. . . ."

30

The instinctive hatred of reality is the outcome of an extreme susceptibility to pain and to irritation, which can no longer endure to be "touched" at all, because every sensation strikes too deep.

The instinctive exclusion of all aversion, of all hostility, of all boundaries and distances in feeling, is the outcome of an extreme susceptibility to pain and to irritation, which regards all resistance, all compulsory resistance as insufferable *anguish* (that is to say, as harmful, as *deprecated* by the self-preservative instinct), and which knows blessedness (happiness) only when it is no longer obliged to offer resistance to anybody, either evil or detrimental, love as the only ultimate possibility of life. . . .

These are the two *physiological realities* upon which and out of which the doctrine of salvation has grown. I call them a sublime further development of hedonism, upon a thoroughly morbid soil. Epicureanism, the pagan theory of salvation, even though it possessed a large proportion of Greek vitality and nervous energy, remains the most closely related to the above. Epicurus was a *typical* decadent: and I was the first to recognise him as such. The terror of pain, even of infinitely slight pain—such a state cannot possibly help culminating in a *religion* of love. . . .

31

I have given my reply to the problem in advance. The prerequisite thereto was the admission of the fact that the type of the Saviour has reached us only in a very distorted form. This distortion in itself is extremely feasible: for many reasons a type of that kind could not be pure, whole, and free from additions. The environment in which this strange figure moved, must have left its mark upon him, and the history, the *destiny* of the first Christian communities must have done so to a still greater degree. Thanks to that destiny, the type must have been enriched retrospectively with features which can be interpreted only as serving the purposes of war and of propaganda. That strange and morbid world into which the gospels lead us—a world which seems to have been drawn from a Russian novel, where the scum and dross of society, diseases of the nerves and "childish" imbecility seem to have given each other rendezvous—must in any case have *coarsened* the type: the first disciples especially must have translated an existence conceived entirely in symbols and abstractions into their own crudities, in order at least to be able to understand something about it, for them the type existed only after it had been cast in a more familiar mould. . . . The prophet, the Messiah, the future judge, the teacher of morals, the thaumaturgist, John the Baptist—all these were but so many opportunities of misunderstanding the type. . . . Finally, let us not underrate the *proprium* of all great and especially sectarian veneration: very often it effaces from the venerated object, all the original and frequently painfully unfamiliar traits and idiosyncrasies—*it does not even see them.* It is greatly to be deplored that no Dostoiewsky lived in the neighbourhood of this most interesting decadent, I mean someone who would have known how to feel the poignant charm of such a mixture of the sublime, the morbid, and the childlike. Finally, the type, as an example of decadence, may actually have been extraordinarily multifarious and contradictory: this, as a possible alternative, is not to be altogether ignored. Albeit, everything seems to point away from it; for, precisely in this case, tradition would necessarily have been particularly true and objective: whereas we have reasons for assuming the reverse. Meanwhile a yawning chasm of contradiction separates the mountain, lake, and pastoral preacher, who strikes us as a Buddha on a soil only very slightly Hindu, from that combative fanatic, the mortal enemy of theologians and priests, whom Renan's malice has glorified as "*le grand maître en ironie.*" For my part, I do not doubt but what the greater part of this venom (and even of *esprit*) was inoculated into the type of the Master only as the outcome of the agitated condition of Christian propaganda. For we have ample reasons for knowing the unscrupulousness of all sectarians when they wish to contrive their own *apology* out of the person of their master. When the first Christian community required a discerning, wrangling, quarrelsome, malicious and hair-splitting theologian, to oppose other theologians, it created its "God" according to its needs; just as it did not hesitate to put upon his lips those utterly unevangelical ideas of "his second coming," the "last judgement"—ideas with which it could not then dispense, and every kind of expectation and promise which happened to be current.

32

I can only repeat that I am opposed to the importation of the fanatic into the type of the Saviour: the word "*impérieux,*" which Renan uses, in itself annuls the type. The "glad tidings" are simply that there are no longer any contradictions, that the Kingdom of Heaven is for the *children;* the faith which raises its voice here is not a faith that has been won by a struggle, it is to hand, it was there from the beginning, it is a sort of spiritual return to childishness. The case of delayed and undeveloped puberty in the organism, as the result of degeneration is at least familiar to physiologists. A faith of this sort does not show anger, it does not blame, neither does it defend itself: it does not bring "the sword," it has no inkling of how it will one day establish feuds between man and man. It does not demonstrate itself, either by miracles, or by reward and promises, or yet "through the scriptures": it is in itself at every moment its own miracle, its own reward, its own proof, its own "Kingdom of God." This faith cannot be formulated—it lives, it guards against formulae. The accident of environment, of speech, of preparatory culture, certainly determines a particular series of conceptions: early Christianity deals only in Judaeo-Semitic conceptions (the eating and drinking at the last supper form part of these, this idea which like everything Jewish has been abused so maliciously by the church). But one should guard against seeing anything more than a language of signs, semeiotics, an opportunity for parables in all this. The very fact that no word is to be taken literally, is the only condition on which this Anti-realist is able to speak at all. Among Indians he would have made use of the ideas of *Sankhyam*, among Chinese, those of *Lao-tze*—and would not have been aware of any difference. With a little terminological laxity Jesus might be called a "free spirit"—he cares not a jot for anything that is established: the word *killeth*, everything fixed *killeth*. The idea, *experience*, "life" as he alone knows it, is, according to him, opposed to every kind of word, formula, law, faith and dogma. He speaks only of the innermost things: "life" or "truth," or "light," is his expression for the innermost thing, everything else, the whole of reality, the whole of nature, language even, has only the value of a sign, of a simile for him. It is of paramount importance not to make any mistake at this point, however great may be the temptation thereto that lies in Christian—I mean to say, ecclesiastical prejudice. Any such essential symbolism stands beyond the pale of all religion, all notions of cult, all history, all natural science, all experience of the world, all knowledge, all politics, all psychology, all books and all Art—for his "wisdom" is precisely the complete ignorance[4] of the existence of such things. He has not even heard speak of *culture*, he does not require to oppose it, he does not deny it. . . . The same holds good of the state, of the whole of civil and social order, of work and of war—he never had any reason to deny the world, he had not the vaguest notion of the ecclesiastical concept "the world. . . ." Denying is precisely what was quite impossible to him. Dialectic is also quite absent, as likewise the idea that any faith, any "truth" can be proved by argument (his proofs are inner "lights," inward feelings of happiness and self-affirmation, a host of "proofs of power"). Neither can such a doctrine contradict, it does not even realise the fact that there are or can be other doctrines, it is absolutely incapable of imagining a contrary judgement. . . . Wherever it encounters such things, from a feeling of profound sympathy it bemoans such "blindness"—for it sees the "light"—but it raises no objections.

33

The whole psychology of the "gospels" lacks the concept of guilt and punishment, as also that of reward. "Sin," any sort of aloofness between God and man, is done away with, *this is precisely what constitutes the "glad tidings."* Eternal bliss is not promised, it is not bound up with certain conditions; it is the only reality—the rest consists only of signs wherewith to speak about it. . . .

The results of such a state project themselves into a new practise of life, the actual evangelical practise. It is not a "faith" which distinguishes the Christians: the Christian acts, he distinguishes himself by means of a *different* mode of action. He does not resist his enemy either by words or in his heart. He draws no distinction between foreigners and natives, between Jews and Gentiles ("the neighbour" really means the co-religionist, the Jew). He is angry with no one, he despises no one. He neither shows himself at the tribunals nor does he acknowledge any of their claims ("Swear not at all"). He never under any circumstances divorces his wife, even when her infidelity has been proved. All this is at bottom one principle, it is all the outcome of one instinct.

The life of the Saviour was naught else than this practise, neither was his death. He no longer required any formulae, any rites for his relations with God—not even prayer. He has done with all the Jewish teaching of repentance and of atonement; he alone knows the *mode* of life which makes one feel "divine," "saved," "evangelical," and at all times a "child of God." *Not* "repentance," *not* "prayer and forgiveness" are the roads to God: the *evangelical mode of life alone* leads to God, it *is* "God." That which the gospels abolished was the Judaism of the concepts "sin," "forgiveness of sin," "faith," "salvation through faith," the whole doctrine of the Jewish church was denied by the "glad tidings."

The profound instinct of how one must live in order to feel "in Heaven," in order to feel "eternal," while in every other respect one feels by *no* means "in Heaven": this alone is the psychological reality of "Salvation." A new life and *not* a new faith. . . .

34

If I understand anything at all about this great symbolist, it is this that he regarded only *inner* facts as facts, as "truths"—that he understood the rest, everything natural, temporal, material and historical, only as signs, as opportunities for parables. The concept "the Son of Man," is not a concrete personality belonging to history, anything individual and isolated, but an "eternal" fact, a psychological symbol divorced from the concept of time. The same is true, and in the highest degree, of the *God* of this typical symbolist, of the "Kingdom of God," of the "Kingdom of Heaven," and of the "Sonship of God." Nothing is more un-Christlike than the *ecclesiastical crudity* of a personal God, of a Kingdom of God that is coming, of a "Kingdom of Heaven" beyond, of a "Son of God" as the second person of the Trinity. All this, if I may be forgiven the expression, is as fitting as a square peg in a round hole—and oh! What a hole! The gospels: a *world-historic* cynicism in the scorn of symbols. . . . But what is meant by the signs "Father" and "Son," is of course obvious—not to everybody, I admit: with the word "Son," *entrance* into the feeling of the general transfiguration of all things (beatitude) is expressed, with the word "Father," *this feeling itself,* the feeling of eternity and of perfection. I blush to have to remind you of what the Church has done with this symbolism: has it not set an Amphitryon story at the threshold of the Christian "faith"? And a dogma of immaculate conception into the bargain? . . . *But by so doing it defiled conception.*

The "Kingdom of Heaven" is a state of the heart—not something which exists "beyond this earth" or comes to you "after death." The whole idea of natural death is lacking in the gospels. Death is not a bridge, not a means of access: it is absent because it belongs to quite a different and merely apparent world the only use of which is to furnish signs, similes. The "hour of death" is not a Christian idea—the "hour," time in general, physical life and its crises do not exist for the messenger of "glad tidings. . . ." The "Kingdom of God" is not something that is expected; it has no yesterday nor any day after tomorrow, it is not going to come in a "thousand years"—it is an experience of a human heart; it is everywhere, it is nowhere. . . .

35

This "messenger of glad tidings" died as he lived and as he taught—*not* in order "to save mankind," but in order to show how one ought to live. It was a mode of life that he bequeathed to mankind: his behaviour before his judges, his attitude towards his executioners, his accusers, and all kinds of calumny and scorn, his demeanour on the *cross*. He offers no resistance; he does not defend his rights; he takes no step to ward off the most extreme consequences, he does more, he provokes them. And he prays, suffers and loves with those, in those, who treat him ill. . . . *Not* to defend one's self, *not* to show anger, not to hold anyone responsible. . . . But to refrain from resisting even the evil one, to *love* him. . . .

36

—Only we spirits that have *become free*, possess the necessary condition for understanding something which nineteen centuries have misunderstood, that honesty which has become an instinct and a passion in us, and which wages war upon the "holy lie" with even more vigour than upon every other lie. . . . Mankind was unspeakably far from our beneficent and cautious neutrality, from that discipline of the mind, which, alone, renders the solution of such strange and subtle things possible: at all times, with shameless egoism, all that people sought was their *own* advantage in these matters, the Church was built up out of contradiction to the gospel. . . .

Whoever might seek for signs pointing to the guiding fingers of an ironical deity behind the great comedy of existence, would find no small argument in the *huge note of interrogation* that is called Christianity. The fact that mankind is on its knees before the reverse of that which formed the origin, the meaning and the *rights* of the gospel; the fact that, in the idea "Church," precisely that is pronounced holy which the "messenger of glad tidings" regarded as *beneath* him, as *behind* him—one might seek in vain for a more egregious example of *world-historic* irony.

37

—Our age is proud of its historical sense: how could it allow itself to be convinced of the nonsensical idea that at the beginning Christianity consisted only of the *clumsy fable of the thaumaturgist and of the Saviour*, and that all its spiritual and symbolic side was only developed later? On the contrary: the history of Christianity—from the death on the cross onwards—is the history of a gradual and ever coarser misunderstanding of an original symbolism. With every extension of Christianity over ever larger and ruder masses, who were ever less able to grasp its first principles, the need of *vulgarising and barbarising* it increased proportionately—it absorbed the teachings and rites of all the *subterranean* cults of the *imperium Romanum*, as well as the nonsense of every kind of morbid reasoning. The fatal feature of Christianity lies in the necessary fact that its faith had to become as morbid, base and vulgar as the needs to which it had to minister were morbid, base and vulgar. *Morbid barbarism* at last braces itself together for power in the form of the Church—the Church, this deadly hostility to all honesty, to all loftiness of the soul, to all discipline of the mind, to all frank and kindly humanity. *Christian* and *noble* values: only we spirits *who have become free* have reestablished this contrast in values which is the greatest that has ever existed on earth!

38

—I cannot, at this point, stifle a sigh. There are days when I am visited by a feeling blacker than the blackest melancholy—the *contempt of man*. And in order that I may leave you in no doubt as to what I despise, *whom* I despise: I declare that it is the man of today, the man with whom I am fatally contemporaneous. The man of today, I am asphyxiated by his foul breath. . . . Towards the past, like all knights of knowledge, I am profoundly tolerant, that is to say, I exercise a sort of *generous* self-control: with gloomy caution I pass through whole millennia of this mad-house world, and whether it be called "Christianity," "Christian Faith," or "Christian Church," I take care not to hold mankind responsible for its mental disorders. But my feeling suddenly changes, and vents itself the moment I enter the modern age, *our* age. Our age *knows.* . . . That which formerly was merely morbid, is now positively indecent. It is indecent nowadays to be a Christian. *And it is here that my loathing begins.* I look about me: not a word of what was formerly known as "truth" has remained standing; we can no longer endure to hear a priest even pronounce the word "truth." Even he who makes but the most modest claims upon truth, *must* know at present, that a theologian, a priest, or a pope, not only errs but actually *lies*, with every word that he utters, and that he is no longer able to lie from "innocence," from "ignorance." Even the priest knows quite as well as everybody else does that there is no longer any "God," any "sinner" or any "Saviour," and that "free will," and "a moral order of the universe" are *lies*. Seriousness, the profound self-conquest of the spirit no longer allows anyone to be *ignorant* about this. . . . All the concepts of the Church have been revealed in their true colours—that is to say, as the most vicious frauds on earth, calculated to *depreciate* nature and all natural values. The priest himself has been recognised as what he is—that is to say, as the most dangerous kind of parasite, as the actual venomous spider of existence. . . . At present we know, our *conscience* knows, the real value of the gruesome inventions which the priests and the Church have made, *and what end they served*. By means of them that state of self-profanation on the part of man has been attained, the sight of which makes one heave. The concepts "Beyond," "Last Judgement," "Immortality of the Soul," the "soul" itself, are merely so many instruments of torture, so many systems of cruelty, on the strength of which the priest became and remained master. . . . Everybody knows this, *and nevertheless everything remains as it was*. Whither has the last shred of decency, of self-respect gone, if nowadays even our statesmen —a body of men who are otherwise so unembarrassed, and such thorough anti-Christians in deed—still declare themselves Christians and still flock to communion?[5] . . . Fancy a prince at the head of his legions, magnificent as the expression of the egoism and self-exaltation of his people, but *shameless* enough to acknowledge himself a Christian! . . . What then does Christianity deny? What does it call "world"? "The world" to Christianity means that a man is a soldier, a judge, a patriot, that he defends himself, that he values his honour, that he desires his own advantage, that he is *proud*. . . . The conduct of every moment, every instinct, every valuation that leads to a deed, is at present anti-Christian: what an *abortion of falsehood* modern man must be, in order to be able *without a blush* still to call himself a Christian!

39

—I will retrace my steps, and will tell you the *genuine* history of Christianity. The very word "Christianity" is a misunderstanding, truth to tell, there never was more than one Christian, and he *died* on the Cross. The "gospel" *died* on the cross. That which thenceforward was called "gospel" was the reverse of that "gospel" that Christ had lived: it was "evil tidings," a *dysangel*. It is false to the point of nonsense to see in "faith," in the faith in salvation through Christ, the distinguishing trait of the Christian: the only thing that is Christian is the Christian mode of existence, a life such as he led who died on the Cross. . . . To this day a life of this kind is still possible; for certain men, it is even necessary: genuine, primitive Christianity will be possible in all ages. . . . *Not* a faith, but a course of action, above all a course of inaction, non-interference, and a different life. . . . States of consciousness, any sort of faith, a holding of certain things for true, as every psychologist knows, are indeed of absolutely no consequence, and are only of fifth-rate importance compared with the value of the instincts: more exactly, the whole concept of intellectual causality is false. To reduce the fact of being a Christian, or of Christianity, to a holding of something for true, to a mere phenomenon of consciousness, is tantamount to denying Christianity. *In fact there have never been any Christians.* The "Christian," he who for two thousand years has been called a Christian, is merely a psychological misunderstanding of self. Looked at more closely, there ruled in him, *notwithstanding* all his faith, only instincts—and *what instincts!* "Faith" in all ages, as for instance in the case of Luther, has always been merely a cloak, a pretext, a *screen,* behind which the instincts played their game, a prudent form of *blindness* in regard to the dominion of *certain* instincts. . . . "Faith" I have already characterised as a piece of really Christian cleverness; for people have always spoken of "faith" and acted according to their instincts. . . . In the Christian's world of ideas there is nothing which even touches reality: but I have already recognised in the instinctive hatred of reality the actual motive force, the only driving power at the root of Christianity. What follows therefrom? That here, even *in psychologicis,* error is fundamental, that is to say capable of determining the spirit of things, that is to say, *substance.* Take one idea away from the whole, and put one realistic fact in its stead, and the whole of Christianity tumbles into nonentity! Surveyed from above, this strangest of all facts, a religion not only dependent upon error, but inventive and showing signs of genius only in those errors which are dangerous and which poison life and the human heart—remains a *spectacle for gods,* for those gods who are at the same time philosophers and whom I met for instance in those celebrated dialogues on the island of Naxos. At the moment when they get rid of their *loathing* (*and we do as well!*), they will be thankful for the spectacle the Christians have offered: the wretched little planet called Earth perhaps deserves on account of *this* curious case alone, a divine glance, and divine interest. . . . Let us not therefore underestimate the Christians: the Christian, false *to the point of innocence in falsity,* is far above the apes, in regard to the Christians a certain well-known theory of Descent becomes a mere good-natured compliment.

40

—The fate of the gospel was decided at the moment of the death, it hung on the "cross. . . ." It was only death, this unexpected and ignominious death; it was only the cross which as a rule was reserved simply for the *canaille,* only this appalling paradox which confronted the disciples with the actual riddle: *Who was that? What was that?* The state produced by the excited and profoundly wounded feelings of these men, the suspicion that such a death might imply the *refutation* of their cause, and the terrible note of interrogation: "why precisely thus?" will be understood only too well. In this case everything *must* be necessary, everything must have meaning, a reason, the highest reason. The love of a disciple admits of no such thing as accident. Only then did the chasm yawn: "who has killed him?" "who was his natural enemy?" this question rent the firmament like a flash of lightning. Reply: *dominant* Judaism, its ruling class. Thenceforward the disciple felt himself in revolt *against* established order; he understood Jesus, after the fact, as one in *revolt against established order.* Heretofore this warlike, this nay-saying and nay-doing feature in Christ had been lacking; nay more, he was its contradiction. The small primitive community had obviously understood *nothing* of the principal factor of all, which was the example of freedom and of superiority to every form of *resentment* which lay in this way of dying. And this shows how little they understood him altogether! At bottom Jesus could not have desired anything else by his death than to give the strongest public *example* and *proof* of his doctrine. . . . But his disciples were very far from *forgiving* this death—though if they had done so it would have been in the highest sense evangelical on their part, neither were they prepared, with a gentle and serene calmness of heart, to *offer* themselves for a similar death. . . . Precisely the most unevangelical feeling, *revenge*, became once more ascendant. It was impossible for the cause to end with this death: "compensation" and "judgement" were required (—and forsooth, what could be more unevangelical than "compensation," "punishment," "judgement"!) The popular expectation of a Messiah once more became prominent; attention was fixed upon one historical moment: the "Kingdom of God" descends to sit in judgement upon his enemies. But this proves that everything was misunderstood: the "Kingdom of God" regarded as the last scene of the last act, as a promise! But the Gospel had clearly been the living, the fulfilment, the *reality* of this "Kingdom of God." It was precisely a death such as Christ's that was this "Kingdom of God." It was only now that all the contempt for the Pharisees and the theologians, and all bitter feelings towards them, were introduced into the character of the Master, and by this means he himself was converted into a Pharisee and a theologian! On the other hand, the savage veneration of these completely unhinged souls could no longer endure that evangelical right of every man to be the child of God, which Jesus had taught: their revenge consisted in *elevating* Jesus in a manner devoid of all reason, and in separating him from themselves: just as, formerly, the Jews, with the view of revenging themselves on their enemies, separated themselves from their God, and placed him high above them. The Only God, and the Only Son of God: both were products of resentment.

41

—And from this time forward an absurd problem rose into prominence: "how *could* God allow it to happen?" To this question the disordered minds of the small community found a reply which in its absurdity was literally terrifying: God gave his Son as a *sacrifice* for the forgiveness of sins. Alas! How prompt and sudden was the end of the gospel! Expiatory sacrifice for guilt, and indeed in its most repulsive and barbaric form, the sacrifice of the *innocent* for the sins of the guilty! What appalling Paganism! For Jesus himself had done away with the concept "guilt"—he denied any gulf between God and man, he *lived* this unity between God and man, it was this that constituted *his* "glad tidings. . . ." And he did *not* teach it as a privilege! Thenceforward there was gradually imported into the type of the Saviour the doctrine of the Last Judgement, and of the "second coming," the doctrine of sacrificial death, and the doctrine of *Resurrection*, by means of which the whole concept "blessedness," the entire and only reality of the gospel, is conjured away—in favour of a state *after* death! . . . St. Paul, with that rabbinic impudence which characterises all his doings, rationalised this conception, this prostitution of a conception, as follows: "if Christ did not rise from the dead, our faith is vain." And, in a trice, the most contemptible of all unrealisable promises, the *impudent* doctrine of personal immortality, was woven out of the gospel. . . . St. Paul even preached this immortality as a reward.

42

You now realise what it was that came to an end with the death on the cross: a new and thoroughly original effort towards a Buddhistic movement of peace, towards real and *not* merely promised *happiness on earth*. For, as I have already pointed out, this remains the fundamental difference between the two religions of *decadence*: Buddhism promises little but fulfils more, Christianity promises everything but fulfils nothing. The "glad tidings" were followed closely by the absolutely *worst* tidings—those of St. Paul. Paul is the incarnation of a type which is the reverse of that of the Saviour; he is the genius in hatred, in the standpoint of hatred, and in the relentless logic of hatred. And alas what did this dysangelist not sacrifice to his hatred! Above all the Saviour himself: he nailed him to *his* cross. Christ's life, his

example, his doctrine and death, the sense and the right of the gospel—
not a vestige of all this was left, once this forger, prompted by his hatred,
had understood in it only that which could serve his purpose. *Not* reality:
not historical truth! . . . And once more, the sacerdotal instinct of the Jew,
perpetrated the same great crime against history, he simply cancelled the
yesterday, and the day before that, out of Christianity; he *contrived of his own
accord a history of the birth of Christianity*. He did more: he once more falsified
the history of Israel, so as to make it appear as a prologue to *his* mission:
all the prophets had referred to *his* "Saviour. . . ." Later on the Church even
distorted the history of mankind so as to convert it into a prelude to
Christianity. . . . The type of the Saviour, his teaching, his life, his death,
the meaning of his death, even the sequel to his death—nothing remained
untouched, nothing was left which even remotely resembled reality. St.
Paul simply transferred the centre of gravity of the whole of that great life,
to a place *behind* this life, in the *lie* of the "resuscitated" Christ. At bottom,
he had no possible use for the life of the Saviour, he needed the death on
the cross, *and* something more. To regard as honest a man like St. Paul
(a man whose home was the very headquarters of Stoical enlightenment)
when he devises a proof of the continued existence of the Saviour out of
a hallucination; or even to believe him when he declares that he had this
hallucination, would amount to foolishness on the part of a psychologist:
St. Paul desired the end, consequently he also desired the means. . . . Even
what he himself did not believe, was believed in by the idiots among whom
he spread *his* doctrine. What he wanted was power; with St. Paul the priest
again aspired to power, he could make use only of concepts, doctrines,
symbols with which masses may be tyrannised over, and with which herds
are formed. What was the only part of Christianity which was subsequently
borrowed by Muhamed? St. Paul's invention, his expedient for priestly
tyranny and to the formation of herds: the belief in immortality—*that is to
say, the doctrine of the "Last Judgement. . . ."*

43

When the centre of gravity of life is laid, *not* in life, but in a beyond—*in
nonentity*, life is utterly robbed of its balance. The great lie of personal
immortality destroys all reason, all nature in the instincts, everything in
the instincts that is beneficent, that promotes life and that is a guarantee
of the future, henceforward aroused suspicion. The very meaning of life
is now construed as the effort to live in such a way that life no longer has
any point. . . . Why show any public spirit? Why be grateful for one's origin

and one's forebears? Why collaborate with one's fellows, and be confident? Why be concerned about the general weal or strive after it? . . . All these things are merely so many "temptations," so many deviations from the "straight path." "One thing only is necessary. . . ." That everybody, as an "immortal soul," should have equal rank, that in the totality of beings, the "salvation" of each individual may lay claim to eternal importance, that insignificant bigots and three-quarter-lunatics may have the right to suppose that the laws of nature may be persistently *broken* on their account, any such magnification of every kind of selfishness to infinity, to *insolence*, cannot be branded with sufficient contempt. And yet it is to this miserable flattery of personal vanity that Christianity owes its *triumph*, by this means it lured all the bungled and the botched, all revolting and revolted people, all abortions, the whole of the refuse and offal of humanity, over to its side. The "salvation of the soul"—in plain English: "the world revolves around me. . . ." The poison of the doctrine "*equal* rights for all"—has been dispensed with the greatest thoroughness by Christianity: Christianity, prompted by the most secret recesses of bad instincts, has waged a deadly war upon all feeling of reverence and distance between man and man—that is to say, the *prerequisite* of all elevation, of every growth in culture; out of the resentment of the masses it wrought its *principal weapons* against us, against everything noble, joyful, exalted on earth, against our happiness on earth. . . . To grant "immortality" to every St. Peter and St. Paul, was the greatest, the most vicious outrage upon *noble* humanity that has ever been perpetrated. And do not let us underestimate the fatal influence which, springing from Christianity, has insinuated itself even into politics! Nowadays no one has the courage of special rights, of rights of dominion, of a feeling of self-respect and of respect for his equals, of *pathos of distance*. Our politics are diseased with this lack of courage! The aristocratic attitude of mind has been most thoroughly undermined by the lie of the equality of souls; and if the belief in the "privilege of the greatest number" creates and will continue *to create revolutions*, it is Christianity, let there be no doubt about it, and Christian values, which convert every revolution into blood and crime! Christianity is the revolt of all things that crawl on their bellies against everything that is lofty: the gospel of the "lowly" *lowers*. . . .

44

—The Gospels are invaluable as a testimony of the corruption which was already persistent *within* the first Christian communities. That which St.

Paul, with the logician's cynicism of a Rabbi, carried to its logical conclusion, was nevertheless merely the process of decay which began with
the death of the Saviour. These gospels cannot be read too cautiously;
difficulties lurk behind every word they contain. I confess, and people will
not take this amiss, that they are precisely on that account a joy of the first
rank for a psychologist, as the reverse of all naïve perversity, as refinement *par excellence*, as a masterpiece of art in psychological corruption.
The gospels stand alone. Altogether the Bible allows of no comparison. The
first thing to be remembered if we do not wish to lose the scent here, is,
that we are among Jews. The dissembling of holiness which, here, literally
amounts to genius, and which has never been even approximately
achieved elsewhere either by books or by men, this fraud in word and pose
which in this book is elevated to an *Art*, is not the accident of any individual gift, of any exceptional nature. These qualities are a matter of *race*.
With Christianity, the art of telling holy lies, which constitutes the whole
of Judaism, reaches its final mastership, thanks to many centuries of Jewish
and most thoroughly serious training and practise. The Christian, this
ultima ratio of falsehood, is the Jew over again—he is even three times a
Jew. . . . The fundamental will only to make use of concepts, symbols and
poses, which are demonstrated by the practise of the priests, the instinctive repudiation of every other kind of practise, every other standpoint of
valuation and of utility—all this is not only tradition, it is *hereditary*: only as
an inheritance is it able to work like nature. The whole of mankind, the
best brains, and even the best ages—(one man only excepted who is perhaps only a monster)—have allowed themselves to be deceived. The
gospels were read as the *book of innocence* . . . this is no insignificant sign of
the virtuosity with which deception has been practised here. Of course, if
we could only succeed in seeing all these amazing bigots and pretended
saints, even for a moment, all would be at an end—and it is precisely
because *I* can read no single word of theirs, without seeing their pretentious poses, *that I have made an end of them.* . . . I cannot endure a certain
way they have of casting their eyes heavenwards. Fortunately for Christianity, books are for the greatest number, merely *literature*. We must not let
ourselves be led away: "judge not!" they say, but they dispatch all those to
hell who stand in their way. Inasmuch as they let God do the judging, they
themselves judge; inasmuch as they glorify God, they glorify themselves;
inasmuch as they *exact* those virtues of which they themselves happen to be
capable—nay more, of which they are in need in order to be able to
remain on top at all; they assume the grand airs of struggling for virtue, of

struggling for the dominion of virtue. "We live, we die, we sacrifice ourselves for the good" ("the Truth," "the Light," "the Kingdom of God"): as
a matter of fact they do only what they cannot help doing. Like sneaks
they have to play a humble part; sit away in corners, and remain obscurely
in the shade, and they make all this appear a *duty*: their humble life now
appears as a duty, and their humility is one proof the more of their
piety. . . . Oh, what a humble, chaste and compassionate kind of falsity!
"Virtue itself shall bear us testimony. . . ." Only read the gospels as books
calculated to seduce by means of morality: morality is appropriated by
these petty people, they know what morality can do! The best way of leading mankind by the nose is with morality! The fact is that the most
conscious *conceit* of people who believe themselves to be *chosen*, here simu-
lates modesty: in this way they, the Christian community, the "good and
the just" place themselves once and for all on a certain side, the side "of
Truth"—and the rest of mankind, "the world" on the other. . . . This was
the most fatal kind of megalomania that had ever yet existed on earth:
insignificant little abortions of bigots and liars began to lay sole claim to
the concepts "God," "Truth," "Light," "Spirit," "Love," "Wisdom," "Life,"
as if these things were, so to speak, synonyms of themselves, in order to
fence themselves off from "the world"; little ultra-Jews, ripe for every kind
of madhouse, twisted values round in order to suit themselves, just as if
the Christian, alone, were the meaning, the salt, the standard and even the
"*ultimate tribunal*" of all the rest of mankind. . . . The whole fatality was
rendered possible only because a kind of megalomania, akin to this one
and allied to it in race, the Jewish kind—was already to hand in the
world: the very moment the gulf between Jews and Judaeo-Christians
was opened, the latter had no alternative left, but to adopt the same self-
preservative measures as the Jewish instinct suggested, even *against* the
Jews themselves, whereas the Jews, theretofore, had employed these same
measures only against the Gentiles. The Christian is nothing more than
an anarchical Jew.

45

—Let me give you a few examples of what these paltry people have stuffed
into their heads, what they have laid *on the lips of their Master*: quite a host
of confessions from "beautiful souls."

"And whosoever shall not receive you, nor hear you, when ye depart
thence, shake off the dust under your feet for a testimony against
them. Verily I say unto you, It shall be more tolerable for Sodom and

Gomorrah in the day of judgement, than for that city." (Mark vi. 11.) —*How evangelical!* ...

"And whosoever shall offend one of these little ones that believe in me, it is better for him that a millstone were hanged about his neck, and he were cast into the sea." (Mark ix. 42.)—How *evangelical!* ...

"And if thine eye offend thee, pluck it out: it is better for thee to enter into the kingdom of God with one eye, than having two eyes to be cast into hell fire: where their worm dieth not, and the fire is not quenched." (Mark ix. 47, 48.)—The eye is not precisely what is meant in this passage. ...

"Verily I say unto you, That there be some of them that stand here, which shall not taste of death, till they have seen the kingdom of God come with power." (Mark ix. 1.)—Well *lied*, lion![6] ...

"Whosoever will come after me, let him deny himself, and take up his cross, and follow me. *For* . . ." (*A psychologist's comment.* Christian morality is refuted by its "For's": its "reasons" refute, this is Christian.) (Mark viii. 34.)

"Judge not, that ye be not judged. For with what judgement ye judge, ye shall be judged." (Matthew vii. 1, 2.)—What a strange notion of justice on the part of a "just" judge! ...

"For if ye love them which love you, what reward have ye? Do not even the publicans the same? And if ye salute your brethren only, what do ye more *than others?* Do not even the publicans so?" (Matthew v. 46, 47.) The principle of "Christian love": it insists upon being *well paid.* ...

"But if ye forgive not men their trespasses neither will your Father forgive your trespasses." (Matthew vi. 15.)—Very compromising for the "Father" in question.

"But seek ye first the kingdom of God, and his righteousness; and all these things shall be added unto you." (Matthew vi. 33.)—"All these things"—that is to say, food, clothing, all the necessities of life. To use a moderate expression, this is an *error.* . . . Shortly before this God appears as a tailor, at least in certain cases. . . .

"Rejoice ye in that day, and leap for joy: for, behold, your reward *is* great in heaven: for in the like manner did their fathers unto the prophets." (Luke vi. 23.)—*Impudent* rabble! They dare to compare themselves with the prophets. . . .

"Know ye not that ye are the temple of God and *that* the Spirit of God dwelleth in you? If any man defile the temple of God, *him shall God destroy;* for the temple of God is holy, which *temple ye are.*" (St. Paul, 1 Corinthians iii. 16, 17.)—One cannot have too much contempt for this sort of thing. . . .

"Do ye not know that the saints shall judge the world? And if the world shall be judged by you, are ye unworthy to judge the smallest matters?" (St. Paul, 1 Corinthians vi. 2.)—Unfortunately this is not merely the speech of a lunatic. . . . This *appalling impostor* proceeds thus: "Know ye not that we shall judge angels? How much more things that pertain to this life?"

"Hath not God made foolish the wisdom of this world? For after that in the wisdom of God, the world by wisdom knew not God, it pleased God by the foolishness of preaching to save them that believe . . . not many wise men after the flesh, not many mighty, not many noble *are called*: But God hath chosen the foolish things of the world to confound the wise; and God hath chosen the weak things of the world to confound the things which are mighty; And base things of the world, and things which are despised, hath God chosen; *yea*, and things which are not, to bring to nought things that are: That no flesh should glory in his presence." (St. Paul, 1 Corinthians i. 20 *et seq.*)—In order to *understand* this passage, which is of the highest importance as an example of the psychology of every Chandala morality, the reader should refer to my *Genealogy of Morals*: in this book, the contrast between a *noble* and a Chandala morality born of *resentment* and impotent revengefulness, is brought to light for the first time. St. Paul was the greatest of all the apostles of revenge. . . .

46

What follows from this? That one does well to put on one's gloves when reading the New Testament. The proximity of so much pitch almost defiles one. We should feel just as little inclined to hobnob with "the first Christians" as with Polish Jews: not that we need explain our objections. . . . They simply smell bad. In vain have I sought for a single sympathetic feature in the New Testament; there is not a trace of freedom, kindliness, openheartedness and honesty to be found in it. Humaneness has not even made a start in this book, while *cleanly* instincts are entirely absent from it. . . . Only evil instincts are to be found in the New Testament, it shows no sign of courage, these people lack even the courage of their evil instincts. All is cowardice, all is a closing of one's eyes and self-deception. Every book becomes clean, after one has just read the New Testament: for instance, immediately after laying down St. Paul, I read with particular delight that most charming and most wanton of scoffers, Petronius, of whom someone might say what Domenico Boccaccio wrote to the Duke of Parma about Caesar Borgia: "*è tutto festo*"—immortally healthy, immortally cheerful and well-constituted. . . . These petty bigots err in their calculations and in the most important thing of all. They certainly attack; but everything they assail is, by that very fact alone, *distinguished*. He whom a "primitive Christian" attacks, is *not* thereby sullied. . . . Conversely it is an honour to be opposed by "primitive Christians." One cannot read the New Testament without feeling a preference for everything in it which is the subject of abuse—not to speak of the "wisdom of this world," which an impudent windbag tries in vain to confound "by the foolishness of preaching." Even the Pharisees and the Scribes derive advantage from such opposition: they must certainly have been worth something in order to have been hated in such a disreputable way. Hypocrisy—as if this were a reproach which the "first Christians" *were at liberty* to make! After all the Scribes and Pharisees were the *privileged ones*: this was quite enough, the hatred of the Chandala requires no other reasons. I very much fear that the "first Christian"—as also the "*last Christian*" *whom I may yet be able to meet*, is in his deepest instincts a rebel against everything privileged; he lives and struggles unremittingly for "equal rights"! . . . Regarded more closely, he has no alternative. . . . If one's desire be personally to represent "one of the chosen of God"—or a "temple of God," or "a judge of angels"—then every *other* principle of selection, for instance that based upon a standard of honesty, intellect, manliness and pride, or upon beauty and freedom of heart, becomes the "world"—*evil in itself*. Moral: every word on the lips of a "first Christian" is a lie, every action he does is an instinctive falsehood, all his values, all his aims are pernicious; but the man he hates, *the thing* he hates, *has value*. . . . The Christian, more particularly the Christian priest, is a *criterion of values*—Do I require to add that in the whole of the New Testament only *one* figure appears which we cannot help respecting? Pilate, the Roman Governor. To take a Jewish quarrel *seriously* was a thing he could not get himself to do. One Jew more or less—what did it matter? . . . The noble scorn of a Roman, in whose presence the word "truth" had been shamelessly abused, has enriched the New Testament with the only saying which *is of value*, and this saying is not only the criticism, but actually the shattering of that Testament: "What is truth!" . . .

47

—That which separates us from other people is not the fact that we can discover no God, either in history, or in nature, or behind nature, but that we regard what has been revered as "God," not as "divine," but as wretched, absurd, pernicious; not as an error, but as a *crime against life*. . . .

426 → FRIEDRICH NIETZSCHE

We deny God as God. . . . If the existence of this Christian God were *proved* to us, we should feel even less able to believe in him. In a formula: *deus qualem Paulus creavit, dei negatio.* A religion such as Christianity which never once comes in touch with reality, and which collapses the very moment reality asserts its rights even on one single point, must naturally be a mortal enemy of the "wisdom of this world"—that is to say, *science.* It will call all those means good with which mental discipline, lucidity and severity in intellectual matters, nobility and freedom of the intellect may be poisoned, calumniated and *decried.* "Faith" as an imperative is a *veto* against science, *in praxi,* it means lies at any price. St. Paul *understood* that falsehood—that "faith" was necessary; subsequently the Church understood St. Paul. That "God" which St. Paul invented for himself, a God who "confounds" the "wisdom of this world" (in a narrower sense, the two great opponents of all superstition, philology and medicine), means, in very truth, simply St. Paul's firm *resolve* to do so: to call his own will "God," *thora*, that is arch-Jewish. St. Paul insists upon confounding the "wisdom of this world": his enemies are the *good old* philologists and doctors of the Alexandrine schools; it is on them that he wages war. As a matter of fact no one is either a philologist or a doctor, who is not also an *Antichrist.* As a philologist, for instance, a man sees *behind* the "holy books," as a doctor he sees *behind* the physiological rottenness of the typical Christian. The doctor says "incurable," the philologist says "forgery."

48

—Has anybody ever really understood the celebrated story which stands at the beginning of the Bible, concerning God's deadly panic over *science?* . . . Nobody has understood it. This essentially sacerdotal book naturally begins with the great inner difficulty of the priest: *he* knows only one great danger, *consequently* "God" has only one great danger.

The old God, entirely "spirit," a high-priest through and through, and wholly perfect, is wandering in a leisurely fashion round his garden; but he is bored. Against boredom even the gods themselves struggle in vain.[7] What does he do? He invents man, man is entertaining. . . . But, behold, even man begins to be bored. God's compassion for the only form of misery which is peculiar to all paradises, exceeds all bounds: so forthwith he creates yet other animals. God's *first* mistake: man did not think animals entertaining, he dominated them, he did not even wish to be an "animal." Consequently God created woman. And boredom did indeed cease from that moment, but many other things ceased as well! Woman was God's *second* mistake. "Woman in her innermost nature is a serpent, Heva"—every priest knows this: "all evil came into this world through woman"—every priest knows this too. "*Consequently science* also comes from woman. . . ." Only through woman did man learn to taste of the tree of knowledge. What had happened? Panic had seized the old God. Man himself had been his *greatest* mistake, he had created a rival for himself, science makes you *equal to God*, it is all up with priests and gods when man becomes scientific! Moral: science is the most prohibited thing of all, it alone, is forbidden. Science is the *first*, the germ of all sins, the original sin. *This alone is morality.* "Thou shalt *not* know": the rest follows as a matter of course. God's panic did not deprive him of his intelligence. How can one *guard* against science? For ages this was his principal problem. Reply: man must be kicked out of paradise! Happiness, leisure leads to thinking, all thoughts are bad thoughts. . . . Man *must* not think. And the "priest-per-se" proceeds to invent distress, death, the vital danger of pregnancy, every kind of misery, decrepitude, and affliction, and above all *disease*, all these are but weapons employed in the struggle with science! Trouble prevents man from thinking. . . . And notwithstanding all these precautions! Oh, horror! The work of science towers aloft, it storms heaven itself, it rings the death-knell of the gods, what's to be done? The old God invents *war*, he separates the nations, and contrives to make men destroy each other mutually (the priests have always been in need of war . . .). War, among other things, is a great disturber of science! Incredible! Knowledge, *the rejection of the sacerdotal yoke*, nevertheless increases. So the old God arrives at this final decision: "Man has become scientific, *there is no help for it, he must be drowned!*" . . .

49

You have understood me. The beginning of the Bible contains the whole psychology of the priest. The priest knows only one great danger, and that is science, the healthy concept of cause and effect. But, on the whole, science flourishes only under happy conditions, a man must have time, he must also have superfluous mental energy in order to "pursue knowledge. . . ." "*Consequently* man must be made unhappy"—this has been the argument of the priest of all ages. You have already divined what, in accordance with such a manner of arguing, must first have come into the world: "sin. . . ." The notion of guilt and punishment, the whole "moral order of the universe," was invented against science, against the deliverance of man from the priest. . . . Man must *not* cast his glance upon the outer world, he must turn it inwards into himself; he must not as a learner look cleverly and cautiously *into* things; he must not see at all: he must *suffer*. . . . And he must suffer, so that he may be in need of the priest every minute. Away with doctors! What is needed is a Saviour! The notion of guilt and punishment, including the doctrine of "grace," of "salvation" and of "forgiveness"—all *lies* through and through without a shred of psychological reality—were invented in order to destroy man's *sense of causality*: they are an attack on the concept of cause and effect! And *not* an attack with the fist, with the knife, with honesty in hate and love! But one actuated by the most cowardly, most crafty, and most ignoble instincts! A *priest's* attack! A *parasite's* attack! A vampyrism of pale subterranean leeches! . . . When the natural consequences of an act are no longer "natural," but are thought to be conjured up by phantom concepts of superstition, by "God," by "spirits," and by "souls," as merely moral consequences, in the form of rewards, punishments, hints, and educational means, then the whole basis of knowledge is destroyed, *then the greatest crime against man has been perpetrated*. Sin, I repeat, this form of self-pollution *par excellence* on the part of man, was invented in order to make science, culture and every elevation and noble trait in man quite impossible; by means of the invention of sin the priest is able to *rule*.

50

—I cannot here dispense with a psychology of "faith" and of the "faithful," which will naturally be to the advantage of the "faithful." If today there are still many who do not know how very *indecent* it is to be a "believer"—*or* to what extent such a state is the sign of decadence, and of the broken will to Life, they will know it no later than tomorrow. My voice can make even those hear who are hard of hearing. If perchance my ears have not deceived me, it seems that among Christians there is such a thing as a kind of criterion of truth, which is called "the proof of power." "Faith saveth; *therefore* it is true." It might be objected here that it is precisely salvation which is not proved but only *promised*: salvation is bound up with the condition "faith"—one *shall* be saved, *because* one has faith. . . . But how prove *that* that which the priest promises to the faithful really will take place, to wit: the "Beyond" which defies all demonstration? The assumed "proof of power" is at bottom once again only a belief in the fact that the effect which faith promises will not fail to take place. In a formula: "I believe that faith saveth; *consequently* it is true." But with this we are at the end of our tether. This "consequently" would be the *absurdum* itself as a criterion of truth. Let us be indulgent enough to assume, however, that salvation is proved by faith (*not* only desired, and *not* merely promised by the somewhat suspicious lips of a priest): could salvation—or, in technical terminology, *happiness*—ever be a proof of truth? So little is it so that, when pleasurable sensations make their influence felt in replying to the question "what is true," they furnish almost the contradiction of truth, or at any rate they make it in the highest degree suspicious. The proof through "happiness," is a proof of happiness—and nothing else; why in the world should we take it for granted that *true* judgements cause more pleasure than false ones, and that in accordance with a pre-established harmony, they necessarily bring pleasant feelings in their wake? The experience of all strict and profound minds teaches the *reverse*. Every inch of truth has been conquered only after a struggle, almost everything to which our heart, our love and our trust in life cleaves, has had to be sacrificed for it. Greatness of soul is necessary for this: the service of truth is the hardest of all services. What then is meant by honesty in things intellectual? It means that a man is severe towards his own heart, that he scorns "beautiful feelings," and that he makes a matter of conscience out of every Yea and Nay! Faith saveth: *consequently* it lies. . . .

51

The fact that faith may in certain circumstances save, the fact that salvation as the result of an *idée fixe* does not constitute a true idea, the fact that faith moves *no* mountains, but may very readily raise them where previously they did not exist—all these things are made sufficiently clear by a mere casual stroll through a *lunatic asylum*. Of course *no* priest would find this sufficient: for he instinctively denies that illness is illness or that lunatic asylums are lunatic asylums. Christianity is in *need* of illness, just as Ancient Greece was in need of a superabundance of health. The actual ulterior motive of the whole of the Church's system of salvation is to *make people ill*. And is not the Church itself the Catholic madhouse as an ultimate ideal? The earth as a whole converted into a madhouse? The kind of religious man which the Church aims at producing is a typical *decadent*. The moment of time at which a religious crisis attains the ascendancy over a people, is always characterised by nerve-epidemics; the "inner world" of the religious man is ridiculously like the "inner world" of over-irritable and exhausted people; the "highest" states which Christianity holds up to mankind as the value of values, are epileptic in character, the Church has pronounced only madmen *or* great swindlers *in majorem dei honorem* holy. Once I ventured to characterise the whole of the Christian training of penance and salvation (which nowadays is best studied in England) as a *folie circulaire* methodically generated upon a soil which, of course, is already prepared for it, that is to say, which is thoroughly morbid. Not every one who likes can be a Christian: no man is "converted" to Christianity, he must be sick enough for it. . . . We others who possess enough courage both for health and for contempt, how rightly *we* may despise a religion which taught men to misunderstand the body! Which would not rid itself of the superstitions of the soul! Which made a virtue of taking inadequate nourishment! Which in health combats a sort of enemy, devil, temptation! Which persuaded itself that it was possible to bear a perfect soul about in a cadaverous body, and which, to this end, had to make up for itself a new concept of "perfection," a pale, sickly, idiotically gushing ideal, so-called "holiness"—holiness, which in itself is simply a symptom of an impoverished, enervated and incurably deteriorated body! . . . The movement of Christianity, as a European movement, was from first to last, a general accumulation of the ruck and scum of all sorts and kinds (and these, by means of Christianity, aspire to power). It does *not* express the downfall of a race, it is rather a conglomerate assembly of all the decadent elements from everywhere which seek each other and crowd together. It was not, as some believe, the corruption of antiquity, of *noble* antiquity, which made Christianity possible: the learned idiocy which nowadays tries to support such a notion cannot be too severely contradicted. At the time when the morbid and corrupted Chandala classes became Christianised in the whole of the *imperium,* the very *contrary type,* nobility, was extant in its finest and maturest forms. The greatest number became master; the democracy of Christian instincts triumphed. . . . Christianity was not "national," it was not determined by race, it appealed to all the disinherited forms of life, it had its allies everywhere. Christianity is built upon the rancour of the sick; its instinct is directed *against* the sound, against health. Everything well-constituted, proud, high-spirited, and beautiful is offensive to its ears and eyes. Again I remind you of St. Paul's priceless words: "And God hath chosen the *weak* things of the world, the *foolish* things of the world; and *base* things of the world, and things which are *despised*": this was the formula, *in hoc signo* decadence triumphed. *God on the Cross*—does no one yet understand the terrible ulterior motive of this symbol? Everything that suffers, everything that hangs on the cross, is *divine.* . . . All of us hang on the cross, consequently we are *divine.* . . . We alone are divine. . . . Christianity was a victory; a *nobler* type of character perished through it, Christianity has been humanity's greatest misfortune hitherto.

52

Christianity also stands opposed to everything happily constituted in the *mind*, it can make use only of morbid reason as Christian reason; it takes the side of everything idiotic, it utters a curse upon "intellect," upon the *superbia* of the healthy intellect. Since illness belongs to the essence of Christianity, the typically Christian state, "faith," *must* also be a form of illness, and all straight, honest and scientific roads to knowledge must be repudiated by the Church as forbidden. . . . Doubt in itself is already a sin. . . . The total lack of psychological cleanliness in the priest, which reveals itself in his look, is a *result* of decadence. Hysterical women, as also children with scrofulous constitutions, should be observed as a proof of how invariably instinctive falsity, the love of lying for the sake of lying, and the inability either to look or to walk straight, are the expression of decadence. "Faith" simply means the refusal to know what is true. The pious person, the priest of both sexes, is false because he is ill: his instinct *demands* that truth should not assert its right anywhere. "That which makes ill is good: that which proceeds from abundance, from superabundance and from power, is evil": that is the view of the faithful. The *constraint to lie*—that is the sign by which I recognise every predetermined theologian. Another characteristic of the theologian is his lack of *capacity* for *philology*. What I mean here by the word philology is, in a general sense to be understood as the art of reading well, of being able to take account of facts *without* falsifying them by interpretation, without losing either caution, patience or subtlety owing to one's desire to understand. Philology as *ephexis*[8] in interpretation, whether one be dealing with books, newspaper reports, human destinies or meteorological records, not to speak of the "salvation of the soul. . . ." The manner in which a theologian, whether in Berlin or in Rome, interprets a verse from the "Scriptures," or an experience, or the triumph of his nation's army for instance, under the superior guiding light of David's Psalms, is always so exceedingly *daring*, that it is enough to make a philologist's hair stand on end. And what is he to do, when pietists and other cows from Swabia explain their miserable everyday lives in their smoky hovels by means of the "Finger of God," a miracle of "grace," of "Providence," of experiences of "salvation"! The most modest effort of the intellect, not to speak of decent feeling, ought at least to lead these interpreters to convince themselves of the absolute childishness and unworthiness of any such abuse of the dexterity of God's fingers. However small an amount of loving piety we might possess, a god who cured us in time of a cold in the nose, or who arranged for us to enter a carriage just at the moment when a cloud burst over our heads, would be such an absurd God, that he would have to be abolished, even if he existed.[9] God as a domestic servant, as a postman, as a general provider, in short, merely a word for the most foolish kind of accidents. . . . "Divine Providence," as it is believed in today by almost every third man in "cultured Germany," would be an argument against God, in fact it would be the strongest argument against God that could be imagined. And in any case it is an argument against the Germans.

53

—The notion that martyrs prove anything at all in favour of a thing, is so exceedingly doubtful, that I would fain deny that there has ever yet existed a martyr who had anything to do with truth. In the very manner in which a martyr flings his little parcel of truth at the head of the world, such a low degree of intellectual honesty and such obtuseness in regard to the question "truth" makes itself felt, that one never requires to refute a martyr. Truth is not a thing which one might have and another be without: only peasants or peasant-apostles, after the style of Luther, can think like this about truth. You may be quite sure, that the greater a man's degree of conscientiousness may be in matters intellectual, the more modest he will show himself on this point. To *know* about five things, and with a subtle wave of the hand to refuse to know *others*. . . . "Truth" as it is understood by every prophet, every sectarian, every free thinker, every socialist and every churchman, is an absolute proof of the fact that these people haven't even begun that discipline of the mind and that process of self-mastery, which is necessary for the discovery of any small, even exceedingly small truth. Incidentally, the deaths of martyrs have been a great misfortune in the history of the world: they led people astray. . . . The conclusion which all idiots, women and common people come to, that there must be something in a cause for which someone lays down his life (or which, as in the case of primitive Christianity, provokes an epidemic of sacrifices), this conclusion put a tremendous check upon all investigation, upon the spirit of investigation and of caution. Martyrs have *harmed* the cause of truth. . . . Even to this day it only requires the crude fact of persecution, in order to create an honourable name for any obscure sect who does not matter in the least. What? Is a cause actually changed in anyway by the fact that someone has laid down his life for it? An error which becomes honourable, is simply an error that possesses one seductive charm the more: do you suppose, dear theologians, that we shall give you the chance of acting the martyrs for your lies? A thing is refuted by being laid respectfully on ice, and theologians are refuted in the same way. This was precisely the world-historic foolishness of all persecutors; they lent the thing they combated a semblance of honour by conferring the fascination of martyrdom upon it. . . . Women still lie prostrate before an error today, because they have been told that someone died on the cross for it. *Is the cross then an argument?* But concerning all these things, one person alone has said what mankind has been in need of for thousands of years, *Zarathustra.*

"Letters of blood did they write on the way they went, and their folly taught that truth is proved by blood.

"But blood is the very worst testimony of truth; blood poisoneth even the purest teaching, and turneth it into delusion and into blood feuds.

"And when a man goeth through fire for his teaching—what does that prove? Verily, it is more when out of one's own burning springeth one's own teaching."[10]

54

Do not allow yourselves to be deceived: great minds are sceptical. Zarathustra is a sceptic. Strength and the *freedom* which proceeds from the power and excessive power of the mind, *manifests* itself through scepticism. Men of conviction are of no account whatever in regard to any principles of value or of non-value. Convictions are prisons. They never see far enough, they do not look down from a sufficient height: but in order to have any say in questions of value and non-value, a man must see five hundred convictions *beneath* him, *behind* him. . . . A spirit who desires great things, and who also desires the means thereto, is necessarily a sceptic. Freedom from every kind of conviction *belongs* to strength, to the *ability* to open one's eyes freely. . . . The great passion of a sceptic, the basis and power of his being, which is more enlightened and more despotic than he is himself, enlists all his intellect into its service; it makes him unscrupulous; it even gives him the courage to employ unholy means; in certain circumstances it even allows him convictions. Conviction as a *means:* much is achieved merely by means of a conviction. Great passion makes use of and consumes convictions, it does not submit to them— it knows that it is a sovereign power. Conversely; the need of faith, of anything either absolutely affirmative or negative, Carlylism (if I may be allowed this expression), is the need of *weakness*. The man of beliefs, the "believer" of every sort and condition, is necessarily a dependent man; he is one who cannot regard *himself* as an aim, who cannot postulate aims from the promptings of his own heart. The "believer" does not belong to himself, he can be only a means, he must be *used up*, he is in need of someone who uses him up. His instinct accords the highest honour to a morality of self-abnegation: everything in him, his prudence, his experience, his vanity, persuade him to adopt this morality. Every sort of belief is in itself an expression of self-denial, of self-estrangement. . . . If one considers how necessary a regulating code of conduct is to the majority of people, a code of conduct which constrains them and fixes them from outside; and how control, or in a higher sense, *slavery*, is the only and ultimate condition under which the weak-willed man, and especially woman, flourish; one also understands conviction, "faith." The man of conviction finds in the latter his *backbone*. To be *blind* to many things, to be impartial about nothing, to belong always to a particular side, to hold a strict and necessary point of view in all matters of values—these are the only conditions under which such a man can survive at all. But all this is the reverse of, the *antagonist* of, the truthful man, of truth. . . . The believer is not at liberty to have a conscience for the question "true" and "untrue": to be upright on *this* point would mean his immediate downfall. The pathological limitations of his standpoint convert the convinced man into the fanatic—Savonarola, Luther Rousseau, Robespierre, Saint-Simon, these are the reverse type of the strong spirit that has become *free*. But the grandiose poses of these *morbid* spirits, of these epileptics of ideas, exercise an influence over the masses, fanatics are picturesque, mankind prefers to look at poses than to listen to reason.

55

One step further in the psychology of conviction of "faith." It is already sometime since I first thought of considering whether convictions were not perhaps more dangerous enemies of truth than lies (*Human, All-Too-Human*, Part 1, Aphs. 54 and 483). Now I would fain put the decisive question: is there any difference at all between a lie and a conviction? All the world believes that there is, but what in Heaven's name does not all the world believe! Every conviction has its history, its preliminary stages, its period of groping and of mistakes: it becomes a conviction only after it has *not* been one for a long time, only after it has *scarcely* been one for a long time. What? Might not falsehood be the embryonic form of conviction? At times all that is required is a change of personality: very often what was a lie in the father becomes a conviction in the son. I call a lie, to refuse to see something that one sees, to refuse to see it exactly *as* one sees it: whether a lie is perpetrated before witnesses or not is beside the point. The most common sort of lie is the one uttered to one's self; to lie to others is relatively exceptional. Now this refusal to see what one sees, this refusal to see a thing exactly as one sees it, is almost the first condition for all those who belong to a *party* in any sense whatsoever: the man who belongs to a party perforce becomes a liar. German historians, for instance, are convinced that Rome stood for despotism, whereas the Teutons introduced the spirit of freedom into the world: what difference is there between this conviction and a lie? After this is it to be wondered at, that all parties, including German historians, instinctively adopt the grandiloquent phraseology of morality, that morality almost owes its *survival* to the fact that the man who belongs to a party, no matter what it may be, is in need of morality every moment? "This is our conviction: we confess it to the whole world, we live and die for it, let us respect everything that has a conviction!"—I have actually heard antisemites speak in this way. On the contrary, my dear sirs! An antisemite does not become the least bit more respectable because he lies on principle. . . . Priests, who in such matters are more subtle, and who perfectly understand the objection to which the idea of a conviction lies open—that is to say of a falsehood which is perpetrated on principle *because* it serves a purpose, borrowed from the Jews the prudent measure of setting the concept "God," "Will of God," "Revelation of God," at this place. Kant, too, with his categorical imperative, was on the same road: this was his *practical* reason. There are some questions in which it is *not* given to man to decide between true and false; all the principal questions, all the principal problems of value, stand beyond human reason. . . . To comprehend the limits of reason—this alone is genuine philosophy. For what purpose did God give man revelation? Would God have done anything superfluous? Man cannot of his own accord know what is good and what is evil, that is why God taught man his will. . . . Moral: the priest does *not* lie, such questions as "truth" or "falseness" have nothing to do with the things concerning which the priest speaks; such things do not allow of lying. For, in order to lie, it would be necessary to know *what* is true in this respect. But that is precisely what man cannot know: hence the priest is only the mouthpiece of God. This sort of sacerdotal syllogism is by no means exclusively Judaic or Christian;

the right to lie and the *prudent measure* of "revelation" belongs to the priestly type, whether of decadent periods or of Pagan times (Pagans are all those who say yea to life, and to whom "God" is the word for the great yea to all things). The "law," the "will of God," the "holy book," and inspiration. All these things are merely words for the conditions under which the priest attains to power, and with which he maintains his power, these concepts are to be found at the base of all sacerdotal organisations, of all priestly or philosophical and ecclesiastical governments. The "holy lie," which is common to Confucius, to the *Law-Book of Manu*, to Muhamed, and to the Christian church, is not even absent in Plato. "Truth is here"; this phrase means, wherever it is uttered: *the priest lies.* . . .

56

After all, the question is, to what *end* are falsehoods perpetrated? The fact that, in Christianity, "holy" ends are entirely absent, constitutes *my* objection to the means it employs. Its ends are only *bad* ends: the poisoning, the calumniation and the denial of life, the contempt of the body, the degradation and self-pollution of man by virtue of the concept sin, consequently its means are bad as well. My feelings are quite the reverse when I read the *Law-Book of Manu*, an incomparably superior and more intellectual work, which it would be a sin against the *spirit* even to *mention* in the same breath with the Bible. You will guess immediately why: it has a genuine philosophy behind it, *in* it, not merely an evil-smelling Jewish distillation of Rabbinism and superstition, it gives something to chew even to the most fastidious psychologist. And, *not* to forget the most important point of all, it is fundamentally different from every kind of Bible: by means of it the *noble classes*, the philosophers and the warriors guard and guide the masses; it is replete with noble values, it is filled with a feeling of perfection, with a saying of yea to life, and a triumphant sense of well-being in regard to itself and to life, the sun shines upon the whole book. All those things which Christianity smothers with its bottomless vulgarity: procreation, woman, marriage, are here treated with earnestness, with reverence, with love and confidence. How can one possibly place in the hands of children and women, a book that contains those vile words: "to avoid fornication, let every man have his own wife, and let every woman have her own husband . . . it is better to marry than to burn."[11] And is it decent to be a Christian so long as the very origin of man is Christianised, that is to say, befouled, by the idea of the *immaculata conceptio*? . . . I know of no book in which so many delicate and kindly things are said to woman, as in the *Law-Book of Manu*; these old grey-beards and saints have a manner of being gallant to women which, perhaps, cannot be surpassed. "The mouth of a woman," says Manu on one occasion, "the breast of a maiden, the prayer of a child, and the smoke of the sacrifice, are always pure." Elsewhere he says: "there is nothing purer than the light of the sun, the shadow cast by a cow, air, water, fire and the breath of a maiden." And finally—perhaps this is also a holy lie: "all the openings of the body above the navel are pure, all those below the navel are impure. Only in a maiden is the whole body pure."

57

The unholiness of Christian means is caught *in flagranti*, if only the end aspired to by Christianity be compared with that of the *Law-Book of Manu*; if only these two utterly opposed aims be put under a strong light. The critic of Christianity simply cannot avoid making Christianity *contemptible*. A law-book like that of Manu comes into being like every good law-book: it epitomises the experience, the precautionary measures, and the experimental morality of long ages, it settles things definitely, it no longer creates. The prerequisite for a codification of this kind, is the recognition of the fact that the means which procure authority for a *truth* to which it has cost both time and great pains to attain, are fundamentally different from those with which that same truth would be proved. A law-book never relates the utility, the reasons, the preliminary casuistry, of a law: for it would be precisely in this way that it would forfeit its imperative tone, the "thou shalt," the first condition of its being obeyed. The problem lies exactly in this. At a certain stage in the development of a people, the most far-seeing class within it (that is to say, the class that sees farthest backwards and forwards), declares the experience of how its fellow-creatures ought to live—i.e., *can* live—to be finally settled. Its object is, to reap as rich and as complete a harvest as possible, in return for the ages of experiment and *terrible* experience it has traversed. Consequently, that which has to be avoided, above all, is any further experimentation, the continuation of the state when values are still fluid, the testing, choosing, and criticising of values *in infinitum*. Against all this a double wall is built up: in the first place, *Revelation*, which is the assumption that the rationale of every law is not human in its origin, that it was not sought and found after ages of error, but that it is divine in its origin, completely and utterly without a history, a gift, a miracle, a mere communication. . . . And secondly, *tradition*, which is the assumption that the law has obtained since the most primeval times, that it is impious and a crime against one's ancestors to attempt to doubt it. The authority of law is established on the principles: God *gave* it, the ancestors *lived* it. The superior reason of such a procedure lies in the intention to draw consciousness off step by step from that mode of life which has been recognised as correct (i.e., *proved* after enormous and carefully examined experience), so that perfect automatism of the instincts may be attained, this being the only possible basis of all mastery of every kind of perfection in the Art of Life. To draw up a law-book like Manu's, is tantamount to granting a people mastership for the future, perfection for the future, the right to aspire to the highest Art of Life. *To that end it must be made unconscious*: this is the object of every holy lie. *The order of castes*, the highest, the dominating law, is only the sanction of a *natural order*, of a natural legislation of the first rank, over which no arbitrary innovation, no "modern idea" has any power. Every healthy society falls into three distinct types, which reciprocally condition one another and which gravitate differently in the physiological sense; and each of these has its own hygiene, its own sphere of work, its own special feeling of perfection, and its own mastership. It is Nature, not Manu, that separates from the rest, those individuals preponderating in intellectual power, those excelling in muscular strength and temperament, and the third class which is distinguished neither in one way nor the other, the mediocre, the latter as the greatest number, the former as the *élite*. The superior caste—I call them the *fewest*, has, as the perfect caste, the privileges of the fewest: it devolves upon them to represent happiness, beauty and goodness on earth. Only the most intellectual men have the right to beauty, to the beautiful: only in them is goodness not weakness. *Pulchrum est paucorum hominum*: goodness is a privilege. On the other hand there is nothing which they should be more strictly forbidden than repulsive manners or a pessimistic look, a look that makes everything *seem ugly*, or even indignation at the general aspect of things. Indignation is the privilege of the Chandala, and so is pessimism. "*The world is perfect*"—that is what the instinct of the most intellectual says, the yea-saying instinct; "imperfection, every kind of *inferiority* to us, distance, the pathos of distance, even the Chandala belongs to this perfection." The most intellectual men, as the *strongest* find their happiness where others meet with their ruin: in the labyrinth, in hardness towards themselves and others, in endeavour; their delight is self-mastery: with them asceticism becomes a second nature, a need, an instinct They regard a difficult task as their privilege; to play with burdens which crush their fellows is to them a *recreation*. . . . Knowledge, a form of asceticism. They are the most honourable kind of men: but that does not prevent them from being the most cheerful and most gracious. They rule, not because they will, but because they *are*; they are not at liberty to take a second place. The second in rank are the guardians of the law, the custodians of order and of security, the noble warriors, the king, above all, as the highest formula of the warrior, the judge, and keeper of the law. The second in rank are the executive of the most intellectual, the nearest to them in duty, relieving them of all that is *coarse* in the work of ruling, their retinue, their right hand, their best disciples. In all this, I repeat, there is nothing arbitrary, nothing "artificial," that which is *otherwise* is artificial, by that which is otherwise, nature is put to shame. . . . The order of castes, and the order of rank merely formulates the supreme law of life itself; the differentiation of the three types is necessary for the maintenance of society, and for enabling higher and highest types to be reared, the *inequality* of rights is the only condition of there being rights at all. A right is a privilege. And in his way, each has his privilege. Let us not underestimate the privileges of the *mediocre*. Life always gets harder towards the summit, the cold increases, responsibility increases. A high civilisation is a pyramid: it can stand only upon a broad base, its first prerequisite is a strongly and soundly consolidated mediocrity. Handicraft, commerce, agriculture, science, the greater part of art, in a word, the whole range of professional and business callings, is compatible only with mediocre ability and ambition; such pursuits would be out of place among exceptions, the instinct pertaining thereto would oppose not only aristocracy but anarchy as well. The fact that one is publicly useful, a wheel, a function, presupposes a certain natural destiny: it is not *society*, but the only kind of *happiness* of which the great majority are capable, that makes them intelligent machines. For the mediocre it is a joy to be mediocre; in them mastery in one thing, a speciality, is a natural instinct. It would be absolutely unworthy of a profound thinker to see any objection in mediocrity per se. For in itself it is the first essential condition under which exceptions are possible; a high culture is determined by it. When the exceptional man treats the mediocre with more tender care than he does himself or his equals, this is not mere courtesy of heart on his part—but simply his *duty*. . . . Whom do I hate most among the rabble of the present day? The socialistic rabble, the Chandala apostles, who undermine the working man's instinct, his happiness and his feeling of contentedness with his insignificant existence, who make him envious, and who teach him revenge. . . . The wrong never lies in unequal rights; it lies in the claim to equal rights. What is *bad*? But I have already replied to this: Everything that proceeds from weakness, envy, and *revenge*. The anarchist and the Christian are offspring of the same womb. . . .

58

In point of fact, it matters greatly to what end one lies: whether one preserves or *destroys* by means of falsehood. It is quite justifiable to bracket the *Christian* and the *Anarchist* together: their object, their instinct, is concerned only with destruction. The proof of this proposition can be read quite plainly from history: history spells it with appalling distinctness. Whereas we have just seen a religious legislation, whose object was to render the highest possible means of making life *flourish*, and of making a grand organisation of society, eternal, Christianity found its mission in putting an end to such an organisation, *precisely because life flourishes through it*. In the one case, the net profit to the credit of reason, acquired through long ages of experiment and of insecurity, is applied usefully to the most remote ends, and the harvest, which is as large, as rich and as complete as possible, is reaped and garnered: in the other case, on the contrary, the harvest is *blighted* in a single night. That which stood there, *aere perennius*, the *imperium Romanum*, the most magnificent form of organisation, under difficult conditions, that has ever been achieved, and compared with which everything that preceded, and everything which followed it, is mere patchwork, gimcrackery, and dilettantism, those holy anarchists made it their "piety," to destroy "the world"—that is to say, the *imperium Romanum*, until no two stones were left standing one on the other, until even the Teutons and other clodhoppers were able to become master of it. The Christian and the anarchist are both decadents; they are both incapable of acting in any other way than disintegratingly, poisonously and witheringly, like *bloodsuckers*; they are both actuated by an instinct of *mortal hatred* of everything that stands erect, that is great, that is lasting, and that is a guarantee of the future. . . . Christianity was the vampire of the *imperium Romanum*, in a night it shattered the stupendous achievement of the Romans, which was to acquire the territory for a vast civilisation which could *bide its time*. Does no one understand this yet? The *imperium Romanum* that we know, and which the history of the Roman province teaches us to know ever more thoroughly, this most admirable work of art on a grand scale, was the beginning, its construction was calculated *to prove* its worth by millenniums, unto this day nothing has ever again been built in this fashion, nor have men even dreamt since of building on this scale *sub specie aeterni!* This organisation was sufficiently firm to withstand bad emperors: the accident of personalities must have nothing to do with such matters—the *first* principle of all great architecture. But it was not sufficiently firm to resist the *corruptest* form of corruption, to resist the Christians. . . . . These stealthy cankerworms, which under the shadow of night, mist and duplicity, insinuated themselves into the company of every individual, and proceeded to drain him of all seriousness for *real* things, of all his instinct for *realities*; this cowardly, effeminate and sugary gang have step by step alienated all "souls" from this colossal edifice, those valuable, virile, and noble natures who felt that the cause of Rome was their own personal cause, their own personal seriousness, their own personal *pride*. The stealth of the bigot, the secrecy of the conventicle, concepts as black as hell such as the sacrifice of the innocent, the *unio mystica* in the drinking of blood, above all the slowly kindled fire of revenge, of Chandala revenge—such things became master of Rome, the same kind of religion on the pre-existent form of which Epicurus had waged war. One has only to read Lucretius in order to understand what Epicurus combated, *not* Paganism, but "Christianity," that is to say the corruption of souls through the concept of guilt, through the concept of punishment and immortality. He combated the *subterranean* cults, the whole of latent Christianity—to deny immortality was at that time a genuine *deliverance*. And Epicurus had triumphed, every respectable thinker in the Roman Empire was an Epicurean: *then St. Paul appeared* . . . St. Paul, the Chandala hatred against Rome, against "the world," the Jew, the eternal Jew *par excellence*, become flesh and genius. . . . What he divined was, how, by the help of the small sectarian Christian movement, independent of Judaism, a universal conflagration could be kindled; how, with the symbol of the "God on the Cross," everything submerged, everything secretly insurrectionary, the whole offspring of anarchical intrigues could be gathered together to constitute an enormous power. "For salvation is of the Jews." Christianity is the formula for the supersession, *and* epitomising of all kinds of subterranean cults, that of Osiris, of the Great Mother, of Mithras for example: St. Paul's genius consisted in his discovery of this. In this matter his instinct was so certain, that, regardless of doing violence to truth, he laid the ideas by means of which those Chandala religions fascinated, upon the very lips of the "Saviour" he had invented, and not only upon his lips, that he *made* out of him something which even a Mithras priest could understand. . . . This was his moment of Damascus: he saw that he had *need* of the belief in immortality in order to depreciate "the world," that the notion of "hell" would become master of Rome, that with a "Beyond" *this life* can be killed. . . . Nihilist and Christian, they rhyme in German, and they do not only rhyme.

59

The whole labour of the ancient world *in vain*: I am at a loss for a word which could express my feelings at something so atrocious. And in view of the fact that its labour was only preparatory, that with adamantine self-consciousness it laid the substructure, alone, to a work which was to last millenniums, the whole *significance* of the ancient world was certainly in vain! . . . What was the use of the Greeks? What was the use of the Romans? All the prerequisites of a learned culture, all the scientific methods already existed, the great and peerless art of reading well had already been established—that indispensable condition to tradition, to culture and to scientific unity; natural science hand in hand with mathematics and mechanics was on the best possible road, the sense for facts, the last and most valuable of all senses, had its schools, and its tradition was already centuries old! Is this understood? Everything *essential* had been discovered to make it possible for work to be begun: methods, and this cannot be said too often, are the essential thing, also the most difficult thing, while they moreover have to wage the longest war against custom and indolence. That which today we have successfully reconquered for ourselves, by dint of unspeakable self-discipline—for in some way or other all of us still have the bad instincts, the Christian instincts, in our body, the impartial eye for reality, the cautious hand, patience and seriousness in the smallest details, complete *uprightness* in knowledge, all this was already there; it had been there over two thousand years before! And in addition to this there was also that excellent and subtle tact and taste! *Not* in the form of brain drilling! *Not* in the form of "German" culture with the manners of a boor! But incarnate, manifesting itself in men's bearing and in their instinct, in short constituting reality. . . . *All this in vain!* In one night it became merely a memory! The Greeks! The Romans! Instinctive nobility, instinctive taste, methodic research, the genius of organisation and administration, faith, the *will* to the future of mankind, the great *yea* to all things materialised in the *imperium Romanum*, become visible to all the senses, grand style no longer manifested in mere art, but in reality, in truth, in *life*. And buried in a night, not by a natural catastrophe! Not stamped to death by Teutons and other heavy-footed vandals! But destroyed by crafty, stealthy, invisible anaemic vampires! Not conquered, but only drained of blood! . . . The concealed lust of revenge, miserable envy become *master*! Everything wretched, inwardly ailing, and full of ignoble feelings, the whole Ghetto-world of souls, was in a trice *uppermost*! One only needs to read anyone of the Christian agitators—St. Augustine, for instance, in order to realise, in order to *smell*, what filthy fellows came to the top in this movement. You would deceive yourselves utterly if you supposed that the leaders of the Christian agitation showed any lack of understanding: Ah! They were shrewd, shrewd to the point of holiness were these dear old Fathers of the Church! What they lack is something quite different. Nature neglected them, it forgot to give them a modest dowry of decent, of respectable and of *cleanly* instincts. . . . Between ourselves, they are not even men. If Islam despises Christianity, it is justified a thousand times over; for Islam presupposes men.

60

Christianity destroyed the harvest we might have reaped from the culture of antiquity, later it also destroyed our harvest of the culture of Islam. The wonderful Moorish world of Spanish culture, which in its essence is more closely related to *us*, and which appeals more to our sense and taste than Rome and Greece, was *trampled to death* (I do not say by what kind of feet), why? Because it owed its origin to noble, to manly instincts, because it said yea to life, even that life so full of the rare and refined luxuries of the Moors! . . . Later on the Crusaders waged war upon something before which it would have been more seemly in them to grovel in the dust, a culture, beside which even our nineteenth century would seem very poor and very "senile." Of course they wanted booty: the Orient was rich. . . . For goodness' sake let us forget our prejudices! Crusades—superior piracy, that is all! German nobility—that is to say, a Viking nobility at bottom, was in its element in such wars: the Church was only too well aware of how German nobility is to be won. . . . German nobility was always the "Swiss Guard" of the Church, always at the service of all the bad instincts of the Church; but it was *well paid for it all.* . . . Fancy the Church having waged its deadly war upon everything noble on earth, precisely with the help of German swords, German blood and courage! A host of painful *questions* might be raised on this point. German nobility scarcely takes a place in the history o higher culture: the reason of this is obvious Christianity, alcohol—the two *great* means of corruption. As a matter of fact, choice ought to be just as much out of the question between Islam and Christianity, as between an Arab and a Jew. The decision is already self-evident; nobody is at liberty to exercise a choice in this matter. A man is either of the Chandala or he is *not*. . . . "War with Rome to the knife! Peace and friendship with Islam": this is what that great free spirit, that genius among German emperors, Frederick the Second, not only felt but also *did*. What? Must a German in the first place be a genius, a free-spirit, in order to have *decent* feelings? I cannot understand how a German was ever able to have *Christian* feelings.

61

Here it is necessary to revive a memory which will be a hundred times more painful to Germans. The Germans have destroyed the last great harvest of culture which was to be garnered for Europe, it destroyed the *Renaissance*. Does anybody at last understand, *will* anybody understand what the Renaissance was? *The transvaluation of Christian values*, the attempt undertaken with all means, all instincts and all genius to make the *opposite* values, the *noble* values triumph. . . . Hitherto there has been only *this* great war: there has never yet been a more decisive question than the Renaissance, *my* question is the question of the Renaissance: there has never been a more fundamental, a more direct and a more severe *attack*, delivered with a whole front upon the centre of the foe. To attack at the decisive quarter, at the very seat of Christianity, and there to place *noble* values on the throne, that is to say, to *introduce* them into the instincts, into the most fundamental needs and desires of those sitting there. . . . I see before me a possibility perfectly magic in its charm and glorious colouring —it seems to me to scintillate with all the quivering grandeur of refined beauty, that there is an art at work within it which is so divine, so infernally divine, that one might seek through millenniums in vain for another such possibility; I see a spectacle so rich in meaning and so wonderfully para-doxical to boot, that it would be enough to make all the gods of Olympus rock with immortal laughter, *Caesar Borgia as Pope*. . . . Do you understand me? . . . Very well then, this would have been the triumph which *I* alone am longing for today: this would have *swept* Christianity *away*! What happened? A German monk, Luther, came to Rome. This monk, with all the vindictive instincts of an abortive priest in his body, foamed with rage over the Renaissance in Rome. . . . Instead of, with the profoundest gratitude, understanding the vast miracle that had taken place, the overcoming of Christianity at its *headquarters*, the fire of his hate knew only how to draw fresh fuel from this spectacle. A religious man thinks only of himself. Luther saw the corruption of the Papacy when the very reverse stared him in the face: the old corruption, the *peccatum originale*, Christianity *no* longer sat upon the Papal chair! But Life! The triumph of Life! The great yea to all lofty, beautiful and daring things! . . . And Luther reinstated the Church; he attacked it. The Renaissance thus became an event without meaning, a great *in vain*! Ah these Germans, what have they not cost us already! In vain—this has always been the achievement of the Germans. The Reformation, Leibniz, Kant and so-called German philosophy, the Wars of Liberation, the Empire—in each case are in vain for something which had already existed, for something which *cannot be recovered*. . . . I confess it, these Germans are my enemies: I despise every sort of uncleanliness in concepts and valuations in them, every kind of cowardice in the face of every honest yea or nay. For almost one thousand years, now, they have tangled and confused everything they have laid their hands on; they have on their conscience all the half-measures, all the three-eighth measures of which Europe is sick; they also have the most unclean, the most incurable, and the most irrefutable kind of Christianity—Protestantism— on their conscience. . . . If we shall never be able to get rid of Christianity, the *Germans* will be to blame.

62

—With this I will now conclude and pronounce my judgement. I *condemn* Christianity and confront it with the most terrible accusation that an accuser has ever had in his mouth. To my mind it is the greatest of all conceivable corruptions, it has had the will to the last imaginable corruption. The Christian Church allowed, nothing to escape from its corruption; it converted every value into its opposite, every truth into a lie, and every honest impulse into an ignominy of the soul. Let anyone dare to speak to me of its humanitarian blessings! To *abolish* any sort of distress was opposed to its profoundest interests; its very existence depended on states of distress; it created states of distress in order to make itself immortal. . . . The cancer germ of sin, for instance: the Church was the first to enrich mankind with this misery! The "equality of souls before God," this falsehood, this *pretext* for the *rancunes* of all the base-minded, this anarchist bomb of a concept, which has ultimately become the revolution, the modern idea, the principle of decay of the whole of social order, this is *Christian* dynamite. . . . The "humanitarian" blessings of Christianity! To breed a self-contradiction, an art of self-profanation, a will to lie at any price, an aversion, a contempt of all good and honest instincts out of *humanitas*! Is this what you call the blessings of Christianity? Parasitism as the only method of the Church; sucking all the blood, all the love, all the hope of life out of mankind with anaemic and sacred ideals. A "Beyond" as the will to deny all reality; the cross as the trade-mark of the most subterranean form of conspiracy that has ever existed, against health, beauty, well-constitutedness, bravery, intellect, kindliness of soul, *against Life itself.* . . .

This eternal accusation against Christianity I would fain write on all walls, wherever there are walls, I have letters with which I can make even the blind see. . . . I call Christianity the one great curse, the one enormous and innermost perversion, the one great instinct of revenge, for which no means are too venomous, too underhand, too underground and too *petty*, I call it the one immortal blemish of mankind. . . .

And *time* is reckoned from the *dies nefastus* upon which this fatality came into being—from the first day of Christianity! *Why not rather from its last day? From today? Transvaluation of All Values!* . . .

ECCE HOMO

TRANSLATED BY
ANTHONY M. LUDOVICI

CONTENTS

ECCE HOMO

PREFACE

1

As it is my intention within a very short time to confront my fellow-men with the very greatest demand that has ever yet been made upon them, it seems to me above all necessary to declare here who and what I am. As a matter of fact, this ought to be pretty well known already, for I have not "held my tongue" about myself. But the disparity which obtains between the greatness of my task and the smallness of my contemporaries, is revealed by the fact that people have neither heard me nor yet seen me. I live on my own self-made credit, and it is probably only a prejudice to suppose that I am alive at all. I do but require to speak to anyone of the scholars who come to the Ober-Engadine in the summer in order to convince myself that I am *not* alive. . . . Under these circumstances, it is a duty—and one against which my customary reserve, and to a still greater degree the pride of my instincts, rebel—to say: *Listen! For I am such and such a person. For Heaven's sake do not confound me with anyone else!*

2

I am, for instance, in no wise a bogey man, or moral monster. On the contrary, I am the very opposite in nature to the kind of man that has been honoured hitherto as virtuous. Between ourselves, it seems to me that this is precisely a matter on which I may feel proud. I am a disciple of the philosopher Dionysus, and I would prefer to be even a satyr than a saint. But just read this book! Maybe I have here succeeded in expressing this contrast in a cheerful and at the same time sympathetic manner—maybe this is the only purpose of the present work.

The very last thing I should promise to accomplish would be to "improve" mankind. I do not set up any new idols; may old idols only learn what it costs to have legs of clay. To overthrow idols (idols is the name I give to all ideals) is much more like my business. In proportion as an ideal world has been falsely assumed, reality has been robbed of its value, its meaning, and its truthfulness. . . . The "true world" and the "apparent world" in plain English, the fictitious world and reality. . . . Hitherto the *lie* of the ideal has been the curse of reality; by means of it the very source of mankind's instincts has become mendacious and false; so much so that those values have come to be worshipped which are the exact *opposite* of the ones which would ensure man's prosperity, his future, and his great right to a future.

3

He who knows how to breathe in the air of my writings is conscious that it is the air of the heights, that it is bracing. A man must be built for it, otherwise the chances are that it will chill him. The ice is near, the loneliness is terrible—but how serenely everything lies in the sunshine! How freely one can breathe! How much, one feels, lies beneath one! Philosophy, as I have understood it hitherto, is a voluntary retirement into regions of ice and mountain peaks—the seeking-out of everything strange and questionable in existence, everything upon which, hitherto, morality has set its ban. Through long experience, derived from such wanderings in forbidden country, I acquired an opinion very different from that which may seem generally desirable, of the causes which hitherto have led to men's moralising and idealising. The secret history of philosophers, the psychology of their great names, was revealed to me. How much truth can a certain mind endure; how much truth can it dare? These questions became for me ever more and more the actual test of values. Error (the belief in the ideal) is not blindness; error is cowardice. . . . Every conquest, every step forward in knowledge, is the outcome of courage, of hardness towards one's self, of cleanliness towards one's self. I do not refute ideals; all I do is to draw on my gloves in their presence. . . . *Nitimur in vetitum*; with this device my philosophy will one day be victorious; for that which has hitherto been most stringently forbidden is, without exception, Truth.

4

In my lifework, my *Zarathustra* holds a place apart. With it, I gave my fellow-men the greatest gift that has ever been bestowed upon them. This book, the voice of which speaks out across the ages, is not only the loftiest book on earth, literally the book of mountain air—the whole phenomenon, mankind, lies at an incalculable distance beneath it—but it is also the deepest book, born of the inmost abundance of truth; an inexhaustible well, into which no pitcher can be lowered without coming up again laden with gold and with goodness. Here it is not a "prophet" who speaks, one of those gruesome hybrids of sickness and Will to Power, whom men call founders of religions. If a man would not do a sad wrong to his wisdom, he must above all give proper heed to the tones—the halcyonic tones—that fall from the lips of Zarathustra:

> The most silent words are harbingers of the storm; thoughts that come on dove's feet lead the world.
> The figs fall from the trees; they are good and sweet, and, when they fall, their red skins are rent.
> A north wind am I unto ripe figs.
> Thus, like figs, do these precepts drop down to you, my friends; now drink their juice and their sweet pulp.
> It is autumn all around, and clear sky, and afternoon.

No fanatic speaks to you here; this is not a "sermon"; no faith is demanded in these pages. From out an infinite treasure of light and well of joy, drop by drop, my words fall out—a slow and gentle gait is the cadence of these discourses. Such things can reach only the most elect; it is a rare privilege to be a listener here; not everyone who likes can have ears to hear Zarathustra. Is not Zarathustra, because of these things, a *seducer*? . . . But what, indeed, does he himself say, when for the first time he goes back to his solitude? Just the reverse of that which any "Sage," "Saint," "Saviour of the world," and other decadent would say. . . . Not only his words, but he himself is other than they.

> Alone do I now go, my disciples! Get ye also hence, and alone! Thus would I have it.
> Verily, I beseech you: take your leave of me and arm yourselves against Zarathustra! And better still, be ashamed of him! Maybe he hath deceived you.
> The knight of knowledge must be able not only to love his enemies, but also to hate his friends.

The man who remaineth a pupil requiteth his teacher but ill. And why would ye not pluck at my wreath?

Ye honour me; but what if your reverence should one day break down? Take heed, lest a statue crush you.

Ye say ye believe in Zarathustra? But of what account is Zarathustra? Ye are my believers: but of what account are all believers?

Ye had not yet sought yourselves when ye found me. Thus do all believers; therefore is all believing worth so little.

Now I bid you lose me and find yourselves; and only when ye have all denied me will I come back unto you.

FRIEDRICH NIETZSCHE

ON THIS PERFECT DAY, WHEN EVERYTHING IS RIPENING, AND NOT ONLY the grapes are getting brown, a ray of sunshine has fallen on my life: I looked behind me, I looked before me, and never have I seen so many good things all at once. Not in vain have I buried my four-and-fortieth year today; I had the *right* to bury it—that in it which still had life, has been saved and is immortal. The first book of the *Transvaluation of All Values*, *The Songs of Zarathustra*, *The Twilight of the Idols*, my attempt to philosophise with the hammer—all these things are the gift of this year, and even of its last quarter. *How could I help being thankful to the whole of my life?*

That is why I am now going to tell myself the story of my life.

WHY I AM SO WISE

1

THE HAPPINESS OF MY EXISTENCE, ITS UNIQUE CHARACTER PERHAPS, consists in its fatefulness: to speak in a riddle, as my own father I am already dead, as my own mother I still live and grow old. This double origin, taken as it were from the highest and lowest rungs of the ladder of life, at once a decadent and a beginning, this, if anything, explains that neutrality, that freedom from partisanship in regard to the general problem of existence, which perhaps distinguishes me. To the first indications of ascending or of descending life my nostrils are more sensitive than those of any man that has yet lived. In this domain I am a master to my backbone—I know both sides, for I am both sides. My father died in his six-and-thirtieth year: he was delicate, lovable, and morbid, like one who is preordained to pay simply a flying visit—a gracious reminder of life rather than life itself. In the same year that his life declined mine also declined: in my six-and-thirtieth year I reached the lowest point in my vitality—I still lived, but my eyes could distinguish nothing that lay three paces away from me. At that time—it was the year 1879—I resigned my professorship at Bâle, lived through the summer like a shadow in St. Moritz, and spent the following winter, the most sunless of my life, like a shadow in Naumburg. This was my lowest ebb. During this period I wrote *The Wanderer and His Shadow*. Without a doubt I was conversant with shadows then. The winter that followed, my first winter in Genoa, brought forth that sweetness and spirituality which is almost inseparable from extreme poverty of blood and muscle, in the shape of *The Dawn of Day*. The perfect lucidity and cheerfulness, the intellectual exuberance even, that this work reflects, coincides,

457

in my case, not only with the most profound physiological weakness, but also with an excess of suffering. In the midst of the agony of a headache which lasted three days, accompanied by violent nausea, I was possessed of most singular dialectical clearness, and in absolutely cold blood I then thought out things, for which, in my more healthy moments, I am not enough of a climber, not sufficiently subtle, not sufficiently cold. My readers perhaps know to what extent I consider dialectic a symptom of decadence, as, for instance, in the most famous of all cases—the case of Socrates. All the morbid disturbances of the intellect, even that semi-stupor which accompanies fever, have, unto this day, remained completely unknown to me; and for my first information concerning their nature and frequency, I was obliged to have recourse to the learned works which have been compiled on the subject. My circulation is slow. No one has ever been able to detect fever in me. A doctor who treated me for some time as a nerve patient finally declared: "No! There is nothing wrong with your nerves, it is simply I who am nervous." It has been absolutely impossible to ascertain any local degeneration in me, nor any organic stomach trouble, however much I may have suffered from profound weakness of the gastric system as the result of general exhaustion. Even my eye trouble, which sometimes approached so parlously near to blindness, was only an effect and not a cause; for, whenever my general vital condition improved, my power of vision also increased. Having admitted all this, do I need to say that I am experienced in questions of decadence? I know them inside and out. Even that filigree art of prehension and comprehension in general, that feeling for delicate shades of difference, that psychology of "seeing through brick walls," and whatever else I may be able to do, was first learnt then, and is the specific gift of that period during which everything in me was subtilised—observation itself, together with all the organs of observation. To look upon healthier concepts and values from the standpoint of the sick, and conversely to look down upon the secret work of the instincts of decadence from the standpoint of him who is laden and self-reliant with the richness of life—this has been my longest exercise, my principal experience. If in anything at all, it was in this that I became a master. Today my hand knows the trick, I now have the knack of reversing perspectives: the first reason perhaps why a *Transvaluation of All Values* has been possible to me alone.

2

For, apart from the fact that I am a decadent, I am also the reverse of such a creature. Among other things my proof of this is, that I always instinctively select the proper remedy when my spiritual or bodily health is low; whereas the decadent, as such, invariably chooses those remedies which are bad for him. As a whole I was sound, but in certain details I was a decadent. That energy with which I sentenced myself to absolute solitude, and to a severance from all those conditions in life to which I had grown accustomed; my discipline of myself, and my refusal to allow myself to be pampered, to be tended hand and foot, and to be doctored—all this betrays the absolute certainty of my instincts respecting what at that time was most needful to me. I placed myself in my own hands, I restored myself to health: the first condition of success in such an undertaking, as every physiologist will admit, is that at bottom a man should be sound. An intrinsically morbid nature cannot become healthy. On the other hand, to an intrinsically sound nature, illness may even constitute a powerful stimulus to life, to a surplus of life. It is in this light that I now regard the long period of illness that I endured: it seemed as if I had discovered life afresh, my own self included. I tasted all good things and even trifles in a way in which it was not easy for others to taste them—out of my Will to Health and to Life I made my philosophy. . . . For this should be thoroughly understood; it was during those years in which my vitality reached its lowest point that I ceased from being a pessimist: the instinct of self-recovery forbade my holding to a philosophy of poverty and desperation. Now, by what signs are Nature's lucky strokes recognised among men? They are recognised by the fact that any such lucky stroke gladdens our senses; that he is carved from one integral block, which is hard, sweet, and fragrant as well. He enjoys that only which is good for him; his pleasure, his desire, ceases when the limits of that which is good for him are overstepped. He divines remedies for injuries; he knows how to turn serious accidents to his own advantage; that which does not kill him makes him stronger. He instinctively gathers his material from all he sees, hears, and experiences. He is a selective principle; he rejects much. He is always in his own company, whether his intercourse be with books, with men, or with natural scenery; he honours the things he chooses, the things he acknowledges, the things he trusts. He reacts slowly to all kinds of stimuli, with that tardiness which long caution and deliberate pride have bred in him—he tests the approaching stimulus; he would not dream of meeting it halfway. He believes neither in "ill-luck" nor "guilt"; he can digest himself and others; he knows how to forget—he is strong enough to make everything turn to his own advantage.

Lo then! I am the very reverse of a decadent, for he whom I have just described is none other than myself.

3

This double thread of experiences, this means of access to two worlds that seem so far asunder, finds in every detail its counterpart in my own nature—I am my own complement: I have a "second" sight, as well as a first. And perhaps I also have a third sight. By the very nature of my origin I was allowed an outlook beyond all merely local, merely national and limited horizons; it required no effort on my part to be a "good European." On the other hand, I am perhaps more German than modern Germans—mere Imperial Germans—can hope to be—I, the last antipolitical German. Be this as it may, my ancestors were Polish noblemen: it is owing to them that I have so much race instinct in my blood—who knows? Perhaps even the *liberum veto*.[1] When I think of the number of times in my travells that I have been accosted as a Pole, even by Poles themselves, and how seldom I have been taken for a German, it seems to me as if I belonged to those only who have a sprinkling of German in them. But my mother, Franziska Oehler, is at any rate something very German; as is also my paternal grandmother, Erdmuthe Krause. The latter spent the whole of her youth in good old Weimar, not without coming into contact with Goethe's circle. Her brother, Krause, the Professor of Theology in Königsberg, was called to the post of General Superintendent at Weimar after Herder's death. It is not unlikely that her mother, my great grandmother, is mentioned in young Goethe's diary under the name of "Muthgen." She married twice, and her second husband was Superintendent Nietzsche of Eilenburg. In 1813, the year of the great war, when Napoleon with his general staff entered Eilenburg on the 10th of October, she gave birth to a son. As a daughter of Saxony she was a great admirer of Napoleon, and maybe I am so still. My father, born in 1813, died in 1849. Previous to taking over the pastorship of the parish of Röcken, not far from Lützen, he lived for some years at the Castle of Altenburg, where he had charge of the education of the four princesses. His pupils are the Queen of Hanover, the Grand-Duchess Constantine, the Grand-Duchess of Oldenburg, and the Princess Theresa of Saxe-Altenburg. He was full of loyal respect for the Prussian King, Frederick William the Fourth, from whom he obtained his living at Röcken; the events of 1848 saddened him extremely. As I was born on the 15th of October, the birthday of the king above mentioned, I naturally received the Hohenzollern names of Frederick William. There was at all events one advantage in the choice of this day: my birthday throughout the whole of my childhood was a day of public rejoicing. I regard it as a great privilege to have had such a father: it even seems to me that this embraces all that I can claim in the matter of privileges—life, the great yea to life, excepted. What I owe to him above all is this, that I do not need any special intention, but merely a little patience, in order involuntarily to enter a world of higher and more delicate things. There I am at home, there alone does my inmost passion become free. The fact that I had to pay for this privilege almost with my life, certainly does not make it a bad bargain. In order to understand even a little of my *Zarathustra*, perhaps a man must be situated and constituted very much as I am myself—with one foot beyond the realm of the living.

4

I have never understood the art of arousing ill-feeling against myself—this is also something for which I have to thank my incomparable father—even when it seemed to me highly desirable to do so. However un-Christian it may seem, I do not even bear any ill-feeling towards myself. Turn my life about as you may, you will find but seldom—perhaps indeed only once— any trace of someone's having shown me ill-will. You might perhaps discover, however, too many traces of *good*-will. . . . My experiences even with those on whom every other man has burnt his fingers, speak without exception in their favour; I tame every bear, I can make even clowns behave decently. During the seven years in which I taught Greek to the sixth form of the College at Bâle, I never had occasion to administer a punishment; the laziest youths were diligent in my class. The unexpected has always found me equal to it; I must be unprepared in order to keep my self-command. Whatever the instrument was, even if it were as out of tune as the instrument "man" can possibly be—it was only when I was ill that I could not succeed in making it express something that was worth hearing. And how often have I not been told by the "instruments" themselves, that they had never before heard their voices express such beautiful things. . . . This was said to me most delightfully perhaps by that young fellow Heinrich von Stein, who died at such an unpardonably early age, and who, after having considerately asked leave to do so, once appeared in Sils-Maria for a three days' sojourn, telling everybody there that it was *not* for the Engadine that he had come. This excellent person, who with all the impetuous simplicity of a young Prussian nobleman, had waded deep into the swamp of Wagnerism (and into that of Dühringism[2] into the bargain!), seemed almost transformed during these three days by a hurricane of freedom, like one who has been suddenly raised to his full height and given wings. Again and again I said to him that this was all owing to the splendid air; everybody felt the same—one could not stand 6000 feet above Bayreuth for nothing—but he would not believe me. . . . Be this as it may, if I have been the victim of many a small or even great offence, it was not "will," and least of all *ill*-will that actuated the offenders; but rather, as I have already suggested, it was goodwill, the cause of no small amount of mischief in my life, about which I had to complain. My experience gave me a right to feel suspicious in regard to all so-called "unselfish" instincts, in regard to the whole of "neighbourly love" which is ever ready and waiting with deeds or with advice. To me it seems that these instincts are a sign of weakness, they are an example of the inability to withstand a stimulus—it is only among decadents that this *pity* is called a virtue. What I reproach the pitiful with is, that they are too ready to forget shame, reverence, and the delicacy of feeling which knows how to keep at a distance; they do not remember that this gushing pity stinks of the mob, and that it is next of kin to bad manners—that pitiful hands may be thrust with results fatally destructive into a great destiny, into a lonely and wounded retirement, and into the privileges with which great guilt endows one. The overcoming of pity I reckon among the noble virtues. In the *Temptation of Zarathustra* I have imagined a case, in which a great cry of distress reaches his ears, in which pity swoops down upon him like a last sin, and would make him break faith with himself. To remain one's own master in such circumstances, to keep the sublimity of one's mission pure in such cases—pure from the many ignoble and more short-sighted impulses which come into play in so-called unselfish actions—this is the rub, the last test perhaps which a Zarathustra has to undergo—the actual proof of his power.

5

In yet another respect I am no more than my father over again, and as it were the continuation of his life after an all-too-early death. Like every man who has never been able to meet his equal, and unto whom the concept "retaliation" is just as incomprehensible as the notion of "equal rights," I have forbidden myself the use of any sort of measure of security or protection—and also, of course, of defence and "justification"—in all cases in which I have been made the victim either of trifling or even *very great* foolishness. My form of retaliation consists in this: as soon as possible to set a piece of cleverness at the heels of an act of stupidity; by this means perhaps it may still be possible to overtake it. To speak in a parable: I dispatch a pot of jam in order to get rid of a bitter experience. . . . Let anybody only give me offence, I shall "retaliate," he can be quite sure of that: before long I discover an opportunity of expressing my thanks to the "offender" (among other things even for the offence)—or of *asking* him for something, which can be more courteous even than giving. It also seems to me that the rudest word, the rudest letter, is more good-natured, more straightforward, than silence. Those who keep silent are almost always lacking in subtlety and refinement of heart; silence is an objection, to swallow a grievance must necessarily produce a bad temper—it even upsets the stomach. All silent people are dyspeptic. You perceive that I should not like to see rudeness undervalued; it is by far the most *humane* form of contradiction, and, in the midst of modern effeminacy, it is one of our first virtues. If one is sufficiently rich for it, it may even be a joy to be wrong. If a god were to descend to this earth, he would have to do nothing but wrong—to take *guilt*, not punishment, on one's shoulders, is the first proof of divinity.

6

Freedom from resentment and the understanding of the nature of resentment—who knows how very much after all I am indebted to my long illness for these two things? The problem is not exactly simple: a man must have experienced both through his strength and through his weakness. If illness and weakness are to be charged with anything at all, it is with the fact that when they prevail, the very instinct of recovery, which is the instinct of defence and of war in man, becomes decayed. He knows not how to get rid of anything, how to come to terms with anything, and how to cast anything behind him. Everything wounds him. People and things draw importunately near, all experiences strike deep, memory is a gathering wound. To be ill is a sort of resentment in itself. Against this resentment the invalid has only one great remedy—I call it *Russian fatalism*, that fatalism which is free from revolt, and with which the Russian soldier, to whom a campaign proves unbearable, ultimately lays himself down in the snow. To accept nothing more, to undertake nothing more, to absorb nothing more—to cease entirely from reacting. . . . The tremendous sagacity of this fatalism, which does not always imply merely the courage for death, but which in the most dangerous cases may actually constitute a self-preservative measure, amounts to a reduction of activity in the vital functions, the slackening down of which is like a sort of will to hibernate. A few steps farther in this direction we find the fakir, who will sleep for weeks in a tomb. . . . Owing to the fact that one would be used up too quickly if one reacted, one no longer reacts at all: this is the principle. And nothing on earth consumes a man more quickly than the passion of resentment. Mortification, morbid susceptibility, the inability to wreak revenge, the desire and thirst for revenge, the concoction of every sort of poison—this is surely the most injurious manner of reacting which could possibly be conceived by exhausted men. It involves a rapid wasting away of nervous energy, an abnormal increase of detrimental secretions, as, for instance, that of bile into the stomach. To the sick man resentment ought to be more strictly forbidden than anything else—it is *his* special danger: unfortunately, however, it is also his most natural propensity. This was fully grasped by that profound physiologist Buddha. His "religion," which it would be better to call a system of hygiene, in order to avoid confounding it with a creed so wretched as Christianity, depended for its effect upon the triumph over resentment: to make the soul free therefrom was considered the first step towards recovery. "Not through hostility is hostility put to flight; through friendship does hostility end": this stands at the beginning of Buddha's teaching—this is not a precept of morality, but of physiology. Resentment born of weakness is not more deleterious to anybody than it is to the weak man himself—conversely, in the case of that man whose nature is fundamentally a rich one, resentment is a superfluous feeling, a feeling to remain master of which is almost a proof of riches. Those of my readers who know the earnestness with which my philosophy wages war against the feelings of revenge and rancour, even to the extent of attacking the doctrine of "free will" (my conflict with Christianity is only a particular instance of it), will understand why I wish to focus attention upon my own personal attitude and the certainty of my practical instincts precisely in this matter. In my moments of decadence I forbade myself the indulgence of the above feelings, because they were harmful; as soon as my life recovered enough riches and pride, however, I regarded them again as forbidden, but this time because they were *beneath* me. That "Russian fatalism" of which I have spoken manifested itself in me in such a way that for years I held tenaciously to almost insufferable conditions, places, habitations, and companions, once chance had placed them on my path—it was better than changing them, than feeling that they could be changed, than revolting against them. . . . He who stirred me from this fatalism, he who violently tried to shake me into consciousness, seemed to me then a mortal enemy—in point of fact, there was danger of death each time this was done. To regard one's self as a destiny, not to wish one's self "different"—this, in such circumstances, is sagacity itself.

7

War, on the other hand, is something different. At heart I am a warrior. Attacking belongs to my instincts. To *be able to be* an enemy, to *be* an enemy—maybe these things presuppose a strong nature; in any case all strong natures involve these things. Such natures need resistance, consequently they go in search of obstacles: the pathos of aggression belongs of necessity to strength as much as the feelings of revenge and of rancour belong to weakness. Woman, for instance, is revengeful; her weakness involves this passion, just as it involves her susceptibility in the presence of other people's suffering. The strength of the aggressor can be measured by the opposition which he needs; every increase of growth betrays itself by a seeking out of more formidable opponents—or problems: for a philosopher who is combative challenges even problems to a duel. The task is not to overcome opponents in general, but only those opponents against whom one has to summon all one's strength, one's skill, and one's swordsmanship—in fact, opponents who are one's equals. . . . To be one's enemy's equal—this is the first condition of an honourable duel. Where one despises, one cannot wage war. Where one commands, where one sees something *beneath* one, one *ought* not to wage war. My war tactics can be reduced to four principles: First, I attack only things that are triumphant—if necessary I wait until they become triumphant. Secondly, I attack only those things against which I find no allies, against which I stand alone—against which I compromise nobody but myself. . . . I have not yet taken one single step before the public eye, which did not compromise me: that is *my* criterion of a proper mode of action. Thirdly, I never make personal attacks—I use a personality merely as a magnifying-glass, by means of which I render a general, but elusive and scarcely noticeable evil, more apparent. In this way I attacked David Strauss, or rather the success given to a senile book by the cultured classes of Germany—by this means I caught German culture red-handed. In this way I attacked Wagner, or rather the falsity or mongrel instincts of our "culture" which confounds the super-refined with the strong, and the effete with the great. Fourthly, I attack only those things from which all personal differences are excluded, in which any such thing as a background of disagreeable

466 → ECCE HOMO

experiences is lacking. On the contrary, attacking is to me a proof of good-will and, in certain circumstances, of gratitude. By means of it, I do honour to a thing, I distinguish a thing; whether I associate my name with that of an institution or a person, by being *against* or *for* either, is all the same to me. If I wage war against Christianity, I feel justified in doing so, because in that quarter I have met with no fatal experiences and difficulties —the most earnest Christians have always been kindly disposed to me. I, personally, the most essential opponent of Christianity, am far from hold-ing the individual responsible for what is the fatality of long ages.

8

May I be allowed to hazard a suggestion concerning one last trait in my character, which in my intercourse with other men has led me into some difficulties? I am gifted with a sense of cleanliness the keenness of which is phenomenal; so much so, that I can ascertain physiologically—that is to say, smell—the proximity, nay, the inmost core, the "entrails" of every human soul. . . . This sensitiveness of mine is furnished with psychological antennae, wherewith I feel and grasp every secret: the quality of concealed filth lying at the base of many a human character which may be the inevi-table outcome of base blood, and which education may have veneered, is revealed to me at the first glance. If my observation has been correct, such people, whom my sense of cleanliness rejects, also become conscious, on their part, of the cautiousness to which my loathing prompts me: and this does not make them any more fragrant. . . . In keeping with a cus-tom which I have long observed—pure habits and honesty towards myself are among the first conditions of my existence, I would die in unclean surroundings—I swim, bathe, and splash about, as it were, incessantly in water, in any kind of perfectly transparent and shining element. That is why my relations with my fellows try my patience to no small extent; my humanity does not consist in the fact that I understand the feelings of my fellows, but that I can endure to understand. . . . My humanity is a perpetual process of self-mastery. But I need solitude—that is to say, recov-ery, return to myself, the breathing of free, crisp, bracing air. . . . The whole of my *Zarathustra* is a dithyramb in honour of solitude, or, if I have been understood, in honour of purity. Thank Heaven, it is not in honour of "pure foolery!"[3] He who has an eye for colour will call him a diamond. The loathing of mankind, of the rabble, was always my greatest danger. . . . Would you hearken to the words spoken by Zarathustra concerning deliv-erance from loathing?

What forsooth hath come unto me? How did I deliver myself from loathing? Who hath made mine eye younger? How did I soar to the height, where there are no more rabble sitting about the well?

Did my very loathing forge me wings and the strength to scent fountains afar off? Verily to the loftiest heights did I need to fly, to find once more the spring of joyfulness.

Oh, I found it, my brethren! Up here, on the loftiest height, the spring of joyfulness gusheth forth for me. And there is a life at the well of which no rabble can drink with you.

Almost too fiercely dost thou rush, for me, thou spring of joyfulness! And ofttimes dost thou empty the pitcher again in trying to fill it.

And yet must I learn to draw near thee more humbly. Far too eagerly doth my heart jump to meet thee.

My heart, whereon my summer burneth, my short, hot, melancholy, over-blessed summer: how my summer heart yearneth for thy coolness!

Farewell, the lingering affliction of my spring! Past is the wickedness of my snowflakes in June! Summer have I become entirely, and summer noontide!

A summer in the loftiest heights, with cold springs and blessed stillness: oh come, my friends, that the stillness may wax even more blessed!

For this is our height and our home: too high and steep is our dwelling for all the unclean and their appetites.

Do but cast your pure eyes into the well of my joyfulness, my friends! How could it thus become muddy! It will laugh back at you with its purity.

On the tree called Future do we build our nest: eagles shall bring food in their beaks unto us lonely ones!

Verily not the food whereof the unclean might partake. They would think they ate fire and would burn their mouths!

Verily, no abodes for the unclean do we here hold in readiness! To their bodies our happiness would seem an ice-cavern, and to their spirits also!

And like strong winds will we live above them, neighbours to the eagles, companions of the snow, and playmates of the sun: thus do strong winds live.

And like a wind shall I one day blow amidst them, and take away
their soul's breath with my spirit: thus my future willeth it.

Verily, a strong wind is Zarathustra to all low lands; and this is his
counsel to his foes and to all those who spit and spew: "Beware
of spitting against the wind!"

WHY I AM SO CLEVER

1

WHY DO I KNOW MORE THINGS THAN OTHER PEOPLE? WHY, IN FACT, AM I
so clever? I have never pondered over questions that are not questions.
I have never squandered my strength. Of actual religious difficulties, for
instance, I have no experience. I have never known what it is to feel
"sinful." In the same way I completely lack any reliable criterion for ascertaining what constitutes a prick of conscience: from all accounts a prick
of conscience does not seem to be a very estimable thing. . . . Once it was
done I should hate to leave an action of mine in the lurch; I should prefer
completely to omit the evil outcome, the consequences, from the problem
concerning the value of an action. In the face of evil consequences one is
too ready to lose the proper standpoint from which one's deed ought to
be considered. A prick of conscience strikes me as a sort of "evil eye."
Something that has failed should be honoured all the more jealously,
precisely because it has failed—this is much more in keeping with my
morality. "God," "the immortality of the soul," "salvation," a "beyond"—to
all these notions, even as a child, I never paid any attention whatsoever,
nor did I waste any time upon them—maybe I was never *naïf* enough for
that? I am quite unacquainted with atheism as a result, and still less as an
event in my life: in me it is inborn, instinctive. I am too inquisitive, too
incredulous, too high spirited, to be satisfied with such a palpably clumsy
solution of things. God is a too palpably clumsy solution of things;
a solution which shows a lack of delicacy towards us thinkers—at bottom
He is really no more than a coarse and rude *prohibition* of us: ye shall not
think! . . . I am much more interested in another question—a question

upon which the "salvation of humanity" depends to a far greater degree than it does upon any piece of theological curiosity: I refer to nutrition. For ordinary purposes, it may be formulated as follows: "How precisely must *thou* feed thyself in order to attain to thy maximum of power, or *virtù* in the Renaissance style—of virtue free from moralic acid?" My experiences in regard to this matter have been as bad as they possibly could be; I am surprised that I set myself this question so late in life, and that it took me so long to draw "rational" conclusions from my experiences. Only the absolute worthlessness of German culture—its "idealism"—can to some extent explain how it was that precisely in this matter I was so backward that my ignorance was almost saintly. This "culture," which from first to last teaches one to lose sight of actual things and to hunt after thoroughly problematic and so-called ideal aims, as, for instance, "classical culture" —as if it were not hopeless from the start to try to unite "classical" and "German" in one concept. It is even a little comical—try and imagine a "classically cultured" citizen of Leipzig! Indeed, I can say, that up to a very mature age, my food was entirely bad—expressed morally, it was "impersonal," "selfless," "altruistic," to the glory of cooks and all other fellow-Christians. It was through the cooking in vogue at Leipzig, for instance, together with my first study of Schopenhauer (1865), that I earnestly renounced my "Will to Live." To spoil one's stomach by absorbing insufficient nourishment—this problem seemed to my mind solved with admirable felicity by the above-mentioned cookery. (It is said that in the year 1866 changes were introduced into this department.) But as to German cookery in general—what has it not got on its conscience! Soup *before* the meal (still called *alla tedesca* in the Venetian cookery books of the sixteenth century); meat boiled to shreds, vegetables cooked with fat and flour; the degeneration of pastries into paperweights! And, if you add thereto the absolutely bestial postprandial drinking habits of the *ancients*, and not alone of the ancient Germans, you will understand where German intellect took its origin—that is to say, in sadly disordered intestines. . . . German intellect is indigestion; it can assimilate nothing. But even English diet, which in comparison with German, and indeed with French alimentation, seems to me to constitute a "return to Nature"—that is to say, to cannibalism—is profoundly opposed to my own instincts. It seems to me to give the intellect heavy feet, in fact, Englishwomen's feet. . . . The best cooking is that of Piedmont. Alcoholic drinks do not agree with me; a single glass of wine or beer a day is amply sufficient to turn life into a valley of tears for me; in Munich live my antipodes. Although I admit that this knowledge came to me somewhat late, it already formed part of my experience even as a child. As a boy I believed that the drinking of wine and the smoking of tobacco were at first but the vanities of youths, and later merely bad habits. Maybe the poor wine of Naumburg was partly responsible for this poor opinion of wine in general. In order to believe that wine was exhilarating, I should have had to be a Christian—in other words, I should have had to believe in what, to my mind, is an absurdity. Strange to say, whereas small quantities of alcohol, taken with plenty of water, succeed in making me feel out of sorts, large quantities turn me almost into a rollicking tar. Even as a boy I showed my bravado in this respect. To compose a long Latin essay in one night, to revise and recopy it, to aspire with my pen to emulating the exactitude and the terseness of my model, Sallust, and to pour a few very strong grogs over it all—this mode of procedure, while I was a pupil at the venerable old school of Pforta, was not in the least out of keeping with my physiology, nor perhaps with that of Sallust, however much it may have been alien to dignified Pforta. Later on, towards the middle of my life, I grew more and more opposed to alcoholic drinks: I, an opponent of vegetarianism, who have experienced what vegetarianism is—just as Wagner, who converted me back to meat, experienced it—cannot with sufficient earnestness advise all more *spiritual* natures to abstain absolutely from alcohol. Water answers the purpose. . . . I have a predilection in favour of those places where in all directions one has opportunities of drinking from running brooks (Nice, Turin, Sils). *In vino veritas*: it seems that here once more I am at variance with the rest of the world about the concept "Truth"—with me spirit moves on the face of the waters. . . . Here are a few more indications as to my morality. A heavy meal is digested more easily than an inadequate one. The first principle of a good digestion is that the stomach should become active as a whole. A man ought, therefore, to know the size of his stomach. For the same reasons all those interminable meals, which I call interrupted sacrificial feasts, and which are to be had at any table d'hôte, are strongly to be deprecated. Nothing should be eaten between meals, coffee should be given up—coffee makes one gloomy. Tea is beneficial only in the morning. It should be taken in small quantities, but very strong. It may be very harmful, and indispose you for the whole day, if it be taken the least bit too weak. Everybody has his own standard in this matter, often between the narrowest and most delicate limits. In an enervating climate tea is not a good beverage with which to start the day: an hour before taking it an excellent thing is to drink a cup of thick cocoa, freed from oil. Remain seated as little as possible, put no trust in any thought that is not born in the open, to the accompaniment of free bodily motion—nor in one in which even the muscles do not celebrate a feast. All prejudices take their origin in the intestines. A sedentary life, as I have already said elsewhere, is the real sin against the Holy Spirit.

2

To the question of nutrition, that of locality and climate is next of kin. Nobody is so constituted as to be able to live everywhere and anywhere; and he who has great duties to perform, which lay claim to all his strength, has, in this respect, a very limited choice. The influence of climate upon the bodily functions, affecting their acceleration or retardation, extends so far, that a blunder in the choice of locality and climate is able not only to alienate a man from his actual duty, but also to withhold it from him altogether, so that he never even comes face to face with it. Animal vigour never acquires enough strength in him in order to reach that pitch of artistic freedom which makes his own soul whisper to him: I, alone, can do that. . . . Ever so slight a tendency to laziness in the intestines, once it has become a habit, is quite sufficient to make something mediocre, something "German" out of a genius; the climate of Germany, alone, is enough to discourage the strongest and most heroically disposed intestines. The tempo of the body's functions is closely bound up with the agility or the clumsiness of the spirit's feet; spirit itself is indeed only a form of these organic functions. Let anybody make a list of the places in which men of great intellect have been found, and are still found; where wit, subtlety, and malice constitute happiness; where genius is almost necessarily at home: all of them rejoice in exceptionally dry air. Paris, Provence, Florence, Jerusalem, Athens—these names prove something, namely: that genius is conditioned by dry air, by a pure sky—that is to say, by rapid organic functions, by the constant and ever-present possibility of procuring for one's self great and even enormous quantities of strength. I have a certain case in mind in which a man of remarkable intellect and independent spirit became a narrow, craven specialist and a grumpy old crank, simply owing to a lack of subtlety in his instinct for climate. And I myself might have been an example of the same thing, if illness had not compelled me to reason, and to reflect upon reason realistically. Now that I have learnt through long practise to read the effects of climatic and meteorological influences, from my own body, as though from a very delicate and reliable instrument, and that I am able to calculate the change in degrees of atmospheric moisture by means of physiological observations upon myself, even on so short a journey as that from Turin to Milan; I think with horror of the ghastly fact that my whole life, until the last ten years—the most perilous years—has always been spent in the wrong, and what to me ought to have been the most forbidden, places. Naumburg, Pforta, Thuringia in general, Leipzig, Bâle, Venice—so many ill-starred places for a constitution like mine. If I cannot recall one single happy reminiscence of my childhood and youth, it is nonsense to suppose that so-called "moral" causes could account for this—as, for instance, the incontestable fact that I lacked companions that could have satisfied me; for this fact is the same today as it ever was, and it does not prevent me from being cheerful and brave. But it was ignorance in physiological matters—that confounded "Idealism"—that was the real curse of my life. This was the superfluous and foolish element in my existence; something from which nothing could spring, and for which there can be no settlement and no compensation. As the outcome of this "Idealism" I regard all the blunders, the great aberrations of instinct, and the "modest specialisations" which drew me aside from the task of my life; as, for instance, the fact that I became a philologist—why not at least a medical man or anything else which might have opened my eyes? My days at Bâle, the whole of my intellectual routine, including my daily time-table, was an absolutely senseless abuse of extraordinary powers, without the slightest compensation for the strength that I spent, without even a thought of what I was squandering and how its place might be filled. I lacked all subtlety in egoism, all the fostering care of an imperative instinct; I was in a state in which one is ready to regard one's self as anybody's equal, a state of "disinterestedness," a forgetting of one's distance from others—something, in short, for which I can never forgive myself. When I had well-nigh reached the end of my tether, simply because I had almost reached my end, I began to reflect upon the fundamental absurdity of my life—"Idealism." It was *illness* that first brought me to reason.

3

After the choice of nutrition, the choice of climate and locality, the third matter concerning which one must not on any account make a blunder, is the choice of the manner in which one *recuperates one's strength*. Here, again, according to the extent to which a spirit is *sui generis*, the limits of that which he can allow himself—in other words, the limits of that which is beneficial to him—become more and more confined. As far as I in

particular am concerned, *reading* in general belongs to my means of recuperation; consequently it belongs to that which rids me of myself, to that
which enables me to wander in strange sciences and strange souls—to
that, in fact, about which I am no longer in earnest. Indeed, it is while
reading that I recover from *my* earnestness. During the time that I am
deeply absorbed in my work, no books are found within my reach; it would
never occur to me to allow anyone to speak or even to think in my presence. For that is what reading would mean. . . . Has anyone ever actually
noticed, that, during the period of profound tension to which the state of
pregnancy condemns not only the mind, but also, at bottom, the whole
organism, accident and every kind of external stimulus acts too acutely
and strikes too deep? Accident and external stimuli must, as far as possible, be avoided: a sort of walling-of-one's-self-in is one of the primary
instinctive precautions of spiritual pregnancy. Shall I allow a strange
thought to steal secretly over the wall? For that is what reading would
mean. . . . The periods of work and fruitfulness are followed by periods
of recuperation: come hither, ye delightful, intellectual, intelligent books!
Shall I read German books? . . . I must go back six months to catch myself
with a book in my hand. What was it? An excellent study by Victor Brochard
upon the Greek sceptics, in which my Laertiana[1] was used to advantage.
The sceptics! The only *honourable* types among that double-faced and
sometimes quintuple-faced throng, the philosophers! . . . Otherwise I
almost always take refuge in the same books: altogether their number is
small; they are books which are precisely my proper fare. It is not perhaps
in my nature to read much, and of all sorts: a library makes me ill. Neither
is it my nature to love much or many kinds of things. Suspicion or even
hostility towards new books is much more akin to my instinctive feeling
than "toleration," *largeur de cœur*, and other forms of "neighbour-love. . . ."
It is to a small number of old French authors, that I always return again
and again; I believe only in French culture, and regard everything else in
Europe which calls itself "culture" as a misunderstanding. I do not even
take the German kind into consideration. . . . The few instances of higher
culture with which I have met in Germany were all French in their origin.
The most striking example of this was Madame Cosima Wagner, by far the
most decisive voice in matters of taste that I have ever heard. If I do not
read, but literally love Pascal, as the most instinctive sacrifice to Christianity, killing himself inch by inch, first bodily, then spiritually, according to
the terrible consistency of this most appalling form of inhuman cruelty; if
I have something of Montaigne's mischievousness in my soul, and—who

knows? Perhaps also in my body; if my artist's taste endeavours to defend the names of Molière, Corneille, and Racine, and not without bitterness, against such a wild genius as Shakespeare—all this does not prevent me from regarding even the latter-day Frenchmen also as charming companions. I can think of absolutely no century in history, in which a netful of more inquisitive and at the same time more subtle psychologists could be drawn up together than in the Paris of the present day. Let me mention a few at random—for their number is by no means small—Paul Bourget, Pierre Loti, Gyp, Meilhac, Anatole France, Jules Lemaître; or, to point to one of strong race, a genuine Latin, of whom I am particularly fond, Guy de Maupassant. Between ourselves, I prefer this generation even to its masters, all of whom were corrupted by German philosophy (Taine, for instance, by Hegel, whom he has to thank for his misunderstanding of great men and great periods). Wherever Germany extends her sway, she *ruins* culture. It was the war which first saved the spirit of France. . . . Stendhal is one of the happiest accidents of my life—for everything that marks an epoch in it has been brought to me by accident and never by means of a recommendation. He is quite priceless, with his psychologist's eye, quick at forestalling and anticipating; with his grasp of facts, which is reminiscent of the same art in the greatest of all masters of facts (*ex ungue Napoleonem*); and, last but not least, as an honest atheist—a specimen which is both rare and difficult to discover in France—all honour to Prosper Mérimée! . . . Maybe that I am even envious of Stendhal? He robbed me of the best atheistic joke, which I of all people could have perpetrated: "God's only excuse is that He does not exist. . . ." I myself have said somewhere— What has been the greatest objection to Life hitherto? God. . . .

4

It was Heinrich Heine who gave me the most perfect idea of what a lyrical poet could be. In vain do I search through all the kingdoms of antiquity or of modern times for anything to resemble his sweet and passionate music. He possessed that divine wickedness, without which perfection itself becomes unthinkable to me—I estimate the value of men, of races, according to the extent to which they are unable to conceive of a god who has not a dash of the satyr in him. And with what mastery he wields his native tongue! One day it will be said of Heine and me that we were by far the greatest artists of the German language that have ever existed, and that we left all the efforts that mere Germans made in this language an incalculable distance behind us. I must be profoundly related to Byron's

Manfred: of all the dark abysses in this work I found the counterparts in my own soul—at the age of thirteen I was ripe for this book. Words fail me, I have only a look, for those who dare to utter the name of *Faust* in the presence of *Manfred*. The Germans are *incapable* of conceiving anything sublime: for a proof of this, look at Schumann! Out of anger for this mawkish Saxon, I once deliberately composed a counter-overture to *Manfred*, of which Hans von Bülow declared he had never seen the like before on paper: such compositions amounted to a violation of Euterpe. When I cast about me for my highest formula of Shakespeare, I find invariably but this one: that he conceived the type of Caesar. Such things a man cannot guess—he either is the thing, or he is not. The great poet draws his creations only from out of his own reality. This is so to such an extent, that often after a lapse of time he can no longer endure his own work. . . . After casting a glance between the pages of my *Zarathustra*, I pace my room to and fro for half an hour at a time, unable to overcome an insufferable fit of tears. I know of no more heartrending reading than Shakespeare: how a man must have suffered to be so much in need of playing the clown! Is Hamlet *understood*? It is not doubt, but certitude that drives one mad. . . . But in order to feel this, one must be profound, one must be an abyss, a philosopher. . . . We all fear the truth. . . . And, to make a confession; I feel instinctively certain and convinced that Lord Bacon is the originator, the self-torturer, of this most sinister kind of literature: what do I care about the miserable gabble of American muddlers and blockheads? But the power for the greatest realism in vision is not only compatible with the greatest realism in deeds, with the monstrous in deeds, with crime—*it actually presupposes the latter*. . . . We do not know half enough about Lord Bacon—the first realist in all the highest acceptation of this word—to be sure of everything he did, everything he willed, and everything he experienced in his inmost soul. . . . Let the critics go to hell! Suppose I had christened my *Zarathustra* with a name not my own—let us say with Richard Wagner's name—the acumen of two thousand years would not have sufficed to guess that the author of *Human, All-Too-Human* was the visionary of *Zarathustra*.

5

As I am speaking here of the recreations of my life, I feel I must express a word or two of gratitude for that which has refreshed me by far the most heartily and most profoundly. This, without the slightest doubt, was my intimate relationship with Richard Wagner. All my other relationships with men I treat quite lightly; but I would not have the days I spent at Tribschen—those days of confidence, of cheerfulness, of sublime flashes, and of profound moments—blotted from my life at any price. I know not what Wagner may have been for others; but no cloud ever darkened *our* sky. And this brings me back again to France—I have no arguments against Wagnerites, and *hoc genus omne*, who believe that they do honour to Wagner by believing him to be like themselves; for such people I have only a contemptuous curl of my lip. With a nature like mine, which is so strange to everything Teutonic, that even the presence of a German retards my digestion, my first meeting with Wagner was the first moment in my life in which I breathed freely: I felt him, I honoured him, as a foreigner, as the opposite and the incarnate contradiction of all "German virtues." We who as children breathed the marshy atmosphere of the fifties, are necessarily pessimists in regard to the concept "German"; we cannot be anything else than revolutionaries—we can assent to no state of affairs which allows the canting bigot to be at the top. I care not a jot whether this canting bigot acts in different colours today, whether he dresses in scarlet or dons the uniform of a hussar.[2] Very well, then! Wagner was a revolutionary—he fled from the Germans. . . . As an artist, a man has no home in Europe save in Paris; that subtlety of all the five senses which Wagner's art presupposes, those fingers that can detect slight gradations, psychological morbidity—all these things can be found only in Paris. Nowhere else can you meet with this passion for questions of form, this earnestness in matters of *mise-en-scène*, which is the Parisian earnestness *par excellence*. In Germany no one has any idea of the tremendous ambition that fills the heart of a Parisian artist. The German is a good fellow. Wagner was by no means a good fellow. . . . But I have already said quite enough on the subject of Wagner's real nature (see *Beyond Good and Evil*, Aphorism 269), and about those to whom he is most closely related. He is one of the late French romanticists, that high-soaring and heaven-aspiring band of artists, like Delacroix and Berlioz, who in their inmost natures are sick and incurable, and who are all fanatics of *expression*, and virtuosos through and through. . . . Who, in sooth, was the first intelligent follower of Wagner? Charles Baudelaire, the very man who first understood Delacroix—that typical decadent, in whom a whole generation of artists saw their reflexion; he was perhaps the last of them too. . . . What is it that I have never forgiven Wagner? The fact that he condescended to the Germans—that he became a German Imperialist. . . . Wherever Germany spreads, she *ruins* culture.

6

Taking everything into consideration, I could never have survived my youth without Wagnerian music. For I was condemned to the society of Germans. If a man wish to get rid of a feeling of insufferable oppression, he has to take to hashish. Well, I had to take to Wagner. Wagner is the counter-poison to everything essentially German—the fact that he is a poison too, I do not deny. From the moment that *Tristan* was arranged for the piano—all honour to you, Herr von Bülow! I was a Wagnerite. Wagner's previous works seemed beneath me—they were too commonplace, too "German. . . ." But to this day I am still seeking for a work which would be a match to *Tristan* in dangerous fascination, and possess the same gruesome and dulcet quality of infinity; I seek among all the arts in vain. All the quaint features of Leonardo da Vinci's work lose their charm at the sound of the first bar in *Tristan*. This work is without question Wagner's *non plus ultra*; after its creation, the composition of the *Mastersingers* and of the *Ring* was a relaxation to him. To become more healthy—this in a nature like Wagner's amounts to going backwards. The curiosity of the psychologist is so great in me, that I regard it as quite a special privilege to have lived at the right time, and to have lived precisely among Germans, in order to be ripe for this work. The world must indeed be empty for him who has never been unhealthy enough for this "infernal voluptuousness": it is allowable, it is even imperative, to employ a mystic formula for this purpose. I suppose I know better than anyone the prodigious feats of which Wagner was capable, the fifty worlds of strange ecstasies to which no one else had wings to soar; and as I am alive today and strong enough to turn even the most suspicious and most dangerous things to my own advantage, and thus to grow stronger, I declare Wagner to have been the greatest benefactor of my life. The bond which unites us is the fact that we have suffered greater agony, even at each other's hands, than most men are able to bear nowadays, and this will always keep our names associated in the minds of men. For, just as Wagner is merely a misunderstanding among Germans, so, in truth, am I, and ever will be. Ye lack two centuries of psychological and artistic discipline, my dear countrymen! . . . But ye can never recover the time lost.

7

To the most exceptional of my readers I should like to say just one word about what I really exact from music. It must be cheerful and yet profound, like an October afternoon. It must be original, exuberant, and tender, and like a dainty, soft woman in roguishness and grace. . . . I shall never admit that a German *can* understand what music is. Those musicians who are called German, the greatest and most famous foremost, are all foreigners, either Slavs, Croats, Italians, Dutchmen—or Jews; or else, like Heinrich Schütz, Bach, and Händel, they are Germans of a strong race which is now extinct. For my own part, I have still enough of the Pole left in me to let all other music go, if only I can keep Chopin. For three reasons I would except Wagner's *Siegfried Idyll*, and perhaps also one or two things of Liszt, who excelled all other musicians in the noble tone of his orchestration; and finally everything that has been produced beyond the Alps—*this side* of the Alps.[3] I could not possibly dispense with Rossini, and still less with my Southern soul in music, the work of my Venetian maëstro, Pietro Gasti. And when I say beyond the Alps, all I really mean is Venice. If I try to find a new word for music, I can never find any other than Venice. I know not how to draw any distinction between tears and music. I do not know how to think either of joy, or of the south, without a shudder of fear.

> On the bridge I stood
> Lately, in gloomy night.
> Came a distant song:
> In golden drops it rolled
> Over the glittering rim away.
> Music, gondolas, lights—
> Drunk, swam far forth in the gloom. . . .
>
> A stringed instrument, my soul,
> Sang, imperceptibly moved,
> A gondola song by stealth,
> Gleaming for gaudy blessedness.
> —Hearkened any thereto?

8

In all these things—in the choice of food, place, climate, and recreation—the instinct of self-preservation is dominant, and this instinct manifests itself with least ambiguity when it acts as an instinct of defence. To close one's eyes to much, to seal one's ears to much, to keep certain things at a distance—this is the first principle of prudence, the first proof of the fact that a man is not an accident but a necessity. The popular word for this instinct of defence is *taste*. A man's imperative command is not only to say "no" in cases where "yes" would be a sign of "disinterestedness," but also to say "no" *as seldom as possible*. One must part with all that which compels one to repeat "no," with ever greater frequency. The rationale of this principle is that all discharges of defensive forces, however slight they may be, involve enormous and absolutely superfluous losses when they become regular and habitual. Our greatest expenditure of strength is made up of those small and most frequent discharges of it. The act of keeping things off, of holding them at a distance, amounts to a discharge of strength—do not deceive yourselves on this point! And an expenditure of energy directed at purely negative ends. Simply by being compelled to keep constantly on his guard, a man may grow so weak as to be unable any longer to defend himself. Suppose I were to step out of my house, and, instead of the quiet and aristocratic city of Turin, I were to find a German provincial town, my instinct would have to brace itself together in order to repel all that which would pour in upon it from this crushed-down and cowardly world. Or suppose I were to find a large German city—that structure of vice in which nothing grows, but where every single thing, whether good or bad, is squeezed in from outside. In such circumstances should I not be compelled to become a hedgehog? But to have prickles amounts to a squandering of strength; they even constitute a twofold luxury, when, if we only chose to do so, we could dispense with them and open our hands instead. . . .

Another form of prudence and self-defence consists in trying to react as seldom as possible, and to keep one's self aloof from those circumstances and conditions wherein one would be condemned, as it were, to suspend one's "liberty" and one's initiative, and become a mere reacting medium. As an example of this I point to the intercourse with books. The scholar who, in sooth, does little else than handle books—with the philologist of average attainments their number may amount to two hundred a day—ultimately forgets entirely and completely the capacity of thinking for himself. When he has not a book between his fingers he cannot think. When he thinks, he responds to a stimulus (a thought he has read)— finally all he does is to react. The scholar exhausts his whole strength in saying either "yes" or "no" to matter which has already been thought out, or in criticising it—he is no longer capable of thought on his own account. . . . In him the instinct of self-defence has decayed, otherwise he would defend himself against books. The scholar is a decadent. With my own eyes I have seen gifted, richly endowed, and free-spirited natures already "read to ruins" at thirty, and mere wax vestas that have to be rubbed before they can give off any sparks—or "thoughts." To set to early in the morning, at the break of day, in all the fulness and dawn of one's strength, and to read a book—this I call positively vicious!

9

At this point I can no longer evade a direct answer to the question, *how one becomes what one is.* And in giving it, I shall have to touch upon that masterpiece in the art of self-preservation, which is *selfishness.* . . . Granting that one's life-task—the determination and the fate of one's life-task—greatly exceeds the average measure of such things, nothing more dangerous could be conceived than to come face to face with one's self by the side of this life-task. The fact that one becomes what one is, presupposes that one has not the remotest suspicion of what one is. From this standpoint even the blunders of one's life have their own meaning and value, the temporary deviations and aberrations, the moments of hesitation and of modesty, the earnestness wasted upon duties which lie outside the actual life-task. In these matters great wisdom, perhaps even the highest wisdom, comes into activity: in these circumstances, in which *nosce teipsum* would be the sure road to ruin, forgetting one's self, misunderstanding one's self, belittling one's self, narrowing one's self, and making one's self mediocre, amount to reason itself. Expressed morally, to love one's neighbour and to live for others and for other things *may* be the means of protection employed to maintain the hardest kind of egoism. This is the exceptional case in which I, contrary to my principle and conviction, take the side of the altruistic instincts; for here they are concerned in subserving selfishness and self-discipline. The whole surface of consciousness—for consciousness *is* a surface—must be kept free from anyone of the great imperatives. Beware even of every striking word, of every striking attitude! They are all so many risks which the instinct runs of "understanding itself" too soon. Meanwhile the organising "idea," which is destined to become master, grows and continues to grow into the depths—it begins to command, it leads you slowly back from your deviations and aberrations, it prepares individual qualities and capacities, which one day will make themselves felt as indispensable to the whole of your task—step by step it cultivates all the serviceable faculties, before it ever whispers a word concerning the dominant task, the "goal," the "object," and the "meaning" of it all. Looked at from this standpoint my life is simply amazing. For the task of *transvaluing values*, more capacities were needful perhaps than could well be found side by side in one individual; and above all, antagonistic capacities which had to be free from the mutual strife and destruction which they involve. An order of rank among capacities; distance; the art of separating without creating hostility; to refrain from confounding things; to keep from reconciling things; to possess enormous multifariousness and yet to be the reverse of chaos—all this was the first condition, the long secret work, and the artistic mastery of my instinct. Its superior guardianship manifested itself with such exceeding strength, that not once did I ever dream of what was growing within me—until suddenly all my capacities were ripe, and one day burst forth in all the perfection of their highest bloom. I cannot remember ever having exerted myself, I can point to no trace of *struggle* in my life; I am the reverse of a heroic nature. To "will" something, to "strive" after something, to have an "aim" or a "desire" in my mind—I know none of these things from experience. Even at this moment I look out upon my future—a *broad* future! As upon a calm sea: no sigh of longing makes a ripple on its surface. I have not the slightest wish that anything should be otherwise than it is: I myself would not be otherwise. . . . But in this matter I have always been the same. I have never had a desire. A man who, after his four-and-fortieth year, can say that he has never bothered himself about *honours, women,* or *money!* Not that they did not come his way. . . . It was thus that I became one day a University Professor—I had never had the remotest idea of such a thing; for I was scarcely four-and-twenty years of age. In the same way, two years previously, I had one day become a philologist, in the sense that my *first* philological work, my start in every way, was expressly obtained by my master Ritschl for publication in his *Rheinisches Museum.*[4] (Ritschl—and I say it in all reverence—was the only genial scholar that I have ever met. He possessed that pleasant kind of depravity which distinguishes us Thuringians, and which makes even a German sympathetic—even in the pursuit of truth we prefer to avail ourselves of roundabout ways. In saying this I do not mean to underestimate in any way my Thuringian brother, the intelligent Leopold von Ranke. . . .)

10

You may be wondering why I should actually have related all these trivial and, according to traditional accounts, insignificant details to you; such action can but tell against me, more particularly if I am fated to figure in great causes. To this I reply that these trivial matters—diet, locality, climate, and one's mode of recreation, the whole casuistry of self-love—are inconceivably more important than all that which has hitherto been held in high esteem. It is precisely in this quarter that we must begin to learn afresh. All those things which mankind has valued with such earnestness heretofore are not even real; they are mere creations of fancy, or, more strictly speaking, *lies* born of the evil instincts of diseased and, in the deepest sense, noxious natures—all the concepts, "God," "soul," "virtue," "sin," "Beyond," "truth," "eternal life. . . ." But the greatness of human nature, its "divinity," was sought for in them. . . . All questions of politics, of social order, of education, have been falsified, root and branch, owing to the fact that the most noxious men have been taken for great men, and that people were taught to despise the small things, or rather the fundamental things, of life. If I now choose to compare myself with those creatures who have hitherto been honoured as the first among men, the difference becomes obvious. I do not reckon the so-called "first" men even as human beings—for me they are the excrements of mankind, the products of disease and of the instinct of revenge: they are so many monsters laden with rottenness, so many hopeless incurables, who avenge themselves on life. . . . I wish to be the opposite of these people: it is my privilege to have the very sharpest discernment for every sign of healthy instincts. There is no such thing as a morbid trait in me; even in times of serious illness I have never grown morbid, and you might seek in vain for a trace of fanaticism in my nature. No one can point to any moment of my life in which I have assumed either an arrogant or a pathetic attitude. Pathetic attitudes are not in keeping with greatness; he who needs attitudes is false. . . . Beware of all picturesque men! Life was easy—in fact easiest—to me, in those periods when it exacted the heaviest duties from me. Whoever could have seen me during the seventy days of this autumn, when, without interruption, I did a host of things of the highest rank—things that no man can do nowadays—with a sense of responsibility for all the ages yet to come, would have noticed no sign of tension in my condition, but rather a state of overflowing freshness and good cheer. Never have I eaten with more pleasant sensations, never has my sleep been better. I know of no other manner of dealing with great tasks, than as *play*: this, as a sign of greatness, is an essential prerequisite. The slightest constraint, a sombre mien, any hard accent in the voice—all these things are objections to a man, but how much more to his work! . . . One must not have nerves. . . . Even to *suffer* from solitude is an objection—the only thing I have always suffered from is "multitude."[5] At an absurdly tender age, in fact when I was seven years old, I already knew that no human speech would ever reach me: did anyone ever see me sad on that account? At present I still possess the same affability towards everybody, I am even full of consideration for the lowest: in all this there is not an atom of haughtiness or of secret contempt. He whom I despise soon guesses that he is despised by me: the very fact of my existence is enough to rouse indignation in all those who have polluted blood in their veins. My formula for greatness in man is *amor fati*: the fact that a man wishes nothing to be different, either in front of him or behind him, or for all eternity. Not only must the necessary be borne, and on no account concealed—all idealism is falsehood in the face of necessity—but it must also be *loved*. . . .

WHY I WRITE SUCH EXCELLENT BOOKS

1

I AM ONE THING, MY CREATIONS ARE ANOTHER. HERE, BEFORE I SPEAK OF the books themselves, I shall touch upon the question of the understanding and misunderstanding with which they have met. I shall proceed to do this in as perfunctory a manner as the occasion demands; for the time has by no means come for this question. My time has not yet come either; some are born posthumously. One day institutions will be needed in which men will live and teach, as I understand living and teaching; maybe, also, that by that time, chairs will be founded and endowed for the interpretation of *Zarathustra*. But I should regard it as a complete contradiction of myself, if I expected to find ears and eyes for my truths today: the fact that no one listens to me, that no one knows how to receive at my hands today, is not only comprehensible, it seems to me quite the proper thing. I do not wish to be mistaken for another—and to this end I must not mistake myself. To repeat what I have already said, I can point to but few instances of ill-will in my life: and as for literary ill-will, I could mention scarcely a single example of it. On the other hand, I have met with far too much *pure foolery*! . . . It seems to me that to take up one of my books is one of the rarest honours that a man can pay himself—even supposing that he put his shoes from off his feet beforehand, not to mention boots. . . . When on one occasion Dr. Heinrich von Stein honestly complained that he could not understand a word of my *Zarathustra*, I said to him that this was just as it should be: to have understood six sentences in that book—that is to say, to have lived them—raises a man to a higher level among mortals than "modern" men can attain. With this feeling of distance how could I even wish to be read by the "moderns" whom I know! My triumph is just the opposite of what Schopenhauer's was—I say "*Non* legor, *non legar.*" Not that I should like to underestimate the pleasure I have derived from the innocence with which my works have frequently been contradicted. As late as last summer, at a time when I was attempting, perhaps by means of my weighty, all-too-weighty literature, to throw the rest of literature off its balance, a certain professor of Berlin University kindly gave me to understand that I ought really to make use of a different form: no one could read such stuff as I wrote. Finally, it was not Germany, but Switzerland that presented me with the two most extreme cases. An essay on *Beyond Good and Evil*, by Dr. V. Widmann in the paper called the *Bund*, under the heading *Nietzsche's Dangerous Book*, and a general account of all my works, from the pen of Herr Karl Spitteler, also in the *Bund*, constitute a maximum in my life—I shall not say of what. . . . The latter treated my *Zarathustra*, for instance, as "*advanced exercises in style*," and expressed the wish that later on I might try and attend to the question of substance as well; Dr. Widmann assured me of his respect for the courage I showed in endeavouring to abolish all decent feeling. Thanks to a little trick of destiny, every sentence in these criticisms seemed, with a consistency that I could but admire, to be an inverted truth. In fact it was most remarkable that all one had to do was to "transvalue all values," in order to hit the nail on the head with regard to me, instead of striking my head with the nail. . . . I am more particularly anxious therefore to discover an explanation. After all, no one can draw more out of things, books included, than he already knows. A man has no ears for that to which experience has given him no access. To take an extreme case, suppose a book contains simply incidents which lie quite outside the range of general or even rare experience— suppose it to be the *first* language to express a whole series of experiences. In this case nothing it contains will really be heard at all, and, thanks to an acoustic delusion, people will believe that where nothing is heard there is nothing to hear. . . . This, at least, has been my usual experience, and proves, if you will, the originality of my experience. He who thought he had understood something in my work, had as a rule adjusted something in it to his own image—not infrequently the very opposite of myself, an "idealist," for instance. He who understood nothing in my work, would deny that I was worth considering at all. The word "Superman," which designates a type of man that would be one of nature's rarest and luckiest strokes, as opposed to "modern" men, to "good" men, to Christians and other Nihilists—a word which in the mouth of Zarathustra, the annihilator of morality, acquires a very profound meaning—is understood almost everywhere, and with perfect innocence, in the light of those values to which a flat contradiction was made manifest in the figure of Zarathustra—that is to say, as an "ideal" type, a higher kind of man, half "saint" and half "genius. . . ." Other learned cattle have suspected me of Darwinism on account of this word: even the "hero cult" of that great unconscious and involuntary swindler, Carlyle—a cult which I repudiated with such roguish malice—was recognised in my doctrine. Once, when I whispered to a man that he would do better to seek for the Superman in a Caesar Borgia than in a Parsifal, he could not believe his ears. The fact that I am quite free from curiosity in regard to criticisms of my books, more particularly when they appear in newspapers, will have to be forgiven me. My friends and my publishers know this, and never speak to me of such things. In one particular case, I once saw all the sins that had been committed against a single book—it was *Beyond Good and Evil*; I could tell you a nice story about it. Is it possible that the *National-Zeitung*—a Prussian paper (this comment is for the sake of my foreign readers—for my own part, I beg to state, I read only *Le Journal des Débats*)—really and seriously regarded the book as a "sign of the times," or a genuine and typical example of Tory philosophy,[1] for which the *Kreuz-Zeitung* had not sufficient courage? . . .

2

This was said for the benefit of Germans: for everywhere else I have my readers—all of them exceptionally intelligent men, characters that have won their spurs and that have been reared in high offices and superior duties; I have even real geniuses among my readers. In Vienna, in St. Petersburg, in Stockholm, in Copenhagen, in Paris, and New York—I have been discovered everywhere: I have not yet been discovered in Europe's flatland—Germany. . . . And, to make a confession, I rejoice much more heartily over those who do not read me, over those who have neither heard of my name nor of the word philosophy. But whithersoever I go, here in Turin, for instance, every face brightens and softens at the sight of me. A thing that has flattered me more than anything else hitherto, is the fact that old market-women cannot rest until they have picked out the sweetest of their grapes for me. To this extent must a man be a philosopher. . . . It is not in vain that the Poles are considered as the French among the Slavs. A charming Russian lady will not be mistaken for a single moment concerning my origin. I am not successful at being pompous, the

488 → ECCE HOMO

most I can do is to appear embarrassed. . . . I can think in German, I can feel in German—I can do most things; but this is beyond my powers. . . . My old master Ritschl went so far as to declare that I planned even my philological treatises after the manner of a Parisian novelist—that I made them absurdly thrilling. In Paris itself people are surprised at "*toutes mes audaces et finesses*"; the words are Monsieur Taine's; I fear that even in the highest forms of the dithyramb, that salt will be found pervading my work which never becomes insipid, which never becomes "German"—and that is, wit. . . . I can do nought else. God help me! Amen. We all know, some of us even from experience, what a "long-ears" is. Well then, I venture to assert that I have the smallest ears that have ever been seen. This fact is not without interest to women—it seems to me they feel that I understand them better! . . . I am essentially the anti-ass, and on this account alone a monster in the world's history—in Greek, and not only in Greek, I am the *Antichrist*.

3

I am to a great extent aware of my privileges as a writer: in one or two cases it has even been brought home to me how very much the habitual reading of my works "spoils" a man's taste. Other books simply cannot be endured after mine, and least of all philosophical ones. It is an incomparable distinction to cross the threshold of this noble and subtle world—in order to do so one must certainly not be a German; it is, in short, a distinction which one must have deserved. He, however, who is related to me through loftiness of will, experiences genuine raptures of understanding in my books: for I swoop down from heights into which no bird has ever soared; I know abysses into which no foot has ever slipped. People have told me that it is impossible to lay down a book of mine—that I disturb even the night's rest. . . . There is no prouder or at the same time more subtle kind of books: they sometimes attain to the highest pinnacle of earthly endeavour, cynicism; to capture their thoughts a man must have the tenderest fingers as well as the most intrepid fists. Any kind of spiritual decrepitude utterly excludes all intercourse with them—even any kind of dyspepsia: a man must have no nerves, but he must have a cheerful belly. Not only the poverty of a man's soul and its stuffy air excludes all intercourse with them, but also, and to a much greater degree, cowardice, uncleanliness, and secret intestinal revengefulness; a word from my lips suffices to make the colour of all evil instincts rush into a face. Among my acquaintances I have a number of experimental subjects, in whom I see depicted all the different, and instructively different, reactions which follow upon a perusal of my works. Those who will have nothing to do with the contents of my books, as for instance my so-called friends, assume an "impersonal" tone concerning them: they wish me luck, and congratulate me for having produced another work; they also declare that my writings show progress, because they exhale a more cheerful spirit. . . . The thoroughly vicious people, the "beautiful souls," the false from top to toe, do not know in the least what to do with my books—consequently, with the beautiful consistency of all beautiful souls, they regard my work as beneath them. The cattle among my acquaintances, the mere Germans, leave me to understand, if you please, that they are not always of my opinion, though here and there they agree with me. . . . I have heard this said even about *Zarathustra*. "Feminism," whether in mankind or in man, is likewise a barrier to my writings; with it, no one could ever enter into this labyrinth of fearless knowledge. To this end, a man must never have spared himself, he must have been hard in his habits, in order to be good-humoured and merry among a host of inexorable truths. When I try to picture the character of a perfect reader, I always imagine a monster of courage and curiosity, as well as of suppleness, cunning, and prudence—in short, a born adventurer and explorer. After all, I could not describe better than *Zarathustra* has done unto whom I really address myself: unto whom alone would he reveal his riddle?

> Unto you, daring explorers and experimenters, and unto all who
>   have ever embarked beneath cunning sails upon terrible seas;
> Unto you who revel in riddles and in twilight, whose souls are lured
>   by flutes unto every treacherous abyss:
> For ye care not to grope your way along a thread with craven fingers; and where ye are able to *guess*, ye hate to *argue*.

4

I will now pass just one or two general remarks about my *art of style*. To communicate a state an inner tension of pathos by means of signs, including the tempo of these signs—that is the meaning of every style; and in view of the fact that the multiplicity of inner states in me is enormous, I am capable of many kinds of style—in short, the most multifarious art of style that any man has ever had at his disposal. Any style is *good* which genuinely communicates an inner condition, which does not blunder over the signs, over the tempo of the signs, or over *moods*—all the laws of phrasing are the outcome of representing moods artistically. Good style, in itself, is a piece of sheer foolery, mere idealism, like "beauty in itself," for instance, or "goodness in itself," or "the thing-in-itself." All this takes for granted, of course, that there exist ears that can hear, and such men as are capable and worthy of a like pathos, that those are not wanting unto whom one may communicate one's self. Meanwhile my Zarathustra, for instance, is still in quest of such people—alas! He will have to seek a long while yet! A man must be worthy of listening to him. . . . And, until that time, there will be no one who will understand the art that has been squandered in this book. No one has ever existed who has had more novel, more strange, and purposely created art forms to fling to the winds. The fact that such things were possible in the German language still awaited proof; formerly, I myself would have denied most emphatically that it was possible. Before my time people did not know what could be done with the German language—what could be done with language in general. The art of grand rhythm, of grand style in periods, for expressing the tremendous fluctuations of sublime and superhuman passion, was first discovered by me: with the dithyramb entitled *The Seven Seals*, which constitutes the last discourse of the third part of *Zarathustra*, I soared miles above all that which heretofore has been called poetry.

5

The fact that the voice which speaks in my works is that of a psychologist who has not his peer, is perhaps the first conclusion at which a good reader will arrive—a reader such as I deserve, and one who reads me just as the good old philologists used to read their Horace. Those propositions about which all the world is fundamentally agreed—not to speak of fashionable philosophy, of moralists and other empty-headed and cabbage-brained people—are to me but ingenuous blunders: for instance, the belief that "altruistic" and "egoistic" are opposites, while all the time the "ego" itself is merely a "supreme swindle," an "ideal. . . ." There are no such things as egoistic or altruistic actions: both concepts are psychological nonsense. Or the proposition that "man pursues happiness"; or the proposition that "happiness is the reward of virtue. . . ." Or the proposition that "pleasure and pain are opposites. . . ." Morality, the Circe of mankind, has falsified everything psychological, root and branch—it has demoralised everything, even to the terribly nonsensical point of calling love "unselfish." A man must first be firmly poised, he must stand securely on his two legs, otherwise he cannot love at all. This indeed the girls know only too well: they don't care two pins about unselfish and merely objective men. . . . May I venture to suggest, incidentally, that I know women? This knowledge is part of my Dionysian patrimony. Who knows? Maybe I am the first psychologist of the eternally feminine. Women all like me. . . . But that's an old story: save, of course, the abortions among them, the emancipated ones, those who lack the wherewithal to have children. Thank goodness I am not willing to let myself be torn to pieces! The perfect woman tears you to pieces when she loves you: I know these amiable Maenads. . . . Oh! What a dangerous, creeping, subterranean little beast of prey she is! And so agreeable withal! . . . A little woman, pursuing her vengeance, would force open even the iron gates of Fate itself. Woman is incalculably more wicked than man, she is also cleverer. Goodness in a woman is already a sign of *degeneration*. All cases of "beautiful souls" in women may be traced to a faulty physiological condition—but I go no further, lest I should become medicynical. The struggle for equal rights is even a symptom of disease; every doctor knows this. The more womanly a woman is, the more she fights tooth and nail against rights in general: the natural order of things, the eternal war between the sexes, assigns to her by far the foremost rank. Have people had ears to hear my definition of love? It is the only definition worthy of a philosopher. Love, in its means, is war; in its foundation, it is the mortal hatred of the sexes. Have you heard my reply to the question how a woman can be cured, "saved" in fact? Give her a child! A woman needs children, man is always only a means, thus spake Zarathustra. "The emancipation of women"—this is the instinctive hatred of physiologically botched—that is to say, barren—women for those of their sisters who are well constituted: the fight against "man" is always only a means, a pretext, a piece of strategy. By trying to rise to "Woman per se," to "Higher Woman," to the "Ideal Woman," all they wish to do is to lower the general level of women's rank: and there are no more certain means to this end than university education, trousers, and the rights of voting cattle. Truth to tell, the emancipated are the anarchists in the "eternally feminine" world, the physiological mishaps, the most deep-rooted instinct of whom is revenge. A whole species of the most malicious "idealism"— which, by the bye, also manifests itself in men, in Henrik Ibsen for instance, that typical old maid—whose object is to poison the clean conscience, the natural spirit, of sexual love. . . . And in order to leave no doubt in your minds in regard to my opinion, which, on this matter, is as honest as it is severe, I will reveal to you one more clause out of my moral code against vice—with the word "vice" I combat every kind of opposition to Nature, or, if you prefer fine words, idealism. The clause reads: "Preaching of chastity is a public incitement to unnatural practises. All depreciation of the sexual life, all the sullying of it by means of the concept 'impure,' is the essential crime against Life—is the essential crime against the Holy Spirit of Life."

6

In order to give you some idea of myself as a psychologist, let me take this curious piece of psychological analysis out of the book *Beyond Good and Evil*, in which it appears. I forbid, by the bye, any guessing as to whom I am describing in this passage.

> The genius of the heart, as that great anchorite possesses it, the divine tempter and born Pied Piper of consciences, whose voice knows how to sink into the inmost depths of every soul, who neither utters a word nor casts a glance, in which some seductive motive or trick does not lie: a part of whose masterliness is that he understands the art of seeming—not what he is, but that which will place a fresh constraint upon his followers to press ever more closely upon him, to follow him ever more enthusiastically and whole-heartedly. . . . The genius of the heart, which makes all loud and self-conceited things hold their tongues and lend their ears, which polishes all rough souls and makes them taste a new longing—to lie placid as a mirror, that the deep heavens may be reflected in them. . . . The genius of the heart which teaches the clumsy and too hasty hand to hesitate and grasp more tenderly; which scents the hidden and forgotten treasure, the pearl of goodness and sweet spirituality, beneath thick black ice, and is a divining rod for every grain of gold, long buried and imprisoned in heaps of mud and sand. . . . The genius of the heart, from contact with which every man goes away richer, not "blessed" and overcome, not as though favoured and crushed by the good things of others; but richer in himself, fresher to himself than before, opened up, breathed upon and sounded by a thawing wind; more uncertain, perhaps, more delicate, more fragile, more bruised; but full of hopes which as yet lack names, full of a new will and striving, full of a new unwillingness and counter-striving. . . .

THE BIRTH OF TRAGEDY

1

In order to be fair to the *Birth of Tragedy* (1872) it is necessary to forget a few things. It created a sensation and even fascinated by means of its mistakes—by means of its application to Wagnerism, as if the latter were the sign of an ascending tendency. On that account alone, this treatise was an event in Wagner's life: thenceforward great hopes surrounded the name of Wagner. Even to this day, people remind me, sometimes in the middle of *Parsifal*, that it rests on my conscience if the opinion, that this movement is of great value to culture, at length became prevalent. I have often seen the book quoted as *The Second Birth of Tragedy from the Spirit of Music*: people had ears only for new formulae for Wagner's art, his object and his mission—and in this way the real hidden value of the book was overlooked. *Hellenism and Pessimism*—this would have been a less equivocal title, seeing that the book contains the first attempt at showing how the Greeks succeeded in disposing of pessimism—in what manner they overcame it. . . . Tragedy itself is the proof of the fact that the Greeks were not pessimists: Schopenhauer blundered here as he blundered in everything else. Regarded impartially, *The Birth of Tragedy* is a book quite strange to its age: no one would dream that it was begun in the thunder of the battle of Wörth. I thought out these problems on cold September nights beneath the walls of Metz, in the midst of my duties as nurse to the wounded; it would be easier to think that it was written fifty years earlier. Its attitude towards politics is one of indifference—"un-German,"[2] as people would say today—it smells offensively of Hegel; only in one or two formulae is it infected with the bitter odour of corpses which is peculiar to Schopenhauer. An idea—the antagonism of the two concepts Dionysian and Apollonian—is translated into metaphysics; history itself is depicted as the development of this idea; in tragedy this antithesis has become unity; from this standpoint things which theretofore had never been face to face are suddenly confronted, and understood and illuminated by each other. . . . Opera and revolution, for instance. . . . The two decisive innovations in the book are, first, the comprehension of the Dionysian phenomenon among the Greeks—it provides the first psychological analysis of this phenomenon, and sees in it the single root of all Greek art; and, secondly, the comprehension of Socraticism—Socrates being presented for the first time as the instrument of Greek dissolution, as a typical decadent. "Reason" *versus* Instinct. "Reason" at any cost, as a dangerous, life-undermining force. The whole book is profoundly and politely silent concerning Christianity: the latter is neither Apollonian nor Dionysian; it denies all aesthetic values, which are the only values that *The Birth of Tragedy* recognises. Christianity is most profoundly nihilistic, whereas in the Dionysian symbol, the most extreme limits of a yea-saying attitude to life are attained. In one part of the book the Christian priesthood is referred to as a "perfidious order of goblins," as "subterraneans."

2

This start of mine was remarkable beyond measure. As a confirmation of my inmost personal experience I had discovered the only example of this fact that history possesses—with this I was the first to understand the amazing Dionysian phenomenon. At the same time, by recognising Socrates as a decadent, I proved most conclusively that the certainty of my psychological grasp of things ran very little risk at the hands of any sort of moral idiosyncrasy: to regard morality itself as a symptom of degeneration is an innovation, a unique event of the first order in the history of knowledge. How high I had soared above the pitifully foolish gabble about Optimism and Pessimism with my two new doctrines! I was the first to see the actual contrast: the degenerate instinct which turns upon life with a subterranean lust of vengeance (Christianity, Schopenhauer's philosophy, and in some respects too even Plato's philosophy—in short, the whole of idealism in its typical forms), as opposed to a formula of the highest yea-saying to life, born of an abundance and a superabundance of life—a yea-saying free from all reserve, applying even to suffering, and guilt, and all that is questionable and strange in existence. . . . This last, most joyous, most exuberant and exultant yea to life, is not only the highest, but also the profoundest conception, and one which is most strictly confirmed and supported by truth and science. Nothing that exists must be suppressed, nothing can be dispensed with. Those aspects of life which Christians and other Nihilists reject, belong to an incalculably higher order in the hierarchy of values, than that which the instinct of degeneration calls good, and *may* call good. In order to understand this, a certain courage is necessary, and, as a prerequisite of this, a certain superfluity of strength: for a man can approach only as near to truth as he has the courage to advance—that is to say, everything depends strictly upon the measure of his strength. Knowledge, and the affirmation of reality, are just as necessary to the strong man as cowardice, the flight from reality—in fact, the "ideal"—are necessary to the weak inspired by weakness. . . . These people are not at liberty to "know"—decadents stand in need of lies—it is one of their self-preservative measures. He who not only understands the word "Dionysian," but understands *himself* that term, does not require any refutation of Plato, or of Christianity, or of Schopenhauer—for his nose *scents decomposition*.

3

The extent to which I had by means of these doctrines discovered the idea of "tragedy," the ultimate explanation of what the psychology of tragedy is, I discussed finally in *The Twilight of the Idols* (Aph. 5, part 10). . . . "The saying of yea to life, and even to its weirdest and most difficult problems: the will to life rejoicing at its own infinite vitality in the sacrifice of its highest types—that is what I called Dionysian, that is what I meant as the bridge to the psychology of the tragic poet. Not to cast out terror and pity, or to purge one's self of dangerous passion by discharging it with vehemence—this was Aristotle's[3] misunderstanding of it—but to be far beyond terror and pity and to be the eternal lust of Becoming itself—that lust which also involves the joy of destruction. . . ." In this sense I have the right to regard myself as the first *tragic philosopher*—that is to say, the most extreme antithesis and antipodes of a pessimistic philosopher. Before my time no such thing existed as this translation of the Dionysian phenomenon into philosophic emotion: tragic wisdom was lacking; in vain have I sought for signs of it even among the great Greeks in philosophy—those belonging to the two centuries before Socrates. I still remained a little doubtful about Heraclitus, in whose presence, alone, I felt warmer and more at ease than anywhere else. The yea-saying to the impermanence and annihilation of things, which is the decisive feature of a Dionysian philosophy; the yea-saying to contradiction and war, the postulation of Becoming, together with the radical rejection even of the concept *Being*—in all these things, at all events, I must recognise him who has come nearest to me in thought hither to. The doctrine of the "Eternal Recurrence"—that is to say, of the absolute and eternal repetition of all things in periodical cycles—this doctrine of Zarathustra's might, it is true, have been taught before. In any case, the Stoics, who derived nearly all their fundamental ideas from Heraclitus, show traces of it.

4

A tremendous hope finds expression in this work. After all, I have absolutely no reason to renounce the hope for a Dionysian future of music.

Let us look a century ahead, and let us suppose that my attempt to destroy two millenniums of hostility to Nature and of the violation of humanity be crowned with success. That new party of life-advocates, which will undertake the greatest of all tasks, the elevation and perfection of mankind, as well as the relentless destruction of all degenerate and parasitical elements, will make that *superabundance of life* on earth once more possible, out of which the Dionysian state will perforce arise again. I promise the advent of a tragic age: the highest art in the saying of yea to life, "tragedy," will be born again when mankind has the knowledge of the hardest, but most necessary of wars, behind it, without, however, suffering from that knowledge. . . . A psychologist might add that what I heard in Wagnerian music in my youth and early manhood had nothing whatsoever to do with Wagner; that when I described Dionysian music, I described merely what *I* personally had heard—that I was compelled instinctively to translate and transfigure everything into the new spirit which filled my breast. A proof of this, and as strong a proof as you could have, is my essay, *Wagner in Bayreuth*: in all its decisive psychological passages I am the only person concerned—without any hesitation you may read my name or the word "Zarathustra" wherever the text contains the name of Wagner. The whole panorama of the *dithyrambic* artist is the representation of the already existing author of *Zarathustra*, and it is drawn with an abysmal depth which does not even once come into contact with the real Wagner. Wagner himself had a notion of the truth; he did not recognise himself in the essay. In this way, "the idea of Bayreuth" was changed into something which to those who are acquainted with my *Zarathustra* will be no riddle—that is to say, into the Great Noon when the highest of the elect will consecrate themselves for the greatest of all duties—who knows? The vision of a feast which I may live to see. . . . The pathos of the first few pages is universal history; the look which is discussed on page 105[4] of the book, is the actual look of *Zarathustra*; Wagner, Bayreuth, the whole of this petty German wretchedness, is a cloud upon which an infinite Fata Morgana of the future is reflected. Even from the psychological standpoint, all the decisive traits in my character are introduced into Wagner's nature— the juxtaposition of the most brilliant and most fatal forces, a Will to Power such as no man has ever possessed—inexorable bravery in matters spiritual, an unlimited power of learning unaccompanied by depressed powers for action. Everything in this essay is a prophecy: the proximity of the resurrection of the Greek spirit, the need of men who will be counter-Alexanders, who will once more tie the Gordian knot of Greek culture, after it has been cut. Listen to the world-historic accent with which the concept "sense for the tragic" is introduced on page 180: there are little else but world-historic accents in this essay. This is the strangest kind of "objectivity" that ever existed: my absolute certainty in regard to what I *am*, projected itself into any chance reality—truth about myself was voiced from out appalling depths. On pages 174 and 175 the style of *Zarathustra* is described and foretold with incisive certainty, and no more magnificent expression will ever he found than that on pages 144–147 for the event for which *Zarathustra* stands—that prodigious act of the purification and consecration of mankind.

THOUGHTS OUT OF SEASON

1

The four essays composing the *Thoughts out of Season* are thoroughly war-like in tone. They prove that I was no mere dreamer, that I delight in drawing the sword—and perhaps, also, that my wrist is dangerously supple. The first onslaught (1873) was directed against German culture, upon which I looked down even at that time with unmitigated contempt. Without either sense, substance, or goal, it was simply "public opinion." There could be no more dangerous misunderstanding than to suppose that Germany's success at arms proved anything in favour of German culture —and still less the triumph of this culture over that of France. The second essay (1874) brings to light that which is dangerous, that which corrodes and poisons life in our manner of pursuing scientific study: Life is diseased, thanks to this dehumanised piece of clockwork and mechanism, thanks to the "impersonality" of the workman, and the false economy of the "division of labour." The object, which is culture, is lost sight of: modern scientific activity as a means thereto simply produces barbarism. In this treatise, the "historical sense," of which this century is so proud, is for the first time recognised as sickness, as a typical symptom of decay. In the third and fourth essays, a signpost is set up pointing to a higher concept of culture, to a re-establishment of the notion "culture"; and two pictures of the hardest self-love and self-discipline are presented, two essentially un-modern types, full of the most sovereign contempt for all that which lay around them and was called "Empire," "Culture," "Christianity," "Bismarck," and "Success," these two types were Schopenhauer and Wagner, *or*, in a word, Nietzsche. . . .

2

Of these four attacks, the first met with extraordinary success. The stir which it created was in every way gorgeous. I had put my finger on the vulnerable spot of a triumphant nation—I had told it that its victory was not a red-letter day for culture, but, perhaps, something very different. The reply rang out from all sides, and certainly not only from old friends of David Strauss, whom I had made ridiculous as the type of a German Philistine of Culture and a man of smug self-content—in short, as the author of that suburban gospel of his, called *The Old and the New Faith* (the term "Philistine of Culture" passed into the current language of Germany after the appearance of my book). These old friends, whose vanity as Würtembergians and Swabians I had deeply wounded in regarding their unique animal, their bird of Paradise, as a trifle comic, replied to me as ingenuously and as grossly as I could have wished. The Prussian replies were smarter; they contained more "Prussian blue." The most disreputable attitude was assumed by a Leipzig paper, the egregious *Grentzboten*; and it cost me some pains to prevent my indignant friends in Bâle from taking action against it. Only a few old gentlemen decided in my favour, and for very diverse and sometimes unaccountable reasons. Among them was one, Ewald of Göttingen, who made it clear that my attack on Strauss had been deadly. There was also the Hegelian, Bruno Bauer, who from that time became one of my most attentive readers. In his later years he liked to refer to me, when, for instance, he wanted to give Herr von Treitschke, the Prussian Historiographer, a hint as to where he could obtain information about the notion "Culture," of which he (Herr von T.) had completely lost sight. The weightiest and longest notice of my book and its author appeared in Würzburg, and was written by Professor Hoffmann, an old pupil of the philosopher von Baader. The essays made him foresee a great future for me, namely, that of bringing about a sort of crisis and decisive turning point in the problem of atheism, of which he recognised in me the most instinctive and most radical advocate. It was atheism that had drawn me to Schopenhauer. The review which received by far the most attention, and which excited the most bitterness, was an extraordinarily powerful and plucky appreciation of my work by Carl Hillebrand, a man who was usually so mild, and the last *humane* German who knew how to wield a pen. The article appeared in the *Augsburg Gazette*, and it can be read today, couched in rather more cautious language, among his collected essays. In it my work was referred to as an event, as a decisive turning point, as the first sign of an awakening, as an excellent symptom, and as an actual revival of German earnestness and of German passion in things spiritual. Hillebrand could speak only in the terms of the highest respect, of the form of my book, of its consummate taste, of its perfect tact in discriminating between persons and causes: he characterised it as the best polemical work in the German language—the best performance in the art of polemics, which for Germans is so dangerous and so strongly to be deprecated. Besides confirming my standpoint, he laid even greater stress upon what I had dared to say about the deterioration of language in Germany (nowadays writers assume the airs of Purists[5] and can no longer even construct a sentence); sharing my contempt for the literary stars of this nation, he concluded by expressing his admiration for my courage— that "greatest courage of all which places the very favourites of the people in the dock. . . ." The after-effects of this essay of mine proved invaluable to me in my life. No one has ever tried to meddle with me since. People are silent. In Germany I am treated with gloomy caution: for years I have rejoiced in the privilege of such absolute freedom of speech, as no one nowadays, least of all in the "Empire," has enough liberty to claim. My paradise is "in the shadow of my sword." At bottom all I had done was to put one of Stendhal's maxims into practise: he advises one to make one's entrance into society by means of a duel. And how well I had chosen my opponent! The foremost freethinker of Germany. As a matter of fact, quite a novel kind of free thought found its expression in this way: up to the present nothing has been more strange and more foreign to my blood than the whole of that European and American species known as *libres penseurs*. Incorrigible blockheads and clowns of "modern ideas" that they are, I feel much more profoundly at variance with them than with any one of their adversaries. They also wish to "improve" mankind, after their own fashion—that is to say, in their own image; against that which I stand for and desire, they would wage an implacable war, if only they understood it; the whole gang of them still believe in an "ideal. . . ." I am the first *Immoralist*.

3

I should not like to say that the last two essays in the *Thoughts out of Season*, associated with the names of Schopenhauer and Wagner respectively, serve any special purpose in throwing light upon these two cases, or in formulating their psychological problems. This of course does not apply to a few details. Thus, for instance, in the second of the two essays, with a profound certainty of instinct I already characterised the elementary factor in Wagner's nature as a theatrical talent which in all his means and inspirations only draws its final conclusions. At bottom, my desire in this essay was to do something very different from writing psychology: an unprecedented educational problem, a new understanding of self-discipline and self-defence carried to the point of hardness, a road to greatness and to world-historic duties, yearned to find expression. Roughly speaking, I seized two famous and, theretofore, completely undefined types by the forelock, after the manner in which one seizes opportunities, simply in order to speak my mind on certain questions, in order to have a few more formulas, signs, and means of expression at my disposal. Indeed I actually suggest this, with most unearthly sagacity, on page 183 of *Schopenhauer as Educator*. Plato made use of Socrates in the same way—that is to say, as a cipher for Plato. Now that, from some distance, I can look back upon the conditions of which these essays are the testimony, I would be loth to deny that they refer simply to me. The essay *Wagner in Bayreuth* is a vision of my own future; on the other hand, my most secret history, my development, is written down in *Schopenhauer as Educator*. But, above all, the *vow* I made! What I am today, the place I now hold—at a height from which I speak no longer with words but with thunderbolts—oh, how far I was from all this in those days! But I saw the land—I did not deceive myself for one moment as to the way, the sea, the danger—*and* success! The great calm in promising, this happy prospect of a future which must not remain only a promise! In this book every word has been lived, profoundly and intimately; the most painful things are not lacking in it; it contains words which are positively running with blood. But a wind of great freedom blows over the whole; even its wounds do not constitute an objection. As to what I understand by being a philosopher—that is to say, a terrible explosive in the presence of which everything is in danger; as to how I sever my idea of the philosopher by miles from that other idea of him which includes even a Kant, not to speak of the academic "ruminators" and other professors of philosophy—concerning all these things this essay provides invaluable information, even granting that at bottom, it is not "Schopenhauer as Educator" but "Nietzsche as Educator," who speaks his sentiments in it. Considering that, in those days, my trade was that of a scholar, and perhaps, also, that I understood my trade, the piece of austere scholar psychology which suddenly makes its appearance in this essay is not without importance: it expresses the feeling of distance, and my profound certainty regarding what was my real life-task, and what were merely means, intervals, and accessory work to me. My wisdom consists in my having been many things, and in many places, in order to become one thing—in order to be able to attain to one thing. It was part of my fate to be a scholar for a while.

HUMAN, ALL-TOO-HUMAN

1

Human, All-Too-Human, with its two sequels, is the memorial of a crisis. It is called a book for free spirits: almost every sentence in it is the expression of a triumph—by means of it I purged myself of everything in me which was foreign to my nature. Idealism is foreign to me: the title of the book means: "Where ye see ideal things I see—human, alas! All-too-human things!" . . . I know men better. The word "free spirit" in this book must not be understood as anything else than a spirit that has become free, that has once more taken possession of itself. My tone, the pitch of my voice, has completely changed; the book will be thought clever, cool, and at times both hard and scornful. A certain spirituality, of noble taste, seems to be ever struggling to dominate a passionate torrent at its feet. In this respect there is some sense in the fact that it was the hundredth anniversary of Voltaire's death that served, so to speak, as an excuse for the publication of the book as early as 1878. For Voltaire, as the opposite of everyone who wrote after him, was above all a grandee of the intellect: precisely what I am also. The name of Voltaire on one of my writings—that was verily a step forward—in my direction. . . . Looking into this book a little more closely, you perceive a pitiless spirit who knows all the secret hiding places in which ideals are wont to skulk—where they find their dungeons, and, as it were, their last refuge. With a torch in my hand, the light of which is not by any means a flickering one, I illuminate this nether world with beams that cut like blades. It is war, but war without powder and smoke, without warlike attitudes, without pathos and contorted limbs—all these things would still be "idealism." One error after the other is quietly laid upon ice; the ideal is not refuted—it freezes. Here, for instance, "genius" freezes; round the corner the "saint" freezes; under a thick icicle the "hero" freezes; and in the end "faith" itself freezes. So-called "conviction" and also "pity" are considerably cooled—and almost everywhere the "thing in itself" is freezing to death.

2

This book was begun during the first musical festival at Bayreuth; a feeling of profound strangeness towards everything that surrounded me there, is one of its first conditions. He who has any notion of the visions which even at that time had flitted across my path, will be able to guess what I felt when one day I came to my senses in Bayreuth. It was just as if I had been dreaming. Where on earth was I? I recognised nothing that I saw; I scarcely recognised Wagner. It was in vain that I called up reminiscences. Tribschen —remote island of bliss: not the shadow of a resemblance! The incomparable days devoted to the laying of the first stone, the small group of the initiated who celebrated them, and who were far from lacking fingers for the handling of delicate things: not the shadow of a resemblance! *What had happened?* Wagner had been translated into German! The Wagnerite had become master of Wagner! *German* art! The German master! German beer! . . . We who know only too well the kind of refined artists and cosmopolitanism in taste, to which alone Wagner's art can appeal, were beside ourselves at the sight of Wagner bedecked with German virtues. I think I know the Wagnerite, I have experienced three generations of them, from Brendel of blessed memory, who confounded Wagner with Hegel, to the "idealists" of the *Bayreuth Gazette*, who confound Wagner with themselves—I have been the recipient of every kind of confession about Wagner, from "beautiful souls." My kingdom for just one intelligent word! In very truth, a blood-curdling company! Nohl, Pohl, and *Kohl*,[6] and others of their kidney to infinity! There was not a single abortion that was lacking among them— no, not even the anti-Semite. Poor Wagner! Into whose hands had he fallen? If only he had gone into a herd of swine! But among Germans! Someday, for the edification of posterity, one ought really to have a genuine Bayreuthian stuffed, or, better still, preserved in spirit—for it is precisely spirit that is lacking in this quarter—with this inscription at the foot of the jar: "A sample of the spirit whereon the 'German Empire' was founded. . . ." But enough! In the middle of the festivities I suddenly packed my trunk and left the place for a few weeks, despite the fact that a charming Parisian lady sought to comfort me; I excused myself to Wagner simply by means of a fatalistic telegram. In a little spot called Klingenbrunn, deeply buried in the recesses of the Böhmerwald, I carried my melancholy and my contempt of Germans about with me like an illness—and, from time to time, under the general title of "The Ploughshare," I wrote a sentence or two down in my notebook, nothing but severe psychological stuff, which it is possible may have found its way into *Human, All-Too-Human.*

3

That which had taken place in me, then, was not only a breach with Wagner—I was suffering from a general aberration of my instincts, of which a mere isolated blunder, whether it were Wagner or my professorship at Bâle, was nothing more than a symptom. I was seized with a fit of impatience with myself; I saw that it was high time that I should turn my thoughts upon my own lot. In a trice I realised, with appalling clearness, how much time had already been squandered—how futile and how senseless my whole existence as a philologist appeared by the side of my life-task. I was ashamed of this false modesty. . . . Ten years were behind me, during which, to tell the truth, the nourishment of my spirit had been at a standstill, during which I had added not a single useful fragment to my knowledge, and had forgotten countless things in the pursuit of a hotch-potch of dry-as-dust scholarship. To crawl with meticulous care and short-sighted eyes through old Greek metricians—that is what I had come to! . . . Moved to pity I saw myself quite thin, quite emaciated: realities were only too plainly absent from my stock of knowledge, and what the "idealities" were worth the devil alone knew! A positively burning thirst overcame me: and from that time forward I have done literally nothing else than study physiology, medicine, and natural science—I even returned to the actual study of history only when my life-task compelled me to. It was at that time, too, that I first divined the relation between an instinctively repulsive occupation, a so-called vocation, which is the last thing to which one is "called," and that need of lulling a feeling of emptiness and hunger, by means of an art which is a narcotic—by means of Wagner's art, for instance. After looking carefully about me, I have discovered that a large number of young men are all in the same state of distress: one kind of unnatural practise perforce leads to another. In Germany, or rather, to avoid all ambiguity, in the Empire,[7] only too many are condemned to determine their choice too soon, and then to pine away beneath a burden that they can no longer throw off. . . . Such creatures crave for Wagner as for an opiate—they are thus able to forget themselves, to be rid of themselves for a moment. . . . What am I saying! For five or six hours.

4

At this time my instincts turned resolutely against any further yielding or following on my part, and any further misunderstanding of myself. Every kind of life, the most unfavourable circumstances, illness, poverty— anything seemed to me preferable to that undignified "selfishness" into which I had fallen; in the first place, thanks to my ignorance and youth, and in which I had afterwards remained owing to laziness—the so-called "sense of duty." At this juncture there came to my help, in a way that I cannot sufficiently admire, and precisely at the right time, that evil heritage which I derive from my father's side of the family, and which, at bottom, is no more than a predisposition to die young. Illness slowly liberated me from the toils, it spared me any sort of sudden breach, any sort of violent and offensive step. At that time I lost not a particle of the good will of others, but rather added to my store. Illness likewise gave me the right completely to reverse my mode of life; it not only allowed, it actually commanded, me to forget; it bestowed upon me the necessity of lying still, of having leisure, of waiting, and of exercising patience. . . . But all this means thinking! . . . The state of my eyes alone put an end to all bookwormishness, or, in plain English—philology: I was thus delivered from books; for years I ceased from reading, and this was the greatest boon I ever conferred upon myself! That nethermost self, which was, as it were, entombed, and which had grown dumb because it had been forced to listen perpetually to other selves (for that is what reading means!), slowly awakened; at first it was shy and doubtful, but at last it *spoke again*. Never have I rejoiced more over my condition than during the sickest and most painful moments of my life. You have only to examine *The Dawn of Day*, or, perhaps, *The Wanderer and his Shadow*,[8] in order to understand what this "return to myself" actually meant: in itself it was the highest kind of recovery! . . . My cure was simply the result of it.

5

Human, All-Too-Human, this monument of a course of vigorous self-discipline, by means of which I put an abrupt end to all the "Superior Bunkum," "Idealism," "Beautiful Feelings," and other effeminacies that had percolated into my being, was written principally in Sorrento; it was finished and given definite shape during a winter at Bâle, under conditions far less favourable than those in Sorrento. Truth to tell, it was Peter Gast, at that time a student at the University of Bâle, and a devoted friend of mine, who was responsible for the book. With my head wrapped in bandages, and extremely painful, I dictated while he wrote and corrected as he went along—to be accurate, he was the real composer, whereas I was only the author. When the completed book ultimately reached me—to the great surprise of the serious invalid I then was—I sent, among others, two copies to Bayreuth. Thanks to a miraculous flash of intelligence on the part of chance, there reached me precisely at the same time a splendid copy of the *Parsifal* text, with the following inscription from Wagner's pen: "To his dear friend Friedrich Nietzsche, from Richard Wagner, Ecclesiastical Councillor." At this crossing of the two books I seemed to hear an ominous note. Did it not sound as if two swords had crossed? At all events we both felt this was so, for each of us remained silent. At about this time the first Bayreuth Pamphlets appeared: and I then understood the move on my part for which it was high time. Incredible! Wagner had become pious.

6

My attitude to myself at that time (1876), and the unearthly certitude with which I grasped my life-task and all its world-historic consequences, is well revealed throughout the book, but more particularly in one very significant passage, despite the fact that, with my instinctive cunning, I once more circumvented the use of the little word "I"—not however, this time, in order to shed world-historic glory on the names of Schopenhauer and Wagner, but on that of another of my friends, the excellent Dr. Paul Rée—fortunately much too acute a creature to be deceived—others were less subtle. Among my readers I have a number of hopeless people, the typical German professor for instance, who can always be recognised from the fact that, judging from the passage in question, he feels compelled to regard the whole book as a sort of superior Réealism. As a matter of fact it contradicts five or six of my friend's utterances: only read the introduction to *The Genealogy of Morals* on this question. The passage above referred to reads: "What, after all, is the principal axiom to which the boldest and coldest thinker, the author of the book *On the Origin of Moral Sensations*" (read Nietzsche, the first Immoralist), "has attained by means of his incisive and decisive analysis of human actions? 'The moral man,' he says, 'is no nearer to the intelligible (metaphysical) world than is the physical man, for there is no intelligible world.' This theory, hardened and sharpened under the hammer-blow of historical knowledge" (read *The Transvaluation of All Values*), "may some time or other, perhaps in some future period—1890! Serve as the axe which is applied to the root of the 'metaphysical need' of man—whether more as a blessing than a curse to the general welfare it is not easy to say; but in any case as a theory with the most important consequences, at once fruitful and terrible, and looking into the world with that Janus-face which all great knowledge possesses."[9]

THE DAWN OF DAY:

THOUGHTS ABOUT MORALITY AS A PREJUDICE

1

With this book I open my campaign against morality. Not that it is at all redolent of powder—you will find quite other and much nicer smells in it, provided that you have any keenness in your nostrils. There is nothing either of light or of heavy artillery in its composition, and if its general end be a negative one, its means are not so—means out of which the end follows like a logical conclusion, *not* like a cannon-shot. And if the reader takes leave of this book with a feeling of timid caution in regard to everything which has hitherto been honoured and even worshipped under the name of morality, it does not alter the fact that there is not one negative word, not one attack, and not one single piece of malice in the whole work—on the contrary, it lies in the sunshine, smooth and happy, like a marine animal, basking in the sun between two rocks. For, after all, I was this marine animal: almost every sentence in the book was thought out, or rather *caught*, among that medley of rocks in the neighbourhood of Genoa, where I lived quite alone, and exchanged secrets with the ocean. Even to this day, when by chance I happen to turn over the leaves of this book, almost every sentence seems to me like a hook by means of which I draw something incomparable out of the depths; its whole skin quivers with delicate shudders of recollection. This book is conspicuous for no little art in gently catching things which whisk rapidly and silently away, moments which I call godlike lizards—not with the cruelty of that young Greek god who simply transfixed the poor little beast; but nevertheless with something pointed—with a pen. "There are so many dawns which have not yet shed their light"—this Indian maxim is written over the doorway of this book. Where does its author seek that new morning, that delicate red, as yet undiscovered, with which another day—ah! A whole series of days, a whole world of new days! Will begin? In the *Transvaluation of All Values,* in an emancipation from all moral values, in a saying of yea, and in an attitude of trust, to all that which hitherto has been forbidden, despised, and damned. This yea-saying book projects its light, its love, its tenderness, over all evil things, it restores to them their soul, their clear conscience, and their superior right and privilege to exist on earth. Morality is not assailed, it simply ceases to be considered. This book closes with the word "or?". It is the only book which closes with an "or?".

2

My life-task is to prepare for humanity one supreme moment in which it can come to its senses, a Great Noon in which it will turn its gaze backwards and forwards, in which it will step from under the yoke of accident and of priests, and for the first time set the question of the Why and Wherefore of humanity as a whole—this life-task naturally follows out of the conviction that mankind does *not* get on the right road of its own accord, that it is by no means divinely ruled, but rather that it is precisely under the cover of its most holy valuations that the instinct of negation, of corruption, and of degeneration has held such a seductive sway. The question concerning the origin of moral valuations is therefore a matter of the highest importance to me because it determines the future of mankind. The demand made upon us to believe that everything is really in the best hands, that a certain book, the Bible, gives us the definite and comforting assurance that there is a Providence that wisely rules the fate of man—when translated back into reality amounts simply to this, namely, the will to stifle the truth which maintains the reverse of all this, which is that hitherto man has been in the *worst possible* hands, and that he has been governed by the physiologically botched, the men of cunning and burning revengefulness, and the so-called "saints"—those slanderers of the world and traducers of humanity. The definite proof of the fact that the priest (including the priest in disguise, the philosopher) has become master, not only within a certain limited religious community, but everywhere, and that the morality of decadence, the will to nonentity, has become morality per se, is to be found in this: that altruism is now an absolute value, and egoism is regarded with hostility everywhere. He who disagrees with me on this point, I regard as infected. But all the world disagrees with me. To a physiologist a like antagonism between values admits of no doubt. If the most insignificant organ within the body neglects, however slightly, to assert with absolute certainty its self-preservative powers, its recuperative claims, and its egoism, the whole system degenerates. The physiologist insists upon the removal of degenerated parts, he denies all fellow-feeling for such parts, and has not the smallest feeling of pity for them. But the desire of the priest is precisely the degeneration of the whole of mankind; hence his preservation of that which is degenerate—this is what his dominion costs humanity. What meaning have those lying concepts, those handmaids of morality, "Soul," "Spirit," "Free will," "God," if their aim is not the physiological ruin of mankind? When earnestness is diverted from the instincts that aim at self-preservation and an increase of bodily energy, i.e., at an *increase of life*; when anaemia is raised to an ideal and the contempt of the body is construed as "the salvation of the soul," what is all this if it is not a recipe for decadence? Loss of ballast, resistance offered to natural instincts, selflessness, in fact—this is what has hitherto been known as morality. With *The Dawn of Day* I first engaged in a struggle against the morality of self-renunciation.

Dawn of Day is a yea-saying book, profound, but clear and kindly. The same applies once more and in the highest degree to *La Gaya Scienza*: in almost every sentence of this book, profundity and playfulness go gently hand in hand. A verse which expresses my gratitude for the most wonderful month of January which I have ever lived—the whole book is a gift—sufficiently reveals the abysmal depths from which "wisdom" has here become joyful.

Thou who with cleaving fiery lances
The stream of my soul from its ice dost free,
Till with a rush and a roar it advances
To enter with glorious hoping the sea:
Brighter to see and purer ever,
Free in the bonds of thy sweet constraint—
So it praises thy wondrous endeavour,
January, thou beauteous saint![10]

Who can be in any doubt as to what "glorious hoping" means here, when he has realised the diamond beauty of the first of Zarathustra's words as they appear in a glow of light at the close of the fourth book? Or when he reads the granite sentences at the end of the third book, wherein a fate for all times is first given a formula? The songs of Prince Free-as-a-Bird, which, for the most part, were written in Sicily, remind me quite forcibly of that Provençal notion of "*Gaya Scienza*," of that union of *singer, knight, and free spirit*, which distinguishes that wonderfully early culture of the Provençals from all ambiguous cultures. The last poem of all, "To the Mistral"—an exuberant dance song in which, if you please, the new spirit dances freely upon the corpse of morality—is a perfect Provençalism.

THUS SPAKE ZARATHUSTRA: A BOOK FOR ALL AND NONE

1

I now wish to relate the history of *Zarathustra*. The fundamental idea of the work, the *Eternal Recurrence*, the highest formula of a Yea-saying to life that can ever be attained, was first conceived in the month of August 1881. I made a note of the idea on a sheet of paper, with the postscript: "Six thousand feet beyond man and time." That day I happened to be wandering through the woods alongside of the Lake of Silvaplana, and I halted not far from Surlei, beside a huge rock that towered aloft like a pyramid. It was then that the thought struck me. Looking back now, I find that exactly two months before this inspiration I had an omen of its coming in the form of a sudden and decisive change in my tastes—more particularly in music. The whole of *Zarathustra* might perhaps be classified under the rubric music. At all events, the essential condition of its production was a second birth within me of the art of hearing. In Recoaro, a small mountain resort near Vicenza, where I spent the spring of 1881, I and my friend and maestro, Peter Gast—who was also one who had been born again, discovered that the phoenix music hovered over us, in lighter and brighter plumage than it had ever worn before. If, therefore, I now calculate from that day forward the sudden production of the book, under the most unlikely circumstances, in February 1883—the last part, out of which I quoted a few lines in my preface, was written precisely in the hallowed hour when Richard Wagner gave up the ghost in Venice—I come to the conclusion that the period of gestation covered eighteen months. This period of exactly eighteen months, might suggest, at least to Buddhists, that I am in reality a female elephant. The interval was devoted to the *Gaya Scienza*, which contains hundreds of indications of the proximity of something unparalleled; for, after all, it shows the beginning of *Zarathustra*, since it presents *Zarathustra's* fundamental thought in the last aphorism but one of the fourth book. To this interval also belongs that *Hymn to Life* (for a mixed choir and orchestra), the score of which was published in Leipzig two years ago by E. W. Fritsch, and which gave perhaps no slight indication of my spiritual state during this year, in which the essentially yea-saying pathos, which I call the tragic pathos, completely filled me heart and limb. One day people will sing it to my memory. The text, let it be well understood, as there is some misunderstanding abroad on this point, is not by me; it was the astounding inspiration of a young Russian lady, Miss Lou von Salome, with whom I was then on friendly terms. He who is in any way able to make some sense of the last words of the poem, will divine why I preferred and admired it: there is greatness in them. Pain is not regarded as an objection to existence: "And if thou hast no bliss now left to crown me—Lead on! Thou hast thy Sorrow still."

Maybe that my music is also great in this passage. (The last note of the oboe, by the bye, is C sharp, not C. The latter is a misprint.) During the following winter, I was living on that charmingly peaceful Gulf of Rapallo, not far from Genoa, which cuts inland between Chiavari and Cape Porto Fino. My health was not very good; the winter was cold and exceptionally rainy; and the small *albergo* in which I lived was so close to the water that at night my sleep was disturbed if the sea was rough. These circumstances were surely the very reverse of favourable; and yet, in spite of it all, and as if in proof of my belief that everything decisive comes to life in defiance of every obstacle, it was precisely during this winter and in the midst of these unfavourable circumstances that my *Zarathustra* originated. In the morning I used to start out in a southerly direction up the glorious road to Zoagli, which rises up through a forest of pines and gives one a view far out to sea. In the afternoon, or as often as my health allowed, I walked round the whole bay from Santa Margherita to beyond Porto Fino. This spot affected me all the more deeply because it was so dearly loved by the Emperor Frederick III. In the autumn of 1886 I chanced to be there again when he was revisiting this small forgotten world of happiness for the last time. It was on these two roads that all *Zarathustra* came to me, above all, Zarathustra himself as a type—I ought rather to say that it was on these walks that *he waylaid me*.

2

In order to understand this type, you must first be quite clear concerning its fundamental physiological condition: this condition is what I call *great healthiness*. In regard to this idea I cannot make my meaning more plain or more personal than I have done already in one of the last aphorisms (No. 382) of the fifth book of the *Gaya Scienza*: "We new, nameless, and unfathomable creatures," so reads the passage,

> . . . we firstlings of a future still unproved—we who have a new end in view also require new means to that end, that is to say, a new healthiness, a stronger, keener, tougher, bolder, and merrier healthiness than any that has existed heretofore. He who longs to feel in his own soul the whole range of values and aims that have prevailed

on earth until his day, and to sail round all the coasts of this ideal "Mediterranean Sea"; who, from the adventures of his own inmost experience, would fain know how it feels to be a conqueror and discoverer of the ideal; as also how it is with the artist, the saint, the legislator, the sage, the scholar, the man of piety and the godlike anchorite of yore; such a man requires one thing above all for his purpose, and that is, *great healthiness*—such healthiness as he not only possesses, but also constantly acquires and must acquire, because he is continually sacrificing it again, and is compelled to sacrifice it! And now, therefore, after having been long on the way, we Argonauts of the ideal, whose pluck is greater than prudence would allow, and who are often shipwrecked and bruised, but, as I have said, healthier than people would like to admit, dangerously healthy, and forever recovering our health—it would seem as if we had before us, as a reward for all our toils, a country still undiscovered, the horizon of which no one has yet seen, a beyond to every country and every refuge of the ideal that man has ever known, a world so overflowing with beauty, strangeness, doubt, terror, and divinity, that both our curiosity and our lust of possession are frantic with eagerness. Alas! How in the face of such vistas, and with such burning desire in our conscience and consciousness, could we still be content with *the man of the present day?* This is bad indeed; but, that we should regard his worthiest aims and hopes with ill-concealed amusement, or perhaps give them no thought at all, is inevitable. Another ideal now leads us on, a wonderful, seductive ideal, full of danger, the pursuit of which we should be loath to urge upon anyone, because we are not so ready to acknowledge any one's *right to it*: the ideal of a spirit who plays ingenuously (that is to say, involuntarily, and as the outcome of superabundant energy and power) with everything that, hitherto, has been called holy, good, inviolable, and divine; to whom even the loftiest thing that the people have with reason made their measure of value would be no better than a danger, a decay, and an abasement, or at least a relaxation and temporary forgetfulness of self: the ideal of a humanly superhuman well-being and goodwill, which often enough will seem inhuman—as when, for instance, it stands beside all past earnestness on earth, and all past solemnities in hearing, speech, tone, look, morality, and duty, as their most lifelike and unconscious parody—but with which, nevertheless, *great earnestness* perhaps alone begins, the first note of interrogation is affixed, the fate of the soul changes, the hour hand moves, and tragedy begins.

3

Has any one at the end of the nineteenth century any distinct notion of what poets of a stronger age understood by the word inspiration? If not, I will describe it. If one had the smallest vestige of superstition left in one, it would hardly be possible completely to set aside the idea that one is the mere incarnation, mouthpiece, or medium of an almighty power. The idea of revelation, in the sense that something which profoundly convulses and upsets one becomes suddenly visible and audible with indescribable certainty and accuracy—describes the simple fact. One hears—one does not seek; one takes—one does not ask who gives: a thought suddenly flashes up like lightning, it comes with necessity, without faltering—I have never had any choice in the matter. There is an ecstasy so great that the immense strain of it is sometimes relaxed by a flood of tears, during which one's steps now involuntarily rush and anon involuntarily lag. There is the feeling that one is utterly out of hand, with the very distinct consciousness of an endless number of fine thrills and titillations descending to one's very toes; there is a depth of happiness in which the most painful and gloomy parts do not act as antitheses to the rest, but are produced and required as necessary shades of colour in such an overflow of light. There is an instinct for rhythmic relations which embraces a whole world of forms (length, the need of a wide-embracing rhythm, is almost the measure of the force of an inspiration, a sort of counterpart to its pressure and tension). Everything happens quite involuntarily, as if in a tempestuous outburst of freedom, of absoluteness, of power and divinity. The involuntary nature of the figures and similes is the most remarkable thing; one loses all perception of what is imagery and metaphor; everything seems to present itself as the readiest, the truest, and simplest means of expression. It actually seems, to use one of Zarathustra's own phrases, as if all things came to one, and offered themselves as similes. ("Here do all things come caressingly to thy discourse and flatter thee, for they would fain ride upon thy back. On every simile thou ridest here unto every truth. Here fly open unto thee all the speech and word shrines of the world, here would all existence become speech, here would all Becoming learn of thee how to speak.") This is my experience of inspiration. I do not doubt but that I should have to go back thousands of years before I could find another who could say to me: "It is mine also!"

4

For a few weeks afterwards I lay an invalid in Genoa. Then followed a melancholy spring in Rome, where I only just managed to live—and this was no easy matter. This city, which is absolutely unsuited to the poet-author of *Zarathustra*, and for the choice of which I was not responsible, made me inordinately miserable. I tried to leave it. I wanted to go to Aquila—the opposite of Rome in every respect, and actually founded in a spirit of hostility towards that city, just as I also shall found a city someday, as a memento of an atheist and genuine enemy of the Church, a person very closely related to me, the great Hohenstaufen, the Emperor Frederick II. But Fate lay behind it all: I had to return again to Rome. In the end I was obliged to be satisfied with the Piazza Barberini, after I had exerted myself in vain to find an anti-Christian quarter. I fear that on one occasion, to avoid bad smells as much as possible, I actually inquired at the Palazzo del Quirinale whether they could not provide a quiet room for a philosopher. In a chamber high above the Piazza just mentioned, from which one obtained a general view of Rome, and could hear the fountains plashing far below, the loneliest of all songs was composed—*The Night-Song*. About this time I was obsessed by an unspeakably sad melody, the refrain of which I recognised in the words, "dead through immortality. . . ." In the summer, finding myself once more in the sacred place where the first thought of *Zarathustra* flashed like a light across my mind, I conceived the second part. Ten days sufficed. Neither for the second, the first, nor the third part, have I required a day longer. In the ensuing winter, beneath the halcyon sky of Nice, which then for the first time poured its light into my life, I found the third *Zarathustra*—and came to the end of my task: the whole having occupied me scarcely a year. Many hidden corners and heights in the country round about Nice are hallowed for me by moments that I can never forget. That decisive chapter, entitled "Old and New Tables," was composed during the arduous ascent from the station to Eza—that wonderful Moorish village in the rocks. During those moments when my creative energy flowed most plentifully, my muscular activity was always greatest. The body is inspired: let us waive the question of "soul." I might often have been seen dancing in those days, and I could then walk for seven or eight hours on end over the hills without a suggestion of fatigue. I slept well and laughed a good deal—I was perfectly robust and patient.

5

With the exception of these periods of industry lasting ten days, the years I spent during the production of *Zarathustra*, and thereafter, were for me years of unparalleled distress. A man pays dearly for being immortal: to this end he must die many times over during his life. There is such a thing as what I call the rancour of greatness: everything great, whether a work or a deed, once it is completed, turns immediately against its author. The very fact that he is its author makes him weak at this time. He can no longer endure his deed. He can no longer look it full in the face. To have something at one's back which one could never have willed, something to which the knot of human destiny is attached—and to be forced thenceforward to bear it on one's shoulders! Why, it almost crushes one! The rancour of greatness! A somewhat different experience is the uncanny silence that reigns about one. Solitude has seven skins which nothing can penetrate. One goes among men; one greets friends: but these things are only new deserts, the looks of those one meets no longer bear a greeting. At the best one encounters a sort of revolt. This feeling of revolt, I suffered, in varying degrees of intensity, at the hands of almost everyone who came near me; it would seem that nothing inflicts a deeper wound than suddenly to make one's distance felt. Those noble natures are scarce who know not how to live unless they can revere. A third thing is the absurd susceptibility of the skin to small pinpricks, a kind of helplessness in the presence of all small things. This seems to me a necessary outcome of the appalling expenditure of all defensive forces, which is the first condition of every *creative* act, of every act which proceeds from the most intimate, most secret, and most concealed recesses of a man's being. The small defensive forces are thus, as it were, suspended, and no fresh energy reaches them. I even think it probable that one does not digest so well, that one is less willing to move, and that one is much too open to sensations of coldness and suspicion; for, in a large number of cases, suspicion is merely a blunder in etiology. On one occasion when I felt like this I became conscious of the proximity of a herd of cows, some time before I could possibly have seen it with my eyes, simply owing to a return in me of milder and more humane sentiments: *they* communicated warmth to me. . . .

6

This work stands alone. Do not let us mention the poets in the same breath: nothing perhaps has ever been produced out of such a superabundance of strength. My concept "Dionysian" here became the *highest* deed; compared with it everything that other men have done seems poor and limited. The fact that a Goethe or a Shakespeare would not for an instant have known how to take breath in this atmosphere of passion and of the heights; the fact that by the side of Zarathustra, Dante is no more than a believer, and not one who first *creates* the truth—that is to say, not a world-ruling spirit, a *Fate*; the fact that the poets of the Veda were priests and not even fit to unfasten Zarathustra's sandal—all this is the least of things, and gives no idea of the distance, of the azure solitude, in which this work dwells. Zarathustra has an eternal right to say: "I draw around me circles and holy boundaries. Ever fewer are they that mount with me to ever loftier heights. I build me a mountain range of ever holier mountains." If all the spirit and goodness of every great soul were collected together, the whole could not create a single one of Zarathustra's discourses. The ladder upon which he rises and descends is of boundless length; he has seen further, he has willed further, and *gone* further than any other man. There is contradiction in every word that he utters, this most yea-saying of all spirits. Through him all contradictions are bound up into a new unity. The loftiest and the basest powers of human nature, the sweetest, the lightest, and the most terrible, rush forth from out one spring with everlasting certainty. Until his coming no one knew what was height, or depth, and still less what was truth. There is not a single passage in this revelation of truth which had already been anticipated and divined by even the greatest among men. Before Zarathustra there was no wisdom, no probing of the soul, no art of speech: in his book, the most familiar and most vulgar thing utters unheard-of words. The sentence quivers with passion. Eloquence has become music. Forks of lightning are hurled towards futures of which no one has ever dreamed before. The most powerful use of parables that has yet existed is poor beside it, and mere child's-play compared with this return of language to the nature of imagery. See how Zarathustra goes down from the mountain and speaks the kindest words to everyone! See with what delicate fingers he touches his very adversaries, the priests, and how he suffers with them from themselves! Here, at every moment, man is overcome, and the concept "Superman" becomes the greatest reality—out of sight, almost far away beneath him, lies all that which heretofore has been called great in man. The halcyonic brightness, the light feet, the presence of wickedness and exuberance throughout, and all that is the essence of the type Zarathustra, was never dreamt of before as a prerequisite of greatness. In precisely these limits of space and in this accessibility to opposites Zarathustra feels himself the *highest of all living things*: and when you hear how he defines this highest, you will give up trying to find his equal.

> The soul which hath the longest ladder and can step down deepest,
> The vastest soul that can run and stray and rove furthest in its own domain,
> The most necessary soul, that out of desire flingeth itself to chance,
> The stable soul that plungeth into Becoming, the possessing soul that must needs taste of willing and longing,
> The soul that flyeth from itself, and overtaketh itself in the widest circle,
> The wisest soul that folly exhorteth most sweetly,
> The most self-loving soul, in whom all things have their rise, their ebb and flow.

But this is the very idea of Dionysus. Another consideration leads to this idea. The psychological problem presented by the type of Zarathustra is, how can he, who in an unprecedented manner says no, and *acts* no, in regard to all that which has been affirmed hitherto, remain nevertheless a yea-saying spirit? How can he who bears the heaviest destiny on his shoulders and whose very life-task is a fatality, yet be the brightest and the most transcendental of spirits—for Zarathustra is a dancer? How can he who has the hardest and most terrible grasp of reality, and who has thought the most "abysmal thoughts," nevertheless avoid conceiving these things as objections to existence, or even as objections to the eternal recurrence of existence? How is it that on the contrary he finds reasons for *being himself* the eternal affirmation of all things, "the tremendous and unlimited saying of Yea and Amen?" . . . "Into every abyss do I bear the benediction of my yea to Life. . . ." But this, once more, is precisely the idea of Dionysus.

7

What language will such a spirit speak, when he speaks unto his soul? The language of the *dithyramb*. I am the inventor of the dithyramb. Hearken unto the manner in which Zarathustra speaks to his soul *Before Sunrise* (iii. 48). Before my time such emerald joys and divine tenderness had found no tongue. Even the profoundest melancholy of such a Dionysus takes shape as a dithyramb. As an example of this I take *The Night-Song*—the immortal plaint of one who, thanks to his superabundance of light and power, thanks to the sun within him, is condemned never to love.

> It is night: now do all gushing springs raise their voices. And my soul too is a gushing spring.
>
> It is night: now only do all lovers burst into song. And my soul too is the song of a lover.
>
> Something unquenched and unquenchable is within me, that would raise its voice. A craving for love is within me, which itself speaketh the language of love.
>
> Light am I: would that I were night! But this is my loneliness, that I am begirt with light.
>
> Alas, why am I not dark and like unto the night! How joyfully would I then suck at the breasts of light!
>
> And even you would I bless, ye twinkling starlets and glowworms on high! And be blessed in the gifts of your light.
>
> But in mine own light do I live, ever back into myself do I drink the flames I send forth.
>
> I know not the happiness of the hand stretched forth to grasp; and oft have I dreamt that stealing must be more blessed than taking.
>
> Wretched am I that my hand may never rest from giving: an envious fate is mine that I see expectant eyes and nights made bright with longing.
>
> Oh, the wretchedness of all them that give! Oh, the clouds that cover the face of my sun! That craving for desire! That burning hunger at the end of the feast!
>
> They take what I give them; but do I touch their soul? A gulf is there 'twixt giving and taking; and the smallest gulf is the last to be bridged.
>
> An appetite is born from out my beauty: would that I might do harm to them that I fill with light; would that I might rob them of the gifts I have given: thus do I thirst for wickedness.
>
> To withdraw my hand when their hand is ready stretched forth like the waterfall that wavers, wavers even in its fall: thus do I thirst for wickedness.
>
> For such vengeance doth my fulness yearn: to such tricks doth my loneliness give birth.

My joy in giving died with the deed. By its very fulness did my virtue
   grow weary of itself.

He who giveth risketh to lose his shame; he that is ever distributing
   groweth callous in hand and heart therefrom.

Mine eyes no longer melt into tears at the sight of the suppliant's
   shame; my hand hath become too hard to feel the quivering of
   laden hands.

Whither have ye fled, the tears of mine eyes and the bloom
   of my heart? Oh, the solitude of all givers! Oh, the silence of
   all beacons!

Many are the suns that circle in barren space; to all that is dark do
   they speak with their light—to me alone are they silent.

Alas, this is the hatred of light for that which shineth: pitiless it
   runneth its course.

Unfair in its inmost heart to that which shineth; cold toward suns—
   thus doth every sun go its way.

Like a tempest do the suns fly over their course: for such is their way.
   Their own unswerving will do they follow: that is their coldness.

Alas, it is ye alone, ye creatures of gloom, ye spirits of the night,
   that take your warmth from that which shineth. Ye alone suck
   your milk and comfort from the udders of light.

Alas, about me there is ice, my hand burneth itself against ice!

Alas, within me is a thirst that thirsteth for your thirst!

It is night: woe is me, that I must needs be light! And thirst after
   darkness! And loneliness!

It is night: now doth my longing burst forth like a spring—for
   speech do I long.

It is night: now do all gushing springs raise their voices. And my
   soul too is a gushing spring.

It is night: now only do all lovers burst into song. And my soul too
   is the song of a lover.

8

Such things have never been written, never been felt, never been *suffered*:
only a God, only Dionysus suffers in this way. The reply to such a dithyramb on the sun's solitude in light would be Ariadne. . . . Who knows, but
I, who Ariadne is! To all such riddles no one heretofore had ever found
an answer; I doubt even whether any one had ever seen a riddle here. One
day Zarathustra severely determines his life-task—and it is also mine. Let

no one misunderstand its meaning. It is a yea-saying to the point of justify-ing, to the point of redeeming even all that is past.

> I walk among men as among fragments of the future: of that future which I see.
> And all my creativeness and effort is but this, that I may be able to think and recast all these fragments and riddles and dismal accidents into one piece.
> And how could I bear to be a man, if man were not also a poet, a riddle reader, and a redeemer of chance!
> To redeem all the past, and to transform every "it was" into "thus would I have it"—that alone would be my salvation!

In another passage he defines as strictly as possible what to him alone "man" can be—not a subject for love nor yet for pity—Zarathustra became master even of his loathing of man: man is to him a thing unshaped, raw material, an ugly stone that needs the sculptor's chisel.

> No longer to will, no longer to value, no longer to create! Oh, that this great weariness may never be mine!
> Even in the lust of knowledge, I feel only the joy of my will to beget and to grow; and if there be innocence in my knowledge, it is because my procreative will is in it.
> Away from God and gods did this will lure me: what would there be to create if there were gods?
> But to man doth it ever drive me anew, my burning, creative will. Thus driveth it the hammer to the stone.
> Alas, ye men, within the stone there sleepeth an image for me, the image of all my dreams! Alas, that it should have to sleep in the hardest and ugliest stone!
> *Now rageth my hammer ruthlessly against its prison.* From the stone the fragments fly: what's that to me?
> I will finish it: for a shadow came unto me—the stillest and lightest thing on earth once came unto me!
> The beauty of the Superman came unto me as a shadow. Alas, my brethren! What are the—gods to me now?

Let me call attention to one last point of view. The line in italics is my pretext for this remark. A Dionysian life-task needs the hardness of the hammer, and one of its first essentials is without doubt the *joy even of destruction*. The command, "Harden yourselves!" and the deep conviction that *all creators are hard*, is the really distinctive sign of a Dionysian nature.

BEYOND GOOD AND EVIL: THE PRELUDE TO A PHILOSOPHY
OF THE FUTURE

1

My work for the years that followed was prescribed as distinctly as possible. Now that the yea-saying part of my life-task was accomplished, there came the turn of the negative portion, both in word and deed: the transvaluation of all values that had existed hitherto, the great war—the conjuring-up of the day when the fatal outcome of the struggle would be decided. Meanwhile, I had slowly to look about me for my peers, for those who, *out of strength*, would proffer me a helping hand in my work of destruction. From that time onward, all my writings are so much bait: maybe I understand as much about fishing as most people? If nothing was *caught*, it was not I who was at fault. *There were no fish to come and bite.*

2

In all its essential points, this book (1886) is a criticism of *modernity*, embracing the modern sciences, arts, even politics, together with certain indications as to a type which would be the reverse of modern man, or as little like him as possible, a noble and yea-saying type. In this last respect the book is a *school for gentlemen*—the term *gentleman* being understood here in a much more spiritual and radical sense than it has implied hitherto. All those things of which the age is proud—as, for instance, far-famed "objectivity," "sympathy with all that suffers," "the historical sense," with its subjection to foreign tastes, with its lying-in-the-dust before *petits faits*, and the rage for science—are shown to be the contradiction of the type recommended, and are regarded as almost ill-bred. If you remember that this book follows upon *Zarathustra*, you may possibly guess to what system of diet it owes its life. The eye which, owing to tremendous constraint, has become accustomed to see at a great distance—*Zarathustra* is even more farsighted than the Tsar—is here forced to focus sharply that which is close at hand, the present time, the things that lie about him. In all the aphorisms and more particularly in the form of this book, the reader will find the same *voluntary* turning away from those instincts which made a *Zarathustra* a possible feat. Refinement in form, in aspiration, and in the art of keeping silent, are its more or less obvious qualities; psychology is handled with deliberate hardness and cruelty—the whole book does not contain one single good-natured word. . . . All this sort of thing refreshes a man. Who can guess the kind of recreation that is necessary after such an expenditure of goodness as is to be found in *Zarathustra*? From a theological standpoint—now pay ye heed; for it is but on rare occasions that I speak as a theologian—it was God Himself who, at the end of His great work, coiled Himself up in the form of a serpent at the foot of the tree of knowledge. It was thus that He recovered from being a God. . . . He had made everything too beautiful. . . . The devil is simply God's moment of idleness, on that seventh day.

THE GENEALOGY OF MORALS: A POLEMIC

The three essays which constitute this genealogy are, as regards expression, aspiration, and the art of the unexpected, perhaps the most curious things that have ever been written. Dionysus, as you know, is also the god of darkness. In each case the beginning is calculated to mystify; it is cool, scientific, even ironical, intentionally thrust to the fore, intentionally reticent. Gradually less calmness prevails; here and there a flash of lightning defines the horizon; exceedingly unpleasant truths break upon your ears from out remote distances with a dull, rumbling sound—until very soon a fierce tempo is attained in which everything presses forward at a terrible degree of tension. At the end, in each case, amid fearful thunderclaps, a new truth shines out between thick clouds. The truth of the first essay is the psychology of Christianity: the birth of Christianity out of the spirit of resentment, not, as is supposed, out of the "Spirit"—in all its essentials, a counter-movement, the great insurrection against the dominion of noble values. The second essay contains the psychology of conscience: this is not, as you may believe, "the voice of God in man"; it is the instinct of cruelty, which turns inwards once it is unable to discharge itself outwardly. Cruelty is here exposed, for the first time, as one of the oldest and most indispensable elements in the foundation of culture. The third essay replies to the question as to the origin of the formidable power of the ascetic ideal, of the priest ideal, despite the fact that this ideal is essentially detrimental, that it is a will to nonentity and to decadence. Reply: it flourished not because God was active behind the priests, as is generally believed, but because it was a *faute de mieux*—from the fact that hitherto it has been the only ideal and has had no competitors. "For man prefers to aspire to nonentity than not to aspire at all."

But above all, until the time of *Zarathustra* there was no such thing as a counter-ideal. You have understood my meaning. Three decisive overtures on the part of a psychologist to a *Transvaluation of All Values*. This book contains the first psychology of the priest.

THE TWILIGHT OF THE IDOLS:

HOW TO PHILOSOPHISE WITH THE HAMMER

1

This work—which covers scarcely one hundred and fifty pages, with its cheerful and fateful tone, like a laughing demon, and the production of which occupied so few days that I hesitate to give their number—is altogether an exception among books: there is no work more rich in substance, more independent, more upsetting—more wicked. If any one should desire to obtain a rapid sketch of how everything, before my time, was standing on its head, he should begin reading me in this book. That which is called "Idols" on the title page is simply the old truth that has been believed in hitherto. In plain English, *The Twilight of the Idols* means that the old truth is on its last legs.

2

There is no reality, no "ideality," which has not been touched in this book (touched! What a cautious euphemism!). Not only the eternal idols, but also the youngest—that is to say, the most senile: modern ideas, for instance. A strong wind blows between the trees and in all directions fall the fruit—the truths. There is the waste of an all-too-rich autumn in this book: you trip over truths. You even crush some to death, there are too many of them. Those things that you can grasp, however, are quite unquestionable; they are irrevocable decrees. I alone have the criterion of "truths" in my possession. I alone *can* decide. It would seem as if a second consciousness had grown up in me, as if the "life-will" in me had thrown a light upon the downward path along which it has been running throughout the ages. The *downward path*—hitherto this had been called the road to "Truth." All obscure impulse—"darkness and dismay"—is at an end, the "*good man*" was precisely he who was least aware of the proper way.[11] And, speaking in all earnestness, no one before me knew the proper way, the way upwards: only after my time could men once more find hope, life-tasks, and roads mapped out that lead to culture—*I am the joyful harbinger of this culture.* . . . On this account alone I am also a fatality.

3

Immediately after the completion of the above-named work, and without letting even one day go by, I tackled the formidable task of the *Transvaluation* with a supreme feeling of pride which nothing could equal; and, certain at each moment of my immortality, I cut sign after sign upon tablets of brass with the sureness of Fate. The preface came into being on 3rd September 1888. When, after having written it down, I went out into the open that morning, I was greeted by the most beautiful day I had ever seen in the Upper Engadine—clear, glowing with colour, and presenting all the contrasts and all the intermediary gradations between ice and the south. I left Sils-Maria only on the 20th of September. I had been forced to delay my departure owing to floods, and I was very soon, and for some days, the only visitor in this wonderful spot, on which my gratitude bestows the gift of an immortal name. After a journey that was full of incidents, and not without danger to life—as for instance at Como, which was flooded when I reached it in the dead of night—I got to Turin on the afternoon of the 21st. Turin is the only suitable place for me, and it shall be my home henceforward. I took the same lodgings as I had occupied in the spring, 6 III Via Carlo Alberto, opposite the mighty Palazzo Carignano, in which Vittorio Emanuele was born; and I had a view of the Piazza Carlo Alberto and above it across to the hills. Without hesitating, or allowing myself to be disturbed for a single moment, I returned to my work, only the last quarter of which had still to be written. On the 30th September, tremendous triumph; the seventh day; the leisure of a god on the banks of the Po.[12] On the same day, I wrote the Preface to *The Twilight of the Idols*, the correction of the proofs of which provided me with recreation during the month of September. Never in my life have I experienced such an autumn; nor had I ever imagined that such things were possible on earth—a Claude Lorrain extended to infinity, each day equal to the last in its wild perfection.

THE CASE OF WAGNER: A MUSICIAN'S PROBLEM

1

In order to do justice to this essay a man ought to suffer from the fate of music as from an open wound. From what do I suffer when I suffer from the fate of music? From the fact that music has lost its world-transfiguring, yea-saying character—that it is decadent music and no longer the flute of Dionysus. Supposing, however, that the fate of music be as dear to man as his own life, because joy and suffering are alike bound up with it; then he will find this pamphlet comparatively mild and full of consideration. To be cheerful in such circumstances, and laugh good-naturedly with others at one's self—*ridendo dicere severum*,[13] when the *verum dicere* would justify every sort of hardness—is humanity itself. Who doubts that I, old artillery-man that I am, would be able if I liked to point my *heavy* guns at Wagner? Everything decisive in this question I kept to myself—I have loved Wagner. After all, an attack upon a more than usually subtle "unknown person" whom another would not have divined so easily, lies in the meaning and path of my life-task. Oh, I have still quite a number of other "unknown persons" to unmask besides a Cagliostro of Music! Above all, I have to direct an attack against the German people, who, in matters of the spirit, grow everyday more indolent, poorer in instincts, and more *honest*; who, with an appetite for which they are to be envied, continue to diet themselves on contradictions, and gulp down "Faith" in company with science, Christian love together with anti-Semitism, and the will to power (to the "Empire"), dished up with the gospel of the humble, without showing the slightest signs of indigestion. Fancy this absence of party-feeling in the presence of opposites! Fancy this gastric neutrality and "disinterestedness!" Behold this sense of justice in the German palate, which can grant equal rights to all—which finds everything tasteful! Without a shadow of a doubt the Germans are idealists. When I was last in Germany, I found German taste striving to grant Wagner and the *Trumpeter of Säkkingen*[14] equal rights; while I myself witnessed the attempts of the people of Leipzig to do honour to one of the most genuine and most German of musicians— using German here in the old sense of the word—a man who was no mere German of the Empire, the master Heinrich Schütz, by founding a Liszt Society, the object of which was to cultivate and spread artful (*listige*[15]) Church music. Without a shadow of doubt the Germans are idealists.

2

But here nothing shall stop me from being rude, and from telling the Germans one or two unpleasant home truths: who else would do it if I did not? I refer to their laxity in matters historical. Not only have the Germans entirely lost the *breadth of vision* which enables one to grasp the course of culture and the values of culture; not only are they one and all political (or Church) puppets; but they have also actually *put a ban upon* this very breadth of vision. A man must first and foremost be "German," he must belong to "*the* race"; then only can he pass judgement upon all values and lack of values in history—then only can he establish them. . . . To be German is in itself an argument, "Germany, Germany above all,"[16] is a principle; the Germans stand for the "moral order of the universe" in history; compared with the Roman Empire, they are the upholders of freedom; compared with the eighteenth century, they are the restorers of morality, of the "Categorical Imperative." There is such a thing as the writing of history according to the lights of Imperial Germany; there is, I fear, anti-Semitic history—there is also history written with an eye to the Court, and Herr von Treitschke is not ashamed of himself. Quite recently an idiotic opinion *in historicis*, an observation of Vischer the Swabian aesthete, since happily deceased, made the round of the German newspapers as a "truth" to which every German *must assent*. The observation was this: "The Renaissance *and* the Reformation only together constitute a whole— the aesthetic rebirth, and the moral rebirth." When I listen to such things, I lose all patience, and I feel inclined, I even feel it my duty, to tell the Germans, for once in a way, all that they have on their conscience. *Every great crime against culture for the last four centuries lies on their conscience.* . . . And always for the same reason, always owing to their bottomless coward- ice in the face of reality, which is also cowardice in the face of truth; always owing to the love of falsehood which has become almost instinctive in them—in short, "idealism." It was the Germans who caused Europe to lose the fruits, the whole meaning of her last period of greatness—the period of the Renaissance. At a moment when a higher order of values, values that were noble, that said yea to life, and that guaranteed a future, had succeeded in triumphing over the opposite values, the values of degenera- tion, in the very seat of Christianity itself—and *even in the hearts of those sitting there*—Luther, that cursed monk, not only restored the Church, but, what was a thousand times worse, restored Christianity, and at a time too when it lay defeated. Christianity, the *Denial of the Will to Live*, exalted to a religion! Luther was an impossible monk who, thanks to his own "impos- sibility," attacked the Church, and in so doing restored it! Catholics would be perfectly justified in celebrating feasts in honour of Luther, and in producing festival plays[17] in his honour. Luther and the "rebirth of moral- ity!" May all psychology go to the devil! Without a shadow of a doubt the Germans are idealists. On two occasions when, at the cost of enormous courage and self-control, an upright, unequivocal, and perfectly scientific attitude of mind had been attained, the Germans were able to discover back stairs leading down to the old "ideal" again, compromises between truth and the "ideal," and, in short, formulae for the right to reject science and to perpetrate falsehoods. Leibniz and Kant—these two great breaks upon the intellectual honesty of Europe! Finally, at a moment when there appeared on the bridge that spanned two centuries of decadence, a superior force of genius and will which was strong enough to consolidate Europe and to convert it into a political and economic unit, with the object of ruling the world, the Germans, with their Wars of Independence, robbed Europe of the significance—the marvellous significance, of Napoleon's life. And in so doing they laid on their conscience everything that followed, everything that exists today—this sickliness and want of reason which is most opposed to culture, and which is called Nationalism —this *névrose nationale* from which Europe is suffering acutely; this eternal subdivision of Europe into petty states, with politics on a municipal scale: they have robbed Europe itself of its significance, of its reason—and have stuffed it into a cul-de-sac. Is there anyone except me who knows the way out of this cul-de-sac? Does anyone except me know of an aspiration which would be great enough to bind the people of Europe once more together?

3

And after all, why should I not express my suspicions? In my case, too, the Germans will attempt to make a great fate give birth merely to a mouse. Up to the present they have compromised themselves with me; I doubt whether the future will improve them. Alas! How happy I should be to prove a false prophet in this matter! My natural readers and listeners are already Russians, Scandinavians, and Frenchmen—will they always be the same? In the history of knowledge, Germans are represented only by doubtful names, they have been able to produce only "*unconscious*" swindlers (this word applies to Fichte, Schelling, Schopenhauer, Hegel, and Schleiermacher, just as well as to Kant or Leibniz; they were all mere *Schleiermachers*).[18] The Germans must not have the honour of seeing the first upright intellect in their history of intellects, that intellect in which truth ultimately got the better of the fraud of four thousand years, reckoned as one with the German intellect. "German intellect" is my foul air: I breathe with difficulty in the neighbourhood of this psychological uncleanliness that has now become instinctive—an uncleanliness which in every word and expression betrays a German. They have never undergone a seventeenth century of hard self-examination, as the French have—a La Rochefoucauld, a Descartes, are a thousand times more upright than the very first among Germans—the latter have not yet had any psychologists. But psychology is almost the standard of measurement for the cleanliness or uncleanliness of a race. . . . For if a man is not even clean, how can he be deep? The Germans are like women, you can scarcely ever fathom their depths—they haven't any, and that's the end of it. Thus they cannot even be called shallow. That which is called "deep" in Germany, is precisely this instinctive uncleanliness towards one's self, of which I have just spoken: people refuse to be clear in regard to their own natures. Might I be allowed, perhaps, to suggest the word "German" as an international epithet denoting this psychological depravity? At the moment of writing, for instance, the German Emperor is declaring it to be his Christian duty to liberate the slaves in Africa; among us Europeans, then, this would be called simply "German. . . ." Have the Germans ever produced even a book that had depth? They are lacking in the mere idea of what constitutes a book. I have known scholars who thought that Kant was deep. At the Court of Prussia I fear that Herr von Treitschke is regarded as deep. And when I happen to praise Stendhal as a deep psychologist, I have often been compelled, in the company of German university professors, to spell his name aloud.

4

And why should I not proceed to the end? I am fond of clearing the air. It is even part of my ambition to be considered as essentially a despiser of Germans. I expressed my suspicions of the German character even at the age of six-and-twenty (see *Thoughts out of Season*, vol. 2. pp. 164, 165)—to my mind the Germans are impossible. When I try to think of the kind of man who is opposed to me in all my instincts, my mental image takes the form of a German. The first thing I ask myself when I begin analysing a man, is, whether he has a feeling for distance in him; whether he sees rank, gradation, and order everywhere between man and man; whether he makes distinctions; for this is what constitutes a gentleman. Otherwise he belongs hopelessly to that openhearted, open-minded—alas! And always very good-natured species, *la canaille*! But the Germans are *canaille*—alas! They are so good-natured! A man lowers himself by frequenting the society of Germans: the German places every one on an equal footing. With the exception of my intercourse with one or two artists, and above all with Richard Wagner, I cannot say that I have spent one pleasant hour with Germans. Suppose, for one moment, that the profoundest spirit of all ages were to appear among Germans, then one of the saviours of the Capitol would be sure to arise and declare that his own ugly soul was just as great. I can no longer abide this race with which a man is always in bad company, which has no idea of nuances—woe to me! I am a nuance—and which has not *esprit* in its feet, and cannot even walk withal! In short, the Germans have no feet at all, they simply have legs. The Germans have not the faintest idea of how vulgar they are—but this in itself is the acme of vulgarity—they are not even ashamed of being merely Germans. They will have their say in everything, they regard themselves as fit to decide all questions; I even fear that they have decided about me. My whole life is essentially a proof of this remark. In vain have I sought among them for a sign of tact and delicacy towards myself. Among Jews I did indeed find it, but not among Germans. I am so constituted as to be gentle and kindly to everyone—I have the right not to draw distinctions—but this does not prevent my eyes from being open. I except no one, and least of all my friends—I only trust that this has not prejudiced my reputation for humanity among them? There are five or six things which I have always made points of honour. Albeit, the truth remains that for many years I have considered almost every letter that has reached me as a piece of cynicism. There is more cynicism in an attitude of goodwill towards me than in any sort of hatred. I tell every friend to his face that he has never thought it worth his while to *study* any one of my writings: from the slightest hints I gather that they do not even know what lies hidden in my books. And with regard even to my *Zarathustra*, which of my friends would have seen more in it than a piece of unwarrantable, though fortunately harmless, arrogance? Ten years have elapsed, and no one has yet felt it a duty to his conscience to defend my name against the absurd silence beneath which it has been entombed. It was a foreigner, a Dane, who first showed sufficient keenness of instinct and of courage to do this, and who protested indignantly against my so-called friends. At what German university today would such lectures on my philosophy be possible, as those which Dr. Brandes delivered last spring in Copenhagen, thus proving once more his right to the title psychologist? For my part, these things have never caused me any pain; that which is *necessary* does not offend me. *Amor fati* is the core of my nature. This, however, does not alter the fact that I love irony and even world-historic irony. And thus, about two years before hurling the destructive thunderbolt of the *Transvaluation*, which will send the whole of civilisation into convulsions, I sent my *Case of Wagner* out into the world. The Germans were given the chance of blundering and immortalising their stupidity once more on my account, and they still have just enough time to do it in. And have they fallen in with my plans? Admirably! My dear Germans. Allow me to congratulate you.

WHY I AM A FATALITY

1

I KNOW MY DESTINY. THERE WILL COME A DAY WHEN MY NAME WILL RECALL the memory of something formidable—a crisis the like of which has never been known on earth, the memory of the most profound clash of consciences, and the passing of a sentence upon all that which theretofore had been believed, exacted, and hallowed. I am not a man, I am dynamite. And with it all there is nought of the founder of a religion in me. Religions are matters for the mob; after coming in contact with a religious man, I always feel that I must wash my hands. . . . I require no "believers," it is my opinion that I am too full of malice to believe even in myself; I never address myself to masses. I am horribly frightened that one day I shall be pronounced "holy." You will understand why I publish this book beforehand—it is to prevent people from wronging me. I refuse to be a saint; I would rather be a clown. Maybe I am a clown. And I am notwithstanding, or rather not *not*withstanding, the mouthpiece of truth; for nothing more blown-out with falsehood has ever existed, than a saint. But my truth is terrible: for hitherto *lies* have been called truth. *The Transvaluation of All Values*, this is my formula for mankind's greatest step towards coming to its senses—a step which in me became flesh and genius. My destiny ordained that I should be the first decent human being, and that I should feel myself opposed to the falsehood of millenniums. I was the first to discover truth, and for the simple reason that I was the first who became conscious of falsehood as falsehood—that is to say, I smelt it as such. My genius resides in my nostrils. I contradict as no one has contradicted hitherto, and am nevertheless the reverse of a negative spirit. I am the harbinger of joy, the like of which has never existed before; I have discovered tasks of such lofty greatness that, until my time, no one had any idea of such things. Mankind can begin to have fresh hopes, only now that I have lived. Thus, I am necessarily a man of Fate. For when Truth enters the lists against the falsehood of ages, shocks are bound to ensue, and a spell of earthquakes, followed by the transposition of hills and valleys, such as the world has never yet imagined even in its dreams. The concept "politics" then becomes elevated entirely to the sphere of spiritual warfare. All the mighty realms of the ancient order of society are blown into space—for they are all based on falsehood: there will be wars, the like of which have never been seen on earth before. Only from my time and after me will politics on a large scale exist on earth.

2

If you should require a formula for a destiny of this kind that has taken human form, you will find it in my *Zarathustra.*

> And he who would be a creator in good and evil—verily, he must
>   first be a destroyer, and break values into pieces.
> Thus the greatest evil belongeth unto the greatest good: but this is
>   the creative good.

I am by far the most terrible man that has ever existed; but this does not alter the fact that I shall become the most beneficent. I know the joy of *annihilation* to a degree which is commensurate with my power to annihilate. In both cases I obey my Dionysian nature, which knows not how to separate the negative deed from the saying of yea. I am the first immoralist, and in this sense I am essentially the annihilator.

3

People have never asked me as they should have done, what the name of Zarathustra precisely meant in my mouth, in the mouth of the first immoralist; for that which distinguishes this Persian from all others in the past is the very fact that he was the exact reverse of an immoralist. Zarathustra was the first to see in the struggle between good and evil the essential wheel in the working of things. The translation of morality into the realm of metaphysics, as force, cause, end-in-itself, is his work. But the very question suggests its own answer. Zarathustra created this most portentous of all errors—morality; therefore he must be the first to expose it. Not only because he has had longer and greater experience of the subject than any other thinker—all history is indeed the experimental refutation of the theory of the so-called moral order of things—but because of the more important fact that Zarathustra was the most truthful of thinkers. In his teaching alone is truthfulness upheld as the highest virtue—that is to say, as the reverse of the cowardice of the "idealist" who takes to his heels at the sight of reality. Zarathustra has more pluck in his body than all other thinkers put together. To tell the truth and to aim straight: that is the first Persian virtue. Have I made myself clear? . . . The overcoming of morality by itself, through truthfulness, the moralist's overcoming of himself in his opposite—in me—that is what the name Zarathustra means in my mouth.

4

In reality two negations are involved in my title Immoralist. I first of all deny the type of man that has hitherto been regarded as the highest—the *good*, the *kind*, and the *charitable*; and I also deny that kind of morality which has become recognised and paramount as morality-in-itself—I speak of the morality of decadence, or, to use a still cruder term, Christian morality. I would agree to the second of the two negations being regarded as the more decisive, for, reckoned as a whole, the overestimation of good-ness and kindness seems to me already a consequence of decadence, a symptom of weakness, and incompatible with any ascending and yea-saying life. Negation and annihilation are inseparable from a yea-saying attitude towards life. Let me halt for a moment at the question of the psychology of the good man. In order to appraise the value of a certain type of man, the cost of his maintenance must be calculated—and the conditions of his existence must be known. The condition of the existence of the *good* is falsehood: or, otherwise expressed, the refusal at any price to see how reality is actually constituted. The refusal to see that this real-ity is not so constituted as always to be stimulating beneficent instincts, and still less, so as to suffer at all moments the intrusion of ignorant and good-natured hands. To consider distress of all kinds as an objection, as something which must be done away with, is the greatest nonsense on earth; generally speaking, it is nonsense of the most disastrous sort, fatal in its stupidity—almost as mad as the will to abolish bad weather, out of pity for the poor, so to speak. In the great economy of the whole universe, the terrors of reality (in the passions, in the desires, in the will to power) are incalculably more necessary than that form of petty happiness which is called "goodness"; it is even needful to practise leniency in order so much as to allow the latter a place at all, seeing that it is based upon a falsification of the instincts. I shall have an excellent opportunity of show-ing the incalculably calamitous consequences to the whole of history, of the credo of optimism, this monstrous offspring of the *homines optimi.* Zarathustra,[19] the first who recognised that the optimist is just as degen-erate as the pessimist, though perhaps more detrimental, says: "*Good men never speak the truth. False shores and false harbours were ye taught by the good. In the lies of the good were ye born and bred. Through the good everything hath become false and crooked from the roots.*" Fortunately the world is not built merely upon those instincts which would secure to the good-natured herd ani-mal his paltry happiness. To desire everybody to become a "good man," "a gregarious animal," "a blue-eyed, benevolent, beautiful soul," or—as Herbert Spencer wished—a creature of altruism, would mean robbing existence of its greatest character, castrating man, and reducing humanity to a sort of wretched Chinadom. *And this some have tried to do! It is precisely this that men called morality.* In this sense Zarathustra calls "the good," now "the last men," and anon "the beginning of the end"; and above all, he considers them as *the most detrimental kind of men,* because they secure their existence at the cost of Truth and at the cost of the Future.

> The good—they cannot create; they are ever the beginning of the end.
> They crucify him who writeth new values on new tables; they sac-rifice *unto themselves* the future; they crucify the whole future of humanity!
> The good—they are ever the beginning of the end.
> And whatever harm the slanderers of the world may do, *the harm of the good is the most calamitous of all harm.*

5

Zarathustra, as the first psychologist of the good man, is perforce the friend of the evil man. When a degenerate kind of man has succeeded to the highest rank among the human species, his position must have been gained at the cost of the reverse type—at the cost of the strong man who is certain of life. When the gregarious animal stands in the glorious rays of the purest virtue, the exceptional man must be degraded to the rank of the evil. If falsehood insists at all costs on claiming the word "truth" for its own particular standpoint, the really truthful man must be sought out among the despised. Zarathustra allows of no doubt here; he says that it was precisely the knowledge of the good, of the "best," which inspired his absolute horror of men. And it was out of this feeling of repulsion that he grew the wings which allowed him to soar into remote futures. He does not conceal the fact that his type of man is one which is relatively superhuman —especially as opposed to the "good" man, and that the good and the just would regard his superman as the *devil*.

"Ye higher men, on whom my gaze now falls, this is the doubt that ye wake in my breast, and this is my secret laughter: methinks ye would call my Superman—the devil! So strange are ye in your souls to all that is great, that the Superman would be terrible in your eyes for his goodness."

It is from this passage, and from no other, that you must set out to understand the goal to which Zarathustra aspires—the kind of man that he conceives sees reality *as it is*; he is strong enough for this—he is not estranged or far removed from it, he is that reality himself, in his own nature can be found all the terrible and questionable character of reality: *only thus can man have greatness.*

6

But I have chosen the title of Immoralist as a surname and as a badge of honour in yet another sense; I am very proud to possess this name which distinguishes me from all the rest of mankind. No one hitherto has felt Christian morality beneath him; to that end there were needed height, a remoteness of vision, and an abysmal psychological depth, not believed to be possible hitherto. Up to the present Christian morality has been the Circe of all thinkers—they stood at her service. What man, before my time, had descended into the underground caverns from out of which the poisonous fumes of this ideal—of this slandering of the world—burst forth? What man had even dared to suppose that they were underground caverns? Was a single one of the philosophers who preceded me a psychologist at all, and not the very reverse of a psychologist—that is to say, a "superior swindler," an "Idealist?" Before my time there was no psychology. To be the first in this new realm may amount to a curse; at all events, it is a fatality: *for one is also the first to despise.* My danger is the loathing of mankind.

7

Have you understood me? That which defines me, that which makes me stand apart from the whole of the rest of humanity, is the fact that I *unmasked* Christian morality. For this reason I was in need of a word which conveyed the idea of a challenge to everybody. Not to have awakened to these discoveries before, struck me as being the sign of the greatest uncleanliness that mankind has on its conscience, as self-deception become instinctive, as the fundamental will to be blind to every phenomenon, all causality and all reality; in fact, as an almost criminal fraud *in psychologicis.* Blindness in regard to Christianity is the essence of criminality —for it is the crime *against* life. Ages and peoples, the first as well as the last, philosophers and old women, with the exception of five or six moments in history (and of myself, the seventh), are all alike in this. Hitherto the Christian has been *the* "moral being," a peerless oddity, and, *as* "a moral being," he was more absurd, more vain, more thoughtless, and a greater disadvantage to himself, than the greatest despiser of humanity could have deemed possible. Christian morality is the most malignant form of all falsehood, the actual Circe of humanity: that which has corrupted mankind. It is not error as error which infuriates me at the sight of this spectacle; it is not the millenniums of absence of "goodwill," of discipline, of decency, and of bravery in spiritual things, which betrays itself in the triumph of Christianity; it is rather the absence of nature, it is the perfectly ghastly fact that *anti-nature* itself received the highest honours as morality and as law, and remained suspended over man as the Categorical Imperative. Fancy blundering in this way, *not* as an individual, *not* as a people, but as a whole species! As *humanity*! To teach the contempt of all the principal instincts of life; to posit falsely the existence of a "soul," of a "spirit," in order to be able to defy the body; to spread the feeling that there is something impure in the very first prerequisite of life—in sex; to seek the principle of evil in the profound need of growth and expansion —that is to say, in severe self-love (the term itself is slanderous); and conversely to see a higher moral value—but what am I talking about? I mean the *moral value* per se, in the typical signs of decline, in the antagonism of the instincts, in "selflessness," in the loss of ballast, in "the suppression of the personal element," and in "love of one's neighbour" (neighbour-itis!). What! Is humanity itself in a state of degeneration? Has it always been in this state? One thing is certain, that ye are taught only the values of decadence as the highest values. The morality of self-renunciation is essentially the morality of degeneration; the fact, "I am going to the dogs," is translated into the imperative, "Ye shall all go to the dogs"—and not only into the imperative. This morality of self-renunciation, which is the only kind of morality that has been taught hitherto, betrays the will to nonentity—it denies life to the very roots. There still remains the possibility that it is not mankind that is in a state of degeneration, but only that parasitical kind of man—the priest, who, by means of morality and lies, has climbed up to his position of determinator of values, who divined in Christian morality his road to power. And, to tell the truth, this is my opinion. The teachers and leaders of mankind—including the theologians—have been, every one of them, decadents: hence their transvaluation of all values into a hostility towards life; hence morality. *The definition of morality*: Morality is the idiosyncrasy of decadents, actuated by a desire *to avenge themselves with success upon life*. I attach great value to this definition.

8

Have you understood me? I have not uttered a single word which I had not already said five years ago through my mouthpiece Zarathustra. The unmasking of Christian morality is an event which is unequalled in history, it is a real catastrophe. The man who throws light upon it is a *force majeure*, a fatality; he breaks the history of man into two. Time is reckoned up before him and after him. The lightning flash of truth struck precisely that which theretofore had stood highest: he who understands what was destroyed by that flash should look to see whether he still holds anything in his hands. Everything which until then was called truth, has been revealed as the most detrimental, most spiteful, and most subterranean form of life; the holy pretext, which was the "improvement" of man, has been recognised as a ruse for draining life of its energy and of its blood. Morality conceived as *Vampirism*. . . . The man who unmasks morality has also unmasked the worthlessness of the values in which men either believe or have believed; he no longer sees anything to be revered in the most venerable man—even in the types of men that have been pronounced holy; all he can see in them is the most fatal kind of abortions, fatal, *because they fascinate*. The concept "God" was invented as the opposite of the concept life—everything detrimental, poisonous, and slanderous, and all deadly hostility to life, was bound together in one horrible unit in Him. The concepts "beyond" and "true world" were invented in order to depreciate the only world that exists—in order that no goal or aim, no sense or task, might be left to earthly reality. The concepts "soul," "spirit," and last of all the concept "immortal soul," were invented in order to throw contempt on the body, in order to make it sick and "holy," in order to cultivate an attitude of appalling levity towards all things in life which deserve to be treated seriously, i.e., the questions of nutrition and habitation, of intellectual diet, the treatment of the sick, cleanliness, and weather. Instead of health, we find the "salvation of the soul"—that is to say, a *folie circulaire* fluctuating between convulsions and penitence and the hysteria of redemption. The concept "sin," together with the torture instrument appertaining to it, which is the concept "free will," was invented in order to confuse and muddle our instincts, and to render the mistrust of them man's second nature! In the concepts "disinterestedness" and "self-denial," the actual signs of decadence are to be found. The allurement of that which is detrimental, the inability to discover one's own advantage and self-destruction, are made into absolute qualities, into the "duty," the "holiness," and the "divinity" of man. Finally—to keep the worst to the last—by the notion of the *good* man, all that is favoured which is weak, ill, botched, and sick-in-itself, which *ought to be wiped out*. The law of selection is thwarted, an ideal is made out of opposition to the proud, well-constituted man, to him who says yea to life, to him who is certain of the future, and who guarantees the future—this man is henceforth called the *evil* one. And all this was believed in as *morality*! *Ecrasez l'infâme*!

9

Have you understood me? *Dionysus* versus *Christ*.

ENDNOTES

INTRODUCTION

[1] *Selected Letters of Friedrich Nietzsche*, ed. and trans. by Christopher Middleton, Indianapolis: Hackett Publishing Company, 1996, letter # 181.

BEYOND GOOD AND EVIL

CHAPTER II

[1] Like the river Ganges: *presto.*
[2] Like the tortoise: *lento.*
[3] Like the frog: *staccato.*

CHAPTER V

[1] Pages 54–55 of Schopenhauer's *Basis of Morality*, translated by Arthur B. Bullock, M.A. (1903).

CHAPTER VII

[1] An expression from Schiller's *William Tell*, Act IV, Scene 3.

CHAPTER IX

[1] Horace's *Epistles*, I, x. 24.
[2] Goethe's *Faust*, Part 2, Act V. The words of Dr. Marianus.

ON THE GENEALOGY OF MORALS

SECOND ESSAY

[1] The German is: "*Sittlichkeit der Sitte.*" H. B. S.
[2] The German world "*schuld*" means both debt and guilt. Cp. the English "owe" and "ought," by which I occasionally render the double meaning. H. B. S.
[3] German: "*Verbrecher.*" H. B. S.
[4] An allusion to *Der Zweck im Recht*, by the great German jurist Professor Ihering.

THIRD ESSAY

[1] An allusion to the celebrated monologue in *William Tell.*
[2] Mistress Sly. TR.
[3] In the German text "*Heiland.*" This has the double meaning of "healer" and "saviour." H. B. S.
[4] "Horrible beast."
[5] "Here I stand! I cannot help myself. God help me! Amen"—were Luther's words before the Reichstag at Worms. H. B. S.
[6] E.g., Lectureships.
[7] An allusion to the well-known patriotic song. H. B. S.

TWILIGHT OF THE IDOLS

MAXIMS AND MISSILES

[1] This is a reference to Seume's poem *Die Gesänge*, the first verse of which is:

> *Wo man singet, lass dich ruhig nieder,*
> *Ohne Furcht, was man im Lande glaubt;*
> *Wo man singet, wird kein Mensch beraubt:*
> *Bösewichter haben keine Lieder.*

(Wherever people sing thou canst safely settle down without a qualm as to what the general faith of the land may be. Wherever people sing, no man is ever robbed; *rascals* have no songs.) Popular tradition, however, renders the lines thus:

> *Wo man singt, da lass dich ruhig nieder;*
> *Böse Menschen* [evil men] *haben keine Lieder.* TR.

THE PROBLEM OF SOCRATES

[1] It should be borne in mind that Nietzsche recognised two types of criminals— the criminal from strength, and the criminal from weakness. This passage alludes to the latter, Aphorism 45, p. 367, alludes to the former. TR.

"REASON" IN PHILOSOPHY

[1] Nietzsche here refers to the concept "free will" of the Christians; this does not mean that there is no such thing as will—that is to say a powerful determining force from within. TR.

HOW THE "TRUE WORLD" BECAME A FABLE

[1] Kant was a native of Königsberg and lived there all his life. Did Nietzsche know that Kant was simply a Scotch Puritan, whose family had settled in Germany?

MORALITY AS THE ENEMY OF NATURE

[1] *Cf.* Spinoza, who says in the *Tractatus politicus* (1677), Chap. 1, § 4: "*Sedulo curavi, humanas actiones non ridere, non lugere, neque detestari, sed intelligere*" ("I have carefully endeavoured not to deride, or deplore, or detest human actions, but to understand them."). TR.

THINGS THE GERMANS LACK

[1] The German national hymn: "*Deutschland, Deutschland über alles.*" TR.
[2] The word *Kultur-Staat* "culture-state" has become a standard expression in the German language, and is applied to the leading European states. TR.

SKIRMISHES IN A WAR WITH THE AGE

[1] The German word *Rausch* as used by Nietzsche here, suggests a blend of our two English words "intoxication" and "elation." TR.
[2] An allusion to a verse in Luther's hymn: "*Lass fahren dahin . . . das Reich muss uns doch bleiben,*" which Nietzsche applies to the German Empire. TR.
[3] A disciple of Schopenhauer who blunted the sharpness of his master's Pessimism and who watered it down for modern requirements. TR.
[4] Quotation from the Libretto of Mozart's *Magic Flute*, Act 1, Sc. 3. TR.
[5] This alludes to Parsifal. See my note on p. 96, vol. 1, *The Will to Power.* TR.
[6] This is a playful adaptation of Max von Schenkendorf's poem *Freiheit*. The proper line reads: "*Freiheit die ich meine*" (The freedom that I do mean). TR.
[7] See *Memoirs of a House of the Dead,* by Dostoiewsky (translation by Marie von Thilo: *Buried Alive*). TR.
[8] Clothilde de Veaux. TR.
[9] See my note on p. 147 of Vol. 1 of the *Will to Power.* TR.

THE ANTICHRIST

[1] The German "*Tüchtigkeit*" has a nobler ring than our word "efficiency." TR.
[2] *Cf.* Disraeli: "But enlightened Europe is not happy. Its existence is a fever which it calls progress. Progress to what?" ("Tancred," Book III, Chap. 7.). TR.
[3] It will be seen from this that in spite of Nietzsche's ruthless criticism of the priests, he draws a sharp distinction between Christianity and the Church.

As the latter still contained elements of order, it was more to his taste than the denial of authority characteristic of real Christianity. TR.

⁴ "*Reine Thorheit*" in the German text, referring once again to Parsifal. TR.

⁵ This applies apparently to Bismarck, the forger of the Ems telegram and a sincere Christian. TR.

⁶ An adaptation of Shakespeare's "Well roared, lion" (*Mid. N. D.*, Act 5, Sc. i.), the lion, as is well known, being the symbol for St. Mark in Christian literature and Art. TR.

⁷ A parody on a line in Schiller's "*Jungfrau von Orleans*" (Act 3, Sc. vi.): "*Mit den Dummheit kämpfen Götter selbst vergebens*" (With stupidity even the gods themselves struggle in vain). TR.

⁸ ἐφεξις = Lat. Retentio, Inhibitio (Stephanus, Thesaurus Graecae Linguae); therefore: reserve, caution. The Greek Sceptics were also called Ephectics owing to their caution in judging and in concluding from facts. TR.

⁹ The following passage from Multatuli will throw light on this passage:

> Father: Behold, my son, how wisely Providence has arranged everything! This bird lays its eggs in its nest and the young will be hatched just about the time when there will be worms and flies with which to feed them. Then they will sing a song of praise in honour of the Creator who overwhelms his creatures with blessings.
> Son: Will the worms join in the song, Dad? TR.

¹⁰ *Thus Spake Zarathustra*. The Priests. TR.

¹¹ 1 Corinthians vii. 2, 9. TR.

ECCE HOMO

WHY I AM SO WISE

¹ The right which every Polish deputy, whether a great or an inferior nobleman, possessed of forbidding the passing of any measure by the Diet, was called in Poland the *liberum veto* (in Polish *nie pozwalam*), and brought all legislation to a standstill. TR.

² Eugen Dühring is a philosopher and political economist whose general doctrine might be characterised as a sort of abstract Materialism with an optimistic colouring. TR.

³ This, of course, is a reference to Wagner's *Parsifal*. See my note on p. 96 of *The Will to Power*, vol. 1. TR.

WHY I AM SO CLEVER

¹ Nietzsche, as is well known, devoted much time when a student at Leipzig to the study of three Greek philosophers, Theognis, Diogenes Laertius, and

Democritus. This study first bore fruit in the case of a paper, *Zur Geschichte der Theognideischen Spruchsammlung*, which was subsequently published by the most influential journal of classical philology in Germany. Later, however, it enabled Nietzsche to enter for the prize offered by the University of Leipzig for an essay, *De fontibus Diogenis Laertii*. He was successful in gaining the prize, and the treatise was afterwards published in the *Rheinisches Museum*, and is still quoted as an authority. It is to this essay, written when he was twenty-three years of age, that he here refers. Tr.

² The favourite uniform of the German Emperor, William II. Tr.

³ In the latter years of his life, Nietzsche practically made Italy his home. Tr.

⁴ See note on page 474.

⁵ The German words are, *Einsamkeit* and *Vielsamkeit*. The latter was coined by Nietzsche. The English word "multitude" should, therefore, be understood as signifying multifarious instincts and gifts, which in Nietzsche strove for ascendancy and caused him more suffering than any solitude. Complexity of this sort, held in check by a dominant instinct, as in Nietzsche's case, is of course the only possible basis of an artistic nature. Tr.

WHY I WRITE SUCH EXCELLENT BOOKS

¹ *Junker-Philosophie*. The landed proprietors constitute the dominating class in Prussia, and it is from this class that all officers and higher officials are drawn. The *Kreuz-Zeitung* is the organ of the Junker party. Tr.

² Those Germans who, like Nietzsche or Goethe, recognised that politics constituted a danger to culture, and who appreciated the literature of maturer cultures, such as that of France, are called *un-deutsch* (un-German) by Imperialistic Germans. Tr.

³ Aristotle's *Poetics*, C. VI. Tr.

⁴ This number and those which follow refer to *Thoughts out of Season*, Part 1 in this edition of Nietzsche's works. Tr.

⁵ The Purists constitute a definite body in Germany, which is called the *Deutscher Sprach-Verein*. Their object is to banish every foreign word from the language, and they carry this process of ostracism even into the domain of the menu, where their efforts at rendering the meaning of French dishes are extremely comical. Strange to say, their principal organ, and their other publications, are by no means free either from solecisms or faults of style, and it is doubtless to this curious anomaly that Nietzsche here refers. Tr.

⁶ Nohl and Pohl were both writers on music; Kohl, however, which literally means cabbage, is a slang expression, denoting superior nonsense. Tr.

⁷ Needless to say, Nietzsche distinguishes between Bismarckian Germany and that other Germany—Austria, Switzerland, and the Baltic Provinces—where the German language is also spoken. Tr.

⁸ *Human, All-Too-Human*, Part 2 in this edition. Tr.

⁹ *Human, All-Too-Human*, vol. 1 Aph. 37.

[10] Translated for *Joyful Wisdom* by Paul V. Cohn. Tr.

[11] A witty reference to Goethe's well-known passage in the Prologue to *Faust*:

> A good man, though in darkness and dismay,
> May still be conscious of the proper way.

The words are spoken by the Lord. Tr.

[12] There is a wonderful promenade along the banks of the Po, for which Turin is famous, and of which Nietzsche was particularly fond. Tr.

[13] The motto of *The Case of Wagner*. Tr.

[14] An opera by Nessler which was all the rage in Germany twenty years ago. Tr.

[15] Unfortunately it is impossible to render this play on the words in English. Tr.

[16] The German National Song (*Deutschland, Deutschland über alles*). Tr.

[17] Ever since the year 1617 such plays have been produced by the Protestants of Germany. Tr.

[18] *Schleiermacher* literally means a weaver or maker of veils. Tr.

[19] Needless to say this is Nietzsche, and no longer the Persian. Tr.

SUGGESTED READING

HEIDEGGER, MARTIN. *Nietzsche, Volumes 1 and 2.* Trans. David Farrell Krell. San Francisco: Harper San Francisco, 1991.

———. *Nietzsche, Volumes 3 and 4.* Trans. David Farrell Krell. San Francisco: Harper San Francisco, 1991.

———. *What Is Called Thinking.* Trans. J. Glenn Gray. New York: Harper Colophon Books, 1968.

———. *The Word of Nietzsche: "God is Dead,"* in *The Question Concerning Technology and Other Essays.* Trans. William Lovitt. New York: Harper Torchbooks, 1977.

NIETZSCHE, FRIEDRICH. *The Birth of Tragedy and The Case of Wagner.* Trans. Walter Kaufmann. New York: Vintage Books, 1967.

———. *The Gay Science.* Trans. Walter Kaufmann. New York: Vintage Books, 1974.

———. *The Portable Nietzsche.* Ed. and trans. Walter Kaufmann. New York: Penguin Books, 1976.

———. *Thus Spoke Zarathustra.* Trans. Walter Kaufmann. New York: Penguin Books, 1982.

———. *Untimely Meditations.* Trans. R. J. Hollingdale. New York: Cambridge University Press, 1992.

PLETSCH, CARL. *Young Nietzsche, Becoming a Genius.* New York: Free Press, 1991.

SCHOPENHAUER, ARTHUR. *The World as Will and Representation, Volumes 1 and 2.* Trans. E. F. J. Payne. New York: Dover Publications, Inc., 1966.